New Approaches in Automation and Robotics

Edited by
Harald Aschemann

Automation and Robotics, New Approaches

Edited by Harald Aschemann

Republished by InTech

Janeza Trdine 9, 51000 Rijeka, Croatia

Additional hard copies can be obtained from orders@intechopen.com

Automation and Robotics, New Approaches, Edited by Harald Aschemann
p. cm.
ISBN 978-3-902613-26-4

For EU product safety concerns:
IN TECH d.o.o., Prolaz Marije Krucifikse Kozulić 3, 51000 Rijeka, Croatia,
info@intechopen.com or visit our website at intechopen.com.

Meet the editor

Harald Aschemann was born in Hildesheim, Germany, on June 27, 1966. He received the Diploma degree in mechanical engineering from the University of Hanover, Hanover, Germany, in 1994 and the Ph.D. degree in the area of optimal trajectory planning and trajectory control of an overhead traveling crane from the University of Ulm, Ulm, Germany, in 2001. After two years working in research and development with a leading company in machine tools, where he worked on automated transfer systems, he joined the Department of Measurement, Control and Microtechnology, University of Ulm, where he was a Research Associate and a Lecturer from 2001 to 2006. Since 2006, he has been a Full Professor and the Head of the Chair of Mechatronics with the University of Rostock, Rostock, Germany. His research interests involve control-oriented modeling, identification, nonlinear control, and simulation of mechatronic, robotic, and thermofluidic systems. Prof. Aschemann was elected as a Corresponding Member of the International Academy of Engineering, Moscow, Russia in October 2011.

where $n(s)$ and $m(s)$ are polynomials and (3) is called polynomial fraction representation of $P_o(s)$. Another way of representing $P_o(s)$ is as the product of a stable transfer function and a transfer function with stable inverse, i.e.,

$$P_o(s) = N(s)M^{-1}(s) \tag{4}$$

where $N(s), M(s) \in \mathcal{RH}_\infty$, the set of stable and proper transfer functions.

In the Single-Input Single-Output (SISO) case, it is easy to get a fractional representation in the polynomial form (3). Let $\delta(s)$ be a Hurwitz polynomial such that $\deg \delta(s) = \deg m(s)$ and set

$$N(s) = \frac{n(s)}{\delta(s)} \qquad M(s) = \frac{m(s)}{\delta(s)} \tag{5}$$

The factorizations to be used will be of a special type called Coprime Factorizations. Two polynomials $n(s)$ and $m(s)$ are said to be coprime if their greatest common divisor is 1 (no common zeros). It follows from Euclid's algorithm – see for example (Kailath, 1980) – that $n(s)$ and $m(s)$ are coprime iff there exists polynomials $x(s)$ and $y(s)$ such that the following identity is satisfied:

$$x(s)m(s) + y(s)n(s) = 1 \tag{6}$$

Note that if z is a common zero of $n(s)$ and $m(s)$ then $x(z)m(z) + y(z)n(z) = 0$ and therefore $n(s)$ and $m(s)$ are not coprime. This concept can be readily generalized to transfer functions $N(s), M(s), X(s), Y(s)$ in $\mathcal{RH}_\infty$. Two transfer functions $M(s), N(s)$ in $\mathcal{RH}_\infty$ are coprime when they do not share zeros in the right half plane. Then it is always possible to find $X(s), Y(s)$ in $\mathcal{RH}_\infty$ such that $X(s)M(s) + Y(s)N(s) = 1$.

When moving to the multivariable case, we also have to distinguish between right and left coprime factorizations since we lose the commutative property present in the SISO case.

The following definitions tackle directly the multivariable case.

Definition 1. (Bezout Identity) Two stable matrix transfer functions N_r and M_r are right coprime if and only if there exist stable matrix transfer functions X_r and Y_r such that

$$\begin{bmatrix} X_r & Y_r \end{bmatrix} \begin{bmatrix} M_r \\ N_r \end{bmatrix} = X_r M_r + Y_r N_r = I \tag{7}$$

Similarly, two stable matrix transfer functions N_l and M_l are left coprime if and only if there exist stable matrix transfer functions X_l and Y_l such that

Preface

The book at hand on "New Approaches in Automation and Robotics" offers in 22 chapters a collection of recent developments in automation, robotics as well as control theory. It is dedicated to researchers in science and industry, students, and practicing engineers, who wish to update and enhance their knowledge on modern methods and innovative applications.

The authors and editor of this book wish to motivate people, especially undergraduate students, to get involved with the interesting field of robotics and mechatronics. We hope that the ideas and concepts presented in this book are useful for your own work and could contribute to problem solving in similar applications as well. It is clear, however, that the wide area of automation and robotics can only be highlighted at several spots but not completely covered by a single book.

The editor would like to thank all the authors for their valuable contributions to this book. Special thanks to Editors in Chief of International Journal of Advanced Robotic Systems for their effort in making this book possible.

Editor
Harald Aschemann
Chair of Mechatronics
University of Rostock
18059 Rostock
Germany
Harald.Aschemann@uni-rostock.de

Contents

1

A Model Reference Based 2-DOF Robust Observer-Controller Design Methodology

Salva Alcántara, Carles Pedret and Ramon Vilanova
Autonomous University of Barcelona
Spain

1. Introduction

As it is well known, standard feedback control is based on generating the control signal u by processing the error signal, $e = r - y$, that is, the difference between the reference input and the actual output. Therefore, the input to the plant is

$$u = K(r - y) \tag{1}$$

It is well known that in such a scenario the design problem has one degree of freedom (1-DOF) which may be described in terms of the stable Youla parameter (Vidyasagar, 1985). The error signal in the 1-DOF case, see figure 1, is related to the external input r and d by means of the sensitivity function $S \doteq (1 + P_o K)^{-1}$, i.e., $e = S(r - d)$.

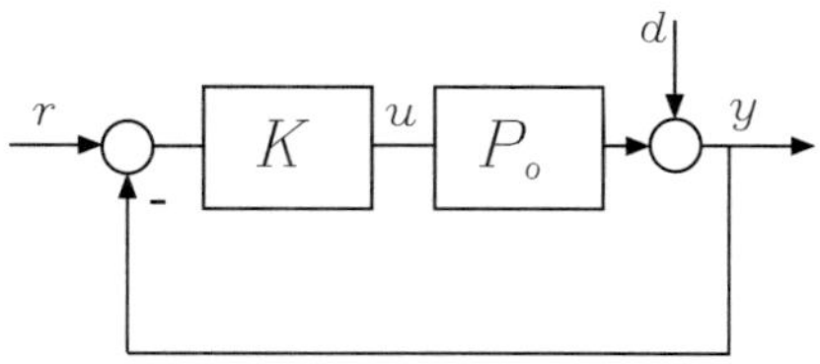

Fig. 1. Standard 1-DOF control system.

Disregarding the sign, the reference r and the disturbance d have the same effect on the error e. Therefore, if r and d vary in a similar manner the controller K can be chosen to minimize e in some sense. Otherwise, if r and d have different nature, the controller has to be chosen to provide a good trade-off between the command tracking and the disturbance rejection responses. This compromise is inherent to the nature of 1-DOF control schemes. To allow independent controller adjustments for both r and d, additional controller blocks have to be introduced into the system as in figure 2.

Two-degree-of-freedom (2-DOF) compensators are characterized by allowing a separate processing of the reference inputs and the controlled outputs and may be characterized by means of two stable Youla parameters. The 2-DOF compensators present the advantage of a complete separation between feedback and reference tracking properties (Youla & Bongiorno, 1985): the feedback properties of the controlled system are assured by a feedback

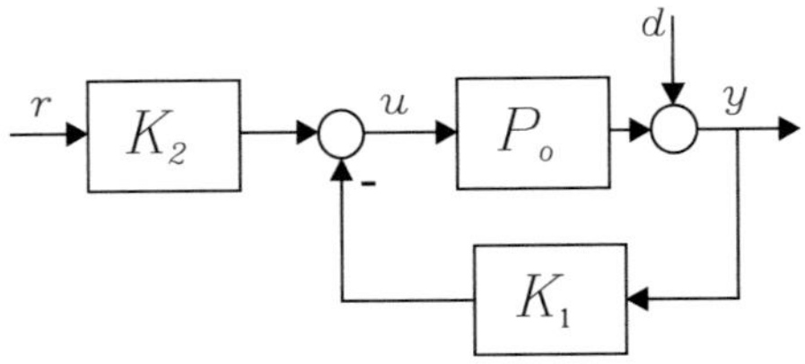

Fig. 2. Standard 2-DOF control configuration.

controller, i.e., the first degree of freedom; the reference tracking specifications are addressed by a prefilter controller, i.e., the second degree of freedom, which determines the open-loop processing of the reference commands. So, in the 2-DOF control configuration shown in figure 2 the reference r and the measurement y, enter the controller separately and are independently processed, i.e.,

$$u = K\begin{bmatrix} r \\ y \end{bmatrix} = K_2 r - K_1 y \tag{2}$$

As it is pointed out in (Vilanova & Serra, 1997), classical control approaches tend to stress the use of feedback to modify the systems' response to commands. A clear example, widely used in the literature of linear control, is the usage of reference models to specify the desired properties of the overall controlled system (Astrom & Wittenmark, 1984). What is specified through a reference model is the desired closed-loop system response. Therefore, as the system response to a command is an open-loop property and robustness properties are associated with the feedback (Safonov et al., 1981), no stability margins are guaranteed when achieving the desired closed-loop response behaviour.

A 2-DOF control configuration may be used in order to achieve a control system with both a performance specification, e.g., through a reference model, and some guaranteed stability margins. The approaches found in the literature are mainly based on optimization problems which basically represent different ways of setting the Youla parameters characterizing the controller (Vidyasagar, 1985), (Youla & Bongiorno, 1985), (Grimble, 1988), (Limebeer et al., 1993).

The approach presented in (Limebeer et al., 1993) expands the role of H_∞ optimization tools in 2-DOF system design. The 1-DOF loop-shaping design procedure (McFarlane & Glover, 1992) is extended to a 2-DOF control configuration by means of a parameterization in terms of two stable Youla parameters (Vidyasagar, 1985), (Youla & Bongiorno, 1985). A feedback controller is designed to meet robust performance requirements in a manner similar as in the 1-DOF loop-shaping design procedure and a prefilter controller is then added to the overall compensated system to force the response of the closed-loop to follow that of a specified reference model. The approach is carried out by assuming uncertainty in the normalized coprime factors of the plant (Glover & McFarlane, 1989). Such uncertainty description allows a formulation of the $\mathcal{H}_\infty$ robust stabilization problem providing explicit formulae.

A frequency domain approach to model reference control with robustness considerations was presented in (Sun et al., 1994). The design approach consists of a nominal design part plus a modelling error compensation component to mitigate errors due to uncertainty.

However, the approach inherits the restriction to minimum-phase plants from the Model Reference Adaptive Control theory in which it is based upon.
In this chapter we present a 2-DOF control configuration based on a right coprime factorization of the plant. The presented approach, similar to that in (Pedret C. et al., 2005), is not based on setting the two Youla parameters arbitrarily, with internal stability being the only restriction. Instead,

1. An observer-based feedback control scheme is designed to guarantee robust stability. This is achieved by means of solving a constrained $\mathcal{H}_\infty$ optimization using the right coprime factorization of the plant in an active way.
2. A prefilter controller is added to improve the open-loop processing of the robust closed-loop. This is done by assuming a reference model capturing the desired input-output relation and by solving a model matching problem for the prefilter controller to make the overall system response resemble as much as possible that of the reference model.

The chapter is organized as follows: section 2 introduces the Observer-Controller configuration used in this work within the framework of stabilizing control laws and the Youla parameterization for the stabilizing controllers. Section 3 reviews the generalized control framework and the concept of $\mathcal{H}_\infty$ optimization based control. Section 4 displays the proposed 2-DOF control configuration and describes the two steps in which the associated design is divided. In section 5 the suggested methodology is illustrated by a simple example. Finally, Section 6 closes the chapter summarizing its content and drawing some conclusions.

2. Stabilizing control laws and the Observer-Controller configuration

This section is devoted to introduce the reader to the celebrated Youla parameterization, mentioned throughout the introduction. This result gives all the control laws that attain closed-loop stability in terms of two stable but otherwise free parameters. In order to do so, first a basic review of the factorization framework is given and then the Observer-Controller configuration used in this chapter is presented within the aforementioned framework. The Observer-Controller configuration constitutes the basis for the control structure presented in this work.

2.1 The factorization framework

A short introduction to the so-called factorization or fractional approach is provided in this section. The central idea is to factor a transfer function of a system, not necessarily stable, as a ratio of two stable transfer functions. The factorization framework will constitute the foundations for the analysis and design in subsequent sections. The treatment in this section is fairly standard and follows (Vilanova, 1996), (Vidyasagar, 1985) or (Francis, 1987).

2.1.2 Coprime factorizations over $\mathcal{RH}_\infty$

A usual way of representing a scalar system is as a rational transfer function of the form

$$P_o(s) = \frac{n(s)}{m(s)} \tag{3}$$

$$\begin{bmatrix} M_l & N_l \end{bmatrix} \begin{bmatrix} X_l \\ Y_l \end{bmatrix} = M_l X_l + N_l Y_l = I \tag{8}$$

The matrix transfer functions X_r, Y_r (X_l, Y_l) belonging to $\mathcal{RH}_\infty$ are called right (left) Bezout complements.

Now let $P_o(s)$ be a proper real rational transfer function. Then,

Definition 2. A right (left) coprime factorization, abbreviated RCF (LCF), is a factorization $P_o(s) = N_r M_r^{-1}$ ($P_o(s) = M_l^{-1} N_l$), where N_r, M_r (N_l, M_l) are right (left) coprime over $\mathcal{RH}_\infty$.

With the above definitions, the following theorem arises to provide right and left coprime factorizations of a system given in terms of a state-space realization. Let us suppose that

$$P_o(s) \doteq \left[\begin{array}{c|c} A & B \\ \hline C & D \end{array}\right] \tag{9}$$

is a minimal stabilisable and detectable state-space realization of the system $P_o(s)$.

Theorem 1. Define

$$\begin{aligned} \begin{bmatrix} M_r & -Y_l \\ N_r & X_l \end{bmatrix} &\doteq \left[\begin{array}{c|cc} A+BF & B & -L \\ \hline F & I & 0 \\ C+DF & -D & I \end{array}\right] \\ \begin{bmatrix} X_r & Y_r \\ -N_l & M_l \end{bmatrix} &\doteq \left[\begin{array}{c|cc} A+LC & -(B+LD) & -L \\ \hline F & I & 0 \\ C & -D & I \end{array}\right] \end{aligned} \tag{10}$$

where F and L are such that $A+BF$ and $A+LC$ are stable. Then, $P_o(s) = N_r(s) M_r^{-1}(s)$ ($P_o(s) = M_l^{-1}(s) N_l(s)$) is a RCF (LCF).

Proof. The theorem is demonstrated by substituting (1.10) into equation (1.7).

Standard software packages can be used to compute appropriate F and L matrices numerically for achieving that the eigenvalues of $A+BF$ are those in the vector

$$p_F = \begin{bmatrix} p_{F_1} \cdots p_{F_n} \end{bmatrix}^T \tag{11}$$

Similarly, the eigenvalues of $A+LC$ can be allocated in accordance to the vector

$$p_L = \begin{bmatrix} p_{L_1} \cdots p_{L_n} \end{bmatrix}^T \tag{12}$$

By performing this pole placement, we are implicitly making active use of the degrees of freedom available for building coprime factorizations. Our final design of section 4 will make use of this available freedom for trying to meet all the controller specifications.

2.2 The Youla parameterization and the Observer-Controller configuration

A control law is said to be stabilizing if it provides internal stability to the overall closed-loop system, which means that we have Bounded-Input-Bounded-Output (BIBO) stability between every input-output pair of the resulting closed-loop arrangement. For instance, if we consider the general control law $u = K_2 r - K_1 y$ in figure 3a internal stability amounts to being stable all the entries in the mapping $(r, d_i, d_o) \rightarrow (u, y)$.

Let us reconsider the standard 1-DOF control law of figure 1 in which $u = K(r - y)$. For this particular case, the following theorem gives a parameterization of all the stabilizing control laws.

Theorem 2. (1-DOF Youla parameterization) For a given plant $P = N_r M_r^{-1}$, let $C_{stab}(P)$ denote the set of stabilizing 1-DOF controllers K_1, that is,

$$C_{stab}(P) \doteq \{K_1 : \text{the control law } u = K_1(r - y) \text{ is stabilizing}\}. \tag{13}$$

The set $C_{stab}(P)$ can be parameterized by

$$C_{stab}(P) = \left\{ \frac{X_r + M_r Q_y}{Y_r - N_r Q_y} : Q_y \in \mathcal{RH}_\infty \right\} \tag{14}$$

As it was pointed out in the introduction of this chapter, the standard feedback control configuration of figure 1 lacks the possibility of offering independent processing of disturbance rejection and reference tracking. So, the controller has to be designed for providing closed-loop stability and a good trade-off between the conflictive performance objectives. For achieving this independence of open-loop and closed-loop properties, we added the extra block K_2 (the prefilter) to figure 1, leading to the standard 2-DOF control scheme in figure 2. Now the control law is of the form

$$u = K_2 r - K_1 y \tag{15}$$

where K_1 and K_2 are to be chosen to provide closed-loop stability and meet the performance specifications. This control law is the most general stabilizing linear time invariant control law since it includes all the external inputs (y and r) in u.

Because of the fact that two compensator blocks are needed for expressing u according to (15), 2-DOF compensators are also referred to as two-parameter compensators. It is worth emphasizing that (15) represents the most general feedback compensation scheme and that, for example, there is no *three-parameter compensator*.

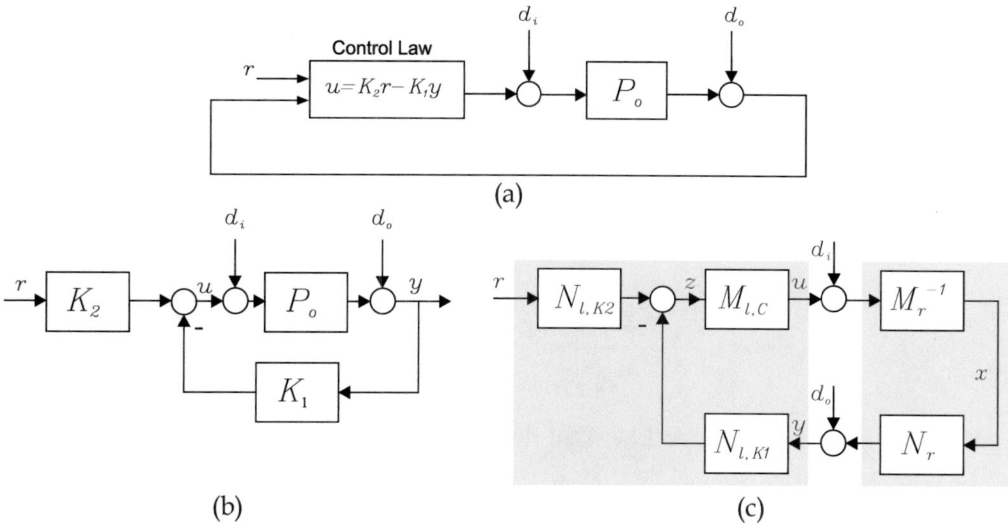

Fig. 3. (a) 2-DOF control diagram. (b) An unfeasible implementation of the 2-DOF control law $u = K_2 r - K_1 y$. (c) A feasible implementation of the control law $u = K_2 r - K_1 y$.

It is evident that if we make $K_1 = K_2 = K$, then we have $u = K(r - y)$ and recover the standard 1-DOF feedback configuration (1 parameter compensator) of figure 1. Once we have designed K_1 and K_2, equation (15) simply gives a control law but it says nothing about the actual implementation of it, see (Wilfred, W.K. et al., 2007). For instance, in figure 3b we can see one possible implementation of the control law given by (15) which is a direct translation of the equation into a block diagram. It should be noted that this implementation is not valid when K_2 is unstable, since this block acts in an open-loop fashion and this would result in an unstable overall system, in spite of the control law being a stabilizing one. To circumvent this problem we can make use of the previously presented factorization framework and proceed as follows: define $C = [K_1 \quad K_2]$ and let $K_1 = M_{l,C}^{-1} N_{l,K1}$ and $K_2 = M_{l,C}^{-1} N_{l,K2}$ such that $(M_{l,C}, [N_{l,K1} \quad N_{l,K2}])$ is a LCF of C. Once $C = [K_1 \quad K_2]$ has been factorized as suggested, the control action in (15) can be implemented as shown in figure 3c. In this figure the plant has been right-factored as $N_r M_r^{-1}$. It can be shown that the mapping $(r, d_i, d_o) \to (z_1, z_2, u, y)$ remains stable (necessary for internal stability) if and only if so it does the mapping $(r, d_i, d_o) \to (u, y)$. The following theorem states when the system depicted in figure 3c is internally stable.

Theorem 3. The system of figure 3c is internally stable if and only if

$$R^{-1} := M_{l,C} M_r + N_{l,K2} N_r \in \mathcal{RH}_\infty, \quad R \in \mathcal{RH}_\infty \tag{16}$$

We can proceed now to announce the 2-DOF Youla Paramaterization.

Theorem 4. (2-DOF Youla parameterization) For a given plant $P = N_r M_r^{-1}$, let $C_{stab}(P)$ denote the set of stabilizing 2-DOF controllers $C = [K_1 \quad K_2]$, that is,

$$C_{stab}(P) \doteq \{C = [K_1, K_2] : \text{the control law } u = K_2 r - K_1 y) \text{ is stabilizing}\}. \tag{17}$$

The set $C_{stab}(P)$ can be parameterized as follows

$$C_{stab}(P) \doteq \left\{ \left(\frac{X_r + M_r Q_y}{Y_r - N_r Q_y} \quad , \quad \frac{Q_r}{Y_r - N_r Q_y} \right) : Q_y, Q_r \in RH_\infty \right\} \tag{18}$$

Proof. Based on theorem 2, it follows that the transfer function R will satisfy theorem 3 if and only if $M_{l,C}^{-1} N_{l,K1}$ equals $(Y_r - Q_y N_r)^{-1}(X_r + Q_y M_r)$ for some Q_y in $\mathcal{RH}_\infty$ such that $|Y_r - Q_y N_r| \neq 0$. Moreover, R is independent of N_{l,K_1}. This leads at once to (18).
Following with figure 3c, let us assume that we take

$$N_{l,K1} = 1, \quad N_{l,K2} = K_1 X_r, \quad M_{l,C} = 1 + K_1 Y_r \tag{19}$$

where $K_1 \in \mathcal{RH}_\infty$. Then the two-parameter compensator can be redrawn as shown in figure 4a. For reasons that will become clear later on, this particular two-parameter compensator is referred to as the Observer-Controller scheme.

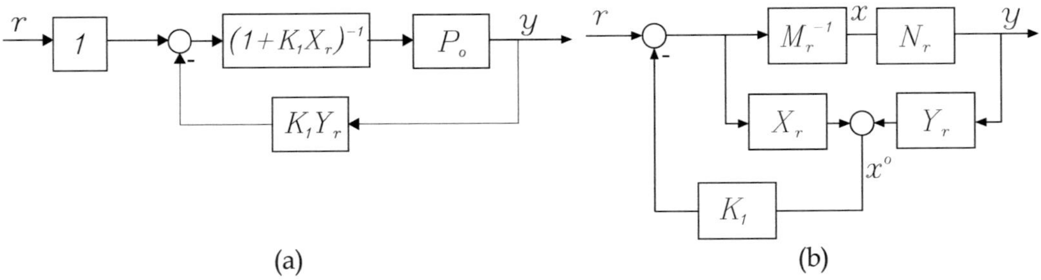

Fig. 4. (a) Observer-Controller in two blocks form. (b) Observer-Controller in three blocks form where $P_o = N_r M_r^{-1}$ is a RCF.

Applying theorem 3 for the particular case at hand the stability condition for the system of figure 4a reduces to

$$R^{-1} = (1 + K_1 X_r) M_r + K_1 Y_r N_r = M_r + K_1 \in \mathcal{RH}_\infty, \quad R \in \mathcal{RH}_\infty \tag{20}$$

It can be verified that the relation between r and y is given by $N_r R$. In order to T_{yr} being stable, we have to require R to be stable. On the other hand, R^{-1} is given by $M_r + K_1$ which

is stable having chosen K_1 stable. Choosing such an R for our design the stability requirements for the overall system to be internally stable are satisfied.
It is easy to see that figure 4a can be rearranged as in figure 4b, where the plant appears in right-factored form ($P_o = N_r M_r^{-1}$). Now it is straightforward to notice that the relation between x and x_o is given by

$$x^o = (X_r M_r + Y_r N_r)x = x \tag{21}$$

where the Bezout identity applies. This way, the X_r and Y_r blocks can be though of as an observer for the fictitious signal x appearing in the middle of the RCF. So, feeding back the observation of x lets to place the close-loop eigenvalues at prescribed locations since the achieved input to output relations is given by $y = N_r R r$ and the stable poles of both N_r and R are freely assignable. This may remind of a basic result coming from state-space control theory associated with observed state feedback: assuming a minimal realization of the plant, state feedback using observers let you change the dynamics of the plant by moving the closed-loop poles of the resulting control system to desired positions in the left half plane. Let us assume the following situation for the figure 4b

$$P = \frac{b}{a},\ M_r = \frac{a}{p_K},\ N_r = \frac{b}{p_K},\ X_r = \frac{n_x}{p_L},\ Y_r = \frac{n_y}{p_L} \tag{22}$$

Now let us take K_1 to be of the form

$$K_1 = \frac{m}{p_K} \tag{23}$$

being m an arbitrary polynomial in s of degree n-1. With p_K and p_L we refer here to monic polynomials in s having as roots the entries of the vectors in (11) and (12), respectively .The dependence of s has been dropped to simplify the notation. By choosing this stable K_1 the relation between the input r and the output y remains as follows

$$T_{yr} = \frac{b}{a+m} \tag{24}$$

So we have achieved a reallocation of the closed-loop poles leaving the zeros of the plant unaltered, as it happens in the context of state-space theory when one makes use of observed state feedback.
What follows is intended to fully understand the relationship between the scheme of figure 4 and conventional state-feedback controllers. For this purpose, we will remind here results

appearing in (Kailath, 1980), among others. Let us assume that the system input-output relation is given in the form

$$y = \frac{b}{a} u \tag{25}$$

One can now replace equation (25) by the following two

$$x_p = \frac{1}{a} u \quad , \quad y = b x_p \tag{26}$$

And choose the following state variables for describing the system in the state space

$$\begin{aligned} x_p &= x_1 \\ \dot{x}_p &= x_2 = \dot{x}_1 \\ &\vdots \\ x_p^{(n-1)} &= x_n = \dot{x}_{n-1} \end{aligned} \tag{27}$$

This leads to the well-known canonical controllable form realization

$$\begin{aligned} \begin{bmatrix} \dot{x}_p \\ \ddot{x}_p \\ \vdots \\ x_p^{(n-1)} \\ x_p^{(n)} \end{bmatrix} &= \begin{bmatrix} 0 & 1 & 0 & \cdots & 0 \\ 0 & 0 & 1 & \cdots & 0 \\ \vdots & \vdots & \vdots & \ddots & \vdots \\ 0 & 0 & 0 & \cdots & 1 \\ -a_0 & -a_1 & -a_2 & \cdots & -a_{n-1} \end{bmatrix} \begin{bmatrix} x_p \\ \dot{x}_p \\ \vdots \\ x_p^{(n-2)} \\ x_p^{(n-1)} \end{bmatrix} + \begin{bmatrix} 0 \\ 0 \\ \vdots \\ 0 \\ 1 \end{bmatrix} u \\ y &= \begin{bmatrix} b_0 - a_0 & b_1 - a_1 & \cdots & b_{n-1} - a_{n-1} \end{bmatrix} \begin{bmatrix} x_p \\ \dot{x}_p \\ \vdots \\ x_p^{(n-1)} \end{bmatrix} + u \end{aligned} \tag{28}$$

The corresponding realization is shown in figure 5a.

The point is that the fictitious signal x_p can be used to determine the complete state (in the controllable canonical form realization) of the system by just deriving it n-1 times. Now suppose that z and w are polynomials such that

$$za + wb = 1 \tag{29}$$

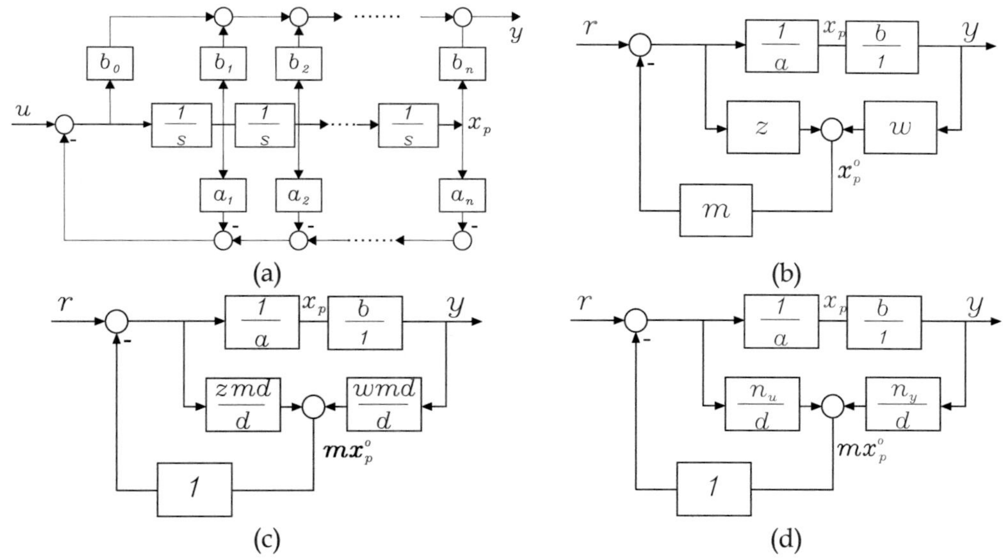

Fig. 5. (a) Controllable canonical form realization of $\frac{b}{a}$. (b) Unfeasible observed-based state-feedback scheme. (c) Towards a feasible observer-controller: part I. (d) Part II.

In figure 5b we can see a way of thinking of a state-feedback controller. Through z and w we observe x_p and by multiplying it by m we achieve an arbitrary linear combination of x_p and its derivatives, that is, a state feedback control law. Obviously, the scheme as such can not be implemented. But it is easy to make it realizable by introducing a nth-order polynomial (the so-called observer polynomial indeed) as in figure 5c, then zmd and wmd can be made of degree equal or less than n - see (Kailath, 1980) - without altering the state feedback gain, leading to n_y and n_u in figure 5d. So figure 5 summarises a procedure entirely based on the transfer function domain (but though at the level of polynomials) to implement a state-feedback control law. However, the scheme in figure 5d is not exactly the one we will work with.

By introducing another nth-degree stable polynomial (a_0) figure 5c can be redrawn as in figure 6a.

By doing this we are considering that our plant is the series connection of two systems, that is $P = P_1 P_2$, where $P_1 = \frac{a_0}{a}$, $P_2 = \frac{b}{a_0}$. So we are considering on purpose a non-minimal realization of the plant. The series connection system is not completely controllable but completely observable. Let denote by A, B, C, D the corresponding realization matrices of P in terms of the realization matrices of $P_1(A_1, B_1, C_1, D_1)$ and $P_2(A_2, B_2, C_2, D_2)$ in controllable canonical form. Then we arrive at the non-minimal realization

$$P \doteq \left[\begin{array}{c|c} A & B \\ \hline C & D \end{array}\right] = \left[\begin{array}{cc|c} A_1 & 0 & B_1 \\ B_2 C_1 & A_2 & B_2 D_1 \\ \hline D_2 C_1 & C_2 & D_2 D_1 \end{array}\right] \tag{30}$$

where the state vector for P is of the form $x = \begin{bmatrix} x_1 & x_2 \end{bmatrix}^T$, being x_1 and x_2 the state vectors of P_1 and P_2, respectively, in controllable canonical form. In more detail, the state matrix A of P is given by

$$A = \left[\begin{array}{ccccc|ccccc} 0 & 1 & 0 & \cdots & 0 & 0 & 0 & 0 & \cdots & 0 \\ 0 & 0 & 1 & \cdots & 0 & 0 & 0 & 0 & \cdots & 0 \\ \vdots & \vdots & \vdots & \ddots & 0 & \vdots & \vdots & 0 & \ddots & \vdots \\ 0 & 0 & 0 & \cdots & 1 & 0 & 0 & 0 & \cdots & 0 \\ -a_0 & -a_1 & -a_2 & \cdots & -a_{n-1} & 0 & 0 & 0 & \cdots & 0 \\ \hline 0 & 0 & 0 & \cdots & 0 & 0 & 1 & 0 & \cdots & 0 \\ 0 & 0 & 0 & \cdots & 0 & 0 & 0 & 1 & \cdots & 0 \\ \vdots & \vdots & \vdots & \ddots & \vdots & \vdots & \vdots & \vdots & \ddots & 0 \\ 0 & 0 & 0 & \cdots & 0 & 0 & 0 & 0 & \cdots & 1 \\ p_{K_0} - a_0 & p_{K_1} - a_1 & p_{K_2} - a_2 & \cdots & p_{K_{n-1}} - a_{n-1} & -p_{K0} & -p_{K1} & -p_{K_2} & \cdots & -p_{K_{n-1}} \end{array}\right] \tag{31}$$

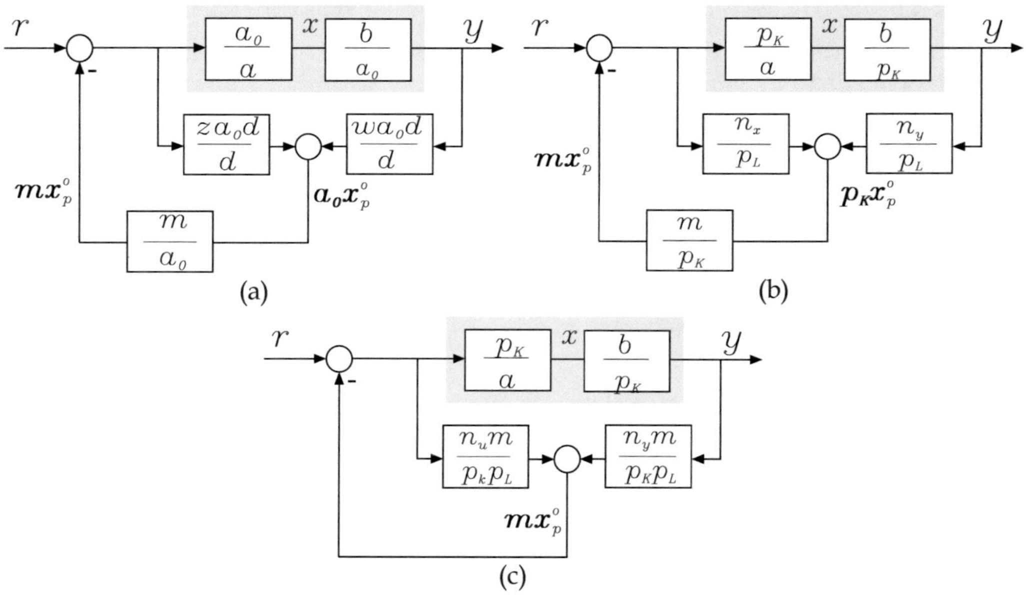

Fig. 6. (a) Non-realizable Observer-Controller configuration. (b) Realizable Observer-Controller configuration. (c) Realizable observer-controller put in the form of a standard observed state feedback (i.e., figure 5d).

Now it is straightforward to see that

$$A' = \left[\begin{array}{c|c} A_1 & 0 \\ \hline 0 & A_2 \end{array}\right] = TAT^{-1} \tag{32}$$

where

$$T = \begin{bmatrix} I_{nxn} & 0_{nxn} \\ -I_{nxn} & I_{nxn} \end{bmatrix}, \quad T^{-1} = \begin{bmatrix} I_{nxn} & 0_{nxn} \\ I_{nxn} & I_{nxn} \end{bmatrix} \tag{33}$$

By using this similarity state transformation the new realization matrices are given by

$$A' = \begin{bmatrix} A_1 & 0_{nxn} \\ 0_{nxn} & A_2 \end{bmatrix}, B' = \begin{bmatrix} 0 \\ \vdots \\ 0 \\ 1 \\ \hline 0_{nx1} \end{bmatrix}, C' = \begin{bmatrix} c_1 \\ \vdots \\ c_n \\ \hline \vdots \\ c_{2n} \end{bmatrix}^T, D' = D \tag{34}$$

where $c_i \neq 0 \ \forall i = 1...2n$.From (34) it is evident that the controllable states are the n first states, which are obtainable through x_p and its n-1 succesive derivatives. Besides, it is easy to see that the similarity transformation employed does not alter the first n state components. The approach taken in this work consists of observing the $2n$ states of the non-minimal realization (34) and consider just the n first states corresponding to the controllable part (this partial vector state of dimension n is equal to the state of $\frac{b(s)}{a(s)}$ in controllable canonical form) for state feedback. By doing this, see figure 6b, we are introducing n extra degrees of freedom (the n roots of the Hurwitz polynomial p_K) into the design. In figures 6b and 6c we have returned to the terminology of section 2.1 when we introduced the coprime factorizations over $\mathcal{RH}_\infty$, with respect to figure 6a the following identities hold: $p_K = a_0$, $p_L = d$. The term *Observer-Controller* is used in this work to make reference to an observed-based state feedback control system designed following this approach. The method presented in section 4 uses the extra freedom which arises from using a non-minimal order observer (see figure 6c, where the observer polynomial $p_K p_L$ has degree $2n$, being n the order of the plant) for trying to meet more demanding objecties.

3. $\mathcal{H}_\infty$-norm optimization based robust control systems design

In this section we review the general method of formulating control problems introduced by (Doyle, 1983). Within this framework, we recall the general method for representing uncertainty for multivariable systems and determine the condition for robust stability in the presence of unstructured additive uncertainty. The presentation is fairly standard, we refer the reader to (Skogestad S., 1997) for a more detailed treatment.

3.1 General control problem formulation

Within the general control configuration (Doyle, 1983) of figure 9, G is referred to as the generalized plant and K is the generalized controller. Four types of external variables are dealt with: exogenous inputs, w, i.e., commands, disturbances and noise; exogenous outputs, z, e.g., error signals to be minimized; controller inputs, v, e.g., commands, measured plant outputs, measured disturbances; and control signals, u.

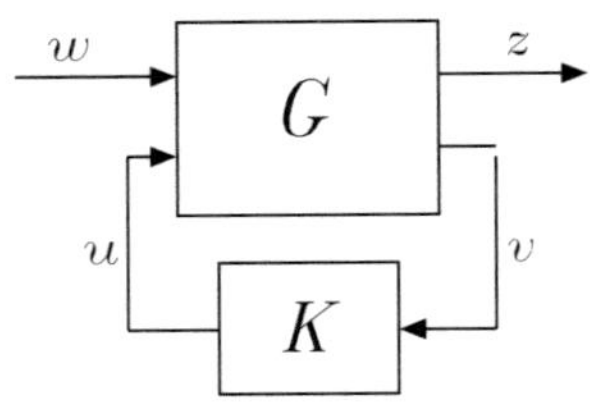

Fig. 7. Generalized plant and controller.

The controller design problem is divided into the analysis and the synthesis phases. The controller K is synthesized such that some measure, mathematically a norm, of the transfer function from w to z is minimized, e.g. the $\mathcal{H}_\infty$ norm.

Definition 3 ($\mathcal{H}_\infty$-norm) The $\mathcal{H}_\infty$-norm of a proper stable system P is given by

$$\|P(s)\|_\infty \doteq \sup_{\omega} \bar{\sigma}\left(P(j\omega)\right) \tag{35}$$

where $\bar{\sigma}(P)$ denotes de largest singular value of the matrix P.

In words, the $\mathcal{H}_\infty$-norm of a dynamic system is the maximum amplification the system can make to the energy of the input signal in any direction. In the SISO case it is equal to the maximum value of the system's frequency response magnitude (the magnitude peak in the Bode diagram). For the general MIMO case it is equal to the system's largest singular value over all the frequencies. From this point on with every mention to a norm we would implicitly be considering the above defined $\mathcal{H}_\infty$ norm, and no further remarks will be made.

The controller design amounts to find a K that minimizes the closed-loop norm from w to z in figure 7. For the analysis phase the designer has to make the actual system meet the form of a generalized control problem according to figure 7. Standard software packages exist that solve numerically the synthesis problem once the problem has been put in the generalized form. In order to get meaningful controller synthesis problems, frequency weights on the exogenous inputs w and outputs z are incorporated to perform the corresponding optimizations over specific frequency ranges.

Once the stabilizing controller K is synthesized, it rests to analyse the closed-loop performance that it provides. In this phase, the controller for the configuration in figure 9 is incorporated into the generalized plant G to form the system $\mathcal{N}$, as shown in figure 11

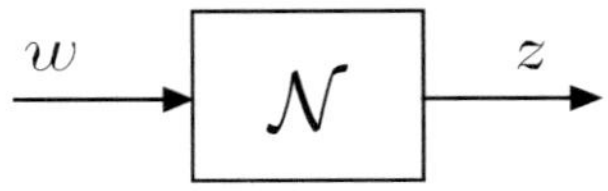

Fig. 8. Relation between w and z in the generalized control problem.

It is relatively straightforward to show that the expression for $\mathcal{N}$ is given by

$$\mathcal{N} = G_{11} + G_{12}K(1 - G_{22}K)^{-1}G_{21} \doteq \mathcal{F}_l(G, K) \tag{36}$$

where $\mathcal{F}_l$ denotes the lower Linear Fractional Transformation (LFT) of G and K. In order to obtain a good design for K, a precise knowledge of the plant is required. The dynamics of interest are modeled but this model may be inaccurate (this is usually the case indeed). To deal with this problem the real plant P is assumed to be unknown but belonging to a class of models built around a nominal model P_o. This set of models is characterized by a matrix Δ, which can be either a full matrix (unstructured uncertainty) or a block diagonal matrix (structured uncertainty), that includes all possible perturbations representing uncertainty to the system. Weighting matrices W_1 and W_2 are usually employed to express the uncertainty in terms of normalized perturbations in such a way that $\|\Delta\|_\infty \leq 1$. The general control configuration in figure 9 may be extended to include model uncertainty as it is shown in figure 9

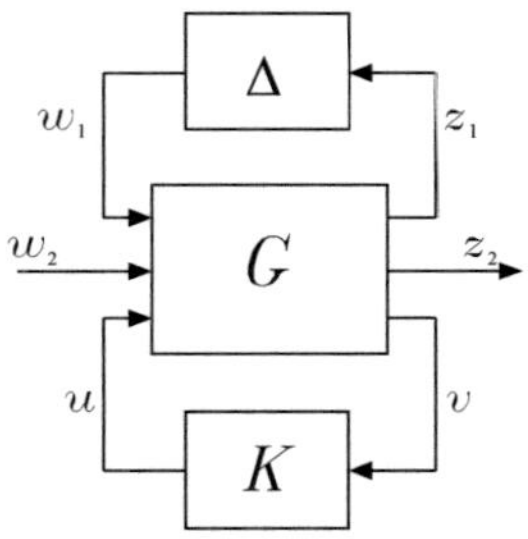

Fig. 9. Generalized control problem configuration.

The block diagram in figure 9 is used to synthesize a controller K. To transform it for analysis, the lower loop around G is closed by the controller K and it is incorporated into the generalized plant G to form the system $\mathcal{N}$ as it is shown in figure 10. The same lower LFT is obtained as if no uncertainty was considered.

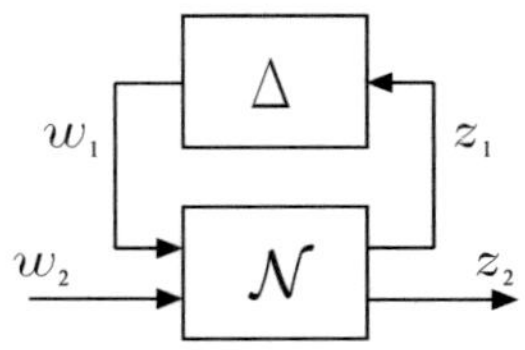

Fig. 10. Generalized block diagram for analysis in the face of uncertainty.

To evaluate the relation from $w = \begin{bmatrix} w_1 & w_2 \end{bmatrix}^T$ to $z = [z_1 \quad z_2]^T$ for a given controller K in the uncertain system, the upper loop around $\mathcal{N}$ is closed with the perturbation matrix Δ. This results in the following upper LFT:

$$\mathcal{F}_u(\mathcal{N}, \Delta) \doteq \mathcal{N}_{22} + \mathcal{N}_{21}\Delta(1 - \mathcal{N}_{11}\Delta)^{-1}\mathcal{N}_{12} \tag{37}$$

and so $z = \mathcal{F}_u(\mathcal{N}, \Delta)w$. To represent any control problem with uncertainty by the general control configuration it is necessary to represent each source of uncertainty by a single perturbation block Δ, normalized such that $\|\Delta\|_\infty \le 1$. We will assume in this work that we can collect all the sources of uncertainties into a single full (unstructured) matrix Δ.

3.2 Uncertainty and robustness

As already commented, an exact knowledge of the plant is never possible. Therefore, it is often assumed that the real plant, denoted by P, is unknown but belonging to a set of class models characterized somehow by Δ and with centre P_o.

Definition 4 (Nominal Stability) The closed-loop system of figure 9 has Nominal Stability (NS) if the controller K internally stabilizes the nominal model P_o ($\Delta = 0$), i.e., the four transfer matrices $\mathcal{N}_{11}, \mathcal{N}_{12}, \mathcal{N}_{21}, \mathcal{N}_{22}$ in the closed-loop transfer matrix $\mathcal{N}$ shown in figure 13 are stable.

Definition 5 (Nominal Performance) The closed-loop system of figure 12 has Nominal Performance (NP) if the performance objectives are satisfied for the nominal model P_o, i.e., $\|\mathcal{N}_{22}\|_\infty < 1$ in figure 10 assuming $\Delta = 0$.

Definition 6 (Robust Stability) The closed-loop system has Robust Stability (RS) if the controller K internally stabilizes the closed-loop system in figure 9 ($\mathcal{F}_u(\mathcal{N}, \Delta)$) for every Δ such that $\|\Delta\|_\infty \le 1$.

We will just consider in this work additive uncertainty, which mathematically is expressed as

$$\mathcal{P}_A = \{P : P = P_o + W_1\Delta\} \tag{38}$$

Being w_A a scalar frequency weight and $\|\Delta\|_\infty \le 1$. Now that we know how to describe the set of plants which our real plant is supposed to lie in the next issue is to answer the question of when a controller stabilizes all the plants belonging to this set.

Theorem 5 (Robust Stability for unstructured uncertainty) Let us assume that we have posed our system in the form illustrated by figure 9. The overall system is robustly stable (see definition 6) iff

$$\|\mathcal{N}_{11}\|_\infty \le 1 \tag{39}$$

where N has been defined in (36), see figure 10.

Robust stability conditions for the different uncertainty representations can be derived by posing the corresponding feedback loops as in figure 9 and then applying theorem 5, also known as the small gain theorem. See (Morari and Zafirou, 1989) for details.

4. The design for the proposed robust 2-DOF Observer-Controller

In this section a methodology for designing 2-DOF controllers is provided. The design is based on the Observer-Controller configuration described in section 2.2. In order to have a 2-DOF scheme a prefilter block (K_2) has been added, leading to the general scheme shown in figure 11

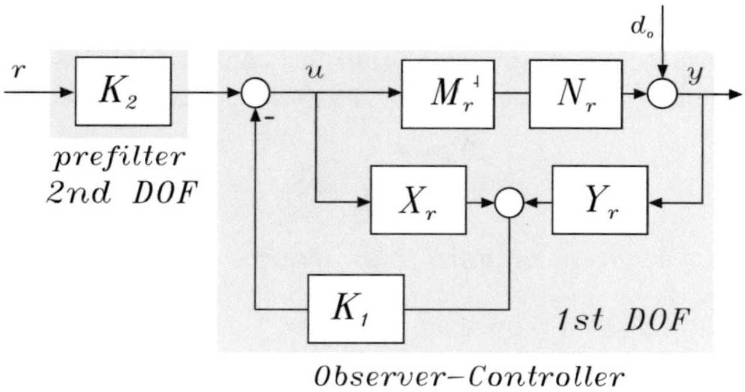

Fig. 11. The proposed 2-DOF control configuration.

The controller blocks X_r, Y_r, K_1 which implicitly fix the Youla parameter Q_y of theorem 5 will be in charge of providing robust stability and good output disturbance rejection. On the other hand, the prefilter K_2 (the Youla parameter Q_r of theorem 5) has to cope with the tracking properties of the system by solving a model matching problem with respect to a specified reference model which describes the desired closed-loop behaviour for the resulting controlled system.

4.1 Step I: Design of the Observer-Controller part through direct search optimization

In section 2.2 we characterized the Observer-Controller configuration in terms of the polynomials p_K, p_L and m. Let us assume without loss of generality that additive output uncertainty (38) is considered. In this first step of the design the objective will be to find convenient p_K, p_L, m, defining entirely X_r, Y_r, K_1 in figure 12. This search will be performed in order to provide robust stability with the best possible output disturbance rejection.

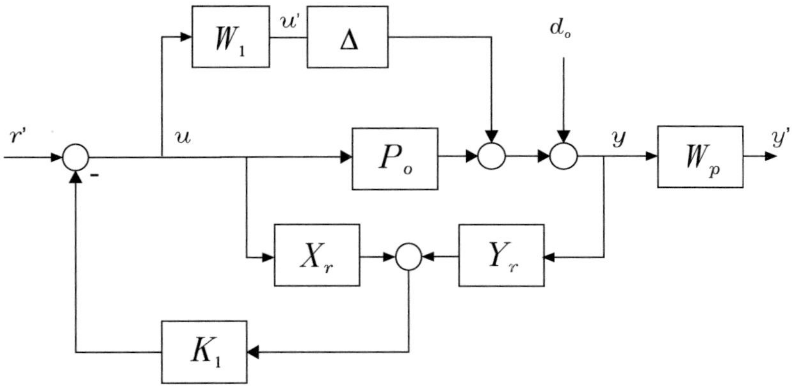

Fig. 12. Observer-Controller part with additive uncertainty.

More specifically, for the scheme in figure 12 the following relations hold

$$\begin{bmatrix} u \\ y' \end{bmatrix} = \begin{bmatrix} M_r\left(1-RM_r\right)Y_r & M_r R \\ W_p\left(1-N_r\left(1-RM_r\right)Y\right)_r & N_r R \end{bmatrix} \begin{bmatrix} d_o \\ r' \end{bmatrix} \tag{40}$$

where all the terms have been defined in section 2.2. It can be proved by applying theorem 5 to figure 12 (once put in the generalized controller configuration of figure 9) that robust stability of the system in figure 12 amounts to satisfy the following inequality

$$\left\| T_{u'd_o} \right\|_\infty \leq 1 \tag{41}$$

The design for the Observer-Controller part reduces finally to solving the following optimization problem

$$\begin{aligned} \min_{p_K, p_L, m} \quad & \left\| W_p \left(1 - N_r \left(1 - RM_r\right) Y_r\right) \right\|_\infty \\ \textit{subject to} \quad & \left\| W_1 \left(M_r \left(1 - RM_r\right) Y_r\right) \right\|_\infty \leq 1 \end{aligned} \tag{42}$$

Direct search techniques - see (Powell, M., 1998) - are suggested for solving the problem (42). Basically they consist of a method for solving optimization problems that does not require any information about the gradient of the objective function. Unlike more traditional optimization methods that use information about the gradient or higher derivatives to search for an optimal point, a direct search algorithm searches a set of points around the current point, looking for one where the value of the objective function is lower than the value at the current point. At each step, the algorithm searches a set of points, called a mesh, around the current point—the point computed at the previous step of the algorithm. The mesh is formed by adding the current point to a scalar multiple of a set of vectors called a pattern. If the pattern search algorithm finds a point in the mesh that improves the objective function at the current point, the new point becomes the current point at the next step of the algorithm. In (Henrion, D., 2006) a recent application of direct search techniques for solving a specific control problem can be consulted.

4.2 Step II: Design of the prefilter controller K_2

In this section we tackle the second step of our design. This step is aimed at designing a prefilter controller for meeting tracking specifications given in terms of a reference model. In order to achieve this goal a model matching problem is posed as in figure 13

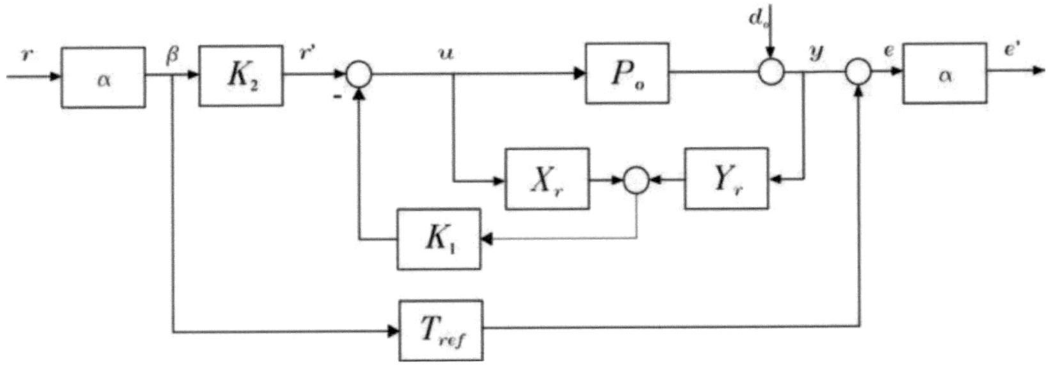

Fig. 13. Model-matching problem arrangement for the design of K_2.

where T_{ref} is the specified reference model for the closed-loop dynamics. The idea is to make use of the general control framework introduced in section 3 and design K_2 so as to minimize the relation from r to e in an $\mathcal{H}_\infty$ sense. In doing so, we also want to have certain control over the amount of control effort employed to make the close loop resemble the model reference. The parameter α will precisely play the role of enabling one to arrive at a compromise between the tracking quality and the amount of energy demanded by the controller, accommodating into the design this practical consideration.

Note that in the nominal case, i.e., $P = P_o$, the prefilter controller K_2 sees just $N_r R$. Therefore, the relation from the reference to the output reads as

$$y = N_r R K_2 r \tag{43}$$

It should be noted that the N_r and R have already been fixed as a result of applying the first step of the design. To include different and independent dynamics for the step response, we have to take advantage of the second degree of freedom that K_2 provides. From the overall scheme in figure 11 we can compute the transfer matrix function that relates the inputs $\begin{bmatrix} d_o & r \end{bmatrix}^T$, i.e., the disturbance d_o and the command signal r, with the outputs $\begin{bmatrix} u' & e \end{bmatrix}^T$, i.e., the weighted control signal u' and the weighted model matching error e.

$$\begin{bmatrix} u' \\ e \end{bmatrix} = \begin{bmatrix} -W_1\left(1 - M_r(X_r + RN_rY_r)\right) & \alpha W_1 M_r \left(1 - RM_r\right) Y_r K_2 \\ N_r\left(X + RN_rY_r\right) & \alpha^2\left(N_r R K_2 - T_{ref}\right) \end{bmatrix} \begin{bmatrix} d_o \\ r \end{bmatrix} \tag{44}$$

The $\mathcal{H}_\infty$-norm of the complete transfer matrix function (44) is minimized to find K_2 without modifying neither the robust stability margins nor the disturbance rejection properties provided by the Observer Controller in the first step of the design. The 2-DOF design problem shown in figure 13 can be easily cast into the general control configuration seen in section 3. Comparing figures 12 and 13 with figure 9 we make the following pairings $w_1 = d_o$, $w_2 = r$, $z_1 = u'$, $z_2 = e'$, $v = \beta$, $u = u$ and $K = K_2$. The augmented plant G and the controller K_2 are related by the following lower LFT:

$$\mathcal{F}_l(G, K_2) \doteq G_{11} + G_{12}K_2(1 - G_{22}K_2)^{-1}G_{21} \tag{45}$$

The corresponding partitioned generalized plant G is:

$$\begin{bmatrix} u' \\ e' \\ \hline \beta \end{bmatrix} = \left[\begin{array}{c|c} G_{11} & G_{12} \\ \hline G_{21} & G_{22} \end{array}\right] \begin{bmatrix} d_o \\ r \\ \hline r' \end{bmatrix}$$
$$= \left[\begin{array}{cc|c} -W_1\left(1 - M_r(X_r + RN_rY_r)\right) & 0 & W_1 M_r R \\ N_r\left(X_r + RN_rY_r\right) & -\alpha^2 T_{ref} & \alpha N_r R \\ \hline 0 & \alpha & 0 \end{array}\right] \begin{bmatrix} d_o \\ r \\ \hline r' \end{bmatrix} \tag{46}$$

Remark. The reference signal r must be scaled by a constant W_r to make the closed-loop transfer function from r to the controlled output y match the desired reference model T_{ref} exactly at steady-state. This is not guaranteed by the optimization which is aimed at minimizing the $\mathcal{H}_\infty$-norm of the error. The required scaling is given by

$$W_r \doteq \left(K_2(0)N_r(0)R(0)\right)^{-1} T_{ref}(0) \tag{47}$$

Therefore, the resulting reference controller is K_2W_r.

5. Illustrative example

In this section we apply the methodology presented in section 4 for designing a 2-DOF controller according to figure 11 for the following nominal plant

$$P_o = \frac{5(s+1.3)}{(s+1)(s+2)} \tag{48}$$

The uncertainty in the model is parameterised using an additive uncertainty description as in (38) with

$$W_1 = \frac{3(s+1)}{(s+20)} \tag{49}$$

Now we initialize the optimization problem (42) with the values $p_{Ko} = \begin{bmatrix}-10 & -10\end{bmatrix}^T, p_{Lo} = \begin{bmatrix}-20 & -20\end{bmatrix}^T, m_o = \begin{bmatrix}1 & 2\end{bmatrix}^T$, where p_{K0} (p_{L0}) contains the initial roots of the polynomials p_K (p_L) and m_o the initial coefficients for the polynomial m.
For this example we have used a non-constrained direct search optimization solver and we have defined as the objective function the same that appears in the problem (42) plus a penalty that acts when the robust stability restriction is not satisfied. In order to have nearly perfect output disturbance rejection in steady state the following weight for the T_{yd_o} relation has been used

$$W_p = \frac{1}{s+0.01} \tag{50}$$

this forces the direct search algorithm to provide small values for the T_{yd_o} magnitude response at dc. The optimization procedure results finally in the following *optimal* controller blocks for the feedback part of the design

$$X_r = \frac{s^2+57.19s-112500}{s^2+35.67s+245}, \quad Y_r = \frac{2.2710s+40190}{s^2+35.67s+245}, \quad K_1 = \frac{0.05355s+0.323}{s^2+24.53s+148.2} \tag{51}$$

or in terms of p_K, p_L, m:

$$p_K = [-10.7774 \quad -13.7519]^T, p_L = [-9.2857 \quad -26.3793]^T, m = [0.0535 \quad 0.3230]^T \qquad (52)$$

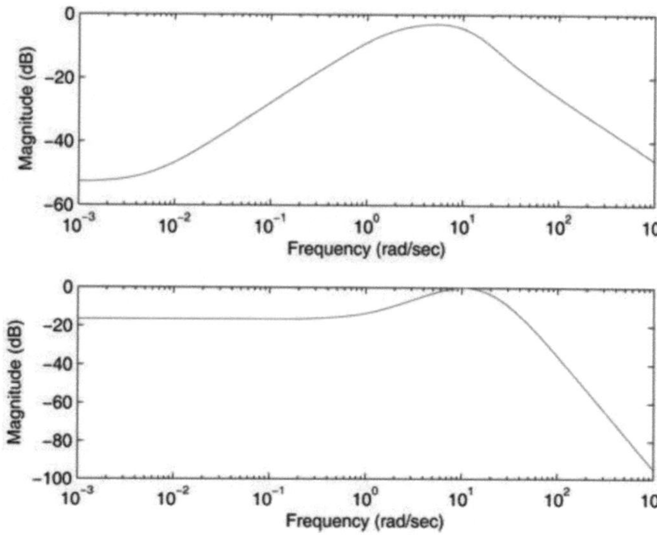

Fig. 14. Top: magnitude response of T_{yd_o}. Bottom: magnitude response of $W_1 T_{ud_o}$ satisfying the robust stability condition.

In figure 14 the finally resulting T_{yd_o} (output disturbance rejection) and $W_1 T_{ud_o}$ magnitude responses are shown, providing the former specially good disturbance rejection at steady state and being the $\mathcal{H}_\infty$-norm of the latter less than one and thus ensuring the robust stability specification.

So far we have obtained the final design for the Observer-Controller part ensuring robust stability and the best achievable output disturbance rejection in a $\mathcal{H}_\infty$ sense. We turn now to the design of the prefilter controller K_2.

Let us assume that we are given the desired closed-loop dynamics in terms of the following reference model

$$T_{ref} = \frac{49}{(s+7)^2} \qquad (53)$$

Such reference model (53) provides second order responses with time constant 1/7 seconds. The second step of the design explained in section 4 results in the prefilter block

$$K_2 = \frac{-0.006051s^3 + 11.65s^2 + 106.8s + 181.7}{s^3 + 28.65s^2 + 184.8s + 508.3} \qquad (54)$$

This prefilter block has been achieved using α =6, see figure 17.
In figure 15 it is shown that the value α =6 provides a tight model matching with the minimum possible control action. Larger values of the α parameter do not improve significantly the model matching and cause the control action to acquire higher values.

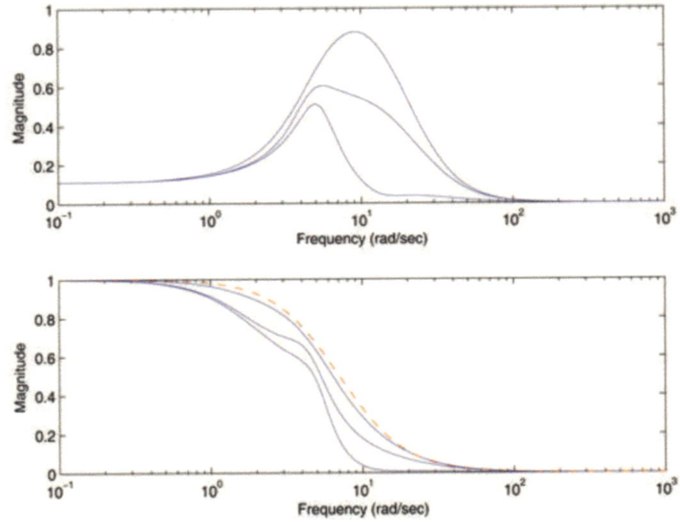

Fig. 15. From bottom to top (in solid), magnitude responses of T_{ur} (top figure) and T_{yr} (bottom figure) for α =1,3,6. In dashed it is shown the response of the target model T_{ref} .

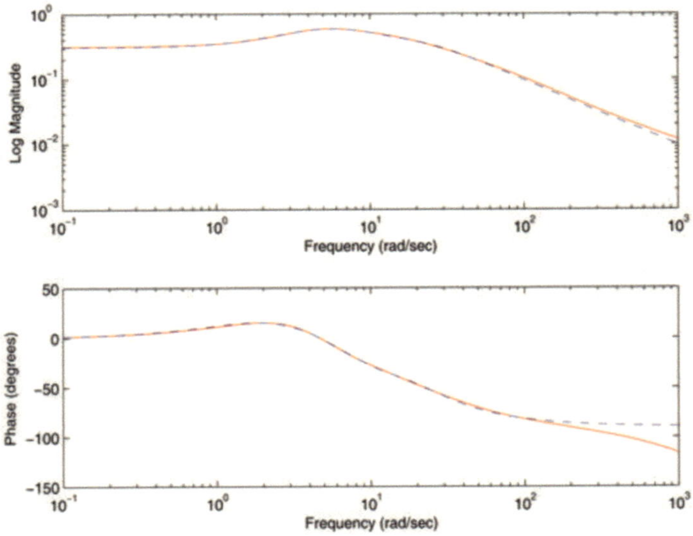

Fig. 16. Bode diagram for the original 11th order prefilter K_2 (dashed) and the 3rd order prefilter K_2 (solid) finally obtained by applying order reduction techniques.

The use of the $\mathcal{H}_\infty$ optimization techniques traditionally results in very high order controllers. In this case, the resulting K_2 is of order eleven. However, standard order

reduction techniques can be applied in order to reduce these orders. For this example, a model reduction based on a balanced realization and the hankel singular values - see (Skogestad S., 1997) - has been performed yielding finally a third order K_2 without sacrificing any significant performance, see figure 16.
To summarize the carried out design, in figure 17 we show the closed-loop final response to a step command set-point change applied at t=0 seconds and a step output disturbance applied at t=3 seconds.

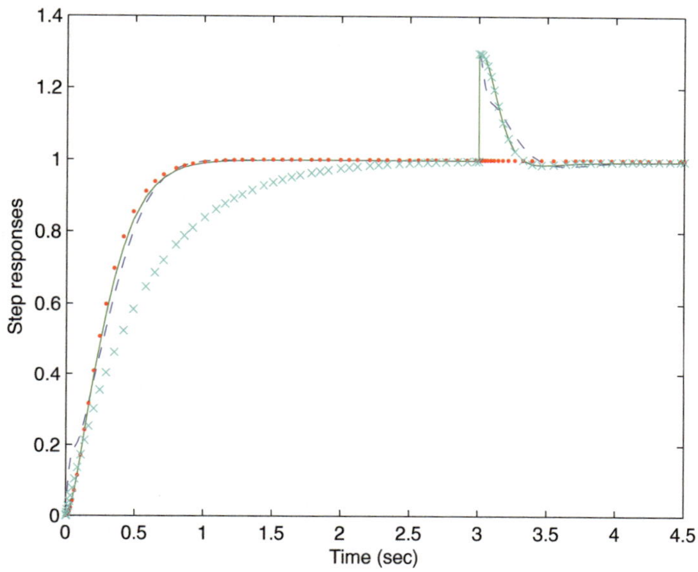

Fig. 17. Time response of the reference model T_{ref} (dotted), nominal controlled system (solid) and uncertain ($\Delta = 0.25$ in (38)) controlled system (dashed). It is also shown the response of the nominal controlled system without making use of the prefilter controller (x-marked).

6. Conclusion

A new 2-DOF control configuration based on a right coprime factorization of the model of the plant has been presented. The approach has been introduced as an alternative to the commonly encountered strategy of setting the two controllers arbitrarily, with internal stability the only restriction, and parameterizing the controller in terms of the Youla parameters.
An non-minimal-observer-based state feedback control scheme has been designed first to guarantee some levels of robust stability and output disturbance rejection by solving a constrained $\mathcal{H}_\infty$ optimization problem for the poles of the right coprime factors X_r, Y_r, N_r, M_r and the polynomial m. After that, a prefilter controller to adapt the reference command and improve the tracking properties has been designed using the generalized control framework introduced in section 3.

7. References

Vidyasagar, M. (1985). *Control System Synthesis. A factorization approach.,* MIT Press. Cambridge, Massachusetts.

Youla, D. C. & Bongiorno, J. J. (1985). A feedback theory of two-degree-of-freedom optimal wiener-hopf design. *IEEE Trans. Automat. Contr.,* 30, 652-665.

Vilanova, R. & Serra, I. (1997). Realization of two-degree-of-freedom compensators, *IEE Proceedings. Part D.* 144(6), 589-596.

Astrom, K.J. & Wittenmark, B. (1984). *Computer Controlled Systems: Theory and Design.,* Prentice-Hall.

Safonov, M.G. ; Laub, A.J. & Hartmann, G.L. (1981). Feedback properties of multivariable systems: The role and use of the return difference matrix. *IEEE Trans. Automat. Contr.,* 26(2), 47-65.

Skogestad, S. & Postlethwaite, I. (1997). *Multivariable Feedback Control.* Wiley.

Grimble, M.J. (1988). Two degrees of freedom feedback and feedforward optimal control multivariable stochastic systems. *Automatica,* 24(6), 809-817.

Limebeer, D.J.N. ; Kasenally, E.M. & Perkins, J.D. (1993). On the design of robust two degree of freedom controllers. *Automatica,* 29(1), 157-168.

McFarlane, D.C. & Glover, K. (1992). A loop shaping design procedure using $\mathcal{H}_\infty$ synthesis. *IEEE Trans. Automat. Contr.,* 37(6), 759-769.

Glover, K. & McFarlane, D. (1989). Robust stabilization of normalized coprime factor plant descriptions with $\mathcal{H}_\infty$ bounded uncertainty. *IEEE Trans. Automat. Contr.,* 34(8), 821-830.

Sun, J. ; Olbrot, A.W. & Polis, M.P. (1994). Robust stabilization and robust performance using model reference control and modelling error compensation. *IEEE Trans. Automat. Contr.,* 39(3), 630-634.

Vilanova, R. (1996). *Design of 2-DOF Compensators: Independence of Properties and Design for Robust Tracking,* PhD thesis. Universitat Autònoma de Barcelona. Spain.

Francis, B.A. (1987). *A course in* $\mathcal{H}^\infty$ *Control theory.,* Springer-Verlag. Lecture Notes in Control and Information Sciences.

Kailath, T. (1980). *Linear Systems.,* Prentice-Hall.

Morari, M. & Zafirou, E. (1989). *Robust Process Control.,* Prentice-Hall. International.

Doyle, J.C. (1983). Synthesis of robust controllers and filters, *Proceedings of the IEEE Conference on Decision and Control,* pp. 109-124.

Powell, M. (1998). Direct search algorithms for optimization calculations. *Acta Numerica.,* Cambridge University Press, 1998, pp. 287-336.

Henrion, D. (2006). Solving static output feedback problems by direct search optimization, *Computer-Aided Control Systems Design,* pp. 1534-1537.

Wilfred, W.K. & Daniel, E.D. (2007). Implementation of stabilizing control laws – How many controller blocks are needed for a universally good implementation ? *IEEE Control Systems Magazine,* 27(1), 55-60.

Pedret, C. ; Vilanova, R., Moreno, R. & Serra, I. (2005). A New Architecture for Robust Model Reference Control, *Decision and Control, 2005 and 2005 European Control Conference. CDC-ECC '05. 44th IEEE Conference on,* pp. 7876-7881.

2

Nonlinear Model-Based Control of a Parallel Robot Driven by Pneumatic Muscle Actuators

Harald Aschemann and Dominik Schindele
Chair of Mechatronics, University of Rostock
18059 Rostock,
Germany

1. Introduction

In this contribution, three nonlinear control strategies are presented for a two-degree-of-freedom parallel robot that is actuated by two pairs of pneumatic muscle actuators as depicted in Fig. 1. Pneumatic muscles are innovative tensile actuators consisting of a fibre-reinforced vulcanised rubber hose with appropriate connectors at both ends. The working principle is based on a rhombical fibre structure that leads to a muscle contraction in longitudinal direction when the pneumatic muscle is filled with compressed air. Pneumatic muscles are low cost actuators and offer several further advantages in comparison to classical pneumatic cylinders: significantly less weight, no stick-slip effects, insensitivity to dirty working environment, and a higher force-to-weight ratio. The achievable closed-loop performance using such actuators has already been investigated experimentally at a linear axis with a pair of antagonistically arranged pneumatic muscles (Aschemann & Hofer, 2004). Current research activities concentrate on the use of pneumatic muscles as actuators for parallel robots, which are known for providing high stiffness, and especially for the capability of performing fast and highly accurate motions of the end-effector. The planar parallel robot under consideration is characterised by a closed-chain kinematic structure formed by four moving links and the robot base, which offers two degrees of freedom, see Fig. 1. All joints are revolute joints, two of which - the cranks - are actuated by a pair of pneumatic muscles, respectively. The coordinated contractions of a pair of pneumatic muscles are transformed into a rotation of the according crank by means of a toothed belt and a pulley. The mass flow rate of compressed air is provided by a separate proportional valve for each pneumatic muscle.

The paper is structured as follows: first, a mathematical model of the mechatronic system is derived, which results in a symbolic nonlinear state space description. Second, a cascaded control structure is proposed: the control design for the inner control loops involves a decentralised pressure control for each pneumatic muscle with high bandwidth, whereas the design of the outer control loop deals with decoupling control of the two crank angles and the two mean pressures of both pairs of pneumatic muscles. For the inner control loops nonlinear pressure controls are designed taking advantage of differential flatness. For the outer control loop three alternative approaches have been investigated: flatness-based control, backstepping, and sliding-mode control. Third, to account for nonlinear friction as well as model uncertainties, a nonlinear reduced order disturbance observer is used in a disturbance compensation scheme. Simulation results of the closed-loop system show excellent tracking performance and high steady-state accuracy.

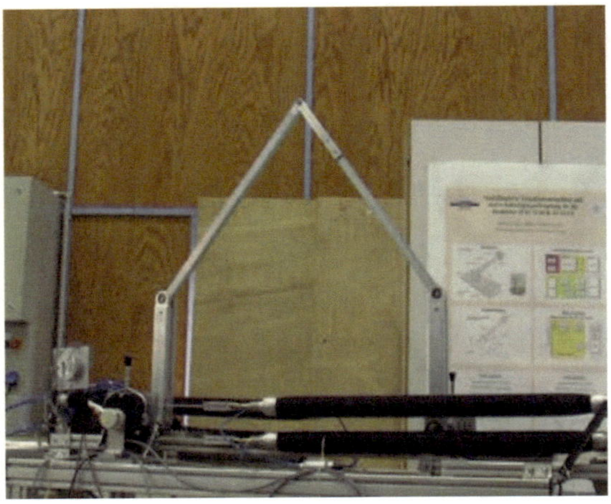

Fig. 1. Test rig.

2. System modelling

The modelling of the pneumatically driven parallel robot involves the mechanical subsystem and the pneumatic subsystem, which are coupled by the torques resulting from the tension forces of a pair of pneumatic muscles, respectively.

2.1 Multibody model of the parallel robot

The control-oriented multibody model of the parallel robot part consists of three rigid bodies (Fig. 2): the two cranks as actuated links with identical properties (mass m_A, reduced mass moment of inertia w.r.t. the actuated axis J_A, centre of gravity distance s_A to the centre of gravity, length of the link l_A, pulley radius r) and the end-effector E (mass m_E), which is modelled as lumped mass.

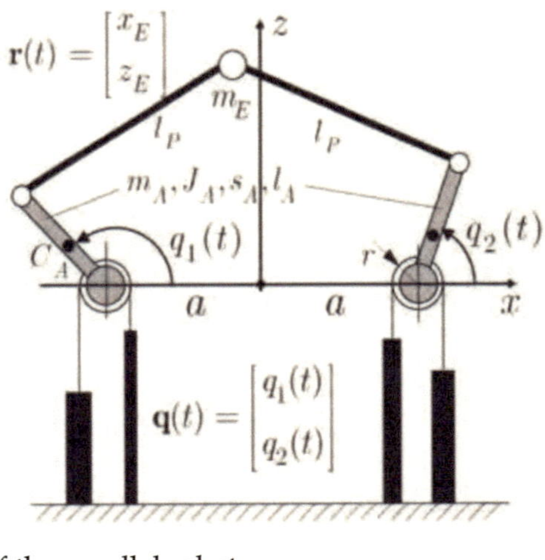

Fig. 2. Multibody model of the parallel robot.

The inertia properties of the remaining two links with length l_P, which are designed as light-weight construction, shall be neglected in comparison to the other links. The inertial xz-coordinate system is chosen in the middle of the straight line that connects both base joints. The motion of the parallel robot is completely described by two generalised coordinates $q_1(t)$ and $q_2(t)$ that denote the two crank angles, which are combined in the vector $\mathbf{q} = [q_1, q_2]^T$. Analogously, the vector of the end-effector coordinates is defined as $\mathbf{r} = [x_E, z_E]^T$.

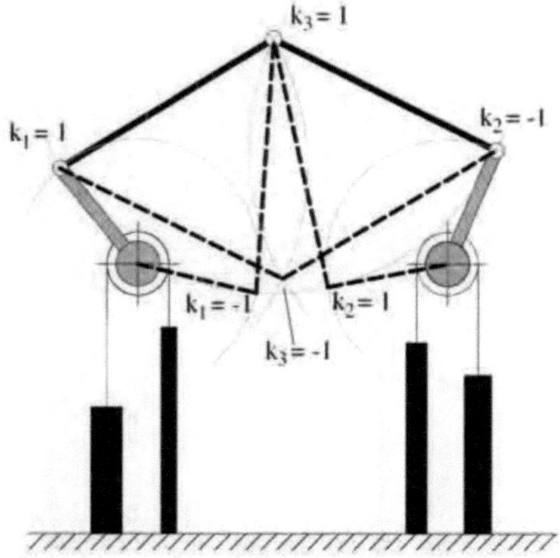

Fig. 3. Ambiguity of the robot kinematics.

The direct kinematics can be stated in symbolic form and describes the vector of end-effector coordinates $\mathbf{r}$ in terms of given crank angles $\mathbf{q}$, i.e.

$$\mathbf{r} = \mathbf{r}(\mathbf{q}, k_3)\,. \tag{1}$$

Here, the configuration parameter k_3 is introduced to cope with two possible configurations, see Fig. 3. The relationship between the corresponding velocities is obtained by differentiation with respect to time

$$\dot{\mathbf{r}} = \mathbf{J}(\mathbf{q}, k_3)\,\dot{\mathbf{q}}, \quad \mathbf{J}(\mathbf{q}, k_3) = \frac{\partial \mathbf{r}(\mathbf{q}, k_3)}{\partial \mathbf{q}^T}, \tag{2}$$

where $\mathbf{J}(\mathbf{q}, k_3)$ denotes the corresponding Jacobian. Here, singularities in the Jacobian can be avoided by model-based trajectory planning. Analogously, the acceleration relationship is given by

$$\ddot{\mathbf{r}} = \mathbf{J}(\mathbf{q}, k_3)\ddot{\mathbf{q}} + \dot{\mathbf{J}}(\mathbf{q}, k_3)\,\dot{\mathbf{q}}\,. \tag{3}$$

For a given end-effector position $\mathbf{r}$ the corresponding crank angles follow from the inverse kinematics

$$\mathbf{q} = \mathbf{q}(\mathbf{r}, k_1, k_2)\,, \tag{4}$$

which can be determined in symbolic form. The given ambiguity is taken into account by introducing two configuration parameters k_1 and k_2 as shown in Fig. 3. The relationships between the corresponding velocities as well as the accelerations follow from direct kinematics

$$\dot{\mathbf{q}} = \mathbf{J}^{-1}(\mathbf{r}, k_3)\,\dot{\mathbf{r}}, \\ \ddot{\mathbf{q}} = \mathbf{J}^{-1}(\mathbf{q}, k_3)\,[\ddot{\mathbf{r}} - \dot{\mathbf{J}}(\mathbf{q}, k_3)\,\dot{\mathbf{q}}]. \tag{5}$$

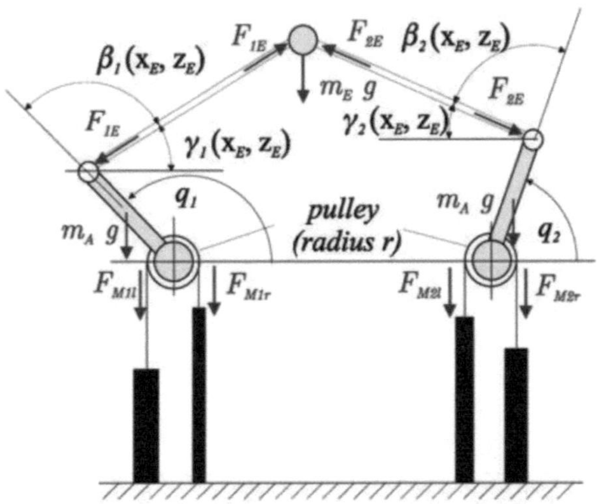

Fig. 4. Free-body diagram of the parallel robot.

The equations of motion for the actuated links can be directly derived from the free-body diagram in Fig. 4 applying the principle of angular momentum

$$J_A \cdot \ddot{q}_1 = \underbrace{r \cdot [F_{M1l} - F_{M1r}]}_{\tau_1} - m_A \cdot g \cdot s_A \cdot \cos q_1 + F_{1E} \cdot l_A \cdot \sin\beta_1 + \eta_1\,, \\ J_A \cdot \ddot{q}_2 = \underbrace{r \cdot [F_{M2l} - F_{M2r}]}_{\tau_2} - m_A \cdot g \cdot s_A \cdot \cos q_2 - F_{2E} \cdot l_A \cdot \sin\beta_2 + \eta_2\,. \tag{6}$$

Here, the driving torque τ_i of drive i depends on the corresponding muscle forces, i.e. $\tau_i = r\,[F_{Mil} - F_{Mir}]$. At this, the indices of all variables describing a particular pneumatic muscle are chosen as follows: the first index $i = \{1, 2\}$ denotes the drive under consideration, described by the generalised coordinate $q_i(t)$, whereas the second index $j = \{l, r\}$ stands for the mounting position, i.e. for the left or the right pneumatic muscle. The disturbance torque η_i accounts for friction effects as well as remaining uncertainties in the muscle force characteristics (13) of drive i, respectively. The coupling forces F_{1E} and F_{2E} are obtained from Newton's second law applied to the end-effector

$$\begin{bmatrix} m_E \cdot \ddot{x}_E \\ m_E \cdot (g + \ddot{z}_E) \end{bmatrix} = \begin{bmatrix} \cos\gamma_1 & -\cos\gamma_2 \\ \sin\gamma_1 & \sin\gamma_2 \end{bmatrix} \begin{bmatrix} F_{1E} \\ F_{2E} \end{bmatrix}. \tag{7}$$

The equations of motion in minimal form for the crank angles can be derived in two steps. First, the last equation has to be solved for the unknown forces

$$\begin{bmatrix} F_{1E} \\ F_{2E} \end{bmatrix} = \begin{bmatrix} \cos\gamma_1 & -\cos\gamma_2 \\ \sin\gamma_1 & \sin\gamma_2 \end{bmatrix}^{-1} \begin{bmatrix} m_E \cdot \ddot{x}_E \\ m_E \cdot (g + \ddot{z}_E) \end{bmatrix}, \tag{8}$$

which then can be eliminated in (6). Second, the substitution of the variables $\gamma_i = \gamma_i(\mathbf{q})$, $\beta_i = \beta_i(\mathbf{q})$, and (3) resulting from direct kinematics leads to the envisaged minimal form of the equations of motion

$$\mathbf{M}(\mathbf{q})\ddot{\mathbf{q}} + \mathbf{k}(\mathbf{q},\dot{\mathbf{q}}) + \mathbf{G}(\mathbf{q}) = \mathbf{Q}(\mathbf{q}), \tag{9}$$

with the mass matrix $\mathbf{M}(\mathbf{q})$, the vector of centrifugal and Coriolis terms $\mathbf{k}(\mathbf{q},\dot{\mathbf{q}})$ and the vector of gravity torques $\mathbf{G}(\mathbf{q})$. The vector of generalised torques $\mathbf{Q}(\mathbf{q})$ contains the corresponding muscle forces times the radius r of the pulley

$$\mathbf{Q}(\mathbf{q}) = r \cdot \begin{bmatrix} F_{M1l} - F_{M1r} \\ F_{M2l} - F_{M2r} \end{bmatrix}. \tag{10}$$

Note that this minimal form of the equations of motions is not compulsory. Instead the corresponding system of differential-algebraic equations can be utilised as well for the flatness-based control design.

2.2 Modelling of the pneumatic subsystem

The parallel robot is equipped with four pneumatic muscle actuators. The contraction lengths of the pneumatic muscles are related to the generalised coordinates, i.e. the crank angles q_i. The position of the crank angle, where the corresponding right pneumatic muscle is fully contracted, is denoted by q_{i0}. Consequently, by considering the transmission consisting of toothed belt and pulley, the following constraints hold for the contraction lengths of the muscles

$$\begin{aligned} \Delta\ell_{Mil}(q_i) &= r \cdot (q_i - q_{i0}), \\ \Delta\ell_{Mir}(q_i) &= \Delta\ell_{M,\max} - r \cdot (q_i - q_{i0}). \end{aligned} \tag{11}$$

Here, $\Delta\ell_{M,\max}$ is the maximum contraction given by 25% of the uncontracted length.
The volume characteristic of the pneumatic muscle (Fig. 5) can be approximated with high accuracy by the following nonlinear function of both contraction length and muscle pressure, where the coefficients in this polynomial approximation have been identified by measurements

$$V(\Delta\ell_{Mij}, p_{Mij}) = \sum_{m=0}^{3} \left(a_m \cdot \Delta\ell_{Mij}^m\right) \cdot \sum_{n=0}^{1} \left(b_n \cdot p_{Mij}^n\right). \tag{12}$$

The force characteristic $F_{Mij}(p_{Mij}, \Delta\ell_{Mij})$ of the pneumatic muscle shown in Fig. 6 describes the resulting static tension force for given internal pressure p_{Mij} as well as given contraction length $\Delta\ell_{Mij}$. This nonlinear force characteristic has been identified by static measurements and, then, approximated by the following polynomial description

$$F_{Mij} = \bar{F}_{Mij}(\Delta\ell_{Mij}) \cdot p_{Mij} - f_{Mij}(\Delta\ell_{Mij}) = \sum_{m=0}^{3} \left(c_m \cdot \Delta\ell_{Mij}^m\right) \cdot p_{Mi} - \sum_{n=0}^{4} \left(d_n \cdot \Delta\ell_{Mij}^n\right). \tag{13}$$

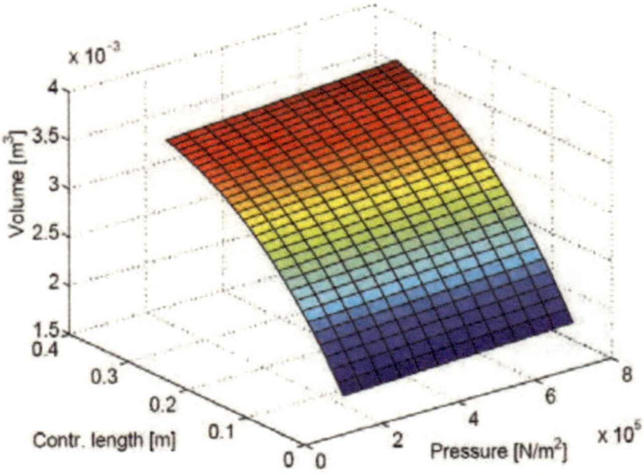

Fig. 5. Volume characteristic of a pneumatic muscle.

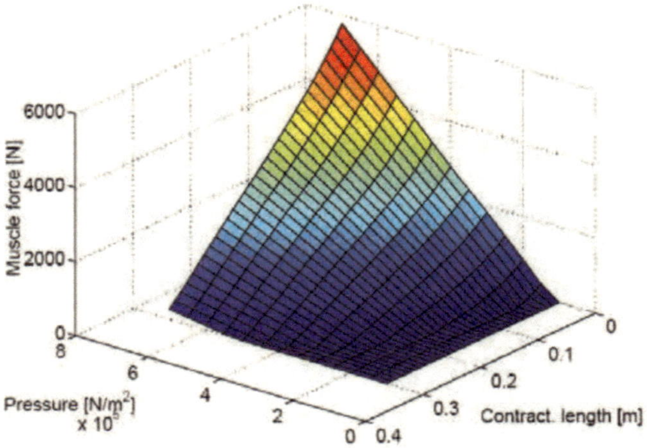

Fig. 6. Force characteristic of a pneumatic muscle.

The dynamics of the internal muscle pressure follows directly from a mass flow balance in combination with the pressure-density relationship. As the maximum internal muscle pressure is limited by a maximum value of $p_{max} = 7$ bar, the ideal gas equation can be utilised as accurate description of the thermodynamic behaviour of the compressed air

$$p_{Mij} = R \cdot T_{Mij} \cdot \rho_{Mij} \,. \tag{14}$$

Here, the density ρ_{Mij}, the gas constant R of air, and the thermodynamic temperature T_{Mij} are introduced. For the thermodynamic process a polytropic change of state is assumed. Thus, the relationship between the time derivative of the pressure and the time derivative of the density results in

$$\dot{p}_{Mij} = n \cdot R \cdot T_{Mij} \cdot \dot{\rho}_{Mij} \,. \tag{15}$$

The mass flow balance for the pneumatic muscle is governed by

$$\dot{\rho}_{Mij} = \frac{1}{V_{Mij}\left(\Delta\ell_{Mij}, p_{Mij}\right)}\left[\dot{m}_{Mij} - \rho_{Mij} \cdot \dot{V}_{Mij}\left(\Delta\ell_{Mij}, p_{Mij}\right)\right]. \tag{16}$$

The resulting pressure dynamics is given by a nonlinear first order differential equation and shall not be neglected as in (Carbonell et. al., 2001)

$$\dot{p}_{Mij} = \frac{1}{V_{Mij} + n \cdot \dfrac{\partial V_{Mij}}{\partial p_{Mij}} \cdot p_{Mij}} \cdot \left[R \cdot T_{Mij} \cdot \dot{m}_{Mij} - \frac{\partial V_{Mij}}{\partial \Delta\ell_{Mij}} \cdot \frac{\partial \Delta\ell_{Mij}}{\partial q_i} \cdot p_{Mij} \cdot \dot{q}_i \right]. \tag{17}$$

The internal temperature T_{Mij} can be approximated with good accuracy by the constant temperature T_0 of the ambiance (Göttert, 2004). Thereby, temperature measurements can be avoided, and the implementational effort is significantly reduced.

3. Control design based on differential flatness

A nonlinear system in state space notation is denoted as differentially flat (Fliess et. al., 1995), if flat outputs

$$\mathbf{y} = \mathbf{y}(\mathbf{x}, \mathbf{u}, \dot{\mathbf{u}}, \ldots, \mathbf{u}^{(\alpha)}), \quad \dim(\mathbf{y}) = \dim(\mathbf{u}) \tag{18}$$

exist that allow for expressing all system states $\mathbf{x}$ and all system inputs $\mathbf{u}$ in the form

$$\begin{aligned} \mathbf{x} &= \mathbf{x}(\mathbf{y}, \dot{\mathbf{y}}, \ldots, \mathbf{y}^{(\beta)}), \\ \mathbf{u} &= \mathbf{u}(\mathbf{y}, \dot{\mathbf{y}}, \ldots, \mathbf{y}^{(\beta+1)}). \end{aligned} \tag{19}$$

As a result, offline trajectory planning considering state and input constraints become possible. Moreover, the stated parametrization of the complete system dynamics by the flat outputs can be exploited for pure feedforward control as well as combined feedforward and feedback control.

3.1 Flatness-based pressure control

The nonlinear state equation (17) for the internal muscle pressure p_{Mij} represents the basis for the decentralized pressure control. It can be re-formulated as

$$\dot{p}_{Mij} = -k_{pij}\left(\Delta\ell_{Mij}, \Delta\dot{\ell}_{Mij}, p_{Mij}\right) \cdot p_{Mij} + k_{uij}\left(\Delta\ell_{Mij}, p_{Mij}\right) \cdot \dot{m}_{Mij}. \tag{20}$$

With the internal muscle pressure as flat output candidate $y_{ijp} = p_{Mij}$, (20) can be solved for the mass flow $\dot{m}_{Mij}$ as control input u_{ijp} and leads to the inverse model for the pressure control

$$\dot{m}_{Mij} = \frac{1}{k_{uij}\left(\Delta\ell_{Mij}, p_{Mij}\right)} \cdot \left[v_{ij} + k_{pij}\left(\Delta\ell_{Mij}, \Delta\dot{\ell}_{Mij}, p_{Mij}\right) \cdot p_{Mij} \right], \tag{21}$$

Since the internal pressure p_{Mij} as state variable is identical to the flat output and $\dim(y_{ijp}) = \dim(u_{ijp}) = 1$ holds, the differential flatness property is proven. The contraction length $\Delta\ell_{Mij}$ as well as its time derivative can be considered as scheduling parameters in a gain-scheduled adaptation of k_{uij} and k_{pij} . With the internal pressure as flat output, its first time derivative is introduced as new control input

$$\dot{p}_{Mij} = v_{ij} \,. \tag{22}$$

Consequently, the state variable of the corresponding Brunovsky form has to be provided by means of measurements, i.e. $z_{ijp} = p_{Mij}$. Each pneumatic muscle is equipped with a pressure transducer mounted at the connection flange that connects the muscle with the toothed belt. For the contraction length and its time derivative either measured or desired values can be employed: in the given implementation, the scheduling parameter $\Delta\ell_{Mij}$ results from the measured crank angle q_i, which is obtained by an encoder providing high resolution. Furthermore, the second scheduling parameter, the contraction velocity, is derived from the crank angle q_i by means of real differentiation using a DT_1-System with the corresponding transfer function

$$G_{DT1}(s) = \frac{s}{T_1 \cdot s + 1} \,. \tag{23}$$

The error dynamics of each muscle pressure p_{Mij} can be asymptotically stabilised by the following control law which is evaluated with the measured pressure. Using this control law all nonlinearities are compensated for. An asymptotically stable error dynamics is obtained by pole placement

$$\left.\begin{aligned} \dot{p}_{Mij} &= v_{ij} \\ v_{ij} &= \dot{p}_{Mijd} + \alpha_{10}(p_{Mijd} - p_{Mij}) \end{aligned}\right\} \Rightarrow \dot{e}_{pij} + \alpha_{10} \cdot e_{pij} = 0 \,, \tag{24}$$

where the constant α_{10} is determined by pole placement. Here, the desired value for the time derivative of the internal muscle pressure can be obtained either by real differentiation of the corresponding control input u_{ij} in (33) or by model-based calculation using only desired values, i.e.

$$\dot{p}_{Mijd} = \dot{p}_{Mijd}(\mathbf{r}, \dot{\mathbf{r}}, \ddot{\mathbf{r}}, p_{Mid}, \dot{p}_{Mid}) \,. \tag{25}$$

The corresponding desired trajectories are obtained from a trajectory planning module that provides synchronous time optimal trajectories according to given kinematic and dynamic constraints (Aschemann & Hofer, 2005). It becomes obvious that a continuous time derivative $\dot{p}_{Mijd}$ requires a three times continuously differentiable desired end-effector trajectory $\mathbf{r}$.

The implementation of the underlying flatness-based pressure control structure for drive i is depicted in Fig. 7. In each input channel, the nonlinear valve characteristic (VC) is compensated by pre-multiplying with its approximated inverse valve characteristic (IVC). This inverse valve characteristic is implemented as look-up-table and depends both on the commanded mass flow and on the measured internal pressure.

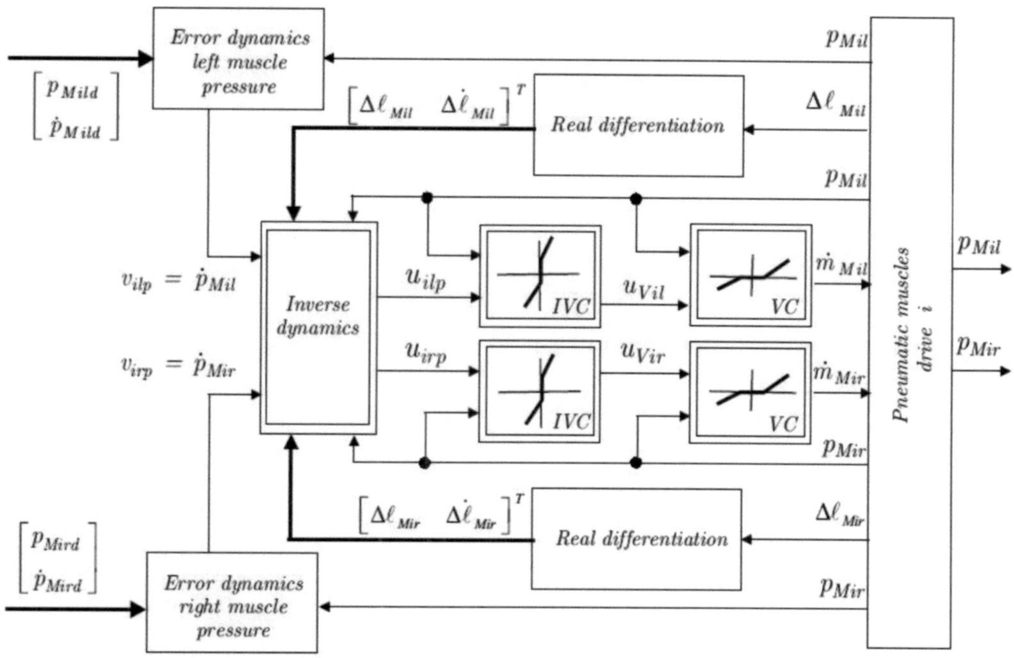

Fig. 7. Implementation of the underlying pressure control structure for drive i.

3.2 Inverse dynamics of the decoupling control

For the outer control loop design the generalised coordinates and the mean muscle pressures are chosen as flat output candidates

$$\mathbf{y} = \mathbf{y}(\mathbf{x},\mathbf{u}) = \begin{bmatrix} q_1 \\ q_2 \\ p_{M1} \\ p_{M2} \end{bmatrix} = \begin{bmatrix} q_1 \\ q_2 \\ \dfrac{p_{M1l}+p_{M1r}}{2} \\ \dfrac{p_{M2l}+p_{M2r}}{2} \end{bmatrix}, \tag{26}$$

where the input vector **u** contains the four muscle pressures

$$\mathbf{u} = \begin{bmatrix} p_{M1l} & p_{M1r} & p_{M2l} & p_{M2r} \end{bmatrix}^T \tag{27}$$

and the state vector **x** consists of the vector of generalised coordinates **q** as well as their time derivatives $\dot{\mathbf{q}}$

$$\mathbf{x} = \begin{bmatrix} \mathbf{q} \\ \dot{\mathbf{q}} \end{bmatrix}. \tag{28}$$

The trajectory control of the mean pressure allows for increasing stiffness concerning disturbance forces acting on the end-effector (Bindel et. al., 1999). As the decentralised pressure controls have been assigned a high bandwidth, these four controlled muscle pressures p_{Mij} can be considered as ideal control inputs of the outer control loop. Subsequent differentiation of the first two flat output candidates until one of the control appears leads to

$$\begin{aligned} y_1 &= q_1 \,, \\ \dot{y}_1 &= \dot{q}_1 \,, \\ \ddot{y}_1 &= \ddot{q}_1(\mathbf{q}, \dot{\mathbf{q}}, p_{M1l}, p_{M1r}), \end{aligned} \tag{29}$$

and

$$\begin{aligned} y_2 &= q_2 \,, \\ \dot{y}_2 &= \dot{q}_2 \,, \\ \ddot{y}_2 &= \ddot{q}_2(\mathbf{q}, \dot{\mathbf{q}}, p_{M2l}, p_{M2r}) \,, \end{aligned} \tag{30}$$

whereas the third and fourth flat output candidates directly depend on the control inputs

$$\begin{aligned} y_3 &= p_{M1} = 0.5 \cdot (p_{M1l} + p_{M1r}), \\ y_4 &= p_{M2} = 0.5 \cdot (p_{M2l} + p_{M2r}). \end{aligned} \tag{31}$$

The differential flatness can be proven as follows: all system states can be directly expressed by the flat outputs and their time derivatives

$$\mathbf{x} = \begin{bmatrix} \mathbf{q} \\ \dot{\mathbf{q}} \end{bmatrix} = \begin{bmatrix} y_1 & y_2 & \dot{y}_1 & \dot{y}_2 \end{bmatrix}^T . \tag{32}$$

The equations of motion (9) are available in symbolic form. Inserting the muscle force characteristics, the internal muscle pressures as control inputs can be parameterized by the flat outputs and their time derivatives

$$\mathbf{u} = \begin{bmatrix} p_{M1l}(\mathbf{q}, \dot{\mathbf{q}}, \ddot{\mathbf{q}}, p_{M1}) \\ p_{M1r}(\mathbf{q}, \dot{\mathbf{q}}, \ddot{\mathbf{q}}, p_{M1}) \\ p_{M2l}(\mathbf{q}, \dot{\mathbf{q}}, \ddot{\mathbf{q}}, p_{M2}) \\ p_{M2r}(\mathbf{q}, \dot{\mathbf{q}}, \ddot{\mathbf{q}}, p_{M2}) \end{bmatrix} = \mathbf{u}(\mathbf{q}, \dot{\mathbf{q}}, \ddot{\mathbf{q}}, p_{M1}, p_{M2}) \,. \tag{33}$$

In the following, three different nonlinear control approaches are employed to stabilize the error dynamics of the outer control loop: flatness-based control, backstepping and sliding-mode control (Khalil, 1996). For all these alternative designs, the differential flatness property proves advantageous (Sira-Ramirez & Llanes-Santiago, 1995; Aschemann et. al., 2007).

3.3 Flatness-based control

In the case of flatness-based control, the inverse dynamics is evaluated with the measured crank angles and the corresponding angular velocities obtained by real differentiation (Aschemann & Hofer, 2005). For the mean pressures, however, desired values are utilized. The second derivatives of the crank angles, the angular accelerations, serve as stabilizing inputs

$$\mathbf{u} = \begin{bmatrix} p_{M1l} & p_{M1r} & p_{M2l} & p_{M2r} \end{bmatrix}^T = \mathbf{u}(\mathbf{q}, \dot{\mathbf{q}}, v_1, v_2, p_{M1d}, p_{M2d}) \,. \tag{34}$$

The inverse dynamics leads to a compensation of all nonlinearities. An asymptotic stabilization is achieved by pole placement with Hurwitz-polynomials for the error dynamics for each drive $i = \{1, 2\}$

$$v_i = \ddot{q}_{id} + \alpha_{i2} \cdot (\dot{q}_{id} - \dot{q}_i) + \alpha_{i1} \cdot (q_{id} - q_i) + \int_0^t \alpha_{i0} \cdot (q_{id} - q_i) d\tau \, . \tag{35}$$

3.4 Backstepping control

The first step of the backstepping control design (Khalil, 1996) involves the definition of the tracking error variable for each drive $i = \{1, 2\}$,

$$e_{i1} = q_{id} - q_i \;\; \Rightarrow \;\; \dot{e}_{i1} = \dot{q}_{id} - \dot{q}_i \, . \tag{36}$$

Next, a first Lyapunov function V_{i1} is introduced

$$V_{i1}(e_{i1}) = \frac{1}{2} e_{i1}^2 > 0 \;\; \Rightarrow \;\; \dot{V}_1(e_{i1}) = e_{i1} \cdot \dot{e}_{i1} = e_{i1} \cdot (\dot{q}_{id} - \dot{q}_i) \overset{!}{=} -c_1 \cdot e_{i1}^2 \tag{37}$$

and the expression for its time derivative is solved for the virtual control input

$$\dot{e}_{i1} = \dot{q}_{id} - \dot{q}_i = -c_1 \cdot e_{i1} \;\; \Rightarrow \;\; \dot{q}_i \approx \alpha_{il}(e_{i1}, \dot{q}_{id}) = \dot{q}_{id} + c_1 \cdot e_{i1} \, . \tag{38}$$

In the second step, the error variable e_{i2} is defined in the following form

$$e_{i2} = \alpha_{il}(e_{i1}, \dot{q}_{id}) - \dot{q}_i = \dot{q}_{id} - \dot{q}_i + c_1 \cdot e_{i1} \;\; \Rightarrow \;\; \dot{e}_{i1} = e_{i2} - c_1 \cdot e_{i1} \tag{39}$$

and its time derivative is computed

$$\dot{e}_{i2} = \ddot{q}_{id} - \ddot{q}_i + c_1 \cdot \dot{e}_{i1} = \ddot{q}_{id} - \ddot{q}_i + c_1 \cdot (e_{i2} - c_1 \cdot e_{i1}) \, . \tag{40}$$

Now, a second Lyapunov function V_{i2} is specified.

$$V_{i2}(e_{i1}, e_{i2}) = \frac{1}{2} e_{i1}^2 + \frac{1}{2} e_{i2}^2 > 0 \;\; \Rightarrow \;\; \dot{V}_{i2}(e_{i1}, e_{i2}) = e_{i1} \cdot \dot{e}_{i1} + e_{i2} \cdot \dot{e}_{i2} \tag{41}$$

The corresponding time derivative

$$\dot{V}_{i2}(e_{i1}, e_{i2}) = -c_1 \cdot e_{i1}^2 + e_{i2} \cdot [\ddot{q}_{id} - v_i + c_1 \cdot (e_{i2} - c_1 \cdot e_{i1}) + e_{i1}] \overset{!}{=} -c_1 \cdot e_{i1}^2 - c_2 \cdot e_{i2}^2 \tag{42}$$

can be made negative definite by choosing the stabilizing control input as follows

$$v_i = \ddot{q}_i = \ddot{q}_{id} + e_{i1} \cdot (1 - c_1^2) + e_{i2} \cdot (c_1 + c_2) \, . \tag{43}$$

Backstepping control design offers several advantages in comparison to flatness based control. It becomes possible to avoid cancellations of useful, i.e. stabilizing nonlinearities. Furthermore, different positive definite functions can be used at control design, e.g. allowing for nonlinear damping.

3.5 Sliding-mode control

For sliding-mode control (Sira-Ramirez & Llanes-Santiago, 1995) the vector of tracking errors is considered

$$\mathbf{z}_i = \begin{bmatrix} q_{id} - q_i \\ \dot{q}_{id} - \dot{q}_i \end{bmatrix} . \tag{44}$$

Based on this error vector $\mathbf{z}_i$, the following sliding surfaces s_i are defined for each drive $i = \{1, 2\}$

$$s_i(\mathbf{z}_i) = \dot{q}_{id} - \dot{q}_i + \beta_{i1} \cdot (q_{id} - q_i) \quad \Rightarrow \quad \dot{s}_i = \ddot{q}_{id} - \ddot{q}_i + \beta_{i1} \cdot (\dot{q}_{id} - \dot{q}_i), \tag{45}$$

where β_{i1} represents a positive gain. The convergence to the corresponding sliding surface is achieved by introducing a discontinuous switching function in the time derivative of a quadratic Lyapunov function

$$V_i(s_i) = \frac{1}{2} s_i^2 \quad \Rightarrow \quad \dot{V}_i(s_i) = s_i \cdot \dot{s}_i \le -\alpha_i \, | s_i | = -\alpha_i \cdot s_i \cdot sign(s_i), \tag{46}$$

with a properly chosen coefficient α_i that dominates remaining model uncertainties. The control design offers flexibility as regards the choice of the sliding surfaces and the reaching laws. For the implementation, however, a smooth switching function is preferred to reduce high frequency chattering. This results in the following stabilizing control law, which leads to a real sliding mode within a boundary layer

$$v_i = \ddot{q}_i = \ddot{q}_{id} + \beta_{i1} \cdot (\dot{q}_{id} - \dot{q}_i) + \alpha_i \cdot \tanh(\frac{s_i}{\varepsilon}). \tag{47}$$

The implemented control structure is depicted in Fig. 8. The desired trajectories are provided from an offline trajectory planning module that calculates time optimal trajectories according to both state constraints and input constraints. This is achieved by proper time-scaling of polynomial functions with free parameters as described in (Aschemann & Hofer, 2005).

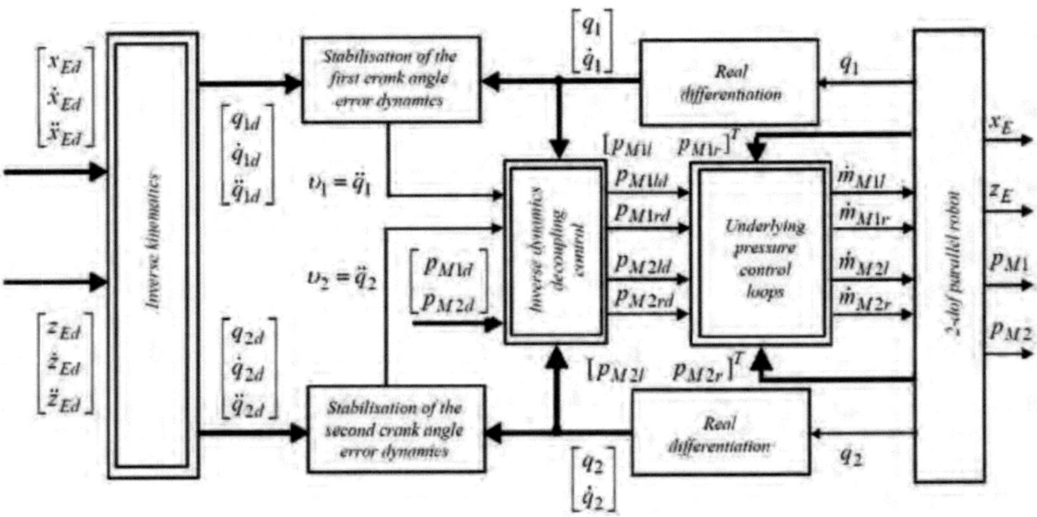

Fig. 8. Implementation of the decoupling control structure.

4. Disturbance observer design

The observer provides a vector $\hat{\mathbf{x}}_2$ of estimated disturbance torques that accounts for both model uncertainties and nonlinear friction. The main idea consists in the extension of the system state equations with the measurable state vector

$$\mathbf{y} = \mathbf{x}_1 = [\mathbf{q}, \dot{\mathbf{q}}]^T \tag{48}$$

by two integrators, which serve as disturbance models (Aschemann et. al., 2007)

$$\begin{aligned} \dot{\mathbf{y}} &= \mathbf{f}(\mathbf{y}, \hat{\mathbf{x}}_2, \mathbf{u}), \quad \dim(\mathbf{y}) = 4, \\ \dot{\hat{\mathbf{x}}}_2 &= \mathbf{0}, \quad \dim(\hat{\mathbf{x}}_2) = 2. \end{aligned} \tag{49}$$

The reduced-order disturbance observer according to (Friedland, 1996) is given by

$$\begin{aligned} \dot{\mathbf{z}} &= \Phi(\mathbf{y}, \hat{\mathbf{x}}_2, \mathbf{u}), \quad \dim(\mathbf{z}) = 2, \\ \hat{\mathbf{x}}_2 &= \begin{bmatrix} \hat{\eta}_1 \\ \hat{\eta}_2 \end{bmatrix} = \mathbf{H}\,\mathbf{y} + \mathbf{z}, \end{aligned} \tag{50}$$

where $\mathbf{H}$ denotes the observer gain matrix and $\mathbf{z}$ the observer state vector. The observer gain matrix is chosen as follows

$$\mathbf{H} = \begin{bmatrix} h_{11} & h_{11} & 0 & 0 \\ 0 & 0 & h_{22} & h_{22} \end{bmatrix}, \tag{51}$$

involving only two design parameters h_{11} and h_{22}. Aiming at an asymptotically stable observer dynamics

$$\lim_{t\to\infty} \mathbf{e} = \lim_{t\to\infty} (\mathbf{x}_2 - \hat{\mathbf{x}}_2) \overset{!}{=} \mathbf{0}, \tag{52}$$

the observer gains are determined by pole placement based on a linearization using the corresponding Jacobian (Friedland, 1996). In Fig. 9 a comparison of simulated disturbance forces and the observed forces provided by the proposed disturbance observer is shown. Here, the resulting tangential force at the pulley with radius r is depicted, which is related to the disturbance torque according to $F_{iU} = \hat{\eta}_i / r$. Obviously, the simulated disturbance forces are reconstructed with high accuracy.

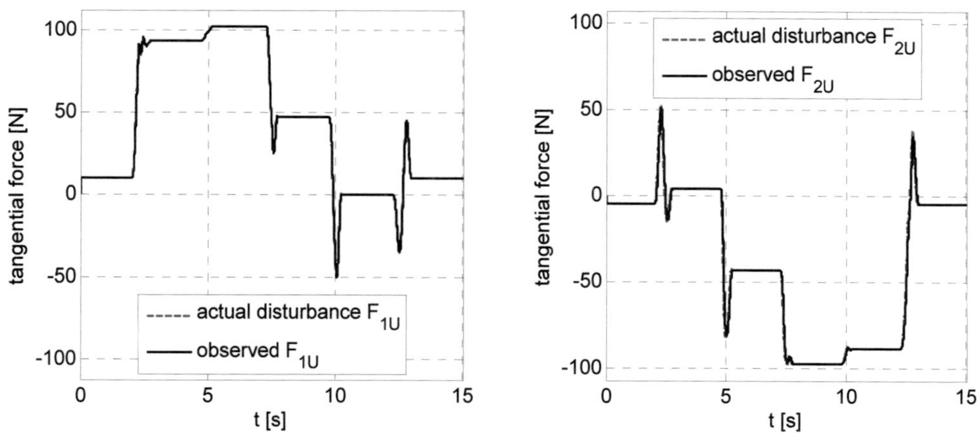

Fig. 9. Comparison of simulated disturbance force and observed disturbance force using the reduced-order disturbance observer.

5. Simulation results

The efficiency of the proposed cascade control structure is investigated using the desired trajectory shown in Fig. 10 with maximum velocities of approx. 0.9 m/s and maximum accelerations of approx. 7 m/s² for each axis.

The first part of the desired trajectory involves the motion on a quarter-circle with the radius 0.2 m from the starting point (x = 0 m, z = 1 m) to the point (x = −0.2 m, z = 0.8 m). The next three movements consist of straight lines: the second part comprises a diagonal movement in the xz-plane to the point (x = −0.1 m, z = 0.6 m), followed by a straight line motion in x-direction to the point (x = 0.1 m, z = 0.6 m). The fourth part is given by a diagonal movement to the point (x = 0.2 m, z = 0.8 m). The fifth part involves the return motion on a quarter-circle to the starting point (x = 0 m, z = 1 m).

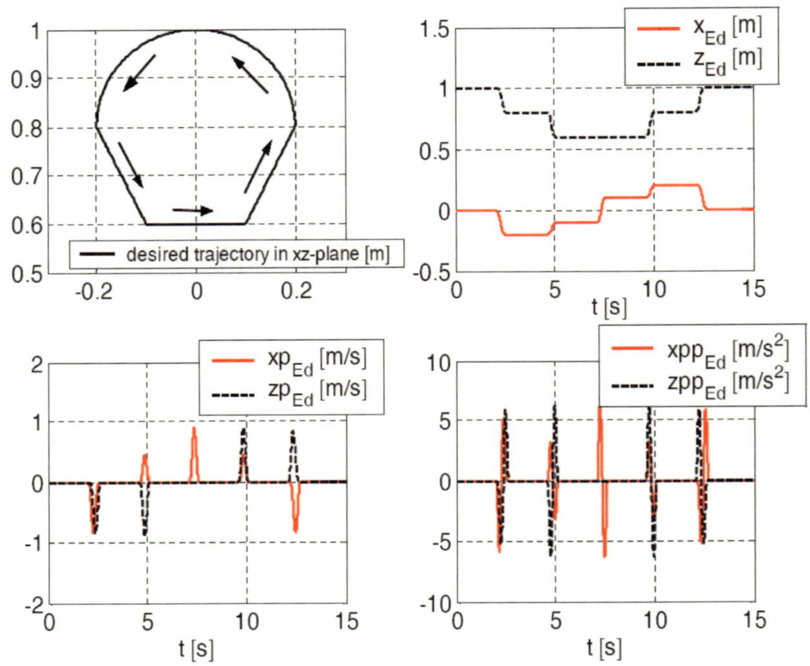

Fig. 10. Desired trajectory in the workspace.

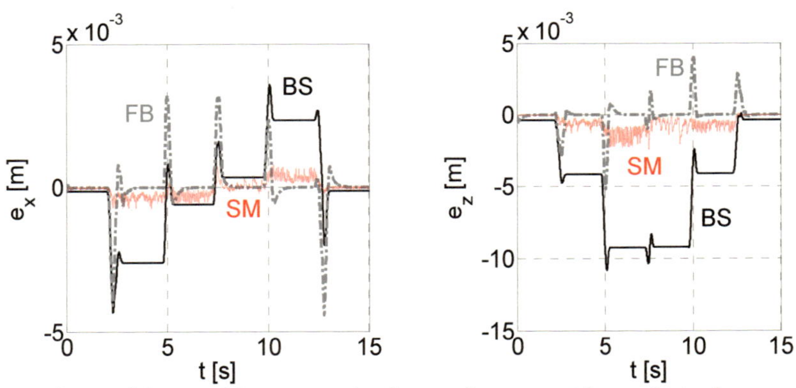

Fig. 11. Comparison of the tracking errors in the workspace without disturbance observer.

Fig. 11 shows a comparison of the resulting tracking errors in the workspace for flatness-based control (FB), backstepping control (BS) and sliding-mode control (SM). Without observer-based disturbance compensation, the best results are obtained using sliding-mode control.

The efficiency of the observer based disturbance compensation is emphasized by Fig. 12. For all considered control approaches a further improvement of tracking accuracy is achieved.

6. Conclusion

In this contribution, a cascaded trajectory control based on differential flatness is presented for a parallel robot with two degrees of freedom driven by pneumatic muscles. The modelling of this mechatronic system leads to a system of nonlinear differential equations of eighth order. For the characteristics of the pneumatic muscles polynomials serve as good approximations. The inner control loops of the cascade involve a flatness-based control of the internal muscle pressure with high bandwidth. For the outer control loop three different control approaches have been investigated leading to a decoupling of the crank angles and the mean pressures as controlled variables. Simulation results emphasize the excellent closed-loop performance with maximum position errors of approx. 1 mm during the movements, vanishing steady-state position error and steady-state pressure error of less than 0.03 bar, which have been confirmed by first experimental results at a prototype system.

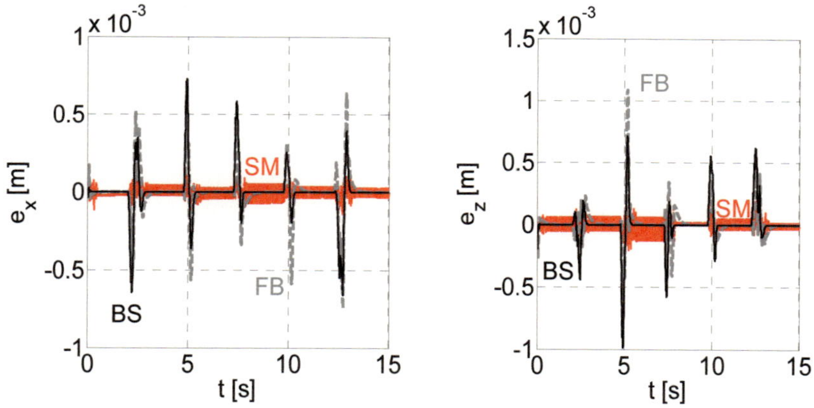

Fig. 12. Tracking errors in the workspace with observer-based disturbance compensation.

7. References

Aschemann H.; Hofer E.P. (2004). *Flatness-Based Trajectory Control of a Pneumatically Driven Carriage with Uncertainties,* CD-ROM-Proc. of NOLCOS, pp. 239 - 244, Stuttgart, September 2004

Aschemann H.; Hofer E.P. (2005). *Flatness-Based Trajectory Planning and Control of a Parallel Robot Actuated by Pneumatic Muscles,* CD-ROM-Proc. of the ECCOMAS Thematic Conference on Multibody Dynamics, Madrid, June 2005

Aschemann H.; Knestel, M.; Hofer E.P. (2007). *Nonlinear Control Strategies for a Parallel Robot Driven by Pneumatic Muscles,* Proc. of 14th Int. Workshop on Dynamics and Control, Moscow, June 2007, Nauka, Moscow

Bindel, R.; Nitsche, R.; Rothfuß, R.; Zeitz, M. (1999). *Flatness Based Control of Two Valve Hydraulic Joint Actuator of a Large Manipulator.* CD-ROM-Proc. of ECC, Karlsruhe, 1999

Carbonell P.; Jian Z.P.; Repperger D. (2001). *Comparative Study of Three Nonlinear Control Strategies for a Pneumatic Muscle Actuator,* CD-Proc. of NOLCOS, Saint-Petersburg, pp. 167 - 172, June 2001

Fliess M.; Levine J.; Martin P.; Rouchon P. (1995). *Flatness and Defect of Nonlinear Systems: Introductory Theory and Examples,* Int. J. of Control, Vol. 61, No. 6, pp. 1327 - 1361

Friedland, B. (1996). *Advanced Control System Design,* Prentice-Hall

Göttert, M. (2004). *Bahnregelung servopneumatischer Antriebe,* Berichte aus der Steuerungs- und Regelungstechnik (in German), Shaker

Khalil, H. K. (1996). *Nonlinear Systems,* 2nd. ed., Prentice-Hall

Sira-Ramirez H.; Llanes-Santiago O. (1995) *Sliding Mode Control of Nonlinear Mechanical Vibrations,* J. of Dyn. Systems, Meas. and Control, Vol. 122, No. 12, pp. 674 - 678

3

Neural-Based Navigation Approach for a Bi-Steerable Mobile Robot

Azouaoui Ouahiba, Ouadah Noureddine,
Aouana Salem and Chabi Djeffer
Centre de Développement des technologies Avancées (CDTA)
Algeria

1. Introduction

Recent developments in robotics have revealed a strong demand for autonomous out-door vehicles capable of some degree of self-sufficiency. These vehicles have many applications in a large variety of domains, from spatial exploration to handling material, and from military tasks to people transportation (Azouaoui &Chohra, 1998; Hong et al., 2002; Kujawski, 1995; Labakhua et al., 2006; Niegel, 1995; Schafer, 2005; Schilling & Jungius, 1995; Wagner, 2006). Most mobile robot missions include autonomous navigation. Thus, vehicle designers search to create dynamic systems able to navigate and achieve intelligent behaviors like human in real dynamic environments where conditions are laborious.

In this context, these last few years small automated and non-pollutant vehicles are developed to perform a public urban transportation task. These vehicles must use advanced control techniques for navigation in dynamic environments especially urban ones. Indeed, several research works have recently emerged to treat this transportation task problem. For instance, the work developed in (Gu & Hu, 2002) presents a path-tracking scheme based on wavelet neural predictive control to model non-linear kinematics of the robot to adapt it to a large operating range. In (Mendes et al., 2003), a path-tracking controller with an anti-collision behavior of a car-like robot is presented. It is based on navigation and anti-collision systems. The first system uses a Fuzzy Logic (FL) to implement the path-tracking while the second system consists of estimating the trajectories and behavior of surrounding objects. Another work developed in (Bento & Nunes, 2004) treats also the path following problem of a cybernetic car. The developed controller with magnetic markers guidance is based on FL and integrates an anti-collision behavior applied to a bi-steerable vehicle. Other works use a visual control to achieve a desired task such as the work proposed in (Avina Cervantes, 2005). It consists to develop a visual-based navigation method for mobile robots using an on-board color camera. The objective is the use of vehicles in agriculture to navigate automatically on a network of roads (to go from a farm to a given field for example).

Although several investigations on the robot navigation problem have been developed (Avina Cervantes, 2005; Azouaoui & Chohra, 2002; Chohra et al., 1998; Gu & Hu, 2002; Kujawski, 1995; Labakhua et al., 2006; Mendes et al., 2003; Niegel, 1995; Schilling & Jungius, 1995; Sorouchyari, 1989), to date further efforts must be made to apprehend and understand the navigation behavior of a vehicle evolving in partially structured and partially known environments such as urban ones.

In this paper, an interesting neural-based navigation approach suggested in (Azouaoui & Chohra, 2002; Chohra et al., 1998) is applied with some modifications to a bi-steerable mobile robot Robucar. Indeed, this approach is based on basic behaviors which are fused under a neural paradigm using Gradient Back-Propagation (GBP) learning algorithm. This navigation is then implemented within a behavioral architecture because of its excellent real-time execution properties (Murphy, 2001).

The aim of this work is to implement a neural-based navigation approach able to provide the Robucar with more autonomy, intelligence, and real-time processing capabilities. In fact, the vehicle relies on its interaction with its environment to extract useful information. In this paper, the used neural navigation approach essentially based on pattern classification (or recognition) (Welstead, 1994) of target localization and obstacle avoidance behaviors is presented. This approach has been developed in (Chohra et al., 1998) for five (05) possible movements of vehicles, while in this paper this number is reduced to three (03) possible movements due to the Robucar structure. Second, simulation results of the neural-based navigation are presented. Finally, an implementation of the neural-based navigation on a real bi-steerable robot Robucar is given leading to a learning vehicle able to behave intelligently faced to unexpected situations.

2. Neural-based navigation approach applied to a bi-steerable mobile robot Robucar in partially structured environnments

To navigate in partially structured environments, the Robucar must reach its target without collisions with possibly encountered obstacles. In other terms, it must have the capability to achieve the target localization, obstacle avoidance, and decision-making and action behaviors. These behaviors are acquired using multilayer feedforward Neural Networks (NN).

This neural navigation is built of three (03) phases as shown in Figure 1. During the phase 1, from the temperature field vector X_T, the robot learns to recognize target location situations T_{j1} (j1 = 1, ..., 5) classifier while it learns to recognize obstacle avoidance situations O_{j2} (j2 = 1, ..., 6) classifier from the distance vector X_O during the phase 2. The phase 3 decides an action A_i (i = 1, ..., 3) from two (02) association stages and their coordination carried out by reinforcement Trial and Error learning.

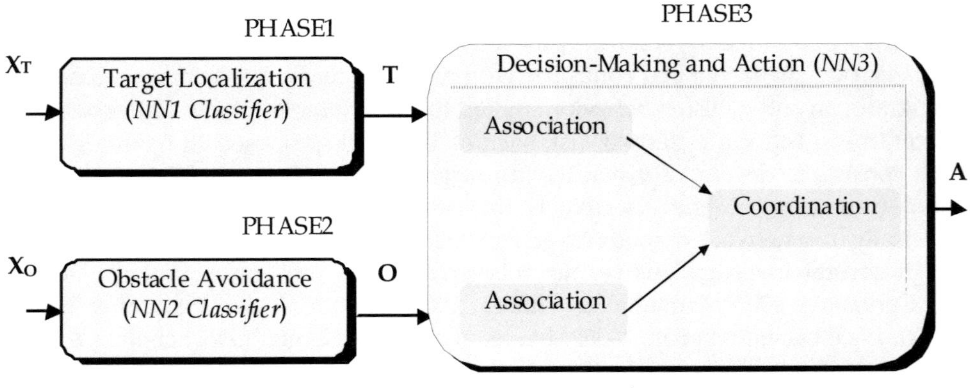

Fig. 1. Neural navigation system synopsis.

2.1 Vehicule and sensor
a) Vehicle.
The Robucar is a non-holonomic robot characterized by its bounded steering angle ($-18° \leq \phi \leq +18°$) and velocity ($0m/s \leq v \leq 5m/s$) (Figure 2(a)). Three movements of the Robucar are defined to ensure safety displacement in the environment. The possible movements are then in three (03) directions consequently three (03) possible actions are defined as action to move left (towards 18°), action to move forward (towards 0°), and action to move right (towards -18°) as shown in Figure 2(b). They are expressed by the action vector $A = [A_1, A_2, A_3]$.

(a) Robucar.

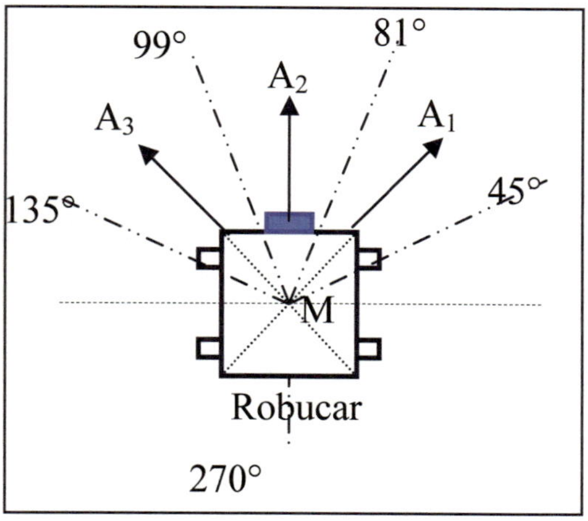

(b) Robot model.

Fig. 2. Robucar and its sensor.
b) Sensor.
The perception system is essentially based on a laser-range finder LMS200 (SICK, 2001). It provides either 100° or 180° coverage with 0.25°, 0.5°, or 1.0° angular resolution. In this paper, the overall coverage area is divided into three sub-areas corresponding to the three possible actions as shown in Figure 2. Thus, to detect possibly encountered obstacles, three (03) areas are defined to get distances (vehicle-obstacle) from 45° to 81°, from 81° to 99°, and from 99° to 135° (see Figure 2). These areas are deduced from the Robucar dimensions to ensure its security.

2.2 Neural-based navigation system
During the navigation, the vehicle must build an implicit internal map (i.e., target, obstacles, and free spaces) allowing recognition of both target location and obstacle avoidance situations. Then, it decides the appropriate action from two association stages and their coordination (Chohra et al., 1998; Sorouchyari, 1989). To achieve this, the neural-based navigation system is used where the only known data are initial and final (i.e., target) positions of the vehicle.
a) Phase 1.
Target Localization (NN1 Classifier). The target localization behavior is based on NN1 classifier trained by the GBP algorithm which must recognize five (05) target location situations, after learning, from data obtained by computing distance and orientation of

robot-target using a temperature field method (Sorouchyari, 1989). This method leads to model the vehicle environment in five (05) areas corresponding to all target locations as shown in Figure 3. These situations are defined with five (05) Classes $T_1, \ldots, T_{j1}, \ldots, T_5$ where ($j1 = 1, \ldots, 5$):

$$\begin{aligned} &\text{If } 45° \leq \gamma < 81° \text{ (Class } T_1\text{)},\\ &\text{If } 81° \leq \gamma < 99° \text{ (Class } T_2\text{)},\\ &\text{If } 99° \leq \gamma < 135° \text{ (Class } T_3\text{)},\\ &\text{If } 135° \leq \gamma < 270° \text{ (Class } T_4\text{)},\\ &\text{If } 270° \leq \gamma < 405° \text{ (Class } T_5\text{)}. \end{aligned} \tag{1}$$

where γ is the angle of the target direction.

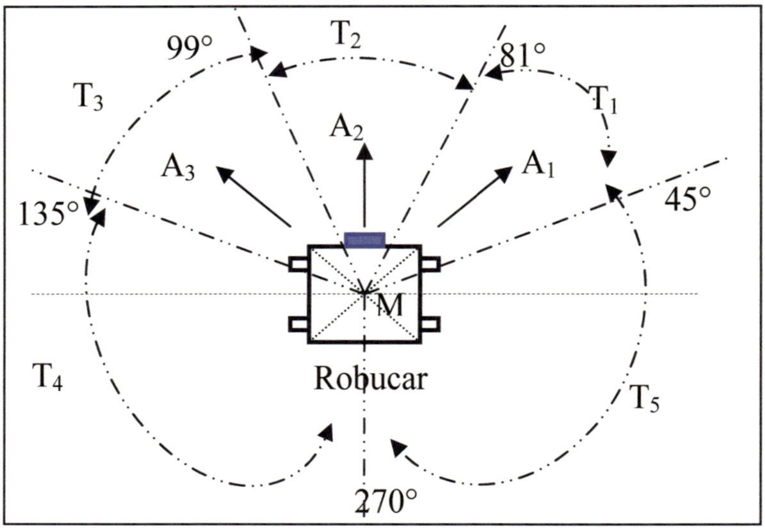

Fig. 3. Target location situations.

Temperatures in the neighborhood of the vehicle are defined by: t_L in direction 18°, t_F in direction 0°, and t_R in direction -18°. These temperatures are computed using sine and cosine functions as follows:

$$\begin{aligned} &\text{If } 45° < \gamma \leq 80° \text{ (Class } T_1\text{)},\\ &\quad \text{Then } T_R = 12\sin(\gamma),\ T_F = 6\cos(\gamma),\ T_L = 6\cos(\gamma),\\ &\text{If } 80° < \gamma \leq 99° \text{ (Class } T_2\text{)},\\ &\quad \text{Then } T_R = 6|\cos(\gamma)|,\ T_F = 12\sin(\gamma),\ T_L = 6|\cos(\gamma)|,\\ &\text{If } 99° < \gamma \leq 135° \text{ (Class } T_3\text{)},\\ &\quad \text{Then } T_R = 6|\cos(\gamma)|,\ T_F = 6|\sin(\gamma)|,\ T_L = 12\sin(\gamma),\\ &\text{If } 135° < \gamma \leq 270° \text{ (Class } T_4\text{)},\\ &\quad \text{Then } T_R = 12|\sin(\gamma)|,\ T_F = 6|\sin(\gamma)|,\ T_L = 12|\sin(\gamma)|,\\ &\text{If } 270° < \gamma \leq 315° \text{ (Class } T_5\text{)},\\ &\quad \text{Then } T_R = 12|\sin(\gamma)|,\ T_F = 6|\sin(\gamma)|,\ T_L = 6\cos(\gamma),\\ &\text{If } 315° < \gamma \leq 360° \text{ (Class } T_5\text{)},\\ &\quad \text{Then } T_R = 12\cos(\gamma),\ T_F = 6\cos(\gamma),\ T_L = 6|\sin(\gamma)|,\\ &\text{If } 360° < \gamma \leq 405° \text{ (Class } T_5\text{)},\\ &\quad \text{Then } T_R = 12\cos(\gamma),\ T_F = 6\cos(\gamma),\ T_L = 6\sin(\gamma). \end{aligned} \tag{2}$$

These components are pre-processed to constitute the input vector X_T of NN1 (Azouaoui & Chohra, 2003; Azouaoui & Chohra, 2002; Chohra et al., 1998) built of input layer, hidden layer, and output layer as shown in Figure 4: architecture of NN1 where $X_i = X_{Ti}$ (i = 1, ..., 3), Y_k (k = 1, ..., 5), $C_j = T_{j1}$ (j = j1 = 1, ..., 5).

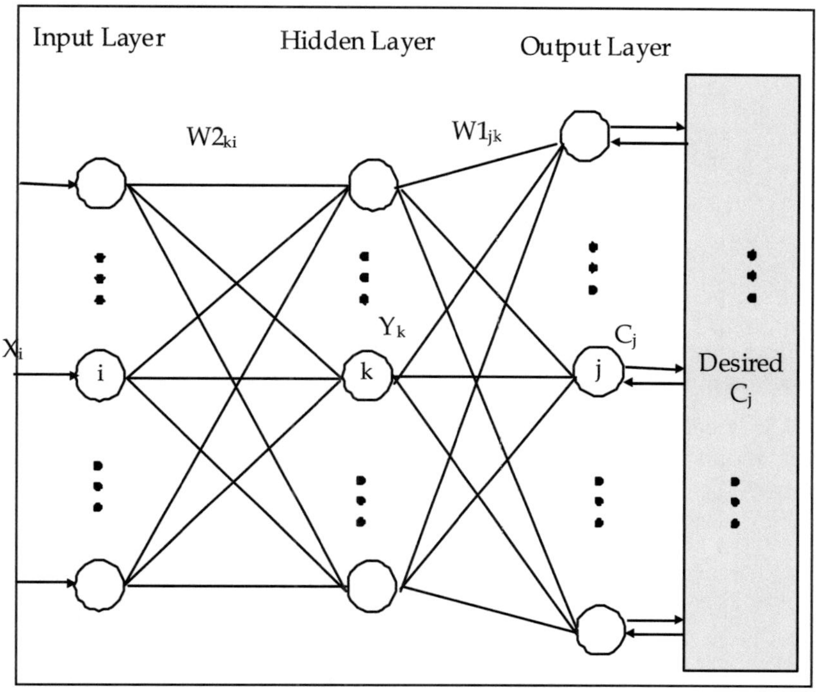

Fig. 4. Architecture of both NN1 and NN2.

After learning, for each input vector X_T, NN1 provides the vehicle with capability to decide its target localization, recognizing target location situation expressed by the highly activated output T_{j1}.

b) Phase 2.

Obstacle Avoidance (NN2 Classifier). The obstacle avoidance behavior is based on NN2 classifier trained by GBP which must recognize obstacle avoidance situations, after learning, from laser sensor data giving robot-obstacle distances. These obstacle avoidance situations are modeled as the human perceives them, that is, as topological situations: corridors, rooms, right turns, etc. (Anderson, 1995; Azouaoui & Chohra, 2003).

The possible movements of the Robucar lead us to structure possibly encountered obstacles in six (06) topological situations as shown in Figure 5. These situations are defined with six (06) Classes O_1, ..., O_{j2}, ..., O_6 where (j2 = 1, ..., 6).

The robot-obstacle minimal distances are defined in the vehicle neighborhood by: d_L in direction 18°, d_F in direction 0°, and d_R in direction -18° as shown in Figure 6. These components are pre-processed to constitute the input vector X_O of NN2 built of input layer, hidden layer, and output layer as shown in Figure 4: architecture of NN2 where $X_i = X_{Oi}$ (i = 1, ..., 3), Y_k (k = 1, ..., 6), $C_j = O_{j2}$ (j = j2 = 1, ..., 6).

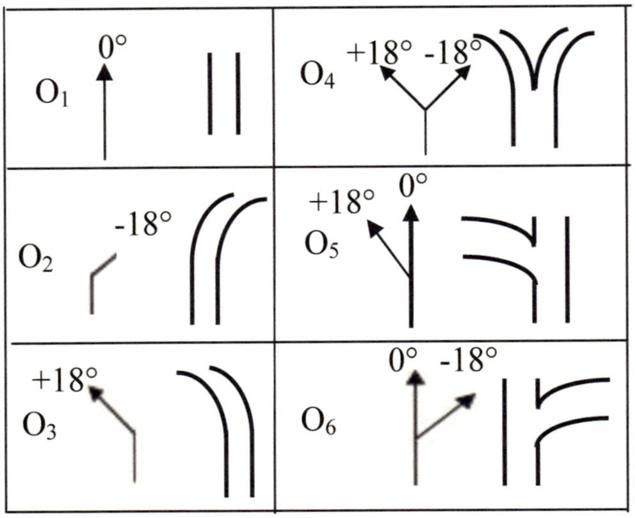

Fig. 5. Obstacle avoidance situations.

After learning, for each input vector X_O, NN2 provides the vehicle with capability to decide its obstacle avoidance, recognizing obstacle avoidance situation expressed by the highly activated output O_{j2}.

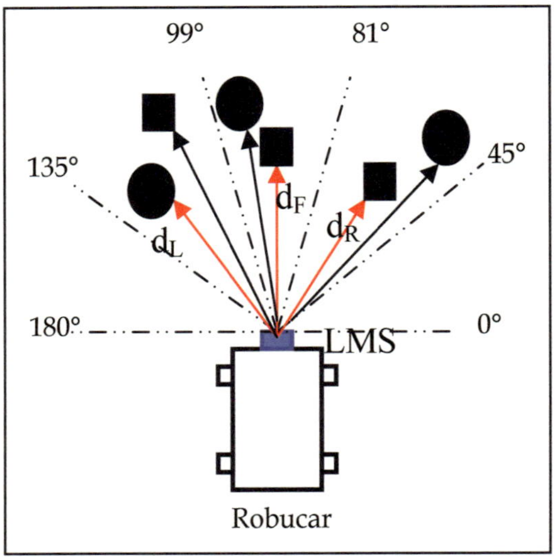

Fig. 6. Laser range areas for obstacle detection.

c) Phase 3.

Decision-Making and Action (NN3). Two (02) association stages between each behavior (target localization and obstacle avoidance) and the favorable actions (among possible actions), and the coordination of these association stages are carried out by NN3. Thus, both situations T_{j1} and O_{j2} are associated by the reinforcement trial and error learning with the favorable actions separately as suggested in (Sorouchyari, 1989). Afterwards, the coordination of the two (02) associated stages allows the decision-making of the appropriate action.

NN3 is built of two layers (input layer and output layer) illustrated in Figure 7.

1) Input Layer.
This layer is the input layer with eleven (11) input nodes receiving the components of T_{j1} and O_{j2} vectors. This layer transmits these inputs to all nodes of the next layer. Each node T_{j1} is connected to all nodes A_i with the connection weights U_{ij1} and each node O_{j2} is connected to all nodes A_i with the connection weights V_{ij2} as shown in Figure 7.
2) Output Layer.
This layer is the output layer with three (03) output nodes which are obtained by adding the contribution of each behavior. The Robucar learns through trial and error interactions with the environment. It learns a given behavior by being told how well or how badly it is performing as it acts in each given situation. As feedback, it receives a single information item from the environment. The feedback is interpreted as positive or negative scalar reinforcement. The goal of the learning system is to maximize positive reinforcement (reward) and/or minimize negative reinforcement (punishment) over time (Sorouchyari, 1989; Sutton & Barto, 1998). By successive trials and/or errors, the Robucar determines a mapping function (see figure 8) which is used for its navigation. The two association stages are obtained as developed in (Chohra et al., 1998).
After learning, NN3 provides the vehicle with capability to decide the appropriate action expressed by the highly activated output A_i.

3. Simulation results

In this section, at first the training processes of NN1, NN2, and NN3 are described. Second, the simulated neural-based navigation is described and simulation results are presented.

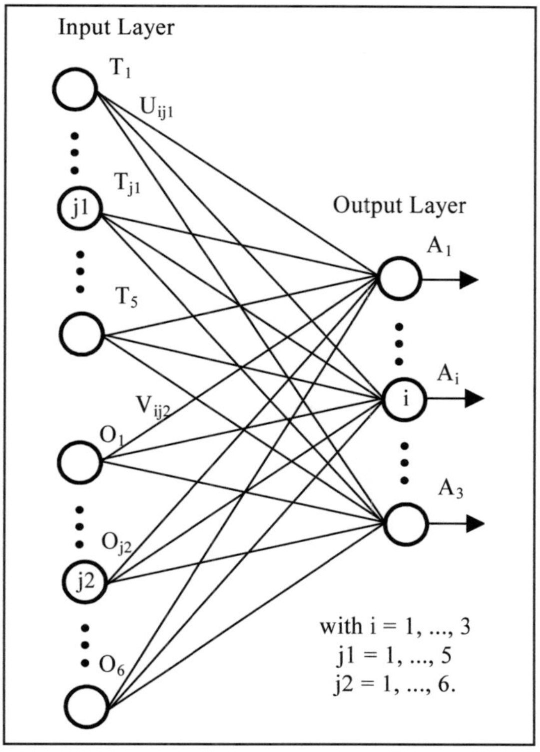

Fig. 7. Architecture of NN3.

3.1 Training of NN1, NN2, and NN3

a) Training of NN1. The used training set is composed of one hundred and nine (109) patterns corresponding to the five (05) target location situations. NN1 classifier yields convergence to the tolerance $Ea_1 = 0.06$ in well with the learning rate $\eta_1 = 0.1$.

b) Training of NN2. The used training set is composed of one hundred and fourteen (115) patterns corresponding to the six (06) obstacle avoidance situations. NN2 classifier yields convergence to the tolerance $Ea_2 = 0.16$ in well with the learning rate $\eta_2 = 0.4$.

c) Training of NN3. This training is achieved with the training of two association stages and their coordination.

1) Association.

In this stage, the training to obtain the weights U_{ij1} and V_{ij2}, constituting the training of NN3, is achieved respectively in an obstacle-free environment (i.e., O = 0) for the target localization behavior and without considering the temperature field (i.e., T = 0) for the obstacle avoidance behavior.

The training results are illustrated in Figure 8 where the weights U_{ij1} and V_{ij2} are adjusted to obtain the reinforced actions among favorable actions. Matrices of the two behaviors are

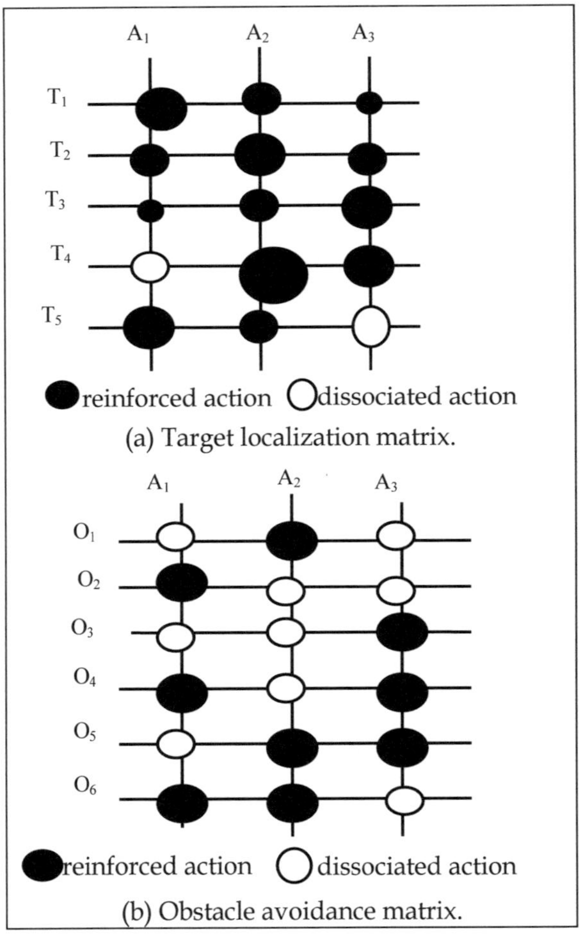

(a) Target localization matrix.

(b) Obstacle avoidance matrix.

Fig. 8. Association matrices.

represented in this figure: solid circles correspond to positive weights which represent favorable actions, indicating reinforced association, where values are proportional to the area of circles and the most reinforced action is the one having the great positive weight. Hollow circles correspond to negative weights which represent dissociated actions.
The choice of the most reinforced action is guided by the principle that the vehicle must avoid obstacles just to avoid collisions for the obstacle avoidance behavior and it must take the straighter action towards its target for the target localization behavior.
2) Coordination.
The coordination of the two association stages is conducted by the fact that actions generated by obstacle avoidance have precedence over those generated by target localization. In fact, the detection of the maximum temperature is interpreted as the goal of the vehicle while the generated actions by the presence of obstacles are interpreted as the reflex of the vehicle.

3.2 Simulation of the neural-based navigation on the Robucar

To reflect the vehicle behaviors acquired by learning, the Robucar navigation is simulated in different static and dynamic partially structured environments. The simulated vehicle has only two known data: its initial and final (target) positions. From these data, it must reach its target while avoiding possibly encountered obstacles using the neural-based navigation approach.
Tested in the environment of Figure 9 corresponding to a corridor of our centre CDTA (Centre de Développement des Technologies Avancées), the vehicle succeeds to avoid walls and obstacles by choosing the appropriate action by steering right or left according to the given situation as shown in Figure 10 where the evolution of v and ϕ is given. At point A, it stops because it finds itself in a blocked situation (walls at both sides and obstacle in front).

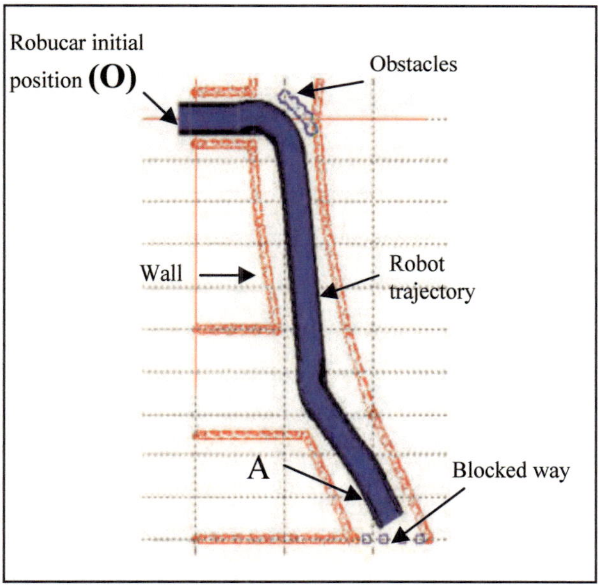

Fig. 9. Corridor environment1 with a blocked way.

The robot at point O in Figure 11 could not reach its target directly because of the wall at its right, so it goes strait until it finds a way to turn right (Figure 11 at point A and Figure 12 at time 1s). Afterwards, it goes strait ahead until point B where it steers to reach its target.

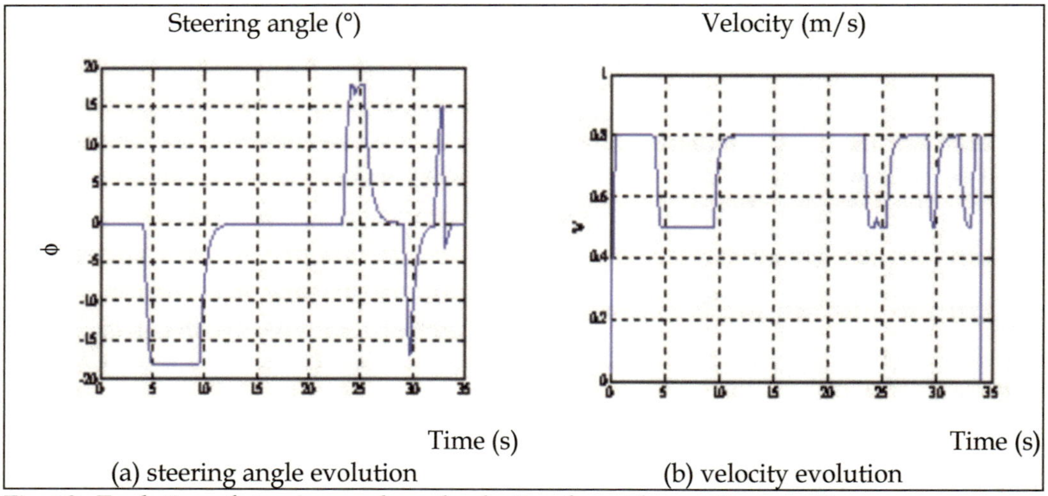

Fig. 10. Evolution of steering angle and velocity of corridor environment1.

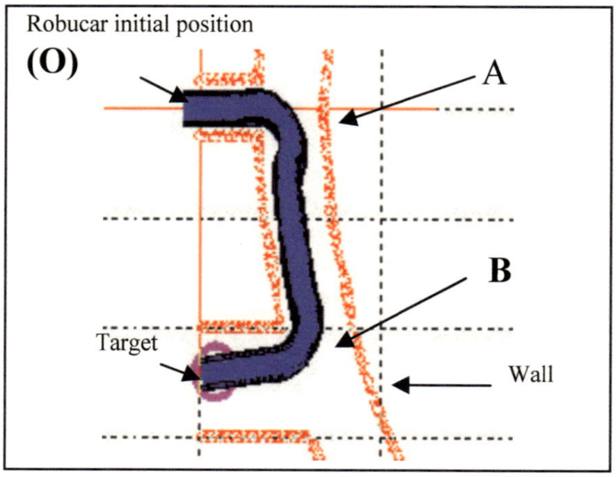

Fig. 11. Corridor environment2.

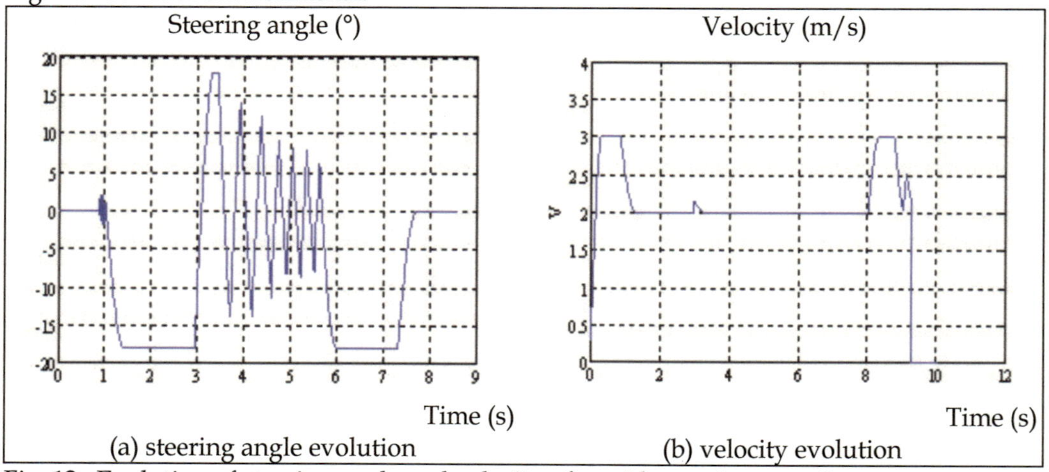

Fig. 12. Evolution of steering angle and velocity of corridor environment2.

The oscillations in Figure 12(a) are due to the fact that the robot tries to point to its target each time it doesn't detect obstacles but the wall pushes it away until point B.

4. Experiments of the neural-based navigation on the Robucar

In this section, experimental results are given for different environments.
Figure 13 corresponds to the confined corridor of CDTA. Obstacle A is put to force the robot to steer right and obstacle B to block a way.
The experiments show that the Robucar behaves intelligently since it moves avoiding collisions with walls (wall1 and wall2) and obstacle A. At this point, it turns right and goes forwards until it detects obstacle B and stops because it finds itself in a dead zone. Note that the same behavior has been observed in the simulation of Figure 9.
Figure 14 (a) gives the trajectory of the Robucar which corresponds to the corridor configuration. The evolution of the steering angle and velocity is illustrated in Figure 14 (b) and (c).
The example of Figure 15 shows a Robucar moving in a dynamic partially structured environment. It avoids the obstacles and reaches its target as shown in Figure 16. At point (c), suddenly an obstacle is put in the robot's trajectory to cause a dead zone and moved after a while (see Figure 16(c) where the velocity between 14s and 19s is equal to zero). The robot stops when it detects the obstacle and restarts when the obstacle is taken out and reaches its target at location (5m, -5m).

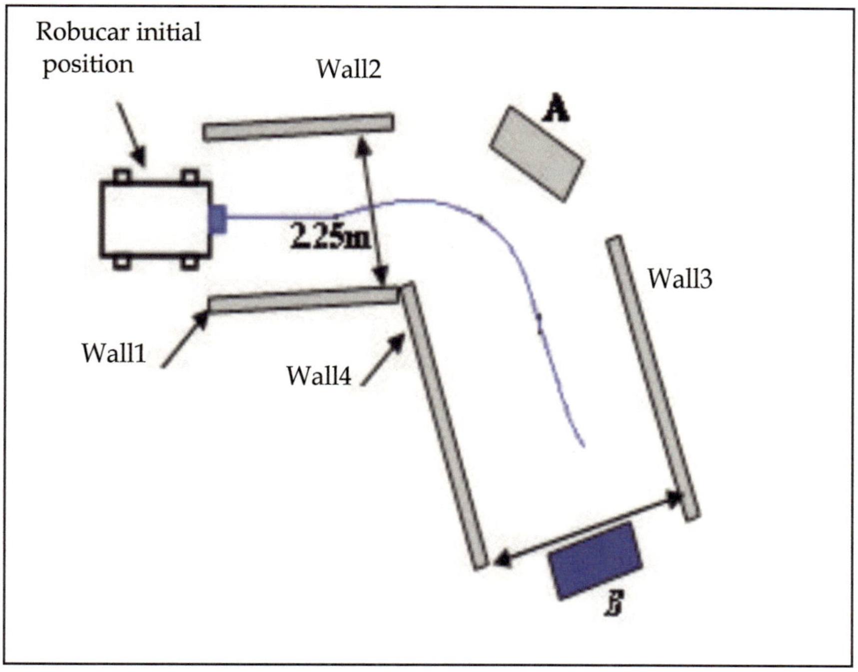

Fig. 13. Internal environment.

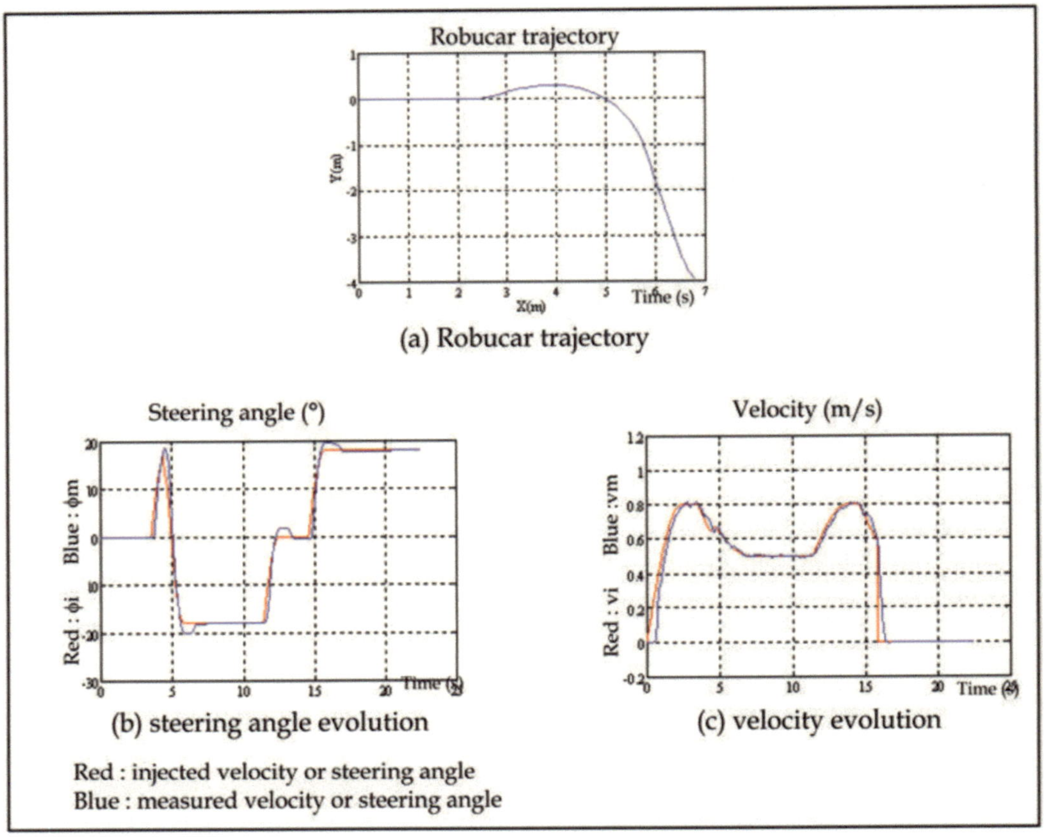

Fig. 14. Robucar trajectory and evolution of steering angle and velocity (internal environment).

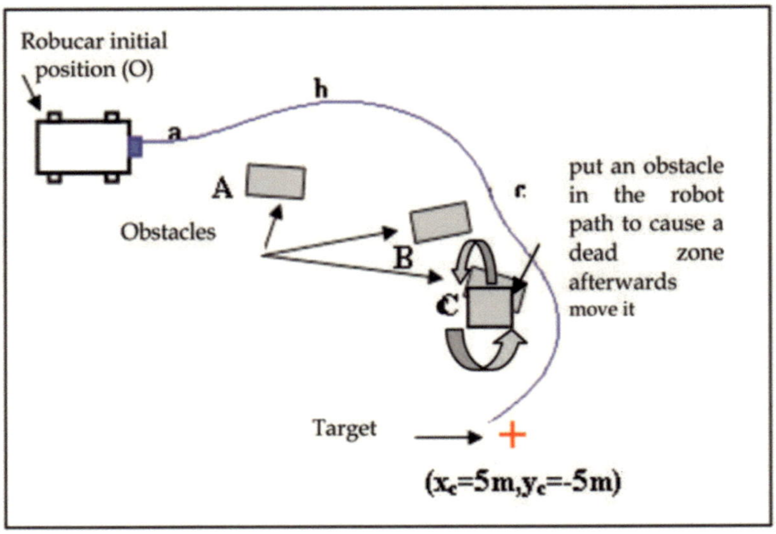

Fig. 15. External environment.

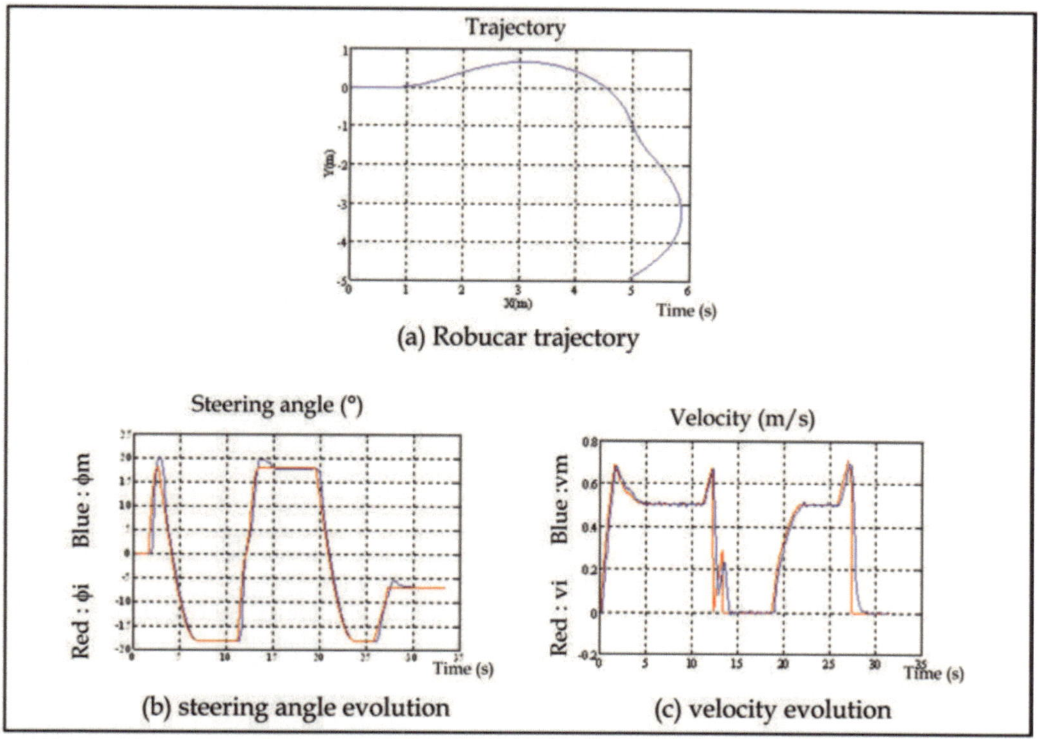

Fig. 16. Robucar trajectory and evolution of steering angle and velocity (external environment).

5. Conclusion

In the implemented neural-based navigation, the two intelligent behaviors necessary to the navigation, are acquired by learning using GBP algorithm. They enable Robucar to be more autonomous and intelligent in partially structured environments. Nevertheless, there are a number of issues that need to be further investigated. At first, the Robucar must be endowed with one or several actions to come back to eliminate a stop in a dead zone situation. Another interesting alternative is the use of a better localization not only based on odometry but by fusing data of other sensors such as laser scanner.

6. References

Anderson, A. (1995). *An Introduction to Neural Networks.* The MIT Press, ISBN: 0262011441, Cambridge, Massachusetts, London, England.

Avina Cervantes, J.G. (2005). *Navigation visuelle d'un robot mobile dans un environnement d'extérieur semi-structuré*, PhD thesis, France.

Azouaoui, O. & Chohra, A. (2003). Pattern classifiers based on soft computing and their FPGA integration for intelligent behavior control of mobile robots, *Proc. IEEE 11th Int. Conf. on Advanced Robotics ICAR'2003*, pp. 148-154, ISBN: 972-96889-9-0, Portugal, June 2003, Universidade de Coimbra Publisher, Coimbra.

Azouaoui, O. & Chohra, A. (2002). Soft computing based pattern classifiers for the obstacle avoidance behavior of Intelligent Autonomous Vehicles (IAV), *Applied Intelligence: The International Journal of Artificial Intelligence, Neural Networks, and Complex*

Problem-Solving Technologies, Vol. 16, N° 3, May/June 2002, pp. 249-271, ISSN: 1573-7497 (online).
Azouaoui, O. & Chohra, A. (1998). Evolution, behavior, and intelligence of Autonomous Robotic Systems (*ARS*), *Proceedings of 3rd Int. IFAC Conf. Intelligent Autonomous Vehicles*, pp. 139-145, Spain, March 1998, Miguel Angel SALICHS and Aarne HALME editors, Madrid.
Bento, L.C. & Nunes, U. (2004). Autonomous navigation control with magnetic markers guidance of a cybernetic car using fuzzy logic, *Machine intelligence and robotic control*, Vol. 6, No.1, March 2004, pp. 1-10, ISSN: 1345-269X.
Chohra, A.; Farah A. & Benmehrez, C. (1998). Neural navigation approach for Intelligent Autonomous Vehicles (*IAV*) in Partially structured Environments, *International Journal of Applied Intelligence: Artificial Intelligence, Neural Networks, and Complex Problem-Solving Technologies*, Vol. 8, No. 3, May 1998, pp. 219- 233, ISSN: 1573-7497 (online).
Gu, D. & Hu, H. (2002). Neural predictive control for a car-like mobile robot, *International Journal of Robotics and Autonomous Systems*, Vol. 39, No. 2-3, May 2002, pp. 73-86, ISSN: 0921-8890.
Hong, T.; Rasmussen, C.; Chang, T. & Shneier, M. (2002). Fusing ladar and color image information for mobile robot feature detection and tracking, Proceedings of *7th International Conference on Intelligent Autonomous Systems*, pp. 124-131, ISBN: 1-58603-239-9, CA, March 2002, IOS Press, Marina del Rey.
Kujawski, C. (1995). Deciding the behaviour of an autonomous mobile road vehicle, *Proceedings of 2nd International IFAC Conference on Intelligent Autonomous Vehicles*, pp. 404-409, Finland, June 1995, Halme and K. Koskinen editors, Helsinki.
Labakhua, L. ; Nunes, U. ; Rodrigues, R. & Leite, F. S. (2006). Smooth trajectory planning for fully automated passengers vehicles, International Conference on Informatics in Control, Automation and Robotics, pp. 89-96, ISBN: 972-8865-60-0, Portugal, August 2006, INSTICC Press, Setubal.
Mendes, A. ; Bento, L.C. & Nunes, U. (2003). Path-tracking controller with an anti-collision behavior of a bi-steerable cybernetic car, *9th IEEE Int. Conference on Emerging Technologies and Factory Automation (ETFA 2003)*, pp. 613-619, ISBN: 0-7803-7937-3, Portugal, September 2003, UNINOVA-CRI and Universidade Nova de Lisboa-FCT-DEE publisher, Lisboa.
Murphy, R. R. (2000). Fuzzy logic for fusion of tactical influences on vehicle speed control, *In: Fuzzy logic techniques for autonomous vehicle navigation*, Dimiter Driankov and Alessandro Saffiotti editors, pp 73-98, Physica-Verlag, ISBN: 978-3-7908-1341-8, New York.
Niegel, W. (1995). Methodical structuring of knowledge used in an intelligent driving system, *Proceedings of 2nd International IFAC Conference on Intelligent Autonomous Vehicles*, pp. 398-403, Finland, June 1995, Halme and K. Koskinen editors, Helsinki.
Schafer, B.H. (2005). Detection of negative obstacles in outdoor terrain, *Technical report*, Kaiserlautern university of technology, 2005.
Schilling, K. & Jungius, C. (1996). Mobile robots for planetary exploration, *PControl Engineering Practice*, Vol. 4, N° 4, April 1996, pp. 513-524, ISSN: 0967-0661.
SICK. (2001). Hardware setup and measurement mode configuration, *Quick manual for LMS communication setup, SICK AG*, Germany, June 2001.
Sorouchyari, E. (1989). Mobile robot navigation: a neural network approach, *In Annales du Groupe CARNAC1 no. S*, pp. 13-24.
Sutton, R.S. & Barto, A. (1998). *Reinforcement Learning : an Introduction.* MA: MIT Press, ISBN-10: 0-262-19398-1, Cambridge.
Wagner, B. (2006). ELROB 2006, *Technical paper*, University of Hannover, May 2006.
Welstead, S. T. (1994). *Neural Network and Fuzzy Logic Applications C/C++*. John Wiley & Sons Inc., ISBN-10: 0471309745, Toronto.

4

On the Estimation of Asymptotic Stability Region of Nonlinear Polynomial Systems: Geometrical Approaches

Anis Bacha, Houssem Jerbi and Naceur Benhadj Braiek
Laboratoire d'Etude et Commande Automatique des Processus-LECAP
Ecole Polytechnique de Tunisie-EPT- La Marsa, B.P. 743,
2078 Tunisia

1. Introduction

In recent years, the problem of determining the asymptotic stability region of autonomous nonlinear dynamic systems has been developed in several researches. Many methods, usually based on approaches using Lyapunov's candidate functions (Davidson & Kurak, 1971) and (Tesi et al., 1996) which altogether allow for a sufficient stability region around an equilibrium point. Particularly, the method of Zubov (Zubov, 1962) is a vital contribution. In fact, it provides necessary and sufficient conditions characterizing areas which are deemed as a region of asymptotic stability around stable equilibrium points.

Such a technique has been applied for the first time by Margolis (Margolis & Vogt, 1963) on second order systems. Moreover, a numerical approach of the method was also handled by Rodden (Rodden, 1964) who suggested a numerical solution for the determination of optimum Lyapunov function. Some applications on nonlinear models of electrical machines, using the last method, were also presented in the Literature (Willems, 1971), (Abu Hassan & Storey, 1981), (Chiang, 1991) and (Chiang et al., 1995). In the same direction, the work presented in (Vanelli & Vidyasagar, 1985) deals with the problem of maximizing Lyapunov's candidate functions to obtain the widest domain of attraction around equilibrium points of autonomous nonlinear systems. Burnand and Sarlos (Burnand & Sarlos, 1968) have presented a method of construction of the attraction area using the Zubov method.

All these methods of estimating or widening the area of stability of dynamic nonlinear systems, called Lyapunov Methods, are based either on the Characterization of necessary and sufficient conditions for the optimization of Lyapunov's candidate functions, or on some approaches using Zubov's digital theorem. Equally important, however, they also have some constraints that prevented obtaining an exact asymptotic stability domain of the considered systems. Nevertheless, several other approaches nether use Lyapunov's functions nor Zubov's which have been dealt with in recent researches. Among these works cited are those based on topological considerations of the Stability Regions (Benhadj Braiek et al., 1995), (Genesio et al., 1985) and (Loccufier & Noldus, 2000).

Indeed, the first method based on optimization approaches and methods using the consideration of Lasalle have been developed to ensure a practical continuous stability

region of the second order systems. Furthermore, other methods based on interpretations of geometric equations of the model have grabbed an increasing attention to the equivalence between the convergence of the linear part of the autonomous nonlinear system model and whether closed Trajectories in the plan exist. An interesting approach dealing with this subject is called trajectory reversing method (Bacha et al. 1997) and (Noldus et al.1995).
In this respective, an advanced reversing trajectory method for nonlinear polynomial systems has been developed (Bacha et al.,2007).Such approach can be formulated as a combination between the algebraic reversing method of the recurrent equation system and the concept of existence of a guaranteed asymptotic stability region around an equilibrium point. The improvement of the validity of algebraic reversing approach is reached via the way we consider the variation model neighbourhood of points determined in the stability boundary's asymptotic region. An obvious enlargement of final region of stability is obtained when compared by results formulated with other methods. This very method has been tested to some practical autonomous nonlinear systems as Van Der Pool.

2. Backward iteration approaches

We attempt to extend the trajectory reversing method to discrete nonlinear systems. In this way, we suggest two different algebraic approaches so as to invert the recurrent polynomial equation representing the discrete-time studied systems. The enlargement and the exactness of the asymptotic stability region will be considered as the main criterion of the comparison of the two proposed approaches applied to an electrical discrete system.

2.1 Description of the studied systems

We consider the polynomial discrete systems described by the following recurrent state equation:

$$X_{k+1} = F\left(X_{k+1}\right) = \sum_{i=1}^{r} F_i . X_k^{[i]} \tag{1}$$

where F_i,$i=1,\ldots,r$ are ($n \times n^{[i]}$) matrices and X_k is an n dimensional discrete-time state vector. $X_k^{[i]}$ designates the ith order of the Kronecker power of the state X_k. The initial state is denoted by X_0. Note that this class of polynomial systems (1) may represent various controlled practical processes as electrical machines and robot manipulators.
It is assumed that system (1) satisfies the known conditions for the existence and the uniqueness of each solution $X(k,X_0)$ for all k, with initial condition $X(k=0)=X_0$.
The origin is obviously an equilibrium point which is assumed to be asymptotically stable.
The region of asymptotic stability of the origin is defined as the set Ω of all points X_0 such that:

$$\forall X_0 \in \Omega,\ \forall k \in \aleph, X\left(k, X_0\right) \in \Re \text{ and } \lim_{k \to \infty} X\left(k, X_0\right) = 0 \tag{2}$$

So, we can find an open invariant set Ω with boundary Γ such that Ω is a region of asymptotic stability (RAS) of system (1) defined by the property that every trajectory starting from $X_0 \in \Omega$ reaches the equilibrium point of the corresponding system.

Note that determining the global stability region of a given system is a difficult task. In this respect, one often has to be satisfied with an approximation that leads to a guaranteed stable region in which all points belong to the entire stability region.
In the forthcoming sections, we try to estimate a stability region of the system (1) included in the entire RAS. The main way to get a stable region Ω is to use the reversing trajectory method called also backward iteration.
For a discrete nonlinear system with a state equation (1) the backward iteration means the running of the reverse of the discrete state equation (1) which requires to explicit the following retrograde recurrent equation:

$$X_k = F^{-1}(X_{k+1}) \tag{3}$$

Note that this reverse system is characterized by the same trajectories in discrete state space as (1). So, it is obvious that the asymptotic behaviour of trajectories starting in the region of asymptotic stability Ω is related to its boundary Γ and always provides information about it.
In order to determine the inverted polynomial recurrent equation, we expose in the next section two dissimilar digital backward iteration approaches by using the Kronecker product form and the Taylor expansion development.

2.2 Proposed approaches for the formulation of the discrete model inversion

The exact determination of the reverse polynomial recurrent equation (3) could not be reached. For the achievement of this target, most of the methods that have been suggested are based on approximation ideas.

- First approach

In the first method, we suggest to use the following approximation:

$$X_k = X_{k+1} + \varepsilon(X_{k+1}) \tag{4}$$

where $\varepsilon(X_{k+1})$ is assumed to be a little term, which we will explicit. This assumption requires a suitable choice of the sampling period. Without loss of generality we will develop the approach of expliciting the term $\varepsilon(X_{k+1})$ for the case r=3. The obtained results can be easily generalized for any polynomial degree r by following the same principle.
So, we consider then the following recurrent equation:

$$X_{k+1} = F_1.X_k + F_2.X_k^{[2]} + F_3.X_k^{[3]} \tag{5}$$

Replacing in (5) X_k by its expression (4) and neglecting all terms $\varepsilon^{[n]}(X_{k+1})$ for n>1, one can easily obtain the following expression of $\varepsilon(X_{k+1})$.

$$\varepsilon(X_{k+1}) = \begin{bmatrix} F_1 + F_2.(X_{k+1} \otimes I_n + I_n \otimes X_{k+1}) + \\ F_3.(X_{k+1} \otimes I_n \otimes X_{k+1} + X_{k+1}^{[2]} \otimes I_n + I_n \otimes X_{k+1}^{[2]}) \end{bmatrix}^{-1} \\ .\left[X_{k+1} - \left(F_1.X_{k+1} + F_2.X_{k+1}^{[2]} + F_3.X_{k+1}^{[3]} + F_4.X_{k+1}^{[4]}\right)\right] \tag{6}$$

Then, the RAS may be well estimated by means of a convergent sequence of simply connected domains generated by the backward iterations (4) and (6).

- Second approach

The second proposed technique of the inversion of the model (1) is made up by the characterization of the reverse model:

$$X_k = F^{-1}(X_{k+1}) = G(X_{k+1}) \tag{7}$$

by a r-polynomial vectorial function G(.) i.e.:

$$X_k = \sum_{i=1}^{r} G_i . X_{k+1}^{[i]} \tag{8}$$

where G_i, i=1,...,r are matrices of (nx $n^{[i]}$) dimensions.
Hence, it is easy to identify the G_i matrices in (8) by writing $F(G(X_{k+1})) = X_{k+1}$ which leads to the following relations:

$$\begin{cases} G_1 = G_1^1 = F_1^{-1} \\ G_2 = G_2^1 = -F_1^{-1} F_2 . G_2^1 \\ \vdots \\ G_r = G_r^1 = -F_1^{-1} \left(\sum_{i=1}^{r-1} F_i . G_r^i \right) \end{cases} \tag{9}$$

where G^i_p, for i=2,...,r and p=2,...,r verify the following recurrent relations:

$$\begin{cases} G_p^2 = \sum_{j=1}^{p-1} \left(G_{p-j}^1 \otimes G_j^1 \right) \\ \vdots \\ G_p^i = \sum_{j=1}^{p-i+1} \left(G_{p-j}^{i-1} \otimes G_j^1 \right) \end{cases} \tag{10}$$

- Evolutionary algorithm of backward iteration method

By using one of the presented approaches of the reversing recurrent equation of system (1) formulated above, the reversing trajectory technique can be run by the following conceptual algorithm.

1. Verify that the origin equilibrium of the system (1) is asymptotically stable i.e. $\|eig(F_1)\| < 1$.
2. Determine a guaranteed stable region (GSR) noted Ω_0 using the theorem 1 proposed in (Benhadj, 1996a) and presented in page 64.
3. Determine the discrete reverse model of the system (1) using the first or the second approach.
4. Apply the reverse model for different initial states belonging to the boundary Γ_0 of the GSR Ω_0.

The application of the backward iteration k times on the boundary Γ_0 leads to a larger stability region Ω_k such that $\Omega_0 \subset \Omega_1 \subset \ldots \subseteq \Omega_{k-1} \subset \Omega_k$.

The performance of the backward iteration algorithm depends on the used inversion technique of the polynomial discrete model among the above two proposed approaches.

In order to compare the two formulated approaches, we propose next their implementation on a synchronous generator second order model.

2.3 Simulation study

We consider the simplified model of a synchronous generator described by the following second order differential equation (Willems, 1971):

$$\frac{d^2\delta}{dt^2} + a\frac{d\delta}{dt} + \sin(\delta + \delta_0) - \sin(\delta_0) = 0 \tag{11}$$

where δ_0 is the power angle and δ is the power angle variation.

The continuous state equation of the studied process for the state vector: $\begin{cases} x_1 = \delta \\ x_2 = \dfrac{d\delta}{dt} \end{cases}$ is given by the following couple of equation:

$$\begin{cases} \dot{x}_1 = x_2 \\ \dot{x}_2 = -ax_2 - \sin(x_1 + \delta_0) + \sin\delta_0 \end{cases} \tag{12}$$

where a is the damping factor.

This nonlinear system can be approached by a third degree polynomial system:

$$X_{k+1} = A_1.X_k + A_2.X_k^{[2]} + A_3.X_k^{[3]} \tag{13}$$

with $$A_1 = \begin{pmatrix} 0 & 1 \\ -\cos\delta_0 & -a \end{pmatrix}, \quad A_2 = \begin{pmatrix} 0 & 0 & 0 & 0 \\ \dfrac{\sin\delta_0}{2} & 0 & 0 & 0 \end{pmatrix}$$

and $$A_3 = \begin{pmatrix} 0 & 0 & \\ & & 0_{2\times 6} \\ \dfrac{\cos\delta_0}{6} & 0 & \end{pmatrix}$$

The discretization of the state equation (13) using Newton-Raphson technique (Jennings & McKeown, 1992), (Bacha et al, 2006a) ,(Bacha et al, 2006b) with a sampling period T leads to the following discrete state equation of the synchronous machine:

$$X_{k+1} = F_1.X_k + F_2.X_k^{[2]} + F_3.X_k^{[3]} \tag{14}$$

with

$$F_1 = \begin{pmatrix} 1 & \mathrm{T} \\ -T\cos\delta_0 & 1-aT \end{pmatrix}, \quad F_2 = \begin{pmatrix} 0 & 0 & 0 & 0 \\ \frac{T.\sin\delta_0}{2} & 0 & 0 & 0 \end{pmatrix}$$

and

$$F_3 = \begin{pmatrix} 0 & 0 & \\ & & 0_{2\times 6} \\ \frac{T.\cos\delta_0}{6} & 0 & \end{pmatrix}$$

With the following parameters: $\begin{cases} \delta_0 = 0.412 \\ a = 0.5 \\ T = 0.05 \end{cases}$

one obtains the following numerical values of the matrices F_i, i=1, 2, 3.

$$F_1 = \begin{pmatrix} 1 & 0.05 \\ -0.0458 & 0.975 \end{pmatrix}, \quad F_2 = \begin{pmatrix} 0 & 0 & 0 & 0 \\ 0.0076 & 0 & 0 & 0 \end{pmatrix}$$

$$F_3 = \begin{pmatrix} 0 & 0 & \\ & & 0_{2\times 6} \\ 0.01 & 0 & \end{pmatrix}$$

One can easily verify that the equilibrium Xe=0 is asymptotically stable since we have $|eig(F_1)| < 1$.

Our aim now is the estimation of a local domain of stability of the origin equilibrium Xe=0. For this goal, we make use of the backward iteration technique with the proposed inversion algorithms of the direct system (14) applied from the boundary Γ_0 of the ball Ω_0 centred in the origin and of radius R_0=0.42 which is a guaranteed stability region (GSR) that characterized the method developed in (Benhadj, 1996a).

- Domain of stability obtained by using the first approach of discrete model inversion :

The implementation of the first approach of the discrete model inversion described by equation (4) leads, after running 2000 iterations, to the region of stability represented in the figure 1.

Figure 2 represents the stability domain of the discrete system (14) obtained after running the backward iteration based on the inversion model (4) 50000 times.

It is clear that the domain obtained after 50000 iterations is larger than that obtained after 2000 iterations and it is included in the exact stability domain of the studied system, which reassures the availability of the first proposed approach of the backward iteration formulation.

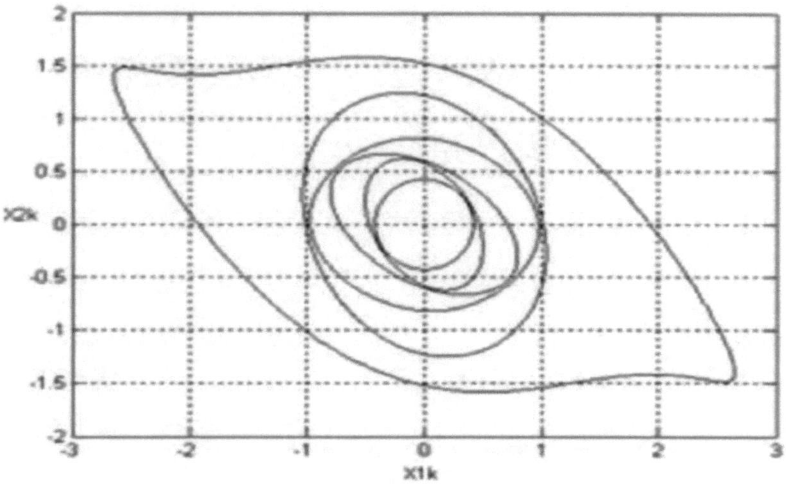

Fig. 1. RAS of discrete synchronous generator model obtained after 2000 backward iterations based on the first proposed approach

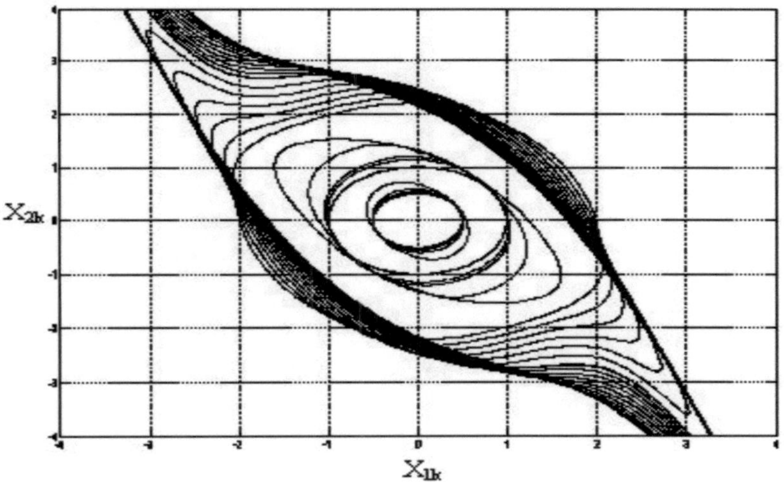

Fig. 2. RAS of discrete synchronous generator model obtained after 50000 backward iterations based on the first proposed approach.

- Domain of stability obtained by using the second approach of discrete model inversion

When applying the discrete backward iteration formulated by using the reverse model (8) we obtain the stability domain shown in figure 3 after 1000 iterations and the domain presented in figure 4 after 50000 iterations.

In figure 4 it seems that the stability domain estimated by the second approach of backward iteration is larger and more precise than that obtained by the first approach. The reached stability domain represents almost the entire domain of stability, which shows the efficiency of the second approach of the backward iteration, particularly when the order of the studied system is not very high as a second order system.

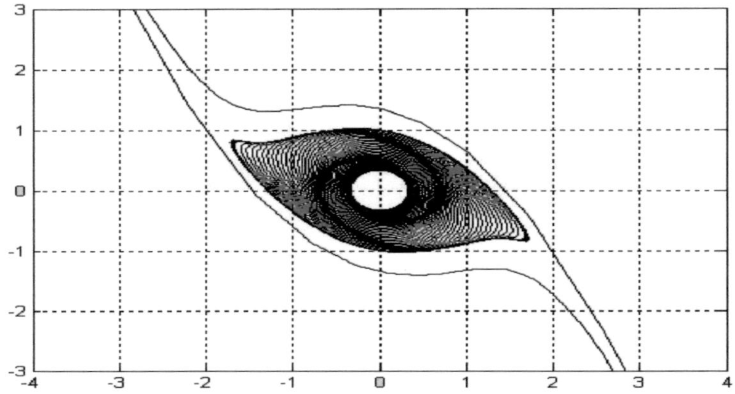

Fig. 3. RAS of discrete synchronous generator model obtained after 1000 backward iterations based on the second proposed approach

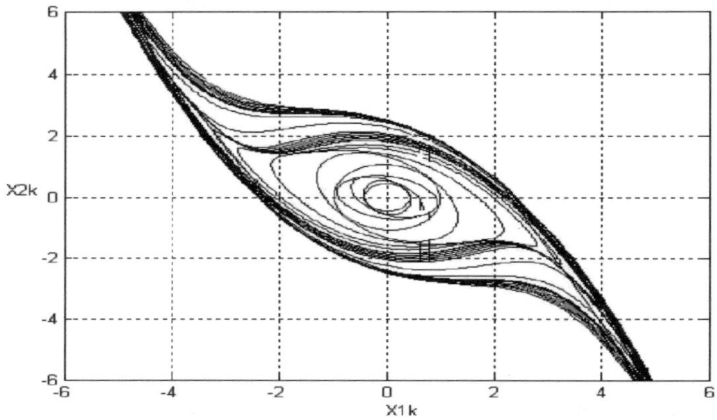

Fig. 4. RAS of discrete synchronous generator model obtained after 50000 backward iterations based on the second proposed approach

2.4 Conclusion

In this work, the extension of the reversing trajectory concept for the estimation of a region of asymptotic stability of nonlinear discrete systems has been investigated.

The polynomial nonlinear systems have been particularly considered.

Since the reversing trajectory method, also called backward iteration, is based on the inversion of the direct discrete model, two dissimilar approaches have been proposed in this work for the formulation of the reverse of a discrete polynomial system.

The application of the backward iteration with both proposed approaches starting from the boundary of an initial guaranteed stability region allows to an important enlargement of the searched stability domain. In the particular case of the second order systems, the studied technique can lead to the entire domain of stability.

The simulation of the developed algorithms on a second order model of a synchronous generator has shown the validity of the two approximation ideas with a little superiority of the second approach of the discrete model inversion, since the RAS obtained by this last one is larger and more precise than the one yielded by the first approximation approach.

3. Technique of a guaranteed stability domain determination

In this part we consider a new advanced approach of estimating a large asymptotic stability domain for discrete time nonlinear polynomial system. Based on the Kronecker product (Benhadj Braiek, 1996a; Benhadj Braiek, 1996b) and the Grownwell-bellman lemma for the estimation of a guaranteed region of stability; the proposed method permits to improve previous results in this field of research.

3.1 Description of the studied systems

We consider the discrete nonlinear systems described by a state equation of the following form

$$X(k+1) = F(x(k)) = \sum_{i=1}^{q} A_i X^{[i]}(k) \tag{15}$$

where k is the discrete time variable, $X(k) \in \Re^n$ is the state vector, $X^{[i]}(k)$ designates the i-th Kronecker power of the vector $X(k)$ and $A_i, i = 1,\dots,q$ are $(n \times n^i)$ matrices. The system (15) can also be written in the following form:

$$X(k+1) = M(X(k)).X(k) \tag{16}$$

where:

$$M(X(k)) = A_1 + \sum_{j=2}^{q} A_j (I_n \otimes X^{[j-1]}(X(k)) \tag{17}$$

where $\otimes$ is the Kronecker product (Benhadj Braiek, 1996a; Benhadj Braiek, 1996b).
Assumption 1: The linear part of the discrete systems (15) is asymptotically stable i.e. all the eigenvalues of the matrix are of module little than 1.

3.2 Guaranteed stability region

Our purpose is to determine a sufficient domain Ω_0 of the initial conditions variation, in which the asymptotic stability of system (15) is guaranteed, according to the following definition:

$$\begin{aligned} &\forall X_0 \in \Omega_0 \quad X(k,k_0,X_0) \in \Re \ \forall k \\ &and \qquad \lim_{k \to +\infty} X(k,k_0,X_0) = 0 \end{aligned} \tag{18}$$

where $X(k,k_0,X_0)$ designates the solution of the nonlinear recurrent equation (15) with the initial condition $X(k_0) = X_0$.

The stability domain that we propose is considered as a ball of radius R_0 and of centre the origin $X = 0$ i.e.,

$$\Omega_0 = \{X_0 \in \Re^n ; \|X_0\| < R_0\} \tag{19}$$

the radius R_0 is called the stability radius of the system (15).

A simple domain ensuring the stability of the system (15) is defined by the following theorem (Benhadj Braiek, 1996b).

Theorem 1. Consider the discrete system (15) satisfying the assumption 1, and let c and α the positive numbers verifying $\alpha \in \left]0 \ 1\right[$,

$$\left\| A_1^{k-k_0} \right\| \le c\alpha^{k-k_0} \forall k \ge k_0 \tag{20}$$

Then this system is asymptotically stable on the domain Ω_0 defined in (19) with R_0 the unique positive solution of the following equation:

$$\sum_{k=2}^{q} \gamma_k R_0^{k-1} - \frac{1-\alpha}{c} = 0 \tag{21}$$

where $\gamma_k, k = 2,\ldots,q$ denote :

$$\gamma_k = c^{k-1} \left\| A_k \right\| \tag{22}$$

Furthermore the stability is exponentially.

Proof. The equation (15) can be written as:

$$X(k+1) = A_1 X(k) + h(X(k))X(k) \tag{23}$$

with

$$h(X(k)) = \sum_{j=2}^{q} A_j (I_n \otimes X^{[j-1]}(k)) \tag{24}$$

Let us consider that:

$$\forall k \ge k_0, \left\| X(k) \right\| \le R \tag{25}$$

then we have, using the matrix norm property of the Kronecker product

$$\left\| h(X(k)) \right\| \le \lambda(R) \tag{26}$$

with:

$$\lambda(R) = \sum_{j=2}^{q} \left\| A_j \right\| R^{j-1} \tag{27}$$

By using the lemma 1(see the appendix), we have:

$$\left\| X(k) \right\| \le c(\alpha + c\lambda(R))^{k-k_0} \left\| X(k_0) \right\| \tag{28}$$

with $g(X) = h(X)X$,we have $\|g(X)\| \le \lambda(R)\|X\|$.
Then, if:

$$\lambda(R) < \frac{1-\alpha}{c} \tag{29}$$

Now, to ensure the hypothesis (25) it is sufficient to have (from (21)):

$$c\|X(k_0)\| \le R_1 \text{ or } \|X(k_0)\| \le R_0 = \frac{R_1}{c} \tag{30}$$

R_1 satisfies the equation (29) implies that R_0 satisfies the equation (21) of the theorem 1.

3.3 Enlargement of the guaranteed stability region (GSR)

Our object in this section is to enlarge the Guaranteed Stability Region Ω_0 characterized in the section 3.2. For this goal, we consider the boundary Γ_0 of the obtained GSR of radius R_0. Let X^i_0 be a point belonging in Γ_0, and X^i_k the image of X^i_0 by the $F(\,.\,)$ function characterizing the considered system, k times.

$$X^i_k = F^k\left(X^i_0\right) \tag{31}$$

X^i_k is then a point belonging in the stability domain Ω_0;

$$\left\|X^i_k\right\| < R_0 \quad , \quad \left\|F^k\left(X^i_0\right)\right\| < R_0 \tag{32}$$

To enlarge the GSR, we will look for a radius $r_{0,i}$ such that for any initial state X_0 verifying

$$\left\|X_0 - X^i_0\right\| \le r_{0,i}$$

one has

$$X_k = F^k\left(X_0\right) \in \Omega_0 \tag{33}$$

and the fact that after k iterations the state of the system attends the domain Ω_0 ensures that X_0 is a state belonging in the stability domain.
Let us note:

$$\delta X_0 = X_0 - X^i_0 \tag{34}$$

And for $k \ge 1$

$$\delta X_k = X_k - X^i_k = F^k\left(X_0\right) - F^k\left(X^i_0\right) \tag{35}$$

δX_k can be expressed in terms of δX_0 as a polynomial function of degree $s=q^k$ where q is the degree of the $F(\,.\,)$ polynomial characterizing the system:

$$\delta X_k = E_1.\delta X_0 + E_2.\delta X_0^{[2]} + ... + E_s.\delta X_0^{[s]}; \quad s = q^k \tag{36}$$

$E_1, E_2..., E_s$ are matrices depending on k and $X^i{}_0$ and they can easily expressed in terms of A_i and $X^i{}_0$.
In the particular case where $q = 3$ and $k = 1$ one has:

$$\begin{aligned}\delta X_1 &= X_1 - X_1^i = F(X_0) - F(X_0^i) \\ &= D_1.\delta X_0 + D_2.\delta X_0^{[2]} + ... + D_r.\delta X_0^{[r]}\end{aligned} \tag{37}$$

where

$$\begin{cases} D_1 = \begin{bmatrix} A_1 + A_2(X_{j,k} \otimes I_n) + A_2(I_n \otimes X_{j,k}) + \\ A_3((X_{j,k} \otimes I_n) \otimes X_{j,k}) + \\ A_3(X_{j,k}^{[2]} \otimes I_n) + \\ A_3((I_n \otimes X_{j,k}) \otimes X_{j,k}) \end{bmatrix} \\ D_2 = \begin{bmatrix} A_2 + A_3((X_{j,k} \otimes I_n) \otimes I_n) + \\ A_3((I_n \otimes X_{j,k}) \otimes I_n) + \\ A_3(I_n^{[2]} \otimes X_{j,k}) \end{bmatrix} \\ D_3 = A_3 \end{cases}$$

From the relation:

$$X_k = \delta X_k + F^k(X_0^i) \tag{38}$$

one has:

$$\|X_k\| \le \|\delta X_k\| + \|F^k(X_0^i)\| \tag{39}$$

From (36) we have:

$$\|\delta X_k\| \le e_1.\|\delta X_0\| + e_2.\|\delta X_0^{[2]}\| + ... + e_s.\|\delta X_0^{[s]}\| \tag{40}$$

with:

$$e_j = \|E_j\|, \quad j = 1, 2, ..., s$$

Hence we have:

$$\begin{aligned} \|X_k\| &\leq \sum_{j=1}^{s} e_j . \left\|\delta X_0^{[j]}\right\| + \left\|F^k\left(X_0^i\right)\right\| \\ &\leq \sum_{j=1}^{s} e_j . r_{0,i}^j + \left\|F^k\left(X_0^i\right)\right\| \end{aligned} \quad (41)$$

Since it is desired that:

$$\|X_k\| \leq R_0; \quad (X_k \in \Omega_0) \quad (42)$$

it will be sufficient to have:

$$\begin{aligned} &\sum_{j=1}^{s} e_j . r_{0,i}^j = R_0 - \left\|F^k\left(X_0^i\right)\right\| \\ &e_1 . r_{0,i} + e_2 . r_{0,i}^2 + \ldots + e_s . r_{0,i}^s = R_0 - \left\|F^k\left(X_0^i\right)\right\| > 0 \end{aligned} \quad (43)$$

which yields:

$$\|\delta X_0\| = \left\|X_0 - X_0^i\right\| \leq r_{0,i} \quad (44)$$

where $r_{0,i}$ is the unique positive solution of the polynomial equation:

$$e_1 . r_{0,i} + e_2 . r_{0,i}^2 + \ldots + e_2 . r_{0,i}^s = R_0 - \left\|F^k\left(X_0^i\right)\right\| \quad (45)$$

and this result can be stated in the following theorem.

Theorem 2

Let the following polynomial discrete system described by:

$$X_{k+1} = F\left(X_k\right) = A_1 . X_k + A_2 . X_k^{[2]} + \ldots + A_r . X_k^{[r]} \quad (46)$$

and let Ω_0 the GSR of radius R_0 given in theorem 1, and Γ_0 the boundary of the GSR, then: For any point $X_0^i \in \Gamma_0$, the ball Ω_i centred on X_0^i and of radius $r_{0,i}$ the unique positive solution of the equation (45) is also a domain of stability of the considered system.

In the particular case where consider *k=1*, one has the following corollary.

Corollary 1

The ball B_i of radius $r_{0,i}$ solution of the equation:

$$\|D_1\| . r_{0,i} + \|D_2\| . r_{0,i}^2 + \ldots + \left\|D_q\right\| . r_{0,i}^q = R_0 - \left\|F\left(X_0^i\right)\right\| > 0 \quad (47)$$

is a domain of asymptotic stability of the considered system.

After considering all the points $X_0^i \in \Gamma_0$ (varying *i*), a new domain of stability is obtained by collecting all the little balls Ω_i to Ω_0 :

$$D = \underset{i}{\cup} \Omega_i \tag{48}$$

For all the considered points X_i^k and the associated balls Ω_i, we can construct a new domain of stability Ω_{i+1} with a boundary Γ_{i+1}, and we have $\Omega_i \subset \Omega_{i+1}$. This procedure can be repeated with these new data Ω_{i+1} and Γ_{i+1} until obtaining a sufficiently large stability domain of the considered system equilibrium points.
This idea is illustrated in Figure 5.

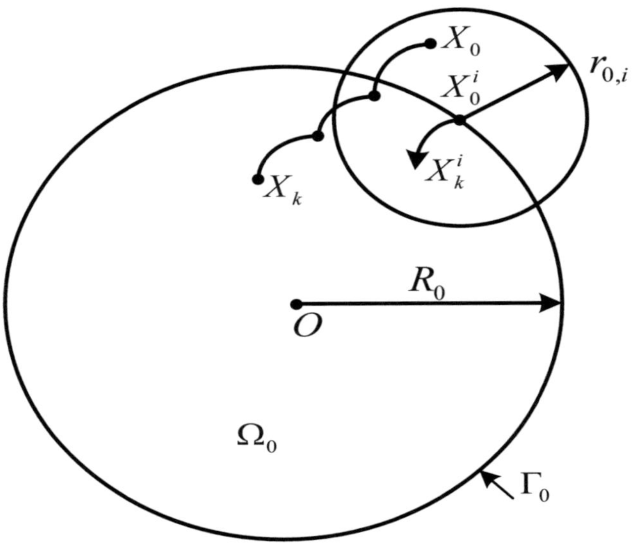

Fig. 5. Illustration of the principle of the proposed method

3.4 Simulation results: application to Van Der pool model

Let us consider the following discrete polynomial Van Der Pool model obtained from the Raphson-newton approximation: (Jening & Mc Keown, 1992)

$$X_{k+1} = A_1 X_k + A_3 X_k^{[3]} \tag{49}$$

Where $X_k = \begin{bmatrix} x_{1k} \\ x_{2k} \end{bmatrix}$ $A_1 = \begin{pmatrix} 0.9988 & -0.0488 \\ 0.0488 & 0.950 \end{pmatrix}$ $A_3 = \begin{pmatrix} 0 & -0.0012 & \\ & & 0_{2\times 6} \\ 0 & 0.0488 & \end{pmatrix}$

Equation (49) has a linear asymptotically stable matrix A_1, which verifies the inequalities (20) with c=1.7 and α=0.65. Then, we may conclude that the origin is exponentially stable for each initial state X_0 included in the disc Ω_0 centered in the origin and of radius R_0=0.33.

Figure 6 shows the guaranteed stability domain Ω_0 obtained by the application of the theorem 1, and the enlarged region resulting from the application of the theorem 2 for one iteration (k=1), and for 22 points X_0^i on the boundary Γ_0. It comes out that the new result stated in the theorem 2 leads to an important enlargement of the guaranteed stability domain.

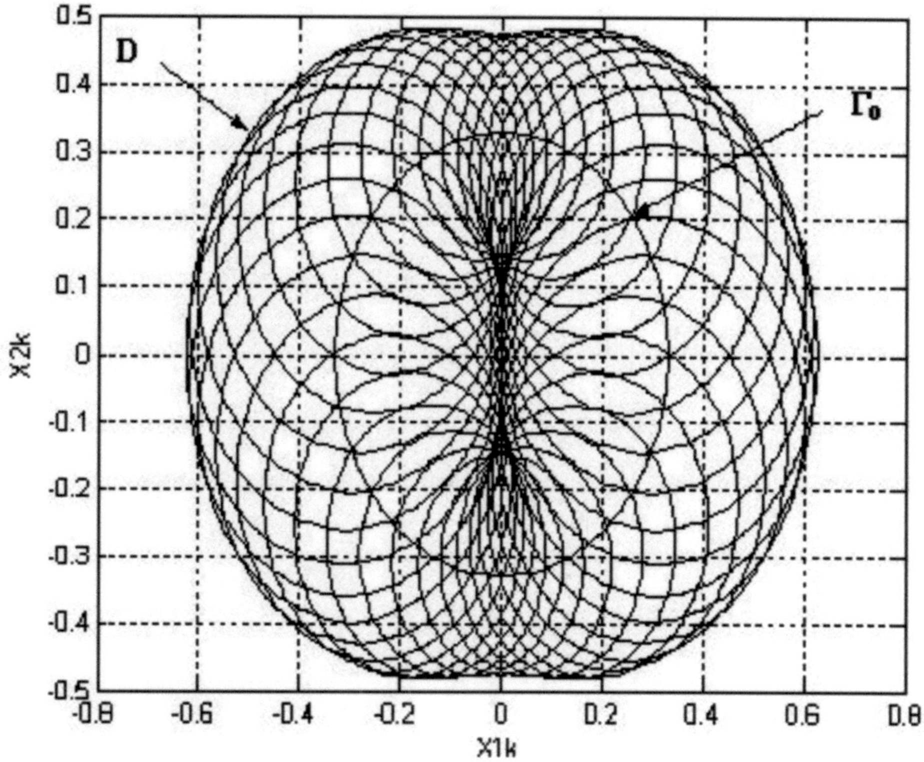

Fig. 6. Enlargement of a guaranteed RAS estimate of Van Der Pool discrete model

4. Conclusion

An advanced discrete algebraic method has been developed to determine and enlarge the region of asymptotic stability for autonomous nonlinear polynomial discrete time systems.
The exactness of the obtained RAS in this case constitutes the main advantage of the proposed approach.
The proposed technique is proved theoretically and tested via numerical simulation on the discrete polynomial Van Der Pool model.
The original discrete developed method is equivalent to the reversing trajectory method which used to determine the RAS for continuous systems.
Further research will be focused on the development and the implementation of an optimal numerical tool which allows to reach the larger region of asymptotic stability for discrete nonlinear systems.

5. Appendix

Lemma 1 (Benhadj Braiek, 1996b):
Let a discrete nonlinear system defined by the state equation:

$$X(k+1) = A_1 X(k) + g(k, X(k)) \tag{50}$$

where the linear part satisfies the assumption 1, and the nonlinear part $g(k, X(k))$ verifies the following inequality :

$$g(k, X(k)) \leq \beta \| X'k) \| \tag{51}$$

where β is a positive constant.
Let $\Phi(k, k_0)$ denotes the transition matrix of the linear part of the discrete system (50):

$$\Phi(k, k_0) = A_1^{k-k_0} \tag{52}$$

and let c and α the positive numbers verifying $\alpha \in \left]0\ 1\right[$,

$$\| \Phi(k, k_0) \| \leq c \alpha^{k-k_0} \qquad \forall k \geq k_0 \tag{53}$$

Then the solution $X(k)$ of the system (50) verifies the following inequality:

$$\| X(k) \| \leq c(\alpha + c\beta)^{k-k_0} \| X(k_0) \| \tag{54}$$

So if $\beta < 1 - \frac{\alpha}{c}$, the system (50) is exponentially stable.

6. References

Abu Hassan M.; Storey C., (1981). Numerical determination of domain of attraction for electrical power systems using the method of Zubov *int. J. Contr*, vol.34, pp.371-381.

Bacha, A.; Jerbi, H. & Benhadj Braiek, N. (2008). A Technique of a stability domain determination for nonlinear discrete polynomial systems, *Proceedings of IFAC 2008*, Seoul South Korea, June 2008, Seoul (submitted and accepted)

Bacha, A.; Jerbi, H. & Benhadj Braiek, N. (2008). Backward iteration approaches for the stability domain estimation of discrete nonlinear polynomial systems, *International Journal of Modelling, Identification and Control IJMIC*, accepted in december 2007, to appear in 2008.

Bacha, A.; Jerbi, H. & Benhadj Braiek, N. (2007a). On the synthesis of a combined discrete reversing trajectory method for the asymptotic stability region estimation of nonlinear polynomial systems, *Proceedings of 13th IEEE IFAC International Conference on Methods and Models in Automation and Robotics, MMAR2007*, pp.243-248, , Poland, August 2007, Szczecin

Bacha, A.; Jerbi, H. & Benhadj Braiek, N. (2007b). A comparative stability study between two new backward iteration approaches of discrete nonlinear polynomial systems, *Proceedings of Fourth International Multi-Conference on Systems, Signals and Devices , SSD2007*, March 19-22, 2007. Hammamet, Tunisia.

Bacha, A.; Jerbi, H. & Benhadj Braiek, N. (2006a). An approach of asymptotic stability domain estimation of discrete polynomial systems. *Proceeding of IMACS Multiconference on Computational Engineering in Systems Applications, Mathematical Modelling, Identification and Simulation, CESA'2006 World Congress* . Vol. 1, pp.288-292, 4-6 October 2006, Beijing, China.

Bacha, A.; Jerbi, H. & Benhadj Braiek, N. (2006b). On the estimation of asymptotic stability regions for nonlinear discrete-time polynomial systems. *Proceeding of International Symposium on Nonlinear Theory and its Applications. NOLTA'2006*. pp.1171-1173, September 2006, Bologna, Italy.

Bacha, A.; Benhadj Braiek, N. & Benrejeb, M. (1997). On the transient stability domain estimation of power systems. *Record of the fth International Middle East power conference. MEPCOM'97*, pp.377- 381, 1997, Alexandria, Egypt.

BenHadj Braiek E., (1996a). A Kronecker product approach of stability domain determination of nonlinear continuous systems. *Journal of Systems Analysis Modeling and Simulation, SAMS*, vol.22, pp.11-16.

BenHadj Braiek E., (1996b). Determination of a stability radius for discrete nonlinear systems. *Journal of Systems Analysis Modeling and Simulation, SAMS.* , vol.22, pp.315-322.

Benhadj Braiek E.; Rotella F. & Benrejeb M., (1995). An algebraic method for global stability analysis of nonlinear systems . *Journal of Systems Analysis Modeling and Simulation, SAMS.* , vol.17, pp.211-227.

Burnand G. & Sarlos G., (1968). Determination of the domain of stability . *J. Math. Anal. Appl.*, vol.23, pp.714-722.

Chiang H.; Chu C. C. & Cauley G., (1995) Direct stability analysis of electric power systems. *Proceeding of the IEEE83*, pp.1497-1529.

Chiang H., (1991). Analytic results on direct methods for power system transient stability analysis. *in Advances in Control and Dynamic Systems*, Vol.43, Academic press, New york, pp.275-334.

Davison E. J. & Kurak E. M., (1971). A computational method for determining quadratic Lyapunov functions for nonlinear systems. *Automatica*, vol.7, p. 627.

Genesio R.; Tartaglia M. & Vicino A., (1985). On the estimation of asymptotic stability regions: State of the art and new proposals *IEEE Trans. Automat. Contr. Syst.*, vol. AC-30,No8, pp.747-755, 1985.

Jenings A. & McKeown J. J., (1992) *Matrix Computation: Second Edition*, Wiley, 1992.

Locufier M. & Noldus E., (2000). A New trajectory reversing method for estimating stability regions of autonomous nonlinear systems, *Nonlinear Dynamics21*, pp.265-288, 2000.

Margolis S. G. & Vogt W. G., (1963). Control engineering applications of V. I. Zubov's construction procedure for Lyapunov functions, *IEEE Trans. Contr.*, vol. AC-8, pp.104-113, Apr 1963.

Noldus E. & Loccufier. M., (1995). A new trajectory reversing method for the estimation of asymptotic stability regions, *International Journal of Control61*, 1995, pp.917-932.

Rodden J. J., (1964). Numerical applications of Lyapunov stability theory, *JACC*, Stanford, CA, pp. 261-268, 1964.

Tesi A.; Villoresi F. & Genesio R., (1996). On the stability domain estimation via quadratic Lyapunov functions: convexity and optimally properties for polynomial functions *IEEE Trans. Automat. Contr.* Vol.41, No.11, pp.1650-1657, November 1996.

Vannelli A. & Vidyasagar, (1985). Maximal Lyapunov functions and domain of attraction for autonomous nonlinear systems, *Automatica,* vol.21, pp.69-80, Jan. 1985.

Willems J. L., (1972). Direct method for transient stability studies in power systems analysis. *IEEE Trans. Automat. Contr.*, vol. AC-16, No.4, Aug.1971.

Zubov V. I, (1962). *Mathematical Methods for the study of Automatic Control Systems.* Israel: Jerusalem Academic Press, 1962.

5

Networked Control Systems for Electrical Drives

Baluta Gheorghe and Lazar Corneliu
"Gh. Asachi" Technical University of Iasi
Romania

1. Introduction

The use of networks as a media to interconnect the different components in an electrical drive control system is increasing in the last decades. Typically, the employ of a network on a control system is desirable when there is a large number of distributed sensors and actuators. Systems designed in this manner allow for easy modification of the control strategy by rerouting signals, having redundant systems that can be activated automatically when component failure occurs, and in general they allow having a high-level supervisor control over the entire plant. The flexibility and ease of maintenance of a system using a network to transfer information is a very appealing goal. Due to these benefits, many industrial companies and institutes apply networks for remote control purposes and factory automation (Yang, 2006), (Lian et al., 2002), (Bushnell, 2001), (Antsaklis & Baillieul, 2004), (Baillieul & Antsaklis, 2004). Control applications utilize networks to connect to Internet in order to perform remote control at much farther distances than in the past without investing on the whole infrastructure.
The connection between new network based control systems and teaching allows many universities to develop virtual and remote control laboratories (Valera et al., 2005), (Casini et al., 2004), (Saad et al., 2001). For several years, at the Departments of Power Electronics and Electrical Drives (Baluta & Lazar, 2007) and Automatic Control and Applied Informatics (Carari et al., 2003), (Lazar & Carari, 2008) from "Gh. Asachi" Technical University of Iasi, virtual and remote laboratories for electrical drive systems and process control have developed using a Networked Control System (NCS).
This chapter presents the experience of the electrical drives control group at the "Gh. Asachi" Technical University of Iasi in developing remote control laboratory for electrical drive systems. A SCADA environment has been chosen to implement the network based control architecture. This architecture allows the user to remotely choose a predefined controller to steer the electrical drives systems or to design a new one. Using SCADA software facilities, students can develop themselves new networked control systems for the set ups from the laboratory. The main advantage of the network based control structure is the user interface, which allows analyze the electrical drives system performances, to tune the controller and to test it through the remote laboratory. During the experiments, it is possible to change the set point, the operating mode and some typical controller parameters. Experimental results can be displayed showing the real running experiment and can be checked through on-line plots.

The chapter is organized as it follows. Section 2 illustrates the main features and the architecture of the networked control system laboratory. In Section 3, typical working sessions are described. Section 4 provides conclusions and future developments.

2. Remote control architecture

In order to achieve the remote control of the electrical drive systems, a Web server is used which assures the process distribution for different users (clients) via Intranet and Internet. The Intranet is the local computer network of the Department of Power Electronics and Electrical Drives from "Gh. Asachi" Technical University of Iasi. The electrical drive systems distribution is realized using a NCS architecture, which implements both configurations: direct structure and hierarchical structure (Tipsuwan, 2003).

2.1 NCS architecture

The developed NCS architecture has the layout from Fig. 1.

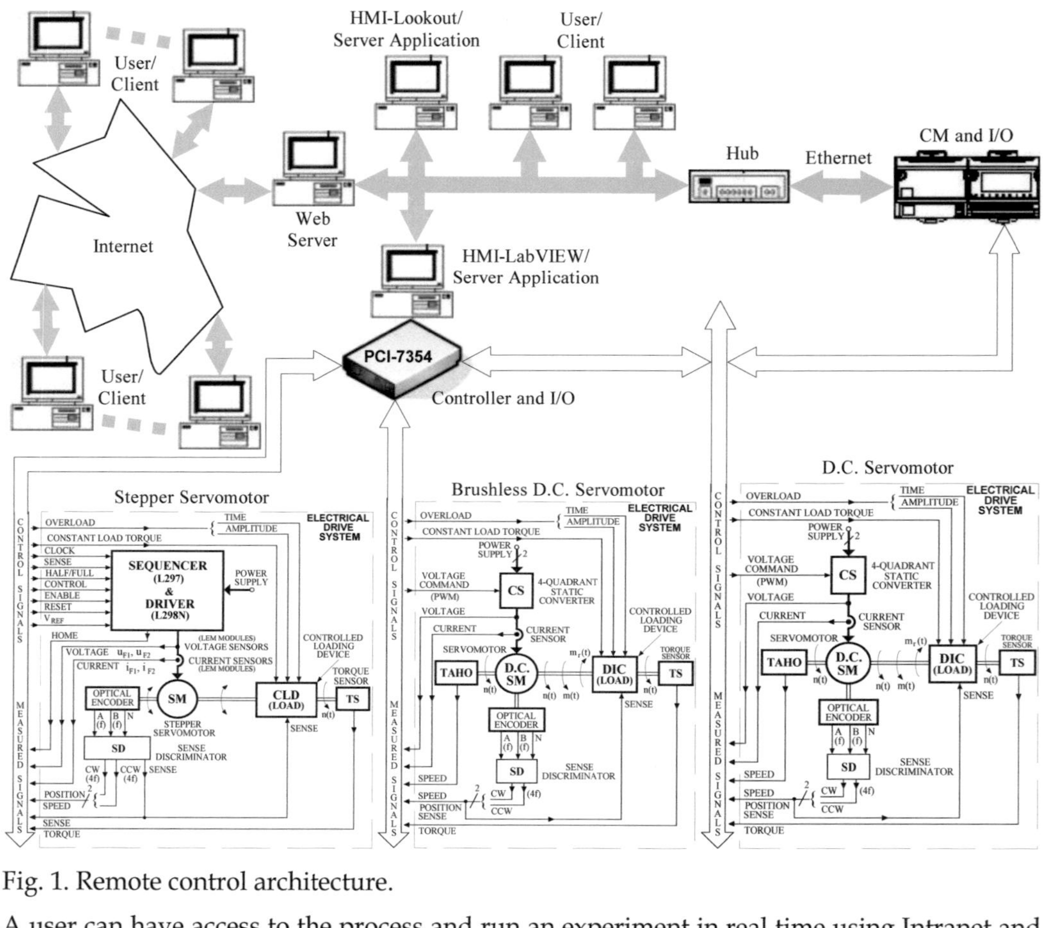

Fig. 1. Remote control architecture.

A user can have access to the process and run an experiment in real time using Intranet and Internet. The user can design and implement different control structures for electrical drive systems employing SCADA software facilities or, for a given control structure, he is able to implement and test PID control algorithms and tuning procedures. SCADA software enables programmers to create distributed control applications having supervisory facilities and a Human-Machine Interface (HMI). As SCADA software, Lookout is used for the direct structure and LabVIEW for the hierarchical structure. All external signals start and arrive at HMI/SCADA computer.

The laboratory architecture allows running experiments while interacting with instruments and remote devices. The I/O remote devices permit data acquisition from sensors and supplying control signals for actuators, using A/D and D/A converters.

The NCS architecture offers the possibility to remotely choose a predefined control structure to handle the electrical drives system variables or to design a new control application, using SCADA software facilities.

In the first case, using the remote control architecture the students have the possibility to practice their theoretical knowledge of electrical drive systems control in an easy way due to process access by a friendly user interface. The second opportunity offered to the students is to design a new networked control architecture which allows creating a new HMI/SCADA application to remotely control a process, using Lookout and, respectively, LabVIEW facilities (Carari et al., 2003).

The software architecture can be split in two parts: one concerns the control of the physical process - server side and the other relates to the user interface - client side. The server runs on the Microsoft Windows NT platform and is based on Lookout for direct structure and, respectively, LabVIEW environment for hierarchical structure.

The server application contains the HMI interface and fulfils the following functions:

- implements the control strategies;
- communicates with I/O devices through object drives;
- records the signals in a database;
- defines the alarms.

The client process contains a HMI interface, similar or not with those from server application, and has the following characteristics:

- allows modifying remotely the parameters defined by application server through a Web site;
- communicates with server application;
- displays the alarms defined by the server application.

The remote control architecture is mainly intended for educational use and it is employed for electrical drive control course. The aim is to allow students to put in practice their knowledge of electrical drives and control theory in an easy way without restrictions due to process availability through laboratory and project works. One of the main features is the possibility of integrating in the control loop of the remote process the user-designed controller. The interface for the controller synthesis is very friendly.

2.2 NCS in the direct structure

The NCS in the direct structure is composed of a computer of the Intranet, called HMI/Lookout that achieves the local communications with the process using Ethernet protocols. The remote electrical drive system, a D.C. brush servomotor, is connected with the communication module (CM) able to transfer data from/to I/O device to/from HMI/SCADA computer via a communication system. The communication module and I/O devices are implemented with National Instruments modules, FP1600 (Ethernet) for communication and, respectively, Dual-Channel Modules for I/O devices. The Lookout environment has been chosen to implement HMI/SCADA application. For D.C. servomotor, a cascade control structure is used in order to control the speed from the primary loop and the current from the secondary loop. The current controller is locally implemented and the speed controller is remotely implemented using Lookout environment. The cascade control structure allows the monitoring of control loops variables and the command of the overload at the servomotor shaft.

2.3 NCS in the hierarchical structure

Hierarchical structure is composed of a computer of the Intranet, called HMI/LabVIEW with a PCI motion controller board (National Instruments PCI-7354) and Analog & Digital I/O devices.
DSP controllers available today are able to perform the computation for high performance digital motion control structures for different motor technologies and motion control configuration. The level of integration is continuously increasing, and the clear trend is towards completely integrated intelligent motion control (Kreidler, 2002). Highly flexible solutions, easy parameterized and "ready-to-run", are needed in the existent "time-to-market" pressing environment, and must be available at non-specialist level.
Basically, the digital system component implements through specific hardware interfaces and corresponding software modules, the complete or partial hierarchical motion control structure, i.e., the digital motor control functionality at a low level and the digital motion control functionality at the higher level (see Fig. 2).

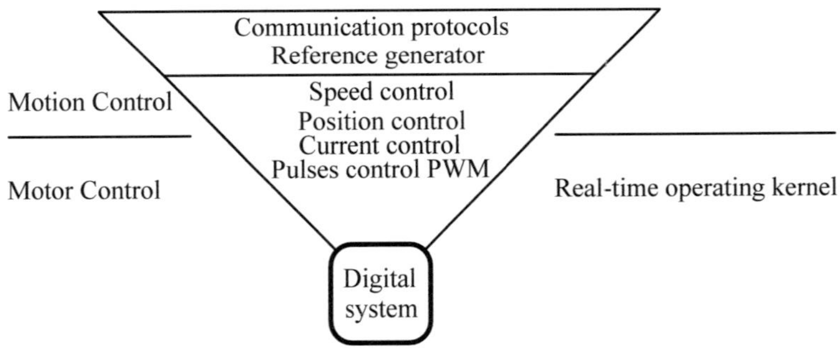

Fig. 2. Motion system structure hierarchy.

The National Instruments PCI-7354 controller is a high-performance 4-axis-stepper/D.C. brush/D.C. brushless servomotors motion controller. This controller can be used for a wide variety of both simple and complex motion applications. It also includes a built-in data acquisition system with eight 16-bit analog inputs as well as a host of advanced motion trajectory and triggering features. Through four axes, individually programmable, the board can control independently or in a coordinated mode the motion. The board architecture, which is build around of a dual-processors core, has own real-time operating system . These board resources assure a high computational power, needed for such real-time control.
Three electrical drive systems, based on a unipolar or bipolar stepper servomotors, D.C. brush servomotors and a D.C. brushless servomotors are linked to the remote control architecture. The connection is achieved with the I/O devices from PCI motion controller

board, which also contains a remote controller implemented using a DSP and real-time operating system, as is presented in Fig. 3.

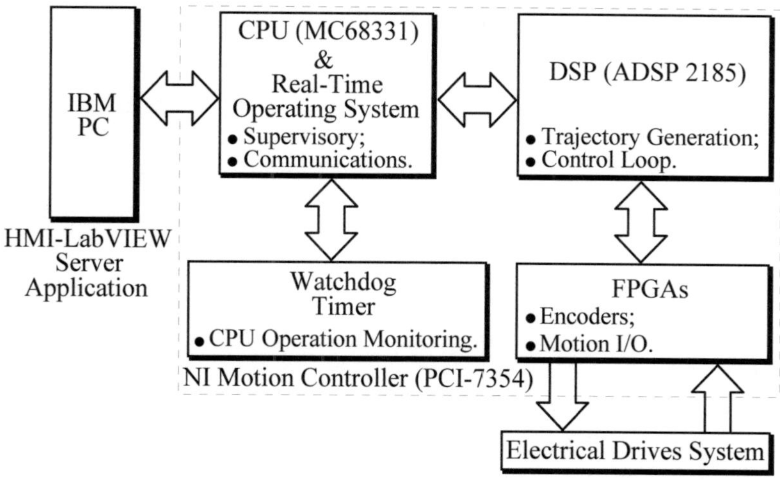

Fig. 3. Motion controller board structure.

Functionally, the architecture of the National Instruments PCI-7354 controller is generally divided into four components (see Fig. 4):

- supervisory control;
- trajectory generator;
- control loop;
- motion I/O.

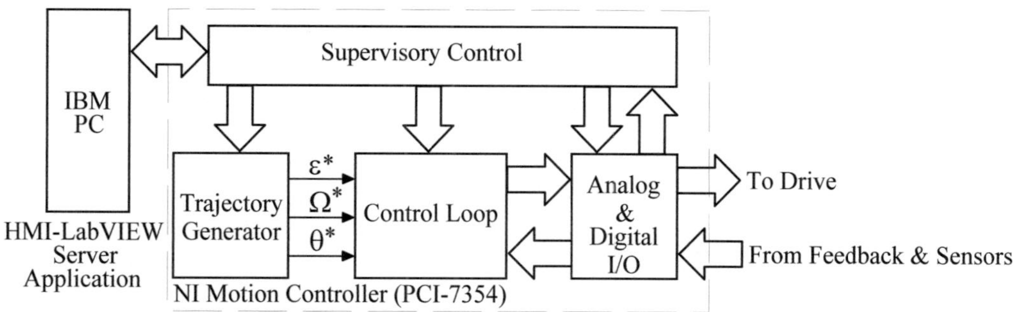

Fig. 4. Functional architecture of the NI PCI-7354.

Supervisory control performs all the command sequencing and coordination required to carry out the specified operation. Trajectory generator provides path planning based on the profile specified by the user, and control loop block performs fast, closed-loop control with simultaneous position, velocity, and trajectory maintenance on one or more axes, based on feedback signals.

The LabVIEW environment has been chosen to implement HMI/SCADA application. The development environment used to complete the applications is LabVIEW 7.0, which beside the graphic implementation that gives easy use and understanding takes full advantage of the networking resources. Using NCS hierarchical structure, control architecture for stepper

servomotors, D.C. brush servomotors and D.C. brushless servomotors supervisory was developed which allows the following functions:
-open-loop control of stepper servomotors using constant frequency or prescribed profile (trapezoidal or S-curve move profile, see Fig. 5);

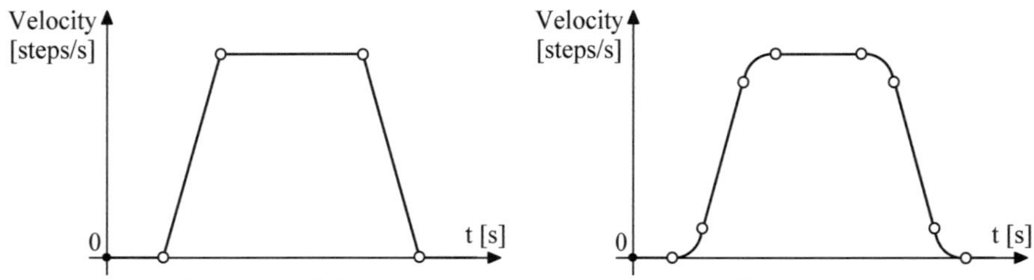

a. Trapezoidal. b. S-Curve.

Fig. 5. Move Profile.

- closed-loop control of stepper servomotors (speed and position);
- the operating mode of the stepper servomotors can be with full step, half step or microstepping mode;
- open-loop control or closed-loop control of D.C. brush servomotors;
- self-commutation control of D.C. brushless servomotor speed, which allows very high speeds;
- sensorless control for D.C. brushless servomotor.

3. Session description

This section presents three examples to illustrate the manipulation of instruments and real devices for low power electrical drives education on the Web. These examples exemplify the laboratory works dedicated to control a D.C. brush servomotor electrical drives system and a stepper servomotor electrical drives system.

3.1 NCS in the direct structure: D.C. brush servomotor electrical drives system

The set-up for D.C. brush servomotor control is presented in Fig. 6 and the layout can be inspected in Fig. 1.
The set-up consists in a D.C. brush servomotor, a D.C. brush generator used as load, an incremental encoder and a tachometer as speed transducer, a controlled loading device and a control block which includes an analogical controller for current loop. The set-up is used to illustrate cascade control and how this structure can reject the load disturbances. The primary variable is the motor speed, the secondary is the armature current and the disturbance is an overload introduced with a D.C. brush generator coupled on the servomotor shaft. The user has to tune the two controllers of the speed and current loops in order to obtain optimal performances and disturbance rejection.
When the application is started, the main panel from Fig. 7 is displayed. The main panel contains in the right side, the layout of the control system, real time data from the sensors and actuator and allows the reference setting, the overload command, the choice of operating mode: manual or automatic and the changing of the tuning parameters of the PI speed controller (Baluta & Lazar, 2007).

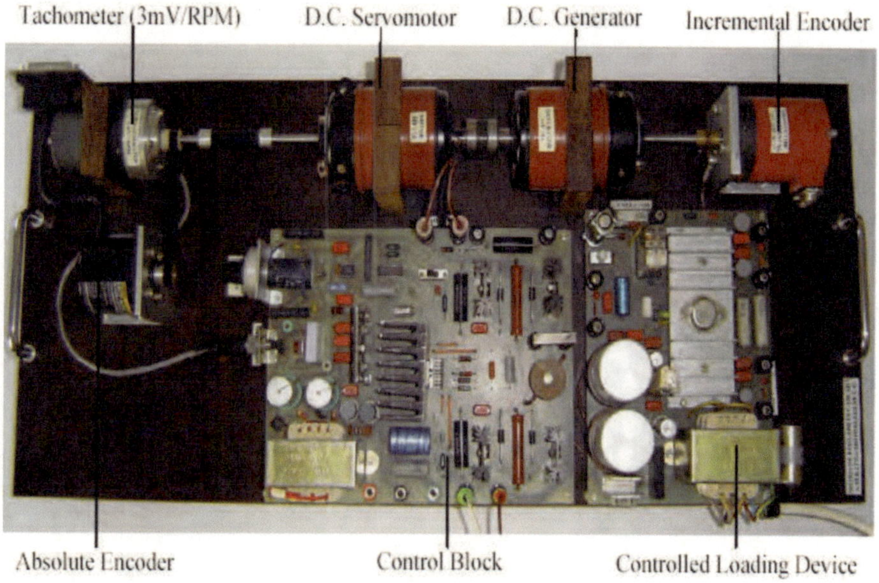

Fig. 6. D.C. brush servomotor electrical drives system.

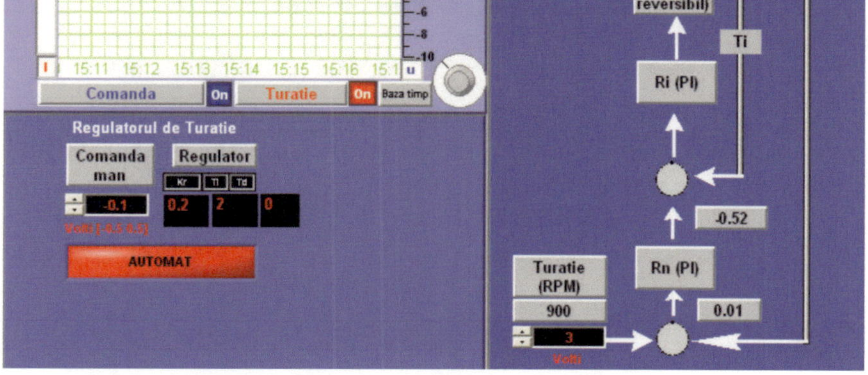

Fig. 7. Main panel for D.C. brush servomotor electrical drives system.

All these commands can be done using the left down side of the main panel. In the left up side, there is a monitor window, which allows the displaying of the main variables of the control loops. The Monitor window has the possibility to represent only the selected signals by using on/off buttons or to stop the variables displaying in order to analyse the signals or to change the time scale through a potentiometer button. All control system real time data are recorded in a database and can be employed for a future analysis (Baluta & Lazar, 2007).

The remote control of the D.C. brush servomotors implements the following functions:

- the reversible speed control;
- the on-line tuning of the parameters of speed controller;
- load command for servomotor shaft.

The monitor window of the main panel from Fig. 7 shows both the speed response for a different set point step variations and the load rejection and the current evolution. Details regarding disturbance rejection are given in Fig. 8. The numerical controller's parameters which have led to such results are Kr=0.2, Ti=2 and Td=0. Due to the well-chosen and adjusted controller, the system's response to a step variation of the set point is very good. At the same time, a good compensation of the disturbance can be noticed (the load torque).

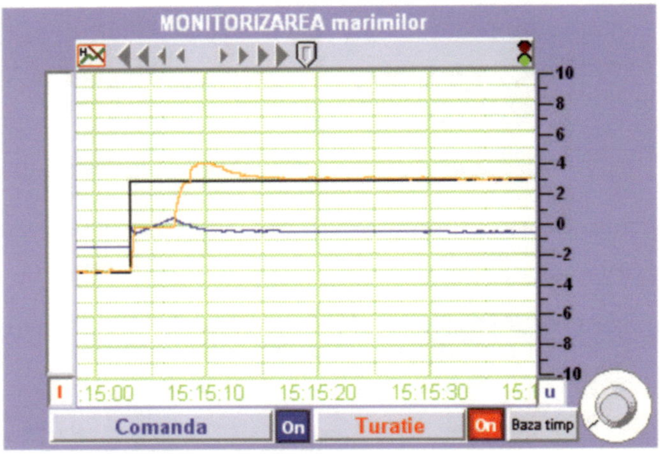

a. Step variation of the set point.

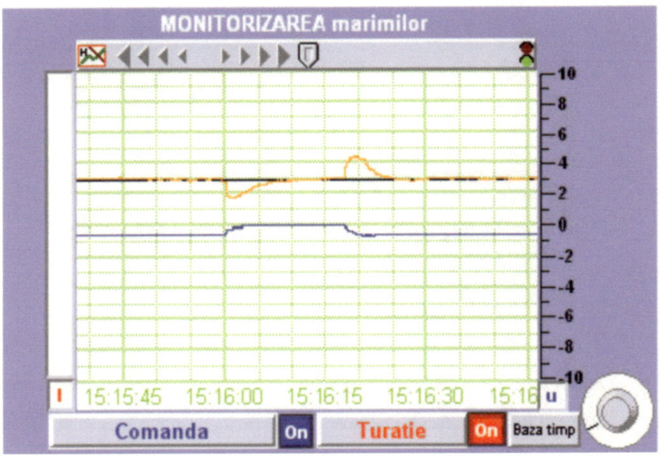

b. Load disturbance rejection.

Fig. 8. Monitoring panel (set point-black, speed-brown, armature current-blue).

3.2 NCS in the hierarchical structure: D.C. brush servomotor electrical drives system

The D.C. brush servomotor has the following features:

- rating armature voltage U_n=20V;

- rating armature current I_n=2A;
- rating speed n_n=2400 rpm;
- armature winding resistance R_a=1.31 Ω;
- armature winding inductance L_a=7.58 mH.

The D.C. brush servomotor is driven by a reversible chopper with the L292 specialized integrated circuit (Baluta, 2004). The motor's shaft is connected with an incremental optical encoder that gives 1000 pulses/rev. (this means 4000 pulses/rev. at the output of the NI PCI-7354 controller). The D.C. brush servomotor is loaded using a controlled loading device. Among the features of the loading system, the authors emphasize (Baluta, 2004):

- the possibility to load the electric drive motor with a reactive load torque in a wide range of speed, including very low speeds;
- the possibility to impose a constant load torque operation mode or an overload operation mode.

The implemented control system uses the algorithm from Fig. 9, which allows to generate in real-time the move trajectory and to change the motion parameters. In order to program the motion control system, the developer employs LabVIEW environment with specific virtual instruments for motion control from the FlexMotion library.

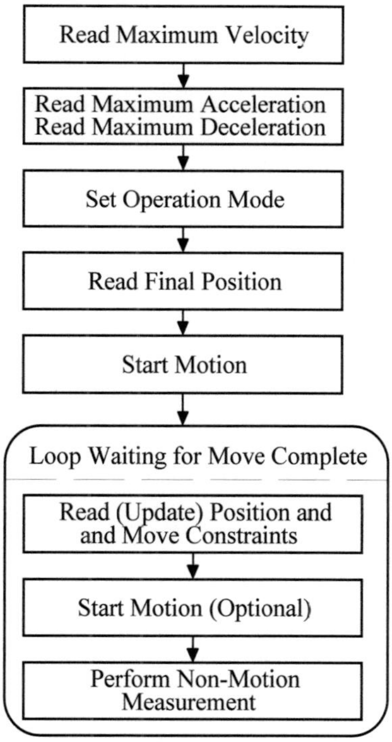

Fig. 9. Position-based straight-line move algorithm.

Within such application, the user has the possibility to study either:

- the command regimes in *speed open-loop*;
- the position control regimes of the positioning system.

The graphic program associated to the first type of study is that shown in Fig. 10. It is structured by means of a single *while ()* loop, preceded by an initialization sequence allowing the configuration of the system (selection of chopper control signal, setting of optical encoder parameters, definition of the speed measurement units). The control elements of the loop creates the possibility that the user could modify the chopper control signal and/or to establish the servomotor loading degree. The measures acquired in view of their graphical representation are the electrical ones (current in the armature winding and supply modulated voltage of the armature winding) as well as the mechanical ones (position and speed of the drive system). Leaving off the application is achieved explicitly, by means the *Stop* push-button, available in the graphical user interface.

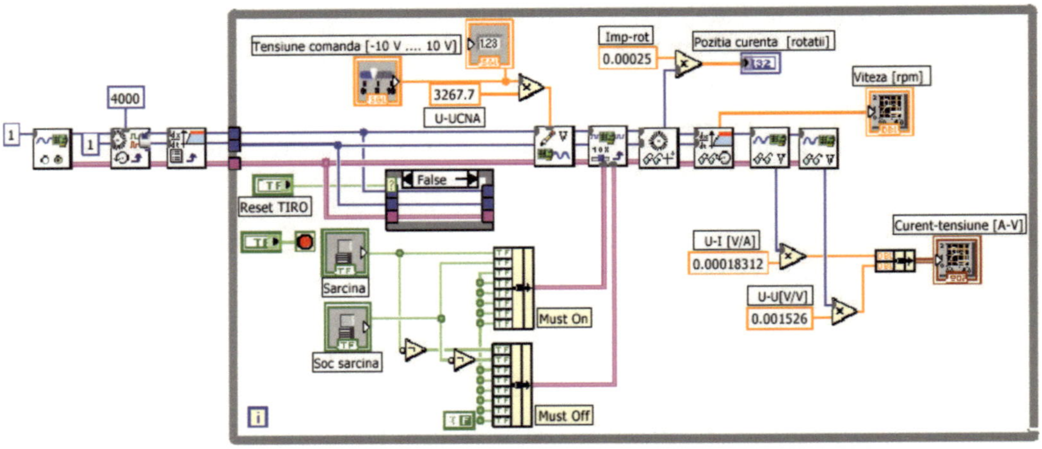

Fig. 10. LabVIEW diagram for the command regimes in speed open-loop.

The vast majority of motion control algorithms employed in industrial applications are of two forms (Ellis & Lorentz, 1999]:

- the well-known PID position loop (Fig. 11a);
- an average velocity loop cascaded with a position loop (Fig. 11b).

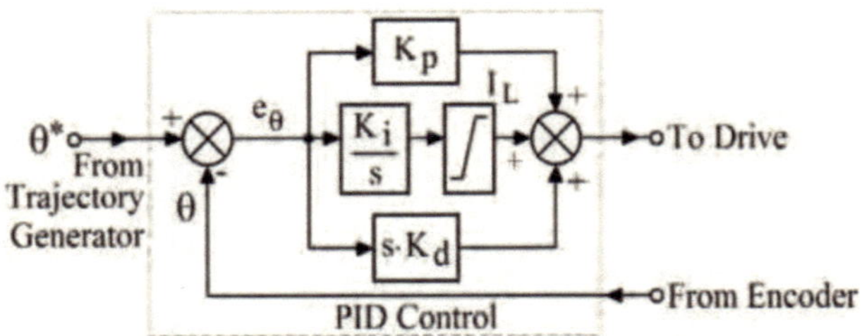

a. PID Servocontrol topology.

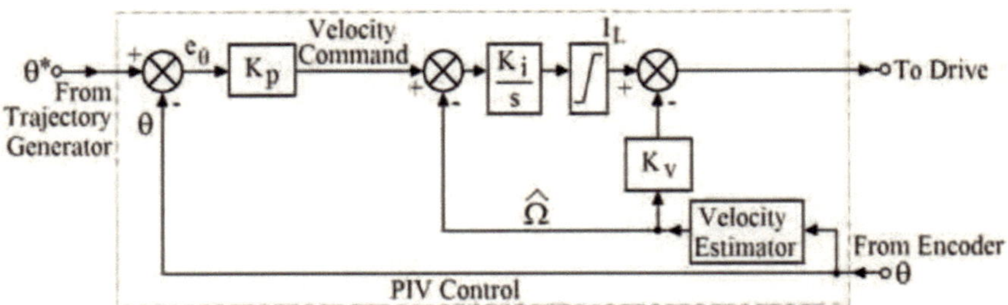

b. PIV. Servocontrol topology.

Fig. 11. Servocontrol topology.

On the other hand, in order to achieve near zero following or tracking error, feedforward control is often employed. A requirement for feedforward control is the availability of both the velocity, $\Omega^*(t)$, and acceleration, $\varepsilon^*(t)$, commands synchronized with the position commands, $\theta^*(t)$.

An example of how feedforward control is used in addition to the second servocontrol topology is shown in Fig. 12. The National Instruments PCI-7354 controller can be configured for any of the above servocontrol topologies.

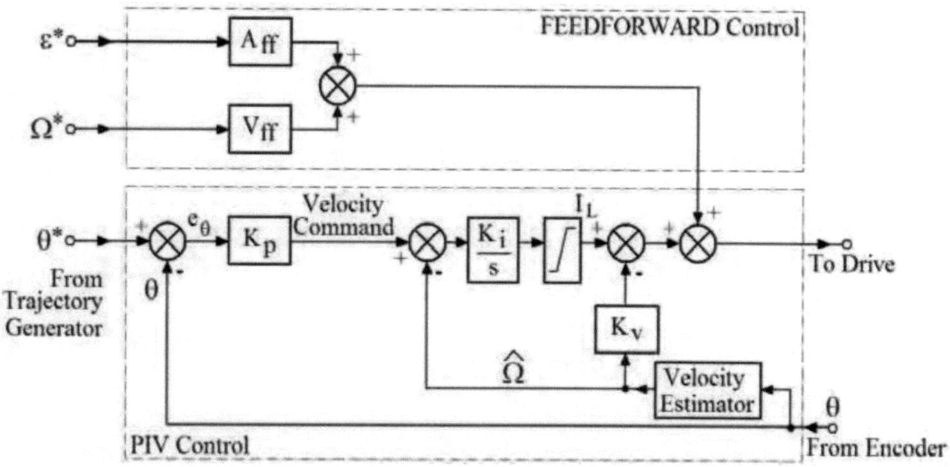

Fig. 12. Basic feedforward and PIV control topology.

In order to build a positioning application, the developer has to follow the stages shown in Fig. 13, which represent the steps required to design a motion application. The learner can also perform the second to fifth stages of motion application design (Bauer & Fedok, 2003) (Fedok & Bauer, 2005), (Saliah et al., 1999).

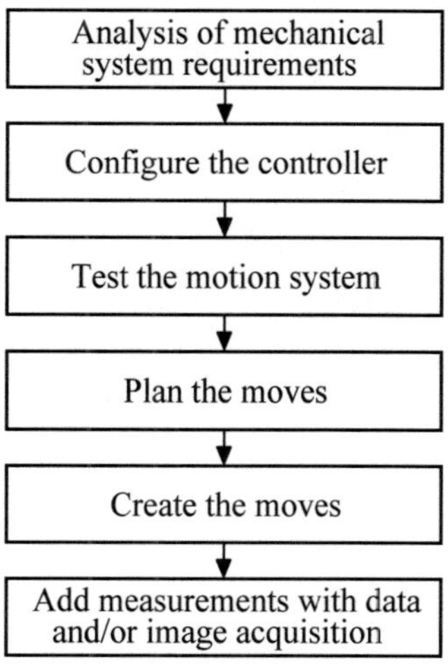

Fig. 13. Generic steps for designing a motion application.

To introduce a student to motor control, the D.C. brush servomotor set-up will provide the opportunity to learn about this motor without ever attending a laboratory session at their institution. Since the majority of students do not have prior technical experience, this remote set-up is very economical and offers students a great tool for learning about the servomechanism and data acquisition.

To ensure proper performance for servomechanism the motion control system must be tuned and tested. Then the type of move profile is planed. Motion constraints are the maximum velocity, acceleration, deceleration and jerk that the system can handle. Trajectory parameters are expressed as a function of motor shaft revolutions. The trajectory generator takes into account the type and the constraints of motion and generates values of instantaneous trajectory parameters in real-time.

Basically, the student can learn about the parameters of the D.C. servomechanism, by tuning the control loop parameters and setting the motion constrains to make execute the operations, i.e., change the rotation direction, position and speed. Also during the experiment, the student can visualise critical input and output points in the D.C. brush servomotor electronic interface using virtual oscilloscopes. Since this system is in real-time mode, the learner observes changes in position, direction, and velocity as the motor rotates after being commanded. Fig. 14 shows the graphical user interface specific to this application.

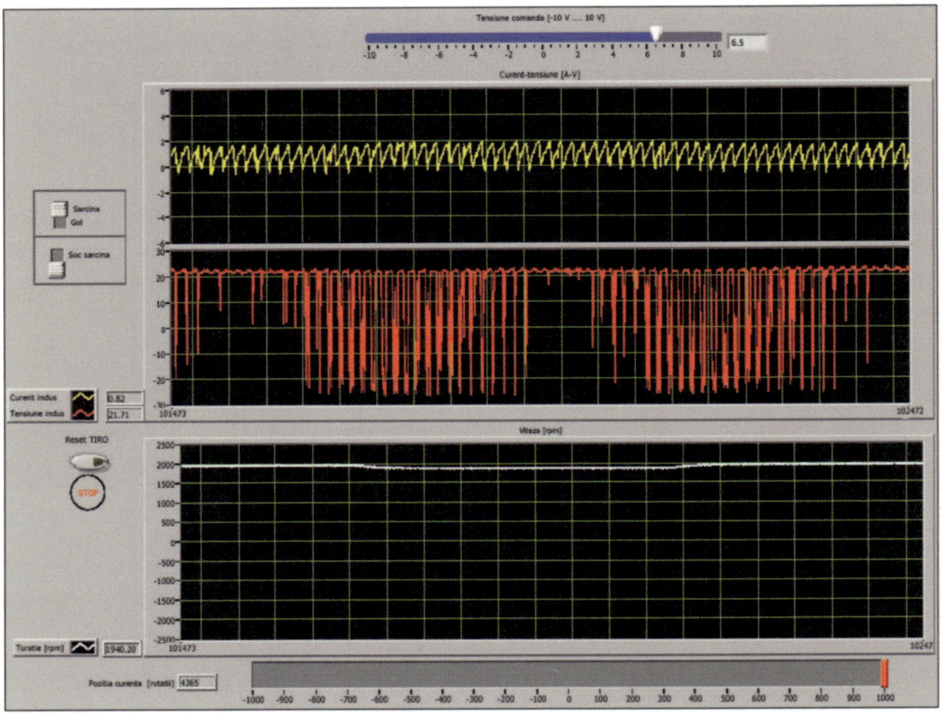

Fig. 14. Main panel for D.C. brush servomotor electrical drives system (open-loop operating mode).

It reveals the experimental results being obtained for the open-loop control of the electrical drives system when the user applies a load torque disturbance to the controlled servomotor shaft. The variations of the armature current and modulated voltage applied to its terminals (for a command signal of 6.5 V) are presented by means of the first virtual oscilloscope. The speed fall caused by the load torque disturbance can be noticed on the second virtual oscilloscope. Thus the user can deduce the causal link between the disturbance acting over the system and its effects over the output measure.

A more complex study can by achieved by means of the second application designed for this stand. This is the control of a positioning system driven by D.C. brush servomotor (the motion control algorithms from Fig. 11 and Fig. 12). The LabVIEW program developed this purpose is shown in Fig. 15. The same as for the application for the position control of the positioning system driven by stepper servomotor, the program is structured into two *while ()* loops (the control algorithm ensures the processing flow described by the same flowchart shown in Fig. 9). The novel element, as compared to the structure of positioning described earlier, is the position and speed controller offering multiple possibilities of configuration for the control topology. Thus, the user can choose to use either a classical structure of position control by means of a *PID controller*, or a *master-slave (cascade)* structure of P-position & PI-speed type. At the same time, either structure can be completed with control elements by *feedforward* in accordance with the speed and/or acceleration references of the trajectory generator. It is obvious that once the topology having been established, the user has to ensure the tuning of the control structure in view of obtaining the desired behavior performances.

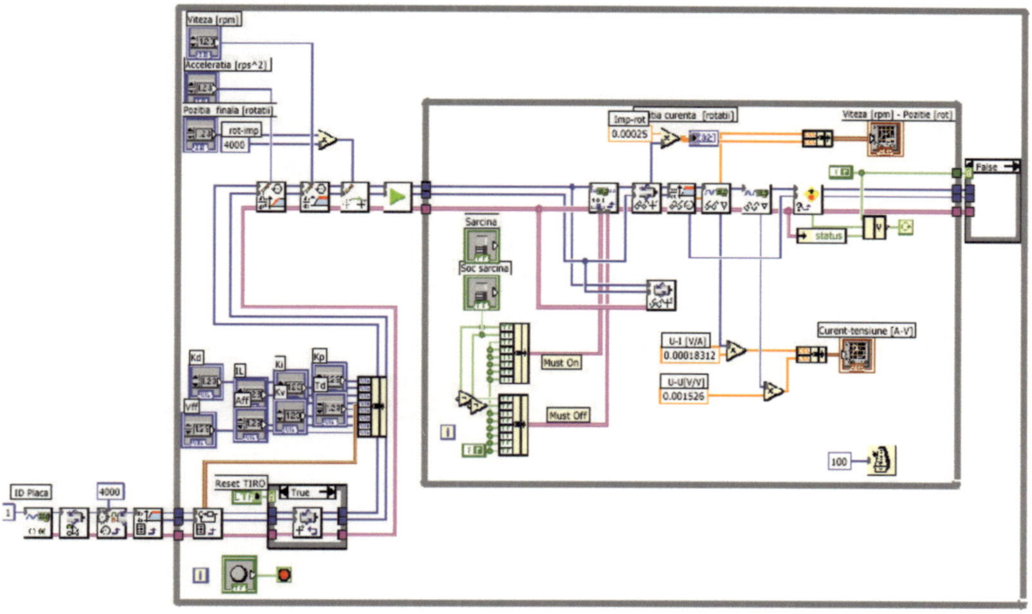

Fig. 15. LabVIEW diagram for single axes positioning system (closed-loop operating mode).

The user graphical interface (see Fig. 16) shows the experimental results obtained for a classical position control structured by using a PID controller. The tuning parameters of the control law are presented in the bottom-left area reserved for the controller settings and those related to the motion in the top-left part. The review of the results certifies the fact that the positioning within the range [0÷1000] rev. is completed in full accordance with the requirements imposed by the motion constraints and with optimal dynamic behavior performances that is little and well harmonized transitory regimes.

Through the graphical user interfaces, the students acquire the following abilities:

- enabling the motor and resetting the control system;
- calibrating a D.C. brush servomechanism;

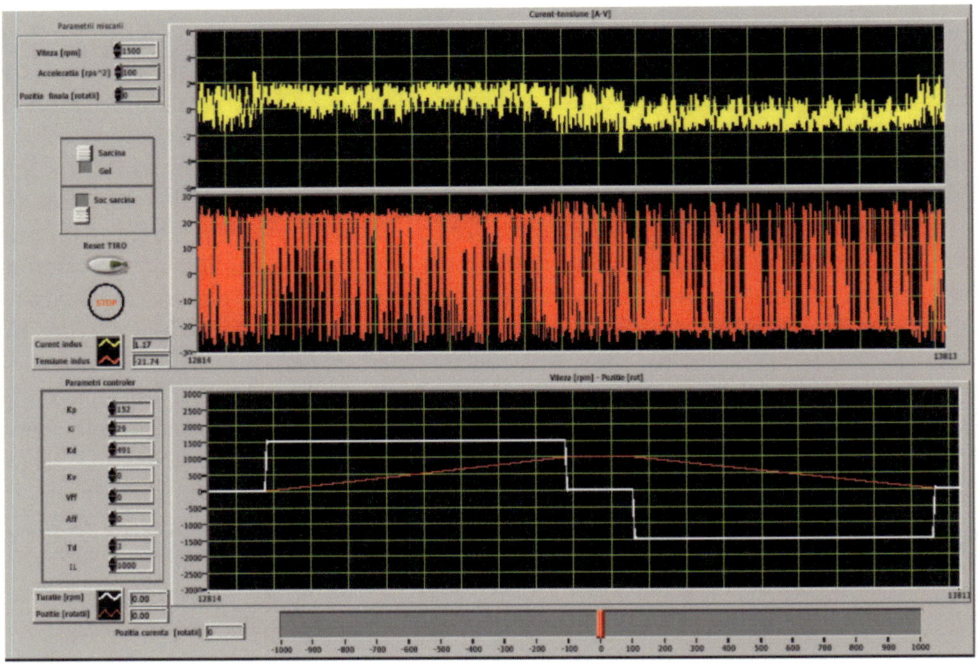

Fig. 16. Main panel for D.C. brush servomotor electrical drives system (closed-loop operating mode).

- controlling the rotation direction of the D.C. brush servomotor;
- moving the servomotor shaft from one arbitrary position to another;
- accelerating the servomotor and maintaining a constant velocity as well as decelerating and bringing it to a complete stop;
- visualizing intermediate motor control and encoder signals;
- understanding the relationship between the external loads and command effort.

3.3 NCS in the hierarchical structure: Stepper servomotor electrical drives system

In order to study positioning application for stepper servomotor electrical drives, the set-up, which is shown in Fig. 17 and has the layer from Fig. 1, is used.
The set-up consists of a stepper servomotor, an optical encoder, a controlled loading device and electronic boards for the delivery of control sequences.
The 2-phase stepper servomotor (made in Italy, type HY 200-2222-100 D 6) has the following features:

- step angle θ_p=1.8 degrees/step (200 steps/revolution);
- rated voltage supply U_n=5V;
- current per phase I_n=1A;
- resistance per phase R_f=5Ω;
- inductance per phase L_m=5.45mH;
- electrical time constant T_e=1.09ms;
- maximum synchronization torque M_{max}=0.3N·m.

The stepper servomotor is driven by two specialized integrated circuits (made by SGS-THOMSON, Microelectronics Company): L297 (stepper servomotor controller) and L298N (dual H-bridge driver). The servomotor's shaft is connected with an incremental optical encoder that gives 250 pulses/rev. (this means 1000 pulses/rev. at the output of the sense discriminator or the NI PCI-7354 controller). Among the features of the loading system, the following ones permit (Baluta et al., 1997), (Baluta, 2003):

Fig. 17. Stepper motor electrical drives system.

- to load the electric drive servomotor with a reactive load torque in a wide range of speed, including very low speeds;
- to impose a constant load torque operation mode or an overload operation mode;
- to prescribe, analogically or numerically, the amplitude and time length of the load torque.

The driven axes with stepper servomotors can be controlled in open-loop using constant frequency or prescribed profile (trapezoidal or S-curve move profile) or closed-loop. In the second case, the user has to initialise the feedback for position and speed variables and to adequately set the control block of the pulse generation for stepper servomotor command. The operating mode of the stepper servomotor can be with full step, half step or microstepping mode. The main function of a motion controller is to assure the desired motion trajectories.

The implemented control system uses the algorithm from Fig. 9, which allows to generate in real-time the move trajectory and to change the motion parameters. In order to program the motion control system, the user employs LabVIEW environment with specific virtual instruments for motion control from the library FlexMotion. The graphic program associated is shown in Fig. 18 (Baluta, 2007).

The processing flow is structured into two loops of *while ()* type. The inner loop, executed for a time period of 1 ms is used to update the temporal trajectories of the measures of interest: electric (phase currents and phase supply voltages) and mechanic (position and speed). The leaving off of the inner loop done as the prescribed position is attained or the follow up speed exceeds a prescribed level. The control outer loop is executed with a period of 1 s and allows or one hand the configuration of the application in relation with the parameters of the drives system (number of stepper steps, number of pulses optical encoder) and on the other hand the definition of the operating regimes and modes and the motion parameters (full steps/half step, open-loop/closed-loop, final position, maximum speed, maximum acceleration and maximum deceleration).

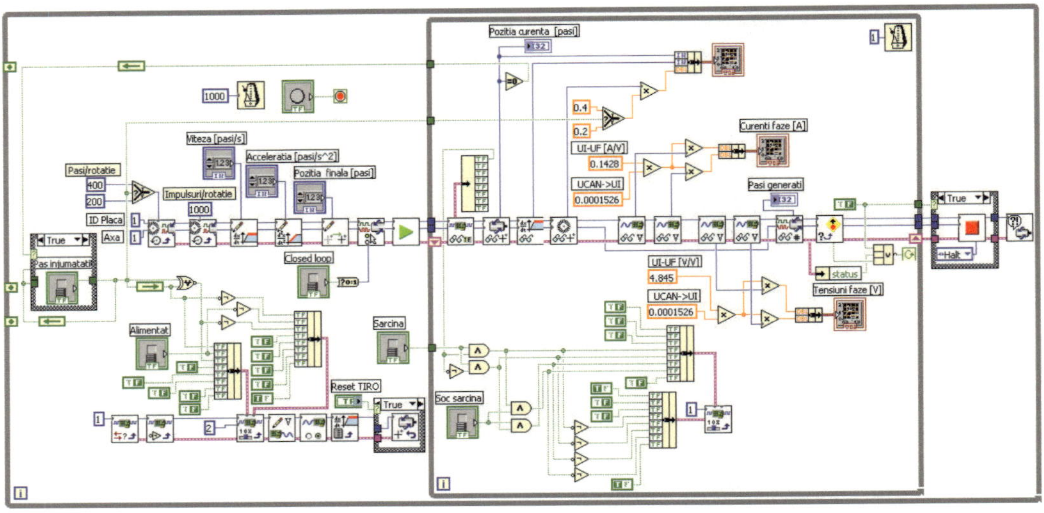

Fig. 18. LabVIEW diagram for single axes positioning system.

The application calculates the error between the prescribed position and real position and, when this error is other than zero, the inner loop is executed until the position error becomes of no value. As one can notice, the program provides two types of configuration:

- implicit configurations, not accessible to user (number of stepper steps, number of pulses/rev. of optical encoder);
- explicit configurations available in the user graphical interface (full steps/half step, open-loop/closed -loop, servomotor loading, position initialisation).

Such configurations are basically achieved when the main loop is executed, therefore after the achieved a motion programmed profile. Nevertheless, in order to ensure to user the possibility of applying an overload when achieving the motion profile, the command of application of the overload was included in the control inner loop.

When the controlling mode of the stepper servomotor (full step/half step) is modified, the settings related of the number of steps that the servomotor is executing during a full revolution must be correlated as well. This is automatically achieved in a transparent manner from the point of view of the user.

The application can be stopped by an explicit control through the *Stop* push-button, involves the leaving off the main loop of the program.

In order to build a positioning application, the developer has to follow the stages shown in Fig. 13, which represent the steps required to design a motion application.

The trajectory generator takes into account the type and the constraints of motion and generates points or instantaneous position in real-time. The control loop converts each instantaneous position to a voltage or to step-and-direction signal, depending on the type of motor is used. Motion constraints are the maximum velocity, acceleration, deceleration and jerk that the system can handle. The trajectory generator creates a velocity profile based on these motion constraints values. Trajectory parameters are expressed as a function of steps numbers. In this case the number of steps depends on the type of the stepper drive and the servomotor that is used.

Basically, the student can learn about the parameters of the stepper servomotor, by changing modes and input settings to make execute the operations, i.e., change the rotation direction, position and speed. Also during the experiment, the student can visualise critical input and output points in the stepper servomotor electronic interface using virtual oscilloscopes. Since this system is in real-time mode, the learner observes changes in position, direction, and velocity as the motor rotates after being stepped through with various frequencies corresponding to increasing or decreasing variations of steps/sec.

The graphical user interfaces for a positioning application of stepper servomotors are presented in:

- Fig. 19 for open-loop control and full step operating mode;
- Fig. 20 for closed-loop control and half step operating mode.

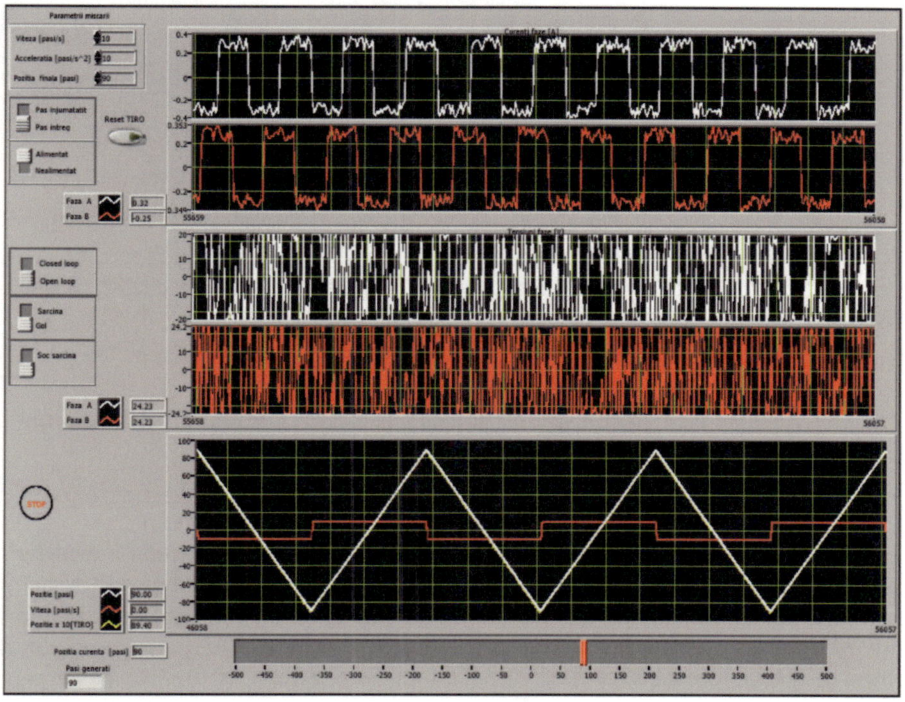

Fig. 19. Main panel for stepper servomotor electrical drives system (open-loop control and full step operating mode).

The graphical interface includes three virtual oscilloscopes allowing the view of the phase currents through the servomotors windings, voltages applied to windings and trajectories of the mechanical measures (prescribed position, measured position, prescribed speed). Additionally, the real position is presented dynamically, by means of a graphical slider too. The instantaneous numerical values of the above measures are also presented using virtual display elements.

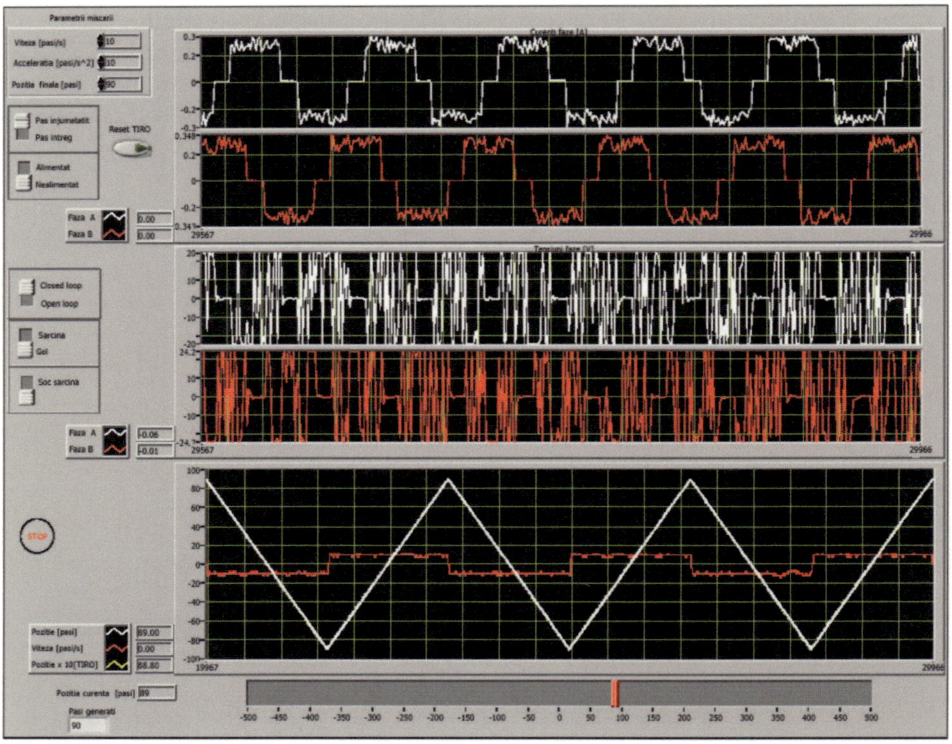

Fig. 20. Main panel for stepper servomotor electrical drives system (closed-loop control and half step operating mode).

The graphical interface offers to the user certain switches, in order to establish the desired operating mode:

- the initialization of the position register of the positioning system is achieved by means of the *Reset TIRO* push-button;
- the *Powered/Unpowered* push-button provides a logical command of activating on the stepper servomotor driver;
- the *Full Step/Half Step* push-button defines the stepper servomotor command mode (full step or half step);
- the positioning system loading is achieved by means of a controlled loading device being controlled through the *Load/Unload* and *Overload* push-buttons.

The parameters and constraints on the motion are defined by means of the introductions elements of numerical values (speed, acceleration, position). After such measures are programmed, the supervision system transfers such measures to the trajectory generator, which, in its turn, supplies suitable references to the control loops. Thus, the user has the possibility to program dynamically the motion parameters, the new values being considered immediately after the completion of the motion current cycle, previously programmed. Fig. 19 shows the experimental results obtained by an *open-loop* control of the position of the positioning system between the extremes [-90÷+90] steps with the maximum speed of 10 steps/s and acceleration/deceleration of 10 steps/s^2. The servomotor command mode is with full step, the positioning system being unloaded.

The temporal trajectories of the electrical and mechanical measures, obtained for three positioning cycles are shown of the virtual oscilloscopes of the user graphical interface. The user has thus the possibility to correlate the command and control measures with the operating regimes and loading modes of the positioning system. Fig. 20 shows, for instance, the operation regime of the positioning system in *closed- loop*. By a comparative study, one can notice that in such case, the reaction measures are easily contaminated by noise. In spite of that, the control block ensures the desired parameters of the motion and guarantees the execution of the positioning without risking of loosing steps.

Through the user interface, the students acquire the following abilities:

- calibrating a stepper servomotor system;
- controlling the rotation direction of the stepper servomotor;
- enabling the motor and resetting the control system;
- understanding the relationship between a step and the number of steps required making one complete 360-degree revolution;
- moving the motor shaft from one arbitrary position to another;
- accelerating the motor and maintaining a constant velocity as well as decelerating and bringing it to a complete stop;
- visualizing intermediate motor control and encoder signals.

The implemented control structure for stepper motors permits the user to get familiarized with solving problems for positioning applications.

4. Conclusions

In this chapter, a remote control laboratory for electrical drive systems is presented. The laboratory allows the students to develop network based control systems using an architecture based on I/O devices, communication modules and server-client application implemented with Lookout and LabVIEW environment facilities and to operate on real electrical drive systems through Intranet and Internet.

Three examples were presented demonstrating the potentiality of the networked control system laboratory to remotely control the electrical drive systems and to develop new network based control system structure.

Work is in progress to upgrade the laboratory with new electrical drive systems: D.C. brushless servomotor electrical drives system.

5. References

Antsaklis, P.J. & Baillieul, J. (2004). Guest Editorial: Special Issue on Networked Control Systems, *IEEE Transactions on Automatic Control*, Vol. 49, No. 9, (September 2004), pp. 1421-1423, ISSN: 0018-9286.

Baillieul, J. & Antsaklis, P.J. (2007). Control and Communication Challenges in Networked Real-Time Systems, *Proceedings of the IEEE*, Vol. 95, No. 1, (January 2007), pp. 9-28, ISSN: 0018-9219.

Baluta, Gh. (2003). *Electrical Drives with Stepper Motors* (in Romanian), Gh. Asachi Publishing House, ISBN: 973-621-034-0, Iasi, Romania.

Baluta, Gh. (2004). *Low Power Electrical Drives. Applications* (in Romanian), Politehnium Publishing House, ISBN: 973-621-072-3, Iasi, Romania.

Baluta, Gh. & Lazar, C. (2007). Remote Control Laboratory Development for Electrical Drive Systems, *Proceedings of the 13-th IEEE/IFAC International Conference on Methods and*

Models in Automation and Robotics, pp. 393–398, ISBN: 978-83-751803-3-6, IEEE Conference Number: 12459, Szczecin, Poland, 27-30 August 2007.

Bauer, P. & Fedak, V. (2003). E-learning for Power Electronics and Electrical Drives, *Proceedings of the 13-th International Conference on Electrical Drives and Power Electronics*, pp. 567-572, ISBN: 80-89061-77-X, High Tatras, Slovak Republic, 24-26 September 2003.

Bushnell, L.G. (2001). Special Section on Networks and Control, *IEEE Control Systems Magazine*, Vol. 21, No. 1, (February 2001), pp. 24-99, ISSN: 0272-1708.

Carari, S.; Chirea, O. & Lazar, C. (2003). Distributed control system for educational training based on Lookout and FieldPoint, *Proceedings of the NIWeek Worldwide Virtual Instrumentation Conference*, Austin, USA, 13-15 August 2003.

Casini, M.; Prattichizzo, D. & Vicino, A. (2004). The Automatic Control Telelab: A Web-based technology for distance learning, *IEEE Control Systems Magazine*, Vol. 24, No. 3, (June 2001), pp. 36-44, ISSN: 0272-1708.

Ellis, G. & Lorentz, R.D. (1999). Comparison of Motion Control Loops for Industrial Applications, *Proceedings of the IEEE IAS Annual Technical Conference*, Vol. 4, pp. 2599-2605, ISBN: 0-7803-5589-X, Phoenix, AZ, USA, 3-7 October 1999.

Fedok, V. & Bauer, P. (2005). E-learning in Education of Electrical Drives and Power Electronics: Opportunities and Challenges, *Proceedings of the 15-th International Conference on Electrical Drives and Power Electronics*, pp. 1-9 (paper E05-L4.pdf), ISBN: 953-6037-43-2, Dubrovnik, Croatia, 26-28 September 2005.

Kreindler, L. (2002). DSP Solution for Digital Motion Control, *Journal of Electrical Engineering*, Vol. 2, (June 2002), pp. 1-9 (paper Kreindler.pdf), ISSN: 1582-4594.

Lian, F.L.; Moyne, J.R. & Tilbury, D.M. (2002). Network Design Consideration for Distributed Control System, *IEEE Transactions on Control Systems Technology*, Vol. 10, No. 2, (March 2002), pp. 297-307, ISSN: 1063-6536.

Lazar, C. & Carari, S. (2008). A Remote Control Engineering Laboratory, *IEEE Transactions on Industrial Electronics*, in press, ISSN: 0278-0046.

Saad, M.; Saliah-Hassane, H.; Hassan, H.; El-Guetioui, Z. & Cheriet, M. (2001). A Synchronous Remote Accessing Control Laboratory on the Internet, *Proceedings of the International Conference on Engineering Education*, Session 8D1, pp. 8D1_30-8D1_33 (paper 321.pdf), ISBN: 1-588-74-091-9, Oslo, Norway, 6-10 August 2001.

Saliah, H.H.; Nurse, E. & Abecassis, A. (1999). Design of a Generic, Interactive, Virtual and Remote Electrical Engineering Laboratory, *Proceedings of the 29-th ASEE/IEEE Frontiers in Education Conference*, Session 12c6, pp. 12c6_18-12c6_23 (paper 1365.pdf), ISBN: 0-7803-5643-8, San Juan, Puerto Rico, 10-13 November 1999.

Tipsuwan, Y. & Chow, M.Y. (2003). Control methodologies in networked control systems. *Control Engineering Practice*, Vol. 11, No. 10, (October 2003), pp. 1099–1111, ISSN: 0967-0661.

Valera, A.; Diez, J.L.; Valles, M. & Albertos, P. (2005). Virtual and Remote Control Laboratory Development, *IEEE Control Systems Magazine*, Vol. 25, No. 1, (February 2005), pp. 35-39, ISSN: 0272-1708.

Yang, T.C. (2006). Networked control system: a brief survey, *IEE Proceedings of Control Theory and Applications*, Vol. 153, No. 4, (10 July 2006), pp. 403-412, ISSN: 1350-2379.

6

Developments in the Control Loops Benchmarking

Grzegorz Bialic and Marian Błachuta
The Opole University of Technology & The Silesian University of Technology
Poland

1. Introduction

The problem of control performance assessment and monitoring is getting more and more significant because control systems have much bigger influence on accomplishing aims determined by companies. These aims mean achieving goals connected with quality, safety and profits. This justify academic and commercial interest in development of methods for analyzing the quality of such systems which allow to avoid unreliable human factor. The control system performance cannot be depicted by means of only one simple statistics. The whole procedure called control loops benchmarking (Harris & Seppala 2002) require much more complicated multi-stage process consisting of: data acquisition, analysis and diagnostics (making the tool based on mathematical model of process, the lower bound estimation, the existing control loop performance assessment, testing of the performance improvement using existing controller structure), retuning or control algorithm replacement.

2. Background of the problem

Complex systems usually are comprised of numerous loops which are controlled by local SISO controllers. Most of this industrial control loops are equipped with PID type controllers whose parameters are usually tuned using classical approach that neglects the disturbance characteristics. The decision to retune or replace any of these controllers should be preceded by an investigation whether and to what extent this would improve performance. Such procedure is referred to benchmarking or control performance assessment (Desborough & Harris 1992) Most of research done so far assume MV (minimum variance) control as the performance lower bound and variance of the system output as basic quantity for control quality assessment. The classical (Huang 2003) performance measure is as follows

$$\eta = \frac{\sigma_{mv}^2}{\sigma_y^2}, \tag{1}$$

where the hypothetical minimum variance, σ^2_{mv} is determined analytically by

$$\sigma_{mv}^2 = \left(f_0^2 + f_1^2 + f_2^2 + \ldots + f_{l-1}^2\right)\sigma_a^2 \tag{2}$$

and defined by impulse response coefficients $f_0, f_1, \ldots\ f_{l-1}$, variance σ_a^2 of the disturbance model driving noise, and discrete-time delay l. It is very important that η can be estimated directly from loop operating data. The exact value of delay l is assumed to be known to the process engineer. Unfortunately, very often there is no pure delay in the process, and the value of delay τ of the frequently used lag-delay model

$$H(s)=\frac{1}{Ts+1}e^{-s\tau} \tag{3}$$

is then used to determine l given sampling period h. As shown in (Błachuta & Bialic 2005), in this case the value of index η may be not very bad even in a relatively purely tuned control system hiding the fact that the best achievable accuracy referring to l=1 can be much better. Moreover MV based benchmark does not take the control effort into account and because of large magnitudes of control signal it is often useless.
In this respect, the modified MV control strategy with bounded control variance is used as benchmark in the chapter. This results in the LQG control algorithm allowing control performance assessment under assumption of the same control effort.

3. Control problem statement

It is assumed that the linear SISO plant is modeled by the following stochastic, continuous-time system

$$\frac{dx(t)}{dt}=Ax(t)+bu(t-\tau)+c\dot{\xi}(t) \tag{4}$$

$$y(t)=d'x(t) \tag{5}$$

where $x(t)$ is p - dimensional state vector, A is $p{\times}p$ - dimensional matrix, b, c and d are p - dimensional vectors. The initial condition x_0 is assumed to be a normal random vector, $x_0 \sim N(0,Q_0)$. $\xi(t)$ is a Wiener process, and var $\xi(t)=\delta(t)$. The time delay is defined as follows:

$$\tau = lh - h + \theta \tag{6}$$

where $l \geq 1$ and $0 < \theta \leq h$. The plant is controlled by the output $u(t)$ of a ZOH device with period h

$$u(t)=u_k,\quad \text{for } t\in(kh,kh+h],\quad k=0,1,\ldots, \tag{7}$$

driven by the digital controller output $u(k)$, which changes its values at discrete time instants t_k=kh, k=0,1,... . The output of the system is assumed to be measured synchronically at instants t_k as:

$$y_k = d'x_k + n_k \tag{8}$$

where n_k is measurement error composed of white noise with zero mean $E[n_k]=0$, and variance $E[n_i^2]=v^2$. The variance of measurement noise characterizes accuracy of the sensor, transmitter and A/D converter.
The aim of the system is to minimize the average value of the system error variance with the control variance limit. The considered problem is equivalent to minimization of the weighted H_2 performance index:

$$I=\lim_{N\to\infty}E\frac{1}{Nh}\int_{0}^{Nh}\left\{y^2(t+\tau)+\lambda u^2(t)\right\}dt \tag{9}$$

This index with controlled output $y(t)$ and control signal $u(t)$ is minimized both for optimal unrestricted LQG and classical restricted structure PID controllers (Grimble 2003) such that the maximum efficiency in terms of disturbance attenuation is achieved under bounded control variance.

4. Control algorithms

4.1 LQG benchmark

Introduce the predictable state

$$x^P(t)=x(t+\tau) \tag{10}$$

The system defined by state equation (4), measurement equation (8), modulation equation (7) and performance index (9) can be described at sampling instants as

$$x_{k+1}^P=Fx_k^P+gu_k+w_k^P \tag{11}$$

$$z_k=d'x_k^P(kh-\tau)+n_k \tag{12}$$

$$I=\lim_{N\to\infty}E\frac{1}{N}\sum_{0}^{N-1}\{x^{P}{}'_k\,Q_1\,x^P{}_k+2x^P{}'_k\,q_{12}u_k+q_2u_k^2+q_w\} \tag{13}$$

where $w_k^P=w(kh+\tau)$ is zero mean Gaussian white noise vector with covariance $E\{w_k^P,w_k^P{}'\}$. Vectors x_0 and $[w_k^P,n_k]$ are uncorrelated for all $k\geq0$. Matrices defining the system (11) -(12) are as follows

$$\left.\begin{aligned}F(h)&=e^{Ah}, & w(h)&=\int_0^h e^{A(h-s)}c\xi(s)ds\\ g(h)&=\int_0^h e^{Av}bdv, & W(h)&=\int_0^h e^{As}cc'e^{A's}ds\end{aligned}\right\} \tag{14}$$

and matrices defining performance criterion (13) are as follows

$$\left.\begin{aligned}Q_1&=\frac{1}{h}\int_0^h F'(\tau)MF(\tau)d\tau,\\ q_{12}&=\frac{1}{h}\int_0^h F'(\tau)Mg(\tau)d\tau,\\ q_2&=\frac{1}{h}\int_0^h g'(\tau)Mg(\tau)d\tau,\\ q_w&=\frac{1}{h}d'\left\{\int_0^h\int_0^\tau F(\tau-s)cc'F'(\tau-s)dsd\tau\right\}d\end{aligned}\right\} \tag{15}$$

The optimal control law minimizing the performance index (13) for the system (11)-(12) is

$$u_k = -k_c{}'\hat{x}^p_{k|k} = -k_c{}'F_p \underbrace{\begin{bmatrix} \hat{x}_{k|k} \\ u_{k-d} \\ \vdots \\ u_{k-2} \\ u_{k-1} \end{bmatrix}}_{\hat{x}^p_{k|k}} = -k_c{}'F_p \underline{\hat{x}}_{k|k} \tag{16}$$

where

$$F_p = \begin{bmatrix} F(\tau) & F(\tau-\theta)g(\theta) & F(lh-2h)g & \cdots & Fg & g \end{bmatrix} \tag{17}$$

$\hat{x}^p_{k|k}$ is an estimate of the state x^p_k using measurements z_k up to and including k. The feedback gain vector depends on the positive solution S of the following algebraic Riccati equation

$$S = Q_1 + F'SF - \frac{(q_{12} + F'Sg)(q_{12} + F'Sg)'}{q_2 + g'Sg} \tag{18}$$

$$k_c = \frac{q_{12} + F'Sg}{q_2 + g'Sg} \tag{19}$$

Stationary Kalman filter (Åström & Wittenmark 1990) for the system (11)-(12) takes the following form

$$\hat{x}_{k|k} = \hat{x}_{k|k-1} + k^f\left(z_k - d'\hat{x}_{k|k-1}\right) \tag{20}$$

$$\hat{x}_{k+1|k} = F\hat{x}_{k|k} + g(h-\theta)u_{k-l+1} + F(h-\theta)g(\theta)u_{k-l} \tag{21}$$

where

$$k^f = \frac{\Sigma d}{v^2 + d'\Sigma d} \tag{22}$$

$$\Sigma = W + F\left(\Sigma - \frac{\Sigma dd'\Sigma'}{v^2 + d'\Sigma d}\right)F' \tag{23}$$

4.2 PID type controllers

The system (4)-(5) controlled by means of discrete time classical PID type controllers is considered. Controller settings are supplied in two ways: as minimization result of the performance index (13), and by means of one of the classical methods called QDR (Quarter Decay Ratio).

The control law for classical controllers is defined by the following equations

-state equation

$$x^c_{k+1} = A^c x^c_k - B^c z_k \tag{24}$$

- and output equation

$$u_k = C^c x_k^c - D^c z_k, \tag{25}$$

where for discrete time PID controller matrices and vectors defining the control law are the following form

$$\left.\begin{array}{ll} A^c = \begin{bmatrix} 1 & 0 \\ 0 & 0 \end{bmatrix}, & C^c = \begin{bmatrix} K_p \dfrac{h}{T_i} & -Kp\dfrac{T_d}{h} \end{bmatrix}, \\ B^c = \begin{bmatrix} 1 \\ 1 \end{bmatrix}, & D^c = \begin{bmatrix} K_p\left(1 + \dfrac{h}{T_i} + \dfrac{T_d}{h}\right) \end{bmatrix}, \end{array}\right\} \tag{26}$$

Since the predictable description of the system (11)-(12) is not useful for the PID control algorithm, the system defined by state equation (4), measurement equation (8), modulation equation (7) and performance index (9) is described at sampling instants in alternative form

$$x_{k+1} = Fx_k + \Gamma_0 u_{k-l+1} + \Gamma_1 u_{k-l} + w_k \tag{27}$$

$$z_k = d' x_k + n_k \tag{28}$$

where

$$\Gamma_1 = e^{A(h-\theta)} \int_0^{\theta} e^{Av} b dv = F(h-\theta) g(\theta), \qquad \Gamma_0 = \int_0^{h-\theta} e^{Av} b dv = g(h-\theta) \tag{29}$$

The corresponding state-space description is as follows

$$\begin{bmatrix} x_{k+1} \\ u_{k-l+1} \\ \vdots \\ u_{k-1} \\ u_k \end{bmatrix} = \underbrace{\begin{bmatrix} F & \Gamma_1 & \Gamma_0 & \cdots & 0 \\ 0 & 0 & 1 & \cdots & 0 \\ \vdots & \vdots & \vdots & \ddots & \vdots \\ 0 & 0 & 0 & \cdots & 1 \\ 0 & 0 & 0 & \cdots & 0 \end{bmatrix}}_{\underline{F}} \underbrace{\begin{bmatrix} x_k \\ u_{k-l} \\ \vdots \\ u_{k-2} \\ u_{k-1} \end{bmatrix}}_{\underline{x}_k} + \underbrace{\begin{bmatrix} 0 \\ 0 \\ \vdots \\ 0 \\ 1 \end{bmatrix}}_{\underline{\Gamma}} u_k + \underbrace{\begin{bmatrix} I \\ 0 \\ \vdots \\ 0 \\ 0 \end{bmatrix}}_{\underline{\Omega}} w_k \tag{30}$$

Introduce the notation

$$\left.\begin{array}{l} \overline{P} = E\{\overline{x}_k, \overline{x}_k'\} = \begin{bmatrix} \overline{P}_{11} & \overline{P}_{12} \\ \overline{P}_{21} & \overline{P}_{22} \end{bmatrix} \\ \overline{x}_k = \begin{bmatrix} \underline{x}_k \\ x^c{}_k \end{bmatrix}, \quad \underline{x}_k = \begin{bmatrix} x_k \\ u_{k-l} \\ \vdots \\ u_{k-2} \\ u_{k-1} \end{bmatrix} \end{array}\right\} \tag{31}$$

Employing (31) and (25), the performance index (13) can be rewritten as

$$\left.\begin{aligned} I = {} & tr\{Q_1 F_p \overline{P}_{11} F_p' + Q_1 W(\tau)\} - tr\{F_p' q_{12} D^c \underline{d}' \overline{P}_{11}\} \\ & - tr\{\underline{d} D^{c}{}' q_{12}' F_p \overline{P}_{11}\} + tr\{q_2 \underline{d} D^{c}{}' D^c \underline{d}' \overline{P}_{11}\} \\ & + tr\{C^{c}{}' q_{12}' F_p \overline{P}_{12}\} - tr\{q_2 C^{c}{}' D^c \underline{d}' \overline{P}_{12}\} \\ & + tr\{F_p q_{12} C^c \overline{P}_{21}\} - tr\{q_2 \underline{d} D^c C^c \overline{P}_{21}\} \\ & + tr\{q_2 C^{c}{}' C^c \overline{P}_{22}\} + tr\{q_2 D^{c}{}' D^c v^2 + q_w\} \end{aligned}\right\} \tag{32}$$

4.3 Output and control variances

The output and control variances at sampling instants for the LQG controller can be calculated from the following expressions

$$\sigma^2_{y_k LQG} = \underline{d}' E\{\underline{x}_k, \underline{x}_k'\} \underline{d} = \underline{d}' \overline{X}(11) \underline{d} \tag{33}$$

$$\sigma^2_{u_k LQG} = k^{c}{}' F_p E\{\underline{\hat{x}}_{k|k}, \underline{\hat{x}}_{k|k}'\} F_p' k^c = k^{c}{}' F_p \overline{X}(22) F_p' k^c \tag{34}$$

where

$$\left.\begin{aligned} & \overline{X} = E\{\overline{x}_k, \overline{x}_k'\} = \begin{bmatrix} \overline{X}(11) & \overline{X}(12) \\ \overline{X}(21) & \overline{X}(22) \end{bmatrix} \\ & \overline{x}_k = \begin{bmatrix} \underline{x}_k \\ \underline{\hat{x}}_{k|k} \end{bmatrix}, \quad \underline{x}_k = \begin{bmatrix} x_k \\ u_{k-l} \\ \vdots \\ u_{k-2} \\ u_{k-1} \end{bmatrix}, \quad \underline{\hat{x}}_k = \begin{bmatrix} \hat{x}_{k|k} \\ u_{k-l} \\ \vdots \\ u_{k-2} \\ u_{k-1} \end{bmatrix} \end{aligned}\right\} \tag{35}$$

and formulas in case of PID type controllers are defined as follows

$$\sigma^2_{y_k PID} = \text{var}\{y_k\} = \underline{d}' \overline{P}_{11} \underline{d} \tag{36}$$

$$\left.\begin{aligned} \sigma^2_{u_k PID} = \text{var}\{u_k\} = {} & C^c \overline{P}_{22} C^{c}{}' - D^c \underline{d}' \overline{P}_{12} C^{c}{}' \\ & - C^c \overline{P}_{21} \underline{d} D^{c}{}' + D^c \underline{d}' \overline{P}_{11} \underline{d} D^{c}{}' + D^c v^2 D^{c}{}' \end{aligned}\right\} \tag{37}$$

5. Trade-off curves

Relationships in two-dimensional space of such criterions as output and control signal variances determine the trade-off curve (Huang & Shah 1999) which separate two regions: achievable (above) and non-achievable (below). On the basis of point location with respect to the trade-off curve one can assess the control performance. Thus the trade-off curve can be defined by means the benchmark which minimizes quadratic performance index in the form of (9). This means that such benchmark acts the lower bound taking the control effort into account.

Since standard deviations better characterize signal magnitudes, in the chapter trade-off curves are drawn on the plane std(y)-std(u).

Therefore the LQG control benchmark for a linear continuous-time plant whose output is corrupted by a stochastic disturbance controlled by a discrete-time controller is proposed. The quality of control systems with PID controllers tuned both classically (QDR-Quarter Decay Ratio) and optimally in such way that disturbance characteristics are taken into account is investigated and, assuming the same control effort, compared with the benchmark. It has been shown that optimal tuning of classical PID controllers improves the disturbance attenuation bringing it closer to the lower bound.

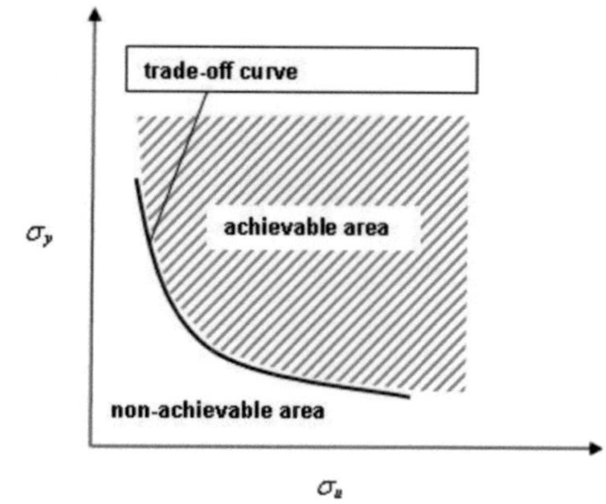

Fig. 1. Trade-off curve

In Fig. 1 standard deviation of output signal against standard deviation of control signal for systems with LQG and optimally tuned PID type controllers is plotted[1]. Optimal values of these parameters were received for varying values of the weighting factor λ.

Results of the minimum variance strategy are plotted as horizontal lines. And results of PID type control with controllers settings supplied by means of QDR method are plotted as points.

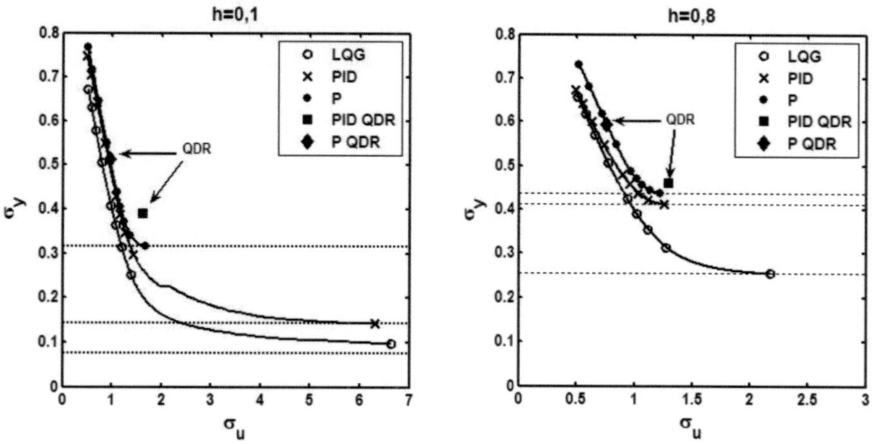

Fig. 2. Standard deviation of output vs control signal (trade-off curve)

[1] Exemplary plant transfer function: $G^P(s) = \frac{1}{(\alpha s + 1)(s + 1)^2}$,

6. Control performance assessment based on lag-delay model

Suitability of control quality assessment based on delay approximation for delay-free plants is investigated in this section. To this end, the LQG control benchmark, which can be seen as a MV benchmark with bounded control variance, is compared for both linear delay-free continuous-time plants with outputs corrupted by a stochastic disturbance and their lag-delay models. Using approximated plant models, the area of achievable accuracy is then defined for control performance assessment.
The transfer function $G^P(s)$[2] is then approximated by the lag-delay transfer function (3)$H^P(s)$. Comparison of their step responses is given in Fig. 3.

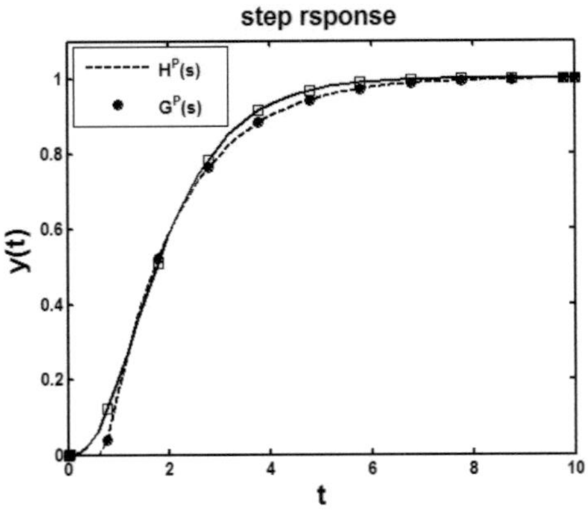

Fig. 3. Step response characteristics of original delay-free plant and its lag-delay model.

In Fig. 4 standard deviations of output signal against standard deviations of control signal for both delayed and non-delayed systems controlled by, respectively, optimal LQG and PID type controllers are plotted. The plots are parametrized by the weighting factor λ. Results of the MV (λ=0) strategy are plotted as horizontal dashed lines and define areas of uncertainty of the performance lower bound when using the lag-delay approximation of non-delayed systems. Results of the benchmark designed for original model with realistic control signal magnitudes (λ=0.001) and PID type control with controllers settings supplied by means of QDR methods are plotted as points.
The MV control strategy used for the delayed model gives lower control quality than the MV algorithm for the delay-free model. Furthermore there is no significant improvement of control quality when optimal settings for classical controllers are used for the delayed model as compared to those obtained by means of QDR method.
Since control signal magnitudes of the lower bound i.e. LQG (λ=0) for lag-delay approximation (3) and those achieved with PID controller are comparable, the most popular MV benchmark η of (1) makes sense when using delayed models, indicating that relatively good performance. It can unfortunately hide the possibility of further performance improvement when delay-free model is used.

---

2 $G^P(s) = \dfrac{1}{(s+1)(0.5s+1)^2}$

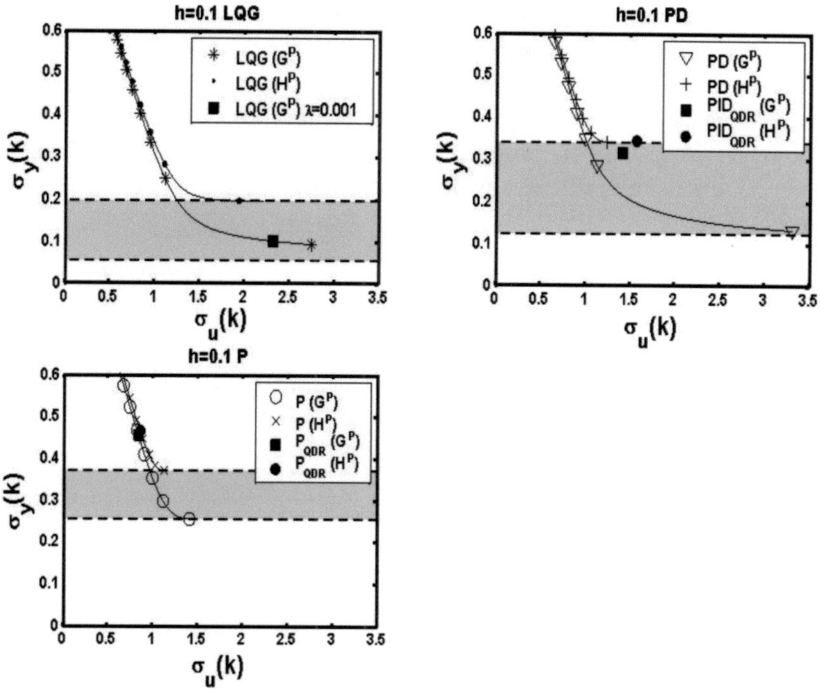

Fig. 4. Areas of achievable accuracy using lag-delay approximation.

Table 1 presents the values of index η and standard deviation of output signal σ_y for the systems with the plant transfer function *$G^P(s)$* and *$H^P(s)$*. Furthermore the value of sqrt(η)*σ_y is shown which is equivalent to standard deviation of the output signal obtained when pure MV Astrom's algorithm is used.

λ=0 h=0.1	η	σ_y	sqrt(η)	sqrt(η)*σ_y
LQG [$G^P(s)$]	0.8421	0.0751	0.9176	0.0689
PD [$G^P(s)$]	0.2668	0.1333	0.5166	0.0689
P [$G^P(s)$]	0.0701	0.2601	0.2648	0.0689
PID_{QDR} [$G^P(s)$]	0.0480	0.3145	0.2088	0.0689
P_{QDR} [$G^P(s)$]	0.0230	0.4545	0.1517	0.0689
LQG [$H^P(s)$]	0.9998	0.2026	0.9999	0.2026
PD [$H^P(s)$]	0.3465	0.3442	0.5886	0.2026
P [$H^P(s)$]	0.2938	0.3738	0.7362	0.2026
PID_{QDR} [$H^P(s)$]	0.3485	0.3432	0.5652	0.2026
P_{QDR} [$H^P(s)$]	0.1900	0.4649	0.4359	0.2026
substitute delay				
LQG [$G^P(s)$]	1.0000	0.0751	1.0000	0.0751
PD [$G^P(s)$]	0.4992	0.1333	0.7065	0.0942
P [$G^P(s)$]	0.4315	0.2601	0.6568	0.1709
PID_{QDR} [$G^P(s)$]	0.2799	0.3145	0.5094	0.1664
P_{QDR} [$G^P(s)$]	0.1773	0.4545	0.2791	0.1914

Table 1. Values of performance measure η and estimated output standard deviation under pure MV Astrom's control algorithm

The bottom part of the table shows the values calculated for the delay-free system, $G^P(s)$, and calculated using the estimated substitute delay. The most important conclusion is that the use of the substitute delay to assess the system control performance often gives unreliable results. Another interesting observation is that the values from the last column belong to the uncertainty area of performance lower bound (see Fig. 3). This can also be seen from Fig. 5s where the estimates of the performance lower bound are plotted when assuming different values of delay *l*.

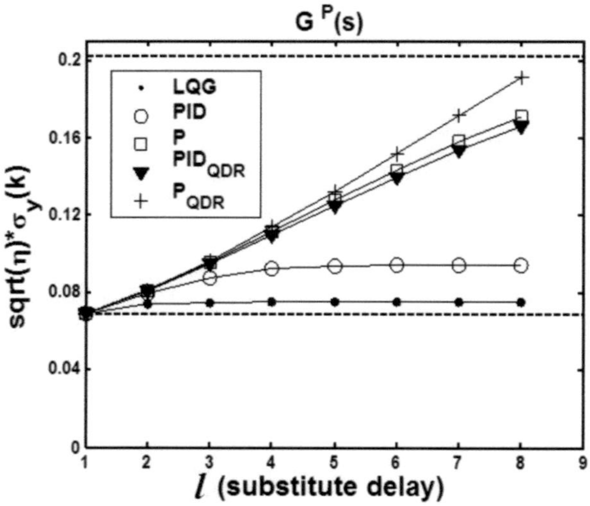

Fig. 5. Areas of achievable accuracy using lag-delay approximation.

7. More complete characteristic of control error

As mentioned in the previous section using more sophisticated original delay-free model additional improvement of control quality can be attained for both PID and LQG controllers. The price paid is much larger control variance. It is interesting to note that while LQG systems remain robust this is not longer valid for PID controllers.

Then in this section comparison of certain time and frequency domain functions will be done to give further insight into assessment of control performance in terms of system robustness.

The notion of 1D-PID will be also used to denote the limited authority tuning of PID controller whose dynamical parameters T_i and T_d are chosen from a popular tuning rule, e.g. the QDR method based on model (3), remain constant, and only the gain K_p is chosen so as to minimize the index in (9).

In Fig. 6. trade-off curves displaying standard deviations of output signals against standard deviations of control signals for the original delay-free system controlled by optimal LQG controller and by optimally tuned 1D-PID controller are plotted. Plots are parameterized by the weighting factor λ, and results of the unrestricted MV-LQG and restricted structure, 1D-PID MV strategies (λ=0) are plotted as horizontal doted lines for both types of controllers. Due to excessive control actions and small increase of control quality MV based benchmarks are not particularly authoritative [3] for non-delayed systems. Therefore, a benchmark which assumes restricted control effort seems to be more suitable for systems controlled by the PID controllers. Points a→a1, b→b1, c→c1 depict correspondence of control systems with the same control effort.

	η	$\sqrt{\eta}$
a	0.4846	0,6961
b	0.3075	0,5545
c	0.3018	0,5494
a1	0.7932	0,8906
b1	0.7071	0,8409
c1	0.5853	0,7650

Table 2. Performance measure for systems in Fig. 6

It is worth noting that for the MV-LQG η=0.9321 (sqrt(η)=0,9655). The almost MV-LQG system represented as a1 has the value of η=0.7932 (sqrt(η)=0,8906), and for a reasonably tuned system represented by c1 there is η=0.5853 (sqrt(η)=0,7650), respectively.

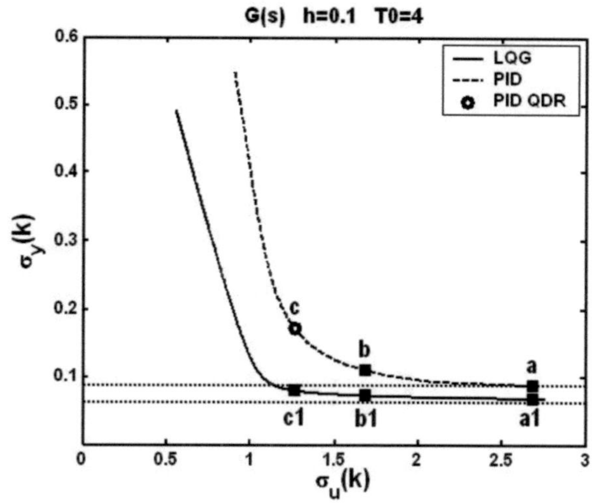

Fig. 6. Standard deviation of output vs control signal for PID and LQG controlled systems.

In Fig. 7-8 PSD[3] functions of output signals of corresponding systems are plotted and compared with the PSDF of disturbance. Important observation is that the optimal PID controller distinguishes itself by very poor robustness both in terms of phase margin and large sensitivity peak. This fact is reflected by the appearance of high frequency peak in PSD function. This is not the case for moderately tuned PID and all LQG controllers.

[3] PSD - Power Spectral Density function

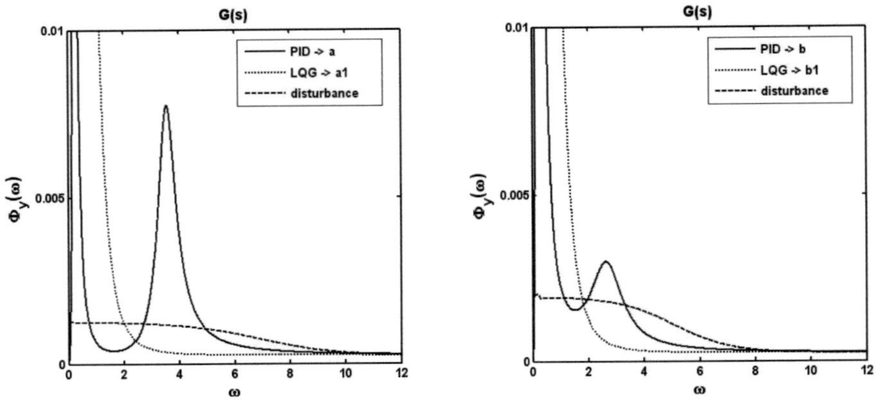

Fig. 7. PSDF of output signals for LQG and PID loop in comparison with PSDF of disturbance corresponding to a, a1, b, b1.

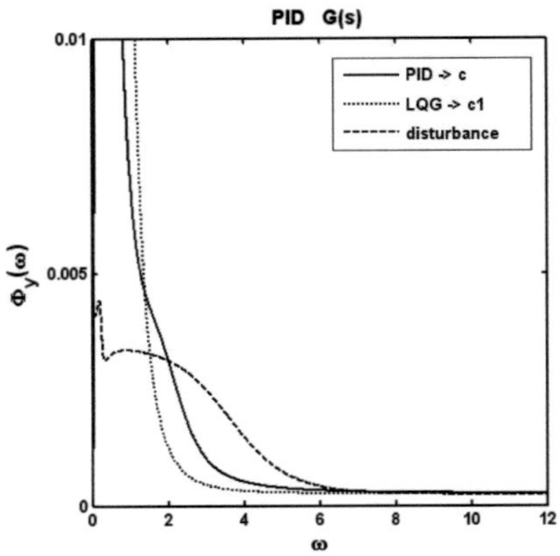

Fig. 8. PSDF of output signals for LQG and PID loop in comparison with PSDF of disturbance; corresponding to c, c1.

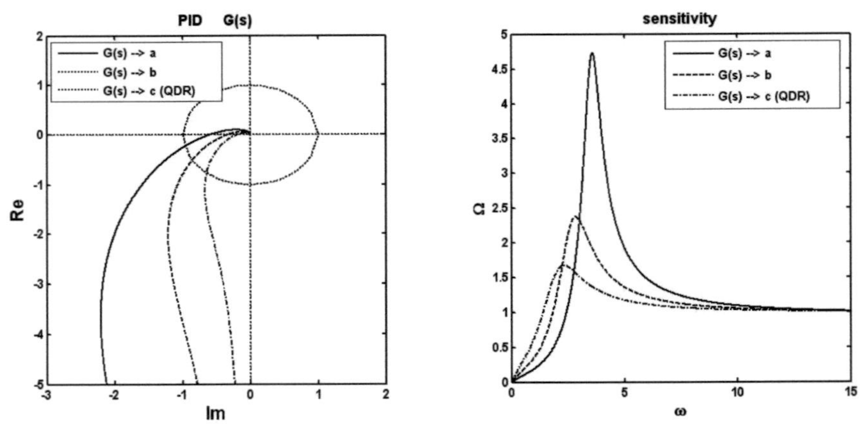

Fig. 9. Nyquist plots of the open loop and the sensitivity function for PID control corresponding to a, b, c.

In Fig. 9-11 Nyquist plots, step responses and sensitivity functions of systems corresponding to points a,b,c and a1, b1, c1 are plotted. The main outcome is that similar efficiency of disturbance attenuation can be attained with both MV-LQG and 1D-PID controllers. Unfortunately, in contrast to LQG, increasing control efficiency results in poorer robustness of 1D -PID MV control systems.

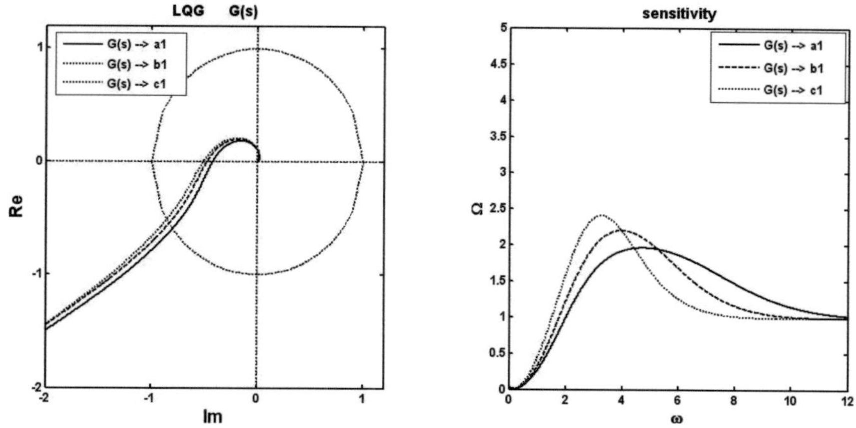

Fig. 10. Nyquist plots of the open loop and the sensitivity function for LQG control corresponding to a1, b1, c1.

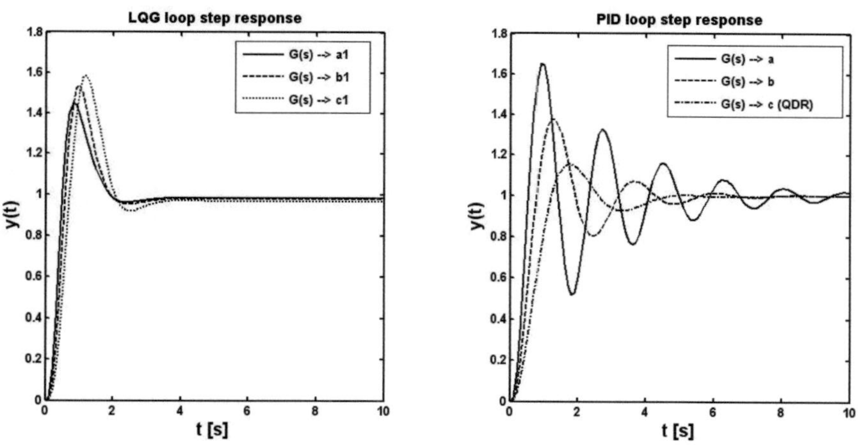

Fig. 11. Step response characteristics of LQG and PID loops corresponding to a, b, c and a1, b1, c1.

8. Remarks on single-stage against multi-stage performance criteria for control benchmarking

The performance measure which takes control effort into account becomes more and more popular. This measure result in solution of GMVC or LQG problem. And this next leads to the minimization of single-stage or computationaly more complicated multi-stage quadratic

performance criteria. The section shows that simple single-stage performance criteria have limited application for unstable and non-minimumphase plants. Further it was shown that for sampled data systems integral performance criterion which takes inter-sample behaviour into account is more suitable.
Single-stage and infinite-horizon performance criteria will be compared due to their use for control system benchmarking. It will be shown that when using simple single-stage cost function, a critical value of control weighting might exist, under which the control system loses its stability. As far as the infinite horizon is concerned, this problem does not exist. Furthermore, if uncontrolled system has unstable discretization zeros, then even a single step cost function can assure stability of the closed loop, provided that the single stage discrete-time performance index is produced by integrating a continuous time index within the sampling period.
To compare the system behaviour under single-stage in contrast to multi-stage criteria standard deviations of output and control signal in sampling instances will be used again. These parameters describe signal magnitudes better then variances and are also useful to assess the control performance.
If the uncontrolled system is unstable or non-minimumphase, controller designed by means of single-stage criterion can be also unstable. This was presented in Fig. 12 and Fig. 13 by means of values of standard deviations of output and control signals.
The examplary uncontrolled first-order unstable system is given by following transfer function:

$$G_1(s) = \frac{1}{(s-1)} \tag{38}$$

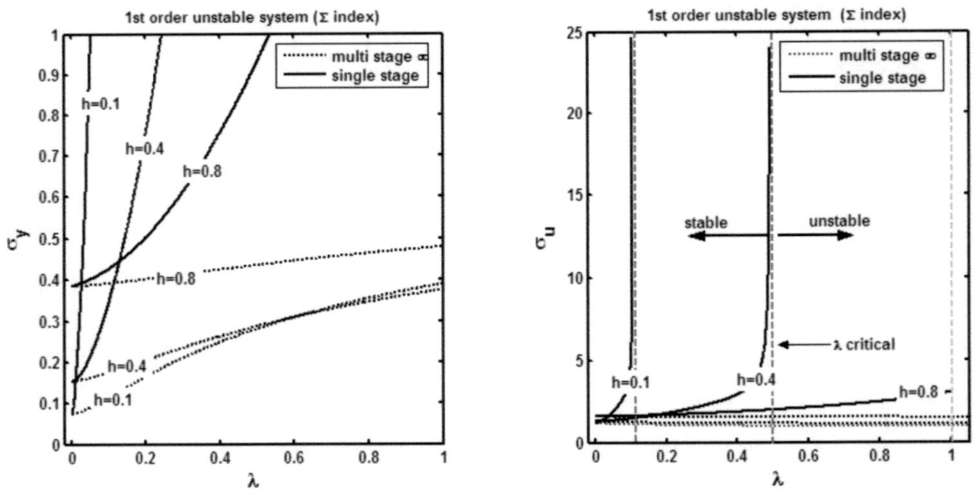

Fig. 12. Standard deviations of output and control signals against weighting factor λ for both single-stage and multi-stage criteria.

Vertical dashed lines represent critical values of weighting factor when the closed loop system controlled by algorithm based on single-stage criteria is unstable. This is not valid for more complicated control algorithm which minimizes multi-stage performance function. Fig. 13 represents results for an exemplary non-minimumphase plant described by following transfer function:

$$G_2(s) = \frac{1}{(s+1)}\left(\frac{1-\alpha s}{1+\alpha s}\right), \quad \alpha = 0.2 \tag{39}$$

The closed loop system with controller designed by means of optimization multi-stage performance index remains stable for all values of λ in contrast to this simple single-stage index.

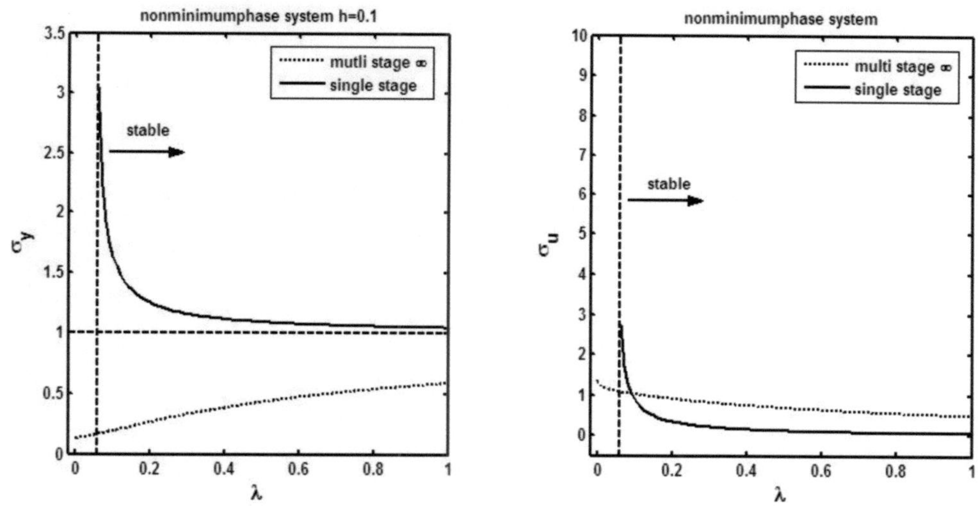

Fig. 12. Standard deviations of output and control signals against weighting factor λ for both single-stage and multi-stage criteria.

8.1 Integral cost function

Next figures illustrate using discrete versus integral cost function for the plant given by following transfer function

$$G_3(s) = \frac{1}{(s+1)} e^{-s\tau} \qquad \tau = 0.7 \qquad h = 0.8 \tag{40}$$

Discretization of the transfer function $G_3(s)$ with period h gives unstable zeros. In contrast to the discrete cost function integral criterion both multi-stage and single-stage provide stable results for the closed loop system.

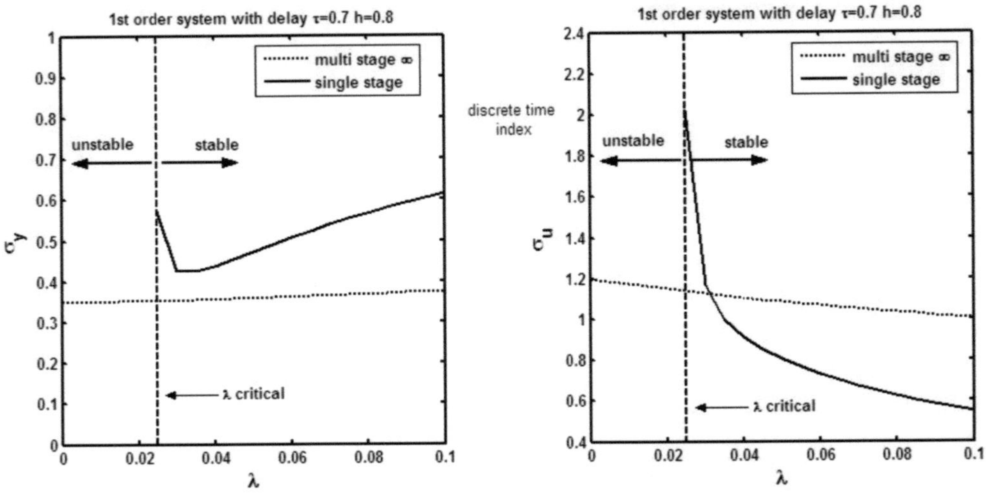

Fig. 13. Standard deviations of output and control signals against weighting factor λ for both single-stage and multi-stage criteria (discrete index).

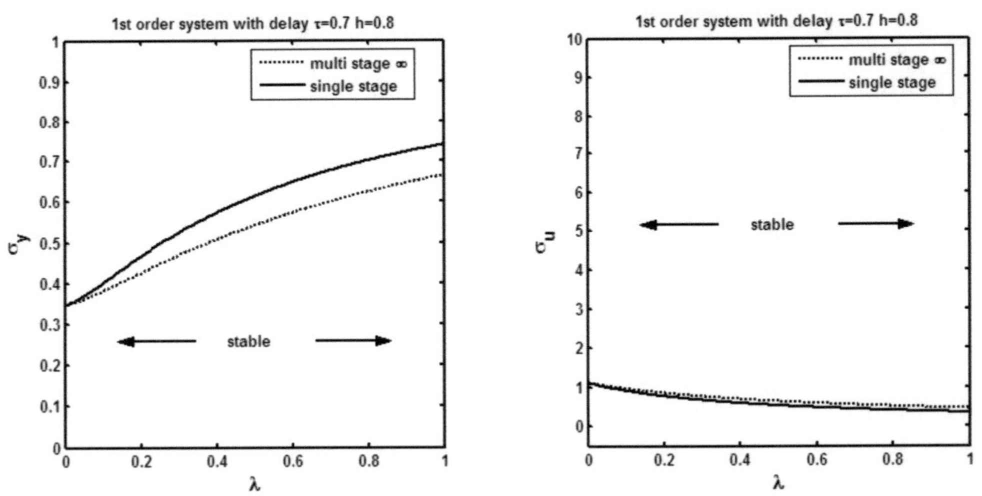

Fig. 14. Standard deviations of output and control signals against weighting factor λ for both single-stage and multi-stage criteria (integral index).

9. Conclusion

In the chapter some developments in the control performance assessment are provided. The solution based on quadratic performance criteria which taking control effort into account was proposed in return for popular MV measure. This further broke about the definition of trade-off curve using standard deviation of both control and error signals. The standard deviation parameter is preferred because better than variance characterize the signal magnitudes. The tool in the form of trade of curve showed to be very useful for the control quality assessment of systems equipped with restricted structure controllers, such as PID type. The area of achievable accuracy, when models with substitute delay is used, was also defined showing the possibility of further improvement of control performance when more sophisticated non-delayed model of plant is applied. The price paid is much larger control variance and loss of robustness in case of the system with PID type controllers. Therefore from the technological point of view the knowledge of control error variance only is not sufficient enough and more complete characteristic which gives further insight into control performance assessment in term of robustness is necessary. In the end the problem of using simple single-stage and computationally more complicated multi-stage quadratic performance criteria was exemplified. That was pointed out existing of the critical value of weighting factor which result in an unstable controller design if uncontrolled system is unstable or non-minimumphase and the simple single-stage cost function is used.

10. References

Åström K., Wittenmark B.: Computer-Controlled Systems: Theory and Design. Prentice-Hall 1990.

Åström K.: Introduction to Stochastic Control Theory. Academic Press, New York, 1970.

Bialic G., Błachuta M.: Models for Performance Assessment of PID Control Loops. 11th IEEE *International Conference on Methods and Models in Automation and Robotics, MMAR 2005*, Międzyzdroje, Poland, pp. 439-444, 2005.

Bialic G., Błachuta M.: Remarks on single-stage against multi-stage performance criteria for control benchmarking. *13 th IEEE IFAC International Conference on Methods and Models in Automation and Robotics, MMAR'2007*, Szczecin, 27-30.08.2007

Błachuta M., Bialic G.: On control performance assessment based on lag-delay models. *IEEE, 24th American Control Conference.*, Portland, Oregon, USA, 8-10 June 2005, pp. 374-379.

Błachuta M., Bialic G.: On the Impact of Plant Model and Controller Sophistication on Performance of Disturbance Attenuation and System Robustness., San Diego, CA, USA, *45th IEEE Conference on Decision and Control* 13-15 December 2006

Chen T., Francis B.: Optimal Control of Sampled-Data Systems. *Springer Verlag* 1995.

Desborough L., Harris T.: Performance assessment measures for univariate feedback control. *The Canadian Journal of Chemical Engineering* vol. 70 December 1992.

Grimble M.J: Restricted structure control loop performance assessment for PID controllers and state-space systems. *Asian Journal of Control.* Vol. 5, pp. 39-57, March 2003.

Harris T.J., Seppala C.T.: Recent Developments in Controller Performance Monitoring and Assessment Techniques. *Chemical Process Control* VI, January 2001, Tuscon, Arizona published A.I.Ch.E Symposium Series: Volume 98 2002.

Huang B.: A pragmatic approach towards assessment of control loop performance. *Int. J. Adap. Control Signal Process.* Vol.17. pp. 589-608, 2003.

Huang B., Shah S.L.: Performance Assessment of Control Loops: Theory and Application. *Springer Verlag* 1999.

Ko B.S., Edgar T.F.: PID control performance assessment: the single loop case. AIChE Journal vol. 50. June 2004.

Lennartson B., Söderström T.: Investigation of the intersample variance in sampled-data control. *Int. J. Control*, vol. 50, no. 5 pp. 1587-1602, 1989.

Lennartson B.: Sampled-Data Control for time-delayed plant. *Int. J. Control*, vol. 49, no. 5 pp. 1601-1614, 1989.

Van Loan C.F.: Computing Integrals Involving the Matrix Exponential. *IEEE Trans. on Auto. Control* AC-23, pp. 395-404, 1978

7

Bilinear Time Series in Signal Analysis

Bielinska Ewa
The Silesian University of Technology
Poland

1. Introduction

Time series models (named also output or signal models), considered in this chapter, are functions of accessible process outputs, observed as a set of uniformly sampled data, which are one and the only information on the process itself. They are mainly applied in signals modeling and prediction. Stochastic time series models, i.e. models that use white noise series as a part of the model, have been used in signal analysis since the sixties of the XX century. Time series modeling consists in fitting a function *f*(·) into a given data set y_i.
The *f* (·) is a function of previous data y_{i-j}, for *j*=*1*,..., *J* and an innovation series w_{i-k}, for *k*=*1*,...,*K*. In general, stochastic time series model has the following form:

$$y_i = f(y_{i-j}, w_{i-k}) + w_i \tag{1}$$

The innovation series w_i use to be assumed either a white noise series e_i, or series of model errors $\varepsilon_i = y_i - \hat{y}_i$. The function *f*(·) may be either linear or nonlinear. Though real processes use to be non-linear and non-Gaussian, they are often modeled as linear ARMA (Box, 1983), (Yaffee, 2000).

$$y_i = \frac{C(D)}{A(D)} e_i = \sum_{k=0}^{dC} c_k e_{i-k} + \sum_{j=1}^{dA} a_j y_{i-j} \tag{2}$$

where:
e_i - Gaussian white noise series,
D - time delay operator: $D^k y_i = y_{i-k}$.
Theory of Gaussian linear time series models, including stability and invertibility conditions, as well as analysis and identification methods, are well established, e.g. (Box, 1983). However, asymmetrical time series or time series that are characterized by data anomalies cannot be modeled as linear. There are a great number of possible nonlinear structures of the function f(·), but the most common one is a nonlinear polynomial structure (3). The model of such form is named nonlinear ARMA model (NARMA).

$$y_i = w_i + \sum_{k=1}^{K} c_k w_{i-k} + \sum_{k_1=1}^{K_1}\sum_{k_2=1}^{K_2} c_{k_1,k_2} w_{i-k_1} w_{i-k_2} + \sum_{k_1=1}^{K_1}\sum_{k_2=1}^{K_2}\sum_{k_3=1}^{K_3} c_{k_1,k_2,k_3} w_{i-k_1} w_{i-k_2} w_{i-k_3} + \ldots$$
$$+ \sum_{j=1}^{J} a_j y_{i-j} + \sum_{j_1=1}^{J_1}\sum_{j_2=1}^{J_2} a_{j_1,j_2} y_{i-j_1} y_{i-j_2} + \sum_{j_1=1}^{J_1}\sum_{j_2=1}^{J_2}\sum_{j_3=1}^{J_3} a_{j_1,j_2,j_3} y_{i-j_1} y_{i-j_2} y_{i-j_3} + \ldots \quad (3)$$

Bilinear ARMA models are a subset of the class of NARMA models, and are described by the following equation:

$$y_i = w_i + \sum_{k=1}^{K} c_k w_{i-k} + \sum_{k=1}^{K}\sum_{l=1}^{L} \beta_{k,l} w_{i-k} y_{i-l} + \sum_{j=1}^{J} a_j y_{i-j} \,. \quad (4)$$

Nonlinear time series analysis, particularly - establishing stability and invertibility conditions, is in general much more complex than analysis of the linear ones. Therefore, only the particular model structures are being analyzed in practice. In 1978, Granger and Andersen derived some interesting properties of the bilinear model with the simplest structure (Granger & Andersen, 1978)

$$y_i = e_i + \beta_{11} e_{i-1} y_{i-1}, \quad (5)$$

where e_i is an independent white noise sequence with zero mean and the variance $m_e^{(2)}$. Since then, simple bilinear models have been also investigated by Martins (Martins, 1997), (Martins, 1999), Berlin Wu (Berlin Wu, 1995), Tong (Tong 1993), Granger and Terasvirta (Granger & Terasvirta, 1993). Opinion on the usefulness of bilinear series vary from a skeptic one "*Using economic data, bilinear models have not been found to be very relevant*", (Tong 1993) to an enthusiastic "*The bilinear model has been used successfully to model time series that have been traditionally difficult to fit with classical linear time series methods*" (Martins, 1999). The aim of the paper is to assume an attitude towards the above statements, especially in the field of technological and medical processes. In the chapter, elementary bilinear model *EB(k,l)*:

$$y_i = w_i + \beta_{kl} w_{i-k} y_{i-l}\,, \quad (6)$$

where $k \le l$, is considered and then applied in signal analysis.

The chapter is organized in the following way:

Section 2 is dedicated to elementary bilinear processes. Analytical relations between process moments and process parameters are presented for diagonal and sub-diagonal elementary bilinear processes. In general, they are valid under assumption that inaccessible process input is uncorrelated and symmetrically distributed.

In *Section 3*, methods of parameters' estimation for elementary bilinear models are presented. Identification algorithms for simple and generalized methods of moments for elementary bilinear models are formulated.

Section 4 is dedicated to application of elementary bilinear models in simulation and prediction. A hybrid linear-bilinear model is introduced and, on its basis, a bilinear minimum-variance prediction algorithm is derived, for model residuum represented by diagonal and sub-diagonal elementary bilinear model.

In *Section 5*, the most important results are summarized.

2. Bilinear time series models

Large amount of dynamical systems may be described with set of conservation equations in the following form:

$$\frac{d\mathbf{x}(t)}{dt} = \mathbf{Ax}(t) + \mathbf{Bu}(t) + \sum_{k=1}^{m} \mathbf{N}_k u_k(t)\mathbf{x}(t), \tag{7}$$

where the last term creates the bilinear part of the equation. Bilinear equations are the natural way of description of a number of chemical technological processes like decantation, distillation, and extraction, as well as biomedical systems, e.g. (Mohler, 1999), (Nise, 2000). Though the nature of many processes is bilinear, identification of the model (7) can be difficult, at least because some of the state or input variables may be immeasurable. This is the case of many biological or biomedical processes. Often, the discrete set of the output observation $\{y_i\}$, for $i=1,\ldots,n$, is the only information on the considered process. In such cases bilinear time series model (8), which explains relation between the set of the output data only, may be considered.

$$A(z^{-1})y_i = C(z^{-1})e_i + \sum_{k=1}^{K}\sum_{l=1}^{L} \beta_{kl} e_{i-k} y_{i-l} \tag{8}$$

Bilinear time series models have been mentioned in control engineering since early seventieth. Schetzen Theorem (Schetzen, 1980) states, that any stable time variant process may be modeled as time invariant bilinear time series. General structure of bilinear time series model (8) is complex enough to make its analysis very difficult. Therefore, in practise the particular model structures are being analysed.
Stochastic processes are completely characterized by their probabilistic structure, i.e. probability or probability density $p(y)$ (e.g. Therrien, 1992). However, in practice, probabilistic structure of a considered system is unknown and, therefore, the system analysis is performed on the ground of its statistical moments. The moments for any stochastic process with any probabilistic density $p(y)$ are expressed as:

$$M_y^{(r)} = E\{y_i^r\} \tag{9}$$

where E is an operator of expected value :

$$E\{y\} = \sum_x yp(y) = \mu\ . \tag{10}$$

Central moments are:

$$M_y^{\prime(r)} = E\{(y_i - \mu)^r\} \tag{11}$$

When the structure of particular bilinear model is simple, the moments and the central moments may be analytically calculated based on the process equation, and the moments' definitions (9), (11). Elementary bilinear time series models, considered in this chapter, in dependence on their structures, are classified as sub diagonal or diagonal.

2.1 Sub diagonal elementary bilinear time series EB(k,l)

When the structure *k,l* of elementary bilinear time series model *EB(k,l)* satisfy relation $k < l$, the model (12) is named sub diagonal.

$$y_i = e_i + \beta_{kl} e_{i-k} y_{i-l}, \tag{12}$$

The model is characterized by two parameters, β_{kl} and m_e^2, related to each other. It may be proven, (e.g. Tong, 1993) that the model (12) is stable when $|\beta_{kl}^2 m_e^{(2)}| < 1$, and is invertible when $|\beta_{kl}^2 m_e^{(2)}| < 0.5$. Time series invertibility means that for a stable time series

$$y_i = f(e_i, e_{i-1}, ..., e_{i-k,} y_{i-1}, ..., y_{i-l}) \tag{13}$$

operation of inversion

$$e_i = f(e_{i-1}, ..., e_{i-k,} y_i, y_{i-1}, ..., y_{i-l}) \tag{14}$$

is stable. The moments and the central moments of *EB(k,l)* may be analytically calculated based on the process equation (12), and the moments' definitions (9), (11). Relations between moments and parameters are given in the table 1. The variance $M_y^{(2)}(0)$ of *EB(k,l)* is bounded when:

$$|\beta_{kl}^2 m_e^{(2)}| < 1. \tag{15}$$

The fourth moment $M_y^{(4)}(0,0,0)$ of *EB(k,l)* is bounded when:

$$|\beta_{kl}^4 m_e^{(4)}| < 1 \tag{16}$$

Irrespective of the probabilistic density of e_i, sub diagonal *EB(k,l)* is non-Gaussian and uncorrelated. Gaussian equivalent of the sub diagonal *EB(k,l)* with a bounded variance is a Gaussian white noise with the first and the second moments the same as the respective moments of the *EB(k,l)*. Comparison of an *EB(2,4)* time series and its Gaussian equivalent is shown in the Fig.(1).

Moments	Formulae
$M_y^{(1)}$	0
$M_y^{(2)}(0)$	$\dfrac{m_e^{(2)}}{1-\beta_{kl}^2 m_e^{(2)}}$
$M_y^{(2)}(m>0)$	0
$M_y^{(3)}(0,0)$	0
$M_y^{(3)}(l_1 \neq k, l_2 \neq l)$	0
$M_y^{(3)}(k,l)$	$\beta_{kl} m_e^{(2)} M_y^{(2)}(0)$
$M_y^{(4)}(0,0,0)$	$\dfrac{m_e^{(4)} + 6\beta_{kl}^2 (m_e^{(2)})^2 M_y^{(2)}(0)}{1-\beta_{kl}^4 m_e^{(4)}}$

Table 1. Relation between moments and *EB(k,l)* parameters

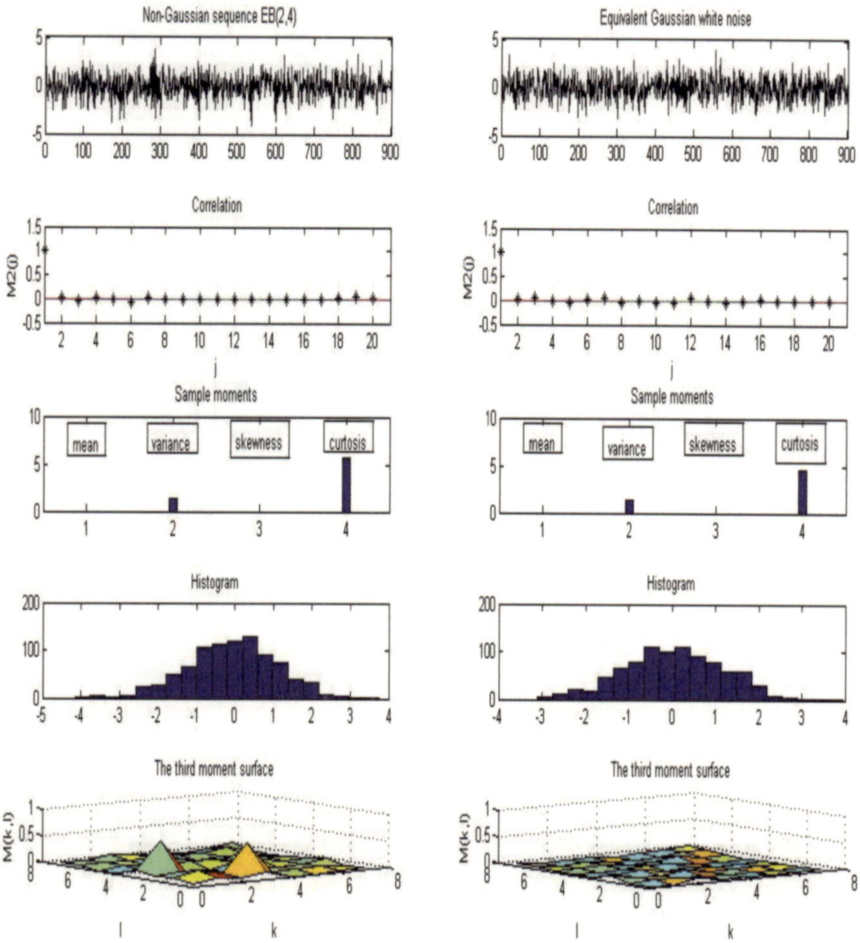

Fig. 1. Comparison of the estimated moments of EB(2,4) and an equivalent white noise

2.2 Diagonal elementary bilinear time series EB(k,k)

Elementary diagonal bilinear time series model, *EB(k,k)* has the following structure:

$$y_i = e_i + \beta_{kk} e_{i-k} y_{i-k}. \tag{17}$$

Properties of the model depend on two parameters, β_{kk} and $m_e^{(2)}$, related to each other.

Stability and invertibility conditions for *EB(k,k)* are the same as for sub diagonal *EB(k,l)* time series model. Having known the process equation (17) and the moments' definitions (9) and (11), moments and central moments of the *EB(k,k)*may be analytically calculated as functions of model parameters. Though *EB(k,l)* and *EB(k,l)* with respect to model equation are similar to each other, their statistical characteristics are significantly different. Relation between succeeding moments and model parameters are given in the table 2. An example of a single realization of EB*(5,5)* series as well as its sampled moments is shown in the the Fig. 2.

Moments	Formulae
$M_y^{(1)}$	$\beta_{kk} m_e^{(2)}$
$M_y^{(2)}(0)$	$\dfrac{m_e^{(2)} + \beta_{kk}^2 (m_e^{(4)} - (m_e^{(2)})^2)}{1 - \beta_{kk}^2 m_e^{(2)}}$
$M_y^{(2)}(m \neq k)$	$\beta_{kk}^2 \left(m_e^{(2)}\right)^2$
$M_y^{(2)}(k)$	$2\beta_{kk}^2 \left(m_e^{(2)}\right)^2$
$M_y^{(3)}(0,0)$	$3\beta_{kk}^2 (m_e^{(2)})^2 + \beta_{kk}^3 \dfrac{m_e^{(6)} - \beta_{kk}^2 m_e^{(2)} m_e^{(6)} + 3\beta_{kk}^2 (m_e^{(4)})^2)}{1 - \beta_{kk}^2 m_e^{(2)}}$
$M_y^{(3)}(k, l < k)$	$2\beta_{kk}^3 \left(m_e^{(2)}\right)^3$
$M_y^{(3)}(k,k)$	$\beta_{kk} m_e^{(4)} + \dfrac{3\beta_{kk}^3 m_e^{(2)} m_e^{(4)}}{1 - \beta_{kk}^2 m_e^{(2)}}$
$M_y^{(3)}(k, l > k)$	$2\beta_{kk}^3 \left(m_e^{(2)}\right)^3$
$M_y^{(3)}(k, 2k)$	$4\beta_{kk}^3 \left(m_e^{(2)}\right)^3$

Table 2. Relations between moments and *EB(k,k)* parameters

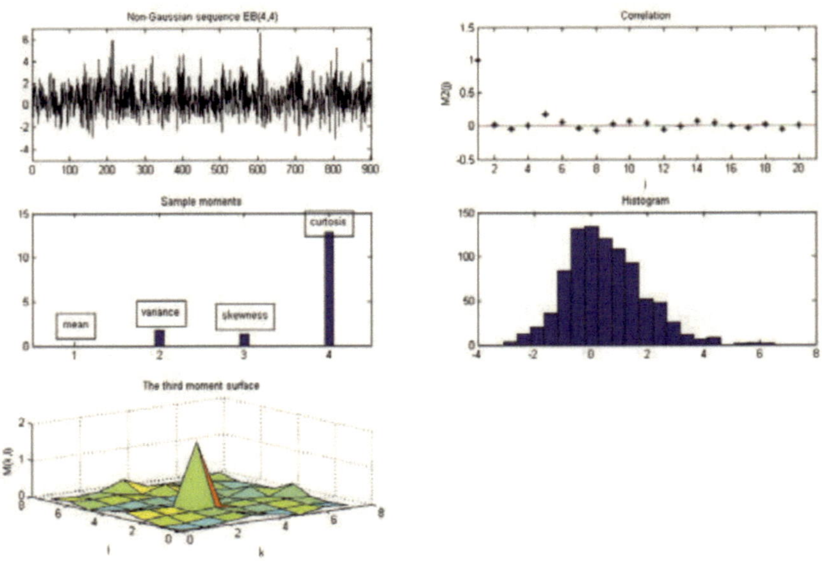

Fig. 2. EB(5,5) sequence and its characteristics

Diagonal *EB(k,k)* time series $\{y_i\}$ has a non-zero mean value, equal to $M_y^{(1)}$. Deviation from the mean $z_i = y_i - M_y^{(2)}$ is a non-Gaussian time series. A Gaussian equivalent of z_i is a *MA(k)* series:

$$z_i = w_i + c_k w_{i-k} \tag{18}$$

where w_i is a Gaussian white noise series. Values of c_k and $m_w^{(2)}$ can be calculated from the set of equations (19):

$$\begin{gathered} \frac{m_e^{(2)}(1+\beta_{kk}^2 m_e^{(2)} + \beta_{kk}^4 (m_e^{(2)})^2)}{1-\beta_{kk}^2 m_e^{(2)}} = m_w^{(2)}(1+c_k^2) \\ \beta_{kk}^2 (m_e^{(2)})^2 = c_k m_w^{(2)} \end{gathered} \tag{19}$$

3. Identification of EB(k,l) models

Under assumption that the model *EB(k,l)* is identifiable, and that the model structure is known, methods of estimation of the model parameters are similar to the methods of estimation of linear model parameters. The similarity stems from that the bilinear model structure, though nonlinear in e_i and y_i, is linear in parameter β_{kl}. A number of estimation methods originate from minimization of a squared prediction error (20). Three of them, which are frequently applied in estimation of bilinear model parameters, will be discussed in the section 3.1.

$$\varepsilon_i = y_i - \hat{y}_{i|i-1} \tag{20}$$

Moments' methods are an alternative way of parameters' estimation. Model parameters are calculated on the base of estimated stochastic moments (Tang & Mohler, 1988). Moments' methods are seldom applied, because hardly ever analytical formulae connecting moments and model's parameters are known. For elementary bilinear time series models the formulae were derived, (see table 1, table 2) and therefore, method of moments and generalized method of moments, discussed in section 3.2, may be implemented to estimate elementary bilinear models parameters.

3.1 Methods originated from minimization of the squared prediction error

Methods that originate from minimization of the squared prediction error (20) calculate model parameters by optimization of a criterion $J(\varepsilon_i^2)$, being a function of the squared prediction error. In this section the following methods are discussed:

- minimization of sum of squares of prediction error,
- maximum likelihood,
- repeated residuum.

a) Minimization of the sum of squares of prediction error

Minimization of the sum of squares of prediction error is one of the simplest and the most frequently used methods for time series model identification. Unfortunately, the method is sensitive to any anomaly in data set applied in model identification (Dai & Sinha, 1989). Generally, filtration of the large data deviation from the normal or common course of time series (removing outliers) precedes the model identification. However, filtration cannot be applied to the bilinear time series, for which sudden and unexpected peaks of data follows from the bilinear process nature, and should not be removed from the data set used for identification. Therefore, the basic *LS* algorithm cannot be applied to elementary bilinear model identification and should be replaced by a modified LS algorithm, resistant to anomalies. Dai and Sinha proposed robust recursive version (RLS) of LS algorithm, where β_{kl} parameter of the model *EB(k,l)* is calculated in the following way:

$$\begin{aligned} b_{kl,i} &= b_{kl,i-1} + k_i\left(y_i - \Phi_i b_{kl,i-1}\right) \\ k_i &= \frac{P_{i-1}\Phi_i}{\alpha_i + \Phi_i^2 p_{i-1}} \\ P_i &= \frac{1}{\alpha_i}\left(P_{i-1} - \frac{P_{i-1}^2\Phi_i^2}{\alpha_i + \Phi_i^2 p_{i-1}}\right) \end{aligned} \tag{21}$$

where:

- $b_{kl,i}$ -- evaluation of model parameter β_{kl} calculated in *i-th* iteration,
- $\Phi_i = \hat{w}_{i-k} y_{i-l}$ -- generalized input,
- $\hat{w}_i = y_i - \Phi_i b_{kl,i-1}$ -- one step ahead prediction error,
- α_i -- coefficient that depends upon the prediction error as follows:

$$\alpha_i = \begin{cases} \dfrac{sign(\hat{w}_i) y_{tresh}}{\hat{w}_i} & \text{for } |\hat{w}_i| > y_{tresh} \\ 1 & \text{for } |\hat{w}_i| \le y_{tresh} \end{cases}$$

y_{tresh} -- a threshold value

b) Maximum likelihood

Maximum likelihood method was first applied to bilinear model identification by Priestley (Priestley, 1980) then Subba (Subba, 1981), and others e.g. (Brunner & Hess, 1995). In this method, elementary bilinear model *EB(k,l)* is represented as a function of two parameters $y_{\text{model}}(b_{kl}, y_{i-k})$:

$$y_{\text{model}} = b_{kl} y_{i-k} w_{i-l} \tag{22}$$

where w_i is an innovation series, equivalent to the model errors:

$$w_i = y_i - y_{\text{model}}(b_{kl}, y_{i-k}). \tag{23}$$

Likelihood is defined as:

$$L = L(b_{kl}, m_w^{(2)}) = \prod_{i=1}^{N} f(b_{kl}, m_w^{(2)}; w_i) \tag{24}$$

Maximization of *L* is equivalent to minimization of *-l=-ln(L)*:

$$-l(b_{kl}, m_w^{(2)}) = -\sum_{i=1}^{N} \ln(f(b_{kl}, m_w^{(2)}; w_i)) \tag{25}$$

Assuming that w_i is a Gaussian series with the mean value equal to zero, and the variance equal to $m_w^{(2)}$, negative logarithm likelihood *-ln(L)* is:

$$-\ln(L) = -l(w_N, w_{N-1}, ..., w_1 \mid b_{kl}, m_w^{(2)}) = \frac{N}{2}\ln(2\pi m_w^{(2)}) + \sum_{i=1}^{N} \frac{w_i^2}{2m_w^{(2)}}. \tag{26}$$

Having assumed initial values $b_{kl,0}$ and $m_{w0}^{(2)}$, parameters b_{kl} and $m_w^{(2)}$ are calculated by minimization of (26). Solution is obtained iteratively, using e.g. Newton-Raphson method. Essential difficulty lies in the fact that w_i is immeasurable and, in each iteration, should be calculated as:

$$w_i = y_i - b_{kl,i-1} w_{i-k} y_{i-l} \tag{27}$$

Obtained estimates of *EB(k,l)* parameters are asymptotically unbiased if w_i is Gaussian (Kramer & Rosenblatt, 1993). For other distributions, Gaussian approximation of the probability density function $f(y_i - y_{\text{model}}(b_{kl}, y_{i-k}))$ causes that the estimated parameters are biased.

c) Repeated residuum method

Alternative estimation method, named repeated residuum method, is proposed in (Priestley, 1980). Implemented to identification of elementary bilinear models, the method may be presented as the following sequence of steps:

1. Model *EB(k,l)* is expressed as:

$$y_i = w_i(1 + b_{kl} y_{i-l} D^k) \tag{28}$$

or equivalently:

$$w_i = \frac{y_i}{1 + b_{kl} y_{i-l} D^k} \tag{29}$$

2. Assuming b_{kl} small, the (29) may be approximated by:

$$w_i = (1 - b_{kl} y_{i-l} D^k) y_i = y_i - b_{kl} y_{i-l} y_{i-k}. \tag{30}$$

Presuming w_i is an identification error, an initial estimate $b_{kl,0}$ of the parameter b_{kl} can be evaluated from the (30), with the use of e.g. LS method.

3. Next, starting from $b_{kl,0}$ and $w_0 = 0$, succeeding w_i can be calculated iteratively:

$$w_i = y_i - b_{kl,0} w_{i-k} y_{i-l} \quad \text{for } i = k, k+1, ..., N. \tag{31}$$

4. Having known y_i and w_i for *i=k,...N*, an improved estimate b_{kl} that minimizes the following sum of squared errors (32) may be calculated.

$$V(b_{kl}) = \sum_{i=k}^{N} (y_i - b_{kl} w_{i-k} y_{i-l})^2. \tag{32}$$

5. The steps 3 and 4 are repeated until the estimate achieves an established value.

3.2 Moments method

With respect to the group of methods that originate from the minimization of the squared prediction error, a precise forms of estimation algorithms can be formulated. On the contrary, for moments method a general idea may be characterized only, and the details depend on a model type and a model structure. Moments method *MM* consists of two stages:

Stage 1: Under the assumption that the model structure is the same as the process structure, moments and central moments $M_y^{(r)}$ are presented as a function of process parameters Θ:

$$M_y^{(r)} = f(\Theta) \tag{33}$$

If it is possible, the moments are chosen such that the set of equations (33) has an unique solution.

Stage 2: In (33) the moments $M_y^{(r)}$ are replaced with their evaluation $\hat{M}_y^{(r)}$, estimated on the base of available data set y_i.

$$\hat{M}_y^{(r)} = f(\Theta) \tag{34}$$

The set of equations (34) is then solved according to the parameters Θ. Taking into consideration particular relation between moments and parameters for elementary bilinear models, *MM* estimation algorithm in a simple and a generalized version can be proposed.

MM - simple version

It is assumed that w_i is a stochastic series, symmetrical distributed around zero, and that the even moments $m_w^{(2r)}$ satisfy the following relations:

$$m_w^{(2r)} = k_{2r}(m_w^{(2)})^r \quad \text{for } r = 1,2,3... \tag{35}$$

Identification of *EB(k,l)* consists of identification of the model structure *(k,l)*, and estimation of the parameters b_{kl} and $m_w^{(2)}$. Identification algorithm is presented below as the sequence of steps:

1. Data analysis:
   a. On the base of data set $\{y_i\}$ for *i=1,...,N*, estimate the following moments:
   $\hat{M}_y^{(1)}$; $\hat{M}_y^{(2)}(m)$ for $m = 0,1,2...$; $\hat{M}_y^{(3)}(l_1,l_2)$ for $l_1,l_2 = 0,1,2...$; $\hat{M}_y^{(4)}(0,0,0)$
   b. Find the values of $l_1 \neq 0$ and $l_2 \neq 0$ ($l_1 \leq l_2$), for which the absolute value of the third moment $\left|\hat{M}_y^{(3)}(l_1,l_2)\right|$ is maximal.
2. Structure identification:
   a. If $l_1 = k,\ l_2 = l$ then subdiagonal model *EB(k,l)* should be chosen.
   b. If $l_1 = k,\ l_2 = k$ then diagonal model *EB(k,k)* should be chosen
3. Checking system identifiability condition:
   If the model *EB(k,l)* was chosen, than:
   a. Calculate an index

$$W_3 = \frac{(\hat{M}_y^{(3)}(k,l))^2}{(\hat{M}_y^{(2)}(0))^3} \tag{36}$$

b. If W_3 <0.25 it is impossible to find a bilinear model *EB(k,l)* that has the same statistical characteristics as the considered process. Nonlinear identification procedure should be stopped. In such case either linear model may be assumed, or another non-linear model should be proposed.

If the model *EB(k,k)* was chosen, than:

a. Calculate an index

$$W_4 = \frac{\hat{M}_y^{(3)}(k,k)}{\hat{M}_y^{(2)}(0)\sqrt{\hat{M}_y^{(2)}(k)}} \tag{37}$$

b. If $\left|W_4 - \frac{3}{\sqrt{2}}\right| < \varepsilon$, where ε is an assumed accuracy, then the model input may be assumed Gaussian.

i. Calculate an index

$$W_5 = \frac{\hat{M}_y^{(3)}(k,k)\hat{M}_y^{(2)}(k)}{\hat{M}_y^{(2)}(0)\hat{M}_y^{(3)}(0,0)} \tag{38}$$

ii. If $W_5 < 0.23$, than the model *EB (k,k)* with the Gaussian input may be applied. If not than linear model *MA(k)* should be taken into account.

c. If $\left|W_4 - \frac{3}{\sqrt{2}}\right| \geq \varepsilon$ than the model input w_i cannot be Gaussian.

4. Estimation of model parameters :

a. When the model *EB(k,l)* was chosen in the step 2:

i. Find the solutions x_1, x_2 of the equation:

$$W_3 = x(1 - x), \tag{39}$$

where $x = b_{kl}^2 m_w^{(2)}$

ii. For each of the solutions x_1, x_2 calculate the model parameters from the following equations:

$$m_w^{(2)} = \hat{M}_y^{(2)}(0)(1 - x), \qquad b_{kl}^2 = \frac{x}{m_w^{(2)}} \tag{40}$$

iii. In general, the model *EB(k,l)* is not parametric identifiable, i.e. there is no unique solution of the equation (39) and (40). Decision on the the final model parameters should be taken in dependance on model's destination. Models applied for control and prediction should be stable and invertible. Models used for simulation should be stable but do not have to be invertible.

b. When in the step 2 the model *EB (k,k)* is chosen:

i. If $\left|W_4 - \frac{3}{\sqrt{2}}\right| \geq \varepsilon$ then $x = \frac{k_4 - W_4\sqrt{2}}{W_4\sqrt{2}(k_4 - 1) - 2k_4}$, where:

$$\text{for } k_4 < 3: \quad \frac{k_4\sqrt{2}}{2} < W_4 < \frac{3\sqrt{2}}{2},$$

$$\text{for } k_4 > 3: \quad \frac{3\sqrt{2}}{2} < W_4 < \frac{k_4\sqrt{2}}{2}.$$

ii. If $W_4 \approx \frac{3}{\sqrt{2}}$, i.e. w_i is Gaussian, then the following equation have to be solved:

$$W_5 = \frac{6x(1 - x)}{3 + 2x + 22x\hat{}2}$$

Because the model EB(k,k) with the Gaussian input is not parametric identifiable, the final model should be chosen according to its destination, taking into account the same circustances as in the paragraph a) -iii.

MM -- generalized version:

Generalized moments method (GMM) (Gourieroux et al., 1996) (Bond et al., 2001), (Faff & Gray 2006), is a numerical method in which model parameters are calculated by minimization of the following index:

$$I = \sum_{j=1}^{J} f_k(y_i, \Theta)^2, \tag{41}$$

where:

Θ -- vector of parameters,

$f_j(y_i, \Theta)$ -- a function of data $y(i)$ and parameters Θ, for which:

$$E\{y_i, \Theta_0\} = 0 \quad \text{when} \quad \Theta = \Theta_0 \tag{42}$$

Θ_0 -- vector of parameters minimizing the index *I*.

Function $f_j(y_i, \Theta)$ for $j=1,2,...,J$ is defined as a difference between analytical moment $M_y^{(k)}(\Theta)$ dependant upon the parameters Θ, and the evaluation $\hat{M}_y^{(k)}$ calculated on the base of y_i for $i=1,...,N$. The number J of considered moments depends on the model being identified.

Identification of the subdiagonal, elementary bilinear model *EB(k,l)* makes use of the four moments. Functions f_j, for $j=1,...,4$ are defined in the following way:

$$f_1(y_i, \Theta) = M_y^{(2)}(0) - \hat{M}_y^{(2)}(0)$$

$$f_2(y_i, \Theta) = M_y^{(3)}(k,l) - \hat{M}_y^{(3)}(k,l)$$

$$f_3(y_i, \Theta) = M_y^{(4)}(0,0,0) - \hat{M}_y^{(4)}(0,0,0)$$

$$f_4(y_i, \Theta) = m_w^{(2)} - \hat{m}_w^{(2)}$$

Diagonal model EB(k,k) is identified on the base of three moments. The functions f_j for $j=1,...,6$ are:

$$f_1(y_i,\Theta) = M_y^{(1)} - \hat{M}_y^{(1)}$$
$$f_2(y_i,\Theta) = M_y^{(2)}(0) - \hat{M}_y^{(2)}(0)$$
$$f_3(y_i,\Theta) = M_y^{(2)}(k) - \hat{M}_y^{(2)}(k)$$
$$f_4(y_i,\Theta) = M_y^{(3)}(0,0) - \hat{M}_y^{(3)}(0,0)$$
$$f_5(y_i,\Theta) = M_y^{(3)}(k,k) - \hat{M}_y^{(3)}(k,k)$$
$$f_6(y_i,\Theta) = m_w^{(2)} - \hat{m}_w^{(2)}$$

For elementary bilinear models vector of parameters contains two elements: $m_w^{(2)}$ and b_{kl}. The parameters are calculated by minimization of the index (41), using e.g. nonlinear least squares method. It is assumed that starting point $\Theta_0 = \left[b_{kl,0}, m_{w0}^{(2)}\right]$ is a solution obtained with the use of the simple method of moments. Minimum of the index I may be searched assuming that the parameters b_{kl} and $m_w^{(2)}$ are constrained. The constrains result from the following attributes:

- The variance $m_w^{(2)}$ of the model input should be positive and less than the output variance, hence:

$$0 < m_w^{(2)} < m_y^{(2)}, \tag{43}$$

- The model should be stable, hence:

$$b_{kl}^2 m_w^{(2)} < 1 \tag{44}$$

3.3 Examples

The methods discussed above were applied to elementary bilinear time series identification under the following conditions:

1. Elementary diagonal and subdiagonal time series were identified.
2. Distribution of the white noise w_i was assumed:
   - Gaussian,
   - even

   with the zero mean and the variance $m_w^{(2)} = 1$.
3. All considered processes were invertible, i.e. the parameters satisfied the following condition: $b_{kl}^2 m_w^{(2)} < 0.5$ (Tong, 1993).
4. Identification was performed for 200 different realizations of the time series consisted of 1000 data.
5. For generalized moments method:

- Minimization of the performance index was carried out with the constrains:

$$\frac{-0.5}{m_y^{(2)}} < \hat{b}_{kl} < \frac{0.5}{m_y^{(2)}}$$
$$0 < m_w^{(2)} < m_y^{(2)}$$

– Starting point was calculated using simple moments method.

Result of conducted investigation may be summarized as follows:

1. Not every invertible elementary bilinear process is identifiable.
2. Correct identification results were obtained for processes, for which $\beta_{kl} \leq 0.4$, what is equivalent to: $\beta_{kl}^2 m_w^{(2)} \leq 0.16$.
3. When $\beta_{kl}^2 m_w^{(2)} > 0.16$ number of process realization, for which elementary bilinear model cannot be identified grows with the growth of $\beta_{kl}^2 m_w^{(2)}$.
4. When $\beta_{kl} \leq 0.4$ all the tested methods give the expected values of identified parameters b_{kl} equal to the truth values β_{kl}.
5. Generalized moments method is somewhat better than other considered methods, because the variances of the estimated parameters are the smallest.
6. For the processes with Gaussian excitation the variances of the identified parameters are greater than for the processes with even distribution of the input signal.

4. Application of EB(k,l) in signal modelling and prediction

Elementary bilinear time series models, which statistical attributes as well as methods of identification have been presented in the previous sections, are fit to modelling a limited class of signals only. However, an idea of using *EB(k,l)* models as a part of a hybrid linear-bilinear model, let to widen the class of signals, for which improving accuracy of modelling and prediction become possible.

4.1 Hybrid linear-bilinear model

Idea of a hybrid linear-bilinear (HLB) model is presented in the Fig. 3. Elementary bilinear model *EB(k,l)*, for which is assumed that $k \leq l$, and $e(i)$ is an independent white noise series, is applied as a part of the HLB. For *k<l* HLB model may be considered as linear autoregressive model stimulated by *EB(k,l)* series. The hybrid model consists of two parts:

– linear, that is built on the original data series $y(i)$:

$$y_i^L = -\sum_{j=1}^{dA} a_j y_{i-j} \tag{45}$$

– nonlinear that is built on the residuum w_i:

$$w_i = y_i - y_i^L \tag{46}$$

Residuum w_i is described in the following way:

$$w_i = \eta_i - \overline{\eta} \tag{47}$$

where:

$$\overline{\eta} = \begin{cases} \beta_{kk} m_e^{(2)} & \text{for } EB(k,k) \text{ model} \\ 0 & \text{for } EB(k,l) \text{ model} \end{cases} \tag{48}$$

and η_i is described by the elementary bilinear model *EB(k,l)* or *EB(k,k)*:

$$\eta_i = \begin{cases} e_i + \beta_{kk} e_{i-k} \eta_{i-k} & \text{for } EB(k,k) \text{ model} \\ e_i + \beta_{kl} e_{i-k} \eta_{i-l} & \text{for } EB(k,l) \text{ model} \end{cases} \tag{49}$$

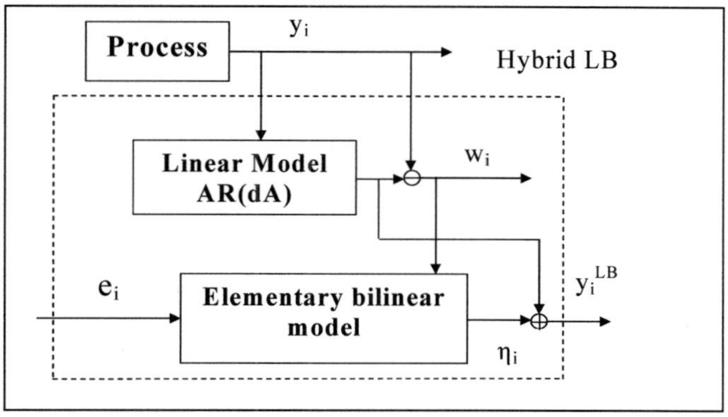

Fig. 3. Hybrid Linear-Bilinear model

The output of the H*LB* model is the following sum:

$$y_i^{LB} = y_i^L + \eta_i \tag{50}$$

Identification of the HLB model is done in three stages.

1. First stage -- data pre-processing -- is optional. If the original data set *{x(i)}* contain linear trends, they are removed according to:

$$z_i = x_i - x_{i-1} \tag{51}$$

If it is necessary, obtained data set z_i may be transformed. One of possible data transformation is:

$$y_i = \frac{z_i - \overline{z}}{\text{var}(z)} \tag{52}$$

2. The second stage -- linear model AR(dA) (53) is identified.

$$A(z^{-1}) y_i = w_i \tag{53}$$

From the experience follows, that the *AR(dA)* models satisfying the coincidence condition:

$$r_j a_j \geq 0 \quad \text{for } j = 1, \ldots, dA \tag{54}$$

where:

$$r_j = \frac{1}{N-j} \sum_{i=1}^{N-j} y_i y_{i-j} \tag{55}$$

are not only parsimonious but also have the better predictive properties than the AR(*dA*) models with the full rank.
3. The third stage -- elementary bilinear time series model is identified for residuum w_i in a way discussed in section 3.

4.2 Prediction

Time series models are mainly applied for signals' prediction. In this section, a prediction algorithm derived on the base of HLB model is presented. As it was discussed in the section 2, elementary bilinear models *EB(k,l)* and *EB(k,k)* have different statistical attributes. Therefore, prediction algorithms, though based on the same *HLB* model, have to be designed separately for residuum represented as *EB(k,l)* and *EB(k,k)*. Minimum variance prediction algorithms have roots in the following theorems.

Theorem 1.

If y_i is a non-Gaussian stochastic time series described by the hybrid model HLB: $A(D)y_i = \eta_i$, *where:*

- *residuum η_i is represented as a sub diagonal model EB(k,l) and k<l:*

$$\eta_i = w_i + b_{kl} w_{i-k} \eta_{i-l} ,$$

- *w_i is an independent white noise series with the variance $m_w^{(2)}$,*

then the h-step prediction according to the algorithm:

$$\hat{y}_{i+h|i} = G(D)y_i + \beta_{kl} F(D)\left(\varepsilon^{\eta}_{i+h-k} \eta_{i+h-l}\right) \tag{56}$$

where:

$$\varepsilon_i^{\eta} = \eta_i - \hat{\eta}_{i|i-h} ,$$

$$\hat{\eta}_{i|i-h} = b_{kl} \varepsilon^{\eta}_{i+h-k} \eta_{i+h-l} ,$$

gives the prediction error $\varepsilon_i^{y} = F(D)w_i$ with the minimal possible variation:

$$E\{\varepsilon_i^y\}^2 = m_w^{(2)} \left(1 + \sum_{i=1}^{h-1} f_i^2\right) \tag{57}$$

In the above equations D – states for a nonlinear delay operator defined as follows:

$$D^k(y_i) = y_{i-k}$$

$$D^k(y_i x_i) = y_{i-k} x_{i-k}$$

$$D^k(y_i)x_i = y_{i-k} x_i ,$$

A(D), F(D), G(D) - are polynomials in D with degrees *dA, h-1, dA-1* respectively. The polynomials are related to each other so to satisfy the following equation:

$$1 = A(D)F(D) + D^h G(D) \tag{58}$$

When residuum is a diagonal *EB(k,k)* process, the following theorem is formulated.
Theorem 2.
If yi is a non-Gaussian stochastic time series described by the hybrid model HLB: $A(D)y_i = z_i$, *where residuum* z_i *may be presented as:*

$$z_i = \eta_i - \overline{\eta},$$

$$\eta_i = w_i + \beta_{kk} w_{i-k} \eta_{i-k},$$

$$\overline{\eta} = \beta_{kk} m_w^{(2)},$$

then the h-step prediction according to the algorithm:

$$\hat{y}_{i+h|i} = G(D)y_i + \beta_{kk} F(D)\left(\varepsilon^{\eta}_{i+h-k} z_i\right) + z_{i+h-k} + \overline{\eta} + \beta_{kk} F(D)\left(\varepsilon^{\eta}_{i+h-k}\overline{\eta}\right) + F(D)\overline{\eta} \tag{59}$$

where:

$$\varepsilon^{\eta}_i = \eta_i - \hat{\eta}_{i|i-h},$$

$$\hat{\eta}_{i|i-h} = b_{kk} \varepsilon^{\eta}_{i+h-k} \eta_{i+h-k},$$

gives the prediction error: $\varepsilon^y_i = F(D)w_i$ *with the minimal possible variation:*

$$E\{\varepsilon^y_i\}^2 = m_w^{(2)}\left(1 + \sum_{i=1}^{h-1} f_i^2\right)$$

Delay operator D and the polynomials *A(D), F(D), G(D)* are defined in the same way as in the Theorem 1.

4.3 Prediction strategy

Prediction strategy means a way of data processing that should be applied to the original data series to obtain the accepted prediction. In this section MV -HLB prediction strategy is formulated. The strategy has the form of an algorithm built of a sequence of the following steps:

1. The original set of data y_i, *i=1,...,N* is divided into two sets:
   - training set, for $i = 1,...,N_{train}$, that is used for model identification,
   - testing set, for $i = 1,...,N_{test}$, on which the prediction algorithm is tested.
2. On the training set, parameters of a linear *AR(dA)* model:

$$y_i = -a_1 y_{i-1} - a_2 y_{i-2} - ... - a_{dA} y_{i-dA} \tag{60}$$

   are estimated. For further consideration, such models that satisfy coincidence condition (54) are accepted only.
3. On the training set the residuum is calculated according to the equation:

$$\eta_i = y_i + a_1 y_{i-1} + a_2 y_{i-2} + ... + a_{dA} y_{i-dA} \tag{61}$$

4. In the following steps *4-7* identification procedures described in details in section 3 are realized.
5. The first, the second, the third and the fourth moments of the residuum η_i are estimated.
6. Identifiability criterion for *EB(k,l)* process is checked for the series of residuum. If fitting elementary bilinear model is possible, one can continue in the step 7. If not, one should move to the step 12.
7. The structure *(k,l)* of the *EB(k,l)* model is established on the base of the third moment for residuum.
8. The values of β_{kl} and $m_w^{(2)}$ are calculated using e.g. one of the moments' methods.
9. For the assumed prediction horizon h and the estimated polynomial *A(D)* the diophantine equation (58) is solved, and the parameters f_k, *k=1,…,h-1* of the polynomial *F(D)* as well as the parameters g_j, *j=1,…,dA-1* of the polynomial *G(D) are* calculated. Then, if the prediction horizon $h \le \min(k,l)$, prediction algorithm is designed either on the base of the Theorem 1 -- for the *EB(k,l)* model of the residuum, or on the base of the Theorem 2 -- for the *EB(k,k)* model of the residuum.
10. The designed prediction algorithm is tested on the testing set. STOP.
11. If $h > \min(k,l)$ then move to the step 12.
12. Design linear prediction algorithm e.g. [1], [4]: $\hat{y}_{i+h|i} = G(D)y_i$
13. Test it on the training set. STOP.

The above prediction strategy was tested for simulated and real world time series. In the next section, the strategy is applied to series of sunspot numbers and MVB prediction is compared with the non-linear prediction performed using the benchmark SETAR model, proposed by Tong (Tong, 1993).

4.4 Sunspot number prediction

Sunspots events have been observed and analysed for more than 2000 years.

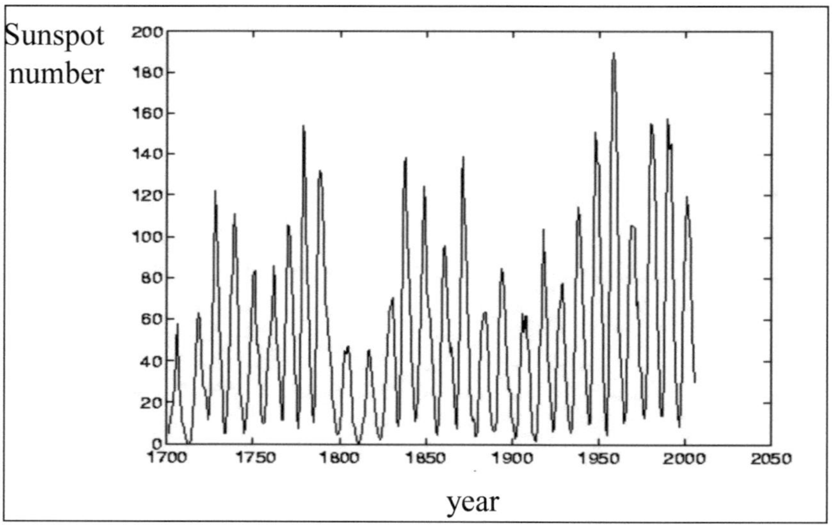

Fig. 4. Sunspot events

The earliest recorded date of a sunspot event was 10 May 28 BC. The solar cycle was first noted in 1843 by the German pharmaceutical chemist and astronomer, Samuel Heinrich Schwabe as a result of 17 years of daily observations. The nature of solar cycle, presented in the Fig. 4 characterized by a number of sunspots that periodically occurs, remains a mystery to date. Consequently, the only feasible method to predict future sunspot number is time series modeling and time series prediction. Linear prediction do not give acceptable results hence, the efforts are made to improve the prediction using nonlinear models and nonlinear methods. Tong (Tong, 1993) has fitted a threshold autoregressive (SETAR) model to the sunspot numbers of the period 1700-1979:

$$Y_i = \begin{cases} 1.92 + 0.84Y_{i-1} + 0.07Y_{i-2} - 0.32Y_{i-3} + 0.15Y_{i-4} - 0.20Y_{i-5} & \\ -0.00Y_{i-6} + 0.19Y_{i-7} - 0.27Y_{i-8} + 0.21Y_{i-9} + 0.01Y_{i-10} + e_i^1 & when\ Y_{i-8} \le 11.93 \\ & \\ 4.27 + 1.44Y_{i-1} - 0.84Y_{i-2} - 0.06Y_{i-3} + e_i^2 & when\ Y_{i-8} > 11.93 \end{cases} \tag{62}$$

The real data were transformed in the following way:

$$Y_i = 2(\sqrt{1+y_i} - 1) \tag{63}$$

where y_i is the sunspot number in the year *1699+i*.

Based on the model (62) prediction for the period 1980-2005 was derived, and used as a benchmark for comparison with the prediction, performed in the way discussed in the paper. The *HLB* model (64) was then fitted to the sunspot numbers, coming from the same period 1700-1979, under the assumption that the linear part of the *HLB* model satisfies the coincidence condition.

$$\begin{aligned} Y_i &= 0.81Y_{i-1} + 0.21Y_{i-8} + \eta_i \\ \eta_i &= e_i + 0.02\eta_{i-7}e_{i-7} \end{aligned} \tag{64}$$

The Y_i is a variable transformed in the same way as in the Tong's model (62), and the variance of residuum is $\mathrm{var}(\eta) = 8.13$.

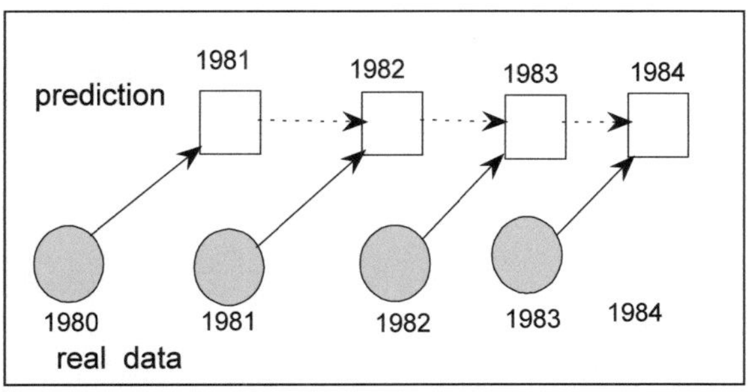

Fig. 5. Scheme of prediction calculation

Sunspot events prediction for the period 1981−2005 was performed according to the scheme showed in the Fig. 5. One step ahead prediction $\hat{y}_{i+1|i}$ calculated at time *i* depends on the previous data and the previous predictions. Prediction algorithm has the form specified in Theorem 2.For the data transformed according to (63) predictions obtained based on Tong's model and the *HLB* model are compared in the Fig. 6.

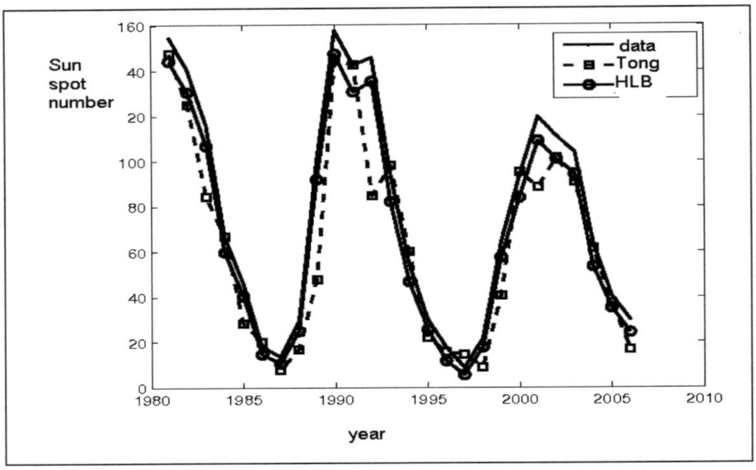

Fig. 6. Prediction for the period 1981-2005 based on Tong's and *HLB* models

The *HLB* prediction is evidently more precise than the one derived on the base of the Tong's model. Sum of squares of the Tong's prediction errors was:

$$S_T = 1.07 \times 10^4 ,$$

while sum of squares of the *HLB* prediction errors was:

$$S_{MLB} = 1.70 \times 10^3$$

Data transformation (63) is not natural for minimum variance prediction. Therefore, *HLB* model was once more identified, for the data transformed in the following way:

$$Y_i = \frac{y_i - \bar{y}}{\mathrm{var}(y)} . \tag{65}$$

This time the following *HLB* model was identified:

$$\begin{aligned} Y_i &= 0.80Y_{i-1} - 0.29Y_{i-7} + 0.52Y_{i-8} + \eta_i \\ \eta_i &= e_i + 0.08\eta_{i-3}e_{i-3} \end{aligned} \tag{66}$$

and variance of the residuum $\mathrm{var}(\eta) = 0.24$. Prediction algorithm was built on the base of model (66) in a way specified in Theorem 2. The sum of squares of the *HLB* prediction errors was this time:

$$S_{MLB} = 30 ,$$

hence, higher quality of the *HLB* prediction was obtained this time than previously. Fig. 7 illustrates prediction for the period 1981-2005, obtained on the base of Tong's model (62), built on the data transformed according to (63), and on the base of *HLB* model (66).

Tong (Tong, 1993) after discussion with Sir David Cox, one of the greatest statisticians in XX century, defined genuine prediction, as the prediction of data that are entirely not known at the stage of prediction establishing. The idea is illustrated in the following scheme, and is known also as a multi-step prediction.

In 1979, genuine prediction of sun spot numbers was established for years 1980−1983 on the base of Tong, and *HLB* models. Sums of squares of the prediction errors were equal to 347 and 342, respectively. The results are showed in the Fig. 9.

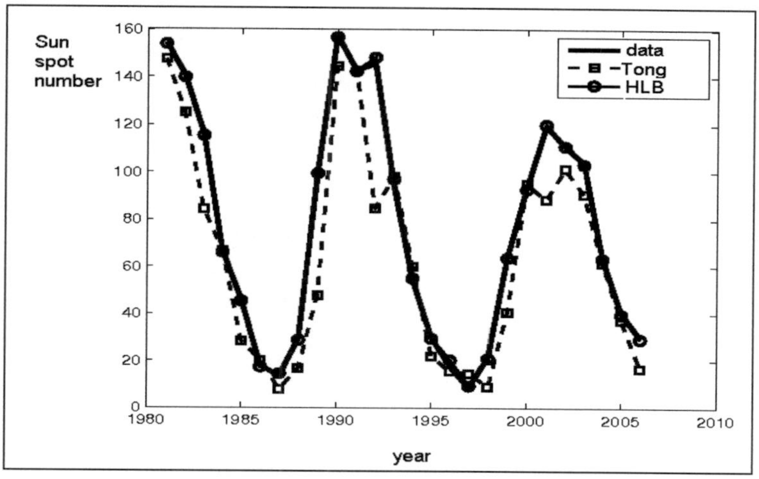

Fig. 7. Prediction for the period 1981-2005 based on Tong's and *HLB* models.

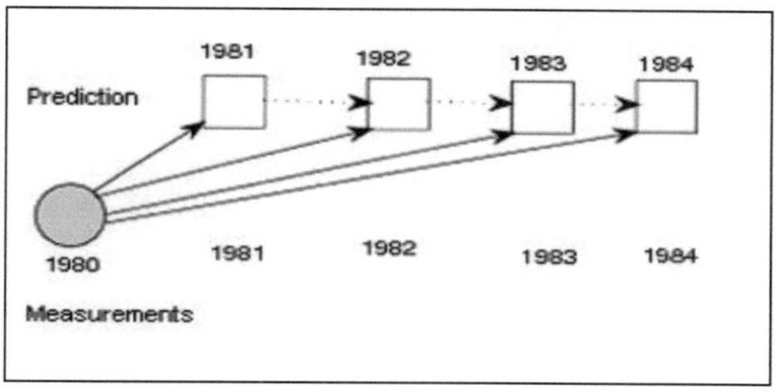

Fig. 8. Illustration of genuine prediction

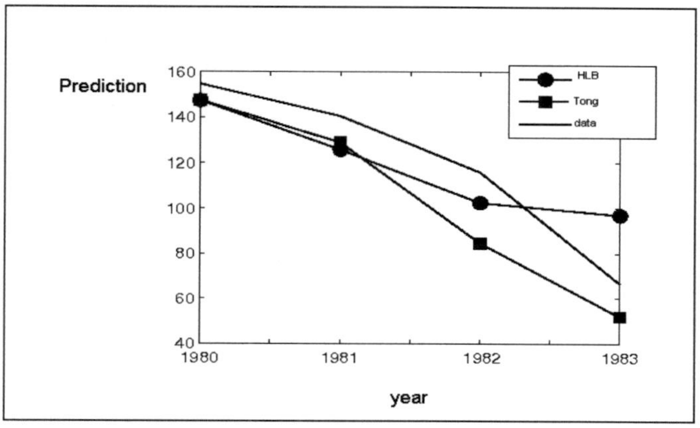

Fig. 9. Genuine prediction for the period 1980-84

5. Resume

In the chapter, a new method of time series analysis, by means of elementary bilinear time series models was proposed. To this aim a new, hybrid linear - elementary bilinear model structure was suggested. The main virtue of the model is that it can be easily identified. Identification should be performed for the linear and the non-linear part of the model separately. Non-linear part of the model is applied for residuum, and has elementary bilinear structure. Model parameters may be estimated using one of the moments' methods, because relations between moments and parameters of elementary bilinear time series models are known.

Based on HLB model, minimum-variance bilinear prediction algorithm was proposed, and the prediction strategy was defined. The proposed prediction strategy was than applied to one of the best-known benchmark - sunspot number prediction. Prediction efficiency obtained with the use of *HLB* model, and bilinear prediction algorithm, in the way described in the paper, occurred much better than the efficiency obtained on the base of SETAR model, proposed by Tong.

6. References

Bond, S.; Bowsher, C. &, Windmeijer F. (2001). Criterion-based inference for GMM in autoregressive panel data models, Economic *Letters*, Vol.73

Brunner, A. & Hess, G. (1995). Potential problems in estimating bilinear time-series models. *Journal of Economic Dynamics & Control*, Vol. 19, Elsevier

Dai, H. & Sinha, N. (1989). Robust recursive least squares method with modified weights for bilinear system identification. *IEE Proceedings*, Vol. 136, No. 3

Faff R. & Gray P. (2006). On the estimation and comparison of short-rate models using the generalised method of moments. *Journal of Banking & Finance*, Vol. 30

Granger, C. & Andersen A., (1978). Nonlinear time series modeling, In: *Applied Time series analysis*, Academic Press.

Granger, C. & Terasvirta, T. (1993). *Modelling nonlinear Economic Relationships,* " Oxford University Press, Oxford

Gourieroux, C.; Monfort A. & Renault E. (1996). Two-stage generalized moment method with applications to regressions with heteroscedasticity of unknown form, Journal *of Statistical Planning and Interference*, Vol.50

Kramer, M. & Rosenblatt, M. (1993). The Gaussian log likehood and stationary sequences, In: *Developments in time series analysis,* Suba Rao, T. (Ed.), Chapman & Hall

Martins, C. (1997). A note on the autocorrelations related to a bilinear model with non-independent shocks. *Statistics & Probability Letters*, Vol. 36

Martins, C. (1999). A note on the third order moment structure of a bilinear model with non independent shocks. *Portugaliae Mathematica*, Vol.56

Mohler, R. (1991). *Nonlinear systems. Vol.II. Applications to bilinear control.* Prentice Hal

Nise, S. (2000). *Control systems engineering.* John Wiley & Sons

Priestley, M. (1980). *Spectral analysis and time series.* Academic Press

Schetzen, M. (1980). *The Volterra & Wiener Theories of Nonlinear Systems.* Wiley-Interscience, New York

Subba Rao, T. (1981). On the theory of bilinear models. *Journal of Royal Statistic Society*, Vol.B, 43

Tang, Z. & Mohler, R. (1988). Bilinear time series: Theory and application. *Lecture notes in control and information sciences*, Vol.106

Therrien, C. (1992). *Discrete random signals and statistical signal processing,* Prentice Hall

Tong, H. (1993). *Non-linear time series.* Clarendon Press, Oxford

Wu Berlin, (1995). Model-free forecasting for nonlinear time series (with application to exchange rates. *Computational Statistics & Data Analysis.* Vol. 19

Yaffee, R. (2000). *Introduction to time series analysis and forecasting,* Academic Press

8

Nonparametric Identification of Nonlinear Dynamics of Systems Based on the Active Experiment

Magdalena Boćkowska and Adam Żuchowski
Szczecin University of Technology
Poland

1. Introduction

Identification is a process (measured experiment and numerical procedure) aiming at determining a quantitative model of the examined object's behaviour. Identification of dynamics is a process which tries to define a quantitative model of variation of system state with time. The goal in the experiment is to measure inputs and outputs of the examined object, the system excitations and reactions. In special cases the model can be treated as a "black box" but it always has to be connected with physical laws and can not be inconsistent with them.

The most commonly used models of system dynamics are differential equations - general nonlinear, partial, often nonlinear ordinary, rarely linear ordinary, additionally non-stationary and with deviated arguments. Sometimes one considers discrete-time models presented in a form of difference equations, which are simplified models of a certain kind. Integral equations, functional equations etc. are models of a different kind.

If a model structure is a priori known or if it can be assumed, the identification consists in determination of model parameters and it is defined as parametric identification. If the full model structure or its part is not known, nonparametric identification has to be used.

In domain of linear models an equivalence of linear ordinary differential equations is transfer function, transient response or frequency response. They can be obtained using experiments of various types: passive - observation of inputs or outputs without interaction upon object or active - excitation of the examined object by special signals (determined: impulse, leap, periodic, a periodic, lottery: white noise, coloured noise, noise with determined spectrum…).

Many possibilities lead to a variety of identification methods. In the last decades various identification methods have been developed. Rich bibliography connected with this thematic includes Uhl's work (Uhl, 1997) which describes computer methods of identification of linear and nonlinear system dynamics, in time domain and also frequency, with short characteristic and a range of their applications.

There are many methods of parametric and nonparametric identifications of linear dynamics of systems (Eykhoff, 1980), (Iserman, 1982), (Söderström & Stoica, 1989). There are fewer useful methods applied for systems with nonlinear dynamics (Billings & Tsang, 1992), (Greblicki & Pawlak, 1994), (Haber & Keviczky, 1999), thereby a presented simple solution

can be very useful in identification of the structure of a model of nonlinear dynamics of 1st and higher orders.
The method of identification has to be adapted to planned and possible experiments and the type of the assumed model structure. Active identification is more precise than that which is based on a passive experiment. A parametric identification connects optimisation with the regression method which allows to decrease the influence of disturbances and consequently increases accuracy of the model parameters. The precision of identification depends on the degree of disturbances elimination, errors of measured methods and accuracy of measuring devices.
The input and output are often measured as disturbed signals. The parametric identification for non-linear systems based on the method of the averaged differentiation with correction was introduced in the paper (Boćkowska, 2003). The method of averaged differentiation allows to filter distorted signals and to obtain their derivatives. Thanks to the correction procedure one can obtain such values of the corrected averaged signals and their derivatives, which are very close to their real values.

2. Averaged differentiation method with correction as regularization filter

The method of averaged differentiation is a regularization filter which allows to determine useful signals and their derivatives based on the disturbed signals available from measurement. Operation of averaged differentiation can be used to evaluate a derivative of any function of signal and time, and averaged signals can be used in estimation of model parameters. Nevertheless its application is not sufficient to determine nonlinearity such as multiplication or other non-linear functions of derivatives with different order. The problem can be solved through connecting the operation with specially designed procedures of correction. Hence one can obtain such values of the corrected averaged signals and their derivatives, which are very close to their real values and so can be used to determine nonlinearity with different structures, good enough to estimate parameters of nonlinear models.

2.1 Definition of averaged differentiation method

If the signal x(t) is passing through the window g(v) with the width ±d starting from the moment t_0, Fig. 1, then the output of the window is the signal (Kordylewski & Wach, 1988):

$$x(t_0)_g = \int_{-d}^{d} x(t_0 + v) \cdot g(v) dv \,. \tag{1}$$

If the function x(t) is differentiable, then it $x(t_0+v)$ can be expanded into Taylor series in the neighbourhood of the point t_0:

$$x(t_0 + v) = \sum_{i=0}^{\infty} \frac{v^i}{i!} \cdot x^{(i)}(t_0) \,. \tag{2}$$

Denoting the moments of the measurement window as:

$$m_i = \int_{-d}^{d} v^i \cdot g(v) dv \tag{3}$$

the window response takes the form:

$$x(t_0)_g = \sum_{i=0}^{\infty} \frac{m_i}{i!} \cdot x^{(i)}(t_0) . \tag{4}$$

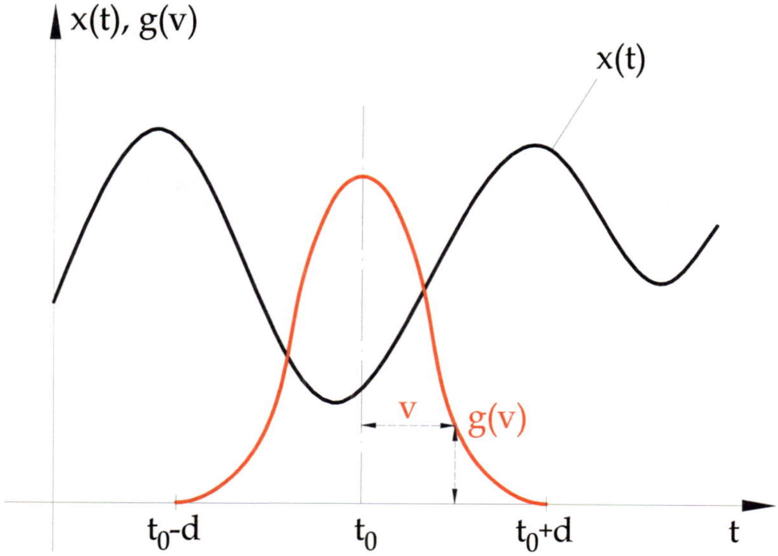

Fig. 1. The measurement window.

In general, we can assume that $x(t)=y^{(n)}(t)$. Using the definition (1) and integrating by parts n-times we get the formula:

$$\int_{-d}^{d} y^{(n)}(t_o + v) \cdot g(v) = y^{(n)}(t_o)_g = (-1)^n \cdot \int_{-d}^{d} y(t_o + v) \cdot g^{(n)}(v) dv + \\ \sum_{i=0}^{n-1} (-1)^i \cdot \left\{ g^{(i)}(d) \cdot y^{(n-i-1)}(t_o + d) - g^{(i)}(-d) \cdot y^{(n-i-1)}(t_o - d) \right\}. \tag{5}$$

If the weight function g(v) satisfies the following conditions:

$$g^{(i)}(-d) = g^{(i)}(d) = 0 \quad \text{for} \quad i = 0,1,2 \ldots n \geq n-1 \ , \tag{6}$$

then Equation (5) can be simplified to the following form:

$$y^{(n)}(t_o)_g = (-1)^n \int_{-d}^{d} y(t_o + v) \cdot g^{(n)}(v) dv . \tag{7}$$

It allows shifting the differentiation from the signal y(t), which is usually disturbed, to the weight function, which is known in an analytical form. In general, this considerably lowers the influence of disturbances on the result of differentiation, all the stronger the greater the measuring window width 2d (Boćkowska, 1998). So the operation of the averaged differentiation can be treated as an equivalent of passing the signal through the measuring window described by the equation:

$$g_n(t) = g^{(n)}(t) \cdot (-1)^n \,. \tag{8}$$

The symmetry and normalisation of the function g(v) are not necessary, but satisfying these conditions is useful for further considerations. Since the function g(v) is an even function

$$g(t)=g(-t), \text{ for } t \in \langle -d, d \rangle \tag{9}$$

the odd moments are always equal to zero $m_{2i+1}=0$ and there are no phase shifts between signals $x(t_0)$ and $x(t_0)_g$. If the normalising condition is satisfied:

$$\int_{-d}^{d} g(v)dv = 1 \,, \tag{10}$$

then the transformation (1) corresponds to the averaging of the signal x(t) with the weight function g(v) in the time interval $\langle t_0 - d, t_0 + d \rangle$:

$$x(t_0)_g = \frac{\int_{-d}^{d} x(t_0 + v) \cdot g(v)dv}{\int_{-d}^{d} g(v)dv} \,. \tag{11}$$

2.2 Optimization of realization of averaged differentiation (Boćkowska, 2005)

The operation (1) as well as (7) can be interpreted as a convolution conducted in a continuous time domain and it is called the convolution integral. Its value at an arbitrary time t is found by integrating the weighted signal by the window g(v) or its derivative in the averaging interval (-d, d). It can be implemented using one of the numerical integration methods with the fixed step being equal to the measuring step T_s or its multiple. Each of them introduces their own errors. The smaller the step size, the more accurate the results. For any given step size, the more computationally complex the method, the more accurate but longer the calculation.

It can be much easier to handle this problem with discrete techniques. The convolution integral can be substituted by the convolution sum:

$$y_z^{(i)}(l_o)_g = \sum_{j=0}^{M-1} h(j) \cdot y_z(l_o - j) \text{ , where } h(j) = (-1)^i \cdot \frac{g^{(i)}(v)}{T_s} \tag{12}$$

and M, l_o are accordingly $2 \cdot d$, t_o divided by the measuring step T_s. If y_z is the measuring signal with N samples the result of the convolution, algebraically the same operation as multiplying the polynomials whose coefficients are the elements of signal and window vectors, is N+M-1 point signal, where the first and last M points may not be useable. The time of completing the convolution in the time domain is directly proportional to the width of the window.

FFT convolution uses the overlap-add method together with the FFT procedure and the principle that multiplication in the frequency domain corresponds to convolution in the time domain and reverse. This operation can be written down as:

$$y_{z\,g}^{(i)} = \mathrm{ifft}\big(\mathrm{fft}(h, M) \cdot \mathrm{fft}(y_z, M)\big) \tag{13}$$

It is faster than standard convolution for the window with the averaging interval longer than 64 points, because its time increases very slowly, only as the logarithm of the window width M. It produces exactly the same result as the corresponding convolution in the time domain and can be more precise, because the round-off error depends on the total number of calculations, which is directly proportional to the computation time. The FFT convolution called high-speed convolution is the best way to complete the operation of the averaged differentiation.

2.3 Form of measurement window and degree of noise attenuation

As a weight function g(v) one can use any even function of the form:

$$g(v) = k(n) \cdot f_1(v) \cdot [f_2(v)]^n \tag{14}$$

if a function $f_2(v)$ is even and satisfies the condition $f_2(\pm d) = 0$, and k(n) is the normalising coefficient. Making the Fourier transformation of the window g(v) one gets the window spectrum $G(j\omega)$:

$$G(j\omega) = \int_{-d}^{d} g(v) \cdot \exp(-j\omega v)dv\,. \tag{15}$$

Since the function g(v) is even its Fourier spectrum contains no imaginary part and can be written in the form:

$$G(j\omega) = \mathrm{Re}\,G(j\omega) = 2 \cdot \int_{0}^{d} g(v) \cdot \cos(\omega v)dv\,. \tag{16}$$

It means that the operation of averaging does not introduce any phase.

If to a weight function g(v) we assign the log magnitude function:

$$G_L(\omega) = 20 \cdot \log_{10}\left|\int_{-d}^{d} g(v) \cdot \exp(-j\omega\, v)dv\right|, \tag{17}$$

then n-th derivative $g^{(n)}(v)$ corresponds to:

$$G_L(\omega)_n = 20 \cdot \log_{10}\left|\omega^n \cdot \int_{-d}^{d} g(v) \cdot \exp(-j\omega\, v)dv\right|. \tag{18}$$

The normalised frequency is introduced for generality:

$$\Omega = \omega \cdot \frac{2 \cdot d}{\pi} . \tag{19}$$

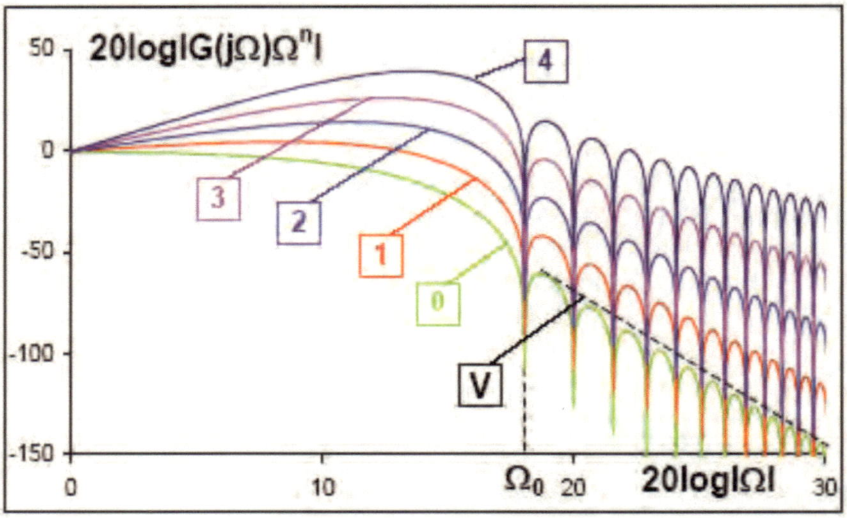

Fig. 2. The logarithmic characteristics of the derivative spectrum of the Nutall window.

The exemplary Bode plots in the logarithmic scale $G_L(\Omega)_n$ for the weight function:

$$g(v) = \frac{k(r)}{d} \cdot \cos^r\left(\frac{\pi \cdot v}{2 \cdot d}\right), \tag{20}$$

which corresponds to the Nuttall window (Nuttall, 1981) with r=6 and the normalising coefficients k(6)=8/5, are shown in Fig. 2. The plots consist of several lobes and because of the normalisation (10) we have G(0)=1 and $G_L(0)_n=0$. Let Ω_0 denote the width of the first lobe and V denote the averaged rate of the decrease of G_L except for the first lobe. The correct reconstruction of the signal $x(t_0)_g$ takes place in the frequency band of the initial part of the main lobe to Ω_0 while the disturbance attenuation - in the frequency band of secondary lobes.

If the signal $y(t_0)$ has the spectrum $Y(j\Omega)$, then the spectrum of the averaged signal $y(t_0)_g$ has the following form:

$$Y(j\Omega)_g = Y(j\Omega) \cdot G(j\Omega) . \tag{21}$$

The error caused by the process of averaging can be evaluated as the deviation of $G(j\Omega)$ from 1. If $Y(j\Omega)$ and $Z(j\Omega)$ denote the spectra of the signal y(t) and disturbances z(t), respectively, then the operation of averaging differentiation of the disturbed signal $y_z(t)=y(t)+z(t)$ is expressed by the equation:

$$y_z^{(n)}(t_0)_g = (-1)^n \cdot \int_{-d}^{d} y(t_0 + v) \cdot g^{(n)}(v)dv + (-1)^n \cdot \int_{-d}^{d} z(t_0 + v) \cdot g^{(n)}(v)dv , \tag{22}$$

which illustrates the process of reducing the effect of disturbances at an adequately selected window g(v). It corresponds to the spectrum:

$$Y_z(j\Omega) = (j \times \Omega)^n \times Y(j\Omega) \times G(j\Omega) + (j \times \Omega)^n \times Z(j\Omega) \times G(j\Omega). \tag{23}$$

If the function $y^{(n)}(t)$ is continuous and differentiable, then we can use its expansion in Taylor series taking into consideration the conditions (6) and (9). Hence we obtain:

$$y^{(n)}(t_0)_g = y^{(n)}(t_0) + \sum_{i=1}^{\infty} \frac{m_{2i}}{(2 \cdot i)!} \cdot y^{(n+2i)}(t_0) + (-1)^n \cdot \int_{-d}^{d} z(t_0 + v) \cdot g^{(n)}(v) dv . \tag{24}$$

This proves that the deformation of the signal $y^{(n)}(t_0)_g$ with regard to the derivative $y^{(n)}(t_0)$ has two components: the first is caused by averaging and the second by the presence of disturbances:

$$y^{(n)}(t_0)_g - y^{(n)}(t_0) = \Delta_1 + \Delta_2 . \tag{25}$$

The first error Δ_1 depends on the smoothness of the signal $y^{(n)}(t_0)$ and on the values of the even moments of the weight function, which for the Nuttall window are given by:

$$m_{2j} = d^{2 \cdot j} \cdot \Theta(2j, r), \tag{26}$$

where Θ are the constant coefficients for the function g(v) in the given form. So it follows that the error Δ_1 can be diminished by decreasing of d or by a suitable choice of the form of weight function g(v), which allows to decrease coefficients Θ. Because of truth of the inequality:

$$\int_{-d}^{d} \{z(t_0 + v)\}^2 \cdot \left\{g^{(n)}(v)\right\}^2 dv \le \{z(t_0 + v)\}^2_{max} \cdot \int_{-d}^{d} \left\{g^{(n)}(v)\right\}^2 dv \tag{27}$$

the influence of disturbances can be evaluated by the following measure:

$$M_n = \sqrt{\int_{-d}^{d} \left\{g^{(n)}(v)\right\}^2 dv} = \frac{\Psi(n,r)}{d^{n+0.5}}, \tag{28}$$

where Ψ is the characteristic coefficient of the weight function g(v), which is growing with the increase of the derivative order n very quickly. The reduction of this error can be done by increasing of d and by a suitable choice of the form of the weight function g(v). So it follows that the greater d the greater Δ_1 and simultaneously the less Δ_2. The interval of averaging and the form of the weight function g(v) should be selected so as to minimise both of these errors. The minimisation of considered errors can be done by a suitable choice of the weight function g(v) so that coefficients Θ and Ψ should be possibly small.

2.4 Designing optimal correction procedure (Boćkowska, 2006)

The form of the known weight function can be corrected through the application of special procedures, which can correspond to the following operation:

$$y(t_o)_k = C_0 \cdot y(t_o)_g + \frac{1}{2}\sum_{i=1}^{n} C_i \cdot \left[y(t_o + T_i)_g + y(t_o - T_i)_g\right] \tag{29}$$

Expanding signals y_g in the Taylor series we obtain the relation:

$$\begin{aligned}
&y(t_o)_k = y(t_o)\cdot(C_0 + C_1 + C_2 + ...)+\\
&y^{(2)}(t_o)\cdot\{m_2\cdot(C_0 + C_1 + C_2 + ...)/2! + C_1\cdot T_1^2 + C_2\cdot T_2^2 + ...\}+\\
&y^{(4)}(t_o)\cdot\{m_4\cdot(C_0 + C_1 + ...) + 4!\cdot m_2\cdot(C_1\cdot T_1^2 + ...)/2!\cdot 2! + C_1T_1^4 + C_2T_2^4 + ...\}/4! +\\
&y^{(6)}(t_o)\cdot\{m_6\cdot(C_0 + C_1 + C_2 + ...) + 6!\cdot m_4\cdot(C_1\cdot T_1^2 + C_2\cdot T_2^2 + ...)/2!\cdot 4! +\\
&6!\cdot m_2\cdot(C_1\cdot T_1^4 + C_2\cdot T_2^4 + ...)/4!\cdot 2! + C_1\cdot T_1^6 + C_2\cdot T_2^6 + ...\}/6! + \dots
\end{aligned} \tag{30}$$

Because of $y_k(t_o) \cong y(t_o)$ the evaluation of the corrector parameters C_i and T_i should be done on the basis of the following system of non-linear equations:

$$\begin{aligned}
&C_0 + C_1 + \ldots + C_n = 1\\
&C_1\cdot T_1^2 + C_2\cdot T_2^2 + \ldots + C_n\cdot T_n^2 = 2!\cdot M_2 = A_2\\
&C_1\cdot T_1^4 + C_2\cdot T_2^4 + \ldots + C_n\cdot T_n^4 = 4!\cdot(M_2^2 - M_4) = A_4\\
&C_1\cdot T_1^6 + C_2\cdot T_2^6 + \ldots + C_n\cdot T_n^6 = 6!\cdot(M_2^3 - 2\cdot M_2\cdot M_4 + M_6) = A_6\\
&C_1\cdot T_1^8 + C_2\cdot T_2^8 + \ldots + C_n\cdot T_n^8 = 8!\cdot(M_2^4 + 2\cdot M_2\cdot M_6 + M_4^2 - 3\cdot M_2^2\cdot M_4 - M_8) = A_8\\
&C_1\cdot T_1^{10} + C_2\cdot T_2^{10} + \ldots + C_n\cdot T_n^{10} = 10!\cdot(M_2^5 - 2\cdot M_2\cdot M_8 - 2\cdot M_4\cdot M_6 + 3\cdot M_2^2\cdot M_6 +\\
&3\cdot M_2\cdot M_4^2 - 4\cdot M_4\cdot M_2^3 + M_{10}) = A_{10}\\
&\ldots
\end{aligned} \tag{31}$$

The system of Equations (31) is non-linear with unknowns C_i, T_i and it is not clear that it has real solutions for arbitrary n and a given window.
In the identification of the system dynamics we want to obtain such values of the corrected averaged signal and their derivatives, which are possibly close to their real values. The corrected signals should be useful to obtain for example the following nonlinearities:

$$y^{(n)}(t)\cdot y^{(k)}(t) \cong y_k^{(n)}(t)\cdot y_k^{(k)}(t) \tag{32}$$

where $y_k^{(n)}(t)$ and $y_k^{(n)}(t)$ are set on the basis of the measured signal y(t). To meet this goal possibly more equations from system (31) must be fulfilled. The first consecutive equations allow to obtain the unknowns C_i (Boćkowska, 2003). The evaluation of the time constants T_i must be done minimizing the rest of equations for a given form of the window, measuring step and the used width d of the averaging interval. The time constants T_i can be expressed depending on the width of the averaging interval d as:

$$T_i = T_{di}\cdot d \tag{33}$$

so T_{di} and corresponding C_i are the corrector parameters. The correction procedure must be unique for different kinds of windows and their chosen order and width. The course of the correction will be considered for the cosine window known as the Max Rolloff 4-Term or Nuttall window of 6th order and the correction procedure of 2nd order in the form:

$$y_k(t_0) = C_0 \cdot y(t_0)_g + \frac{1}{2}\sum_{i=1}^{2} C_i \cdot \left[y(t_0 + T_i)_g + y(t_0 - T_i)_g\right]. \tag{34}$$

The corrector parameters C_i are determined by the following relations:

$$\begin{aligned} C_1 &= \left(A_2 \cdot T_2^2 - A_4\right) / \left(T_1^2 \cdot T_2^2 - T_1^4\right) \\ C_2 &= \left(A_4 - A_2 \cdot T_1^2\right) / \left(T_2^4 - T_1^2 \cdot T_2^2\right) \\ C_0 &= 1 - C_1 - C_2 \end{aligned} \tag{35}$$

which follow from the first three equations of the system (31). The determination of the time constants T_i requires optimisation. After introduction of two auxiliary variables:

$$x = T_1^2 \quad \text{and} \quad y = T_2^2 \tag{36}$$

the next equation can be written as a relation, which is linear and symmetrical in regards to x and y:

$$f(x,y) = y \cdot A_4 - y \cdot x \cdot A_2 + x \cdot A_4 - A_6 = 0 \tag{37}$$

As it is shown in Figure 3 Equation (37) is never satisfied for the positive x and y and has to be omitted. The fifth equation from the system (31) is a quadratic equation with two roots:

$$g(x,y) = y^2 \cdot A_4 - y^2 \cdot x \cdot A_2 + y \cdot x \cdot A_4 - y \cdot x^2 \cdot A_2 + x^2 \cdot A_4 - A_8 = 0 \tag{38}$$

The positive one can be taken into consideration. It can be written as the next function:

$$\begin{aligned} x(y) = \Big[&-y^2 \cdot A_2 + y \cdot A_4 - \left(y^4 \cdot A_2^2 + 2 \cdot y^3 \cdot A_2 \cdot A_4 - 3 \cdot y^2 \cdot A_4^2 \right. \\ &\left. - 4 \cdot y \cdot A_2 \cdot A_8 + 4 \cdot A_4 \cdot A_8\right)^{1/2}\Big] / 2 \cdot \left(y \cdot A_2 - A_4\right) \end{aligned} \tag{39}$$

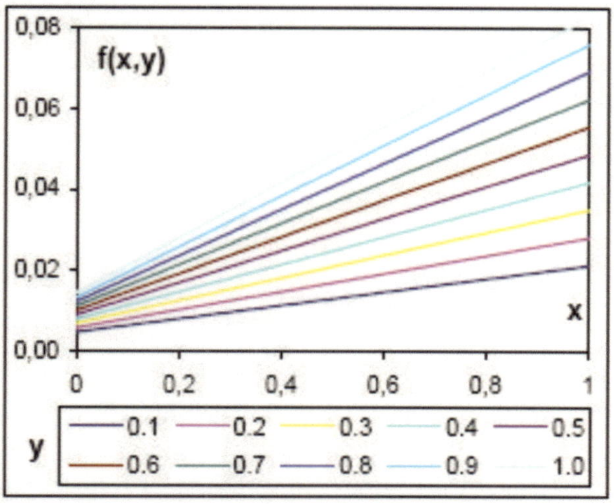

Fig. 3. Relation f(x,y) defined by Equation (37).

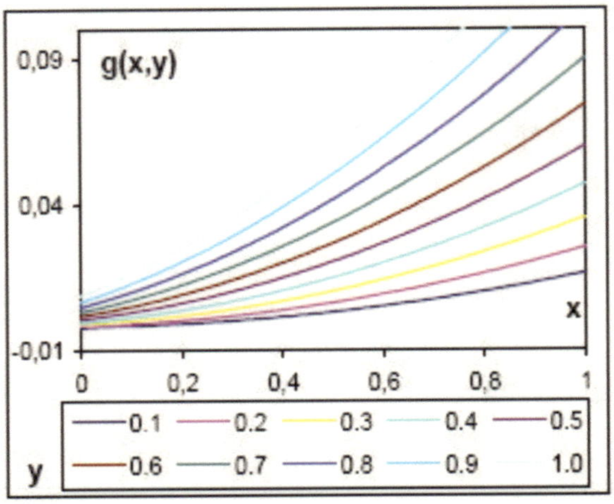

Fig. 4. Relation g(x,y) defined by Equation (38).

which allows us to obtain the allowed interval of the variability of y and x, because their changes are symmetrical. The additional condition is needed to obtain both x and y:

$$|C_0| + |C_1| + |C_2| = \min \tag{40}$$

which follows from the postulate of the minimal increase of the disturbances participation. Taking into consideration (35) and (39) it can be written down as the function of y:

$$h(y) = \left| \frac{y \cdot A_2 - A_4}{x(y) \cdot (y - x(y))} \right| + \left| \frac{x(y) \cdot A_2 - A_4}{y \cdot (y - x(y))} \right| + \left| \frac{x(y) \cdot A_2 - A_4 + y \cdot A_2 - x(y) \cdot y}{x(y) \cdot y} \right| \tag{41}$$

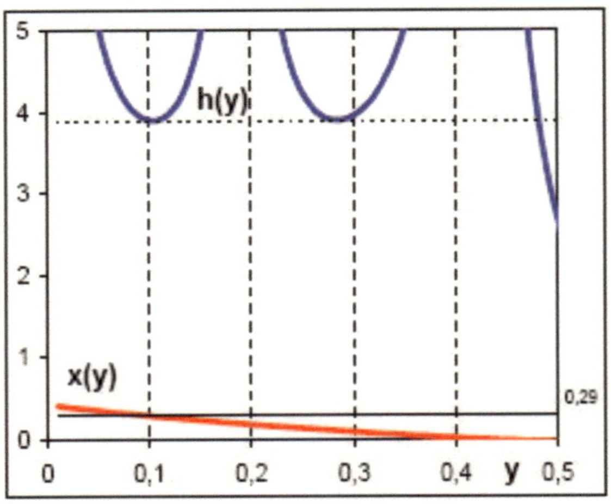

Fig. 5. Variability of the auxiliary variable x and function h(y).

The above derivation is valid for corrector of 2nd order of any window, but presented graphs correspond to Nuttall window of 6th order. The determined values of the coefficients $A_{2,4,6,8}$ and corrector parameters $C_{0,1,2}$ and $T_{1,2}$ for the Nuttall window of 1st to 6th order are shown in Table 1. The presented values are obviously functions of the window width d.

R	A_2	A_4	A_6	A_8	C_0	C_1	C_2	T_{d1}	T_{d2}
1	-0.189	0.137	-0.207	0.547	1.773	0.21	-0.983	1.139	0.686
2	-0.131	0.061	-0.058	-0.091	1.878	0.251	-1.129	0.89	0.54
3	-0.099	0.034	-0.023	0.025	1.977	0.265	-1.242	0.75	0.447
4	-0.08	0.022	-0.011	0.009	2.013	0.316	-1.329	0.648	0.4
5	-0.067	0.015	-0.006	0.004	2.108	0.29	-1.398	0.589	0.346
6	-0.057	0.011	-0.004	0.002	2.119	0.330	-1.449	0.533	0.323

Table 1. The coefficients A and corrector parameters C and T for the Nuttall window of 1st to 6th order.

Figure 5 shows the variability of the slack variables x, y and thereby the time constants T_1 and T_2. The minimum of function h(y) is for $y \cong 0.29$ or 0.10 and consequently $T_2 \cong 0.53$ and 0.32. The time constant T_1 obtained from Equations (41) and (36) is $T_1=0.32$ or 0.53. Because the product of the time constants and the width d of the averaging interval expressed in the samples must be integer, so they have to be recalculated using the following relation:

$$T_{rdi} = \frac{\text{round}(T_{di} \cdot d)}{d} \tag{42}$$

The correction procedure of 2nd order corresponds to the change of the basic window spectrum to the following form:

$$G_z(\omega) = G(\omega) \cdot G_k(\omega) = G(\omega) \cdot \left[C_0 + \sum_{i=1}^{2} C_i \cdot \cos(\omega \cdot T_i) \right] \tag{43}$$

Introducing the auxiliary variable:

$$u = \frac{\pi \cdot v}{2 \cdot d} \tag{44}$$

the definition (15) can be rewritten in the following form:

$$G(\Omega) = \frac{\pi}{d} \cdot \int_0^{\pi/2} g(u) \cdot \cos(\Omega \cdot u) du \tag{45}$$

and the spectrum of the corrected window assumes the form:

$$G_z(\Omega) = \frac{\pi}{d} \cdot \left[C_0 + \sum_{i=1}^{2} C_i \cdot \cos(\Omega \cdot T_{ui}) \right] \cdot \int_0^{\pi/2} g(u) \cdot \cos(\Omega \cdot u) du \tag{46}$$

The relation (46) allows to obtain the maximum normalised frequency Ω_α, which can be transferred with the assumed accuracy α through the corrected window, solving the following equation:

$$\alpha = 1 - G_z(\Omega) \tag{47}$$

The evaluation of the corrector parameters C_i and T_i should be done on the basis of two criteria: the minimisation of the deviation $G(j\Omega)$ from 1 in the pass band and the magnitude

$\Omega^n G(j\Omega)$ in the stop band. The application of the procedures is a trial of the window approach to the ideal window with wall spectral properties.
The correct evaluation of the pass band frequency f_p is the next important problem, which decides about the correctness of the processing of the measured signals and has big influence on the quality of the identification. The pass band frequency is a filter feature and for a low-pass filter assigns the maximum frequency, which as a component of a useful signal is transferred without deformation. It determines the transfer band frequency being its upper limit. It is a basis to determine the filter parameters and proper choice of corrector parameters, if a valuable information of signal is lost or if a processed signal is deformed by noise. It decides about the credibility of processed signals as the material for identification of dynamics of systems. The pass band frequency f_p can be determined on the basis of the output spectrum which is more complex than the input spectrum, because of the influence of the system's dynamics.

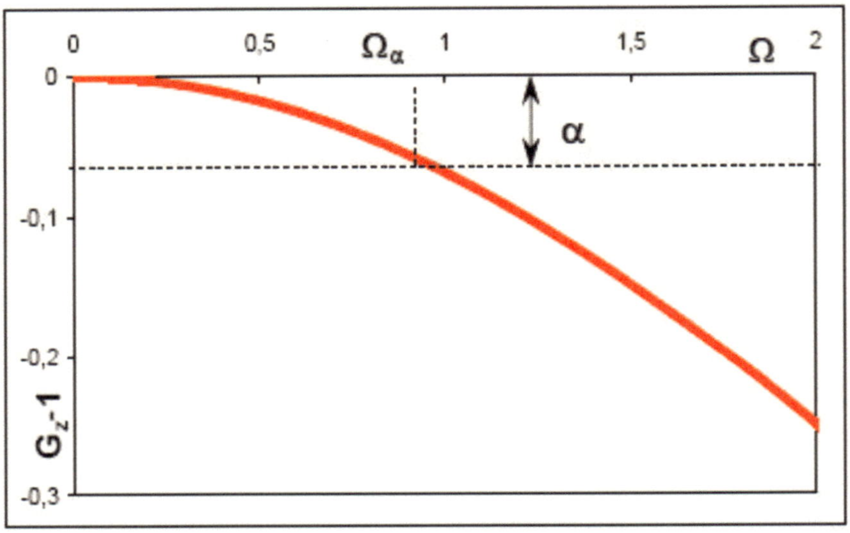

Fig. 6. Accuracy α of transmission of frequencies lower than Ω_α by the corrected window with spectrum $G_z(\Omega)$.

If a measurement experiment is carried out on the same examined system using the same instruments, but input with different parameters, then one can use the power spectral density of outputs assigned for two extremes of inputs. The power spectral density is suggested in order to increase the spectrum resolution and is defined as follows:

$$GWM = Y \cdot \mathrm{conj}(Y), \tag{48}$$

and the frequency axis is defined in Hz according to $f=(0:N-1)/(N \cdot T_s)$,where N is the number of samples, T_s - time step between consecutive samples. The frequencies of dominant peaks can be determined through an analysis of the graph of the difference of power spectral density both of outputs.

$$\Delta G = GWM_1 - GWM_2 \,. \tag{49}$$

If Ω_α and f_p are known then the required width of the measurement window can be calculated according to the following relation:

$$d_{opt} = \frac{\Omega_\alpha}{4 \cdot f_p}. \tag{51}$$

The determination of Ω_α can be done very easily and quickly if the analytical relation Ω_α=f(α) fulfilled for small α, for example $0,01 \le \alpha \le 0,1$, for a given kind of the measurement window is known. An example of such relation for a given window is shown below. Allowing for the correction procedure of 2nd order defined by (34) the spectrum of the corrected window of *r* order gets the form:

$$G(\Omega) = \frac{\left[\frac{2}{\pi \cdot \Omega} \cdot \sin\left(\frac{\pi \cdot \Omega}{2}\right)\right]^{1-\mathrm{mod}(r,2)} \cdot \left[\cos\left(\frac{\pi \cdot \Omega}{2}\right)\right]^{\mathrm{mod}(r,2)} \cdot \left[C_0 + \sum_{i=1}^{2} C_i \cdot \cos(\Omega \cdot T_{ui})\right]}{\prod_{n=1}^{r}\left[1-\left(\frac{\Omega}{n}\right)^2\right]^{[1-\mathrm{mod}(r,2)-\mathrm{mod}(n,2)]}} \tag{52}$$

and corresponding plots for *r*=1÷6 are shown in Figure 7.
Figure 8 presents variability of Ω_α versus α in the range $0.01 \le \alpha \le 0.1$. The relationship Ω_α=f(α) in an analytical form is needed to calculate quickly the optimal width of the measurement window d for a given output and its pass band frequency f_p according to (51). The approximation of this relation can be evaluated using (51) and (47). The courses in the given range were approximated by an exponential function:

$$\Omega_{\alpha\, apr} = S \cdot \alpha^P \tag{53}$$

with very good fitting using the regression method. The results: the values of the coefficients *S* and *P* as well as correlation coefficients *R* are shown in Table 2. The mean value of the exponent P_m is equal to 0.197 and was accepted as constant. The new values of coefficients S_m for P_m are also presented in Table 2. For S_m and *r* the quadratic dependence was found as it is shown in Figure 9.

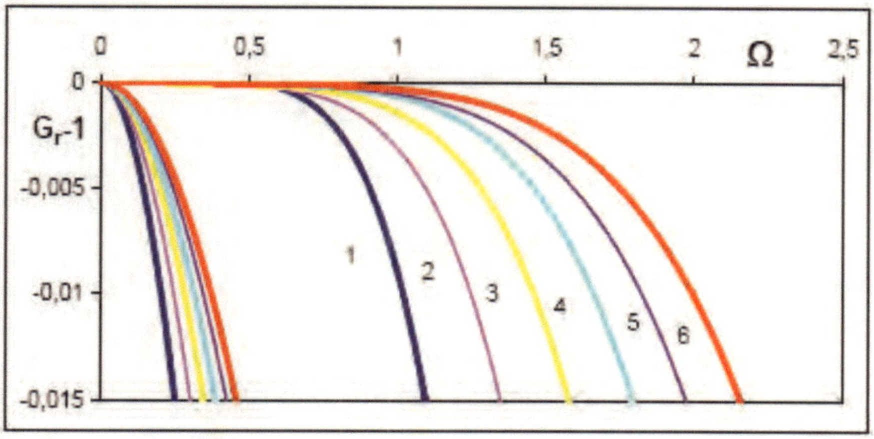

Fig. 7. The spectrum of the corrected Nuttall window of 1st to 6th order versus Ω.

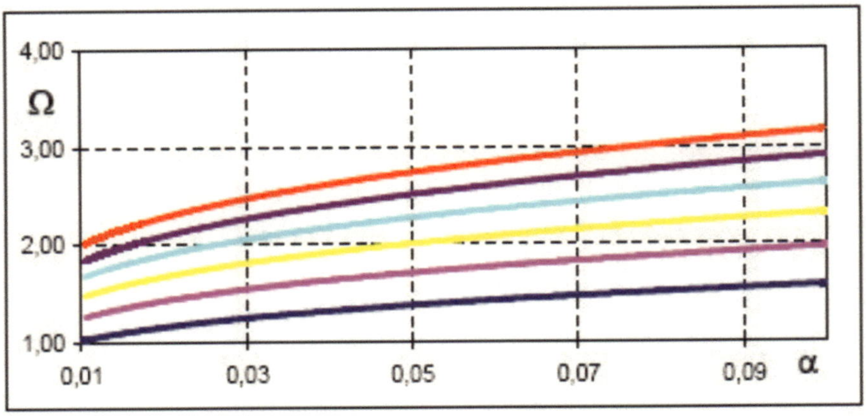

Fig. 8. The normalised frequency Ω versus the accuracy α of transmission of the useful signal.

r	1	2	3	4	5	6
S	4.9755	4.5838	4.1065	3.6324	3.0745	2.4184
P	0.1991	0.2006	0.1971	0.1982	0.1961	0.1882
R	0.9997	0.9997	0.9996	0.9997	0.9998	0.9995
S_m	4.941	4.529	4.105	3.618	3.083	2.49

Table 2. Parameters of the approximate exponential function to the order r of the measurement window.

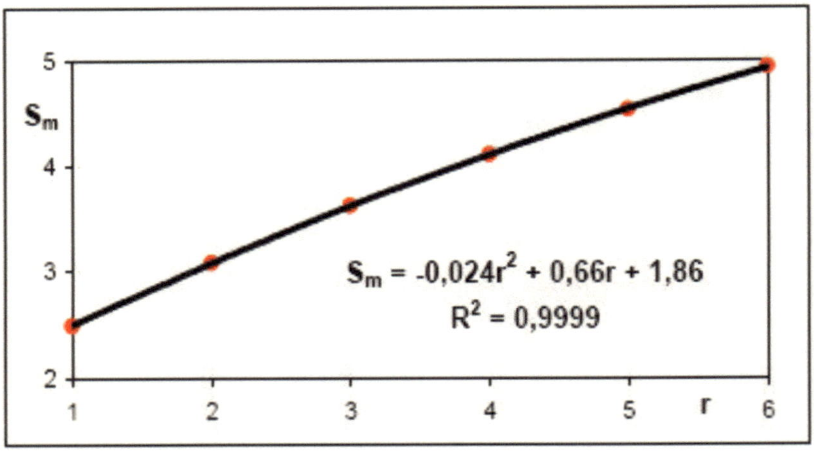

Fig. 9. Variability of S_m versus r.

The result approximate relation, who determines the variability of Ω_α versus r, is as follows:

$$\Omega_{\alpha\,apr} = (-0.024 \cdot r^2 + 0.66 \cdot r + 1.86) \cdot \alpha^{0.197} \tag{54}$$

The correlation coefficients between the data, which was obtained on the basis of the corrected window spectrum and the other calculated on the basis of the above mentioned

Equation (53), are still close to unity. The needed width of the measurement window can be expressed in seconds, using (54) and measurement step relating to:

$$d_{opt} = \frac{(-0.024 \cdot r^2 + 0.66 \cdot r + 1.86) \cdot \alpha^{0.197}}{(4 \cdot f_p \cdot step)} . \tag{55}$$

3. Identification of non-linear system dynamics

3.1 Parametric identification

The proposed procedure, the averaged differentiation operation with correction, can be applied to evaluation of the parameters of the model of the system dynamics if the model structure is known and corresponds in general to the differential equations of the kind:

$$y^{(n)}(t) = F\left(y, y^{(1)}, ..., y^{(n-1)}, x, x^{(1)}, ..., x^{(n)}, A_0, ..., B_0, ..., D\right) \tag{56}$$

which can be written down as the following equation:

$$y^{(n)}(t) = \sum_{j=0}^{n} A_j \cdot F_{jx}\left(y, \dots y^{(n-1)}, x, \dots x^{(n)}\right) \cdot x^{(j)} - \sum_{j=0}^{n-1} B_j \cdot F_{jy}\left(y, \dots y^{(n-1)}, x, \dots x^{(n)}\right) \cdot y^{(j)} + D \tag{57}$$

Taking into account all the measured data samples N, to which the model with the parameters A_j, B_j and D must be fitted we can present the system in the matrix form:

$$Yn = XY \cdot PAR, \quad \text{where } Yn = \begin{bmatrix} y_1^{(n)} \\ y_2^{(n)} \\ \dots \\ y_N^{(n)} \end{bmatrix}, \ PAR = \begin{bmatrix} A_0 \\ \dots \\ A_n \\ B_0 \\ \dots \\ B_{n-1} \\ D \end{bmatrix},$$

$$XY = \begin{bmatrix} F_{0x,1} \cdot x_1 & \dots & F_{nx,1} \cdot x_1^{(n)} & F_{0y,1} \cdot y_1 & \dots & F_{ny,1} \cdot y_1^{(n-1)} & 1 \\ F_{0x,2} \cdot x_2 & \dots & F_{nx,2} \cdot x_2^{(n)} & F_{0y,2} \cdot y_2 & \dots & F_{ny,2} \cdot y_2^{(n-1)} & 1 \\ \dots & \dots & \dots & \dots & \dots & \dots & \dots \\ F_{0x,N} \cdot x_N & \dots & F_{nx,N} \cdot x_N^{(n)} & F_{0y,N} \cdot y_N & \dots & F_{ny,N} \cdot y_N^{(n-1)} & 1 \end{bmatrix} \tag{58}$$

The system (58) with respect to some or all parameters A_j, B_j and D can be non-linear or quite linear. In case of nonlinearity, non-linear optimisation has to be applied, for instance by the simplex search method. An initial estimation of the parameters can be carried out either by omitting nonlinearities, if this is possible, or by using another estimation procedure. It is advisable to try several sets of starting values to make sure that the solution gives relatively consistent results. The obtained result for a given optimal averaging width d_{opt} of the measurement window g(v) does not have to be an optimum. The verification of the result of the identification, the model parameters, can be done through the determination of the mean square deviation between the output signal y and the model response obtained through the simulation y_s for the assigned parameters:

$$J = \sum_{i=1}^{N} (y_s - y)^2 = \|y_s - y\|^2 . \tag{59}$$

Both signals y and y_s must be averaged and corrected. The minimum of criteria J proves the result of non-linear optimisation and correctness of the choice of d_{opt}.

3.2 Nonparametric identification of nonlinear dynamics of 1st order of systems based on the active experiment (Boćkowska & Żuchowski, 2007)

Despite the fact that the presented method is nonparametric, its usefulness is limited to systems dynamics with structure described by the following differential equation:

$$y^{(1)} \cdot \varphi(x,y) + y \cdot f(x,y) = x . \tag{60}$$

Thanks to the fact that the measured window is an even function, the method of the averaged differentiation does not introduce any time shift between signals: the signals measured for example $y^{(1)}(t_0)$ and those who were averaged $y^{(1)}(t_0)_g$. The corrected signals are not shifted in relation to the measured signals, because the correction procedure is also even.

An active experiment ensures that a rich spectrum signal is fed into the system input. A rich spectrum can be achieved when a periodic signal with a modulated amplitude and frequency is applied, for example:

$$x(t) = A(t) \cdot \sin(t \cdot \omega(t) + \phi_0) . \tag{61}$$

Averaged and corrected courses of signals x(t), y(t) and $y^{(1)}(t)$ should be obtained and the plots of these courses created. The time moments for which $y^{(1)}(t)=0$ can be easily obtained and correspond to the points of the static characteristics of the examined object:

$$y \cdot f(x,y) = x . \tag{62}$$

Next, the values of the second unknown function φ(t) can be defined using all the values of both averaged and corrected signals.

The goal of the presented method is not the determination of the static characteristic, but that of the function f(x,y). These two can produce the same or similar graphs, but they are not always the same mathematically. It means that the structure of the function f(x,y) can not be concluded from the relation y(x) without additional assumptions. The functions f and φ can be the functions only of x or y or of both signals together. Hence, various models can be created and some of them differ from the true model. The regression method should be used in order to determine the functions f and φ on the basis of the plots of the following relations:

$$f(x,y) = z_1 = \frac{x}{y}, \quad \varphi(x,y) = z_2 = \frac{x - y \cdot f(x,y)}{y^{(1)}} \tag{63}$$

in the co-ordinate system x, y, z_1 and x, y, z_2. An input with a rich spectrum enables to obtain a big collection of different points x, y, z_1, z_2.

The examined object can have the dynamics of an order higher than one. In this case the obtained static characteristic is different from the real one and the change of the form of the signal x(t) leads to other results. Hence, it is a good control test of the correctness of the dynamics order.
The identified model should be obviously verified using numerical simulation. A comparison between simulation results and measured data should also be carried out.

3.3 Nonparametric identification of nonlinear dynamics of 2nd order of systems

The consideration relates to the models of system dynamics with the following structure:

$$y^{(2)} \cdot F_2\left(x, y, y^{(1)}\right) + y^{(1)} \cdot F_1\left(x, y, y^{(1)}\right) + F_0\left(x, y, y^{(1)}\right) = x. \tag{64}$$

The averaged corrected values of signals x, y, $y^{(1)}$ and $y^{(2)}$ are used. At first the relation corresponding to static characteristics should be determined – a steady state, when $y^{(1)}(t)=0$, $y^{(2)}(t)=0$ and x(t)=x=const.:

$$F_0(x, y, 0) = x. \tag{65}$$

Usually the function $F_0(x,y)$ is independent at $y^{(1)}(t)$, hence the substitute relation can be obtained:

$$y = \phi(x). \tag{66}$$

Next, the values of x, y corresponding to the extreme values of the first derivative should be chosen, for which:

$$y^{(2)}(t) = 0. \tag{67}$$

The knowledge of the function $F_0(x,y)$, which was determined in the first step and multiple chosen values of $y^{(1)}{}_{ex}$ in the second step allow us to evaluate the structure of the function $F_1(x,y,y^{(1)})$:

$$F_1\left(x, y, y^{(1)}\right) = \frac{x - F_0(x, y)}{y^{(1)}{}_{ex}}. \tag{68}$$

In a particular case, if $F_1(x,y,y^{(1)})$ is the function only of the output, the relation (68) is obtained uniquely:

$$F_1(y) = \frac{x - F_0(x, y)}{y^{(1)}{}_{ex}}. \tag{69}$$

In different cases the additional conditions should be assumed a priori.
The finding of the values of x, y and $y^{(2)}$ for $y^{(1)}(t)=0$ allows us to choose the structure of the last function:

$$F_2(y) = \frac{x - F_0(x, y)}{y^{(2)}}. \tag{70}$$

The result of non-parametric identification is unique if the model of system dynamics can be described by the following differential equation:

$$y^{(2)} \cdot F_2(y) + y^{(1)} \cdot F_1(y) + F_0(y) = x\,. \tag{71}$$

The accuracy of this process is defined by the accuracy of the operation of averaged differentiation with correction.

3.4 Nonparametric identification of nonlinear dynamics of order higher than 2nd

For the systems, which model has the analogue structure to (71) but is the higher order the parametric identification is necessary. Let us now consider:

$$y^{(3)} \cdot F_3(y) + y^{(2)} \cdot F_2(y) + y^{(1)} \cdot F_1(y) + F_0(y) = x\,. \tag{72}$$

After the determination of the static characteristics and definition of the relation:

$$F_0(y) = x \tag{73}$$

the values of x, y corresponding to the extreme values of the first or second derivative should be chosen, because both of these conditions are fulfilled very rarely. Supposing that $y^{(3)}(t)=0$ we obtain:

$$y^{(2)}{}_{ex} \cdot F_2(y) + y^{(1)} \cdot F_1(y) = x - F_0(y)\,. \tag{74}$$

The structure of the functions F_2 and F_1 can be assumed as follows:

$$F_2(y) = \sum_{i=0}^{n} a_i \cdot y^i,\quad F_1(y) = \sum_{i=0}^{m} b_i \cdot y^i \tag{75}$$

and obtained using the regression. However if $y^{(2)}(t)=0$ we obtain:

$$y^{(3)}{}_{ex} \cdot F_3(y) + y^{(1)} \cdot F_1(y) = x - F_0(y) \tag{76}$$

and the function F_1 can be treated as determined. Consequently, the form of the function F_3 can be found. In case of models of a higher order the procedure can be analogous.

3.5 An optimal degree of complexity of a model

In all the cases described above the analytical form of the functions F_0, F_1, … F_k is evaluated using the appropriate set of data, supporting the base functions:

$$F_k(y) = \sum_{i=0}^{n} c_i \cdot f_i(y) \tag{77}$$

and regression method remembering that the variables x and y are known with the certain accuracy Δx and Δy. If the measured accuracy of variables can be obtained the optimal degree of complexity of the model can be determined. Assuming that the model with the degree of complexity n in the form:

$$F_n(y) = \sum_{i=0}^{n} c_i \cdot y^i \tag{78}$$

was determined by regression based on the minimisation of the error:

$$D^2(c_i) = \int_y \left\{ F(y) - \sum_{i=0}^{n} c_i \cdot y^i \right\}^2 \cdot dy\,, \tag{79}$$

hence the following equations are satisfied for i=0,1,...,n:

$$\frac{\partial D^2(c_i)}{\partial c_i} = 0 = -2 \cdot \int_y \left\{ F(y) - \sum_{i=0}^{n} c_i \cdot y^i \right\} \cdot y^i \cdot dy\,. \tag{80}$$

If the values of y are known with the accuracy Δy=const or $\Delta_1 = \Delta y / y$=const then the application of the model (78) is connected with the additional error, for the small Δy defined by the relation:

$$F_n(y + \Delta y) = F_n(y) + \Delta y \cdot \frac{dF_n(y)}{dy} = F_n(y) + \Delta y \cdot \sum_{i=0}^{n} i \cdot c_i \cdot y^{i-1} \tag{81}$$

or

$$F_n(y + \Delta y) = F_n(y) + \Delta y \cdot \frac{dF_n(y)}{dy} = F_n(y) + \Delta_1 \cdot \sum_{i=0}^{n} i \cdot c_i \cdot y^i\,. \tag{82}$$

The square error is as follows:

$$D_a^2(n) = (\Delta y)^2 \int_y \left\{ \sum_{i=0}^{n} c_i \cdot y^{i-1} \right\}^2 \cdot dy \quad \text{or} \quad D_a^2(n) = \Delta_1^2 \int_y \left\{ \sum_{i=0}^{n} c_i \cdot y^i \right\}^2 \cdot dy\,, \tag{83}$$

A total model error:

$$D^2(n) = D_{min}^2(n) + D_a^2(n)\,, \tag{84}$$

depends on its degree of complexity n. If for the supported Δy or Δ_1 as a result of the calculations one gets $D^2(n+1) \geq D^2(n)$, then the degree of model complexity n is optimal.

4. Conclusion

The presented method can be useful in identification of the structure of a model of nonlinear dynamics of 1st and higher orders. The advantage of the proposed solution is its simplicity and possibility of evaluation of its accuracy. The application of the averaged differentiation with correction ensures one to evaluate an averaged signal and its derivatives close to their real values. A novelty is the proposed procedure of the correction of the averaged differentiation. The method allows to obtain a structure of the model of the nonlinear dynamics of 1st or 2nd order. The advantage of this identification is the fact that it can be used even if the measured signals are disturbed and the dynamics is nonlinear. In case of dynamics of a higher order the application of parametric identification to define a part of model structure is the solution.

5. References

Billings, S.A. & Tsang, K.M. (1992). Reconstruction of linear and non-linear continuous time models from discrete time sampled-data systems, *Mech. Systems and signal Processing*, Vol. 6, No. 1, pp. 69-84

Boćkowska, M. (1998). *Reconstruction of input of a measurement system with simultaneous identification of its dynamics in the presence of intensive, random disturbances*, Ph.D. thesis, Technical University of Szczecin

Boćkowska, M. (2003). Application of the averaged differentiation method to the parameter estimation of non-linear systems. *Proceedings of the 9th IEEE International Conference on Methods and Models in Automation and Robotics*, pp. 695-700, Technical University of Szczecin, Międzyzdroje, 2003

Boćkowska, M. (2005). Corrector design for the window-fft processing during the parametric identification of non-linear systems, *Proceedings of the 11th IEEE International Conference on Methods and Models in Automation and Robotics*, pp. 461-466, Technical University of Szczecin, Międzyzdroje, 2005

Boćkowska, M. (2006). Identification of system dynamics using the averaged differentiation with correction adapted to output spectrum, *Proceedings of the 12th IEEE International Conference on Methods and Models in Automation and Robotics*, pp. 461-466, Technical University of Szczecin, Międzyzdroje, 2006

Boćkowska, M. & Żuchowski, A. (2007). Application of the averaged differentiation method to the parameter estimation of non-linear systems, *Proceedings of the 13th IEEE International Conference on Methods and Models in Automation and Robotics*, pp. 461-466, Technical University of Szczecin, Szczecin, 2007

Eykhoff, P. (1980). *Identification in dynamics systems*, PWN, Warsaw

Greblicki, W. & Pawlak, M. (1994). Cascade nonlinear system identification by a nonparametric method, *Int. Journal of System Science*, Vol. 25, No 1, pp. 129-153

Haber, R. & Keviczky, L. (1999). *Nonlinear system identification – input – output modelling approach*. Kluwer Academic Publishers

Iserman, R. (1982). *Identifikation dynamischer Systeme*, Springer Verlag, Berlin

Kordylewski, W. & Wach, J. (1988). Averaged differentiation of disturbed measurement signals. *PAK*, No. 6

Nuttall, A.H. (1981). Some windows with very good sidelobe behaviour. *IEEE Trans. On Acoustic, Speech and Signal Processing 29*, No 1, pp. 84-91

Söderström, V.T. & Stoica, P. (1989). *System identification*, Englewood Clifs, NJ: Prentice Hall

Uhl, T. (1997). *Computer aided identification of models of mechanical constructions*, WNT, Warsaw

9

Group Judgement with Ties. Distance-Based Methods

Hanna Bury and Dariusz Wagner
Systems Research Institute of the Polish Academy of Sciences
Poland

1. Introduction

Problems of determining group judgement have been widely explored and many methods have been proposed (Nurmi, 1987). It is due to the fact that there is no "ideal" method satisfying all the requirements formulated. Hence new methods – possessing desirable properties and avoiding deficiencies of the previous ones – have been developed.

To efficiently analyse and solve problems of determining group judgement usually some simplifying assumption are introduced.

Very often it is assumed that no equivalent alternatives can appear in experts' judgements. Such an assumption is adopted, despite of the fact that in real life problems experts are not always able to uniquely determine the order of alternatives with respect to the given criterion or set of criteria.

Almost all the methods of determining group judgement are based on the assumption that there are no ties in this judgement. This assumption seems to be more restrictive than the previous one, and may strongly influence the solution obtained. This is specially important in the case of distance-based methods i.e. making use of the concept of distance among preference orders (Cook, 2006; Cook et al., 1997; Cook & Seiford, 1978).

In further considerations experts' judgements given in the form of preference orders are taken into account only.

One of the methods making it possible to overcome the problem of ties is to use the approach proposed by Armstrong et al. (1982).

It will be shown that some distance-based methods of group judgement derived for the case of no ties can be extended to the case of ties in experts opinion as well as in group judgement.

2. Positions taken by alternatives and the table of structures

Assume that there is a set of n alternatives $\boldsymbol{O} = \{O_1, \ldots, O_n\}$ and K experts, who are asked to order this set with respect to a given criterion (or criteria). Expert present their judgements in the form of preference orders

$$P^k = \{O_{i_1}, \ldots, O_{i_n}\}, \; k=1, \ldots, K, \tag{1}$$

where an alternative regarded as the best one takes the first position and that regarded as the worst one takes the last position.

This preference order can be also written as a ranking:

$$P^k = \{q_1^k, \ldots, q_n^k\}, \tag{2}$$

where q_i^k denotes the position taken by the i-th alternative in k-th expert's judgement.

One can also assume that in an expert judgement as well as in the group judgement more than one alternative can be put in the same position, i.e. ties can occur. In this case a preference order may be given as follows

$$O_{i_1}, \ldots, (O_{i_p}, \ldots, O_{i_{p+r}}), \ldots, O_{i_n} \text{ , r tied alternatives are given in brackets.} \tag{3}$$

Example 1.
$P = \{ O_2, (O_1, O_3, O_4), O_5 \}$ may be written as $P = \{ 2, 1, 2, 2, 3 \}$. We shall refer to this notation as to the classical one. It is sometimes called a dense ranking.
Cook & Seiford (1978) proposed to apply fractional ranking, i.e. when r alternatives are placed in the same - called it p - position, it is assumed that they take positions (p, p+1, …, p+r-1) and the fractional position assigned to them is the mean

$$t = \frac{p + (p+1) + \ldots + (p+r-1)}{r} = \frac{2p + (r-1)}{2r} r = p + \frac{r-1}{2}. \tag{4}$$

It should be emphasized that the expression obtained is of the form v+½ for any even r and is an integer otherwise; where p, r, v are integer numbers.
For the preference order given in Example 1 one has $P = \{ 3, 1, 3, 3, 5 \}$.
Hence in the fractional notation alternatives can take positions from the following set:

$$\Psi = \{ 1, 1½, 2, 2½, 3, 3½, \ldots, n-1, n-½, n\}. \tag{5}$$

One should notice that there may be positions with no alternatives assigned to.
The number of positions (with respect to classical notation) is increased almost twice (2n-1), but for given n it is fixed. This property is important for construction of the table of structures described later on. An example explaining the use of this notation is given in Table 1 (Σ denotes the sum of the positions).

Preference orders		Positions			
		classical notation	Σ	fractional notation	Σ
P^1:	O_2, O_3, O_4, O_1, O_5	4, 1, 2, 3, 5	15	4, 1, 2, 3, 5	15
P^2:	$(O_2, O_3), O_4, (O_1, O_5)$	3, 1, 1, 2, 3	10	4½, 1½, 1½, 3, 4½	15
P^3:	$O_2, (O_1, O_3, O_4), O_5$	2, 1, 2, 2, 3	10	3, 1, 3, 3, 5	15
P^4:	$O_2, (O_1, O_3, O_4, O_5)$	2, 1, 2, 2, 2	9	3½, 1, 3½, 3½, 3½	15

Table 1. Classical and fractional notation of positions of alternatives.

It can be easily shown that the number of equivalent alternatives taking a given position t can be different.
Assume the number of position is t=4.
Let's consider the following preference orders of seven elements:

1. $(O_1, O_2, O_3, O_4, O_5, O_6, O_7)$ $t_1 = (1+2+3+4+5+6+7)/7 = 4$
2. $O_1, (O_2, O_3, O_4, O_5, O_6), O_7$ $t_2 = (2+3+4+5+6)/5 = 4$
3. $O_1, O_2, (O_3, O_4, O_5), O_6, O_7$ $t_3 = (3+4+5)/3 = 4$.
4. $O_1, O_2, O_3, O_4, O_5, O_6, O_7$ $t_4 = 4$.

Hence for all the preference orders tied alternatives take the fourth position. In order to precise the number of equivalent alternatives taking a given position one has to provide an additional information on a position (in the sense of (4)) taken by the first alternative from the group of equivalent ones. This position is called *level* and is denoted by ℓ . It is evident that ℓ = 1, …,n.

The level ℓ=1 is assigned to the group of equivalent alternatives such that the first alternative is located in the first position. The level ℓ=2 defines such groups of equivalent alternatives for which the first alternative takes the second position, etc.

This approach makes it possible to define the concept of structure.

A group of positions (in the sense of (4)) taken by equivalent alternatives is called structure and is denoted by $S^{\ell t}$, because it depends on the position t as well as on the level ℓ . The number of positions corresponding to a given structure is denoted as $s_{\ell t}$. It is evident that $1 \le s_{\ell t} \le n$. The concept introduced is, in the authors opinion, more useful for solving the problem under consideration than that given in (Armstrong et al., 1982).

The application of structures $S^{\ell t}$ enables one to define a table whose rows correspond to structures related to a given level ℓ =1, ..., n and columns to a given position t=1; 1½,..., n.

In a preference order with ties positions taken by alternatives are of the form "an integer or an integer + ½". Hence it is easy to transform them into the integer domain (needed to formulate integer programming problem (Section 5); the numbers of positions are doubled (T=2t). The numbers in the shaded area denote positions (in the classical sense) that can be taken by alternatives.

T	2	3	4	5	6	7	8	9	10
t	1	1,5	2	2,5	3	3,5	4	4,5	5
ℓ=1	1	(1,2)	(1,2,3)	(1,2,3,4)	(1,2,3,4,5)	(1,2,3,4,5,6)	(1,2,3,4,5,6,7)	(1,2,3,4,5,6,7,8)	(1,2,3,4,5,6,7,8,9)
ℓ=2			2	(2,3)	(2,3,4)	(2,3,4,5)	(2,3,4,5,6)	(2,3,4,5,6,7)	(2,3,4,5,6,7,8)
ℓ=3					3	(3,4)	(3,4,5)	(3,4,5,6)	(3,4,5,6,7)
ℓ=4							4	(4,5)	(4,5,6)
ℓ=5									5

Table 2 . The table of structures $S^{\ell t}$ for ℓ=5 and t=1, 1½,...,10.

The bottom edges of shaded area, for t being integer, correspond to preference orders with no ties. The detailed description of the table of structures introduced is given in (Bury & Wagner, 2007a).

It should be emphasized that one of the structures from the level 1 must appear in the preference order. Moreover, it should be noted that for any level ℓ >1 only one structure, if any, can be taken into account. The latter holds true also for any position t. It is worth to note that at a given level ℓ the alternatives can take positions T=2ℓ, ..., n+ℓ and the number of positions $s_{\ell T}$ to be taken into account for given ℓ and T is equal to

$$s_{\ell T} = T - 2\ell + 1, \text{ for } \underline{\ell}_T \le \ell \le \overline{\ell}_T, \tag{6}$$

where

$$\underline{\ell}_T = \max(1, T-n), \quad \overline{\ell}_T = [T/2]. \tag{7}$$

The number of levels at which alternatives can be placed depends on the number of alternatives considered n and position T.

T	2	3	4	5	6	7	8	9	10
$\underline{\ell}_T$	1	1	1	1	1	2	3	4	5
$\overline{\ell}_T$	1	1	2	2	3	3	4	4	5

Table 3. The levels that should be taken into account for subsequent positions T for n=5.

For given T, ℓ and n one can determine structures and number of positions to be considered.

T	2	3	4	5	6	7	8	9	10
t	1	1,5	2	2,5	3	3,5	4	4,5	5
ℓ=1	1	2	3	4	5				
ℓ=2			1	2	3	4			
ℓ=3					1	2	3		
ℓ=4							1	2	
ℓ=5									1

Table 4. Values of $s_{\ell T}$ for n=5.

For the preference order P^1={O_2, O_3, O_4, O_1, O_5} the table of structures is as follows

t	1	1,5	2	2,5	3	3,5	4	4,5	5
ℓ=1	O_2								
ℓ=2			O_3						
ℓ=3					O_4				
ℓ=4							O_1		
ℓ=5									O_5

Table 5. Positions and levels of alternatives for the preference order P^1.

3. Determining group opinion

Methods of group judgement based on the concept of distance consist in determining a preference order $\hat{P}$ that is the closest one – in the sense of a distance assumed - to the given set of expert judgements presented in the form of preference orders. In general one has to solve the following problem

$$\min_{P}\sum_{k=1}^{K} d(P^k, P) \rightarrow \hat{P}. \tag{8}$$

This problem can be solved by means of searching over the set of all the preference orders that can be regarded as a group judgement and choosing one (ones) that minimizes the distance assumed. However, this approach is limited by the total number s_n of preference orders to be considered. It is growing fast with n and equals to

$$s_n = \sum_{k=1}^{n} k!\,S_{n,k}, \tag{9}$$

where $S_{n,k}$ is the Stirling number of the second kind (Lipski & Marek, 1985).
This number can be estimated (Bailey, 1998) as

$$s_{n+1} = \frac{(n+1)}{\log 2} s_n = 1{,}442695(n+1)s_n. \tag{10}$$

No of alternatives	No of preference orders - no ties	s_n - total number of preference orders
3	6	13
4	24	75
5	120	541
6	720	4 683
7	5 040	47 293
8	40 320	545 835
9	362 880	7 087 261
10	3 628 800	102 247 563

Table 6. Number of preference orders to be considered with respect to the number of alternatives with no ties or with ties allowed.

For n=17 the total number of the preference orders to be considered is expressed by 18-digits number. Hence instead of searching through all the preference orders, it is worth to apply more specialized approach, e.g. to formulate a constrained optimization problem which can be regarded as a modification of the linear assignment problem.

If ties are allowed in the group judgement then the problem is to be modified according to the table of structures related to the problem under consideration. Moreover, some additional constraints are to be added. The optimization problem with ties was investigated by Cook & Seiford (1978), Armstrong et al. (1982) and Bury and Wagner (2007a, b).

The framework described in Section 4 was applied to formulate and solve the problem of determining the Cook-Seiford median, the Litvak median as well as the Kemeny median. The results are presented in Section 5. For the first two problems the distance is defined with respect to the positions of alternatives. For the Kemeny median the distance is based on pairwise comparisons of alternatives and differs significantly from the previous ones. However a general framework formulated can be applied in all the cases mentioned.

4. Framework for preference structure description

The following binary variables are to be introduced:

$$y_{iT}^{\ell} = \begin{cases} 1 & \text{if } O_i \text{ takes the position T at the level } \ell \text{ in the preference order P} \\ 0 & \text{otherwise} \end{cases} \tag{11}$$

$$y_{iT} = \begin{cases} 1 & \text{if } O_i \text{ takes the position T in the preference order P} \\ 0 & \text{otherwise} \end{cases} \tag{12}$$

$$\gamma_{\ell T} = \begin{cases} 1 & \text{if the structure } S^{\ell T} \text{ appears in the preference order P} \\ 0 & \text{otherwise} \end{cases} \tag{13}$$

$$\Lambda_{\ell} = \begin{cases} 1 & \text{if a structure from the level } \ell \text{ appears in the preference order P} \\ 0 & \text{otherwise} \end{cases} . \tag{14}$$

It follows from table of structures that for a given position T structures can be chosen from levels ℓ such that $\underline{\ell}_T \le \ell \le \overline{\ell}_T$, $\underline{\ell}_T, \overline{\ell}_T$ are given by (7) and

$$y_{iT} = \sum_{\ell=\underline{\ell}_T}^{\overline{\ell}_T} y_{iT}^{\ell} . \tag{15}$$

The constraints are as follows:

$$\underset{i=1,\dots,n}{\forall} \sum_{T=2}^{2n} y_{iT} = 1, \tag{16}$$

i.e. a given alternative can be placed in one position only.

$$\underset{T=2,\dots,2n}{\forall} \; \underset{\ell=\underline{\ell}_T \dots \overline{\ell}_T}{\forall} \sum_{i=1}^{n} y_{iT}^{\ell} = s_{\ell T}\gamma_{\ell T} , \tag{17}$$

i.e. the number of alternatives that can be placed in a given position T on a given level ℓ is equal to zero or $s_{\ell T}$, where $s_{\ell T}$ (6) is the number of positions corresponding to a given structure $S^{\ell t}$.

$$\underset{i=1,\dots,n}{\forall} \; \underset{T=2,\dots,2n}{\forall} \sum_{\ell=\underline{\ell}_T}^{\overline{\ell}_T} y_{iT}^{\ell} = y_{iT} , \tag{18}$$

i.e. for a given position an alternative can be placed at one level at least.

$$\underset{\ell=1,\dots,n}{\forall} \Lambda_{\ell} = \sum_{T=2\ell}^{n+\ell} \gamma_{\ell T} , \tag{19}$$

i.e. for a given level ℓ, $\ell > 1$ only one structure, if any, can be taken into account.
For one of the structures from level $\ell = 1$ must appear in the preference order, then $\Lambda_1 = 1$ and

$$\underset{\ell=2,\ldots,n}{\forall} \quad \Lambda_\ell = \sum_{\lambda=1}^{\ell-1} \gamma_{\lambda,\lambda+\ell-1} \text{ for } \ell = 2, \ldots, n, \tag{20}$$

i.e. the possibility of the occurrence of ℓ-level structure is determined by the structures chosen on preceding levels.

It is worth to note that if for any reason no tied alternatives should occur in group judgement it suffices to impose $\Lambda_\ell = 1$ for $\ell = 1, \ldots, n$ in (20).

5. Optimization problem

As it was mentioned in Section 3 the group judgement based on the concept of distance is to be derived as the solution of an optimization problem (8). A solution obtained depends upon the assumed definition of the distance as well as of the form of the preference order $\hat{P}$ searched for.

The median distance is understood as a l^1 norm defined in an adequate space. Three cases are to be considered:

- the space of positions taken by alternatives for the Cook-Seiford median,
- the space of preference vectors for the Litvak median
- the space of pairwise comparisons for the Kemeny median.

This problem will be analyzed for two cases:

a) there are no ties in expert as well as in group judgement *(complete ordering)*,

b) tied alternatives can occur both in expert and in group judgement *(weak ordering)*.

The CPLEX optimization software was used to solve discrete optimization problems formulated.

5.1 No ties case

For the case of no ties in expert opinion as well as in group judgement the optimization problem (8) can be formulated as follows (Cook & Seiford, 1978; Hwang & Lin, 1987; Nurmi, 1987; Bury & Wagner, 2000):

minimize the distance defined subject to following constraints:

- any given alternative O_i (i=1, …, n) can be placed in one position only, (21)
- the number of alternatives that can be placed in a given position is equal to one. (22)

To avoid ambiguity it is assumed that positions the alternatives can take in experts' judgements are denoted as j, j=1, …, n.

The assumption of no ties in expert judgement will be relaxed for the Litvak and for the Kemeny median.

5.1.1 The Cook–Seiford median

Definition (Cook & Seiford, 1978)

The distance between two preference orders is defined in terms of positions taken by alternatives

$$d(P^{k_1}, P^{k_2}) = \sum_{i=1}^{n} \left| q_i^{k_1} - q_i^{k_2} \right| \tag{23}$$

where q_i^k denotes the position taken by the i-th alternative in k-th expert's opinion.

It can be shown that the distance defined in such a way satisfies all the axioms describing the measure of closeness (Cook & Seiford, 1978; Cook, 2006).

The distance of a preference vector P from the set of experts' judgements $\{P^k\}$is as follows

$$d(P,P^{(k)}) = \sum_{k=1}^{K} d(P,P^k) = \sum_{k=1}^{K}\sum_{i=1}^{n} \left| q_i^k - q_i \right| \tag{24}$$

where q_i denotes the position of an alternative O_i in the preference order P.
The optimization problem can be formulated as follows.
Find such a preference order $\hat{P}$ that

$$d(\hat{P},P^{(k)}) = \min_P \sum_{k=1}^{K} d(P^k,P) = \min_P \sum_{k=1}^{K}\sum_{i=1}^{n} \left| q_i^k - q_i \right| . \tag{25}$$

If one assumes that the alternative O_i can take the j-th position in the preference order P, (j = 1, …, n), the distance (24) can be written in the form

$$d(P^k,P) = \sum_{i=1}^{n}\sum_{j=1}^{n} d_{ij} y_{ij} . \tag{26}$$

where

$$d_{ij} = \sum_{k=1}^{K} \left| q_i^k - j \right| \tag{27}$$

and y_{ij} is defined as (12).
The matrix of d_{ij} coefficients is denoted as D. d_{ij} expresses the aggregated difference between the position of the i-th alternative in the preference order P and its positions in the preference orders P^k, k=1, …, K. The distance matrix D is of the form

$$D = \begin{array}{c} \\ O_1 \\ O_2 \\ \vdots \\ O_n \end{array} \begin{array}{c} \begin{array}{cccc} j=1 & j=2 & \cdots & j=n \end{array} \\ \begin{bmatrix} d_{11} & d_{12} & \cdots & d_{1n} \\ d_{21} & d_{22} & \cdots & d_{2n} \\ \vdots & \vdots & \ddots & \vdots \\ d_{n1} & d_{n2} & \cdots & d_{nn} \end{bmatrix} \end{array} . \tag{28}$$

The lower bound of the distance (26) is equal

$$C = \sum_{i=1}^{n} d_{i\,min} \text{ , where } d_{i\,min} = \min_j [d_{i1},\ldots,d_{in}] . \tag{29}$$

The value of C is of importance for estimation how close is the group judgement derived to an "ideal" judgement.
The minimization problem (25) can be rewritten as a linear assignment problem

$$\min_{y_{ij}} \sum_{i=1}^{n}\sum_{j=1}^{n} d_{ij} y_{ij} , \tag{30}$$

subject to

$$\underset{i=1,\dots,n}{\forall} \sum_{j=1}^{n} y_{ij} = 1, \tag{31}$$

i.e. an alternative can be placed at one position only and

$$\underset{j=1,\dots,n}{\forall} \sum_{i=1}^{n} y_{ij} = 1, \tag{32}$$

i.e. only one alternative can be placed at a given position.
The latter constraint can be easily derived from (17) in the structure framework.
Summing (17) over ℓ, $\ell = \underline{\ell_T},\dots,\overline{\ell_T}$ and taking into account (15) one obtains

$$\underset{T=2,\dots,2n}{\forall} \sum_{\ell=\underline{\ell_T}}^{\overline{\ell_T}} \sum_{i=1}^{n} y_{iT}^{\ell} = \sum_{i=1}^{n} \sum_{\ell=\underline{\ell_T}}^{\overline{\ell_T}} y_{iT}^{\ell} = \sum_{i=1}^{n} y_{iT} = \sum_{\ell=\underline{\ell_T}}^{\overline{\ell_T}} s_{\ell T} \gamma_{\ell T}\,. \tag{33}$$

For the case of no ties one has T=2, 4, …, 2n (j=1, 2, …n).
From the table of structures (Table 5) it can be seen that $s_{jj}=1$ and $\gamma_{jj}=1$. Finally one gets $\underset{j=1,\dots,n}{\forall} \sum_{i=1}^{n} y_{ij} = 1$.
This problem was described in details e.g. in Bury & Wagner, (2000) and Cook, (2006).

5.1.2 The Litvak median

Litvak (1982) introduced the notion of so called preference vector. For the preference order given by k-th expert the preference vector is defined as follows:

$$\pi^k = [\pi_1^k,\dots,\pi_n^k], \tag{34}$$

where π_i^k is equal to the number of alternatives preceding the i-th one in this preference order.
Under assumptions taken

$$\pi_i^k = q_i^k - 1, \tag{35}$$

where q_i^k denotes the position taken by the i-th alternative in the k-th expert's opinion.
Example 3.
For a preference order P^1 from Table 1, $P^1 = \{O_2, O_3, O_4, O_1, O_5\}$ one has $\pi^1 = [3, 0, 1, 2, 4]$.
The distance between preference orders is expressed in terms of corresponding preference vectors.
Definition (Litvak, 1982).
Given two preference vectors π^{k_1} i π^{k_2} of the preference orders P^{k_1} and P^{k_2} respectively. The distance between these two preference orders is defined as

$$d\left(P^{k_1}, P^{k_2}\right) = \sum_{i=1}^{n} \left|\pi_i^{k_1} - \pi_i^{k_2}\right|. \tag{36}$$

It can be shown that the distance defined in such a way satisfies all the axioms describing the measure of closeness (Litvak, 1982).

Definition (Litvak, 1982).
The distance of a preference order P from the set of experts' preference orders $\{P^k\}$ is as follows

$$d\left(P,P^{(k)}\right)=\sum_{k=1}^{K}\sum_{i=1}^{n}\left|\pi_i^P-\pi_i^k\right|. \tag{37}$$

$$\text{Let } h_i^{k(j)}=\left|\pi_i^{P(j)}-\pi_i^k\right| \quad i=1,\ldots,n;\ j=1,\ldots,n;\ k=1,\ldots K, \tag{38}$$

where $\pi_i^{P(j)}$ is the number of alternatives preceding O_i if O_i takes the j-th position in the preference order P.
Summing $h_i^{k(j)}$ (38) over k (k=1,...,K) one obtains $h_i^{(j)}$

$$h_i^{(j)}=\sum_{k=1}^{K}h_i^{k(j)} \tag{39}$$

The distance (37) may be written as follows

$$d(P,P^{(k)})=\sum_{i=1}^{n}\sum_{j=1}^{n}\sum_{k=1}^{K}\left|\pi_i^{P(j)}-\pi_i^k\right|y_{ij}=\sum_{i=1}^{n}\sum_{j=1}^{n}h_i^{(j)}y_{ij} \tag{40}$$

where y_{ij} is defined by (12).
The matrix of $h_i^{(j)}$ coefficients is denoted as H, $h_i^{(j)}$ expresses the aggregated difference between the position of the i-th alternative in the preference order P and its positions in the preference orders P^k, k=1, ..., K.
The distance matrix H is of the form

$$H=\begin{array}{c} \\ O_1 \\ O_2 \\ \vdots \\ O_n \end{array}\begin{array}{c}\begin{array}{cccc} j=1 & j=2 & \cdots & j=n\end{array}\\ \begin{bmatrix} h_1^{(1)} & h_1^{(2)} & \cdots & h_1^{(n)} \\ h_2^{(1)} & h_1^{(2)} & \cdots & h_2^{(n)} \\ \vdots & \vdots & \ddots & \vdots \\ h_n^{(1)} & h_1^{(2)} & \cdots & h_n^{(n)} \end{bmatrix}\end{array}. \tag{41}$$

The lower bound of the distance (40) is equal (Litvak (1982))

$$G=\sum_{i=1}^{n}h_{i\,min}\text{, where } h_{i\,min}=\min_j[h_i^{(1)},\ldots,h_i^{(n)}] \tag{42}$$

The problem of determining the Litvak median can be formulated as the following binary optimization problem (Litvak, 1982; Bury & Wagner, 2000)

$$\min_{y_{ij}}\sum_{i=1}^{n}\sum_{j=1}^{n}h_i^{(j)}y_{ij} \tag{43}$$

subject to (31)÷(32).

One should note that in the case when in expert judgement tied alternatives can occur the definition of preference vector makes it easy to determine its components and the distance matrix. The preference vector for expert judgement with ties is of the same form for classical as well as for fractional position system. Hence it may be applied for the optimization problem formulated (43).
Example 2.
For a preference order P^2 from Table 1, $P^2 = \{(O_2, O_3), O_4, (O_1, O_5)\}$ one has $\pi^2 = \{3, 0, 0, 2, 3\}$.

5.1.3 The Kemeny median

The distance for the Kemeny median method is defined with the use of pairwise comparison matrices (Kemeny, 1959; Kemeny & Snell, 1960).
For a given preference order of n alternatives presented by the k-th expert (k=1,...,K)
P^k: $O_{i_1}, O_{i_2}, \ldots, O_{i_n}$ the matrix of pairwise comparisons can be constructed as follows (e.g. Litvak, 1982); it is assumed that in expert judgement ties can occur.

$$\mathbf{A}^k = \begin{bmatrix} a_{11}^k, & \ldots, & a_{1n}^k \\ \vdots & \ddots & \vdots \\ a_{n1}^k, & \ldots, & a_{nn}^k \end{bmatrix}, \text{ where } a_{il}^k = \begin{cases} 1 & \text{for } O_i \succ O_l \\ 0 & \text{for } O_i \approx O_l \\ -1 & \text{for } O_i \prec O_l \end{cases}, \ a_{ii}^k \triangleq 0 \tag{44}$$

i=1, …n, l=1, …, n.
The notation $O_i \succ O_l$ ($O_i \approx O_l$) should be read as follows: the i-th alternative O_i is better than (equivalent to) the l-th alternative O_l with respect to a chosen criterion (a set of criteria). Assume that two preference orders P^{k_1} and P^{k_2} are given. The distance between these two preference orders is defined as follows (e.g. Litvak, 1982; Bury & Wagner, 2000)

$$d(P^{k_1}, P^{k_2}) = \frac{1}{2}\sum_{i=1}^{n}\sum_{l=1}^{n}\left|a_{il}^{k_1} - a_{il}^{k_2}\right|. \tag{45}$$

It can be shown that the distance defined in such a way satisfies all the axioms describing the measure of closeness (Litvak, 1982).
The distance between a given preference order P and a set of preference orders given by the experts is defined as

$$d = d(P, P^{(k)}) = \frac{1}{2}\sum_{i=1}^{n}\sum_{l=1}^{n}\sum_{k=1}^{K}\left|a_{il}^{P} - a_{il}^{k}\right|. \tag{46}$$

The following equality holds

$$\left|a_{il}^{k} - a_{il}^{P}\right| + \left|a_{li}^{k} - a_{li}^{P}\right| = 2\left|a_{il}^{k} - a_{il}^{P}\right| = 2\left|a_{li}^{k} - a_{li}^{P}\right| \tag{47}$$

so the expression (46) can be rewritten as follows

$$d = \sum_{\substack{i \\ (i,l)\in I_P^{(1)}}}\sum_{l}\sum_{k=1}^{K}\left|a_{il}^{k} - a_{il}^{P}\right| + \sum_{\substack{i \\ (i,l)\in I_P^{(2)}}}\sum_{l}\sum_{k=1}^{K}\left|a_{il}^{k} - a_{il}^{P}\right| \tag{48}$$

where

$I_P^{(1)}$ -the set of indices (i,l) for which $O_i \succ O_l$ in the preference order P, i.e. $a_{il}^P = 1$. (49)

$I_P^{(2)}$ -the set of indices (i,l) for which $O_i \approx O_l$ in the preference order P, i.e. $a_{il}^P = 0$. (50)

Assume that in the preference order P $O_i \succ O_l$, i.e. $a_{il}^P = 1$. In order to determine the distance of this preference order from a given set $\{P^k\}$, use can be made of coefficients defined as follows

$$r_{il} = \sum_{k=1}^{K} d_{il}\left(P, P^{(k)}\right) = \sum_{k=1}^{K} \left|a_{il}^k - a_{il}^P\right| = \sum_{k=1}^{K} \left|a_{il}^k - 1\right|. \tag{51}$$

They are called the loss coefficients and the matrix $R=[r_{il}]$ is called the loss matrix (Litvak,1982). It is assumed that $r_{il}=0$ for all i=l. It should be noted that elements of the matrix R depend upon the form of preference orders P^k (k=1,...,K) only and are independent of position system assumed (classical as well as fractional - if applicable).
Making use of the coefficients r_{il} (i,l=1,...,n) the formulae (48) can be rewritten in the following form (Bury & Wagner, 2000; Litvak, 1982):

$$d = \sum_{\substack{i \\ (i,l)\in I_P^{(1)}}} \sum_{l} r_{il} + \sum_{\substack{i \\ (i,l)\in I_P^{(2)}}} \sum_{l} \sum_{k=1}^{K} \left|a_{il}^k\right|. \tag{52}$$

If in the group judgement ties are not allowed, then $I_P^{(2)} = \{i,i\}$, i=1,...,n. In this case we have (Litvak, 1982)

$$d = \sum_{(i,l)\in I_P^{(1)}} r_{il}. \tag{53}$$

This formula can be used to determine the lower bound E of the distance (53). Litvak has shown that in the case under consideration the following theorem is satisfied.
Theorem (Litvak, 1982).

$$E = \sum_{i=1}^{n-1} \sum_{l=i+1}^{n} \min\left(r_{il}, r_{li}\right). \tag{54}$$

These results make it possible to propose some heuristic algorithms for determining the Kemeny median (Bury & Wagner, 2000; Litvak, 1982).
The distance (53) can be written in the form

$$d(P, P^{(k)}) = \sum_{i=1}^{n} \sum_{l=1}^{n} r_{il} x_{il}, \tag{55}$$

where

$$x_{il} = \begin{cases} 1 & \text{for } O_i \succ O_l \text{ in the preference order P} \\ 0 & \text{otherwise} \end{cases} \tag{56}$$

The problem of determining a group judgement that minimizes the distance (55) can be formulated as follows

$$\min_{x_{il}} \sum_{i=1}^{n} \sum_{l=1}^{n} r_{il} x_{il} , \tag{57}$$

It should be emphasized that this problem (even if ties are not allowed in group judgement) cannot be solved within the framework presented in this subsection. It needs to be formulated within the framework of structures presented for the case of ties.

5.2 The case of ties in group judgement

For this case the fractional notation is to be used i.e.

$$t \in \Psi = \{1, 1½, 2, 2½, 3, 3½, \ldots, n\text{-}1, n\text{-}½, n\}.$$

5.2.1 The Cook–Seiford median

The problem (30) ÷ (32) is to be modified (double positions T are applied).

The distance matrix $\bar{D}$ is of the form

$$\bar{D} = \begin{array}{c} \\ O_1 \\ O_2 \\ \vdots \\ O_n \end{array} \begin{array}{c} \begin{array}{ccccc} T=2 & T=3 & T=4 & \cdots & T=2n \end{array} \\ \left[\begin{array}{ccccc} \bar{d}_{12} & \bar{d}_{13} & \bar{d}_{14} & & \bar{d}_{1\,2n} \\ \bar{d}_{22} & \bar{d}_{23} & \bar{d}_{12} & & \bar{d}_{12} \\ \vdots & \vdots & \vdots & \ddots & \bar{d}_{12} \\ \bar{d}_{n2} & \bar{d}_{n3} & \bar{d}_{12} & & \bar{d}_{12} \end{array} \right] \end{array} , \tag{58}$$

where

$$\bar{d}_{iT} = \sum_{k=1}^{K} \left| 2q_i^k - T \right| , \tag{59}$$

and q_i^k is the number of fractional position taken by an alternative O_i in the preference order P^k given by the k-th ekspert.

The optimization problem is as follows

$$\min_{y_{iT}} \sum_{i=1}^{n} \sum_{T=2}^{2n} \bar{d}_{iT} y_{iT} , \tag{60}$$

with the constraints (15)÷(20).

5.2.2 The Litvak median

For the case of ties it is worth to notice that the number of alternatives preceding a given i-th one in the preference order is determined by the level ℓ this alternative takes in the table of structures and equals (ℓ -1). This means that alternatives from the first level are preceded by zero alternatives, alternatives from the second level are preceded by one alternative, etc.

The following example shows this observation.

Example 3.

For a preference order P^2 from Table 1, $P^2 = \{(O_2, O_3), O_4, (O_1, O_5)\}$ one has

$$P^2 = \{4½, 1½, 1½, 3, 4½\}.$$

Hence

- (O_2, O_3) are placed in the positions 1½, 1½ on the level ℓ =1; it is evident there are no alternatives preceding those ones, $\pi_2^2 = 0$, $\pi_3^2 = 0$,
- O_4 takes the 3rd position on the level ℓ =3, it is preceded by two alternatives, $\pi_4^2 = 2$,
- (O_1, O_5) are placed in the positions 4½, 4½ on the level ℓ =4, they are preceded by three alternatives, $\pi_1^2 = 3$, $\pi_5^2 = 3$.

It may be shown that the components of a preference vector for a respective preference order P may be determined as follows

$$\pi_i^{P(\ell)} = (\ell - 1)\Lambda_\ell, \ \ell = 1, \ldots, n, \tag{61}$$

where Λ_ℓ is given by (14).

The preference order $P^2=\{(O_2,O_3), O_4, (O_1, O_5)\}$ presented with the use of the table of structures is as follows

	T	2	3	4	5	6	7	8	9	10
	t	1	1,5	2	2,5	3	3,5	4	4,5	5
Λ_1=1	ℓ =1		(O_2, O_3)							
Λ_2=0	ℓ =2									
Λ_3=1	ℓ =3					O_4				
Λ_4=1	ℓ =4								(O_1, O_5)	
Λ_5=0	ℓ =5									

Table 7. Positions and levels of alternatives for the preference order P^2.

For a preference order P^2 given above one has

$$\pi_2^{P(1)} = (1-1)\Lambda_1 = 0, \ \pi_3^{P(1)} = 0,$$

$$\pi_4^{P(3)} = (3-1)\Lambda_3 = 2,$$

$$\pi_1^{P(4)} = (4-1)\Lambda_4 = 3, \ \pi_5^{P(4)} = 3,$$

hence $\Lambda = [1, 0, 1, 1, 0]$, $\pi^2 = [3, 0, 0, 2, 3]$.

The coefficients $h_i^{k(\ell)}$ of distance matrix $\overline{H}$ are of the form:

$$h_i^{k(\ell)} = \left|\pi_i^{P(\ell)} - \pi_i^k\right| \quad i=1,\ldots,n; \ k=1,\ldots K; \ \ell=1,\ldots,n. \tag{62}$$

Summing coefficients $h_i^{k(\ell)}$ (62) over k (k=1,...,K) one gets

$$h_i^{(\ell)} = \sum_{k=1}^{K} h_i^{k(\ell)}. \tag{63}$$

It should be emphasized that the components of preference vectors result from the table of structure, i.e. they depend on position as well as on the level a given alternative is located.

As components of preference vectors π^k, k=1, ..., K are the same regardless of the notation of positions applied, it can be seen that H = $\overline{H}$. The bar over H indicates another way of defining the components of preference vector only. One has

$$\overline{H} = \begin{array}{c} \\ O_1 \\ O_2 \\ \vdots \\ O_n \end{array} \begin{array}{c} \begin{array}{cccc} \ell=1 & \ell=2 & \cdots & \ell=n \end{array} \\ \begin{bmatrix} \overline{h}_1^{(1)} & \overline{h}_1^{(2)} & \cdots & \overline{h}_1^{(n)} \\ \overline{h}_2^{(1)} & \overline{h}_1^{(2)} & \cdots & \overline{h}_2^{(n)} \\ \vdots & \vdots & \ddots & \vdots \\ \overline{h}_n^{(1)} & \overline{h}_1^{(2)} & \cdots & \overline{h}_n^{(n)} \end{bmatrix} \end{array} . \tag{64}$$

The optimization problem for Litvak median is as follows:

$$\min_{y_{iT}^{\ell}} \sum_{i=1}^{n} \sum_{T=2}^{2n} \sum_{\ell=\underline{\ell_T}}^{\overline{\ell_T}} \overline{h}_i^{(\ell)} y_{iT}^{\ell} \tag{65}$$

subject to (15)÷(20).

5.2.3 The Kemeny median

If ties can occur in the group judgement, an optimization problem to be solved is more difficult. As it was mentioned before, the Kemeny median is defined with the use of pairwise comparisons. To solve the problem of determining group judgement one has to introduce some additional constraints.

The problem of finding a preference order $\hat{P}$ such that the distance (52) is minimized can be formulated as follows:

$$\min_{x_{il}, z_{il}} \left(\sum_{i=1}^{n} \sum_{l=1}^{n} r_{il} x_{il} + \sum_{i=1}^{n-1} \sum_{l=i+1}^{n} b_{il} z_{il} \right), \tag{66}$$

where

x_{il} is given by (56),

$$z_{il} = \begin{cases} 1 & \text{for } O_i \approx O_l \text{ in the preference order P} \\ 0 & \text{otherwise} \end{cases} \tag{67}$$

$$b_{il} = \left(\sum_{k=1}^{K} \left| a_{il}^{k} \right| \right) \tag{68}$$

r_{il} is given by (51),

subject to a specially defined set of constraints. This set can be divided into two groups. First one contains those resulting from the table of structure. The second one consists of constraints resulting from the definition of the Kemeny median.

The following binary variables are introduced:

$$x_{il}^{\ell} = \begin{cases} 1 & \text{if } O_i \text{ located on the level } \ell \text{ is such that } O_i \succ O_l \text{ in the preference order P,} \\ & \text{for } O_l \text{ from an arbitrary level } \lambda > \ell \\ 0 & \text{otherwise} \end{cases} \tag{69}$$

$$z_{il}^{\ell} = \begin{cases} 1 & \text{if } O_i \approx O_l \text{ on the level } \ell \text{ in the preference order P} \\ 0 & \text{otherwise} \end{cases} . \quad (70)$$

The constraints are as follows
for ℓ =1, …, n-1, i = 1, …, n, l = 1, …, n:

$$x_{il} = \sum_{\ell=1}^{n-1} x_{il}^{\ell} \quad (71)$$

$$z_{il} = \sum_{\ell=1}^{n-1} z_{il}^{\ell} . \quad (72)$$

It should be noticed that

$$x_{il}^{\ell} = 1 \quad \text{iff} \quad \left(\underbrace{\sum_{T=2\ell}^{n+\ell-1} y_{iT}^{\ell} = 1}_{\substack{\text{preceding} \\ \text{alternative}}} \right) \wedge \left(\underbrace{\sum_{\lambda=\ell+1}^{n} \sum_{T=2\lambda}^{n+\lambda} y_{lT}^{\lambda} = 1}_{\substack{\text{preceded} \\ \text{alternative}}} \right) \quad (73)$$

and

$$z_{il}^{\ell} = 1 \quad \text{iff} \quad \left(\sum_{T=2\ell+1}^{n+\ell} y_{iT}^{\ell} = 1 \right) \wedge \left(\sum_{T=2\ell+1}^{n+\ell} y_{lT}^{\ell} = 1 \right) \quad (74)$$

For the case of binary minimization problem (66) with positive coefficients of the objective function, in order to satisfy this condition the following inequalities should hold true

$$x_{il}^{\ell} \geq \underbrace{\sum_{T=2\ell}^{n+\ell-1} y_{iT}^{\ell}}_{\substack{\text{preceding} \\ \text{alternative}}} + \underbrace{\sum_{\lambda=\ell+1}^{n} \sum_{T=2\lambda}^{n+\lambda} y_{lT}^{\lambda}}_{\substack{\text{preceded} \\ \text{alternative}}} - 1 \quad (75)$$

and

$$z_{il}^{\ell} \geq \sum_{T=2\ell+1}^{n+\ell} \left(y_{iT}^{\ell} + y_{lT}^{\ell} \right) - 1 . \quad (76)$$

Hence the optimization problem becomes:
solve (66) subject to the constraints (67) ÷ (76) and (15)÷(20).

6. Numerical examples

6.1 The Cook-Seiford median

Example 4.
Given the set of five alternatives and eleven experts' judgements.
There are no ties in experts' judgements.

$P^1 = \{O_4, O_1, O_3, O_2, O_5\}$
$P^2 = \{O_3, O_1, O_5, O_2, O_4\}$
$P^3 = \{O_3, O_1, O_5, O_2, O_4\}$
$P^4 = \{O_2, O_1, O_5, O_4, O_3\}$
$P^5 = \{O_1, O_5, O_4, O_3, O_2\}$
$P^6 = \{O_3, O_5, O_2, O_4, O_1\}$
$P^7 = \{O_4, O_1, O_3, O_5, O_2\}$
$P^8 = \{O_1, O_3, O_5, O_2, O_4\}$
$P^9 = \{O_5, O_1, O_2, O_4, O_3\}$
$P^{10} = \{O_1, O_2, O_3, O_5, O_4\}$
$P^{11} = \{O_1, O_5, O_2, O_3, O_4\}$

The lower bound C (29) of the distance is equal to 51.
If ties are not allowed in group judgement the solutions obtained are

$$\{O_1, O_3, O_5, O_2, O_4\}$$
$$\{O_1, O_5, O_3, O_2, O_4\}$$

and the distance (30) from the set of preference orders given by experts is equal to 58.
The group judgement with ties is $\{O_1, (O_2, O_3, O_5), O_4\}$.
The distance (60) from the set of preference orders given by experts is equal to 56.
Example 5.
Given the set of five alternatives and eleven experts' judgements.
Ties are allowed in experts' judgements.

$P^1 = \{O_3, (O_4, O_5), (O_1, O_2)\}$
$P^2 = \{(O_1, O_2, O_3), (O_4, O_5)\}$
$P^3 = \{O_3, O_2, (O_1, O_4, O_5)\}$
$P^4 = \{O_2, (O_1, O_5), (O_3, O_4)\}$
$P^5 = \{(O_1, O_4), O_3, O_5, O_2\}$
$P^6 = \{(O_2, O_4), (O_1, O_5), O_3\}$
$P^7 = \{(O_1, O_2, O_3, O_5), O_4\}$
$P^8 = \{O_5, (O_1, O_3), O_4, O_2\}$
$P^9 = \{O_2, (O_1, O_3, O_4), O_5\}$
$P^{10} = \{O_1, O_2, (O_3, O_4, O_5)\}$
$P^{11} = \{O_1, (O_2, O_3), (O_4, O_5)\}$

The lower bound C (29) of the distance is equal to 52.
If ties are allowed in experts' judgements only then the solutions obtained are as follows

$$\{O_1, O_2, O_3, O_5, O_4\}$$
$$\{O_2, O_1, O_3, O_5, O_4\}$$

and the distance (30) from the preference orders given by experts is equal to 66.
The group judgement with ties is $\{(O_1, O_2, O_3), (O_4, O_5)\}$.
The distance (60) from the set of preference orders given by experts is equal to 60.

6.2 The Litvak median

Example 6.

Given the set of six alternatives and eleven experts' judgements.
There are no ties in experts' judgements.

$P^1 = \{O_2, O_1, O_3, O_5, O_6, O_4\}$
$P^2 = \{O_1, O_3, O_2, O_5, O_6, O_4\}$
$P^3 = \{O_4, O_5, O_6, O_3, O_1, O_2\}$
$P^4 = \{O_5, O_1, O_4, O_6, O_2, O_3\}$
$P^5 = \{O_5, O_4, O_2, O_6, O_1, O_3\}$
$P^6 = \{O_2, O_5, O_4, O_6, O_3, O_1\}$
$P^7 = \{O_1, O_5, O_2, O_4, O_3, O_6\}$
$P^8 = \{O_6, O_1, O_2, O_5, O_3, O_4\}$
$P^9 = \{O_2, O_5, O_6, O_4, O_3, O_1\}$
$P^{10} = \{O_4, O_2, O_6, O_1, O_3, O_5\}$
$P^{11} = \{O_4, O_5, O_6, O_1, O_2, O_3\}$

The lower bound G (40) of the distance is equal to 82.
If ties are not allowed in group judgement the solutions obtained are

$\{O_4, O_5, O_2, O_6, O_1, O_3\}$
$\{O_2, O_5, O_4, O_6, O_1, O_3\}$

The distance (43) from the set of preference orders given by experts is equal to 98.
The group judgement with ties is $\{(O_2, O_4, O_5), O_6, O_1, O_3\}$
The distance (65) from the set of preference orders given by experts is equal to 96.

Example 7.

Given the set of six alternatives and eleven experts' judgements.
Ties are allowed in experts' judgements.

$P^1 = \{O_1, O_6, O_4, (O_2, O_3), O_5\}$
$P^2 = \{(O_1, O_2), O_4, O_6, (O_3, O_5)\}$
$P^3 = \{O_4, (O_1, O_2), O_5, (O_3, O_6)\}$
$P^4 = \{(O_2, O_3, O_6), O_4, O_1, O_5\}$
$P^5 = \{(O_3, O_5), (O_1, O_2, O_6), O_4\}$
$P^6 = \{(O_2, O_4, O_5), (O_3, O_6), O_1\}$
$P^7 = \{O_3, (O_4, O_5, O_6), (O_1, O_2)\}$
$P^8 = \{O_1, (O_3, O_6), (O_2, O_4, O_5)\}$
$P^9 = \{(O_1, O_5), O_3, (O_2, O_6), O_4\}$
$P^{10} = \{(O_3, O_6), O_2, O_4, O_5, O_1\}$
$P^{11} = \{O_1, O_2, (O_3, O_4, O_5), O_6\}$

The lower bound G (42) of the distance is equal to 95.
The solutions obtained for the case of no ties in group judgement are

$\{O_1, O_3, O_2, O_6, O_4, O_5\}$, $\{O_1, O_3, O_2, O_6, O_5, O_4\}$
$\{O_1, O_3, O_2, O_4, O_6, O_5\}$, $\{O_1, O_2, O_3, O_6, O_4, O_5\}$
$\{O_1, O_2, O_3, O_6, O_5, O_4\}$, $\{O_1, O_2, O_3, O_4, O_6, O_5\}$

The distance (43) from the set of preference orders given by experts is equal to 116.
The group judgement with ties is $\{(O_1, O_2, O_3, O_4, O_5, O_6)\}$.
The distance (65) from the set of preference orders given by experts is equal to 97. It is worth to note that in this example making all the alternatives equivalent significantly improved the distance.

6.3 The Kemeny median

Example 8.
Given the set of seven alternatives and eleven experts' judgements.
There are no ties in experts' judgements.

$P^1 = \{O_1, O_2, O_6, O_7, O_5, O_3, O_4\}$
$P^2 = \{O_2, O_6, O_4, O_5, O_1, O_7, O_3\}$
$P^3 = \{O_3, O_2, O_6, O_1, O_7, O_4, O_5\}$
$P^4 = \{O_4, O_1, O_6, O_5, O_3, O_2, O_7\}$
$P^5 = \{O_4, O_6, O_1, O_3, O_7, O_5, O_2\}$
$P^6 = \{O_4, O_2, O_7, O_6, O_1, O_3, O_5\}$
$P^7 = \{O_4, O_7, O_6, O_1, O_3, O_2, O_5\}$
$P^8 = \{O_6, O_3, O_7, O_1, O_2, O_4, O_5\}$
$P^9 = \{O_2, O_5, O_7, O_1, O_3, O_4, O_6\}$
$P^{10} = \{O_7, O_6, O_2, O_5, O_3, O_4, O_1\}$
$P^{11} = \{O_6, O_3, O_1, O_2, O_7, O_4, O_5\}$

The lower bound E (54) of the distance is equal to 166.
If ties are not allowed in group judgement the solutions are

$\{O_6, O_1, O_2, O_7, O_3, O_4, O_5\}$, $\{O_6, O_1, O_3, O_2, O_7, O_4, O_5\}$

and the distance (55) from the set of preference orders given by experts is equal to 170.
The group judgement derived for the problem (66) ÷ (76) (with ties assumed) is $\{O_6, O_1, O_2, O_7, O_3, O_4, O_5\}$.It is worth to note that it doesn't contain tied alternatives even though ties were allowed.
The distance (66) from the set of preference orders given by experts is equal to 170.
Example 9.
Given the set of seven alternatives and eleven experts' judgements.
Ties are allowed in experts' judgements.

$P^1 = \{O_1, O_2, O_4, O_7, (O_3, O_5, O_6)\}$
$P^2 = \{(O_4, O_6), O_7, O_5, (O_2, O_3), O_1\}$
$P^3 = \{O_4, O_7, (O_1, O_2, O_6), (O_3, O_5)\}$
$P^4 = \{O_2, O_3, (O_4, O_5, O_6), O_7, O_1\}$
$P^5 = \{(O_3, O_5, O_6, O_7), (O_1, O_4), O_2\}$
$P^6 = \{O_4, O_6, (O_1, O_2), (O_3, O_5), O_7\}$
$P^7 = \{O_1, (O_3, O_4, O_5, O_7), (O_2, O_6)\}$
$P^8 = \{O_4, (O_3, O_6), O_7, (O_1, O_2), O_5\}$
$P^9 = \{O_5, O_6, O_4, O_2, O_3, (O_1, O_7)\}$

$P^{10} =$ $\{O_5, O_1, O_3, (O_2, O_4, O_6), O_7\}$

$P^{11} =$ $\{(O_1, O_2), (O_3, O_4), (O_5, O_6), O_7\}$

The lower bound E (52) of the distance is equal to 187.

If ties are not allowed in group judgement the solutions obtained are

$$\{O_4, O_6, O_1, O_2, O_3, O_5, O_7\}, \qquad \{O_4, O_6, O_1, O_2, O_5, O_3, O_7\}$$

and the distance (55) from the set of preference orders given by experts is equal to 187.

The group judgement with ties is $\{O_4, (O_1, O_2, O_3, O_5, O_6), O_7\}$

and the distance (66) from the set of preference orders given by experts is equal to 177.

7. Concluding remarks

In the paper it is shown that the fractional notation and the structure table can be successfully applied to find the group judgement with ties for the distance defined as the Cook-Seiford, Litvak and Kemeny median. On the basis of results obtained it seems reasonable to make an attempt at applying the approach discussed to the other methods of determining group judgement with ties or in the case when some alternatives are not comparable.

8. References

Armstrong R.D.; Cook W.D. & Seiford L.M. (1982). Priority ranking and consensus formation: The case of ties. Management Science, 28, no 6, 638-645

Bailey R.W (1998). The number of weak orderings of a finite set. Social Choice and Welfare, vol.15, pp.559-562

Bury H. & Wagner D. (2000). The use of Kemeny median for group decision making. Integer programming approach, *Proceedings of 6th International Conference on Methods and Models in Automation and Robotics MMAR 2000*, Międzyzdroje, Poland, 193-198

Bury H., Wagner D. (2007a). Determining group judgement when ties can occur, *Proceedings of 13th IEEE IFAC International Conference on Methods and Models in Automation and Robotics MMAR 2007*, Szczecin, Poland, 779-784

Bury H., Wagner D. (2007b). Determining the Litvak median with ties (in Polish), Studia i Materiały Polskiego Stowarzyszenia Zarządzania Wiedzą, 10, Bydgoszcz, 19-34.

Cook W.D. & Seiford L.M. (1978). Priority ranking and consensus formation. Management Science, 24, no 16, 1721-1732

Cook W.D.; Kress M. & Seiford L.M. (1997). A general framework for distance-based consensus in ordinal ranking models. European Journal of Operational Research, 96, issue 2, 392-397

Cook W.D. (2006). Distance-based and ad hoc consensus models in ordinal preference ranking. European Journal of Operational Research, 172, 369-385

Hwang C.-L., Lin M.-J. (1987). Group decision making under multiple criteria, Springer Verlag, Berlin, Heidelberg

Kemeny J. (1959). Mathematics without numbers, Daedalus, 88, 571-591

Kemeny J., Snell L. (1962). Mathematical Models in the Social Sciences, Ginn. Boston

Lipski W., Marek W. (1985). Combinatorial Analysis (in Polish), PWN Warszawa

Litvak B.G. (1982). Ekspertnaja informacija. Mietody połuczienija i analiza (in Russian), Radio i Swjaz, Moskwa

Nurmi H. (1987). Comparing voting systems, Kluwer, Dordrecht/ Boston/ Lancaster, Tokio

10

An Innovative Method for Robots Modeling and Simulation

Laura Celentano
Dipartimento di Informatica e Sistemistica
Università degli Studi di Napoli Federico II
Napoli,
Italy

1. Introduction

The robot dynamics modeling and simulation problem has been studied for the last three decades intensively.

In particular, the forward dynamics problem of a robot is a very relevant issue, which there is still to say about in terms of efficient computation algorithms, that can be also simple to understand, to develop and to implement, above all for practical robots, robots with many links and/or with flexible links (Featherstone, 1987), (Featherstone & Orin, 2000), (Sciavicco & Siciliano, 2000), (Khalil & Dombre, 2002).

Indeed, in these cases the methods based on the classical Lagrange formulation give rise to an analytical model with numerous terms that may be difficult to use. The methods based on the Newton-Euler formulation are not very easy to apply and do not provide easily manageable analytical formulae, even if they are efficient from a computational point of view (Featherstone, 1987).

An important contribution to solve the previous problems is given (Celentano, 2006), (Celentano & Iervolino, 2006), (Celentano & Iervolino, 2007) by a new, simple and efficient methodology of analysis, valid for all of robots, that makes use of a mathematical model containing a lower number of algebraic terms and that allows computing, with a prescribed maximum error, the gradient of the kinetic energy starting from the numerical knowledge of the only inertia matrix rather than using, as usually found in the literature, complex analytical calculations of the closed-form expression of this matrix.

This result is very strong because it allows solving the forward dynamics problem of a robot in a simple and efficient manner, by analytically or numerically computing the inertia matrix and the potential energy gradient only.

Moreover, this method allows students, researchers and professionals, with no particular knowledge of mechanics, to easily model planar and spatial robots with practical links.

From this methodology follows also a simple and efficient algorithm for modeling flexible robots dividing the links into rigid sublinks interconnected by equivalent elastic joints and approximating and/or neglecting some terms related to the deformation variables.

In this chapter some of the main results stated in (Celentano, 2006), (Celentano & Iervolino, 2006), (Celentano & Iervolino, 2007) are reported.

In details, in Section II the new integration scheme for robots modeling, based on the knowledge of the inertia matrix and of the potential energy only, is reported (Celentano & Iervolino, 2006).
In Section III, for planar robots with revolute joints, theorems can be introduced and demonstrated to provide a sufficiently simple and efficient method of expressing both the inertia matrix and the gradient of the kinetic energy in a closed and elegant analytical form. Moreover, the efficiency of the proposed method is compared to the efficiency of the Articulated-Body method, considered one of the most efficient Newtonian methods in the literature (Celentano & Iervolino, 2006).
In Section IV, for spatial robots with generic shape links and connected, for the sake of brevity, with spherical joints, several theorems are formulated and demonstrated in a simple manner and some algorithms that allow efficiently computing, analytically the inertia matrix, analytically or numerically the gradient of the kinetic and of the gravitational energy are provided. Furthermore, also in this case a comparison of the proposed method in terms of efficiency with the Articulated-Body one is reported (Celentano & Iervolino, 2007).
In Section V some elements of flexible robots modeling, that allow obtaining, quite simply, accurate and efficient, from a computational point of view, finite-dimensional models, are provided. Moreover, a significant example of implementation of the proposed results is presented (Celentano, 2007).
Finally, in Section VI some conclusions and future developments are reported.

2. A new formulation of the Euler-Lagrange equation

In the following a new formulation of the dynamic model of a robot mechanism in a more efficient form (for its analytical and/or numerical study) is presented.
It is well known that the usual form of the Euler-Lagrange equation for a generic robot with n degrees of freedom, which takes on the form (De Wit et al., 1997)

$$\frac{d}{dt}\frac{\partial T}{\partial \dot{q}} - \frac{\partial T}{\partial q} = \gamma + \eta + u_a + u\,, \tag{1}$$

where: q is the vector of the Lagrangian coordinates; T is the kinetic energy, given by $T = \frac{1}{2}\dot{q}^T B(q)\dot{q}$, being B the robot inertia matrix; γ is the vector of the gravity forces, η is the vector of the elasticity forces and u_a is the non-conservative generalised forces (e.g. damping torques), which are usually function of q and $\dot{q}$ only, and u is the vector of the actuation generalised forces, is typically rewritten as

$$B(q)\ddot{q} + C(q,\dot{q})\dot{q} = \gamma + \eta + u_a + u\,, \tag{2}$$

in which an expression of matrix C is the following:

$$C(q,\dot{q}) = \sum_{i=1}^{n}\frac{\partial B}{\partial q_i}\dot{q}_i - \frac{1}{2}\begin{bmatrix} \dot{q}^T \dfrac{\partial B}{\partial q_1} \\ \vdots \\ \dot{q}^T \dfrac{\partial B}{\partial q_n} \end{bmatrix}. \tag{3}$$

By setting $B=\{b_{ij}\}, C=\{c_{ij}\}$, it is also

$$c_{ij}=\sum_{k=1}^{n}\left(\frac{\partial b_{ij}}{\partial q_k}-\frac{1}{2}\frac{\partial b_{ik}}{\partial q_i}\right)\dot{q}_k . \tag{4}$$

Alternatively, an equivalent matrix $C_c=\{c_{cij}\}$, i.e. such that $C_c\dot{q}=C\dot{q}$, that makes uses of the Christoffell's symbols (Sciavicco & Siciliano, 2000), is given by

$$c_{cij}=\sum_{k=1}^{n}\frac{1}{2}\left(\frac{\partial b_{ij}}{\partial q_k}+\frac{\partial b_{ik}}{\partial q_j}-\frac{\partial b_{jk}}{\partial q_i}\right)\dot{q}_k . \tag{5}$$

There are various methods to calculate both $B(q)$ and $C(q,\dot{q})$. The simplest one, from a conceptual point of view, based on analytical expressions, is extremely complex and onerous, even if symbolic manipulation languages are employed. Other methods do require a more in-depth knowledge of mechanics (De Wit et al., 1997).

The next theorem provides an innovative, efficient and simple method for modeling and simulating a robot.

Theorem 1. If the Euler-Lagrange equation is rearranged as follows:

$$\frac{d}{dt}(B\dot{q})=c+\gamma+\eta+u_a+u , \tag{6}$$

where c is the gradient of the kinetic energy with respect to q, namely

$$c=\frac{\partial T}{\partial q}, \tag{7}$$

then it can be efficiently integrated according to the innovative integration scheme of Fig. 1, where $\dot{q}_g=B\dot{q}$ and F is a suitable function that allows computing $\dot{q}$ and $\ddot{q}_g$ from u, q and $\dot{q}_g$.

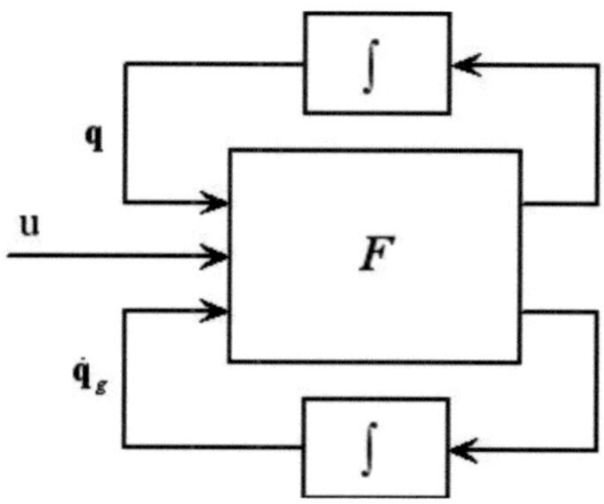

Fig. 1. Block diagram for the robot forward dynamics integration.

Proof. It is easy to verify that the algorithm that describe the function F of the block scheme of Fig. 1 is:

Step 1. Compute $B(q)$ by applying one of the classic methods proposed in the literature (see also Theorems 2 and 3 and (30) in Section 3).

Step 2. Compute $\dot{q}$ through the relationship $\dot{q} = B^{-1}\dot{q}_g$.

Step 3. Compute $c(q,\dot{q})$ and u_a.

Step 4. Compute $\frac{d}{dt}(B\dot{q}) = \ddot{q}_g = c + \gamma + \eta + u_a + u$.

Remark 1. The proposed method allows avoiding the computation of the first term on the right hand-side of (4) or of the first two terms on the right-hand side of (5). Such saving is significant because the computational burden relative to this term is not negligible with respect to the one required by the calculation of $B^{-1}\dot{q}_g$.

This clearly emerges from Fig. 2, where the percentages of saved flops vs. the number of flops required to compute $B^{-1}\dot{q}_g$ are evaluated (in MATLAB™ environment) with reference to the coefficients in (4), for a considerable number of cases of robots with random and anyhow realistic links parameters.

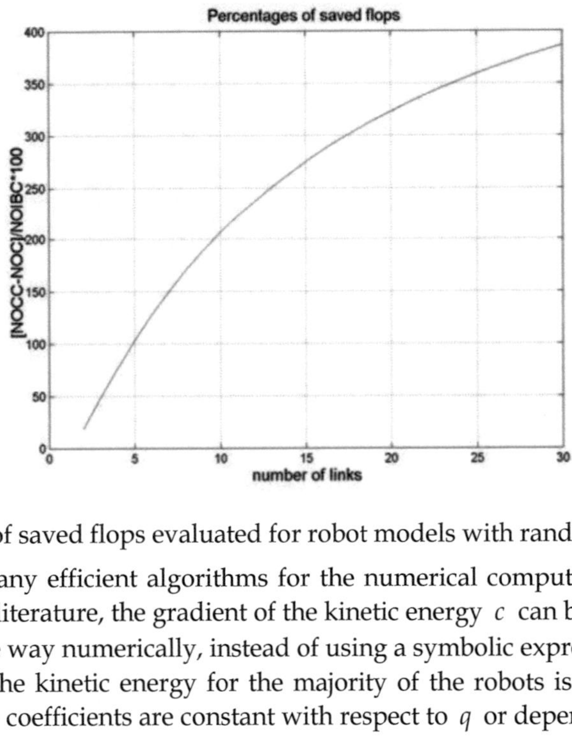

Fig. 2. Percentages of saved flops evaluated for robot models with random links parameters.

Remark 2. Since many efficient algorithms for the numerical computation of the matrix B are available in the literature, the gradient of the kinetic energy c can be computed in a very simple and accurate way numerically, instead of using a symbolic expression.

To this end, since the kinetic energy for the majority of the robots is a quadratic function respect to $\dot{q}$, whose coefficients are constant with respect to q or depend on q_i according to terms of the type $\sin(aq_i + \varphi)$, the following lemma is useful.

Lemma 1. The derivative of $\sin(aq_i)$ can be numerically computed by a two [three] points formula:

$$\frac{d}{dq_i}\sin(aq_i) = \frac{\sin[a(q_i+\Delta)] - \sin(aq_i)}{\Delta} \quad \left[\frac{d}{dq_i}\sin(aq_i) = \frac{\sin[a(q_i+\Delta)] - \sin[a(q_i-\Delta)]}{2\Delta}\right] \tag{8}$$

with error:

$$e_2 = -\frac{1}{2}a^2 \sin(a\chi)\Delta, \; |e_2| \le a^2 \frac{\Delta}{2}, \quad \chi \in (q_i, q_i + \Delta)$$
$$\left[e_3 = -\frac{1}{6}\Delta^2 a^3 \cos(a\chi), \; |e_3| \le a^3 \frac{\Delta^2}{6}, \; \chi \in (q_i - \Delta, q_i + \Delta) \right]. \tag{9}$$

Proof. See any numerical computation book.

In view of Lemma 1 it is possible to compute, with a prescribed maximum error, the gradient of the kinetic energy starting from the numerical knowledge of the inertia matrix B rather than using, as usually found in literature, complex analytical calculations of the analytical expression of B. In details, for practical precision purposes, a good value of $\partial T/\partial q$ can be obtained using a two [three] points formula with $\Delta = 10^{-3} \div 10^{-4}$ [with $\Delta = 10^{-2} \div 10^{-3}$] and evaluating n-1 [2(n-1)] times the inertia matrix B numerically.

3. Planar robot modeling

In the case of planar robots with revolute joints, theorems can be introduced and demonstrated to provide a sufficiently simple and efficient method of expressing both the inertia matrix and the gradient of the kinetic energy in a closed and elegant analytical form.

3.1 Hypotheses and notations

In the following it is considered the case of a generalised planar robot constituted by n links, each of them with parallel rotation axes C^-, C^+ and center of mass G belonging to the plane containing the two relative rotation axes (see Fig. 3). In Fig. 4 a planar robot with three links and a horizontal work plane is shown.

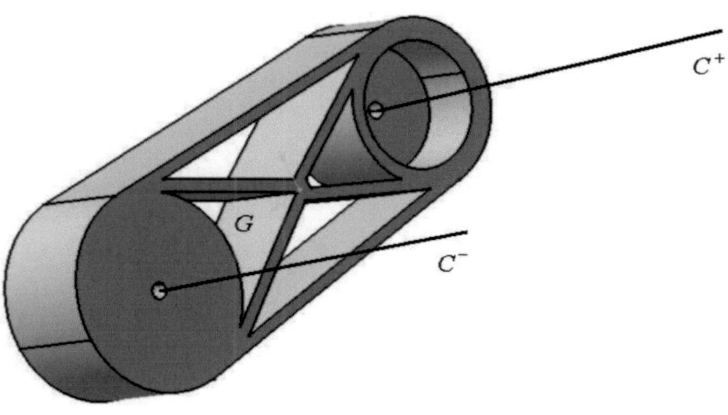

Fig. 3. The generic link of the considered generalised planar robot.

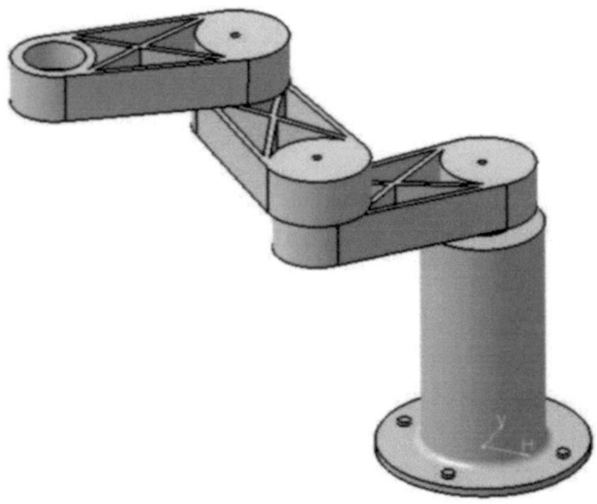

Fig. 4. The considered generalised planar robot with three links and horizontal work plane.

Referring to Figs. 5 and 6 the next notations are also employed:

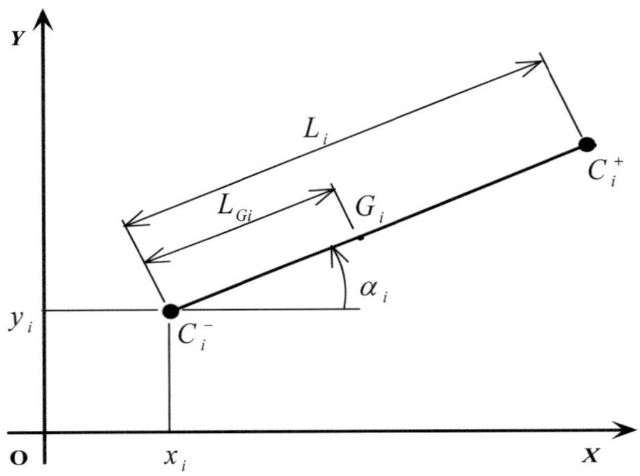

Fig. 5. Geometric characteristics of the *i*-th link.

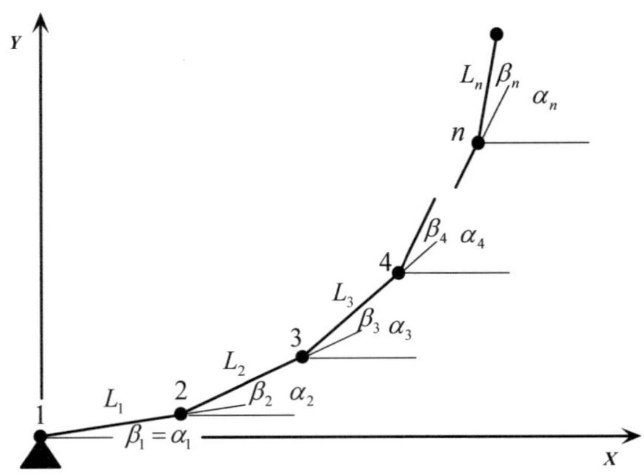

Fig. 6. Schematic representation of a planar robot with n links.

q_i = $[x_i\ y_i\ \alpha_i]^T$ = absolute coordinates of the i-th link,

I_i = inertia matrix of the i-th link in terms of the coordinates q_i,

M_i = total mass of the i-th link,

J_i, ρ_i = inertia moment and radius of the i-th link with respect to the rotation axis C_i^-,

N_i = static moment of the i-th link with respect to the plane containing C_i^- and orthogonal to the plane passing through C_i^- and C_i^+,

L_{Gi} = distance of the center of mass G_i of the i-th link from the axis C_i^-,

$\alpha_{1...i}$ = $[\alpha_1\ \alpha_2\ ...\ \alpha_i]^T$ = vector of the absolute angular coordinates of the chain constituted by the first i links,

$\beta_{1...i}$ = $[\beta_1\ \beta_2\ ...\ \beta_i]^T$ = vector of the relative angular coordinates of the chain constituted by the first i links,

A_i = inertia matrix of the i-th link in terms of the coordinates $\alpha_{1...i}$,

B_i = inertia matrix of the i-th link in terms of the coordinates $\beta_{1...i}$,

α = $[\alpha_1\ \alpha_2\ ...\ \alpha_n]^T$ = vector of the absolute angular coordinates of the robot,

β = $[\beta_1\ \beta_2\ ...\ \beta_n]^T$ = vector of the relative angular coordinates of the robot,

A = inertia matrix of the robot in terms of the coordinates α,

B = inertia matrix of the robot in terms of the coordinates β.

3.2 Main results

Consider a generic link of a planar robot, with revolute joints. The following theorem can be stated.

Theorem 2. The kinetic energy T_i of the link of a planar robot, whose rotation axes are parallel and center of mass belongs to the plane that contains the respective rotation axes (see Figs. 3 and 5) can be calculated by the relationship

$$T_i = \frac{1}{2}\dot{q}_i^T I_i \dot{q}_i, \tag{10}$$

where

$$I_i = \begin{bmatrix} M_i & 0 & -N_i \sin\alpha_i \\ 0 & M_i & N_i \cos\alpha \\ -N_i \sin\alpha_i & N_i \cos\alpha_i & J_i \end{bmatrix} = M_i \begin{bmatrix} 1 & 0 & -L_{Gi}\sin\alpha_i \\ 0 & 1 & L_{Gi}\cos\alpha_i \\ -L_{Gi}\sin\alpha_i & L_{Gi}\cos\alpha_i & \rho_i^2 \end{bmatrix}. \tag{11}$$

Proof. By omitting subscript i, the coordinates of a generic point P of link L are (see Fig. 7)

$$\begin{aligned} x_p &= x + \xi\cos\alpha - \eta\sin\alpha \\ y_p &= y + \xi\sin\alpha + \eta\cos\alpha, \end{aligned} \tag{12}$$

from which it is easy to prove that the square of the velocity of P is

$$\begin{aligned} V_p^2 &= \dot{x}_p^2 + \dot{y}_p^2 = \dot{x}^2 + \dot{y}^2 + \dot{\alpha}^2(\xi^2+\eta^2) - 2\dot{x}\dot{\alpha}(\xi\sin\alpha + \eta\cos\alpha) + 2\dot{y}\dot{\alpha}(\xi\cos\alpha - \eta\sin\alpha) \\ &= V_{C^-}^2 + \dot{\alpha}^2 d^2 - 2\dot{x}\dot{\alpha}(\xi\sin\alpha + \eta\cos\alpha) + 2\dot{y}\dot{\alpha}(\xi\cos\alpha - \eta\sin\alpha). \end{aligned} \tag{13}$$

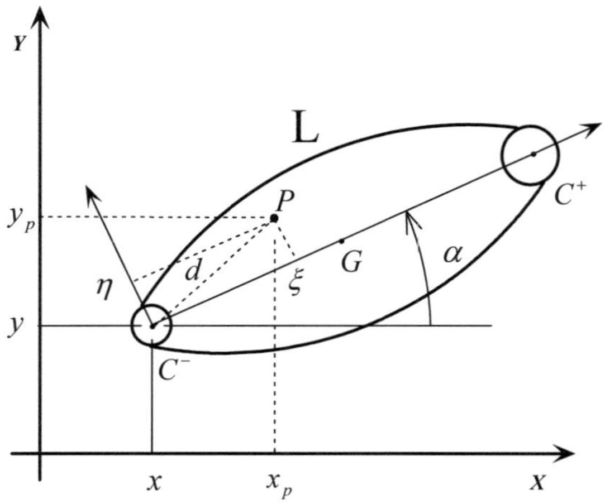

Fig. 7. Determination of the coordinates of a generic point *P* of the link L.

Since the kinetic energy of link L is $T = \frac{1}{2}\int_L V_p^2 dm$, and for the hypothesis made about the characteristics of the link, the proof of the theorem easily follows.

Consider a planar robot with *n* links (see Fig. 6). The following theorem holds:

Theorem 3. The kinetic energy of the *i*-th link of a generic planar robot can be calculated by the relationship

$$T_i = \frac{1}{2}\dot{\alpha}_{12...i}^T A_i \dot{\alpha}_{12...i}, \tag{14}$$

where the inertia matrix in terms of the angular coordinates $\alpha_{1...i}$, expressed by $A_i = \{a_{i,hk}\}$, can be calculated by using the formula:

$$A_i = R_i^T I_i R_i, \tag{15}$$

in which

$$R_i = \begin{bmatrix} -L_1 \sin\alpha_1 & -L_2 \sin\alpha_2 & . & -L_{i-1}\sin\alpha_{i-1} & 0 \\ L_1\cos\alpha_1 & L_2\cos\alpha_2 & . & L_{i-1}\cos\alpha_{i-1} & 0 \\ 0 & 0 & . & 0 & 1 \end{bmatrix} \tag{16}$$

or more directly by the formulae:

$$a_{i,hh} = \begin{cases} M_i L_h^2, & if \;\; h < i \\ J_i = M_i \rho_i^2, & if \;\; h = i, \end{cases} \tag{17a}$$

$$a_{i,hk} = \begin{cases} M_i L_h L_k \cos(\alpha_k - \alpha_h), & if \;\; h < k < i \\ M_i L_h L_{Gi} \cos(\alpha_i - \alpha_h), & if \;\; h < k = i. \end{cases} \tag{17b}$$

An alternative equivalent and more mnemonic expression for (17a)-(17b) is

1) $\forall\, h \le i$,

$$a_{i,hh} = M_i \tilde{L}_h^2,\; \tilde{L}_h = \begin{cases} L_h \;, \; if \;\; h < i \\ \rho_i \;, \; if \;\; h = i, \end{cases} \tag{18a}$$

2) $\forall\, h < k \le i$,

$$a_{i,hk} = M_i \tilde{L}_h \tilde{L}_k \cos(\alpha_k - \alpha_h),\; \tilde{L}_{h,k} = \begin{cases} L_{h,k}, \; if \;\; h,k < i \\ L_{Gi}, \; if \;\; h,k = i. \end{cases} \tag{18b}$$

Proof. For the generic *i*-th link, in the hypothesis that $x_1 = y_1 = 0$, it is

$$\begin{aligned} x_i &= L_1 \cos\alpha_1 + L_2 \cos\alpha_2 + \ldots + L_i \cos\alpha_i \\ y_i &= L_1 \sin\alpha_1 + L_2 \sin\alpha_2 + \ldots + L_i \sin\alpha_i \\ \alpha_i &= \alpha_i, \end{aligned} \tag{19}$$

from which

$$\begin{aligned} \dot{x}_i &= -\dot{\alpha}_1 L_1 \sin\alpha_1 - \dot{\alpha}_2 L_2 \sin\alpha_2 - \ldots - \dot{\alpha}_i L_i \sin\alpha_i \\ \dot{y}_i &= \dot{\alpha}_1 L_1 \cos\alpha_1 + \dot{\alpha}_2 L_2 \cos\alpha_2 + \ldots + \dot{\alpha}_i L_i \cos\alpha_i \\ \dot{\alpha}_i &= \dot{\alpha}_i, \end{aligned} \tag{20}$$

or

$$\dot{q}_i = R_i \dot{\alpha}_{1\ldots i}\,. \tag{21}$$

It follows that

$$T_i = \frac{1}{2}\dot{q}_i^T I_i \dot{q}_i = \frac{1}{2}\dot{\alpha}_{12\ldots i}^T R_i^T I_i R_i \dot{\alpha}_{1\ldots i} \tag{22}$$

and hence (15).
From (15) it is:
1) $\forall h \le k < i$

$$a_{i,hk} = \begin{bmatrix} -L_h \sin\alpha_h & L_h \cos\alpha_h & 0 \end{bmatrix} \cdot \begin{bmatrix} M_i & 0 & -N_i \sin\alpha_i \\ 0 & M_i & N_i \cos\alpha \\ -N_i \sin\alpha_i & N_i \cos\alpha_i & J_i \end{bmatrix} \cdot \begin{bmatrix} -L_k \sin\alpha_k \\ L_k \cos\alpha_k \\ 0 \end{bmatrix} = M_i L_h L_k \cos(\alpha_k - \alpha_h)\,; \tag{23}$$

2) $\forall h < k = i$

$$a_{i,hi} = \begin{bmatrix} -L_h \sin\alpha_h & L_h \cos\alpha_h & 0 \end{bmatrix} \cdot \begin{bmatrix} M_i & 0 & -N_i \sin\alpha_i \\ 0 & M_i & N_i \cos\alpha \\ -N_i \sin\alpha_i & N_i \cos\alpha_i & J_i \end{bmatrix} \cdot \begin{bmatrix} 0 \\ 0 \\ 1 \end{bmatrix} = L_h N_i \cos(\alpha_i - \alpha_h); \tag{24}$$

3) $h = k = i$

$$a_{i,ii} = \begin{bmatrix} 0 & 0 & 1 \end{bmatrix} \cdot \begin{bmatrix} M_i & 0 & -N_i \sin \alpha_i \\ 0 & M_i & N_i \cos \alpha \\ -N_i \sin \alpha_i & N_i \cos \alpha_i & J_i \end{bmatrix} \cdot \begin{bmatrix} 0 \\ 0 \\ 1 \end{bmatrix} = J_i \tag{25}$$

and hence (17a), (17b).
In view of Theorem 3, the kinetic energy of the robot is

$$T = T_1 + T_2 + \ldots + T_n = \frac{1}{2} \dot{\alpha}^T A \dot{\alpha} , \tag{26}$$

where

$$\alpha = \alpha_{1 \ldots n} = [\alpha_1 \; \alpha_2 \; \ldots \; \alpha_n]^T , \tag{27}$$

and the inertia matrix $A = A(\alpha)$ of the robot in terms of the angular coordinates α is obtained by assembling the matrices A_i as illustrated in Fig. 8 (namely, by summing to all the principal minors of A_n of order $i<n$ the respectie A_i's).

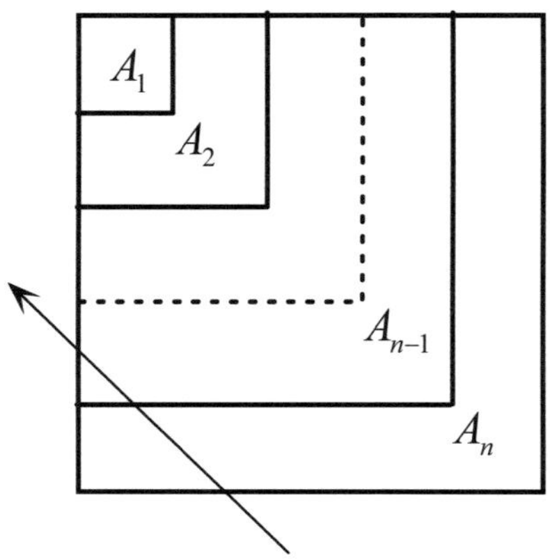

Fig. 8. Graphical representation of the algorithm that computes the robot inertia matrix.

In MATLAB-like instructions the algorithm to calculate the inertia matrix is:

```
A=An;
for i=n-1:-1:1
A(1:i,1:i)=A(1:i,1:i)+Ai;
end.
```

Moreover, since $\alpha = U\beta$, where

$$U = \begin{bmatrix} 1 & 0 & . & 0 \\ 1 & 1 & . & 0 \\ . & . & . & . \\ 1 & 1 & 1 & 1 \end{bmatrix} , \tag{28}$$

the kinetic energy of the robot can be calculated by using the relationship alternatively

$$T = \frac{1}{2}\dot{\beta}^T B \dot{\beta}, \tag{29}$$

where the inertia matrix $B = B(\beta)$ of the robot in terms of the angular coordinates β is obtained by

$$B = U^T A(\alpha) U = U^T A(U^{-1}(\beta)) U . \tag{30}$$

Note that the computation of the inertia matrix is performed by jointly using the absolute and relative coordinates. This allows simplifying, in a natural manner, the algebraic expression of the analytical model.

Clearly, if for a given β and hence for a given $\alpha = U\beta$ the interest is only about the numerical value of B, it is possible to numerically compute the matrix A preliminarily (from α by using Theorem 3 and the algorithm illustrated in Fig. 7) and then the matrix B through the relationship $B=U^TAU$ or through the following algorithm described in MATLAB-like instructions:

```
for i=n-1:-1:1
    A(:,i)=A(:,i)+A(:,i+1);
end
for i=n-1:-1:1
    A(1:i,i+1)=A(i+1,1:i)';
    A(i,1:i)=A(i,1:i)+A(i+1,1:i);
end
B=A.
```

Remark 3. It is important to note that, although by virtue of Theorem 3 the analytical expression of A_i is relatively simple, the analytical expression of A is quite complex and, as a result, the expression of B is extremely complex (e.g. the entry $B(1,1)$ of B is the sum of all the elements of all the matrices A_i !).

Once the inertia matrix B is obtained, the dynamic model of the robot can be derived by the Euler-Lagrange equation in the usual form (1) or in the alternative form (6). In the case of a planar robot, with link characteristics as required by Theorem 2, the efficiency of the method illustrated in Theorem 1 can be further improved by using the following result.

Theorem 4. The gradient of the kinetic energy of the *i*-th link in terms of $\alpha_{12\ldots i}$ $\left[\beta_{12\ldots i}\right]$ can be calculated by the relationship

$$\frac{\partial T_i}{\partial \beta_{12\ldots i}} = c_i = -\begin{bmatrix} 0 \\ M_i \sum\limits_{h<k:\text{var}\,\beta_2} \tilde{L}_h \dot{\alpha}_h \tilde{L}_k \dot{\alpha}_k \sin(\alpha_k - \alpha_h) \\ M_i \sum\limits_{h<k:\text{var}\,\beta_3} \tilde{L}_h \dot{\alpha}_h \tilde{L}_k \dot{\alpha}_k \sin(\alpha_k - \alpha_h) \\ \vdots \\ M_i \sum\limits_{h<k:\text{var}\,\beta_i} \tilde{L}_h \dot{\alpha}_h \tilde{L}_k \dot{\alpha}_k \sin(\alpha_k - \alpha_h) \end{bmatrix},$$

$$\frac{\partial T_i}{\partial \beta_{12\ldots i}} = c_i = -\begin{bmatrix} 0 \\ M_i \sum_{h<k:\mathrm{var}\,\beta_2} \tilde{L}_h \sum_{p=1}^{h} \dot{\beta}_p \tilde{L}_k \sum_{q=1}^{k} \dot{\beta}_q \sin(\sum_{r=h+1}^{k} \beta_r) \\ M_i \sum_{h<k:\mathrm{var}\,\beta_3} \tilde{L}_h \sum_{p=1}^{h} \dot{\beta}_p \tilde{L}_k \sum_{q=1}^{k} \dot{\beta}_q \sin(\sum_{r=h+1}^{k} \beta_r) \\ \vdots \\ M_i \sum_{h<k:\mathrm{var}\,\beta_i} \tilde{L}_h \sum_{p=1}^{h} \dot{\beta}_p \tilde{L}_k \sum_{q=1}^{k} \dot{\beta}_q \sin(\sum_{r=h+1}^{k} \beta_r) \end{bmatrix}, \tag{31a}$$

where

$$\tilde{L}_m = \begin{cases} L_m, & if\ m < i \\ L_{Gi}, & if\ m = i \end{cases}, \quad m = \{h, k\}, \tag{31b}$$

and the notation $h < k : \mathrm{var}\,\beta_l$, $l = 2,\ldots,i$, indicates the set of the pairs h, k, with $h < k$, such that the angle $\alpha_{hk} = \alpha_k - \alpha_h = \beta_{h+1} + \beta_{h+2} + \ldots + \beta_k$ between the links h and k varies with β_l.

Proof. In view of Theorem 3, the kinetic energy of the generic i-th link is

$$\begin{aligned} T_i &= \frac{1}{2} M_i \sum_{h=1,\ldots,i-1} L_h^2 \dot{\alpha}_h^2 + \frac{1}{2} M_i \dot{\alpha}_i^2 + M_i \sum_{\substack{h=1,\ldots,i-1 \\ k=h+1,\ldots,i}} \tilde{L}_h \tilde{L}_k \dot{\alpha}_h \dot{\alpha}_k \cos(\alpha_k - \alpha_h) \\ &= T_c + M_i \sum_{\substack{h=1,\ldots,i-1 \\ k=h+1,\ldots,i}} \tilde{L}_h \tilde{L}_k \dot{\alpha}_h \dot{\alpha}_k \cos(\alpha_k - \alpha_h), \end{aligned} \tag{32}$$

where T_c is the portion of kinetic energy that is independent of $\alpha_{12\ldots i}$.

From (32) the expression (31a) of the gradient of T_i in terms of $\alpha_{12\ldots i}$ [$\beta_{12\ldots i}$] easily follow.

The vector c can be simply obtained by suitably assembling the various vectors c_i (i.e. by progressively summing to the first i components of c_n, $i<n$, the respective c_i's).

In MATLAB-like instructions:

```
c=cn;
for i=n-1:-1:2
c(1:i)=c(1:i)+ci;
end.
```

Finally, it is important to note that if the work plane of the robot is vertical, the gravitational torques can be calculated by using the following result.

Theorem 5. If the work plane of the robot is vertical, the weight of the i-th link originates a torque on the k-th joint, $k \le i$:

$$\gamma_k = M_i g \sum_{m=k}^{i} \tilde{L}_m \cos \alpha_m, \tag{33}$$

where g is the gravitational acceleration and the lengths $\tilde{L}_m$ are given by (31b).

Proof. The proof easily follows by considering Fig. 6.
Remark 4. The proposed method efficiency has been explicitly compared to the Articulated Body approach efficiency in terms of number of flops (in Matlab™ environment), for executing the same elementary integration step by using the absolute Lagrangian coordinates (see Fig. 9). From this figure it results that, for industrial robots with a limited number of links, the proposed method is more efficient.

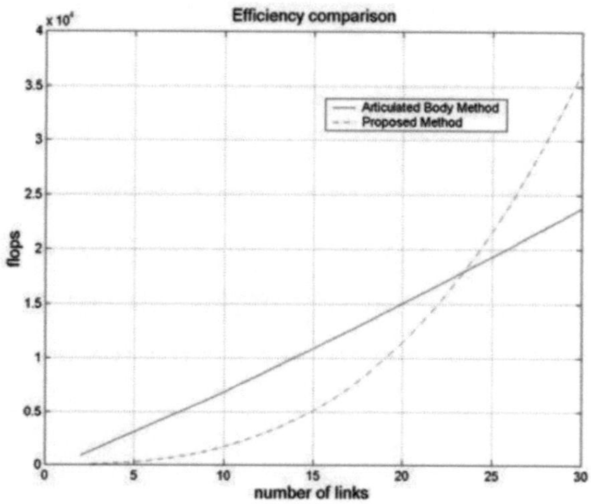

Fig. 9. Efficiency comparison between the Articulated Body method and the proposed method.

Remark 5. The above-derived analytical expressions, in explicit form, of B, c and γ are useful for speeding up the simulation, for comparing them to the proposed numerical approach and for finally evaluating which terms can be simplified or neglected in the case of robots with many and/or flexible links. Thus, for instance, for flexible link robots models, obtained via discretization of the links, the terms relative to the deformation angles can be simplified by substituting the *sine* function with the respective argument or even be completely neglected, considering the terms relative to the motion only.

4. Spatial robot modeling

For spatial robots with generic shape links and connected, for the sake of brevity, with spherical joints, several theorems are formulated and demonstrated in a simple manner and some algorithms that allow computing in an efficient way analytically or numerically both the inertia matrix and the gradient of the potential energy are provided.

4.1 Hypotheses and notations

In the following, for brevity, only spatial robots constituted by n links of generic shape, connected by spherical joints are considered.
Moreover, the following notations will be used (see Fig. 10):

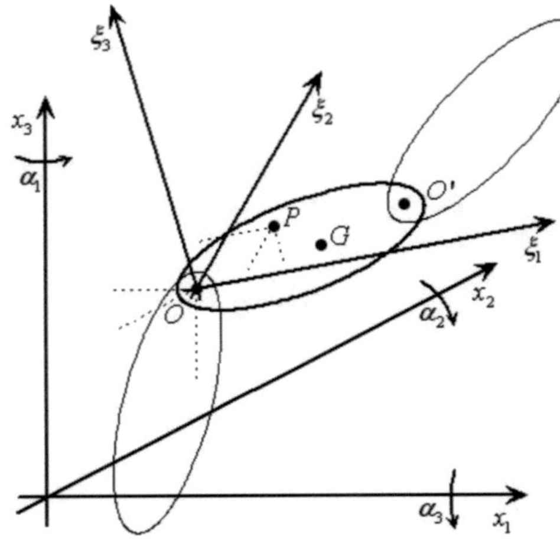

Fig. 10. Coordinates of the generic point P of a link with respect to the body frame and to the inertial frame.

$\mathbf{q}_i = [\mathbf{x}_{Oi}^T \;\; \boldsymbol{\alpha}_i^T\,]^T = [x_{O1i} \;\; x_{O2i} \;\; x_{O3i} \;\; \alpha_{1i} \;\; \alpha_{2i} \;\; \alpha_{3i}]^T$ = *"absolute coordinates" of the i-th link,*

$I_i = \{I_{ihk}\}$ = *inertia matrix of the i-th link with respect to the axes* ξ_1, ξ_2, ξ_3,

$\boldsymbol{\xi}_{Gi} = [\xi_{G1i} \;\; \xi_{G2i} \;\; \xi_{G3i}]^T$ = *coordinates of the center of mass* G_i *in the body frame,*

$\boldsymbol{\xi}_{O'i} = [\xi_{O'1i} \;\; \xi_{O'2i} \;\; \xi_{O'3i}]^T$ = *coordinates of the rotation center* O'_i *in the body frame,*

M_i = *total mass of the i-th link,*

$\boldsymbol{\alpha}_{1\ldots i} = [\boldsymbol{\alpha}_1^T \;\; \boldsymbol{\alpha}_2^T \;\; \ldots \;\; \boldsymbol{\alpha}_i^T]^T$ = *"angular absolute coordinates" of the chain constituted by the first i links,*

$\Re_i(\boldsymbol{\alpha}_i)$ = *rotation matrix of the i-th link,*

$$R_{ih} = \frac{\partial \Re_i(\boldsymbol{\alpha}_i)}{\partial \alpha_{ih}},$$

A_i = *inertia matrix of the i-th link with respect to the coordinates* $\boldsymbol{\alpha}_{1\ldots i}$,

$\boldsymbol{\alpha} = \boldsymbol{\alpha}_{1\ldots n}$ = *"absolute angular coordinates" of the robot,*

A = *inertia matrix of the robot with respect to the coordinates* $\boldsymbol{\alpha}$,

I = *identity matrix of order 3,*

$s_{hi} = \sin(\alpha_{hi})$,

$c_{hi} = \cos(\alpha_{hi})$.

4.2 Main results

Let us consider a generic link of a generic shape of a spatial robot with spherical joints.
The following theorems and algorithms for the computation of the kinetic energy T_i of the *i*-th link first as a function of the absolute coordinates $\mathbf{q}_i$ of the *i*-th link and then as a function of the absolute angular coordinates $\boldsymbol{\alpha}_{1\ldots i}$ of the chain constituted by the first i links are provided.

Theorem 6. The kinetic energy of the *i*-th link may be calculated by means of the relationship

$$T_i = \frac{1}{2}\dot{\mathbf{q}}_i^T \Im_i \dot{\mathbf{q}}_i \,, \tag{34}$$

where

$$\Im_i = \begin{bmatrix} M_i I & M_i \sum_h R_{hi}\xi_{Ghi} \\ M_i \sum_h R_{hi}^T \xi_{Ghi} & \sum_{h,k} R_{hi}^T R_{ki} I_{hki} \end{bmatrix}. \tag{35}$$

Proof. By omitting subscript i, the coordinates of the generic point P of the link in the fixed frame (see Fig. 10) are given by

$$\mathbf{x}_P = \mathbf{x}_O + \Re(\boldsymbol{\alpha})\boldsymbol{\xi}_P \,, \tag{36}$$

where $\Re$ is the rotation matrix of the body frame with respect to the fixed frame and $\boldsymbol{\xi}_P$ is the vector of the coordinates of the generic point P of the link in the body frame.
From (36) it follows

$$\dot{\mathbf{x}}_P = \dot{\mathbf{x}}_O + \sum_h R_h \xi_{Ph} \dot{\boldsymbol{\alpha}} \,, \tag{37}$$

where

$$R_h = \frac{\partial \Re}{\partial \alpha_h}, h = 1, 2, 3 \,. \tag{38}$$

From (37) it is

$$V^2 = \dot{\mathbf{x}}_P^T \dot{\mathbf{x}}_P = \dot{\mathbf{x}}_0^T \dot{\mathbf{x}}_0 + \dot{\boldsymbol{\alpha}}^T \sum_{h,k} R_h^T R_k \xi_{Ph} \xi_{Pk} \dot{\boldsymbol{\alpha}} + 2\dot{\mathbf{x}}_0^T \sum_h R_h \xi_{Ph} \dot{\boldsymbol{\alpha}} \,, \tag{39}$$

from which

$$\begin{aligned} T &= \frac{1}{2}\int V^2 dm = \\ &= \frac{1}{2} M \dot{\mathbf{x}}_0^T \dot{\mathbf{x}}_0 + \frac{1}{2}\dot{\boldsymbol{\alpha}}^T \sum_{h,k} R_h^T R_k I_{hk} \dot{\boldsymbol{\alpha}} + M \dot{\mathbf{x}}_0^T \sum_h R_h \xi_{Gh} \dot{\boldsymbol{\alpha}} = \\ &= \frac{1}{2}\begin{pmatrix} \dot{\mathbf{x}}_0^{\mathrm{T}} & \dot{\boldsymbol{\alpha}}^{\mathrm{T}} \end{pmatrix} \begin{bmatrix} MI & M\sum_h R_h \xi_{Gh} \\ M\sum_h R_h^T \xi_{Gh} & \sum_{h,k} R_h^T R_k I_{hk} \end{bmatrix} \begin{pmatrix} \dot{\mathbf{x}}_0 \\ \dot{\boldsymbol{\alpha}} \end{pmatrix} \end{aligned} \tag{40}$$

and hence the proof.
Remark 6. The vector of the coordinates of the center of mass $\boldsymbol{\xi}_{G_i}$ and the inertia matrix $\{I_{hk}\}$ of the i-th link, in the case of a complex structure, may be easily evaluated by making use of software packages, such as CATIA™.
Theorem 7. If the Euler angles of the i-th link $\boldsymbol{\alpha}_i = [\alpha_{1i} \quad \alpha_{2i} \quad \alpha_{3i}]^T$ are the ZYX angles, also called RPY angles (*Roll-Pitch-Yaw*), (see Fig. 10), by omitting subscript i, the matrices R_h result:

$$R_1 = \begin{bmatrix} -s_1c_2 & -s_1s_2s_3 - c_1c_3 & -s_1s_2c_3 + c_1s_3 \\ c_1c_2 & c_1s_2s_3 - s_1c_3 & c_1s_2c_3 + s_1s_3 \\ 0 & 0 & 0 \end{bmatrix} \tag{41}$$

$$R_2 = \begin{bmatrix} -c_1s_2 & c_1c_2s_3 & c_1c_2c_3 \\ -s_1s_2 & s_1c_2s_3 & s_1c_2c_3 \\ -c_2 & -s_2s_3 & -s_2c_3 \end{bmatrix} \tag{42}$$

$$R_3 = \begin{bmatrix} 0 & c_1s_2c_3 + s_1s_3 & -c_1s_2s_3 + s_1c_3 \\ 0 & s_1s_2c_3 - c_1s_3 & -s_1s_2s_3 - c_1c_3 \\ 0 & c_2c_3 & -c_2s_3 \end{bmatrix}. \tag{43}$$

Proof. The rotation matrix $\Re_i(\boldsymbol{\alpha}_i)$ of the *i*-th link, by omitting subscript *i*, results (43)

$$\Re(\boldsymbol{\alpha}) = \begin{bmatrix} c_1c_2 & c_1s_2s_3 - s_1c_3 & c_1s_2c_3 + s_1s_3 \\ s_1c_2 & s_1s_2s_3 + c_1c_3 & s_1s_2c_3 - c_1s_3 \\ -s_2 & c_2s_3 & c_2c_3 \end{bmatrix}, \tag{44}$$

from which, for (38), the proof.

The computation of the matrices $\Im_i$ may be sped up by the following algorithm, where subscript *i* has been omitted.

Algorithm 1.

Step 1. Compute

$$s_1, s_2, s_3; \quad c_1, c_2, c_3. \tag{45}$$

Step 2. Compute

$$\begin{array}{ll} s_1s_2, s_1s_3, s_2s_3; & c_1c_2, c_1c_3, c_2c_3; \\ s_1c_2, s_1c_3, s_2c_3; & c_1s_2, c_1s_3, c_2s_3; \\ (s_1s_2)s_3, (s_1s_2)c_3; & (s_1c_2)s_3, (s_1c_2)c_3; \\ (c_1c_2)s_3, (c_1c_2)c_3; & (c_1s_2)s_3, (c_1s_2)c_3. \end{array} \tag{46}$$

*Step 3.*Compute

$$R_1^T R_1, R_1^T R_2, R_1^T R_3; \quad R_2^T R_2, R_2^T R_3; \quad R_3^T R_3. \tag{47}$$

If the axis ξ_{1i} of the body frame is chosen such as to contain the center of gravity G_i and it results principal of inertia then, by choosing the other two axes parallel to the other inertia principal axes, the computation of the matrix $\Im_i$ may be further sped up, as it results from the following theorem.

Theorem 8. If the body reference axes of the *i*-th link are parallel to the inertia principal axes and the center of gravity G_i belong to the axis ξ_{1i}, the matrix $\Im_i$ results

$$\Im_i = \begin{bmatrix} M_i I & M_i R_{1i}\xi_{G1i} \\ M_i R_{1i}^T \xi_{G1i} & \sum_h R_{hi}^T R_{hi} I_{hhi} \end{bmatrix}. \tag{48}$$

Proof. The proof easily follows from (35) and from

$$\xi_{G2i} = 0, i = 2,3; \quad I_{hki} = 0, h = 1,2, k = h+1,3 . \tag{49}$$

Let us consider now a robot with n links (see Fig. 11). The following theorems and algorithms for the computation of the inertia matrix A of the whole robot, as a function of the absolute angular coordinates $\boldsymbol{\alpha}$ of the robot, hold.

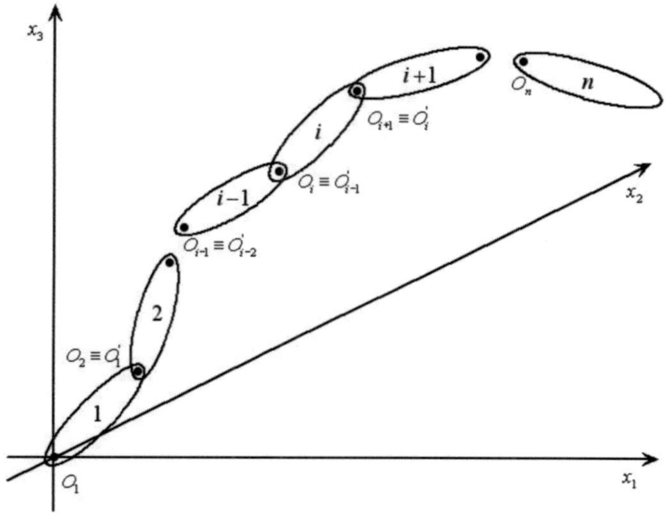

Fig. 11. Schematic representation of a spatial robot with n links.

Theorem 9. The kinetic energy of the i-th link of a generic spatial robot may be computed by means of the relationship

$$T_i = \frac{1}{2}\dot{\boldsymbol{\alpha}}_{1...i}^T A_i \dot{\boldsymbol{\alpha}}_{1...i}, \tag{50}$$

where

$$A_i = \begin{cases} \Im_{221}, \text{ if } i=1 \\ \begin{bmatrix} M_i V_{1...i-1}{}^T V_{1...i-1} & V_{1...i-1}{}^T \Im_{12i} \\ \Im_{12i}^T V_{1...i-1} & \Im_{22i} \end{bmatrix}, \text{ if } i = 2,3,...,n \end{cases} \tag{51}$$

in which:

$$\Im_{12i} = M_i \sum_h R_{hi}\xi_{Ghi}, \quad \Im_{22i} = \sum_{h,k} R_{hi}^T R_{ki} I_{hki}$$
$$V_{1...i-1} = [V_1 \quad V_2 \quad \cdots \quad V_{i-1}], \; V_j = \sum_h R_{hj}\xi_{O'hj}, \; j = 1,2,...,i-1 . \tag{52}$$

Proof. From the following relationships (see Fig. 11 and (37))

$$\dot{\mathbf{x}}_{Oi} = \dot{\mathbf{x}}_{O'i-1} = \dot{\mathbf{x}}_{Oi-1} + \sum_h R_{hi-1}\xi_{O'hi-1}\dot{\boldsymbol{\alpha}}_{i-1}, \quad i = 2,\ldots,n, \quad \dot{\mathbf{x}}_{O1} = 0, \tag{53}$$

it is

$$\dot{\mathbf{x}}_{Oi} = \begin{bmatrix} V_1 & V_2 & \cdots & V_{i-1} \end{bmatrix} \begin{bmatrix} \dot{\boldsymbol{\alpha}}_1 \\ \dot{\boldsymbol{\alpha}}_2 \\ \vdots \\ \dot{\boldsymbol{\alpha}}_{i-1} \end{bmatrix} = V_{1\ldots i-1}\dot{\boldsymbol{\alpha}}_{1\ldots i-1}, \tag{54}$$

from which

$$\dot{\mathbf{q}}_i = \begin{bmatrix} \dot{\mathbf{x}}_{Oi} \\ \dot{\boldsymbol{\alpha}}_i \end{bmatrix} = \begin{bmatrix} V_{1\ldots i-1}\dot{\boldsymbol{\alpha}}_{1\ldots i-1} \\ \dot{\boldsymbol{\alpha}}_i \end{bmatrix} = \begin{bmatrix} V_{1\ldots i-1} & 0 \\ 0 & I \end{bmatrix} \dot{\boldsymbol{\alpha}}_{1\ldots i}. \tag{55}$$

By substituting (55) in (34), it is

$$\begin{aligned} T_i &= \frac{1}{2}\dot{\mathbf{q}}_i^T \Im_i \dot{\mathbf{q}}_i = \\ &= \frac{1}{2}\dot{\boldsymbol{\alpha}}_{1\ldots i}^T \begin{bmatrix} V_{1\ldots i-1}{}^T & 0 \\ 0 & I \end{bmatrix} \begin{bmatrix} M_i I & \Im_{12i} \\ \Im_{12i}^T & \Im_{22i} \end{bmatrix} \begin{bmatrix} V_{1\ldots i-1} & 0 \\ 0 & I \end{bmatrix} \dot{\boldsymbol{\alpha}}_{1\ldots i} = \\ &= \frac{1}{2}\dot{\boldsymbol{\alpha}}_{1\ldots i}^T \begin{bmatrix} M_i V_{1\ldots i-1}{}^T V_{1\ldots i-1} & V_{1\ldots i-1}{}^T \Im_{12i} \\ \Im_{12i}^T V_{1\ldots i-1} & \Im_{22i} \end{bmatrix} \dot{\boldsymbol{\alpha}}_{1\ldots i} \end{aligned} \tag{56}$$

from which the proof follows.
The next theorem, similar to Theorem 8, is useful to simplify the computation of the matrices A_i.

Theorem 10. If the axes of the body frame of link *j*, $j = 1,2,\ldots,i-1$, are parallel to the inertia principal axes and the centers of gravity G_j and the rotation centers O_j' belong to the axis ξ_{1j}, matrices (52) may be more easily calculated by the relations:

$$\Im_{12i} = M_i R_{1i}\xi_{G1i}, \quad \Im_{22i} = \sum_h R_{hi}^T R_{hi} I_{hhi}, \tag{57}$$

$$V_{1\ldots i-1} = \begin{bmatrix} V_1 & V_2 & \cdots & V_{i-1} \end{bmatrix}, \; V_j = R_{1j}\xi_{O'1j}, \; j = 1,2,\ldots,i-1. \tag{58}$$

Proof. The proof easily follows from Theorem 8 and from the fact that

$$\xi_{O'hj} = 0, \quad h = 2,3, \; j = 1,2,\ldots,i-1. \tag{59}$$

The following theorems may be effectively used to compute the gradient of the gravitational potential energy.

Theorem 11. The gradient of the gravitational potential energy of the *i*-th link U_i with respect to the angular coordinates $\boldsymbol{\alpha}_{1\ldots i}$ may be calculated by the formula

$$\frac{\partial U_i}{\partial \boldsymbol{\alpha}_{1\ldots i}} = \boldsymbol{\gamma}_i = \\ -M_i[R_{11}\xi_{0_1'} \ R_{21}\xi_{0_1'} \ R_{31}\xi_{0_1'} \ R_{12}\xi_{0_2'} \ R_{22}\xi_{0_2'} \ R_{32}\xi_{0_2'} \cdots \\ \cdots R_{1i}\xi_{G_i} \ R_{2i}\xi_{G_i} \ R_{3i}\xi_{G_i}]^T \mathbf{g}, \tag{60}$$

where $\mathbf{g}$ is the gravity acceleration vector in the inertial frame.

Proof. It is easy to verify that the gravitational potential energy of the generic i-th link results

$$U_i = -M_i \mathbf{g}^T (\Re_1(\boldsymbol{\alpha}_1)\xi_{O_1'} + \Re_2(\boldsymbol{\alpha}_2)\xi_{O_2'} + \cdots + \Re_i(\boldsymbol{\alpha}_i)\xi_{G_i}). \tag{61}$$

Relation (60) easily follows from (61).

The next theorem is useful to simplify the computation of $\frac{\partial U_i}{\partial \boldsymbol{\alpha}_{1\ldots i}}$.

Theorem 12. If the x_3-axis of the inertial frame is vertical and upwards oriented, the rotation centers O_j' of the j-th links, $j = 1,2,\ldots,i-1$, belong to the axes ξ_{1j} of the body frames, the center of gravity G_i of the i-th link belongs to the axis ξ_{1i} and the Euler angles of the j-th links, $j = 1,2,\ldots,i$, are the ZYX angles, the gradient $\frac{\partial U_i}{\partial \boldsymbol{\alpha}_{1\ldots i}}$ may be calculated much more easily by the relationship

$$\frac{\partial U_i}{\partial \boldsymbol{\alpha}_{1\ldots i}} = \boldsymbol{\gamma}_i = \\ = M_i g \begin{bmatrix} 0 & c_{21}\xi_{O_1'1} & 0 & 0 & c_{22}\xi_{O_2'1} & 0 & \cdots & 0 & c_{2i}\xi_{G_i1} & 0 \end{bmatrix}^T. \tag{62}$$

Proof. Since the x_3-axis is vertical and upwards oriented it is $\mathbf{g} = \begin{bmatrix} 0 & 0 & -g \end{bmatrix}^T$, where g is the gravity acceleration. Moreover, since $O_j' \in \xi_{1j}$, $j = 1,2,\ldots,i-1$, $G_i \in \xi_{1i}$:

$$\xi_{O_i'} = \begin{bmatrix} \xi_{O_i'1} & 0 & 0 \end{bmatrix}^T, \ \xi_{G_i} = \begin{bmatrix} \xi_{G_i1} & 0 & 0 \end{bmatrix}^T, i = 1\ldots n. \tag{63}$$

The proof easily follows from (41)-(43), (60), (63).

4.3 Application of the main results

On the base of Theorem 9 the kinetic energy of the whole robot is

$$T = T_1 + T_2 + \ldots + T_n = \frac{1}{2}\dot{\boldsymbol{\alpha}}^T A \dot{\boldsymbol{\alpha}}, \tag{64}$$

where the *inertia matrix* $A = A(\boldsymbol{\alpha})$ is obtained by assembling the matrices A_i according to the following efficient algorithm written in Matlab-like language:

```
A=An;
for i=n-1:-1:1
A(1:3*i,1:3*i)=A(1:3*i,1:3*i)+Ai;
end.
```

Once the vectors $\gamma_i, i=1,2,...,n,$ have been computed by the (60) or the (62), the gradient of the gravity energy γ is obtained by assembling the γ_i according to the following efficient algorithm written in Matlab-like language:

```
γ = γ n;
for i=n-1:-1:1
γ (1:i)= γ (1:i)+ γ i;
end.
```

Finally, by using the efficient integration scheme shown in Fig. 1 (Celentano & Iervolino, 2006), it is possible to get the dynamic model of the robot in a simple way.

4.4 Comparison in terms of efficiency with the articulated-body method

The efficiency of the method of modeling and simulation proposed for spatial robots has been explicitly compared to the efficiency of a Newtonian method of order N considered one of the most efficient methods in the literature, i.e. the Articulated-Body Method (Featherstone, 1987), (Featherstone & Orin, 2000).
More in details, such comparison has been executed in terms of number of flops (in MATLAB™ environment), for the execution of the same integration step (see Table 1).

Number of links	Flops of the proposed method	Flops of the Articulated-Body method
1	362	1269
2	2459	7168
3	8400	13758
4	21451	20804
5	45868	28252

Table 1. Efficiency comparison between the proposed method and the Articulated-Body method.

From Table 1 it results that for practical spatial robots (which of course have a limited number of links), the proposed method is more efficient when $n < 4$, although spatial robots with three degrees of freedom spherical joints have been considered. Moreover, it is important to note that the great easiness of the proposed method with respect to the Articulated-Body one is an important index of its efficiency.
However, the authors have the plan to continue and to improve this comparison.

5. Elements of flexible robots modeling

5.1 Methodology

The results stated in the previous sections allow obtaining, quite simply, accurate and efficient, from a computational point of view, finite-dimensional models.
These models, for rectilinear links, can be obtained approximating the *i*-th link as follows:

1. in order to compute the kinetic energy and, therefore, the inertia matrix and the gradient of the kinetic energy, with ν_i+1 rigid sublinks with lengths $L_{1i},...,L_{\nu_i+1,i}$, interconnected by relative angles $\beta_{1i},...,\beta_{\nu_i i}$ (see Fig. 12);
2. in order to compute the elastic energy, with ν_i flexible sublinks joined and deformable such that their axes make a suitable spline tangent to the axes of the intermediate rigid sublinks in the extreme points of the link and to the intermediate rigid sublinks in suitable interior points (see Fig. 12).

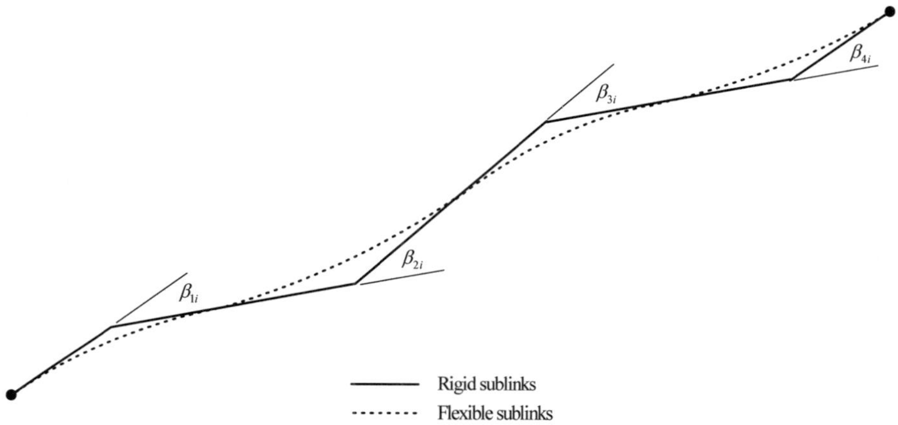

Fig. 12. Approximation of a flexible link with $\nu_i+1=5$ rigid sublinks and with $\nu_i=4$ flexible sublinks congruent to each other at the end.

In this way, neglecting, about the computation of the kinetic energy, the deformation angles respect to the angles of motion, it is easy to verify, from the results of Sections 2 and 3, that the inertia matrix can be computed as follows:

$$\begin{aligned} B &= B(\beta_2, ..., \beta_n) = \\ &= B_1 + B_2\cos\beta_2 + ... + B_n\cos\beta_n + B_{23}\cos(\beta_2+\beta_3) + B_{24}\cos(\beta_2+\beta_3+\beta_4) + ... + B_{n-1,n}\cos(\beta_{n-1}+\beta_n), \end{aligned} \tag{65}$$

where β_i is the angle of motion between the $(i-1)$-th link and the i-th link, $i=2,...,n$ (see Fig. 13).

From (65) it is easy to compute also the gradient of the kinetic energy respect to $\beta=\lfloor\beta_1\ \beta_{11}...\beta_{\nu_1 1}\ \beta_2\ \beta_{12}...\beta_{\nu_2 2}\ \beta_n\ \beta_{1n}...\beta_{\nu_n n}\rfloor^T$ using the following relation

$$c=\frac{1}{2}\begin{bmatrix}0_{1,\nu_1+1} & \dot\beta^T\frac{\partial B}{\partial\beta_2}\dot\beta & ... & 0_{1,\nu_{n-1}} & \dot\beta^T\frac{\partial B}{\partial\beta_n}\dot\beta & 0_{1,\nu_n}\end{bmatrix}^T. \tag{66}$$

There are different ways of approximating a flexible link using a chain of rigid sublinks and flexible sublinks congruent to each other at the end (Celentano, 2007).

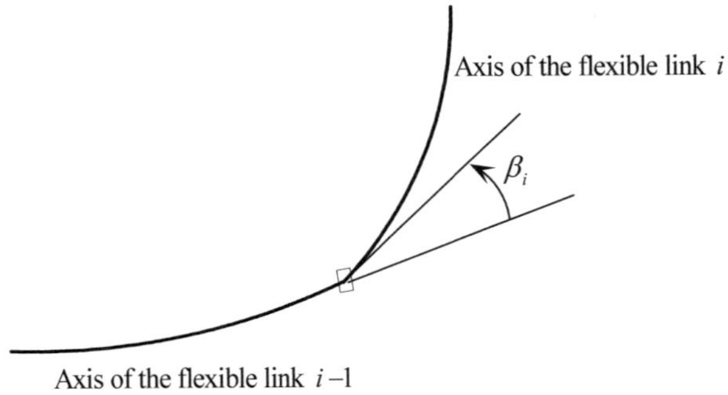

Fig. 13. Angle of motion between two flexible consecutive links.

In the hypothesis that the stiffness of the i-th link is uniform, a very efficient way for the choice of the sublinks is to consider the intermediate rigid sublinks with a length of L_i/ν_i, the extreme ones with an half length, the flexible sublinks with a length of L_i/ν_i and deformable as parabolic arcs. Consequetly the elastic energy of the i-th link results

$$U_i = \frac{1}{2}K_i(\beta_{1i}^2 + \cdots + \beta_{\upsilon_i i}^2), \tag{67}$$

where

$$K_i = \frac{E_i I_i}{L_i/\nu_i} \tag{68}$$

is the stiffness of the flexible sublinks.

Therefore the vector of the elastic torques is

$$\gamma = [0\ K_1\beta_{11}\ K_1\beta_{21}\cdots K_1\beta_{\nu_1 1}\ 0\ K_2\beta_{12}\ K_2\beta_{22}\cdots K_2\beta_{\nu_2 2}\cdots 0\ K_n\beta_{1n}\ K_n\beta_{2n}\cdots K_n\beta_{\nu_n n}]^T. \tag{69}$$

Remark 7. The proposed method is simple to apply, is very efficient from a computational point of view and it provides a model with null error when the control and disturbance torques are constant. For control actions and disturbances, also in forces, with a fixed and limited band-pass, this model provides an error strongly decreasing when the number of sublinks increase. This fact clearly emerges from the following example.

5.2 Example: Modeling of a Single-Link Flexible Arm

Consider a flexible robot with a single flexible link (see Fig. 14).

If the link is a steel bar with a length of $L = 2m$ and with a squared section of side $l = 0.01m = 1cm$, the first five frequencies computed with the theoretic formulae:

$$f_i = \sqrt{\frac{EI}{m}}\frac{\pi}{32L^2}(4i+1)^2, \quad i = 1,2,\cdots,5 \tag{70}$$

where E is the modulus of elasticity of Joung ($\cong 10^{11} N/m^2$), $I = l^4/12$ is the moment of inertia of the section respect to the deflection axis and $m \cong 7876 l^2 Kg/m$ is the mass per unit length of the link, are:

$$f = 6.31,\ 20.4,\ 42.7,\ 73.0,\ 111.3\ Hz. \tag{71}$$

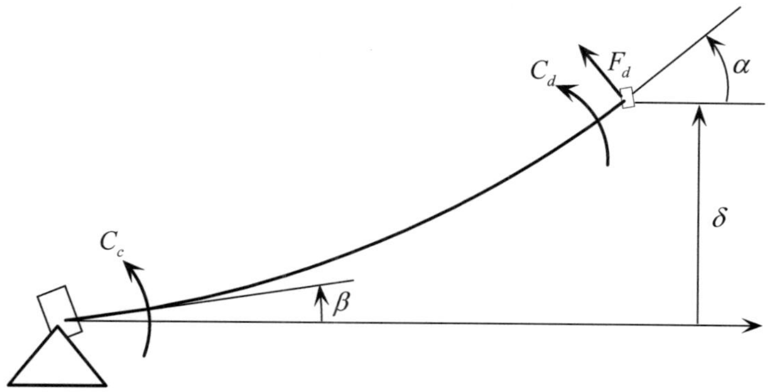

Fig. 14. Schematic representation of a single-link flexible arm.

The frequencies obtained with the proposed method, dividing the link into five and ten flexible sublinks, respectively result:

$$f = 6.31,\ 20.4,\ 41.9,\ 65.6,\ 90.8\text{Hz} \tag{72}$$

$$f = 6.31,\ 20.4,\ 42.6,\ 72.77,\ 110.5\text{Hz}. \tag{73}$$

Stressing the link with $C_c = -1Nm, C_d = 1Nm, F_d = 0N$, if $\beta = 0$, the theoretic values of α and δ are:

$$\alpha = \frac{L}{EI} C_d = 1.375°,\ \delta = \frac{L^2}{2EI} C_d = 2.40cm. \tag{74}$$

It is worth noting that these values and the ones obtained using the proposed method are coincident $\forall \nu \geq 1$ (Celentano, 2007).

Applying to the link $C_c = -2Nm, C_d = 0Nm, F_d = 1N$, if $\beta = 0$, the theoretic values of α and δ result:

$$\alpha = \frac{L^2}{2EI} F_d = 1.375°,\ \delta = \frac{L^3}{3EI} F_d = 3.20cm. \tag{75}$$

The first value (the orientation angle of payload due to the arm deflection) and the ones computed with the proposed method $\forall \nu \geq 1$ are coincident, while the second value (the motion of the payload due to the arm deflection) obtained using the proposed method has a relative error of (Celentano, 2007)

$$\varepsilon_\delta = -\frac{1}{4\nu^2} = \begin{cases} -0.01 = 1\%, & if\ \nu = 5 \\ -0.0025 = 0.25\%, if & \nu = 10. \end{cases} \tag{76}$$

6. Conclusion

In this chapter an innovative method for robots modeling and simulation, based on an appropriate mathematical formulation of the relative equations of motion and on a new integration scheme, has been illustrated. The proposed approach does require the calculation of the inertia matrix and of the gradient of the kinetic energy only. It provides a new analytical-numerical methodology, that has been shown to be simpler and numerically more efficient than the classical approaches, requires no a priori specialized knowledge of the dynamics of mechanical systems and is formulated in order to allow students, researchers and professionals to easily employ it for the analysis of manipulators with the complex-shaped links commonly used in industry.

In the case of planar robots with revolute joints, theorems have been stated and proved that offer a particularly simple and efficient method of computation for both the inertia matrix and the gradient of the kinetic energy. Then a comparison has been made in terms of efficiency between the proposed method and the Articulated-Body one.

Moreover, for spatial robots with generic shape links and connected, for the sake of brevity, with spherical joints, several theorems have been formulated and demonstrated in a simple manner and some algorithms that allow efficiently computing, analytically the inertia matrix, analytically or numerically the gradient of the kinetic and of the gravitational energy have been provided. Furthermore, also in this case a comparison of the proposed method in terms of efficiency with the Articulated-Body one has been reported.

Finally, a methodology for flexible robots modeling, that allow obtaining, quite simply, accurate and efficient, from a computational point of view, finite-dimensional models, has been provided. This method is illustrated with a very significant example.

7. References

Celentano, L. (2007). An Innovative and Efficient Method for Flexible Robots Modeling and Simulation. *Internal Report,* Dipartimento di Informatica e Sistemistica, Università degli Studi di Napoli Federico II, Napoli, Italy, October 2007

Celentano, L. and Iervolino, R. (2007). A Novel Approach for Spatial Robots Modeling and Simulation. *MMAR07, 13th IEEE International Conference on Methods and Models in Automation and Robotics,* pp. 1005-1010, Szczecin, Poland, 27-30 August 2007

Celentano, L. and Iervolino, R. (2006). A New Method for Robot Modeling and Simulation. *ASME Journal of Dynamic Systems, Measurement and Control,* Vol. 128, December 2006, pp. 811-819

Celentano, L. (2006). Modellistica e Controllo dei Sistemi Meccanici Rigidi e Flessibili. *PhD Thesis,* Dipartimento di Informatica e Sistemistica, Università degli Studi di Napoli Federico II, Napoli, Italy, November 2006

De Wit, C.C., Siciliano, B. and Bastin, G. (1997). *Theory of Robot Control,* (2nd Ed.) Springer-Verlag, London, UK

Featherstone, R. and Orin, D.E. (2000). Robot Dynamics: Equations and Algorithms. *Proceedings of the 2000 IEEE International Conference on Robotics and Automation,* pp. 826-834

Featherstone, R. (1987). *Robot Dynamics Algorithms,* Kluwer Academic Publishers, Boston/ Dordrecht/ Lancaster

Khalil, W. and Dombre, E. (2002). *Modelling, Identification and Control of Robots,* Hermes Penton Science, London, UK

Sciavicco, L. and Siciliano, B. (2000). *Modeling and Control of Robot Manipulators,* (2nd Ed.) Springer-Verlag, London, UK

11

Models for Simulation and Control of Underwater Vehicles

Jorge Silva[1] and João Sousa[2]
[1]*Engineering Institute of Porto*
[2]*University of Porto*
Portugal

1.Introduction

Nowadays, the computational power of the average personal computer provides to a vast audience the possibility of simulating complex models of reality within reasonable time frames. This chapter presents a review of modelling techniques for underwater vehicles with fixed geometry, giving emphasis on their application to real-time or faster than real-time simulation.

In the last decade there was a strong movement towards the development of Autonomous Underwater Vehicles (AUV) and Remotely Operated Vehicles (ROV). These two classes of underwater vehicles are intended to provide researchers with simple, long-range, low-cost, rapid response capability to collect pertinent environmental data. There are numerous applications for AUV and ROV, including underwater structure inspection, oceanographic surveys, operations in hazardous environments, and military applications. In order to fulfil these objectives, the vehicles must be provided with a set of controllers assuring the desired type of autonomous operation and offering some aid to the operator, for vehicles which can be teleoperated.

The design and tuning of controllers requires, on most methodologies, a mathematical model of the system to be controlled. Control of underwater vehicles is no exception to this rule. The most common model in control theory is the classic system of differential equations, where x and u are denominated respectively state vector and input vector:

$$\dot{x} = f(x,u) \tag{1}$$

In this framework, the most realistic models of underwater vehicles require f(x,u) to be a nonlinear function. However, as we will see, under certain assumptions, the linearization of f(x,u) may still result in an acceptable model of the system, with the added advantage of the analytic simplicity.

On the other hand, simulation, or more specifically, numerical simulation, does not require a model with the conceptual simplicity of Eq.(1). In this case, we are not concerned with an analytic proof of the system's properties. The main objective is to compute the evolution of a set of state variables, given the system's inputs.

The hydrodynamic effects of underwater motion of a rigid body are well described by the Navier-Stokes equations. However, these equations form a system of nonlinear partial differential equations whose solution is very hard to compute for general problems. Computational fluid dynamics deal with the subject of solving these equations. However, even with today's computer technology and software packages, the time to obtain the solution on average computer, even for simple scenarios, is still far from real-time. This kind of simulation may return very accurate results, but the computation times are not acceptable if simulation of long term operation is desired. These models are just too complex for control design and approximations are used for this purpose.

If near, or faster than, real-time simulations are desired, acceptable results can be obtained by simulating the model employed in the control design. Real-time response is most useful when teleoperation simulation is desired. In this case, as in car or flight simulators, the user interacts with the underwater vehicle simulator by setting references or direct actuator commands on a graphical user interface.

Usually we are interested in checking the performance of the vehicle's controllers in a set of operation scenarios. This is done because the control design may involve certain simplifications or heuristic methods which make it difficult to analytically characterize certain parameters of the system's response, such as settling time or peak values (overshoots) during transient phases of operation. Simulation is an important tool for controller tuning and for exposing certain limit situations (e.g., actuator saturation) that may be hard to describe analytically on the model employed for control design.

The typical design cycle involves the test of different control laws and navigation schemes. In most cases, the control system must be replicated in a simulation environment, usually on a different language. Even when that is done correctly, it is difficult to keep consistency between that implementation and the final control system, which may be subject to updates from other sources. It is possible, as described in (Silva et al. 2007), to have a single implementation of the control software to function unmodified in both real-life and simulated environments. Instead of writing separate code first for a prototyping environment and then for the final version, this approach allows the employment of the stable/final software in the overall design cycle. Therefore, the simulation may be seen also as a debugging tool of the overall software design process. Underwater vehicle's mission management, with special regards to autonomous operation, may involve complex logic, besides the continuous control laws. It is of the major importance to test the implementation of that logic, namely switching between manoeuvres, manoeuvre coordination, event detection, etc. Since real-life missions may last for some hours, it is quite useful to simulate these missions in compressed simulated time.

The literature from naval architecture proposes several models for underwater vehicles following the structure of Eq.(1). The main difference between these models is the way how the hydrodynamic phenomena associated with underwater rigid body motion is modelled. The model described in (Healey & Lienard, 1993) is used in many works. These authors refine a model that can be traced back to 1967 (Gertler & Hagen, 1967) in order to describe a box shaped AUV. Most recent works use the framework presented on (Fossen, 1994) which, while less descriptive than the one of (Healey & Lienard, 1993), is more amenable to direct application of tools from nonlinear control. Recent research on underwater vehicle's motion equations can still be found, for instance on (Nahon, 2006).

However, in general, the literature only provides the general equations of the models. These models are parametrized by tens (sometimes over one hundred) of coefficients. Some of these coefficients can be easily computed based on direct physical measurements (mass, length, etc.). However, the computation of the coefficients related to hydrodynamic effects is not a straightforward task. When considering new designs, the accurate estimation of some of the coefficients, mainly those associated with hydrodynamic phenomena, usually requires hydrodynamics tests. Although ingenious techniques can be used, see for instance (von Ellenrieder, 2006), these tests are usually expensive or involve an apparatus which is not justifiable for every institution.

Certain software packages can be used to obtain more accurate parameters. For instance, (Irwin & Chavet, 2007) present a study comparing results obtained with Computational Fluid Dynamics with those of classical heuristic formulas. However, software packages for this purpose are usually expensive, or of limited accessibility.

The simplest alternative approaches rely on empirical formulas, or on adapting the coefficients from well-proved models from similar vehicles. In fact, empirical results show that, for vehicles of the same shape, the hydrodynamic effects can be normalized as a function of scale and vehicle's operating speed. For instance, the work of (Healey & Lienard, 1993) presents the complete set of numeric parameters for the model proposed by the authors on that work. However, the later method is suitable only for vehicles with similar shape to those whose models are known and the former requires the vehicle being modelled to follow closely the assumptions of the empirical formulas.

In what follows, we review a standard nonlinear model derived from (Fossen, 1994), describe further aspects of the hydrodynamic phenomena, and explain how the symmetries of the vehicle can be explored in order to reduce the number of considered coefficients.

The final conclusions are drawn based on our experiments with the Light Autonomous Underwater Vehicle (LAUV) designed and built at University of Porto (see Fig. 1). LAUV is a torpedo shaped vehicle, with a length of 1.1 meters, a diameter of 15 cm and a mass of approximately 18 kg. The actuator system is composed of one propeller and 3 or 4 control fins (depending on the vehicle version), all electrically driven. We compare trajectories logged during the operation of the LAUV with trajectories obtained by simulation of the vehicle's mathematical model.

Fig. 1. Light Autonomous Underwater Vehicle (LAUV) designed and built at University of Porto.

2. Underwater vehicle dynamics

When discussing underwater vehicle dynamics we typically consider two coordinate frames: the Earth-Fixed Frame and the Body-Fixed Frame.

The Earth-Fixed Frame defines a coordinate system with origin fixed to an arbitrary point on the surface of the Earth and following the north-east-down convention: x points due North, y points due East, and z points toward the center of the Earth. For marine applications, this frame is considered the inertial frame.
In the Body-Fixed Reference Frame the origin and axes of the coordinate system are fixed with respect to the (nominal) geometry of the vehicle. The orientation of the axes is as shown on Fig. 2: if the underwater vehicle has a plane of symmetry (and we will assume here that they all do) then x_B and z_B lie in that plane of symmetry. x_B is chosen to point forward and z_B is chosen to point downward. Usually the body axes coincide with the principal axes of inertia of the vehicle. Fig. 2 shows one possibility. The origin of the body-fixed frame is frequently chosen to coincide with the center of gravity. This is a natural choice given the equations of rigid body motion. However, in many situations, most remarkably during prototyping, the center of mass may be changing relatively to the vehicle's geometry. That makes necessary to recalculate the moments due some of the forces involved on vehicle's motion (e.g., forces due to the actuators). Therefore, in those cases, a more useful choice would be a point relative to the vehicle's shape such as the center of pressure (described later) or simply the geometrical center.

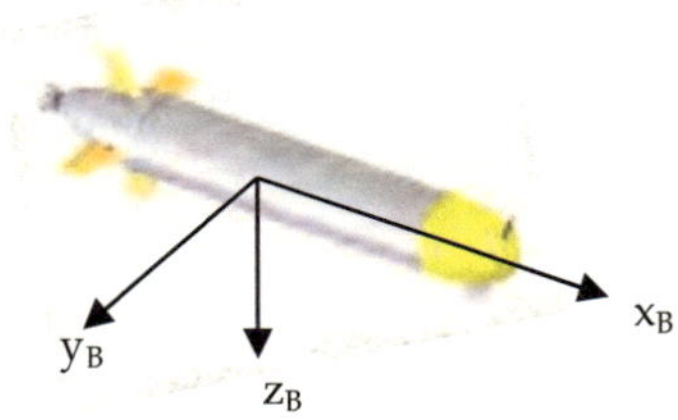

Fig. 2. Body-Fixed Reference Frame.

The minimum set of variables that completely describe the vehicle's position, orientation, and linear and angular velocities is called vehicle state. The most commonly chosen state variables are the inertial position and orientation of the vehicle, and its body-fixed linear and angular velocities. The orientation of the vehicle with respect to inertial space can be described by the Euler angles. These angles are termed yaw angle (ψ), pitch angle (θ) and roll angle (ϕ). This implies three different rotations will be needed (one for each axis). The order in which these rotations are carried out is not arbitrary. The standard coordinate systems and rotations (Lewis, 1989), are as defined in Fig. 3. In what follows, the notation from the Society of Naval Architects and Marine Engineers (SNAME) is used (Lewis, 1989). The motions in the body-fixed frame are described by 6 velocity components u, v, w, p, q and r. Let us define the following vectors:

$$\nu_1 = [u \quad v \quad w]^T \tag{1}$$

$$\nu_2 = [p \quad q \quad r]^T \tag{2}$$

$$\nu = [\nu_1^T \quad \nu_2^T]^T \tag{3}$$

The body fixed linear velocities u, v and w are termed, respectively, surge, sway and heave. We adopt the following convention: when considering slow varying ocean currents, these velocities are relative to a coordinate frame moving with the ocean current.

The vehicle's position and orientation in the inertial frame are defined by the following vectors:

$$\eta_1 = [x \quad y \quad z]^T \tag{4}$$

$$\eta_2 = [\phi \quad \theta \quad \psi]^T \tag{6}$$

$$\eta = [\eta_1^T \quad \eta_2^T]^T \tag{5}$$

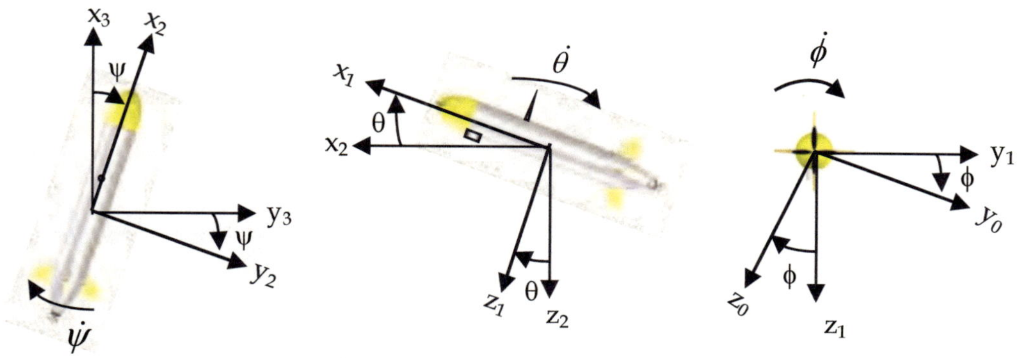

Fig. 3. Euler angles definition: yaw, pitch and roll.

The twelve basic states of an underwater vehicle may therefore be written as (again, this is just one possible choice, but it is the standard one):

Name	Description	Unit
u	Linear velocity along body-fixed x-axis (surge)	m/s
v	Linear velocity along body-fixed y-axis (sway)	m/s
w	Linear velocity along body-fixed z-axis (heave)	m/s
p	Angular velocity about body-fixed x-axis	rad/s
q	Angular velocity about body-fixed y-axis	rad/s
r	Angular velocity about body-fixed z-axis	rad/s
ψ	Heading angle with respect to the reference axes	rad
θ	Pitch angle with respect to the reference axes	rad
ϕ	Roll angle with respect to the reference axes	rad
x	Position with respect to the reference axes (North)	m
y	Position with respect to the reference axes (East)	m
z	Position with respect to the reference axes (Down)	m

Table 1. Vehicle States

2.1 Dynamic equations

The evolution of η is defined by the following kinematic equation:

$$\dot{\eta} = J(\eta_2)\nu \tag{6}$$

This equation defines the relationship between the velocities on both reference frames, with the term $J(\eta_2)$ given as follows:

$$J_1(\eta_2)=\begin{bmatrix}\cos\theta\cos\psi & (-\cos\phi\sin\psi+\sin\phi\sin\theta\cos\psi) & (\sin\phi\sin\psi+\cos\phi\sin\theta\cos\psi)\\ \cos\theta\sin\psi & (\cos\phi\cos\psi+\sin\phi\sin\theta\sin\psi) & (-\sin\phi\cos\psi+\cos\phi\sin\theta\sin\psi)\\ -\sin\theta & \cos\theta\sin\psi & \cos\theta\cos\phi\end{bmatrix} \quad (7)$$

$$J_2(\eta_2)=\left(\frac{1}{\cos\theta}\right)\begin{bmatrix}\cos\theta & \sin\phi\sin\theta & \cos\phi\sin\theta\\ 0 & \cos\phi\cos\theta & -\sin\phi\cos\theta\\ 0 & \sin\phi & \cos\phi\end{bmatrix} \quad (8)$$

$$J(\eta_2)=\begin{bmatrix}J_1(\eta_2) & 0\\ 0 & J_2(\eta_2)\end{bmatrix} \quad (9)$$

Note that there is a singularity in Eq. (8) when the pitch angle is ±90°. Underwater vehicles typically do not operate close to this singularity. If we want to consider operation in that zone, one possible alternative to the Euler angles is the quaternion representation. For further details see, for instance, (Fossen, 1994).

For most marine control applications it is valid to assume the principle of superposition can be applied when considering environmental disturbances. For underwater vehicles operating far from the surface, the main environmental disturbance to be considered is due to marine currents. Ocean and river currents arise due to a multitude of factors but, in the generality of the operations, they have a low spatial and temporal rate of change with respect to the vehicle dynamics. Therefore we can incorporate the effect of currents in the vehicle model by considering that ν is relative to a frame moving with the water current velocity ν_c, where $\nu_c = [v_{cx}, v_{cy}, v_{cz}, 0, 0, 0]$ is the earth-fixed current velocity vector. The only change to the previously defined model will be in the kinematic equations which will come as follows:

$$\dot{\eta}=J(\eta_2)\nu+\nu_c \quad (10)$$

The equations of motion are composed of the standard terms for the motion of an ideal rigid body plus the terms due to hydrodynamic forces and moments and the terms due to propulsive forces. The usual approach to model the hydrodynamic terms consists of considering the following effects: restoring forces, the simplest one, which depends only on the vehicle weight, buoyancy and relative positions of the centers of gravity and buoyancy; added mass, which describes the pressure induced forces/moments due to forced harmonic motion of the body; drag, caused by skin friction (either laminar or turbulent) and vortex shedding; and lift, due to the fluid flow whose direction is changed perpendicularly to vehicle's linear velocity vector. As hinted in the introduction, added mass, drag and lift are very hard to describe accurately by theoretical methods. An extensive discussion about the added mass effect is presented in (Brennen, 1982).

The drag effect is modelled as a force opposing to the vehicle's velocity. The lift effect is modelled as a force perpendicular to the vehicle's velocity. Both forces act on the center of pressure of the vehicle and are a function of the vehicles' shape and of the square of its velocity. The center of pressure is also strongly dependent on vehicle's shape. For a more in-depth analysis of this subject see, for instance, (Hoerner, 1992).

With the exception of the gravity and buoyancy forces, these effects are best described in the Body-Fixed Frame. Therefore, the remaining equations of motion, describing the vehicle's kinetics, can be presented in the following compact form:

$$M\dot{\nu} + C(\nu)\nu + D(\nu)\nu + g(\eta) = \tau_{act} \quad (11)$$

M is the constant inertia and added mass matrix of the vehicle, $C(\nu)$ is the Coriolis and centripetal matrix, $D(\nu)$ is the Damping matrix, $g(\eta)$ is the vector of restoring forces and moments and τ_{act} is the vector of body-fixed forces from the actuators. We follow the common formulation where the lift and drag terms are both accounted in the damping matrix.

For vehicles with a streamlined shape, theoretical and empirical formulas may be used. However, it must be remarked that in practice these vehicles are not quite as regular as assumed in the formulas usually employed for added mass, drag and lift: they have antennas, transducers and other protuberances that affect those effects, with special incidence on the drag terms. Therefore we should look at the formulas as giving underestimates of the true values of the coefficients.

In certain situations it may be useful to consider the following simplifications: if the vehicle's weight equals its buoyancy and the center of gravity is coincident with the center of buoyancy, $g(\eta)$ is null; for an AUV with port/starboard, top/bottom and fore/aft symmetries, M and $D(\nu)=D_1(\nu)+D_2(\nu)$ are diagonal. In the later case, the damping matrix has the following form:

$$D_1(\nu) = \text{diag}(X_u, Y_v, Z_w, K_p, M_q, M_q) \quad (12)$$

$$D_2(\nu) = \text{diag}(X_{u|u|}|u|, Y_{v|v|}|v|, Z_{w|w|}|w|, K_{p|p|}|p|, M_{q|q|}|q|, N_{r|r|}|r|) \quad (13)$$

For low velocities, the quadratic terms on Eq. 13, such as $Y_{v|v|}|v|$, may be considered negligible. However, in practice, the fore/aft symmetry is rarely verified and non-diagonal terms should be considered. Even so, certain simplifications can be further considered. For instance, in torpedo shaped vehicles, some of the coefficients affecting the motion on the vertical plane are the same as those affecting the motion on the horizontal plane, reducing the number of different coefficients that must be estimated.

Some of the models found in the literature, e.g. (Prestero 2001; Leonard & Graver, 2001; Conte & Serrani, 1996; Ridley et al., 2003), do not consider the linear damping terms contained on $D_1(\nu)$. These terms may play an important role in the design of the control system, namely on local stability analysis. For low velocities scenarios the quadratic damping terms become very small. If the linear damping is ignored, the linearization of the system model around the equilibrium point may falsely reveal a locally unstable system. This leads the control system designer to counteract by adding linear damping in the form of velocity feedback, which potentially could be unnecessary, leading to conservative designs. In fact, it is possible to find examples in the literature where the authors perform a worst case analysis, by totally disregarding the damping matrix (Leonard 1996; Chyba 2003).

2.2 Actuators

In the last years there has been a trend in the research of biologically inspired actuators for underwater vehicles, see for instance (Tangorra, 2007). The development of vehicles employing variable buoyancy and center of mass (e.g., gliders) is also underway (Bachmayer, 2004). However, the preferred types of actuators for small size AUVs still are electrically driven propellers and fins, due to its simplicity, robustness and low cost.

When high manoeuvrability is desired, full actuation is employed (for instance, with two longitudinal thrusters, two lateral thrusters and two vertical thrusters). For over-actuated vehicles, thruster allocation schemes may be applied in order to optimize performance and power consumption. However, for a broad range of applications the cost effectiveness of under-actuated vehicles is still a factor of preference. In those cases, a smaller number of thrusters, eventually coupled with fins, is employed. This approach is applied in most torpedo-like AUVs: there is a propeller for actuation in the longitudinal direction and fins for lateral and vertical actuation. In this case, τ_{act} depends only on 3 parameters: propeller velocity, horizontal fin inclination and vertical fin inclination.

Dynamic models for propellers can be found in (Fossen, 1994) and this is still an active area of research (D'Epagnier, 2006). However, the dynamics of the thruster motor and fin servos are generally faster than the remaining dynamics. Therefore, they can be frequently excluded from the model, namely when operation at steady speed is considered as opposed to dynamic positioning, or station keeping.

2.3 Simplified models

For a large class of underwater vehicles it is usual to consider decoupled modes of operation, see for instance (Healey & Lienard, 1993), the most common being motion on the horizontal plane, involving changes on x, y, ψ, v, and motion on the vertical plane aligned with the body fixed x-z axes, involving changes on z, θ, w and q. In the later mode, assuming small deviations from 0 on the pitch angle, a linearized model can be used without introducing significant error (the a_{ij}, k_w and k_q coefficients can be calculated as a function of the coefficients of the full nonlinear model):

$$\begin{bmatrix} \dot{z} \\ \dot{\theta} \\ \dot{w} \\ \dot{q} \end{bmatrix} = \begin{bmatrix} 0 & -u & 1 & 0 \\ 0 & 0 & 0 & 1 \\ 0 & a_{32} & a_{33} & a_{34} \\ 0 & a_{42} & a_{43} & a_{44} \end{bmatrix} \begin{bmatrix} z \\ \theta \\ w \\ q \end{bmatrix} + \begin{bmatrix} v_{cz} \\ 0 \\ k_w \tau_w \\ k_q \tau_q \end{bmatrix} \tag{14}$$

For the purpose path planning on the horizontal plane with piecewise continuous velocity, a simple kinematic model can be used:

$$\begin{cases} \dot{x} = u\cos(\psi) - v\sin(\psi) + v_{cx} \\ \dot{y} = v\cos(\psi) + u\sin(\psi) + v_{cx} \\ \dot{\psi} = r \end{cases} \tag{15}$$

For the purpose of path planning, it is considered that the actuators produce the desired velocities instantaneously. The allowable ranges for u, v and r must be the same as the ones verified for the full dynamic model, or measured in real operation. While this model introduces some errors that must be compensated later by the on-line control system, this is very useful for the general path planning algorithms. If the vehicle does not possess lateral actuation, such as a torpedo, the model drops the terms on v and becomes the well-known unicycle model.

3. Results and discussion

In (Silva et al., 2007) we describe a simulation environment which allows us to simulate AUV operation in real-time and with direct interaction with the control software. All software was written in C++ and is based on the Dune framework, also developed at the University of Porto. Using this framework, the control software and simulation engine may run either on a desktop computer or on the final target computer. Our results show that realistic real-time and faster than real-time simulation of underwater vehicles is quite feasible in today's computers. The trajectories obtained with the exact same inputs as those used in experiments in the water differ slightly from the real trajectories. However, in what concerns simulation of closed-loop operation, the feedback employed on the control laws smoothes out the effects of parameter uncertainty. Therefore it is possible to observe a good correlation between the performance of the controlled system in simulation and that obtained in real operation. This conclusion is drawn using the exact same controllers and timings on simulation and real operation. This result is not as assuring as a complete analytical proof but, then again, none of the currently employed models are perfect descriptions of the reality therefore, even an analytical study does not guarantee the planned behaviour when the respective implementation comes to real life operation.

The available methods are quite satisfactory for high level mission planning and already provide a good basis for initial controller tuning. However, additional tuning is still required when it comes to real life vehicle operation. Research on models whose simulation can be done in reasonable time while providing an increasing level of adherence to reality should continue.

4. References

Bachmayer, R.; Leonard, N.E.; Graver, J.; Fiorelli, E.; Bhatta, P. & Paley, D. (2004). Underwater gliders: recent developments and future applications, *Proceedings of the 2004 International Symposium on Underwater Technology*, pp. 195-200, Taipei, Taiwan, April 2004

Brennen, C.E (1982). *A review of added mass and fluid internal forces*, Naval Civil engineering laboratory, California

Chyba, M.; Leonard, N. E. & Sontag, E. (2003). Singular trajectories in multi-input time-optimal problems: Application to controlled mechanical systems, *Journal of Dynamical and Control Systems*, Vol. 9, No. 1, pp. 73-88

Conte, G. & Serrani, A. (1996) Modelling and simulation of underwater vehicles, *Proceedings of the 1996 IEEE International Symposium on Computer-Aided Control System Design*, pp. 62-67, Dearborn, Michigan, September 1996

D'Epagnier, K. P. (2006). AUV Propellers: Optimal Design and Improving Existing Propellers for Greater Efficiency, *Proceedings of the OCEANS 2006 MTS/IEEE Conference*, Boston, Massachusetts USA, September 2006

Fossen, T.I. (1994). *Guidance and Control of Ocean Vehicles*, John Wiley and Sons, Inc., New York

Gertler, M. & Hagen, G. R. (1967). *Standard equations of motion for submarine simulation*, Naval Ship Research and Development Center, Report 2510.

Healey, A. J. & Lienard, D. (1993). Multivariable Sliding Mode Control for Autonomous Diving and Steering of Unmanned Underwater Vehicles, *IEEE Journal of Oceanic Engineering*, Vol. 18, No. 3, pp. 1-13

Leonard, N. E. (1996). Stabilization of steady motions of an underwater vehicle, *Proceedings of the 1996 IEEE Conference on Decision and Control*, pp. 961-966, Kobe, Japan, December 1996

Leonard, N. E. & Graver, J. G. (2001). Model-based feedback control of autonomous underwater gliders, *IEEE Journal of Oceanic Engineering (Special Issue on Autonomous Ocean-Sampling Networks)*, Vol. 26, No. 4, pp. 633-645

Lewis, E. (Ed.) (1989). *Principles of Naval Architecture (2nd revision)*, Society of Naval Architects and Marine Engineers, Jersey City, New Jersey

Hoerner, S. F. & Borst H. V. (1992). *Fluid Dynamic Lift (second edition)*, published by author, ISBN 9998831636

Irwin, R. P. & Chauvet, C. (2007). Quantifying Hydrodynamic Coefficients of Complex Structures, *Proceedings of the IEEE/OES OCEANS 2007 - Europe*, pp. 1-5, Aberdeen, Scotland, June 2007

Nahon, M. (2006). A Simplified Dynamics Model for Autonomous Underwater Vehicles, *Journal of Ocean Technology*, Vol. 1, No. 1, pp. 57-68

Prestero, T. J. (2001). Development of a six-degree of freedom simulation model for the remus autonomous underwater vehicle, *Proceedings of the OCEANS 2001 MTS/IEEE Conference and Exhibition*, pp. 450-455, Honolulu, Hawaii, November 2001

Ridley, P.; Fontan, J. & Corke, P. (2003). Submarine dynamic modelling, *Proceedings of the Australian Conference on Robotics and Automation*, Brisbane, Australia, December 2003

Silva, J.; Terra, B.; Martins R. & Sousa, J. (2007). Modeling and Simulation of the LAUV Autonomous Underwater Vehicle, *Proceedings of the 13th IEEE IFAC International Conference on Methods and Models in Automation and Robotics*, pp. 713-718, Szczecin, Poland, August 2007

Tangorra, J. L.; Davidson, S. N.; Hunter, I. W.; Madden, P. G. A.; Lauder, G. V.; Dong, H.; Bozkurttas, M. & Mittal, R. (2007). The Development of a Biologically Inspired Propulsor for Unmanned Underwater Vehicles, *IEEE Journal of Oceanic Engineering*, Vol. 32, No. 3, pp. 533-550

von Ellenrieder, K. D. & Ackermann, L. E. J. (2006). Force/flow measurements on a low-speed, vectored-thruster propelled UUV," *Proceedings of the OCEANS 2006 MTS/IEEE Conference*, Boston, Massachusetts USA, September 2006

12

Fuzzy Stabilization of Fuzzy Control Systems

Mohamed M. Elkhatib and John J. Soraghan
University of Strathclyde
United Kingdom

1. Introduction

Recently there has been significant growth in the use of fuzzy logic in industrial and consumer products (J. Yen 1995). However, although fuzzy control has been successfully applied to many industrial plants that are mostly nonlinear systems, many critics of fuzzy logic claim that there is no such thing as a stability proof for fuzzy logic systems in closed-loop control (Reznik 1997; Farinwata, Filev et al. 2000). Since fuzzy logic controllers are classified as "non-linear multivariable controllers" (Reznik 1997; Farinwata, Filev et al. 2000), it can be argued that all stability analysis methods applicable to these controller types are applicable to fuzzy logic controllers. Unfortunately, due to the complex non-linearities of most fuzzy logic systems, an analytical solution is not possible. Furthermore, it is important to realize that real, practical problems have uncertain plants that inevitably cannot be modelled dynamically resulting in substantial uncertainties. In addition the sensors noise and input signal level constraints affect system stability. Therefore a theory that is able to deal with these issues would be useful for practical designs. The most well-known time domain stability analysis methods include Lyapunov's direct method (Wu & Ch. 2000; Gruyitch, Richard et al. 2004; Rubio & Yu 2007) which is based on linearization and Lyapunov's indirect method (Tanaka & Sugeno 1992; Giron-Sierra & Ortega 2002; Lin, Wang et al. 2007; Mannani & Talebi 2007) that uses a Lyapunov function which serves as a generalized energy function. In addition many other methods have been used for testing fuzzy systems stability such as Popov's stability criterion (Katoh, Yamashita et al. 1995; Wang & Lin 1998), the describing function method (Ying 1999; Aracil & Gordillo 2004), methods of stability indices and systems robustness (Fuh & Tung 1997; Espada & Barreiro 1999; Zuo & Wang 2007), methods based on theory of input/output stability (Kandel, LUO et al. 1999), conicity criterion (Cuesta & Ollero 2004). Also there are methods based on hyper-stability theory (Piegat 1997) and linguistic stability analysis approach (Gang & Laijiu 1996).

Fuzzy logic uses approximate reasoning and in this chapter a practical algorithm to improve system stability by using a fuzzy stabilizer block in the feedback path is introduced. The fuzzy stabilizer is tuned such that its nonlinearity lies in a bounded sector resulting from the circle criterion theory (Safonov 1980). The circle criterion presents the sufficient condition for absolute stability (Vidyasagar 1993). An appealing aspect of the circle criterion is its geometric nature, which is reminiscent of the Nyquist criterion. It is a frequency domain method for stability analysis and has been used by Ray et al (1984) to ensure fuzzy system stability (Ray, Ghosh et al. 1984; Ray & Majumderr 1984).

Throughout this chapter we use a practical approach to stabilize fuzzy systems with the aid of the circle criterion theory using a Takagi-Sugeno fuzzy block in the feedback loop of the closed system. The new technique is used to ensure stability for the proposed robot fuzzy controller. Furthermore, the study indicates that the fuzzy stabilizer can be integrated, with minor modifications, into any fuzzy controller to enhance its stability. As a result, the proposed design is suitable for hardware implementation even permitting relatively simple modification of existing designs to improve system stability. In addition an extension to the approach to stabilize MIMO (Multi-input Multi-output) systems is also presented.

2. Problem formulation and analysis

This chapter concentrates on the stability of a closed loop nonlinear system using a Takagi-Sugeno (T-S) fuzzy controller. Fuzzy control based on Takagi-Sugeno (T-S) fuzzy model (Babuska, Roubos et al. 1998; Buckley & Eslami 2002) has been used widely in nonlinear systems because it efficiently represents a nonlinear system by a set of linear subsystems. The main feature of the T-S fuzzy model is that the consequents of the fuzzy rules are expressed as analytic functions. The choice of the function depends on its practical applications. Specifically, the T-S fuzzy model is an interpolation method, which can be utilized to describe a complex or nonlinear system that cannot be exactly modelled mathematically. The physical complex system is assumed to exhibit explicit linear or nonlinear dynamics around some operating points. These local models are smoothly aggregated via fuzzy inferences, which lead to the construction of complete system dynamics.

Takagi-Sugeno (T-S) fuzzy controller is used in the feedback path as shown in Fig.1, so that it can change the amount of feedback in order to enhance the system performance and its stability.

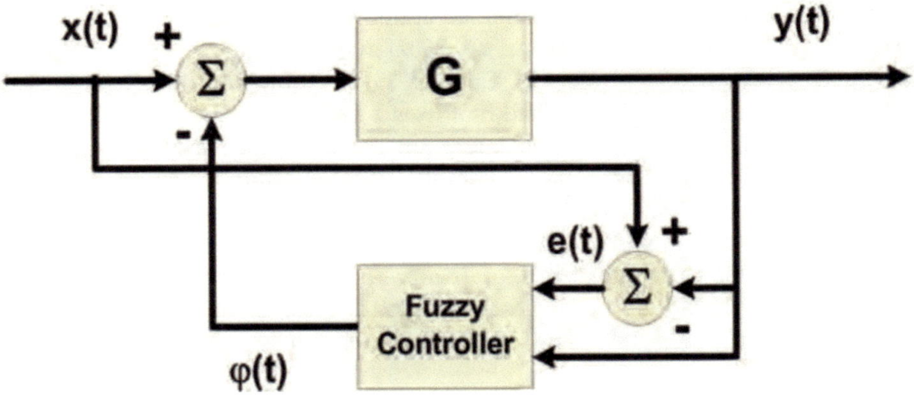

Fig. 1 The proposed System block diagram

The proposed fuzzy controller is a two-input one-output system: the error e(t) and the output y(t) are the controller inputs while the output is the feedback signal φ(t). The fuzzy controller uses symmetric, normal and uniformly distributed membership functions for the rule premises as shown in Fig.2(a) and 2(b). Labels have been assigned to every membership function such as NBig (Negative Big) and PBig (Positive Big) etc. Notice that the widths of the membership functions of the input are parameterized by L and h which are used to tune the controller and limited by the physical limitations of the controlled system.

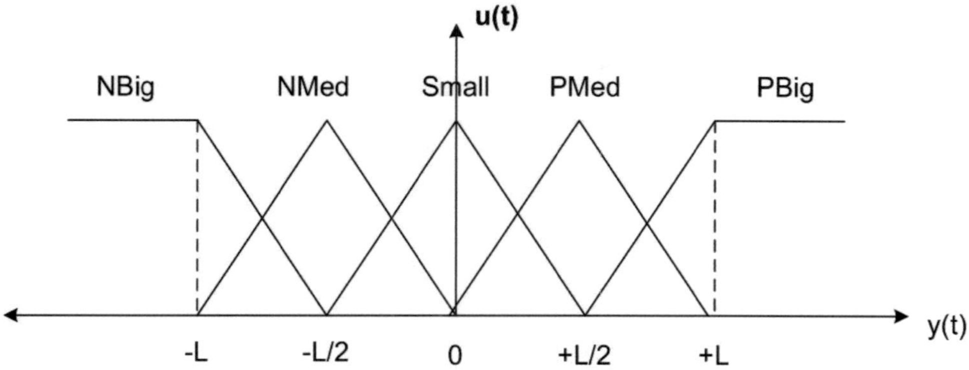

Fig. 2 (a) The membership distribution of the 2nd input, open loop output y(t)

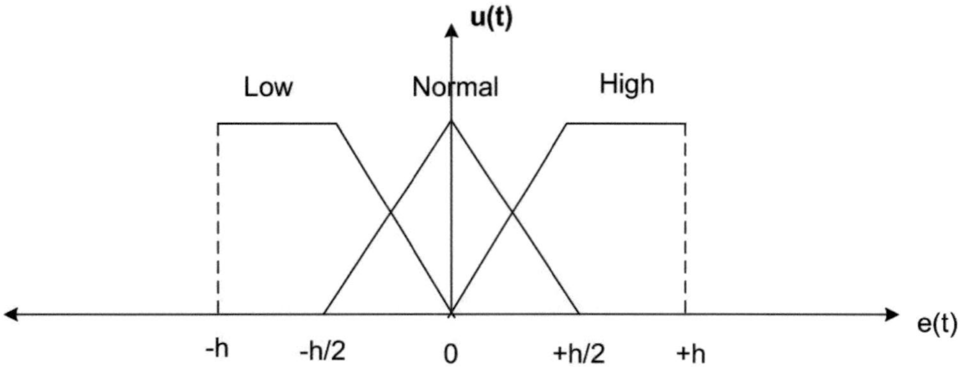

Fig. 2 (b) The membership distribution of the 1st input, the error e(t)

While using the T-S fuzzy model (Buckley & Eslami 2002), the consequents of the fuzzy rules are expressed as analytic functions which are linearly dependent on the inputs. In present case, three singleton fuzzy terms are assigned to the output such that the consequent part of the ith rule φ^c_i is a linear function of one input y(t) which can be expressed as:

$$\varphi_i^c(t) = r_i \, M \, y(t) \tag{1}$$

where r_i takes the values -1, 0, 1 (depends on the output's fuzzy terms)
$y(t)$ is the 2nd input to the controller
M is a parameter used to tune the controller.

The fuzzy rules are formulated such that the output is a feedback signal inversely proportional to the error signal as follow:

IF	the error	is	High	THEN	$\varphi_1^c = M\, y(t)$
IF	the error	is	Normal	THEN	$\varphi_2^c = 0$
IF	the error	is	Low	THEN	$\varphi_3^c = -M\, y(t)$

The fuzzy controller is adjusted by changing the values of L, h and M which affect the controller nonlinearity map. Therefore, the fuzzy controller implements these values equivalent to the saturation parameters of standard saturation nonlinearity (Jenkins & Passino 1999).

Before studying the system stability, a general model of a Sugeno fuzzy controller is defined (Thathachar & Viswanath 1997; Babuska, Roubos et al. 1998; Buckley & Eslami 2002) as follows:

For a two-input T-S fuzzy system; let the system state vector at time t be:

$$z = \begin{bmatrix} z_1 \\ z_2 \end{bmatrix}$$

where z_1, and z_2 are the state variable of the system at time t.

A T-S fuzzy system is defined by the implications such that:

$$\begin{aligned} R_i &: \textit{if} \quad (z_1 \textit{ is } S_1^i \textit{ AND } \quad z_2 \textit{ is } S_2^i) \quad \textit{then} \\ \dot{z} &= A_n z + B_n \end{aligned}$$

and for the proposed system where B_n is taken as a zero matrix and n = 2 for the two-input system, then:

$$\begin{aligned} R_i &: \textit{if} \quad (z_1 \textit{ is } S_1^i \textit{ AND } \quad z_2 \textit{ is } S_2^i) \quad \textit{then} \\ \dot{z} &= A_1 z_1 + A_2 z_2 \end{aligned}$$

for $i = 1 \ldots\ldots N$,

where S^i_1, S^i_2 are the fuzzy set corresponding to the state variables z_1, z_2 and R_i.

$A_n=[A_1, A_2]$, are the characteristic matrices which represent the fuzzy system.

However the truth value or weight of the implication R_i at time t denoted by $w_i(z)$ is defined as:

$$w_i(z) = \wedge(\mu_{S_1^i}(z_1), \mu_{S_2^i}(z_2))$$

where

$\mu_S(z)$ is the membership function value of fuzzy set S at position z

$\wedge$ is taken to be the min operator

Then the system state is updated according to (Reznik 1997):

$$\dot{z} = \frac{\sum_{i=1}^{N} w_i(z) A_i z}{\sum_{i=1}^{N} w_i(z)} = \sum_{i=1}^{N} \delta_i(z) A_i z \tag{2}$$

where $\delta_i(z) = \dfrac{w_i(z)}{\sum_{p=1}^{N} w_p(z)}$

However, the consequent part of the proposed system rules is a linear function of only one input y(t) as mentioned in the pervious section, and therefore the output of the fuzzy controller is of the form:

$$\dot{y} = \sum_{i=1}^{N} \delta_i(y) M_i y \tag{3}$$

where N is the number of the rules

M_i is a parameter used for the ith rule to tune the controller

Notice that Eq. 3 directly depends on the input y(t) and indirectly depends on e(t) which affects the weights δ_i. Thus the proposed system can be redrawn as shown in Fig. 3

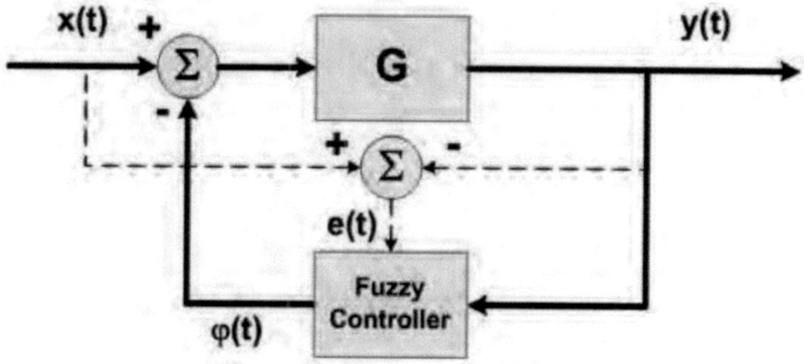

Fig. 3 The equivalent block diagram of the proposed system

The stability analysis of the system considers the system nonlinearities and uses circle criterion theory to ensure stability.

3. Stability analysis using circle criterion

In this section the circle criterion (Ray, Ghosh et al. 1984; Ray & Majumderr 1984; Vidyasagar 1993; Jenkins & Passino 1999) will be used for testing and tuning the controller in order to ensure the system stability and improve its output response. The circle criterion was first used in (Ray, Ghosh et al. 1984; Ray & Majumderr 1984) for stability analysis of fuzzy logic controllers and as a result of its graphical nature; the designer is given a physical feel for the system.

The output of the system given by Eq. 3 can be rewritten as follow:

$$\dot{y} = \sum_{i=1}^{N} \{M_i y - [(1-\delta_i(y))M_i y]\} \tag{4}$$

This comprises a separate linear part and nonlinear part denoted as φ(t) that can be expressed by (Vidyasagar 1993; Cuesta, Gordillo et al. 1999):

$$\varphi = \sum_{i=1}^{N} [(1-\delta_i(y))M_i y] \tag{5}$$

As a result a T-S fuzzy system can be represented according to a LUR'E system (Vidyasagar 1993; Cuesta, Gordillo et al. 1999). Consider a closed loop system, Fig. 4, given a linear time-invariant part G (a linear representation of the process to be controlled) with a nonlinear feedback part φ(t) (represent a fuzzy controller).

The function φ(t) represents memoryless, time varying nonlinearity with:

$$\varphi : [0,\infty) \times \Re \rightarrow \Re$$

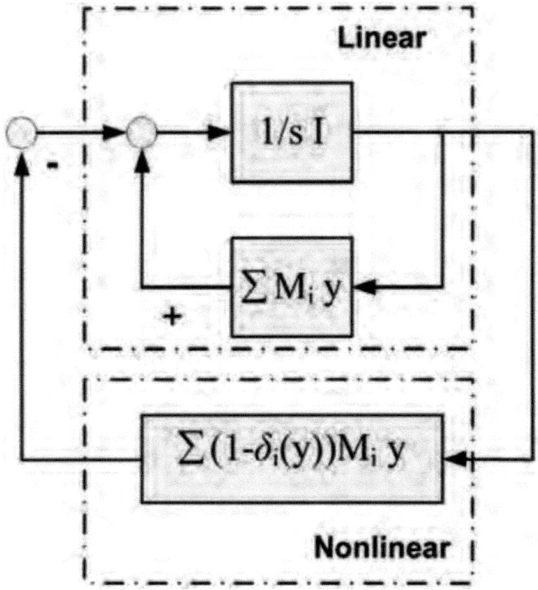

Fig. 4 T-S Fuzzy System according to the structure of the problem of LUR'E

If φ is bounded within a certain region as shown in Fig. 5 such that there exist:

α, β, a, b, ($\beta>\alpha$, $a<0<b$) for which:

$$\alpha y \leq \varphi(y) \leq \beta y \tag{6}$$

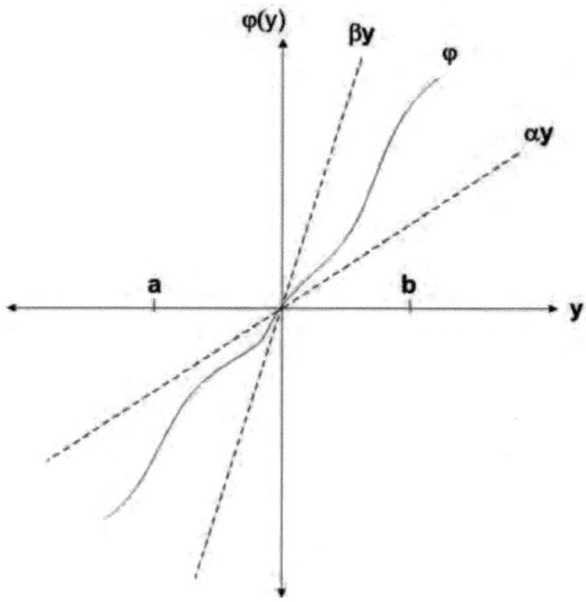

Fig. 5 Sector Bounded Nonlinearity

for all $t \geq 0$ and all $y \in [a, b]$ then: $\varphi(y)$ is a "Sector Nonlinearity":

If $\alpha y \le \varphi(y) \le \beta y$ is true for all y ∈ (-∞,∞) then the sector condition holds globally and the system is "absolutely stable". The idea is that no detailed information about nonlinearity is assumed, all that known it is that φ satisfies this condition (Vidyasagar 1993).

Let D(α, β) denote the closed disk in the complex plane centred at $-\frac{(\alpha+\beta)}{2\alpha\beta}$, with radius $\frac{|\alpha-\beta|}{2|\alpha\beta|}$ and the diameter is the line segment connecting the points $\frac{-1}{\alpha}+j0$ and $\frac{-1}{\beta}+j0$.

The circle criterion states that when φ satisfies the sector condition Eq.6 the system in Fig.3 is absolutely stable if one of following conditions are met (Vidyasagar 1993):

- If 0 < α < β, the Nyquist Plot of G(jw) is bounded away from the disk D(α, β) and encircles it m times in the counter clockwise direction where m is the number of poles of G(s) in the open right half plane(RHP).
- If 0 = α < β, G(s) is Hurwitz (poles in the open LHP) and the Nyquist Plot of G(jw) lies to the right of the line $s = \frac{-1}{\beta}$.
- If α < 0 < β, G(s) is Hurwitz and Nyquist Plot of G(jw) lies in the interior of the disk D(α, β) and is bounded away from the circumference of D(α, β).

For the fuzzy controller represented by Eq. 2, we are interested in the first two conditions (Ray & Majumderr 1984), and it can be sector bounded in the same manner (Jenkins & Passino 1999) as described next.

Consider the fuzzy controller as a nonlinearity φ and assume that there exist a sector (α, β) in which φ lies, then use the circle criterion to test the stability. Simply, using the Nyquist plot, the sector bounded nonlinearity of the fuzzy logic controller will degenerate, depending on its slope *a* that is always zero (Jenkins & Passino 1999) and the disk to the straight line passing through $\frac{-1}{\beta}$ and parallel to the imaginary axis as shown in Fig.6 In such case the stability criteria will be modified as follows (Vidyasagar 1993):

Definition: A single-input single-output (SISO) system will be globally and asymptotically stable provided the complete Nyquist locus of its transfer function does not enter the forbidden region left to the line passing through $\frac{-1}{\beta}$ in an anticlockwise direction as shown in Fig. 6.

The fuzzy controller is tuned until its parameters lie in the bounded sector, so that the fuzzy system nonlinearity is bounded in this sector. In fact, even if the function φ is approximately linear, the saturation outside this region causes φ to be always nonlinear.

From the above discussion, we conclude that to ensure stability for a closed loop system with known transfer function or nonlinearity sector, one can add a fuzzy block (stabilizer) in the feedback loop tuned in the manner described above and under the condition that the stabilizer block is faster than the controlled system. This concept is used to enhance the performance of existing control systems especially for systems controlled using fuzzy controller in the forward loop. In such cases the feedback fuzzy stabilizer can be integrated in the main fuzzy controller as explained in the next section.

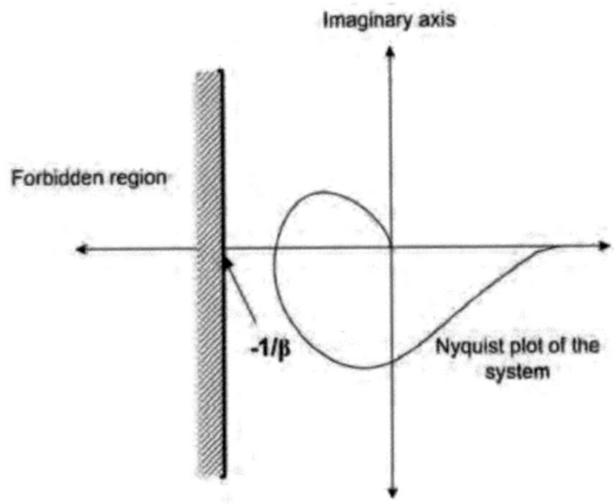

Fig. 6 Nyquist plot with fuzzy feedback system (Ray & Majumderr 1984).

4. Self stabilized fuzzy controller

Figure 7 comprises a plant controlled by a SISO fuzzy controller. In order to guarantee the system stability, a fuzzy stabilizer has been added in the feedback path.

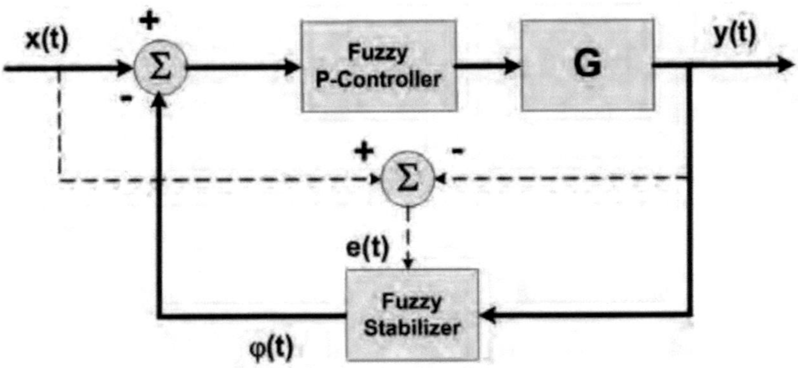

Fig. 7 Block Diagram of the system with Fuzzy-P controller

Only, minor changes are necessary to the above analysis in order to include the SISO fuzzy controller nonlinearities if these have not been included in the previously calculated sector. As a result, the fuzzy stabilizer will be retuned to the new sector which will be the minimum intersection between the fuzzy controller nonlinearity sector and the sector results using the circle criterion. This is understandable as the fuzzy controller represents an odd function (Reznik 1997; Jenkins & Passino 1999) (i.e. $\varphi(-y) = -\varphi(y)$) , so that fuzzy controller can be in the feedback path rather than the feed forward path. Therefore, the dominant nonlinear sector will be the minimum sector. Consequently from analysis, the feedback stabilizer can be built in each fuzzy controller to improve its performance by adding an extra input and modifying the original fuzzy rule base by adding the stabilization rules.

Generally, there are many types of fuzzy reasoning that can be employed in fuzzy control applications, the most commonly used types are Mamdani and Takagi-Sugeno (T-S) type. For Mamdani fuzzy systems (Farinwata, Filev et al. 2000), the same structure can be used except for the addition of another input y(t) and three extra rules to the rule base as shown in Fig. 8.

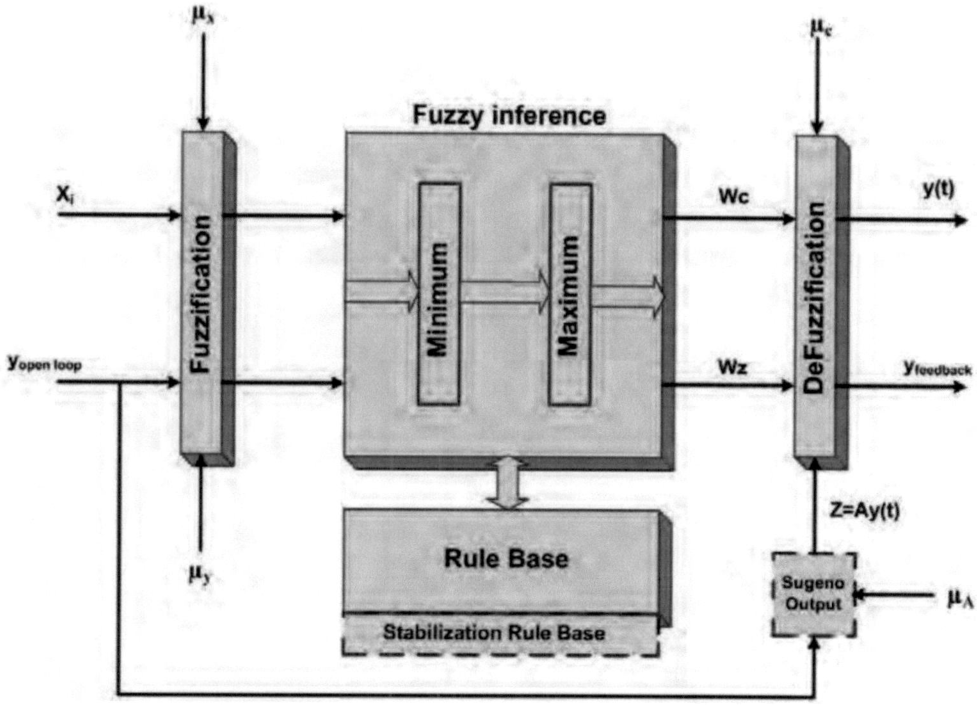

Fig. 8 The modification to the fuzzy system structure

Where μ_x, μ_c are the input and output fuzzy sets for Mamdani fuzzy system
μ_y, μ_A are the input and output fuzzy sets for fuzzy stabilizer system

Consequently, less modification is required for T-S type fuzzy systems.

The main reason for integrating the stabilizer into the normal structure of fuzzy controllers is to make them suitable for hardware and software implementation. The same design of the circuits or algorithms will be used without significant modifications.

5. Examples and simulation results

A plant with transfer function:

$$G(s) = \frac{400}{s^3 + 10.4s^2 + 8s + 40},$$

is used to demonstrate the performance of fuzzy stabilizer. The Nyquist plot of G(jw) is shown in Fig. 9.

The system is unstable and has closed loop poles at -12.6 and 1.08± j 5.82, with a gain margin of -19.3dB. If we consider the fuzzy stabilizer as a nonlinearity φ as shown in Fig. 5, then the disk D(α, β) is the line segment connecting the points $\frac{-1}{\alpha} + j0$ and $\frac{-1}{\beta} + j0$. Applying the Circle Criterion and because $a = 0$ the second condition will be used. To find a sector (a, β)

in which φ lies, the system Nyquist plot Fig. 9 is analyzed. The Nyquist plot does not satisfy the second condition as it intersects with the line drawn at $\frac{-1}{\beta} = -9.259$. In order to meet the second condition of the theory the line drawn at $\frac{-1}{\beta}$ will be moved to be at $\frac{-1}{\beta} = -27.5$ such that the Nyquist plot lies to the right of it. As a result, the fuzzy controller will be tuned by choosing M, and L such that its nonlinearities lies in the sector (0,0.036).

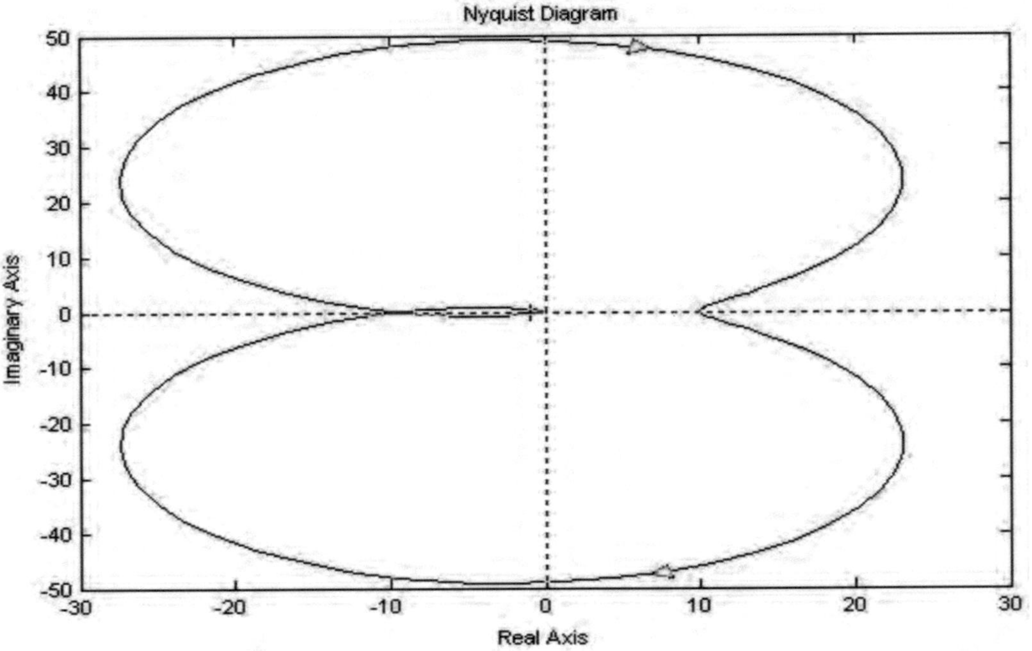

Fig. 9 The plant Nyquist plot

In order to satisfy the circle criterion condition, the ratio M/L will be kept less than β (i.e M/L < 0.036) by choosing M = 0.68 and L = 20 .

A traditional fuzzy like proportional controller (Reznik 1997) is used to control the system with a normal feedback loop as we saw in Fig. 7 in order that a comparison can be made between the results with and without a fuzzy stabilizer in the feedback loop. In order to retune the fuzzy stabilizer, the fuzzy P-controller has a ratio M_c/L_c or $\beta_c = 1$.

However $\beta = 0.036$ for the plant, and therefore the minimum sector for the stabilizer to be tuned is: $(a, \beta) = (0, 0.036)$.

The system step response (solid line) results with and without the use of the stabilizer (dashed line) are shown Fig. 10. The results shows that the system with the fuzzy P-controller in Fig. 7 yields an unstable output (dashed line) while the use of the stabilizer produces a stable output.

The approach described has provided a quick and easy stabilization process which can allow designers to fine tune their controller's performance without at the same time, being worried about stability issues.

In Fig. 11 (a), and (b), the step responses for different systems, according to the setup in Fig. 3, are shown. The simulations show the tested system for a normal feedback without the stabilizer and with adding the stabilizer in the feedback loop as in illustrated in Fig. 3.
Using the same algorithm given a transfer function, a nonlinearity sector and the tuned values of M and L of the fuzzy stabilizer, the stabilizer has been tuned.

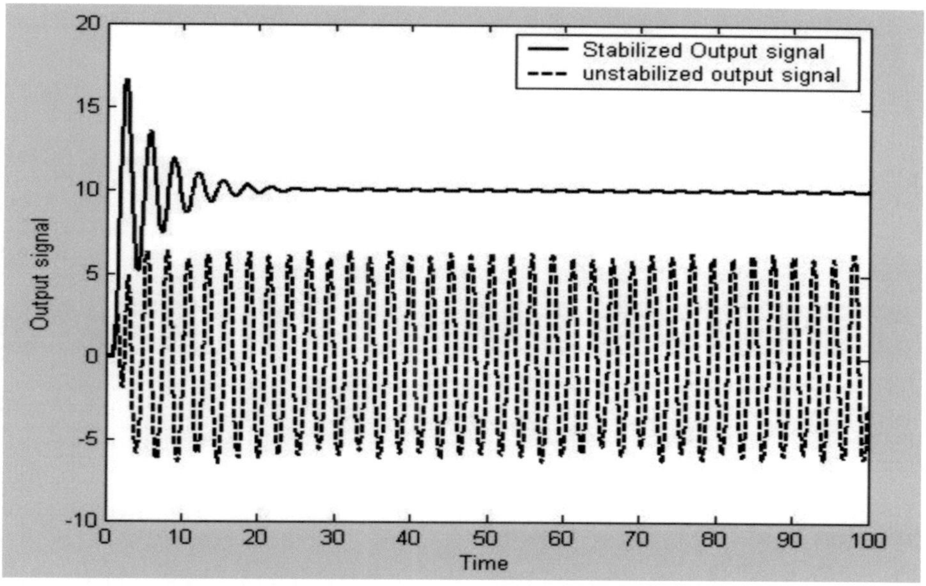

Fig. 10 The simulated step response of the two compared systems

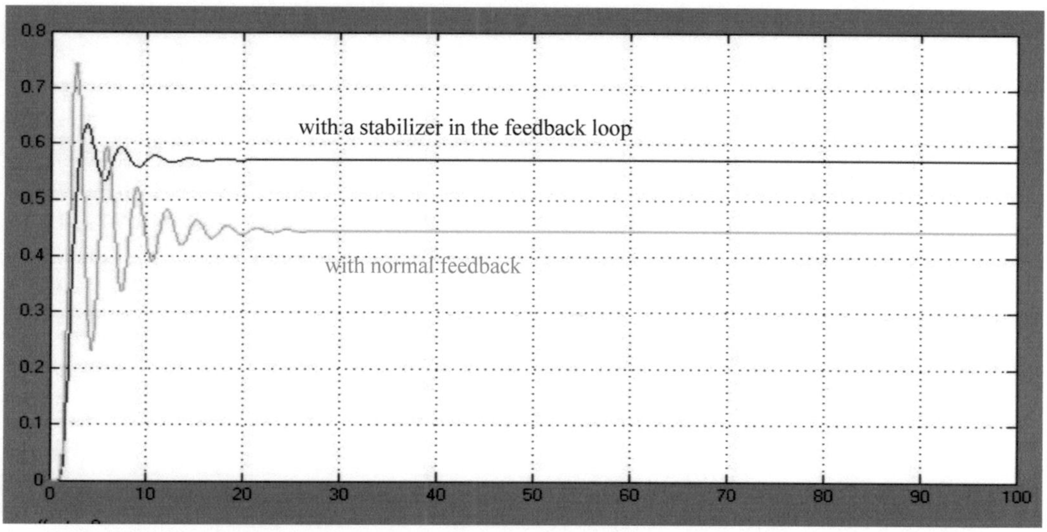

Fig. 11(a) The step Response of the controller with following parameters (Black curve):

$G(s) = \frac{12}{s^3 + 7s^2 + 7s + 15}$, (α, β)=(0, 0.3), L=1, M= 0.3

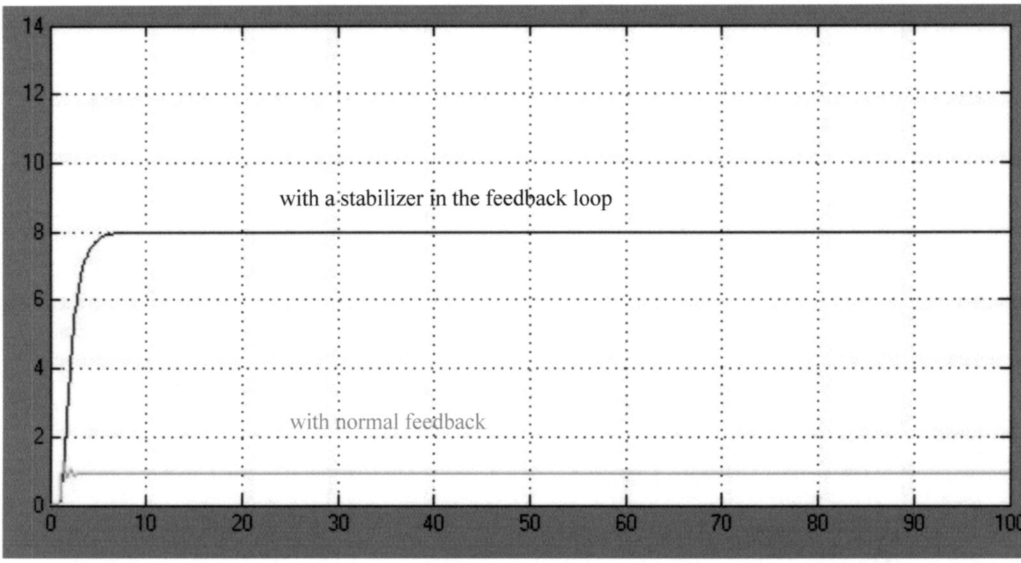

Fig. 11(b) The step Response of the controller with following parameters (Black curve):

$$G(s) = \frac{40}{s^2 + 4s + 3}, \ (\alpha, \beta) = (0, 1.3), \ L=1, M = 1.3$$

6. Extension to MIMO fuzzy systems

The stability analysis of multi-inputs multi-outputs (MIMO) is a nontrivial task due to the complexity of the system (Safonov 1980), however, many algorithms have been proposed to tackle the problem; K. Ray and D. Majumder (Ray & Majumderr 1984) extended their approach of using circle criteria to MIMO systems but restricted the result to square systems only. The conicity theory has been used by others (Kang, Kwon et al. 1998; Cuesta, Gordillo et al. 1999; Cuesta & Ollero 2004) to study the stability of MIMO fuzzy systems but it suffers from the nontrivial problem of determining the candidate centre. Linear matrix inequalities (LMI) technique is also used (Wang, Tanaka et al. 1996; Lam & Seneviratne 2007) but has the disadvantage of high number of LMI used which make the analysis more complicated (Cuesta, Gordillo et al. 1999). The description function is also used to study the stability of MIMO systems (Abdelnour, Cheung et al. 1993; Aracil & Gordillo 2004).

6.1 Stability analysis of open loop MIMO systems

In order to extend the proposed approach fuzzy stabilizer to MIMO (Multi-input Multi-output) systems, an additively decomposition technique (Ying 1996) is used. According to the structure of the classical problem of LUR'E (Vidyasagar 1993; Cuesta, Gordillo et al. 1999) shown in Fig. 4 , and referring to the analysis in section 3, a T-S fuzzy system can be represented as linear and nonlinear part as follows:
Consider a T-S fuzzy system with N rules (Cuesta, Gordillo et al. 1999):

$$R_r : if \ (z_1 \ is \ S_1^i \ AND \ z_2 \ is \ S_2^j) \ then$$
$$\dot{z} = M_{ij} z$$

with:

$$M_{ij} = \begin{bmatrix} a_i & b_j \\ c_i & d_j \end{bmatrix} \text{ and } z = \begin{bmatrix} z_1 \\ z_2 \end{bmatrix}$$

for r = 1 ..... m×n, where
S^i_1, S^j_2 are the fuzzy membership function corresponding to the state variables
z_1, z_2, which represented by linguistic terms with membership functions such that:

$$\mu_{S^1_p}(z_1 = 0) = 1, \quad \mu_{S^1_i}(z_1 = 0) = 0$$

$$i \neq p, i = 1, \ldots, m$$

and

$$\mu_{S^2_q}(z_2 = 0) = 1, \quad \mu_{S^2_j}(z_2 = 0) = 0$$

$$j \neq q, j = 1, \ldots, n$$

and $M_{ij} \in R^{2\times2}$, is the characteristic matrices which represents the fuzzy system.
Similar to the analysis in section 2, the system state is updated according to:

$$\dot{z} = \sum_{i=1}^{m}\sum_{j=1}^{n} \delta_{ij}(z) M_{ij} z \tag{7}$$

where $\delta_{ij}(z) = \dfrac{w_{ij}(z)}{\sum_{k=1}^{m}\sum_{p=1}^{n} w_{kp}(z)}$

and $w_{ij}(z)$ is the truth value or weight of the implication R_{ij} at time t
Then Eq. 7 can be rewritten as:

$$\dot{z} = \sum_{i=1}^{m}\sum_{j=1}^{n} \left\{ M_{ij} z - \left[\left(1 - \delta_{ij}(z) \right) M_{ij} z \right] \right\} \tag{8}$$

Eq. 8 shows the system has been split into linear and nonlinear part, Fig. 4. Notice that the first column of M_{ij} depends on i while the second column depends on j Hence, the resulting nonlinear part φ(z) such that:

$$\varphi(z) = \sum_{i=1}^{m}\sum_{j=1}^{n} \left(1 - \delta_{ij}(z) \right) M_{ij} z \tag{9}$$

is additively decomposable (Cuesta, Gordillo et al. 1999), that is:

$$\varphi(z) = \varphi(z_1, z_2) = \varphi(z_1, 0) + \varphi(0, z_2) \tag{10}$$

(see (Cuesta, Gordillo et al. 1999) for the proof)

Eq. 10 implies that the nonlinear part φ is additively decomposable, and therefore techniques used for stability analysis of SISO system can be used to stabilize the multi-input multi-output systems. This can be done by adding a number of small fuzzy systems equal to the number of the output variables in the feedback loop of the MIMO system for each input variable as shown in Fig. 12. In this way all the nonlinearities of the fuzzy system can be included within a bounded sector.

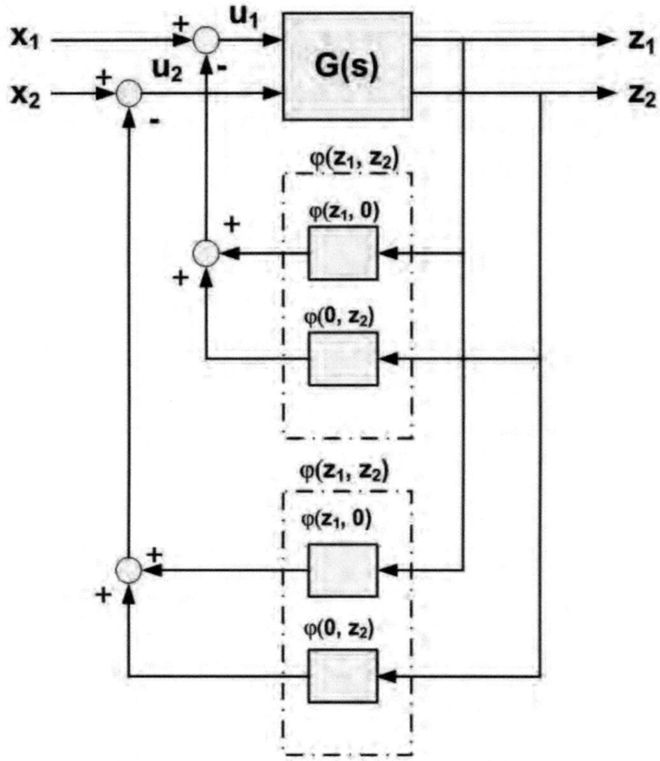

Fig. 12 The proposed MIMO fuzzy feedback system

6.2 Stability analysis of closed loop MIMO system

A simple stability analysis for closed loop system is shown in Fig. 13 (a). In this system the proposed fuzzy stabiliser is placed on each feedback loop for each input as shown in Fig. 13(b). That includes all the nonlinearities of the system.

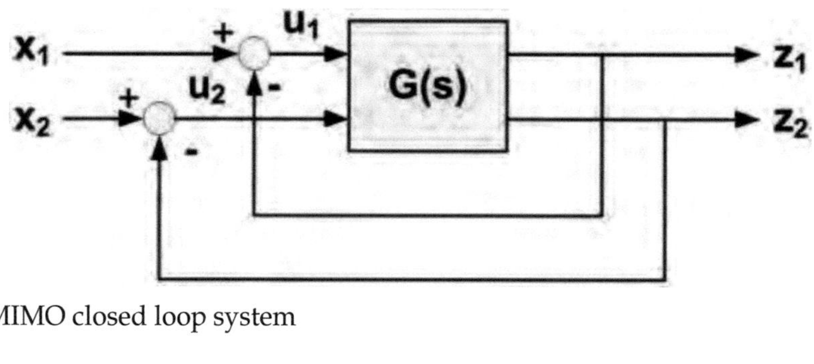

Fig. 13.(a) MIMO closed loop system

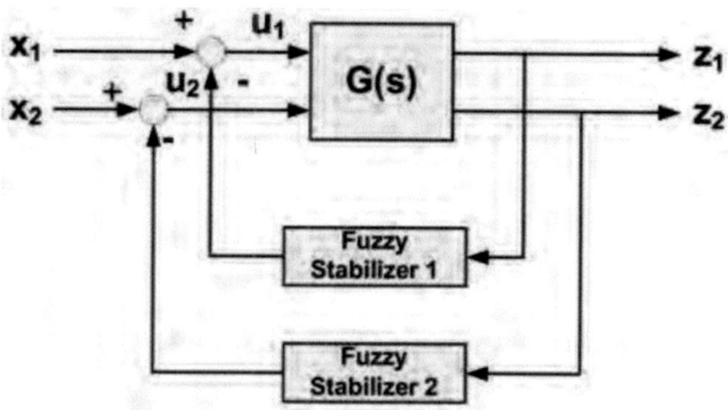

Fig. 13.(b) MIMO closed loop system with fuzzy stabilizers

6.3 Simulation example

Consider a MIMO system with a state space representation:

$$\begin{bmatrix}\dot{x}_1\\ \dot{x}_2\\ \dot{x}_3\end{bmatrix}=\begin{bmatrix}-7 & -7 & -50\\ 1 & 0 & 0\\ 0 & 1 & 0\end{bmatrix}\begin{bmatrix}x_1\\ x_2\\ x_3\end{bmatrix}+\begin{bmatrix}1 & 0\\ 0 & 1\\ 0 & 0\end{bmatrix}\begin{bmatrix}u_1\\ u_2\end{bmatrix}$$

$$\begin{bmatrix}y_1\\ y_2\end{bmatrix}=\begin{bmatrix}-1 & 0 & 0\\ 0 & 1 & 0\end{bmatrix}\begin{bmatrix}x_1\\ x_2\\ x_3\end{bmatrix}$$

In our problem we will find a transfer function of the model of the form:

$$\begin{bmatrix}y_1\\ y_2\end{bmatrix}=\begin{bmatrix}G_{11} & G_{12}\\ G_{21} & G_{22}\end{bmatrix}\begin{bmatrix}u_1\\ u_2\end{bmatrix}$$

where $G_{11}=\dfrac{s^2}{s^3+7s^2+7s+50}$

$$G_{21}=\frac{-s}{s^3+7s^2+7s+50}$$

$$G_{12}=\frac{7s+50}{s^3+7s^2+7s+50}$$

$$G_{22}=\frac{s^2+7s}{s^3+7s^2+7s+50}$$

Using the analysis described in section 5 and by aid of Nyquist plot of the system as shown in Fig. 14 we can determine $-\frac{1}{\beta}=-6.45$, as a result $M/L\leq 0.155$.

Note that, for all the components of the system (G11, G12, G21, and G22), the denominator in each case remains the same, since it holds the key to the system stability.

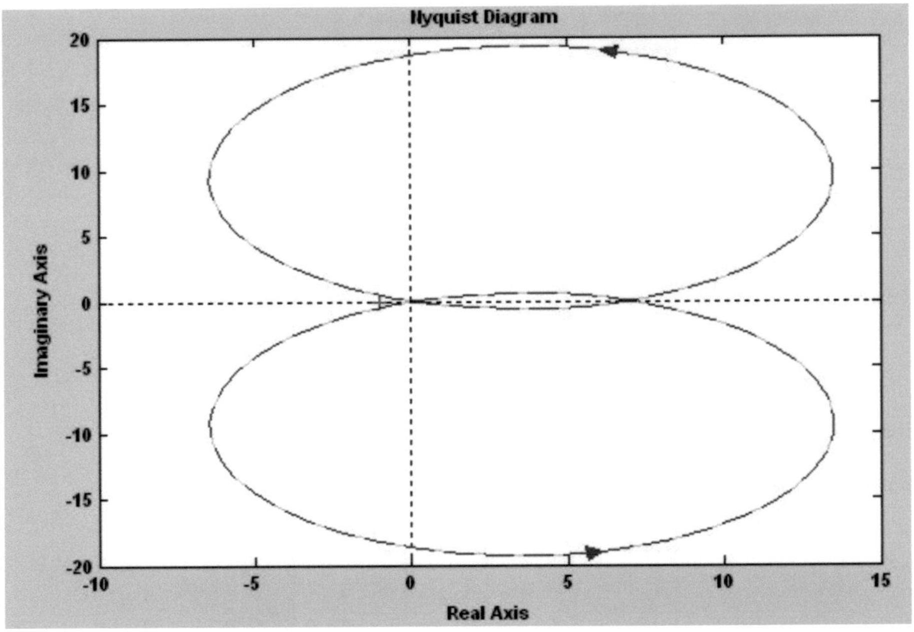

Fig. 14 The Nyquist plot of the simulated system

The outputs of the open loop system show the system instability as shown in Fig. 15.

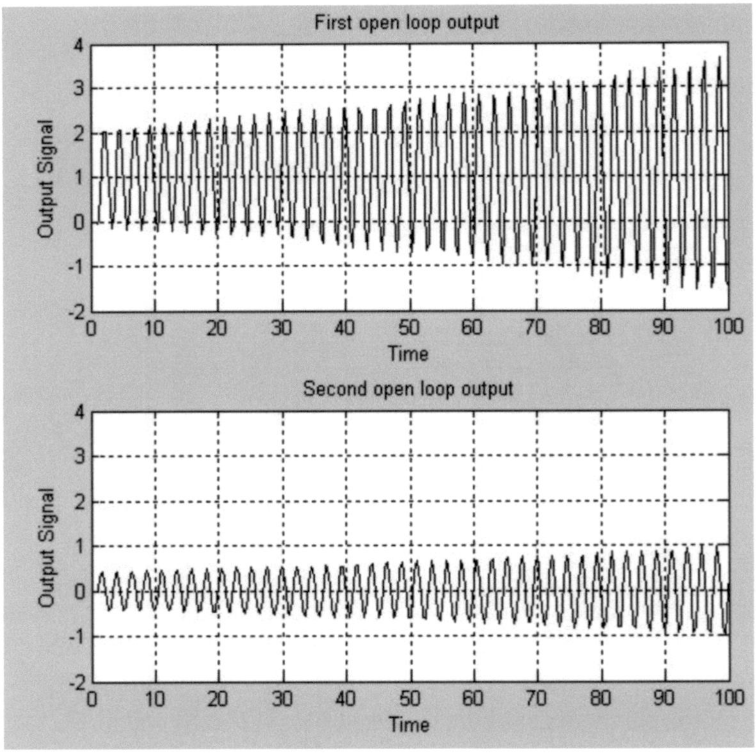

Fig. 15 The open loop response of the simulated system

When the fuzzy stabilizers are added to the system according to Fig. 12 and the fuzzy parameters are set such that the ratio $M/L \le 0.007$ is kept the same as follow:

Stabilizer (1) M11= 3.1 , L11= 25
Stabilizer (2) M12= 1.8 , L12= 12
Stabilizer (3) M21= 0.031 , L21= 0.25
Stabilizer (4) M22= 0.018 , L22= 0.12

The simulation results in Fig. 16 show the output of the stabilized system.

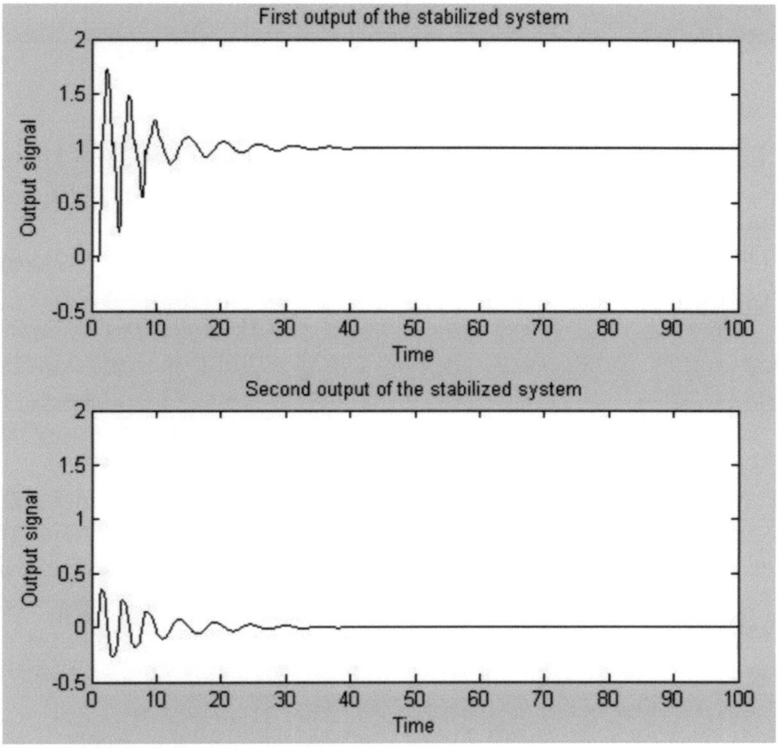

Fig. 16 The outputs of the stabilized simulated system

The proposed technique has the advantage of keeping the system stable even if the system nonlinearities have been changed provided that they still remain within the bounded sector proposed.

7. Conclusion

This chapter presented a practical approach to stabilize fuzzy systems based on adaptive nonlinear feedback using a fuzzy stabilizer in the feedback loop. For this we needed to identify the nonlinearity range of the system. The fuzzy stabilizer is tuned so that the system nonlinearities lie in a bounded sector as delivered by using the circle criterion theory. Because of circle criterion's graphical nature; the designer is given a physical feel for the system. The concept has been used to ensure stability of a car-like robot controller. In addition, the idea has been extended to stabilize MIMO systems based on the additively decomposition technique.

The advantage of the proposed approach is the simplicity of the design procedure especially for the MIMO systems analysis and implementation. The use of the fuzzy system to control the feedback loop using its approximate reasoning algorithm gives a good opportunity to handle the practical system uncertainty. The approach described have provided a quick and easy stabilization process which can allow designers to fine tune their controllers performance without at the same time, worrying about stability issues It is also shown that the fuzzy stabilizer can be integrated, with small modifications, in any fuzzy controller to enhance its stability. As a result it is suitable for hardware implementation or even to modify existence software and hardware design if required to ensure system stability.

8. References

Abdelnour, G., J. Y. Cheung, et al. (1993). "Application of Describing Functions in the Transient Respose Analysis of Three Term Fuzzy Controller." IEEE Transaction on System, Man and Cybernetics **23**: 603-606.

Aracil, J. and F. Gordillo (2004). "Describing function method for stability analysis of PD and PI fuzzy controllers." Fuzzy Sets and Systems **143**: 233-249.

Babuska, R., J. Roubos, et al. (1998). Identification of MIMO systems by input-output TS fuzzy models. In the proceedings of The 1998 IEEE International Conference on Fuzzy systems, IEEE World Congress on Computational Intelligence.

Buckley, J. J. and E. Eslami (2002). An Introduction to Fuzzy Logic and Fuzzy Sets, Phydica-Verlag Heidelberg.

Cuesta, F., F. Gordillo, et al. (1999). "Stability Analysis of Nonlinear Multivariable Takagi–Sugeno Fuzzy Control Systems." IEEE Transaction on Fuzzy Systems **7**(5): 508-520.

Cuesta, F. and A. Ollero (2004). "Fuzzy control of reactive navigation with stability analysis based on conicity and Lyapunov theory." Journal of Control Engineering Practice **12**: 625-638.

Espada, A. and A. Barreiro (1999). "Robust stability of fuzzy control systems based on conicity conditions." Automatica **35**: 643-654.

Farinwata, S. S., D. Filev, et al. (2000). Fuzzy Control: Synthesis and Analysis, John Wiley & Sons Ltd.

Fuh, C.-C. and P.-C. Tung (1997). "Robust stability analysis of fuzzy control systems." Fuzzy Sets and Systems **88**: 289-298.

Gang, J. and C. Laijiu (1996). "Linguistic stability analysis of fuzzy closed loop control systems." Fuzzy Sets and Systems **82**: 27-34.

Giron-Sierra, J. M. and G. Ortega (2002). A Survey of Stability of Fuzzy Logic Control with Aerospace Applications. 15th Triennial World Congress. Barcelona, Spain.

Gruyitch, L., J.-P. Richard, et al. (2004). Stability Domains, Chapman& Hall/CRC.

J. Yen, R. L., and L. A. Zadeh (1995). Industrial applications of fuzzy logic and intelligent systems, IEEE Press.

Jenkins, D. and K. M. Passino (1999). "An Introduction to Nonlinear Analysis of Fuzzy Control Systems." Journal of Intelligent and Fuzzy Systems, **17**(1): 75–103.

Kandel, A., Y. LUO, et al. (1999). "Stability analysis of fuzzy control systems." Fuzzy Sets and Systems **105**: 33-48.

Kang, H.-J., C. Kwon, et al. (1998). "Robust Stability Analysis and Design Method for the Fuzzy Feedback Linearization Regulator." IEEE Transaction on Fuzzy Systems **6**(4): 464-472.

Katoh, R., T. Yamashita, et al. (1995). "Stability analysis of control system having PD type of fuzzy controller." Fuzzy Sets and Systems **74**: 321-334.

Lam, H. K. and L. D. Seneviratne (2007). "LMI-based stability design of fuzzy controller for nonlinear systems." IET Control Theory Appl. **1**(1): 393-401.

Lin, C., Q.-G. Wang, et al. (2007). "Stability conditions for time-delay fuzzy systems using fuzzy weighting-dependent approach." IET Control Theory Appl. **1**(1): 127-132.

Mannani, A. and H. A. Talebi (2007). "A Fuzzy Lyapunov-Based Control Strategy for a Macro–Micro Manipulator: Experimental Results." IEEE Transactions on Control Systems Technology **15**(2): 375-383.

Piegat, A. (1997). Hyperstability of fuzzy-control systems and degrees of freedom. In the proceedings of EUFIT'97.

Ray, K. S., A. M. Ghosh, et al. (1984). "L2-Stability and the related design concept for SISO linear systems associated with fuzzy logic controllers." IEEE Transactions on Systems, Man, and Cybernetics **SMC-14**(6): 932–939.

Ray, K. S. and D. D. Majumderr (1984). "Application of circle criteria for stability analysis of linear SISO and MIMO systems associated with fuzzy logic controllers." IEEE Transactions on Systems, Man, and Cybernetics **SMC-14**(2): 345–349.

Reznik, L. (1997). Fuzzy Contollers, Newnes.

Rubio, J. d. J. and W. Yu (2007). "Stability Analysis of Nonlinear System Identification via Delayed Neural Networks." IEEE TRANSACTIONS ON CIRCUITS AND SYSTEMS-II: EXPRESS BRIEFS **54**(2): 161-165.

Safonov, M. G. (1980). Stability and Roboustness of Multivariable Feedback Systems. Unites State of America, The Massachusetts Institute Of Technology.

Safonov, M. G. (1980). Stability and Robustness of Multivariable Feedback systems, The Massachusetts Institute of Technology.

Tanaka, K. and M. Sugeno (1992). "Stability analysis and design of fuzzy control systems." Fuzzy Sets and Systems **45**: 135-156.

Thathachar, M. A. L. and P. Viswanath (1997). "On the stability of fuzzy systems." IEEE Transaction on Fuzzy Systems **5**(1): 145-151.

Vidyasagar, M. (1993). Nonlinear Systems Analysis. Englewood, Cliffs, New Jersey, Prentice Hall, Inc.

Wang, H. O., K. Tanaka, et al. (1996). "An Aproach to Fuzzy Control of Nonlinear Systems: Stability and Design Issues." IEEE Trans. Fuzzy Systems **4**: 14-23.

Wang, W. J. and H. R. Lin (1998). "Fuzzy control design for the trajectory tracking in phase plane." IEEE Transaction on System, Man and Cybernetics, part A **28**(5): 710-719.

Wu, S. J. and T. L. Ch. (2000). "Optimal fuzzy controller design: Local concept approach." IEEE Trans. Fuzzy Systems **8**(2): 171-185.

Ying, H. (1996). "Structure Decomposition of the General MIMO Fuzzy Systems." International Journal of Intelligent Control and Systems **1**(3): 327-337.

Ying, H. (1999). "Analytical analysis and feedback linearization tracking control of the general Takagi-Sugeno fuzzy dynamic systems." IEEE Transaction on system, Man and Cybernetics, part C **29**(2): 290-298.

Zuo, Z. and Y. Wang (2007). "Robust stability and stabilisation for nonlinear uncertain time-delay systems via fuzzy control approach." IET Control Theory Appl. **1**(1): 422-429.

13

Switching Control in the Presence of Constraints and Unmodeled Dynamics

Vojislav Filipovic
Regional center for talents, Loznica
Serbia

1. Introduction

Recently there has been increased research interest in the study of the hybrid dynamical systems (Sun & Ge, 2005) and (Li et al., 2005). These systems involve the interaction of discrete and continuous dynamics. Continuous variables take the values from the set of real numbers and the discrete variables take the values from finite set of symbols. The hybrid systems have the behaviour of an analog dynamic system before certain abrupt structural or operating conditions are changed. The event driven dynamics in hybrid control systems can be described using different frameworks from discrete event systems (Cassandras & Lafortune, 2008) such as timed automata, max-plus algebra or Petry nets. For dynamic systems whose component are dominantly discrete event, main tools for analysis and design are representation theory, supervisory control, computer simulation and verification. From the clasical control theory point of view, hybrid systems may be considered as a switching control between analog feedback loops. Generally, hybrid systems can achieve better performance then non-switching controllers because they can to reconfigure and reorganize their structures. For that is necessery correct coordination of discrete and analog control variables.

The mathematical model for real process, generally, has the Hammerstein-Wiener form (Crama & Atkins, 2001) and (Zhao & Chen, 2006). It means that on the input and output of the process are present nonlinear elements (actuator and sensor). Here we will consider Hammerstein model which has the input saturation as nonlinear element. That is the most frequent nonlinearity encountered in practice (Hippe, 2006). Also, unmodeled dynamics with matching condition is present. As a control strategy will be used switching control. The switched systems can be viewed as higher abstraction of hybrid systems.

The design of switching controllers having guaranted stability, known as the picewise linear LQ control (PLC), is first considered in (Wredenhagen & Belanger, 1994). The picewise linear systems are systems that have different linear dynamics in different regions of the continuous state space (Johansson, 2003). The PLC control has the associated switching surfaces in form of positively invariant sets and yields a relatively low-gain controller. In the LHG (low-and-high gain) design a low gain feedback law is first designed in such a way

that the actuator does not saturate in magnitude and the closed - loop system remains linear. The low gain enlarge the region in which the closed-loop system remains linear and enlarge the basin of attraction of the closed-loop systems (Lin, 1999). After that, using appropriate Lyapunov function for the closed-loop system, under this low gain feedback control law, a linear high gain feedback law is designed and added to the low gain feedback control. Combination of LHG and PLC gives the robust controllers with fast transience. The key feature of PLC/LHG controllers is that the saturation level is avoided. But, it has been recognized in references (Lin et al., 1997) and (De Dona et al., 2002) that the performance of closed-loop system can be further improved by forcing the control into saturation. Such controller increases the value of the switching regions so that each linear controller is able to act in a region where a degree of over-saturation is reached. The over-saturation means that the controller demands for input level is greater than the avaliable range.
The actuator rate saturation, also, is important problem. Namely, the phase lag associated with saturation rate has a destabilizing effect (Saberi et al., 2000). The problem is more severe when the actuator is, also, subject to magnitude saturation since small actuator output results in small stability margin even in the absence of rate saturation (Lin et al., 1997).
The problem is more complex in the presence of delay in the system. The paper (Tarbouriech & da Silva, 2000) deals with the synthesis of stabilizing controllers for linear systems with state delay and saturation controls. Performance guided hybrid LQ controller for discrete time-delay systems is considered in (Filipovic, 2005). In (Wu et al., 2007) the method for designing an output feedback law that stabilize a linear system subject to actuator saturation with large domain of attraction is considered. It is usually true that higher performance levels are associated with pushing the limits (Goodwin et al., 2005). That is motivation to operate the system on constraint bounderies. It means that problem with actuator saturation can be considered as optimisation with constraints.
In this paper the robustness of picewise linear LQ control with prescribed degree of stability using switching, low-and-high gain and over-saturation is considered. The process is described with linear uncertain dynamic system in the state space form. Structure of the uncertaintes is defined with matching conditions. By the Lyapunov stability criterion (Michel et al., 2008) it is shown that a robust PLC/LHG controller with allowed over-saturation, can exponentially stabilize linear uncertain systems with prescribed exponential rate. This approach is different in comparison with (De Dona et al., 2002) where the Riccati equation approach is used.

2. Switching controller with prescribed degree of stability

The dynamic system subject to input saturation can be described in the next form

$$\dot{x}(t) = Ax(t) + B\,\mathrm{sat}_{\Delta}u(t),\; x(t_0) = x_0 \in X \subset R^n \tag{1}$$

Where $x \in R^n$ and $u \in R^m$. Nonlinear input function (saturation function) is defined as

$$\mathrm{sat}_{\Delta} : R^m \to R^m$$

$$\Delta = [\Delta_1, \cdots, \Delta_m] \ , \ \Delta_i > 0 \ , \ i = 1,2,\cdots,m$$

$$sat_\Delta(u) = [sat_{\Delta_1}(u_1), \cdots, sat_{\Delta_m}(u_m)]^T$$

$$sat_{\Delta_i}(u_i) \overset{\Delta}{=} sign(u_i)\min(|u_i|, \Delta_i) \tag{2}$$

The u_i is the ith element of vector u. As in (Wredenhagen & Belanger, 1994) we take a sequence $\{\rho_i\}_{i=1}^N$ such that $\rho_1 > \rho_2 \cdots > \rho_N > 0$ and matrix $Q > 0$. Then that one can to define matrix

$$R_i = diag[r_i^1, r_i^2, \cdots, r_i^m], \quad r_i^j > 0, \ j = 1,2,\cdots,m \tag{3}$$

Design of optimal LQ regulator with prescribed degree of stability is based on minimization of next functional

$$J(x_0, \alpha) = \int_{t_0}^{\infty} e^{2\alpha t}[x^T(t)Qx(t) + v^T(t)R_i v(t)]dt \tag{4}$$

The quantity α in (4) defines the degree of system stability for the feedback control systems. From (4) for every R_i we can get matrices P_i and K_i from equations

$$(A + \alpha I)^T P_i + P_i(A + \alpha I) - P_i B R_i^{-1} B^T P_i + Q = 0 \tag{5}$$

$$K_i = R_i^{-1} B^T P_i \tag{6}$$

where P_i is the positive solution of the algebraic Riccati equation (5) for the optimal LQ problem. Matrix K_i is gain of the controller.
The switching surfaces are ellipsoids defined by

$$E_i = E_i(P_i, \rho_i) \overset{\Delta}{=} \{x : x^T e^{-2\alpha t} P_i x \le \rho_i\} \quad i = 1,2\cdots,N \tag{7}$$

Elements of matrix R_i are chosen, for a given q_i, to be the largest so that is satisfied

$$|v_j| = \left|\frac{1}{r_i^j} b_j^T P_i x\right| \le (1 + \beta_j)\Delta_j, \quad \forall x \in E_i(P_i, \rho_i) \ , \tag{8}$$

$$j = 1, \cdots, m_i$$

where v_j is the j th element of $v = -K_i x$, b_j is the j th column of matrix B.
The ellipsoids in the sequence $\{E_i\}_{i=1}^N$ are nested, i.e.

$$E_{i+1} \subset E_i \ , \ i = 1,2\cdots,N-1 \tag{9}$$

he state space region contained in the biggest ellipsoid can be devided into N cells $\{C_i\}_{i=1}^{N}$

$$C_i = E_i / E_{i-1} \ , \ C_N = E_N \tag{10}$$

Now, the controller based on the switching strategy is given in the next form

$$v = -K_i x \ , \ x \in C_i \ , \ i = 1,2...,N \tag{11}$$

The controller (5), (6) and (11) for $\alpha = 0$ is originally proposed in (Tarbouriech & da Silva, 2000). This controller is known as the picewise linear LQ contoller (PLC). Associated switching surfaces to PLC strategy are positively invariant sets (Blanchini, 1999) and (Blanchini & Miani, 2008) given by nested ellipsoids.
The PLC strategy which is proposed in (Lin, 1999) is low-gain controller. Such controller underutilize the available control capacity and the resulting convergence of the regulation error to zero is very slow although saturation is avoided.
Remark 1. Recent advances in miniaturizing, communication, sensing and actuation have made it feasible to envision large numbers of autonomous vehicles working cooperatively to accomplish an objective (Ren & Beard, 2008). The communication band and power constraints preclude centralized command and control. As a result a critical problem for cooperative control is to design distributed algorithms such that the group of vehicles can reach consensus on the shared information in the presence of limited and unreliable information exchange and dynamically changing interaction topologies. For the switching information exchange topologies the convergence of consensus protocol is proved (Ren & Atkins, 2007). As a controller the dwell time controller (switching controller) is used. From the stability of switched system follows that consensus can be achieved asymptotically. That is the new interesting application of hybrid systems.
In the next section will be considered switching control strategy which leads to better closed-loop performance.

3. Robust switching controller

A common feature for controllers which are described in (Hippe, 2006) is that the saturation levels are avoided. Because such controllers are low-gain controllers. It has been discovered in (De Dona et al., 2002) and (Lin et al., 1997) that the performance of closed loop system can be improved by forcing the controls into the saturation. In (De Dona et al., 2002) is shown that combination of switching, scaling and over-saturation has a superior performance then in the case where each is used seperetly.
In this section, we define a class of uncertain linear systems

$$\dot{x}(t) = [A + \Delta A(\omega(t))]x(t) + [B + \Delta B(\omega(t))]u(t) \tag{12}$$

The matrices A and B are the nominal system and input matrices respectively and $\Delta A(\omega)$ and $\Delta B(\omega)$ are uncertain matrices which depend continuosly on the uncertainty vector $\omega(t)$

$$\omega(t) \in \Omega \subset R^p \ , \quad t \in [0, \infty) \tag{13}$$

We will suppose that the following assumptions are satisfied

A.1) (A,B) is controllable

A.2) $\Omega \in R^{P}$ is a compact set

A.3) There are continuous mappings

$$D(\cdot):\omega \to R^{m\times n} \ , \ E(\cdot):\omega \to R^{m\times m}$$

$$\Delta A(\omega)=BD(\omega) \ , \ \Delta B(\omega)=BE(\omega), \forall \omega \in \Omega$$

Assumption A.3) is known as matching contition . This assumption can be relaxed using the notion of mismatching threshold (Barmish & Leitmann, 1982).
In the control law (11) a high-gain component is incorporated by multiplying the gains with a scaling factor $(1+k)$ with $k \geq 0$. The PLC control law with low-and-high gain has the form

$$u(t)=(1+k)K_i x(t) \ , \ x \in C_i \ , \ i=1,2,..,N \tag{14}$$

where is k design parameter.
We, also, can to introduce the over-saturation index as in (De Dona et al., 2002). Let us define the function $\beta_i(t)$ as

$$\beta_i(t)=\begin{cases} \dfrac{v_i(t)-\text{sat}\Delta_i(v_i(t))}{\text{sat}\Delta_i(v_i(t))} & , \ v_i(t)\neq 0 \\ 0 & , \ v_i(t)=0 \end{cases} \tag{15}$$

The over-saturation index is a constant $\overline{\beta}_i$ such that

$$\|\beta_i(t)\|_\infty \leq \overline{\beta}_i \tag{16}$$

In the case of over-saturation elements of matrix R_i are chosen to be the largest so that is satisfied

$$|v_{j_s}|=\left|\frac{1}{r_i^j}b_j^T P_i x\right| \leq (1+\overline{\beta}_j)\Delta_j \ , \ \forall x \in E_i(P_i q_i) \tag{17}$$

Now we will formulate theorem which defines the conditions under which control system which is described with relations (12) and (14) – (17) is exponentially stable.
Theorem 1. Let us suppose that the closed loop system described with (12) and (14) – (17) for wich together with assumptions A.1) - A.3), also, are satisfied

A.4) R_i is positive definite matrix

$$R_i=\begin{bmatrix} r_1^i & & D \\ & \ddots & \\ D & & r_i^m \end{bmatrix} > 0 \ , \ i=1,2,...,N$$

A.5) $\lambda_{min}\{Q-2D^T(\omega)B^TP_i-aK_i^TR_iK_i\}>0$

For precomputed gains

$$K_i \quad , \quad i=1,2..,N$$

$$a\in(0,1) \quad \text{for} \quad \|D(\omega)\|>0 \quad , \quad \|E(\omega)\|>0$$

$$a=0 \quad \text{for} \quad \|D(\omega)\|=\|E(\omega)\|=0$$

A.6) $\lambda_{min}\{E(\omega)+I\}>1-a \quad , \quad \forall\omega\in\Omega$

A.7) The allowed over-saturation for each element v_i of the control vector v is

$$[\beta_{max}]_j=\min_{i=1,2,..,N}\sqrt{1+\frac{4\lambda_{min}\{Q-2D^T(\omega)B^TP_i-aK_i^TR_iK_i\}}{\lambda_{min}\{E(\omega)+I_m\}\left(\sum_{Q=p+1}^{m}r_i^{j_1}\right)\left\|K_i^{j_s}\right\|^2}}$$

where k_i^j is the j th row of matrix K_i

Then feedback (14)-(17) exponentially stabilize system (12) with exponential speed α for $\forall\omega\in\Omega$ and $x\in E_1$.

Proof: In the control systems (12) and (14)-(17) the continuous states $x(t)$ and discrete state (relating to the switching paradigm) are present and we choose a piecewise quadratic Lyapunov function

$$V(x)=x^TP_ix, \qquad x\in C_i\,,\; i=1,2...,N \tag{18}$$

Using relation (12) we have

$$\dot{V}(x)=\dot{x}^TP_ix+x^TP_i\dot{x}=[(A+\Delta A(\omega))x+(B+\Delta B(\omega))]^T\cdot$$

$$\cdot P_ix+x^TP[(A+\Delta A(\omega))x+(B+\Delta B(\omega))sat_\Delta(u)]=$$

$$=[x^T(A+BD(\omega))^T+(sat_\Delta(-(1+k)K_ix))^T(B+BE(\omega))]^T\cdot$$

$$P_ix+x^TP_i[(A+BD(\omega))x+(B+BE(\omega))sat_\Delta(-(1+k)K_ix)]=$$

$$x^T[(A+BD(\omega))^TP_i+P_i(A+BD(\omega))]x+$$

$$+(sat_\Delta(-(1+k)K_ix))^T(B+BE(\omega))^TP_ix+x^TP_i\cdot$$

$$\cdot(B+BE(\omega))sat_\Delta(-(1+k)K_ix) \tag{19}$$

From relation (5) we have

$$A^T P_i + P_i A = P_i B R_i^{-1} B^T P_i - 2\alpha P_i - Q \tag{20}$$

Using relation (20) the first term in (19) becames

$$x^T \left[(A + BD(\omega))^T P_i + P_i (A + BD(\omega))\right] x =$$

$$x^T \left(A^T P_i + P_i A\right) x + x^T D^T(\omega) B^T P_i x + x^T P_i D(\omega) x =$$

$$= x^T P_i B R_i^{-1} B^T P_i x - 2\alpha x^T P_i x - x^T Q x + \; + x^T D^T(\omega) B^T P_i x + x^T P_i B D(\omega) x =$$

$$= -x^T P_i B v - 2\alpha V(x) - x^T Q x + x^T D^T(\omega) B^T(\omega) \cdot P_i x + x^T P_i B D(\omega) x =$$

$$= v^T P_i v - 2\alpha V(x) - x^T Q x - x^T D^T(\omega) R_i v - v^T R_i D(\omega) x \tag{21}$$

Also, one can get

$$x^T Q x + x^T D^T(\omega) R_i v + v^T R_i D(\omega) x - a v^T R_i v - a v^T R_i v =$$

$$= x^T Q x - 2 x^T D^T(\omega) B^T P_i x - a x K_i^T R_i K_i x + a v^T R_i v =$$

$$= x^T \left(Q - 2D^T(\omega) B^T P_i - a K_i^T R_i K_i\right) x + a v^T R_i v \tag{22}$$

For a second and third terms in relation (19) we have

$$(\mathrm{sat}_\Delta(-(1+k)K_i x))^T (B + BE(\omega))^T P_i x + \; x^T P_i (B + BE(\omega)) \mathrm{sat}_\Delta(-(1+k)K_i x) =$$

$$(\mathrm{sat}_\Delta(-(1+k)K_i))^T B^T P_i x + (\mathrm{sat}_\Delta(-(1+k)K_i))^T E^T(\omega) B^T P_i x + B x^T P_i B \mathrm{sat}_\Delta(-(1+k)K_i x) +$$

$$x^T P_i B + BE(\omega) \mathrm{sat}_\Delta(-(1+k)K_i x) = -\mathrm{sat}_\Delta(-(1+k)K_i x)^T R_i v - (\mathrm{sat}_\Delta(-(1+k)K_i x))^T E^T(\omega) R_i v -$$

$$- v^T R_i \mathrm{sat}_\Delta(-(1+k)K_i x) - v^T R_i E(\omega) \mathrm{sat}_\Delta(-(1+k)K_i x) =$$
$$= -(\mathrm{sat}_\Delta(-(1+k)K_i x))^T \left[E^T(\omega) + I\right] R_i v - v^T R_i \left[E^T(\omega) + I\right] \mathrm{sat}_\Delta(-(1+k)K_i x)$$

$$= -2 v^T R_i \left[E^T(\omega) + I\right] \mathrm{sat}_\Delta(-(1+k)K_i x) \le -2\lambda_{min}\{E(\omega) + I\} v^T R_i \mathrm{sat}_\Delta(-(1+k)k_i x)$$

$$\le -2\lambda_{min}\{E(\omega) + I\} v^T R_i \mathrm{sat}_\Delta(-(1+k)k_i x) \tag{23}$$

From (19) and (21)-(23) and assumption A6) of Theorem follows

$$\dot V(x) \le (1+a) v^T R_i v - 2\alpha V(x) - x^T \left(Q - 2D^T(\omega) B^T P_i - a K_i^T R_i K_i\right) x -$$

$$- 2\lambda_{min}\{E(\omega) + I\} v^T R_i \mathrm{sat}_\Delta(-(1+k)k_i x) \le -2\alpha V(x) + \lambda_{min}\{E(\omega) + I\} v^T R_i v - x^T \cdot$$

$$\left(Q-2D^T(\omega)B^TP_i-aK_i^TR_iK_i\right)x-2\lambda_{min}\{E(\omega)+I\}v^TR_i sat_\Delta(-(1+k)k_ix)=$$

$$-2\alpha V(x)-x^T\left(Q-2D^T(\omega)B^TP_i-aK_i^TR_iK_i\right)x++\lambda_{min}\{E(\omega)+I\}\cdot$$

$$\cdot\left[\sum_{j=1}^{m} r_i^j\left|v_j\right|\left(\left|v_j\right|-2sat_{\Delta_j}\left((1+k)K_i\left|v_j\right|\right)\right)\right] \tag{24}$$

In last relation is the v_j is the j th element of $v_i=-K_ix$ i.e.

$$v_j=-\frac{1}{r_i^j}b_j^TP_ix=-k_i^jx \tag{25}$$

From relation (17) one can get

$$\left|v_j\right|\le\left(1+\overline{\beta}\right)\Delta_j\le\left(1+[\beta_{max}]_j\right)\quad,\quad\forall x\in C_i\subset E_i\quad,\quad j=1,2,\ldots,m \tag{26}$$

and $[\beta_{max}]_j$ is defined in the assumption A.7) of Theorem.

For the $x\ne 0$ we have two posibilites

$$\left|v_{j_s}\right|\le 2\Delta_{j_s}\quad,\quad j_s\in S_1\quad,\quad S_1=\{j_1,j_2,\cdots,j_p\} \tag{27}$$

and

$$2\Delta_{j_s}<\left|v_{j_s}\right|\le\left(1+[\beta_{max}]_{j_s}\right)\Delta_{j_s}\quad,\quad j_s\in S_2\quad,\quad S_2=\{j_{p+1},\cdots,j_m\} \tag{28}$$

whereby

$$0\le p\le m\quad,\quad S_1\cup S_2=\{1,2,..,m\}\quad,\quad S_1\cap S_2=\phi$$

Using argument as in (De Dona et al., 2002) one can get

$$x^Tx>\sum_{s=p+1}^{m}\frac{r_i^{j_s}}{\left(\sum_{l=p+1}^{m}r_i^{j_l}\right)}\frac{4\Delta_{j_s}^2}{\left\|k_i^{j_s}\right\|} \tag{29}$$

From (24) and (29) follows

$$\dot{V}(x)-2\alpha V(x)+\lambda_{min}\{E(\omega)+I\}\cdot\left\{\sum_{s=1}^{p}r_i^{j_s}\left|v_{j_s}\right|\left[\left|v_{j_s}\right|-2sat_{\Delta_{j_s}}\left((1+k)\left|v_{j_s}\right|\right)\right]+\sum_{s=p+1}^{m}r_i^{j_s}\cdot\right.$$

$$\cdot\left[\left|v_{j_s}\right|^2 - 2\left|v_{j_s}\right|\Delta_{j_s} - A_1\right]\Big\}A_1 = \frac{4\lambda_{min}\left\{Q - 2D^T(\omega)B^T P_i - aK_i^T R_i K_i\right\}\Delta_{j_s}^2}{\lambda_{min}\{E(\omega)+I\}\left(\sum_{l=p+1}^{m} r_i^{j_l}\right)\left\|K_i^{j_s}\right\|^2} \tag{30}$$

According to relation (27) first term in (30) is always nonpositive, i.e.

$$\left|v_{j_s}\right| - 2sat_{\Delta_{js}}\left((1+k)\left|V_{j_s}\right|\right) \le 0 \quad , \quad \forall k \ge 0 \tag{31}$$

It is well known fact that quadratic polinomial

$$z^2 + p_1 z + p_2 \quad , \quad z \in R^1$$

is negative if zeros belong to the interval

$$\left(\frac{-p_1 - \sqrt{D}}{2}, \frac{-p_1 + \sqrt{D}}{2}\right) \quad , \; D = p_2^2 - 4p_2$$

Using those facts it is possible to conclude that second term in relation (30) is nonpositive if

$$\left|v_{j_s}\right| \le \left(1 + \sqrt{1 + \frac{4\lambda_{min}\left\{Q - 2D^T(\omega)B^T P_i - aK_i^T R_i K_i\right\}}{\lambda_{min}\{E(\omega)+I\}\left(\sum_{l=p+1}^{m} r_i^{j_l}\right)\left\|K_i^{j_s}\right\|^2}}\right)\Delta_{j_s}$$

This is true because from the definition of elipsoid E_i fallows

$$\left|v_{j_s}\right| \le \left(1 + [\beta_{max}]_{j_s}\right)\Delta_{j_s} \quad , \quad j_s \in S_1 \cup S_2 \tag{32}$$

whereby $[\beta_{max}]_{j_s}$ is defined in the assumption A7) of Theorem.
From relation (31)-(32) follows

$$\dot{V}(x) < -2\alpha V(x), \; \forall x \ne 0 \; , \; x \in C_i \; , i = 1,2,\ldots,N \tag{33}$$

It means that closed-loop system is exponentially stable. Namely

$$\left\|x(t_j)\right\| \le k_e \left\|x(t_1)\right\| \exp\{-\alpha(t_2 - t_1)\}, \forall x \ne 0 \, , \; x \in C_i \tag{34}$$

whereby

$$k_1 = \sqrt{\frac{\lambda_{max}\{P_i\}}{\lambda_{min}\{P_i\}}} \quad , \quad i = 1,2,\ldots,N \tag{35}$$

The trajectories in each cell C_i approach the origin with a exponential decrease in $V(x)$ along the trajectory. According with the philosophy of control strategy, the trajectories will enter the smallest ellipsoid corresponding to ρ_N. The exponential stability is assured by (33).

Remark 2. In the paper (De Dona et al., 2004) is considered the case when in the model (12) uncertainty matrix $\Delta B(w) = 0$ and the degree of prescribed stability $\alpha = 0$. Also, in that reference the Riccati equation approach is used until in this paper the Lyapunov approach is used.

Remark 3. When unmodeled dynamic is absent, i.e. in the Theorem 1

$$a = 0 \;, \quad \|D(w)\| = \|E(w)\| = 0$$

the conditions A.5) and A.7) in the Theorem have the form

$$\lambda_{min}\{Q\} > 0$$

$$[\beta_{max}]_{js} = \min_{i=1,2,\ldots,N} \sqrt{1 + \frac{4\lambda_{min}\{Q\}}{\left(\sum_{l=p+1}^{m} r_i^{j_l}\right) \left\|K_i^{js}\right\|^2}}$$

These assumption are identical with the assumptions in reference (De Dona et al., 2002).

4. Conclusion

In this paper the switching controller with low-and-high gain and alloved over-saturation for uncertain system is considered. The unmodeled dynamics satisfies matching conditions. Using picewise quadratic Lyapunov function it is proved the exponential stability of the closed loop system.

It would be interesting to develop the theory for output case and for the descrete-time case. Also, extremely is important application of hybrid systems in distributed coordination problems (multiple robots, spacecraft and unmanned air vehicles).

8. References

Anderson, B.D.O. & Moore, J.B. (1989). *Optimal Control. Linear Quadratic Methods,* Prentice-Hall, 0-13-638651-2, New Jersey

Barmish, B.R. & Leitmann, G. (1982). On ultimate boundedness control of uncertain system in the absence of matching conditions. *IEEE Trans. Automatic Control,* Vol. 27, No. 2, (Feb. 1982) 153-158

Blanchini, F. (1999). Set invariance in control a – survey. *Automatica,* Vol.35, No. 11, (Nov. 1999) 1747-1767

Blanchini, F. & Miani, S. (2008). *Set –Theoretic Methods on Control,* Birkhauser, 978-0-8176-3255-7, Basel

Cassandras, C.G. & Lafortune, S. (2008). *Introduction to Discrete – Event Systems*, Springer Verlag, , 978-0-387-33332-8, Berlin

De Dona. J.A., Goodwin, G.C. & Moheimani, S.O.R. (2002). Combining switching, over - saturation and scaling to optimize control performance in the presence of model uncertainty and input saturation. *Automatica*, Vol. 38, No.11, (Nov. 2002) 1153-1162

Crama, P. & Schoukens, J. (2001). Initial estimates of Wiener and Hammerstein Systems using multisine excitation. *IEEE Trans. Instrum Measure.*, vol. 50, No. 6, (Dec. 2005) 1791-1795

Filipovic, V.Z. (2005). Performance guided hybrid LQ controller for time-delay systems. *Control Engineering and Applied Informatics*. Vol. 7, No. 2, (Mar. 2005) 34-44

Goodwin, G.C., Seron, M.M. & De Dona, J.A. (2005). *Constrained Control and Estimation. An optimization Approach*, Springer Verlag, 1-85233-548-3, Berlin

Johansson, M. (2003). *Picewise Linear Control Systems*, Springer-Verlag, 3-54044-124—7, Berlin

Hippe, P. (2006). *Windup in Control*, Springer Verlag, 1-84628-322-1, Berlin

Li, Z., Soh, Y. & Wen, C (2005). *Switched and Impulsive Systems. Analysis, Design and Applications*, Springer Verlag, 3-540-23952-9, Berlin

Lin, Z., Pachter, M, Banda, S. & Shamash,Y. (1997). Stabilizing feedback design for linear systems with rate limited actuators, In *Control of Uncertain Systems with Bounded Inputs*, Tarbouriech, S. & Garcia, G. (Ed.), pp. 173-186, Springer Verlag, 3-540-761837, Berlin

Lin, Z. (1999). *Low Gain Feedback*, Springer Verlag, 1-85233-081-3, Berlin

Michel, A., Hou, L. & Liu, D. (2008). *Stability of Dynamical Systems: Continuous, Discontinuous and Discrete Systems*, Birkhauser, 978-0—8176-4486-4, Basel

Ren, W. & Atkins, E. (2007). Distributed multi-vehicle coordinated control via local information exchangle. *International Journal of Robust and Nonlinear Control*, Vol. 17, No. 10-11 , (July, 2007) 1002-1033

Ren, W. & Beard, R.W. (2008). *Distributed Consensus in Multi-vehicle Cooperative Control. Theory and Applications*, Springer Verlag, 978-1-84800-014-8, Berlin

Saberi, A., Stoorvogel, A.A. & Sannuti, P. (2000). *Control of Linear Systems with Regulation and Input Constraints*. Springer Verlag, 1-85233-153-4, Berlin

Sun, Z. & Ge, S.S. (2005). *Switched Linear Systems. Control and Design*, Springer Verlag, 1-85233-893-8, Berlin

Tarbouriech, S. & Da Silva, J.M.G. (2000). Sinthesis of controllers for continuous – time delay systems with saturating control via LMI's. *IEEE Trans. Automatic Control*, Vol. 45, No. 1, (Jan. 2000) 105-111

Tsay, S.C. (1991). Robust control for linear uncertain systems via linear quadratic state feedback, *Systems and Control Letters*, Vol.15, No. 2, (Feb. 1991) 199-205

Wredenhagen, G.F. & Belanger, P.R. (1994). Picewise linear L Q control for systems with input constraints. *Automatica*, Vol.30, No. 3, (Mar. 1994) 403-416

Wu, F., Lin, Z. & Zheng, Q. (2007). Output feedback stabilization. *IEEE Trans. Automatic Control*, Vol. 45, No. 1, (Jan. 2007) 122-128

Zhao, W.X. & Chen, H.F. (2006). Recursive identification for Hammerstein system with ARX subsystem. *IEEE Trans. Automatic Control,* vol. 51, No. 12, (Dec. 2006) 1966-1974

14

Advanced Torque Control

C. Fritzsche and H.-P. Dünow
Hochschule Wismar – University of Technology, Business and Design
Germany

1. Introduction

Torque is one of the fundamental state variables in powertrain systems. The quality of motion control highly depends on accuracy and dynamics of torque generation. Modulation of the air massflow by opening or closing a throttle is the classical way to control the torque in gasoline combustion engines.
In addition to the throttle and the advance angle several other variables are available to control the torque of modern engines - either directly by control of mixture or indirectly by influence on energy efficiency. The coordination of the variables for torque control is one of the major tasks of the electronic control unit (ECU).
In addition to the generation of driving torque other objectives (emission threshold, fuel consumption) have to be taken into account. The large number of variables and pronounced nonlinearities or interconnections between sub-processes makes it more and more difficult to satisfy requirements in terms to quality of control by conventional map-based control approaches. For that reason the investigation of new approaches for engine control is an important research field (Bauer 2003).
In this approach substitute variables instead of the real physical control variables are used for engine torque control. The substitute variables are used as setpoints for subsidiary control systems. They can be seen as torque differences comparative to a torque maximum (depending on fresh air mass). One advantage of this approach is that we can describe the controlled subsystems by linear models. So we can use standard design methods to construct the torque controller. Of course we have to consider variable constraints. Due to the linearization the resulting control structure can be used in conventional controller hardware.
For the superordinate controller a Model Predictive Controller (MPC) based on state space models is used because with this control approach constraints, and also setpoint- and disturbance progressions respectively, are considered.
In chapter 2 we briefly explain the most important engine processes and the main torque control variables. The outcome of this explanations is the use of a linear multivariable model as a bases for the design of the superordinate torque controller. The MPC- algorithm and its implementation are specified in chapter 3. Chapter 4 contains several examples of use.
In this chapter it is also shown how the torque controller can change to a speed- or acceleration controller simply by manipulation of some weighting parameters.

2. Process and torque generation

Combustion and control variables: In figure 1 the four cycles of a gasoline engine are shown in a pressure/volume diagram. The mean engine torque results from the difference energy explained by the two closed areas in the figure.
The large area describes the relation of pressure and volume during compression and combustion. The charge cycle is represented by the smaller area.
For good efficiency the upper area should be as large as possible and the area below should be minimal (for a given gas quantity). The best possible efficiency in theory is represented by the constant-volume cycle (or Otto cycle) (Grohe 1990, Urlaub 1995, Basshuysen 2002).

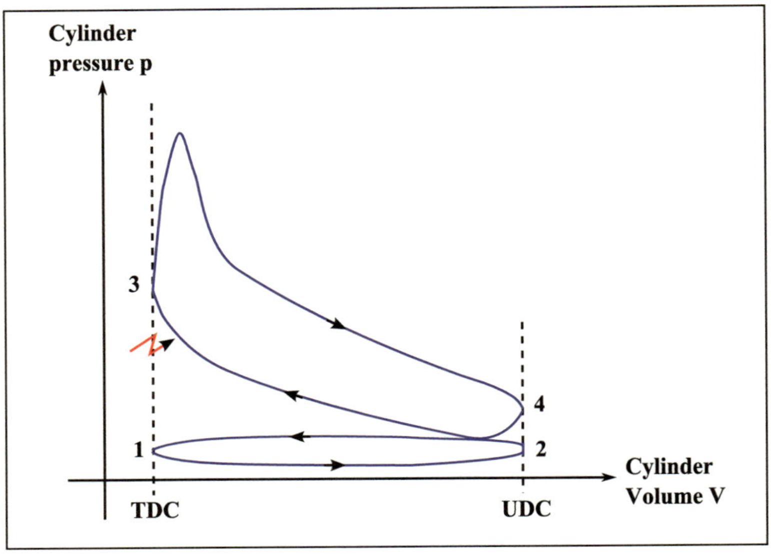

Fig. 1. p-V-Diagram (gasoline engine)

The maximum torque of the engine basically depends on the fresh air mass which is reaching the combustion chamber during the charge cycle. A desired air/fuel mixture can be adjusted by injecting an appropriate fuel quantity. The air/fuel-ratio is called lambda (λ). If the mass of fresh air corresponds to the mass of fuel (stoichiometric ratio) the lambda parameter is one (λ=1). By several reasons the combustion during the combustion cycle is practically never complete. So after the cycle there remain some fresh air and also unreacted particles of fuel. A more complete reaction of the air can be reached by increasing fuel mass (λ<1). This results in rising head supply and hence to an increase of the potential engine torque. The maximum of torque is reached by approximately λ=0.9. The torque decreases more and more if lambda increases. So one can realize fast torque changes for direct injection engines by modulation of the fuel.
The maximum of lambda is bounded by combustibility of the mixture (depends on operating conditions). For engine concepts with lean fuel-air ratio (λ>1) the fuel feed is the main variable for torque control. Because of the exhaust after treatment λ=1 is requested for most gasoline engines at present. In case of weighty demands however it is possible to change lambda temporary.

In addition to air and fuel the torque can be controlled by a number of other variables like the advance angle or the remaining exhaust gas which can be adjusted by the exhaust gas recirculation system.
For turbocharged engines the air flow depends in addition to the throttle position on turbocharger pressure which can be controlled by compressors or by exhaust gas turbines.
Pressure charging leads to an increase of the maximum air mass in the combustion chamber and hence to an increasing maximum of torque even if the displaced volume of the engine is small (downsizing concepts).
Because of the mass inertia of the air system it takes time until a desired boost pressure is achieved. The energy for the turbocharging process is taken from the flue gas stream. This induces a torque load which can result in nonminimumphase system behaviour.
In addition to the contemplated variables there are further variables imaginable which influence the torque (maximum valve opening, charge-motion valve, variable compression ratio, etc.).
Furthermore the total torque of the engine can be influenced by concerted load control. For example one can generate a negative driving torque by means of the load of the electric generator. The other way around one can generate a fast positive difference torque by abrupt unloading. This torque change can be much faster than via throttle control.
In hybrid vehicles we have a number of extra control variables and usable parameters for torque control.
More details on construction and functionality of internal combustion engines are described by Schäfer and Basshuysen 2002, Guzella and Onder 2004 and Pulkrabeck 2004.
For control engineering purposes the torque generation process of a gasoline engine is multivariable and nonlinear. It has a large number of plant inputs, a main variable to be controlled (the torque) and some other aims of control like the quality of combustion concerning emission and efficiency.
Considerable differences in the dynamic behaviour of the subsystems generate further problems particularly for the implementation of the control algorithms. For example we can change the torque very fast by modulation of the advance angle (compared to the throttle). Normally the value that causes the best efficiency is used for the advance angle. However to obtain the fastest torque reduction it can be helpful to degrade the efficiency and so the engine torque is well directed by the advance angle. Fast torque degradation is required e. g. in case of a gear switching operation. For the idle speed control mode fast torque interventions can be useful to enhance the stability and dynamics of the closed loop. Fast load changes also necessitate to generate fast torque changes. In many cases the dynamic of sub-processes depends on engine speed and load.
Whether the torque controller uses fast- or slow-acting variables depends on dynamic, efficiencies and emission requirements. Mostly the range of the manipulated variables is bounded.
In the normally used "best efficiency" mode one can only degrade the torque by the advanced angle. For special cases (e. g. idle speed mode) the controller chooses a concerted permanent offset to the optimal advance angle. So a "boost reserve" for fast torque enhancement occurs. Because of the efficiency this torque difference is as small as possible and we have a strong positive (and changeable) bound for the control variable. This should be considered in the control approach. The main target variables and control signals are pictured in figure 2.

We can summarize: The torque control of combustion engine is a complex multivariable problem. In addition to the torque we have to control other variables like lambda, the efficiency, EGR , etc. The sub-processes are time variant, nonlinear and coupled. The control variables are characterized by strong bounds.

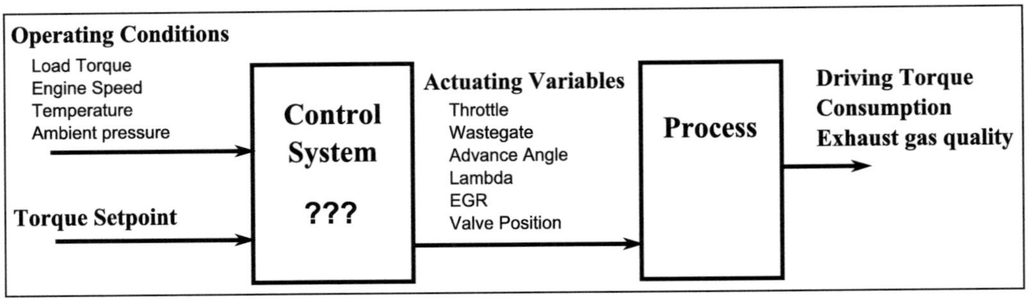

Fig. 2. Actuating and control variables

Torque control: Below we describe the most important variables for torque control and the effect chain.

a.) fresh air mass:

As aforementioned the engine torque mainly depends on the fresh air mass as the base for the maximum fuel mass. Classical the air mass is controlled by a throttle within the intake. In supercharged engines the pressure in front of the throttle can be controlled by a turbocharger or compressor. The result of supercharging is a higher maximum of fresh air mass in the combustion chamber. This leads to several benefits. In addition to the throttle or charging pressure the air mass flow can also be controlled by a variable stroke of the inlet valve.

It is not expedient to use all variables of the air system for torque control directly. For the torque generation the air mass within the cylinder is mainly important (not the procedure of the adjustion). Hence it is more clever to use the setpoint for the fresh air mass as the plant input for the torque controller. This can be realized by the mentioned control variables with a the aforementioned sub-control system. One advantage of the approach is, that the sub-control system at large includes measures for the linearization of the air system. Furthermore the handling of bounds is a lot easier in this way.

b.) exhaust gas recirculation (EGR):

By variable manipulating of the in- and outlet valves it is possible to arrange, that both valves are simultaneously open during the charge cycle (valve lap). So in addition to the fresh air some exhaust gas also remains the combustion chamber. This is advantageous for the combustion and emission. In case of valve lap the throttle valve must be more open for the same mass of fresh air. This is another benefit because the wastage caused by the throttle decreases. The EGR can also be realized by an extern return circuit. Here we only consider the case of internal EGR. The EGR induced a deviation from the desired set point of fresh air. This deviation usually will be corrected by a controller via the throttle. As aforementioned this correction is relatively slow. If the mechanism for the valve lap allows fast shifting we can realize fast torque adjustments because the change of air mass by the valve lap occurs immediately.

c.) advance angle:

An important parameter for the efficiency of the engine is the initiation of combustion. The point of time mainly depends on the advance angle. The ignition angle which leads to the best efficiency is called the optimized advance angle. It depends on engine speed and the amount of mixture. A delay in the advance angle leads to less efficiency and to the decrease of engine torque. The relation between advance angle and torque is nonlinear.

d.) lambda:

The amount of fuel determines (for a given fresh air mass) the torque significantly. As aforementioned bounded we can manipulate the torque by lambda. For direct injection concepts the torque changes immediately if lambda is modified. Torque control by means of lambda is limited for engine concepts with λ=1.

e.) other variables

The quality of mixture has also an effect on the efficiency and so on the torque. For the quality several construction parameters are important. Further the quality depends on adjustable variables like fuel pressure, point of injection or the position of a charge-motion valve. The setpoints for these parameters are primarily so chosen that we obtain best mixture efficiency.

In figure 3 the main variables and the effects on the process are outlined.

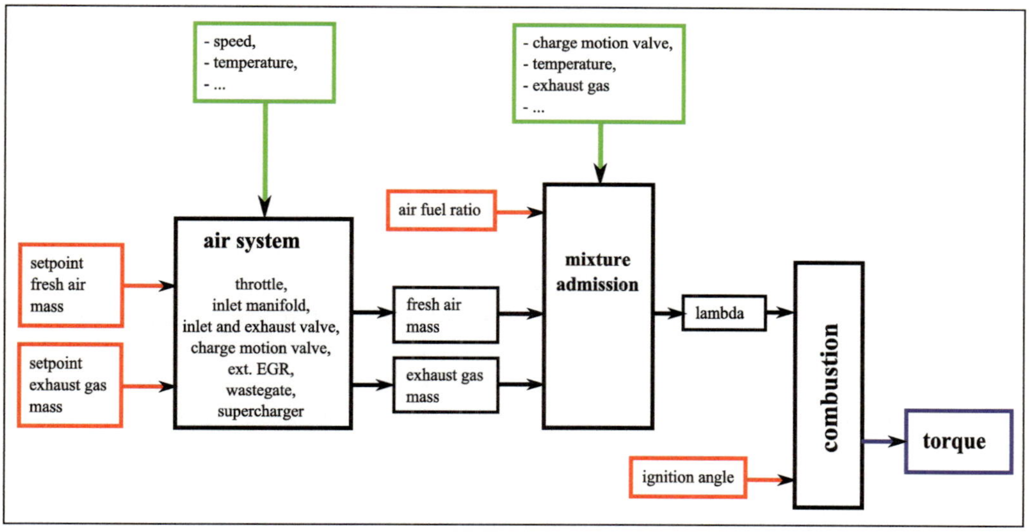

Fig. 3. Main variables to influence the energy conversion and the torque generation

From the explanation up to now we can deduce appropriate variables for torque control:

- fresh air mass in the combustion chamber (adjustable via charge pressure, throttle, valve aperture and valve lap),
- fuel, lambda (adjustable by injection valve),
- advance angle,
- internal exhaust gas recirculation (adjustable via valve lap)

All variables are bounded.

Subsidiary control systems: For simplification of the torque control problem it is expedient to divide the process in to several sub-control circuits. The following explanations are aimed to gasoline engines with turbo charging, internal EGR, direct injection and homogeneous engine operation (λ=1).

The sub-control circuits are outlined in figure 4. The most complicated problem is the design of the subsystem for fresh air control. Because of the strong connection of fresh air and EGR it makes sense to control both simultaneously in one sub-system. The control system has to consider or compensate a number of effects and nonlinear dependences.

The main task is to control the fresh air mass and the desired amount of exhaust gas which reaches the combustion chamber during the charge cycle. The control system should reject disturbances and adjust new setpoint values well (fast, small overshoot). Another requirement is that it should be possible to describe the complete control circuit by a linear model.

For the control structure we propose a reference-model controller (figure 5). One of the aims of this control structure is to achieve a desired dynamic behaviour for the circuit. The mentioned requirement for simplification of the modelling is implicitly given in this way. Nonlinear effects can be compensated by appropriate inverted models.

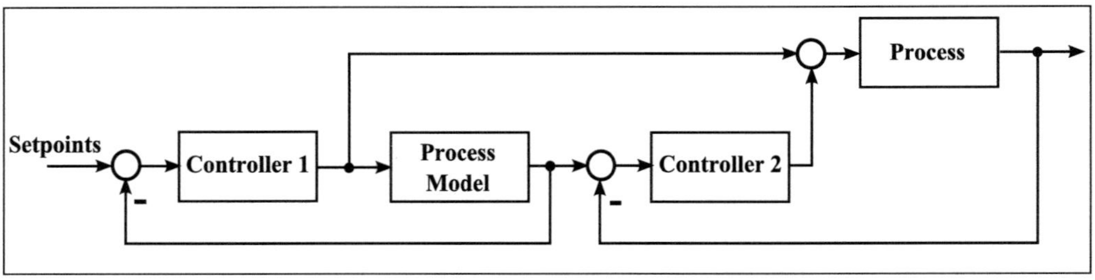

Fig. 4. Model Following Control (MFC)

In the explained approach the fresh air mass is used as the main control variable. From this air mass results the maximum possible torque with approximately λ = 0.9.

In case of modification of the exhaust gas portion we only consider the influence on the fresh air. The influence on combustion quality is disregarded. Increasing of exhaust gas portion leads to decreasing of fresh air and so to reduction of torque. This influence is compensated by a special controller so that the action of EGR on the engine torque is comparable to the characteristic of a high-pass filter. An advantage is obtained if the acting effect from EGR-setpoint to the fresh air is faster than via the throttle. In this case it is possible to realize fast (but transient) changes of the torque.

For torque manipulation via the advance angle it is not necessary to use a feedback system. The influence on the efficiency of the engine can be modelled by a characteristic curve. So for this control path a feedforward control action is adequate. We can find the same conclusion for lambda.

Second-level control system: By means of the described sub-control systems the actuating variables of the torque control system can be defined. The main variables are the setpoints of the fresh air mass, the exhaust gas, the advance angle and the setpoint for lambda. The relation between the torque and the mentioned variables is nonlinear. Following the torque controller also had to be nonlinear and the controller design could be difficult.

A more convenient way is to linearize the sub-control systems first by stationary functions at the in and outputs. In the described control approach the control variables are substituted by a number of partial torque setpoints (delta torques). The partial torques represent the

influence of the used control variables to the whole engine torque. The over-all behaviour of the system to be controlled is linear (widely).
Base control variable is the theoretical maximum of the torque for a given fresh air mass. The other variables can be seen as desired torque differences to a reference point (the maximum of torque). That means if the delta variables all set to zero, the maximum of torque for the given fresh air mass should be generated by the engine.
The difference variables are both: actuation variables for the torque and variables to be controlled. In this way it is possible to adjust stationary other setpoints for lambda, the residual exhaust gas or the advance angle.
We can find the bounds for the substituted variables from the physical bounds also by using the linearization functions. It is assumed that the nonlinear functions are monotone in the considered range.
From the explanations above the total control structure follows (figure 5). The plant for the torque controller consists of the sub-control-systems (fresh air, residual exhaust gas, and lambda and advance angle) and the stationary linearization systems. The whole system can be described by a linear multivariable model. Only the bounds of the input variables have to be taken into account. The plant outputs are the engine torque and the difference variables. Other plant outputs could be estimated values for exhaust gas emission or for fuel consumption (can be estimated by simplified models).
The setpoints for the torque are generated by the driver or by other ECU-functions (e.g. for changing gears). For the realization one can find different requirements.
For example we have to realize a requested torque as fast as possible. For other situations the time could be less important and one wish to realize a desired torque with a minimum of consumption. The control system should be able to handle all the different requirements.
The control variables are not available at all time. In general the range of the control variables is bounded. Sometimes they may not differ from the setpoint. The torque controller should consider this variability of bounds.
An appropriate control principle with the ability to solve this problem is the well known model predictive controller (MPC). This approach can handle variable bounds as well as known future setpoints and disturbances. Future setpoints are known for instance for changing gears. Switch-on of the air conditioning system is an example for known future disturbances. Matching to miscellaneous priorities is possible by appropriate weighting matrices in the control algorithm.
The model structures for the superordinate torque control system can be explained from figure 5.
For example we can arrange the model equation

$$\begin{bmatrix} y_1 \\ y_2 \\ y_3 \\ y_4 \end{bmatrix} = \begin{bmatrix} G_{11}(s) & G_{12}(s) & G_{13}(s) & G_{14}(s) \\ 0 & G_{22}(s) & 0 & 0 \\ 0 & 0 & G_{33}(s) & 0 \\ 0 & 0 & 0 & G_{44}(s) \end{bmatrix} \cdot \begin{bmatrix} u_1 \\ u_2 \\ u_3 \\ u_4 \end{bmatrix} \tag{1}$$

if we use all of the aforementioned control variables (fresh air, residual exhaust gas, lambda and advance angle). The output signals of the model are the engine torque (y_1) and the three difference control variables which appear in fact ($y_2 \ldots y_4$).

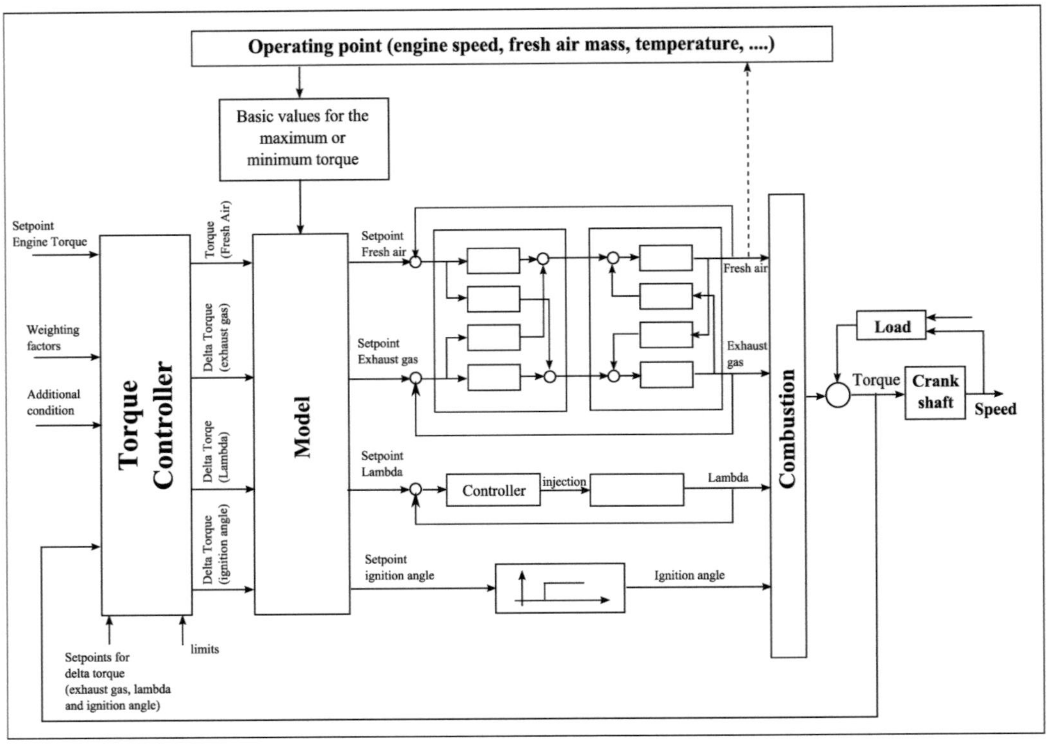

Fig. 5. Two layer control approach

The engine torque (y_1) depends on all actuating variables. $G_{11}(s)$ describes the effect of the fresh air path to the engine torque, $G_{12}(s)$ models the effect of the exhaust gas path on the engine torque, $G_{13}(s)$ describes the behaviour of the torque depending on lambda and $G_{14}(s)$ the effect of the ignition angle path. We may assume, that the output variables y_2 ... y_4 are only dependent on the corresponding setpoints because of the decoupling effects of the sub-control circuits. $G_{22}(s)$, $G_{33}(s)$ and $G_{44}(s)$ are simple low-order transfer functions.

If we have (in addition to the torque setpoint) other control requirements (e.g. consumption) it is easy to extend the model by appropriate transfer functions for the estimation of the control variable effects on the considered output variables. For exhaust gas emission and fuel consumption this results in a model as follows:

$$\begin{bmatrix} y_1 \\ y_2 \\ y_3 \\ y_4 \\ y_5 \\ y_6 \end{bmatrix} = \begin{bmatrix} G_{11}(s) & G_{12}(s) & G_{13}(s) & G_{14}(s) \\ 0 & G_{22}(s) & 0 & 0 \\ 0 & 0 & G_{33}(s) & 0 \\ 0 & 0 & 0 & G_{44}(s) \\ G_{51}(s) & G_{52}(s) & G_{53}(s) & G_{54}(s) \\ G_{61}(s) & G_{62}(s) & G_{63}(s) & G_{64}(s) \end{bmatrix} \cdot \begin{bmatrix} u_1 \\ u_2 \\ u_3 \\ u_4 \end{bmatrix} \tag{2}$$

The extension of the model is possible by using any other variable of the engine as plant output signals. Possibilities are, for instance, the engine speed or the acceleration.

In this way we can consider the torque and the speed simultaneously. The model has to be completed to:

$$\begin{bmatrix} \vdots \\ y_7 \end{bmatrix} = \begin{bmatrix} \vdots & \vdots & \vdots & \vdots \\ G_{71}(s) & G_{72}(s) & G_{73}(s) & G_{74}(s) \end{bmatrix} \cdot \begin{bmatrix} \vdots \\ u_4 \end{bmatrix} \quad . \tag{3}$$

y_7 describes the engine speed. The transfer functions of the lower line describe the effects of all inputs on the speed.
Certainly, it is not possible to adjust torque and speed independently. The structure allows however to switch between torque and speed control smoothly. This can be done by the weighting parameters of the MPC. In the same way it is feasible to extend the model by a line which describes the acceleration depending on the input signals. A disadvantage of the model extensions is the increasing complexity.

3. MPC-algorithm and implementation

3.1 Approach

As mentioned the model predictive control concept seems to be an appropriate approach for torque control. In the following we describe the basics of this control concept. The explanations are focused mainly on a state space solution.
MPC is widely adopted in industries, primarily in chemical engineering processes. This control principle is an established method to deal with large constrained multivariable control problems (Dittmar 2004, Dünow 2004, Grimble 2001, Maciejowsky 2002, Salgado et al. 2001). The main idea of MPC is to precalculate the control action by repeatedly solving of an optimization problem (see figure 6). The optimization aims to minimize a performance criterion during a time-horizon subject to selected control and plant signals. An appropriate and usual criterion is the quadratic cost function

$$J(k)=\sum_{i=0}^{H_p}(\hat{y}(k+i\,|\,k)-r(k+i))^T Q_i (\hat{y}(k+i\,|\,k)-r(k+i))+\sum_{i=0}^{H_u-1}\Delta\hat{u}^T(k+i\,|\,k)R_i\Delta\hat{u}(k+i\,|\,k). \tag{4}$$

$\hat{y}(k+i\,|\,k)$ denotes the predicted output for the time $k+i$ calculated at the time instant k.
$\Delta\hat{u}$ denotes the difference control signal. Q and R are the weighting matrices for the input and the output variables of the process. H_p and H_u are prediction and control horizons. The use of difference control signals for the cost function leads to better control structuring and inhibits high-frequency signals. Unlike huge computing potential in other application fields of MP-Controllers the hardware capacity of engine control systems is limited in memory and computing power. For this reason we implemented a MPC-algorithm which is suitable for realtime application in engine control units. As minimum requirements the control algorithm should allow the application to multivariable systems with variable constraints in the control output. A main design requirement was the achievement of reasonable computing efforts.
For the MP-Controller we use a set of linear constant time-discrete state-space process models of the form

$$
\begin{aligned}
x(k+1) &= Ax(k) + Bu(k) \\
y(k) &= Cx(k)
\end{aligned}
\tag{5}
$$

(u-input signal, y-output signal, x-state of the system, A-system matrix, B-input- and C-output matrix).

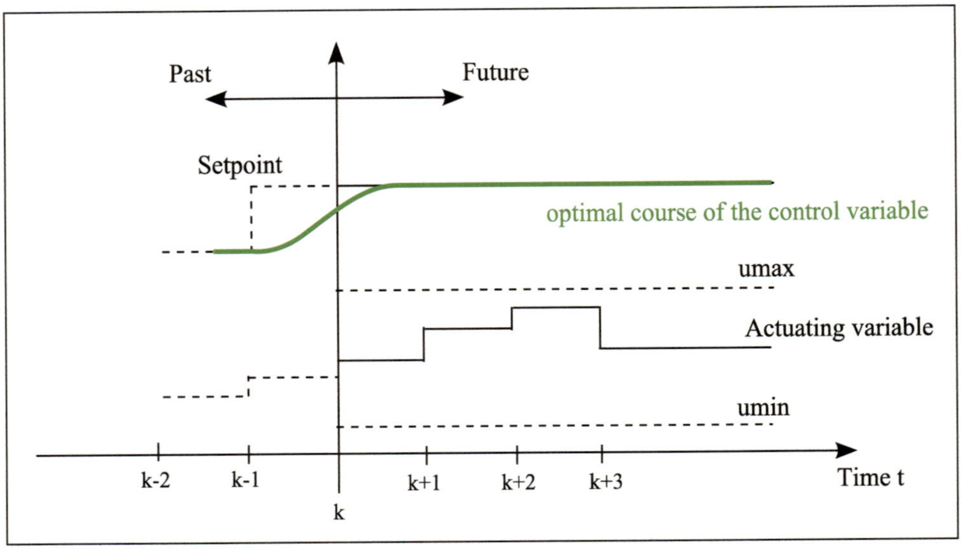

Fig. 6. Predictive Control: The basic idea

In case of control signal constraints we have to consider the conditions

$$
\begin{array}{ccccc}
u_{\min}(k) & \leq & u(k \mid k) & \leq & u_{\max}(k) \\
u_{\min}(k+1) & \leq & u(k+1 \mid k) & \leq & u_{\max}(k+1) \\
\vdots & & \vdots & & \vdots \\
u_{\max}(k+H_u-1) & \leq & u(k+H_u-1 \mid k) & \leq & u_{\max}(k+H_u-1)
\end{array}
\tag{6}
$$

From the model we obtain the prediction for the output of the system for a horizon of H_p steps at time k.

$$
\begin{bmatrix} \hat{y}(k+1 \mid k) \\ \vdots \\ \hat{y}(k+H_p \mid k) \end{bmatrix}
=
\begin{bmatrix} CA \\ \vdots \\ CA^{H_u} \\ CA^{H_u+1} \\ \vdots \\ CA^{H_p} \end{bmatrix} x(k)
+
\begin{bmatrix} CB \\ \vdots \\ C\sum_{i=0}^{H_u-1} A^i B \\ C\sum_{i=0}^{H_u} A^i B \\ \vdots \\ C\sum_{i=0}^{H_p-1} A^i B \end{bmatrix} u(k-1)
+
\begin{bmatrix} CB & \cdots & 0 \\ C(AB+B) & \cdots & 0 \\ \vdots & \ddots & \vdots \\ C\sum_{i=0}^{H_u-1} A^i B & \cdots & CB \\ C\sum_{i=0}^{H_u} A^i B & \cdots & C(AB+B) \\ \vdots & \vdots & \vdots \\ C\sum_{i=0}^{H_p-1} A^i B & \cdots & C\sum_{i=0}^{H_p-H_u} A^i B \end{bmatrix}
\begin{bmatrix} \Delta\hat{u}(k \mid k) \\ \Delta\hat{u}(k+1 \mid k) \\ \vdots \\ \Delta\hat{u}(k+H_u-1 \mid k) \end{bmatrix}
\tag{7}
$$

$$
= y(k) = \Psi x(k) + \Upsilon u(k-1) + \Theta \Delta U(k) \tag{8}
$$

With the setpoint signal $r(k+i\,|\,k)$, $i=0\ldots H_p$, the equation

$$\varepsilon(k)=\begin{bmatrix} r(k\,|\,k) \\ r(k+1\,|\,k) \\ \vdots \\ r(k+H_p\,|\,k) \end{bmatrix} - \Psi x(k) - \Upsilon u(k-1) \tag{9}$$

and the weight matrices

$$Q=\begin{bmatrix} Q(0) & 0 & \cdots & 0 \\ 0 & Q(1) & \cdots & 0 \\ \vdots & \vdots & \ddots & \vdots \\ 0 & 0 & \cdots & Q(H_p) \end{bmatrix} \quad \textit{respectively} \quad R=\begin{bmatrix} R(0) & 0 & \cdots & 0 \\ 0 & R(1) & \cdots & 0 \\ \vdots & \vdots & \ddots & \vdots \\ 0 & 0 & 0 & R(H_u-1) \end{bmatrix} \tag{10 and 11}$$

the cost functional (4) becomes to

$$J(k) = -\Delta U(k)^T G + \Delta U^T H \Delta U(k) \tag{12}$$

with

$$G = 2\Theta^T Q \varepsilon(k) \quad \textit{and} \quad H = \Theta^T Q \Theta + R \tag{13 and 14}$$

The constraint conditions from equation 6 we can formulate as a linear matrix inequation like

$$A\Delta U(k) \le U_{constraint} \tag{15}$$

with

$$A=\begin{bmatrix} 1 & 0 & 0 & \cdots & 0 \\ 1 & 1 & 0 & \cdots & 0 \\ \vdots & \vdots & \vdots & \ddots & \\ 1 & 1 & 1 & \cdots & 1 \\ -1 & 0 & 0 & \cdots & 0 \\ -1 & -1 & 0 & \cdots & 0 \\ \vdots & \vdots & \vdots & \ddots & \vdots \\ -1 & -1 & -1 & \cdots & -1 \end{bmatrix} \quad \textit{and} \quad U_{constraint}=\begin{bmatrix} u_{max}(k)-u(k-1) \\ u_{max}(k+1)-u(k-1) \\ \vdots \\ u_{max}(k+H_u-1)-u(k-1) \\ -u_{min}(k)+u(k-1) \\ -u_{min}(k+1)+u(k-1) \\ \vdots \\ -u_{min}(k+H_u-1)+u(k-1) \end{bmatrix} \tag{16 and 17}$$

The main problem of the model predictive controller is to minimize the cost function 12 subject to the constraints expressed in inequation 15. To solve this standard convex optimization problem (which is summarized in figure 7) efficient numerical procedures (quadratic programming (QP)) are available. For the realtime application we developed a computing time optimized QP program which uses an active set algorithm (Dünow et al. 2005, Lekhadia et al. 2004, Lekhadia 2004a). We implemented this optimization algorithm for Mathworks xPC-Target and for an Infineon TriCore microcontroller board. This microcontroller is actually also used in ECU-Systems.

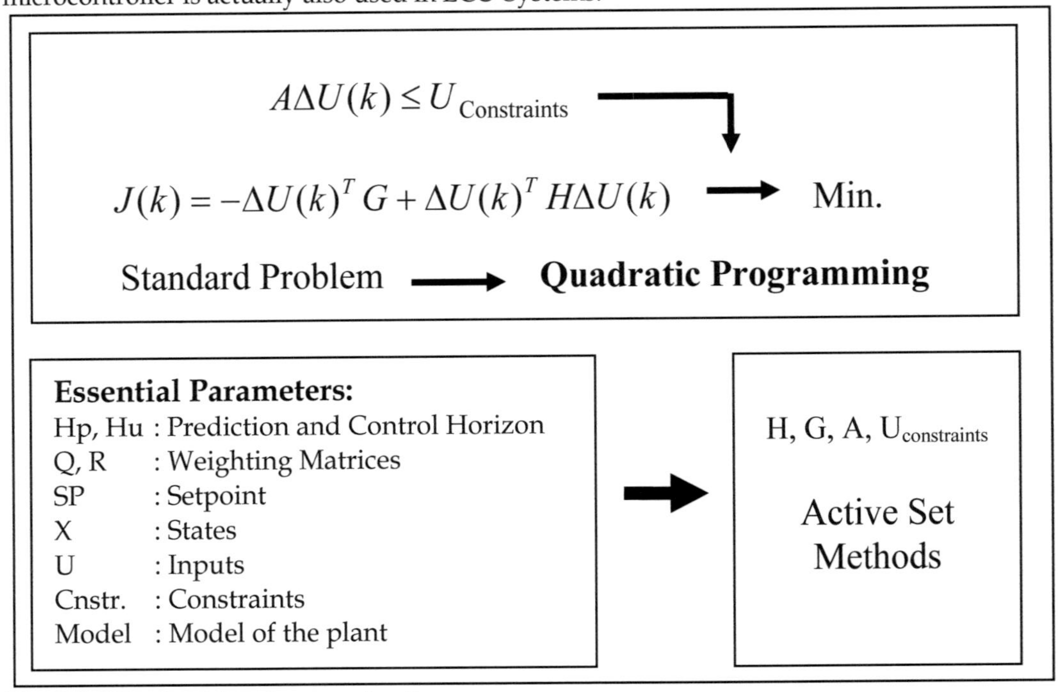

Fig. 7. MPC-algorithm (summarized)

3.2 Implementation

The model predictive controller was implemented by means of the packages LAPACK and BLAS for C-language (Dünow et al. 2005). These Libraries are efficient concerning the computing effort and widely used in research and industrial applications. The MPC-algorithm was implemented by a C-S-function for Matlab / Simulink to use it on a xPC Target system. Because of the limited capabilities of the ECU the implemented control algorithm should need less computing time and memory space. For the unconstraint case we can find a constant MPC solution. Here the bounds will be ignored. The optimal $\Delta U(k)$ for the unconstrained case we find by

$$(dJ/d\Delta U) = \nabla_{\Delta U(k)} J = -G + 2H\Delta U(k) = 0 \tag{18}$$

From equation 18 follows the optimal set of control variables:

$$\Delta U(k)_{opt} = \frac{1}{2} H^{-1} G \tag{19}$$

Condition 16 minimizes the cost function because of the fact that

$$\frac{\partial_2 J}{\partial \Delta U(k)^2} = 2H = 2 \cdot \left(\Theta^T Q \Theta + R\right) \tag{20}$$

is positive defined if $Q \geq 0$ and $R > 0$. In figure 8 the unconstrained case is summarized in a block diagram. The implementation of a controller which based on equation 19 is outlined in figure 9. Here the controller consists of a linear state space model, three constant gains and a simple wind up clipping structure (Dünow et al. 2005).

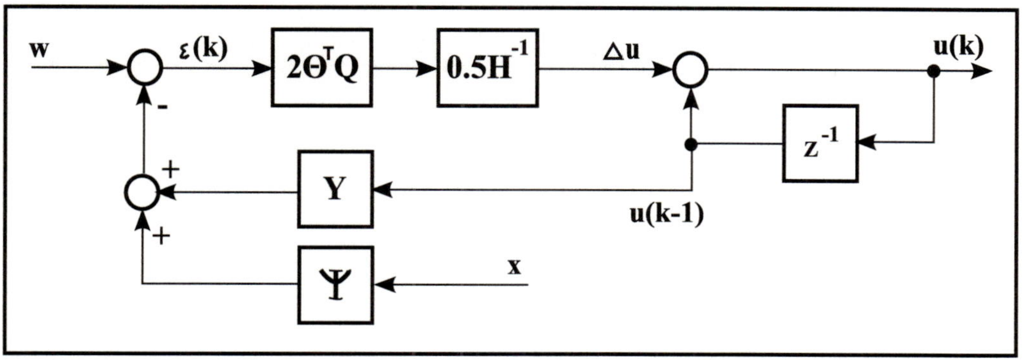

Fig. 8. Block diagram of the unconstrained case

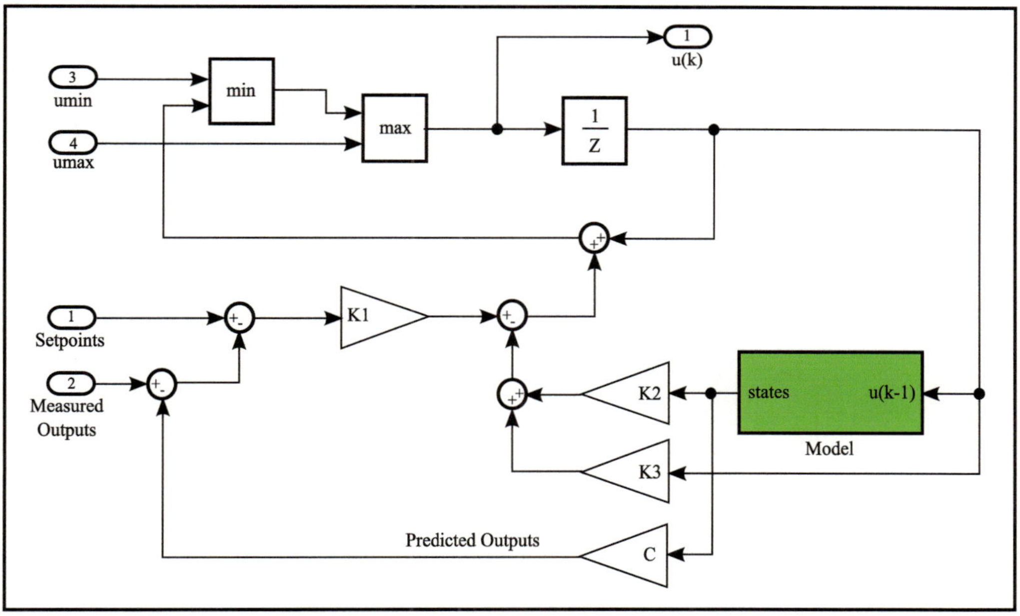

Fig. 9. Implementation of the constant Controller in Matlab/Simulink (Dünow et al. 2005)

For the constrained case we have to minimize the cost function (see equation 12) regarding to the controller constraints output marked in equation 15. With the help of active set methods we solved this standard quadratic programming optimization problem. In figure 10 the flow chart, which based on Fletscher 1997, Gill et al. 1991 and Maciejowski 2002, of the optimization algorithm is shown. The active set method involves two phases. At first a feasible point is calculated. The second phase involves the generation of an iterative sequence of feasible points that converge to the solution. The λ-check below in figure 10 is a test for Karush-Kuhn-Tucker condition for a global optimum (Fletscher 1987).

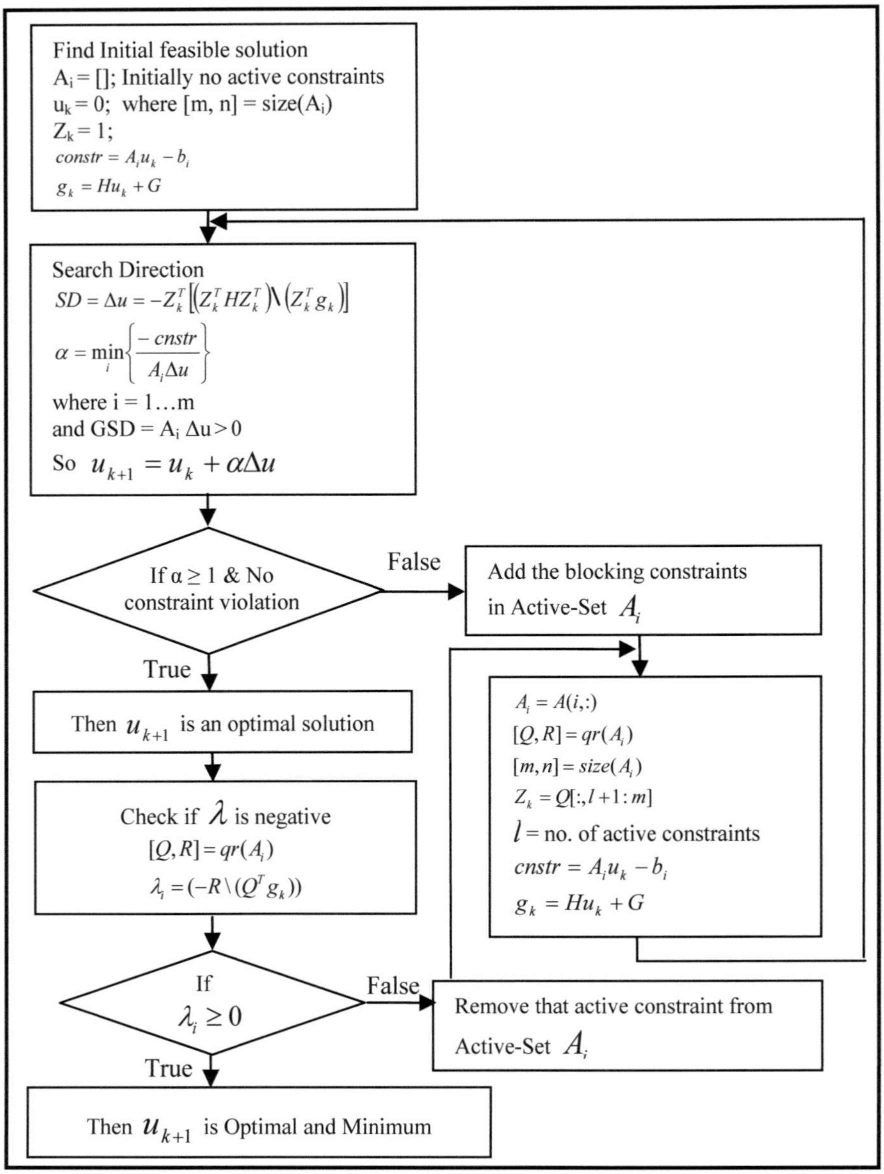

Fig. 10. Flow chart of the implemented active set algorithm (Dünow et al. 2005 and Lekhadia 2004a)

4. Practical applications and results

In this section we will investigate practical aspects of the described approach. As a test environment we used a complex nonlinear model of a four-cylinder direct injection engine. This model includes the physical elements of the engine as well as the necessary ECU-functions for torque control. The model is usable at Matlab/Simulink. The model is briefly depicted in figure 11.

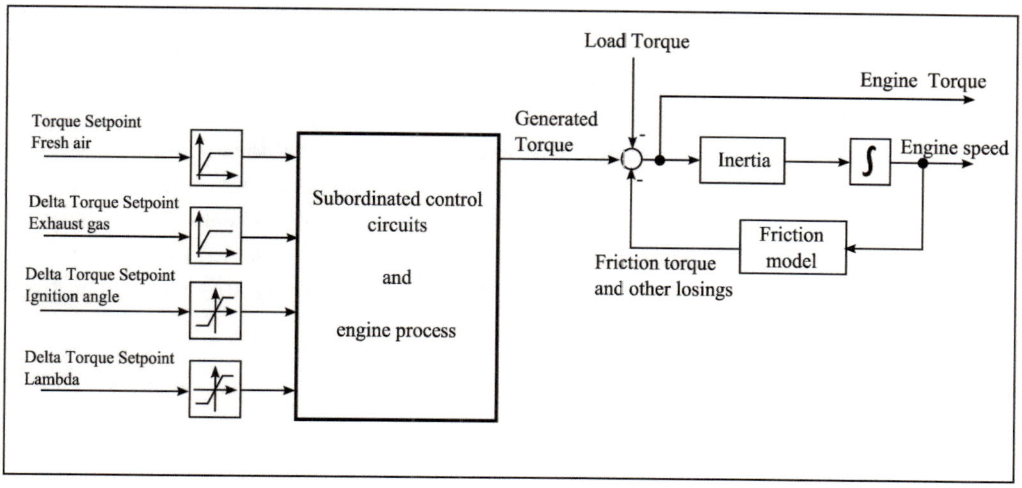

Fig. 11. Engine model (simplified)

The model was completed by a part for exhaust gas emission and one part for fuel consumption.

Because of the different dynamics of the control pathways the sampling time is relatively small. This results in a corresponding large prediction horizon of the MPC. Regarding the control horizon we btained the best compromise between performance and computational effort for $H_u = 5$.

Figure 12 foreshadows the structure of the simulation system. We used a state space method for the modelling and solution of the control problem. The MPC-Block in the left of the simulink-model includes the control solution explained in section 3. The process model can be seen as an alternative to a real engine. The background of the model was illustrated in section 1 and 2. The model in the controller block is conform to equation 2.

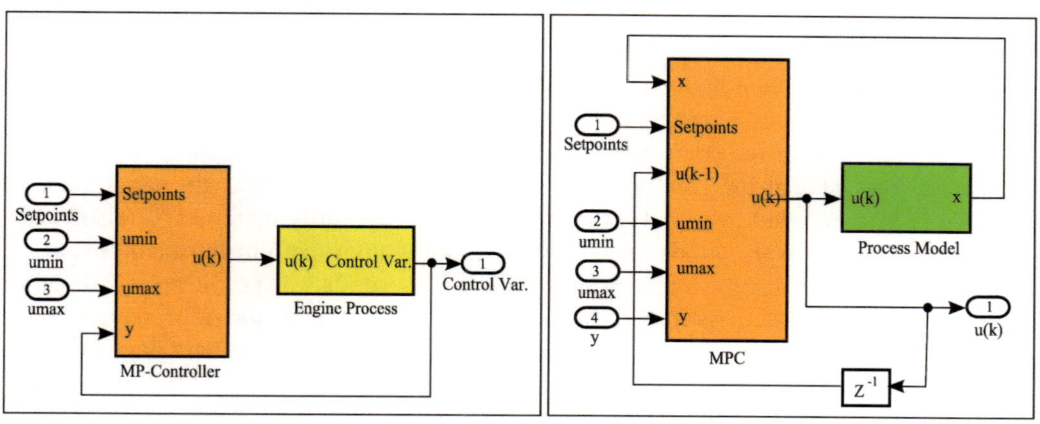

a) MPC and engine process b) Optimization and internal model

Fig. 12. Simulation environment

In figures 13a to 13d an application case of the torque controller is shown. The main objective of the control process in this example is to follow the torque setpoint as accurately as possible. The upper figure (13a) shows the setpoint and the real values of the torque. Below (13a) the four control variables are pictured. At about 1.5 seconds we have a setpoint step. At 2.5 seconds a load step occurs. This load step is predictable (turn-on procedure of the air conditioner). In the example the setpoints for the delta torques of the ignition and exhaust gas path are zero. The setpoint for the lambda torque path is here about -8 Nm. This corresponds to $\lambda=1$. The torque value of 8 Nm can be seen as a "reserve" and the MPC can boost the total engine torque due to the fuel path immediately by this value. The upper bound for the delta torque via the fuel path is zero in the example.

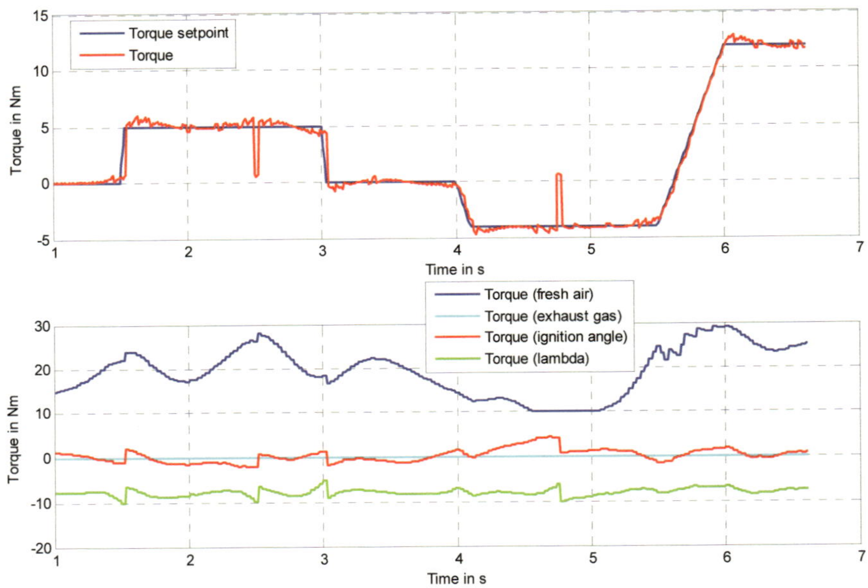

Fig. 13a. Results – max torque priority

The upper and lower bounds for the exhaust gas path in the example are equal (zero). That means the MPC must not use this variable for torque control until the constraints are changing. The value of the controller output always is equal to the setpoint (as required). Because of the fact that the controller outputs for the delta torques at the same time are variables to be controlled these outputs are used only temporarily by the MPC (also visible in figure 13b). The lower bounds for the fuel and the ignition path in the example are -15 Nm. The setpoint step for the total engine torque at 1.5 seconds was predictable. It is visible that the MPC automatically prepared this action. The maximum torque (represented by the air path) increases. The available delta variables (fuel and ignition path) are decreasing. So the total torque doesn't change up to 1.5 seconds. In this way the MPC builds up a torque reserve which can be used (temporarily) to advance the setpoint adjustment.

The compensation of a predictable load step (in the example about at 2.5 seconds) occurs in the same way. Figure 13b and 13d give a zoomed view to the load compensation. The controller is able to readjust the torque very fast due to the torque reserve.

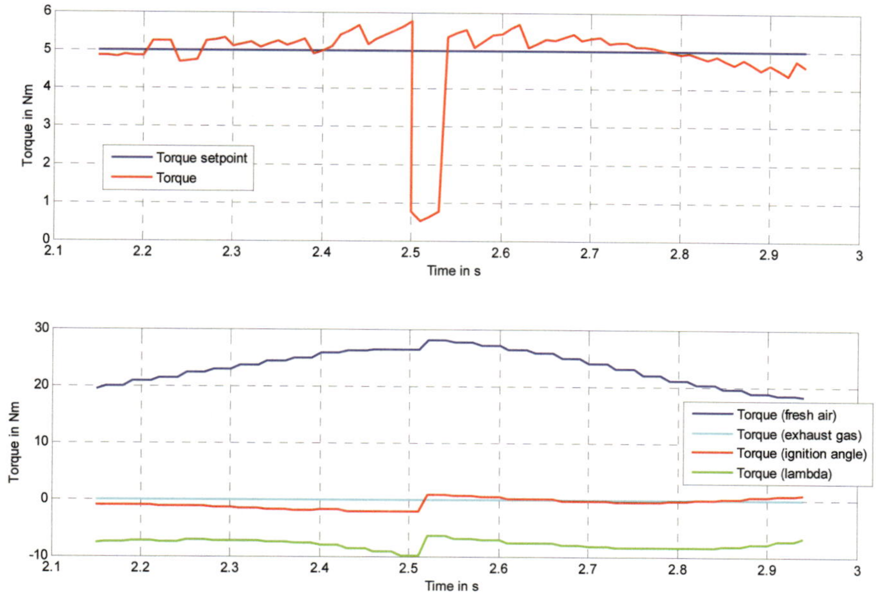

Fig. 13b. Results - max torque priority

In the example above the control request was focused mainly to minimize the engine torque deviation from the desired setpoint. This was achieved by appropriate weighting variables within the model predictive control algorithm.

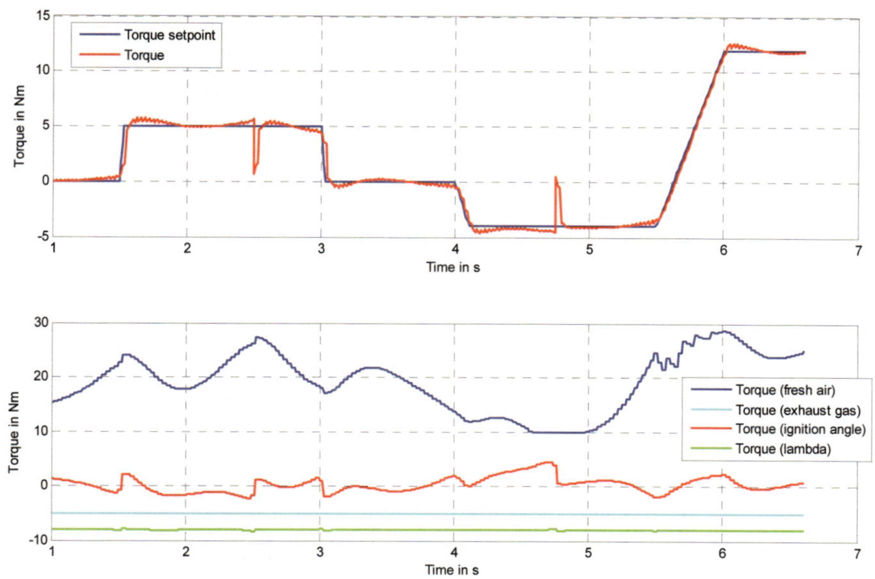

Fig. 13c. Results - min torque priority

By changing the weighting factors it is also possible to shift the focus more towards other attributes. For instance one can achieve a reduction of the waste gas emission by a setpoint for corresponding λ=1 and increasing the weighting factors of the lambda path.
The results are shown in figure 13c for the same setpoint and load steps as in the example above. It is visible that the torque adjustment is (compared to figure 13a) slower and the controller output for the fuel path is used only marginally.

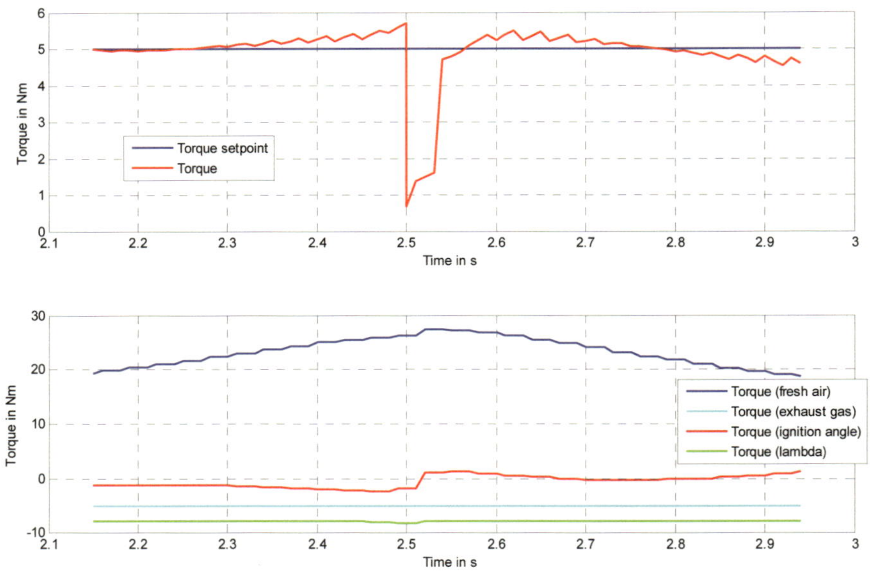

Fig. 13d. Results – min torque priority

As mentioned in section 2 the described control approach allows to switch smoothly between torque, speed or acceleration control. This can be simply achieved by the model extension (described in section 2, equation 3) and appropriate weighting parameters for the MPC. Only by shifting the weighting factors one can switch from speed control to torque control and back.
The plots in figure 14 demonstrate how this control mode works. In this example we used only the fresh air and the ignition path for torque control. Up to 3 seconds the controller should work as a speed controller. From then it should work as a torque controller. At approximately 6 seconds the weighting factors where switched back to speed control mode values. Equation 21 represents the linear model which is used internally by the MPC for this example.

$$\begin{pmatrix} \text{Engine Torque} \\ \text{Engine Speed} \\ \Delta Torque_{\text{Ignition Angle}} \end{pmatrix} = \begin{pmatrix} G_{11}(s) & G_{12}(s) \\ G_{21}(s) & G_{22}(s) \\ 0 & G_{32}(s) \end{pmatrix} \cdot \begin{pmatrix} Torque_{\text{Fresh Air Setpoint}} \\ \Delta Torque_{\text{Ignition Angle Setpoint}} \end{pmatrix} \tag{21}$$

Switching between speed and torque control can simply be realized by changing some weighting factors. The behaviour of the MPC changes automatically. This is a very convenient way to change for instance to the idle speed control mode and back to torque control.

In figure 14 first the speed control is active. The speed follows the desired characteristic whereas the torque is different from the corresponding setpoint. After changing the weighting factors the torque will be adjusted to the setpoint and the engine speed is only marginally considered by the controller.

Time period in s	**Active Control**	**Torque weighting factor**	**Speed weighting factor**
0 ... 2.5	Speed control	0	1
2.5 ...6	Torque control	1	0
6 ... 8.5	Speed control	0	1

Table 1. Enabled control

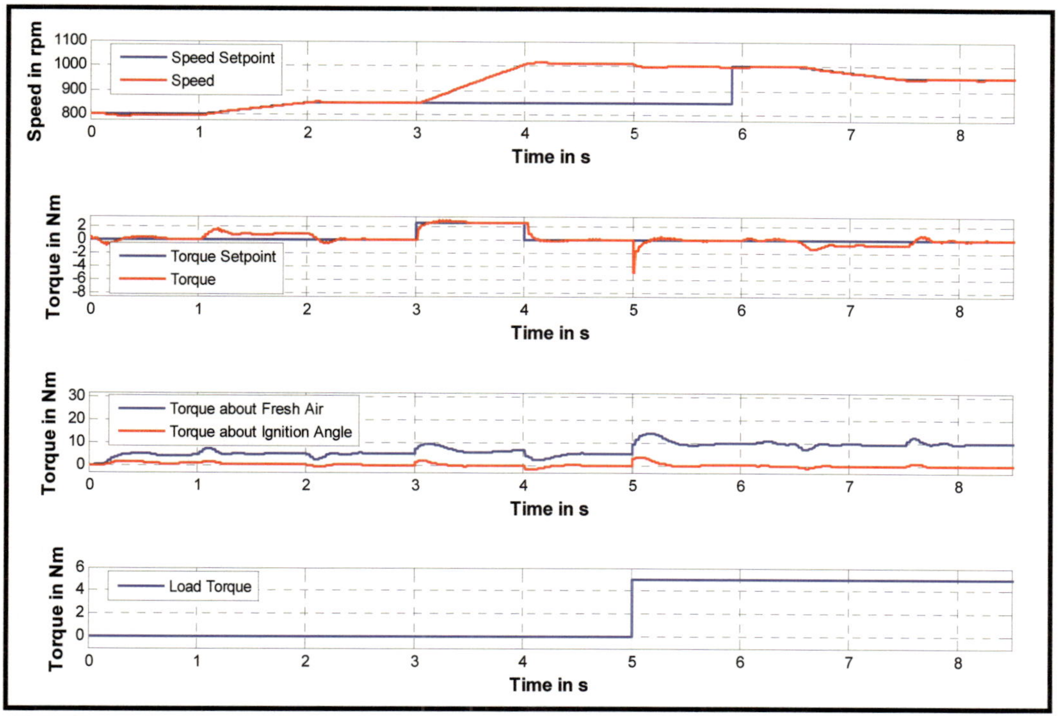

Fig. 14. Speed and Torque Control

At approximately 6 seconds the engine speed control mode was activated again. The speed should decrease here from the current value smoothly along a given trajectory. It is visible in figure 14 that the controller solves the differing control tasks properly. In the third plot (from the top) one can see also that the ignition path control variable is used transient by the controller. Stationary the setpoint is adjusted.

5. Conclusion

In the chapter we discussed a control approach for torque control of gasoline engines. Because of several actuating variables and control requirements the process to be controlled is multivariable. The actuating variables are usually bounded and the effects on the engine torque are nonlinear. Hence direct use of the actuator variables for torque control generally produces plenty of problems.

The two layer approach described in the chapter allows the application of standard control methods. The main idea of the control structure is to compensate or alleviate the nonlinearity behaviour by subordinate control circuits. All the physical actuating variables are substituted by setpoints of the subordinate systems. The torque controller so can be designed on base of linear models. Additionally only bounds of some control variables have to be considered.

An appropriate standard control concept for the superordinate torque controller is the model predictive control principle. For the implementation we used a state space approach. The optimization problem is solved by the active set algorithm. For lower computation effort a solution with constant parameters was introduced. But this solution doesn't consider constraints and loss performance can occur.

The three examples in section 4 show the capability of the control concept. The extension of the control structure is possible simply by completing the model and appropriate weighting parameters. In this way the controller should be able to handle more actuating variables or other requirements.

The control quality depends on the quality of the model. Although the subordinate control circuits contribute to the linearization of the process behaviour the dynamic parameters may be dependent on engine speed or load. For that case a set of linear models could be useful.

The control approach described in this chapter demonstrates that modern control approaches have considerable potential to improve the performance of embedded control systems. In addition to better performance also the variability of the systems and the ability to handle different control requirements could improve.

6. References

Auckenthaler, T.S. (2005). Modelling and Control of Three-Way Catalytic Converters, Institute of Technology, Zürich, Dissertation

Back, M. (2005). Prädiktive Antriebsregelung zum energieoptimalen Betrieb von Hybridfahrzeugen, Institut für Regeluns- und Steuerungssysteme Universität Karlsruhe, Dissertation

Bauer, H. (2003): Ottomotor-Management: Systeme und Komponenten, Friedr. Vieweg & Sohn Verlagsgesellschaft mbH

Brand, D. (2005). Control-Oriented Modeling of NO Emissions of SI Engines, Institute of Technology, Zürich, Dissertation

Basshuysen, R. van; Schäfer, F. (2002): Handbuch Verbrennungsmotor - Grundlagen, Komponenten, Systeme und Perspektiven, Vieweg und Sohn Verlagsgesellschaft mbH, Braunschweig/Wiesbaden

Dittmar, R.; Pfeiffer, B. (2004). Modellbasierte prädiktive Regelung, Oldenbourg Verlag München, Wien

Dünow, H.-P. (2004). Anwendung Modellprädiktiver Regelungen, Forschungsbericht, Hochschule Wismar, Fachhochschule für Technik, Wirtschaft und Gestaltung - Fachbereich Elektrotechnik und Informatik

Dünow, H.-P.; Lekhadia, K.N.; Köller, M.; Jeinsch, T. (2005). Model based predictive control of spark ignition engine, *Proceedings of MMAR*

Fletscher, R.R (1987). Practical Methods of Optimization, Wiley, 2nd edition

Fritzsche, C.; Dünow, H.-P.; Lampe, B.; Schultalbers, M. (2007). Torque Coordination of Spark Ignition Engines based on Predictive Control, *Proceedings of MMAR*, Szczecin, Poland

Gill, P.E.; Murray, W.; Wright, M.H. (1991). Numerical Linear Algebra and Optimization, Volume 1, Addison Wesley

Grimble, M.J. (2001). Industrial Control Systems Design, John Willey & Sons, LDT Chichester, New York, Weinheim, Brisbane, Singapore and Toronto

Grohe, Heinz (1990). Otto- und Dieselmotoren, Vogel Fachbuchverlag, Auflage 9, Würzburg, Germany

Guzella, L. and Onder, C.H. (2004). Introduction to Modeling and Control of Internal Combustion Engine Systems, Springer Verlag Berlin, Heidelberg, Germany

Johansen, T.A. (1994). Operating Regime based Process Modelling and Identification, PhD Thesis, Department of Engineering Cybernetics - The Norwegian Institute of Technology - University of Trondheim

Johansen, T.A.; Murray-Smith, R. (1997). Multiple Model Approaches to Modelling and Control, Taylor & Francis London

Kristoffersson, I. (2006). Model Predictive Control of a Turbocharged Engine, School of Electrical Engineering and Information Technology, Stockholm

Lekhadia, K.N.; Dünow, H.-P.; Jeinsch, T. (2004). Active Set Method Approach for Real Time Model Predictive Engine Control, In: Modellierung, Regelung und Diagnose von Verbrennungsmotorprozessen, 2. ASIM Workshop Wismar

Lekhadia, K.N. (2004a). Development of OP Algorithms for Real-Time Predictive Control Systems, Master Thesis, FH Darmstadt

Maciejowski, J.M. (2002). Predictive Control with constraints, Prentice Hall

Pulkrabek, Willard (2004). Engineering Fundamentals of the Internal Combustion Engine, Prentice Hall

Rückert, J.; Richert, F.; Schlosser, A.; Abel, D.; Herrmann, O.; Pfeifer, A.; Pischinger, S. (2003). Konzepte zur Regelung von Ladedruck und AGR-Rate beim Nutzfahrzeug-Dieselmotor, GMA-Kongress - VDI-Berichte 1756, VDI-Verlag Düsseldorf

Salgado, M.E.; Godwin, G.C.; Greabe, S.F. (2001). Control System Design, Prentice Hall London

Urlaub, Alfred (1995). Verbrennungsmotoren - Grundlagen, Verfahrenstheorie, Konstruktion, Springer Verlag Berlin, Heidelberg, Germany

15

Design, Simulation and Development of Software Modules for the Control of Concrete Elements Production Plant

Georgia Garani and George K. Adam
Technological Educational Institute of Larissa
Dept. of Informatics and Telecommunications
41110 Larissa
Greece

1. Introduction

Manufacturing and control procedures for automation require many different technologies. The last decade has seen computer technology applied widely in industrial production, particularly in manufacturing processes not generally associated with high technology. The technology used in the automated production of moulded concrete elements for the architectural and building industry has changed dramatically in recent years. The introduction of Computer Integrated Manufacturing (CIM) between 1960 and 1980 (Trybula & Goodman, 1989), e.g., numerically controlled machines, followed in the 1980 to 1990 developments in robotics, e.g., advanced robotics (Shell & Hall, 2000) had a significant impact on automating the production of moulded concrete elements.

The types of system that produce concrete elements are mainly machines using hydraulic compression and extraction. This is the most common method used to form the complex product shapes required by the architectural and building industry. These machines can be either stationary, or they can be mobile, with automated mobile machines being the machine of preference these days. Other relevant ancillary equipment used in the automated production of concrete elements are aggregate mixers, material storage silos and conveyors.

The concrete elements required by architects and builders often include complex geometric shapes; it is for this reason that the central process in their production is the hydraulic press. Complex geometric shapes in concrete and their quality control can only produced using automated compression machinery (Isayev, 1987; Reinhart, 1987). The various phases of this process are (1) material mixture; aggregates of variable form tightly compressed into a mould and (2) compression to form and extract the desired product.

The application of computer aided systems to hydraulic press machines has increased the range and variety of concrete elements that these machines can produce for the architectural and building industry (e.g., ZENITH, KNAUER, BESSER, etc.). The consistency and quality control of landscape and architectural products, such as concrete blocks, curb stones, palisades, paving stones, etc., has improved through introducing computer aided systems. Computer-control systems, teleoperation and automation technology, modelling and simulation tools are some of the technologies and techniques used to acquire the desired

functionality in operation control and quality in production (Chryssolouris, 1992; Gutta & Sinha, 1996; Marvel & Bloemer, 2000).
However, quite often various problems arise during the attempt of systems modelling and control, in most cases due to insufficient structuring of the system in the real world. In these cases, usually artificial intelligence techniques are being applied (Fishwick & Luker, 1991; Hwang et. al., 1995). For this reason, the design and control of automated production system requires an effective development system that enables the design specifications to be implemented and tested prior to the actual implementation and control of the production system. The generation and implementation of such systems has become essential to the development of automated production systems (Rao et al., 1993; Nise, 1995; Shetty & Kolk, 1997; Srovnal & Pavliska, 2002).
Qualitative modelling approaches have been applied for a long period of time with quite successful results in most of the cases (Forbus, 1984; Groumpos & Krauth, 1997; de Kleer & Brown, 1984; Trave-Massuyes, 1992; Garani & Adam, 2007). One of the aims of this research was to accomplish an adequate control structure for a synchronised co-operation of the plant machines. Previous work on applications of qualitative modelling techniques (Adiga & Gadre, 1990; Lamperti & Zanella, 2003; Mak et. al., 1999; Zhang et. al., 1990) shows that there is still further need of work to be carried out for the development of highly intelligent qualitative modelling approaches.
This chapter presents the application of design, simulation and software development techniques for the operation and control of a concrete elements production plant and particularly, an automated mobile press machine (RoboPress). Teleoperation is required in operating the mobile press machine for performing the actual production procedures. The plant is consisted of various machines such as a press machine for concrete elements production, a mixing machine for aggregates mixing, aggregates storage silos, transport buckets and conveyors, etc. The design, operation and control of a concrete mixer machine and an autonomous mobile hydraulic press machine are discussed in detail. The whole system automates the production of moulded concrete elements for architectural and building projects. The research work demonstrates how the design of a state-of-the-art industrial plant can be optimised by using qualitative modelling and simulation from artificial intelligence and other engineering software tools. Further on, it shows how an efficient control algorithm for operating the group of machines can be derived from a qualitative modelling approach.
The rest of this chapter is structured as follows: the following section describes the application environment of this research; in section 3 a detailed description of the overall plant control system is provided; section 4 provides details of the modelling and simulation techniques used for the development and verification of the overall system's operation and control algorithm prior to its implementation; in section 5 details are given for the system performance evaluation and implementation procedures of the software control modules and algorithms. The chapter is concluded in section 6, which presents the outcomes and future research work.

2. Application environment

The concrete plant under investigation and control is consisted of a group of machines including a mobile press machine for the concrete elements production, an aggregates' mixing machine, aggregates' storage silos, a forklift loader, feeding conveyors, etc. Other

basic machine components include the electronic control board based on a Hitachi EC series programmable logic controller of type EC-60HRP. That unit offers up to 60 I/O points, direct PC connection (RS232) and monitoring. A number of solid state inductive proximity sensors of Telemecanique type XS7C40NC440 for industrial applications and PLC compatible are employed, in perfect compatibility with the electronic automated system for presence detection. The overall control is based on a closed-loop control system, with the PLC unit to control real-time processes, under the operator's control. The driving force behind the above control system is the control software, the creation of which is based on the construction and execution of descriptive qualitative models.
The concrete elements production of the plant varies from 6000 blocks per day (8hours) up to 14000. Two of the main machines of interest, press and mixer machine, are shown in Fig. 1 while an overall configuration of the concrete plant is shown schematically in Fig. 2.

Fig. 1. Press and mixer machines

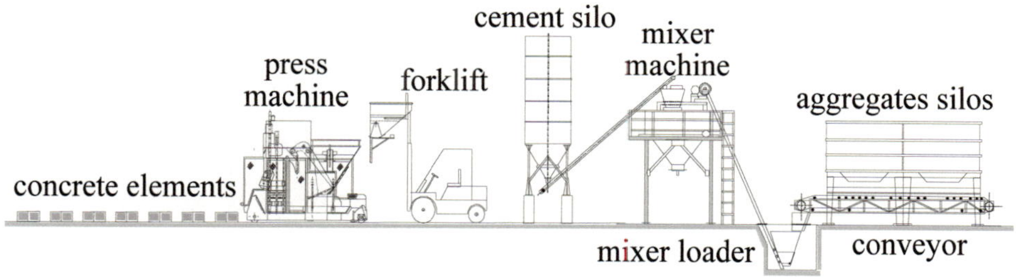

Fig. 2. Concrete plant configuration

The press and mixer machines are constructed mainly of mechanical and electrical parts and devices, incorporating electrical boards, PLC units and other electronic equipment. Basically, the plant operates as follows: aggregates from the storage silos are being supplied through a feeding conveyor into the mixer machine and the wet concrete produced is transported by a forklift loader into the press machine for the actual production of the concrete elements. A simplified functional diagram of plant's overall operation cycle is shown in Fig. 3.

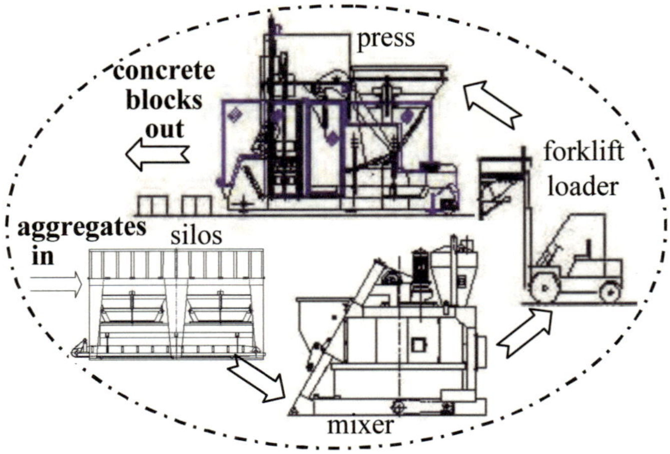

Fig. 3. Plant's operation cycle

2.1 The mobile press machine

The press machine is one of the most important production units of the concrete plant (Fig. 4). The machine produces a variety of concrete products such as blocks, curbs, paving stones, etc. It is consisted mainly of mechanical and electrical parts and devices, the electrical board and the electronic control system based on a PLC unit (Hitachi EC series) and other electronic equipment. The machine is mobile, based on a four wheels metallic base. Other basic machine components include a mould table and a tamper head fitted with a pair of vibrators each, the aggregates' hopper, the oil pump system, the electro-valves and the hydraulic pump system. The mould and tamper units lie on an anti-vibrating mounting system to reduce the wear of moulds.

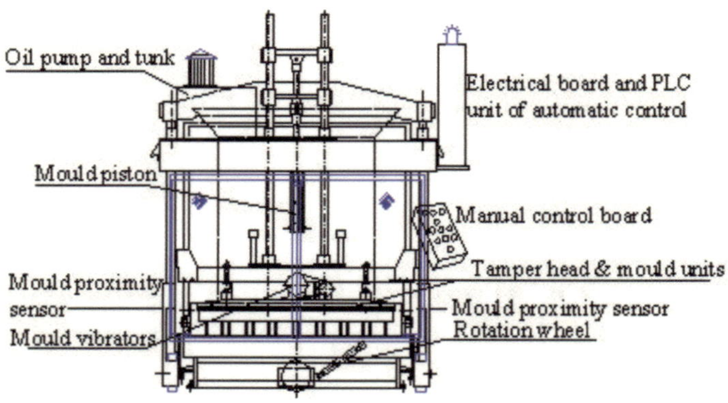

Fig. 4. Schematic representation of the autonomous mobile press machine (RoboPress)

The machine is electrically operated of hydraulic functioning, with automatic control based on the PLC unit. The machine operates on a concrete floor slab, inside or outside a building. Concrete elements are demoulded directly onto the concrete floor slab during a vibrating (starting and main vibration) and compressing cycle. The machine is equipped with a bilateral track corrector, with automatic track collision detection and avoidance, automatic concrete feeding control and automatic shutdown in interfering with safety grates. The machine's motion is enabled by an electro-motor device in conjunction with a mechanism of cogs at the back of the machine. The machine can move in a bidirectional route (forward-backward) in two gear speeds, or turn (left/right) using a fifth wheel. The speed that develops is within the range of 10km/h (first gear speed) to 20km/h (second). The electro-motor (reductor) is of 2kw power. The operation of the machine is performed in automatic (or semi-automatic) mode, driven by an electro-hydraulic control system based on electro-valves and the PLC control unit.

2.2 The mixer machine

The mixer is planetary of roughly mixing vertical high resistant steel shaft fitted with mixing blades of strong-wearing cast-iron. The machine is equipped with a turnover feeding bucket, an electronic cement weighing mechanism, an electro-reductor for bucket's elevation with brakes and two spiral drums for wire rope wrapping. The machine performs the mixing of the mineral aggregates with water and produces the wet concrete that is fed (through a forklift loader) to the mould of the press machine, where is vibrated and compacted. A portion of the plant with the mixer platform and materials storage and feeding system is shown in Fig. 5.

Fig. 5. The materials feeding and mixing platform

2.3 Press and mixer machine operation

In order to describe the dynamic configuration of the machines' processes, prior to the actual specification of the control structures, basic details on machines' requirements and activities have to be defined. In consequence, using that information a system's control model is constructed and executed. The resulted performance of the model is analysed and accordingly in cases that is necessary, its design structure is modified. Finally, the appropriate structure of the control algorithm is implemented.

There are various machine processes and activities under control (Fig. 6), such as the aggregates mixing process, mixer feeding process, concrete transfer process and concrete elements production process, and activities such as aggregates bucket fill operation, aggregates drawer transfer motion (backwards/forwards), tamper head and mold table motion (up/down), the hydraulic arms actuators motion, vibrators operation, etc.

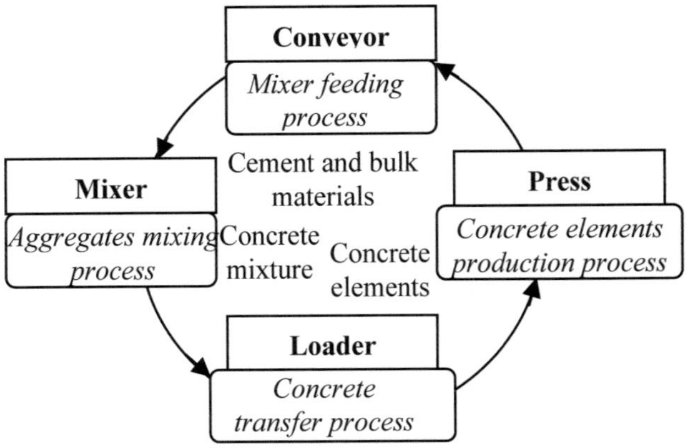

Fig. 6. Plant's operation cycle

Beyond the above machine processes, an important machine function under strict control is press movement along a trajectory path (forward/backward route and left/right turns) and its correcting maneuvers according to sensors input, in order to avoid collision with any obstacles. A generalised view of the control algorithms of those structural processes is presented in Fig. 7. In particular, the left part of the figure is a diagrammatic form of the

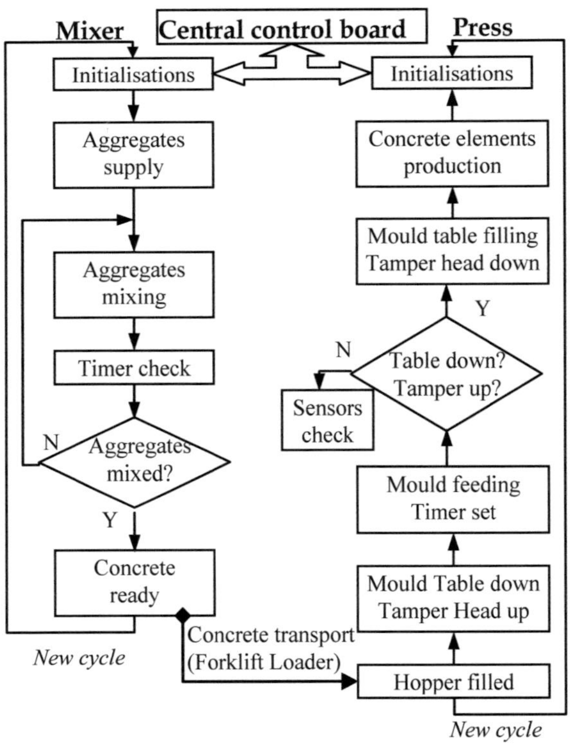

Fig. 7 Generalisations of press and mixer machine operation algorithms

basic processes running in the mixer machine, while the right part of the processes running in the press machine. The communication link between the processes is established through a transport loader. In both diagrams, the processes are running on cycles. On each machine operation cycle, certain initialisations (or re-calibrations) are carried out, materials and parts positions are checked (e.g. aggregates mixture state, mold table and tamper head position), until the final output is produced (e.g. concrete extraction and concrete block elements, respectively).

3. Control system

This section provides details of the control structures and algorithms developed and used for data acquisition and process monitoring for the overall plant control and operation. Particular details are provided for the automatic control of the mobile press machine that performs (in cooperation with the mixer machine) the production of moulded concrete elements for architectural and building projects.

The overall monitoring and control is based on a closed-loop control system with the human in the control loop, for establishing the most optimum control operation. The central control board (based on a PLC unit - Hitachi EM-II series) monitors the machines' operations which provide feedback in the form of analog input signals through the electrical data transmission lines, installed for this purpose. The PLC is programmed to process the data signals acquired. All the electronics for the control of the mixer and aggregates feeding systems are incorporated into a control console which is pushbutton operated. The mobile press machine has its own separate electric control board, with the PLC unit incorporated into the main panel and a receiver (antenna) for remote operation (start, stop and turn manoeuvres).

3.1 Data acquisition and control

The data acquisition and control system is consisted of sensor devices for detecting and transmitting in real-time signals about the processes status, such as aggregates' level and status, as analog/digital signals into the programmable control unit for processing. Solid state proximity sensors (of inductive type and PLC compatible) are employed for presence detection. The central control board (based on the PLC unit) processes the inputs and controls the equipment by producing analog control signals in outputs. The end-receiver of those control signals are the electrical valves actuators, which control (open/close) the fluid rate of hydraulic valves that activate the silos openings, the mixer machine rotation and other processes. The driving force behind the above data acquisition and control system is the control software programmes, installed using a combination of programming packages.

3.2 Press machine remote control and operation

The control system is based on a Hitachi EC series programmable logic controller of type EC-60HRP that offers up to 60I/O points and direct PC connection (RS232) and monitoring. The actual programming of the machine control unit is carried out using the Hitachi PLC programming software (ActGraph, Actron A.B. Co.) for EC PLC series. The program stored is processed in a cycle with an execution speed of 1.5μs per basic instruction. All the logic program functions of the overall machine control are controlled by that PLC unit.

A number of solid state inductive proximity sensors of type Telemecanique XS7C40NC440 for industrial applications and PLC compatible are employed, in perfect compatibility with

the electronic automated system, for presence detection. The usable sensing range and response time is 0-15mm (.47"), appropriate for metallic targets passing the sensors at durations that are not critical. The use of sensors is essential for the accurate control of the various machine operations and processes. The PLC reads the status of the inputs, solves the logic programmed and updates the outputs.
The overall machine remote control and operation could be summarised in four stages: cart and mould filling operations, compression molding (pressurisation) and mould extraction operation. Compression molding basically involves the pressing of wet concrete mixture (aggregates) between two halves of a mould (tamper and table) to fill the material in the mould form. Compression pressure varies from 150 bar to 200 bar. That functionality of the sensory system is shown in Fig. 8.

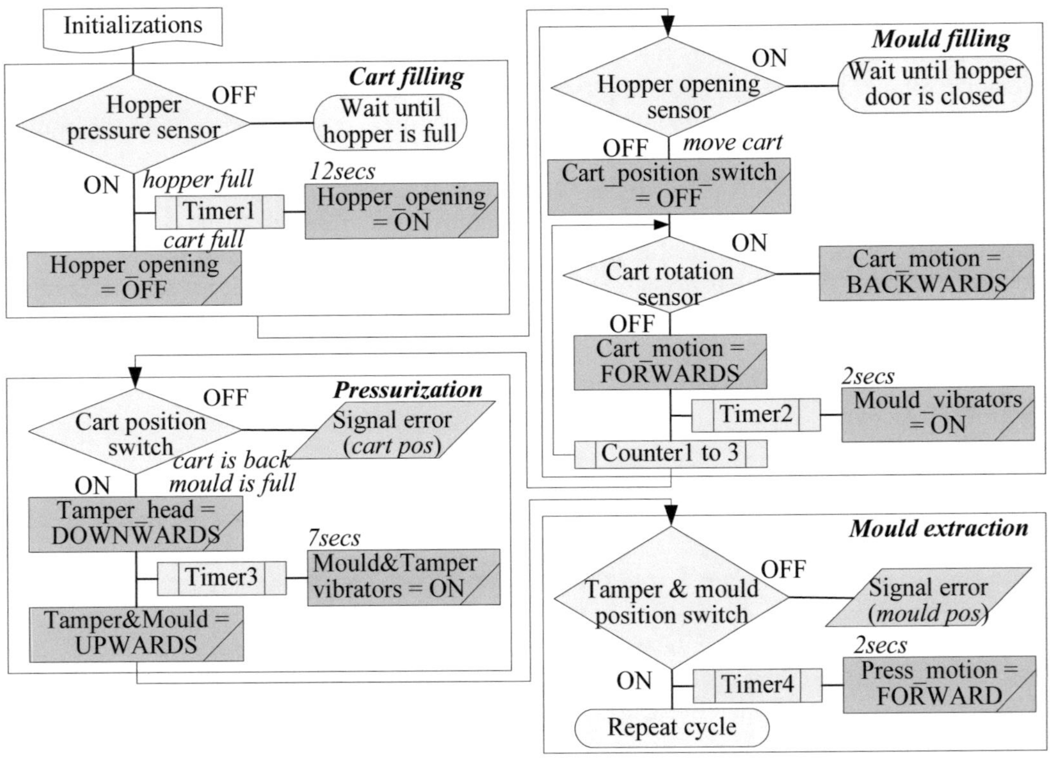

Fig. 8. Simplified sensory system operation flowchart

The study of the machine's overall operation has enabled the specification of the sensory information required. A schematic view of the sensory system developed is shown in Fig. 9. The machine's hopper is periodically supplied with aggregates (wet concrete mixture), the level of which is sensed with a pressure sensor. Once the hopper is filled with aggregates, the door opens (hopper opening sensor turns ON) for certain time interval (materials flow timer T1: 12secs), so that the aggregates transfer-cart to the mould gets filled. Then, the door closes (hopper opening sensor turns OFF) and the transfer-cart moves forward (in a reciprocal way) in order to fill the mould. Each time the transfer-cart moves forward, a sensor is activated and the cart starts to move backwards. This is repeated three times (cart pass counter C1: 3). However, after the second pass, a vibrator on the mould is activated (timer T2: 2secs) for the mixture to be distributed equally in the mould. Then, a third pass of the cart follows and the mould is filled. Once the cart is back (cart position switch is ON) and the mould is filled with wet aggregates, the tamper-head begins to move downwards squeezing the mixture in the mould. At the same time, two sets of pairs of vibrators (one pair in the tamper and the other in the mould table) are activated (until the tamper goes up, about 7secs) in order for the concrete product to become denser. The overall pressurising procedure lasts about 10secs. After that, the tamper-head and the mould-table move up and the machine moves forward (~1m) to the next production point.

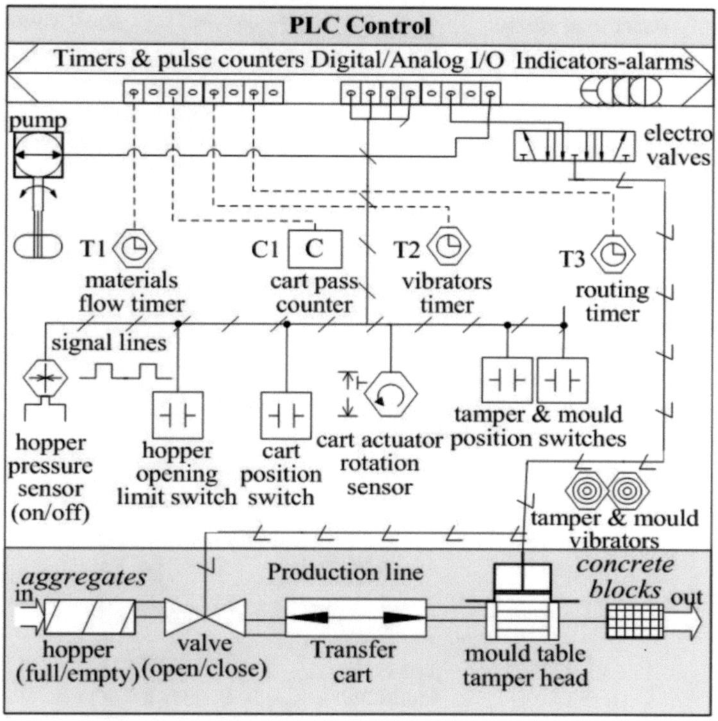

Fig. 9. Sensory system

It is evident that the sensory system plays an important role in the overall operation of the compression press machine. The normal operation of the machine is based on correct sensory information. In case an error is detected (sensor signal error), the machines fall into a faulty state. A schematic description of the machine states taking in consideration the functionality of the sensory system, is given in Fig. 10. Based on that functionality the control software is created and downloaded to the PLC unit.

The mobile press machine is also equipped with a receiver (antenna) for remote control of its operation. Beyond the start and stop operations, teleoperation of the machine is required in performing the manoeuvres necessary to proceed with the next production line. During the navigation along a production line, the machine follows the route automatically based on the mounted sensors. If necessary (in case of the machine falling out of the specified linear trajectory), automatic route correction is carried out based on the lateral sensors signals the machine is equipped with and using the fifth wheel for performing the actual correction manoeuvres. A schematic diagram of the mobile press navigation terrain is shown in Fig. 11.

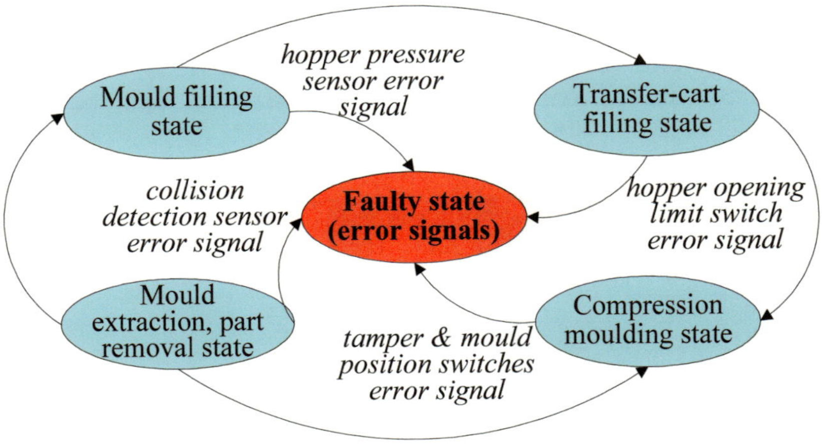

Fig. 10. Normal operation and faulty states diagram

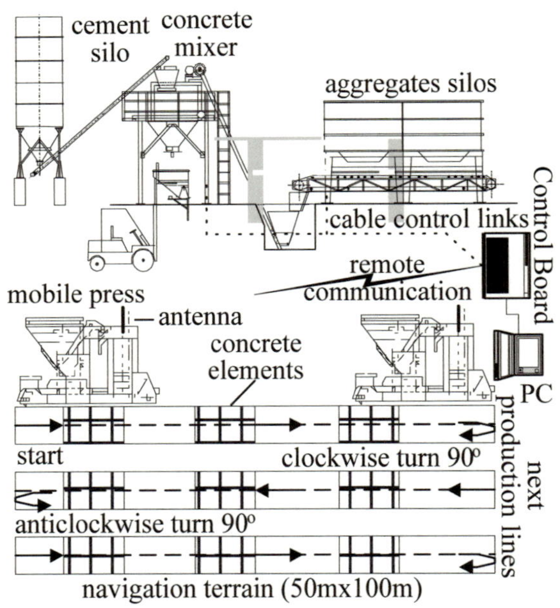

Fig. 11. Press machine navigation and remote control

3.3 Mixer remote control and operation

The mixer is loaded periodically with a specific volume of aggregates and cement which are mixed with water for a certain period of time (~15min). The aggregates silos and the feeding conveyor (of the bucket that loads the mixer with aggregates) are controlled manually from the central control console. However, the cement and water volumes fed into the mixer are controlled automatically, once a certain load is achieved. At this stage, mixing operation starts automatically. In case of insufficient material volume or weight, the mixing operation does not start and the corresponding indicators are illuminated at the control console.

3.4 Overall plant remote control and diagnosis

The overall plant monitoring and control is carried out through the central board of control (Fig. 12). The board of plant control presents an operating and monitoring system. This is consisted of a panel of push buttons, key switches and lamp indicators for immediate visualisation of the processing signals. The operation of the plant from the central board is based on indicating and alarm elements. In order to make the operation simple, a graphic plan (mimic diagram) of the plant under control is integrated within the control board, which shows at each time point the visualisation of operations flow.

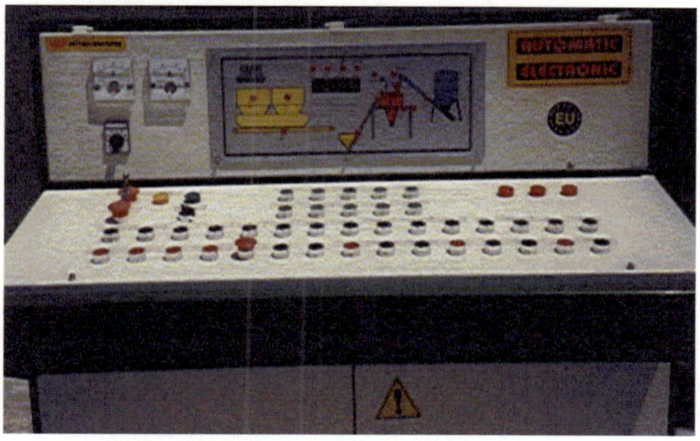

Fig. 12. The central board of plant control and monitoring

In addition, an external PC is connected directly (through RS232C) to the central control board in order to perform regular maintenance tasks (e.g., programming the internal PLC unit) and collect statistical results about the values of specific parameters (e.g., aggregates' flow) for further analysis and diagnosis of the plants' operation.

4. Modelling and simulation

This section describes the modelling and simulation techniques used for the development and verification of the overall plant's operation and control prior to its implementation. Considering the complexity of the concrete plant machines' operations, MATLAB Simulink simulation tools were considered to describe and analyse its performance. However, although quantitative modelling techniques provide much of the required information to describe a manufacturing system (e.g., using MATLAB SimMechanics), they are often too complex for real-time dynamic systems. For this reason, in addition to the above, QMTOOL, a qualitative modelling and simulation tool already applied successfully in robotics research (Adam & Grant, 1994), was used to overcome the shortcomings, due to systems complexity and extensive numerical computations. Using that tool, we have dealt successfully with some of the uncertainties in the positioning of the various machine parts and the control of press machine processes. Prior to the actual implementation of the control structure and machine operation, qualitative models are generated describing the functionality of the processes involved and tested for their effectiveness. The qualitative models are introduced at a high-level abstraction form, using relatively small amount of information, similar to human reasoning on studying complex system's behaviour.

4.1 MATLAB Simulink model

The design and control of such an automated plant requires an efficient development system that would enable the design specifications to be implemented and tested prior to the actual development. In order to describe the machines' operation with MATLAB Simulink models, several factors have to be considered. This is because there are various machine processes and activities under control, such as the aggregates input/output operation, the linear movement of aggregates' transfer drawer, the concurrent movements of tamper head and mold table during moulding, vibrators operation, etc.
Provided that the press machine's overall operation could be described in operational states, as shown in a diagrammatic form in Fig. 13, a working model was created. The equations that describe the machines' states are given by the following relationships:

$$\begin{aligned} ST\_A &= (ST\_A + ST\_C \cdot Mv_{off}) \cdot ST\_A \cdot Mf_{off} \\ ST\_B &= (ST\_B + ST\_A \cdot Mf_{off}) \cdot ST\_B \cdot Mp_{off} \\ ST\_C &= (ST\_C + ST\_B \cdot Mp_{off}) \cdot ST\_C \cdot Mv_{off} \end{aligned} \quad (1)$$

where:
ST_0: Initial conditions machine state
ST_A: State of aggregates filling
ST_B: State of machine press up/down
ST_C: State of machine route
ST_E: State of machine fault operation
Mf: Variable of ST_A (on-off)
Mp: Variable of ST_B (on-off)
Mv: Variable of ST_C (on-off)
Merror: Machine error
Mferror: Mould filling fault
Mperror: Aggregates pressing fault
Mverror: Machine route fault

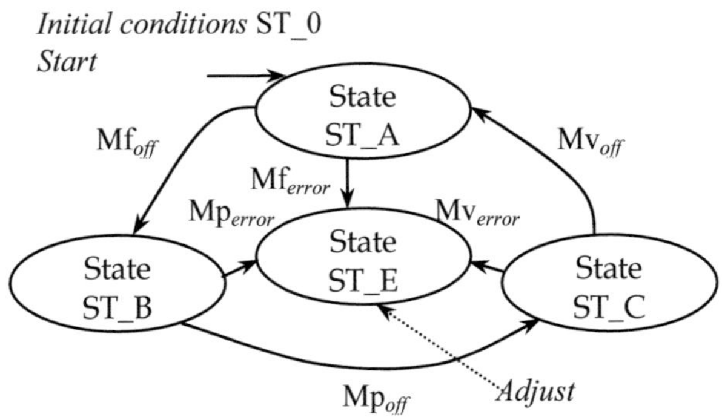

Fig. 13. States diagram of the press machine control and operation algorithm

A partial view of the overall press machine operation structure, using Matlab-Simulink, is given in Fig. 14.

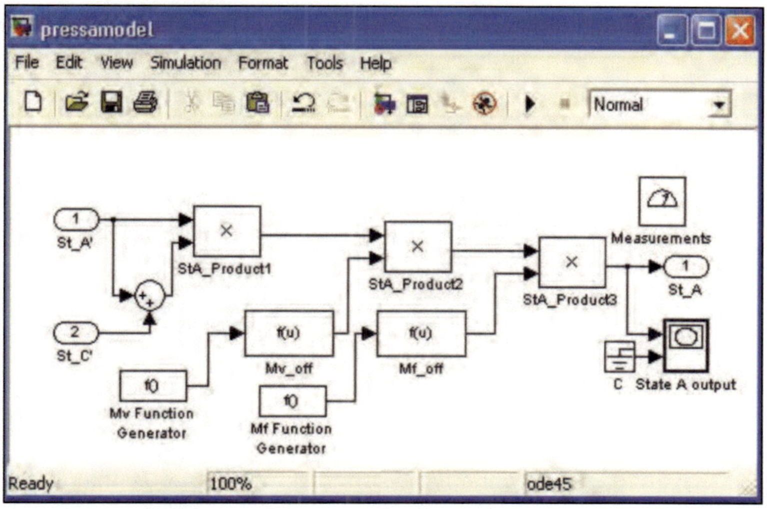

Fig. 14. Partial view of Simulink-based control system model of press machine

Particularly, for the description of the compression molding operation and the creation of models for simulation analysis, the hydraulic driving units had to be studied. The use of hydraulic actuators is of main importance in the overall machine operation, particularly for compression molding. So, one of the main goals in compression molding modelling is to verify the design and operation of the pressurisation system. For this purpose, a motion controller was developed to regulate the pressure (up/down) in the actuators valves of the mould units for simulating the action of compression molding. The final position of the hydraulic piston is monitored. A ramp reference input was used to evaluate the tracking ability of the subsystems in the model. The actual pressurisation subsystem (see Fig. 15) enables to control and monitor the operation pressure which is supplied to the molding system (tamper head and mould table) actuators. The control pressure generated is proportional to the area and the mass of the hydraulic cylinder piston under control.

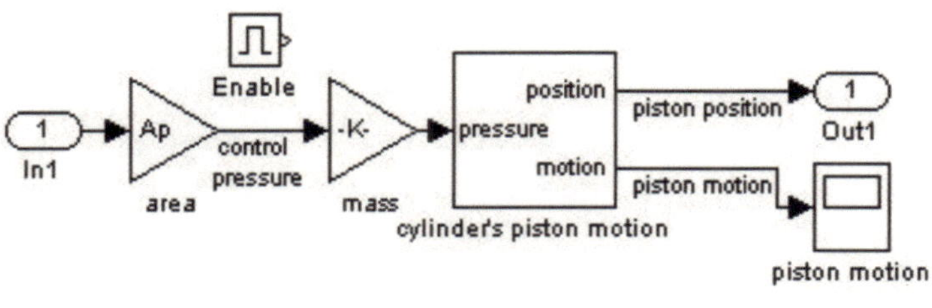

Fig. 15. Pressurisation subsystem

Another goal is to verify the design and operation of the sensory system. For this purpose, a sensor cell subsystem was developed that emulates the behaviour of a proximity sensor. In particular, an inductive proximity sensor senses the proximity of a metal object using an oscillator principle. It is essentially comprised of an oscillator whose windings constitute the fencing face and where an electromagnetic field is generated. When a metal object is positioned within this field, the resulting currents induced into the target form an additional load and the oscillations cease. This causes the output driver to operate, producing an ON or OFF output signal. Based on this principle of operation, a basic sensor cell subsystem was created (Fig. 16), upon which the overall sensory system model was build. A simple function called *turn_sensor(mode)*, where mode is {ON, OFF}, is created to simulate the sensor state status.

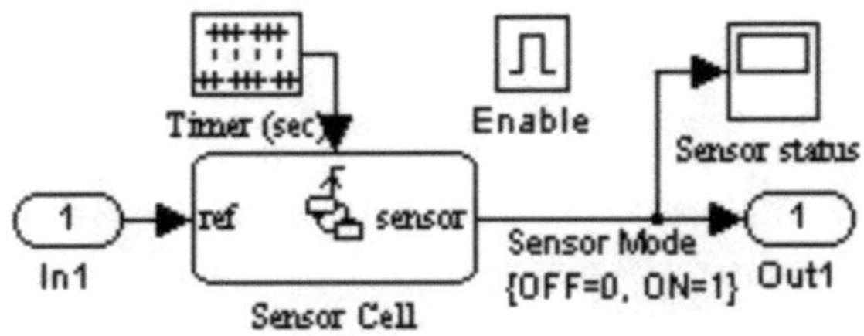

Fig. 16. Sensor cell subsystem

4.2 QMTOOL model

One of the key advantages of qualitative reasoning in general, is that it can work with partial knowledge and information, thus overcoming some of the difficulties of quantitative modelling. Although in most of the manufacturing cases predominate the dynamic continuous systems, however most of them could be described in a discrete-event manner. This is because, in most of the cases, their status changes instantaneously at specific time points or time intervals at which events take place, triggered by some actions or activities. For example, the operation of the industrial compression molding press machine, although it is continuous in time, its individual compression actions (e.g., mould actuators pressure up and down) could be described as being executed at specific or separate time points. In other words, a discrete-event simulation model could be build and executed, although it is also known, that a discrete model is not always used to describe a discrete system and vice versa. In addition, their operation usually involves an unknown number of input parameters that change in a random way, which is difficult to describe analytically.

In order to test and validate the operation and control of the press and mixer machines, prior to their actual operation control implementation, simulation models were build, based on given set of parameters and associated relationships.

4.2.1 QMTOOL model construction

It is important to determine the appropriate control and operation algorithm of the machines (in synchronisation) prior to their installation in plant and cooperation with the rest of the machines' group. It is also necessary to find the tools to test and modify such a control structure, even at the design specification level, without an in-depth requirement for programming skills.

QMTOOL is used to produce working models of the machines under control and test them in order to acquire the desired functionality. The main focus is in the processes running in press and mixer machine. This modelling tool, based on object-oriented techniques methods and objects, provides an interactive environment that eases the modelling process. During the modelling phase, system models are created by simply connecting *input*, *state* and *output* variables (represented as objects) and assigning to them and their connections qualitative values of their magnitudes and relationships. Providing that a physical system is given, the user selects from a type menu the types of variables needed to define the model and to describe sufficiently the structure of the model. The individual attributes for each variable, such as name, initial value, operating range limits (min, max), etc., are assigned from a data menu.

During the execution phase, the system converts qualitative attributes into numerical data in order for the appropriate simulations' calculations to take place. This conversion is based on qualitative to numerical values conversion tables, describing basic numerical factors such as the operating range of the main variables (machine parameters) in a machine process, etc. An example of such a qualitative to numerical values conversion table is shown below in Table 1.

Max Min Sign	+++	+-+
Range	Max - Min	Max
Step	(Range/5)*Sign	(Range/5)*Sign
Nvalue'	QVal * Step	QVal * Step
Upper Lim	Min + Nvalue'	Nvalue'
Lower Lim	Upper - Step	Upper - Step
NValue	(Upper+Lower)/2	(Upper+Lower)/2

Table 1. Qualitative to numerical values conversion table of variables relationships

The operating range of a variable (Range) is determined and divided (qualitative partitioning) by the amount of qualitative values this variable can obtain (e.g., in our case: xl, l, m, s, xs). Then, after is taken in consideration the actual sign of the qualitative value the variable is assigned to, the numerical value (Nvalue') is determined by multiplying that value with a numerical factor that corresponds to this qualitative value (QVal). This numerical factor ranges from 1 to 5, respectively for xs (extra small), xl (extra large) and 0 (zero). However, in practice it was determined, that the final numerical value (Nvalue) should actually be between its respective step-range determined by the Upper and Lower limit values.

In order to clarify the above and understand the role of the qualitative to numerical values conversion table, lets examine the following single-variable case example. Suppose that a variable is assigned a large qualitative value (numerical factor 4), with a positive sign (+) and an operation range defined between 0 (Min) and 100 (Max). Then, according to the conversion table, it's numerical value (Nvalue') would be determined by the following set of equations:

$$\begin{aligned} &\text{Range} = \text{Max} - \text{Min} &&\Rightarrow \text{Range} = 100 \\ &\text{Step} = (\text{Range}/5) * \text{Sign} &&\Rightarrow \text{Step} = 20 \\ &\text{Nvalue}' = \text{QVal} * \text{Step} &&\Rightarrow \text{Nvalue}' = 80 \end{aligned} \tag{2}$$

However, as it was mentioned above, this value should be between its respective step-range (determined by the Upper and Lower limit values), namely equal to 1/2 of that range. As a result in this example, the actual numerical value will be determined by the following equations:

$$\begin{aligned} &\text{Upper} = \text{Min} + \text{Nvalue}' &&\Rightarrow \text{Upper} = 80 \\ &\text{Lower} = \text{Upper} - \text{Step} &&\Rightarrow \text{Lower} = 60 \\ &\text{NValue} = (\text{Upper}+\text{Lower})/2) &&\Rightarrow \text{NValue} = 70 \end{aligned} \tag{3}$$

The above conversion process is being carried out similarly for all the qualitative values described in each system's model until they have been converted to quantitative values.

4.2.2 QMTOOL model simulation

A QMTOOL system model is defined as a structure of interconnected components (machine's activities and processes) presented as input, state and output objects and their relationships presented as connection objects.

The system model of the press machine is based on the given set of parameters and associated relationships, examined by the control algorithm. It is build using the types of variables that correspond to the following machine parameters:

- Input variables: initial values of parts' positions, sensors, etc.
- State variables: machines bucket feed rate, tamper head and mold table states, etc.
- Output variables: machine move, concrete elements production rate, etc.

Similarly, the system model of the mixer machine is based on the given set of parameters and associated relationships examined by the control algorithm and build using the types of variables that correspond to the following machine parameters:

- Input variables: initial values of aggregates conditions, etc.
- State variables: machines bucket elevation rate, mixture state, bucket door state, etc.
- Output variables: concrete production rate, etc.

Qualitative values are assigned to the components (parameters) and their relationships, in order to describe how these variables are linked together, interactively. The system objects have already embedded behavioural rules and functionality as (prolog) predicates, which however could be easily modified (menu-driven properties) according to the specific model construction requirements. Using relatively a small amount of qualitative information to define the structure and behaviour of the machines being modeled (symbolic computation), prototype models were created and executed (Fig. 17), in order to produce the dynamic machine behaviour that reflects the functional requirements for the system. This simulation model is a decision-support tool. It presents the dynamic behaviour of the machines and reflects the functional requirements for the concrete plant system. It enabled to test and redefine the machines operation control models prior to their application, in order to verify and finally achieve the desired overall control system cooperative functionality.

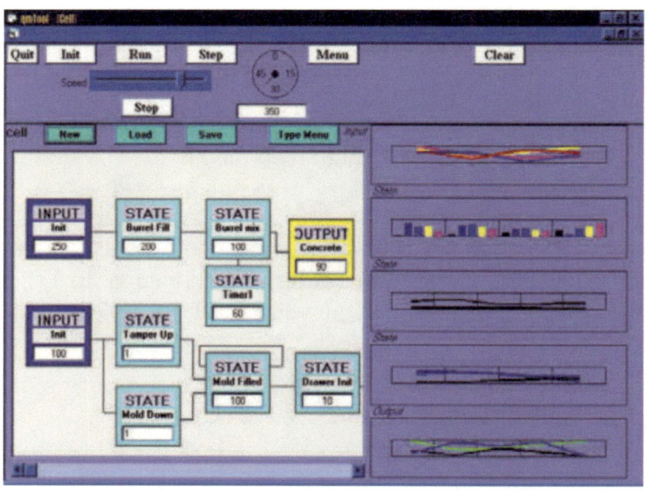

Fig. 17. Partial view of QMTOOL-based control system models of press and mixer machines

In order to show how the actual relations between the input, state and output variables are represented qualitatively, the following notation is used:

$$M+(Stvar,Invar),\ M-(Stvar,Stvar),\ f(Outvar,Stvar) \quad (4)$$

where M+, M- and f simply indicate that there is a relationship (influence), positive or negative (qualitative terms representing the magnitude of the functional relationship) between these variables.

The actual value calculation of the State variable is based on its current value (State(t)) plus a sum of values (Influences) of the preceding variables (predecessors), namely:

$$State(t)=State(t+1)+Influences(i) \quad (5)$$

A single influence is calculated taking in consideration the value of the predecessor PredVal and the magnitude ConMag of this connection, expressed in qualitative terms (i.e. 0 (zero), s (small), m (medium), etc.), namely:

$$Influence=f(Predval,ConMag) \quad (6)$$

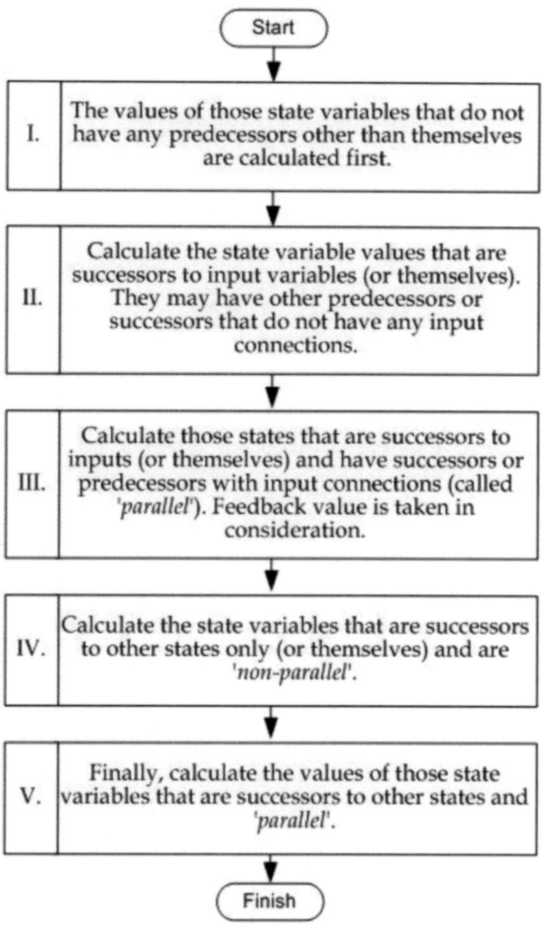

Fig. 18. State variables calculation order algorithm

In order for state variables' values to be calculated appropriately at the correct time interval, the system arranges them in a specific order according to their interconnections within the structure of the model. To achieve this, a set of rules is defined that determines the order in which the state variables should be calculated. The order of calculations is defined by the algorithm given in Fig. 18.

The mapping of mathematical equations (relationships) into qualitative descriptions is carried out using functional M+, M-, arithmetic add, minus, etc. and derivative incr, steady, decr, etc. constraints. For instance, the press machine's movement (Mv) is in functional relationship with the mold table and tamper head states positions (TTp) and the sensors input (Ps), expressed in the following way:

$$\begin{array}{l} \text{PressMachineMovement: M+\{Ps\},M+\{TTp\}} \\ \text{MoldTable FeedRate: M+\{Ds\}} \end{array} \quad (7)$$

Internally, qualitative modelling involves the interpretation and execution of such equations, based on qualitative methods for modelling physical systems (Pearce et. al., 1989; Kuipers, 1986). A graphical representation of these constraints, indicating the functional relationships between the parameters of interest, is shown in Fig. 19.

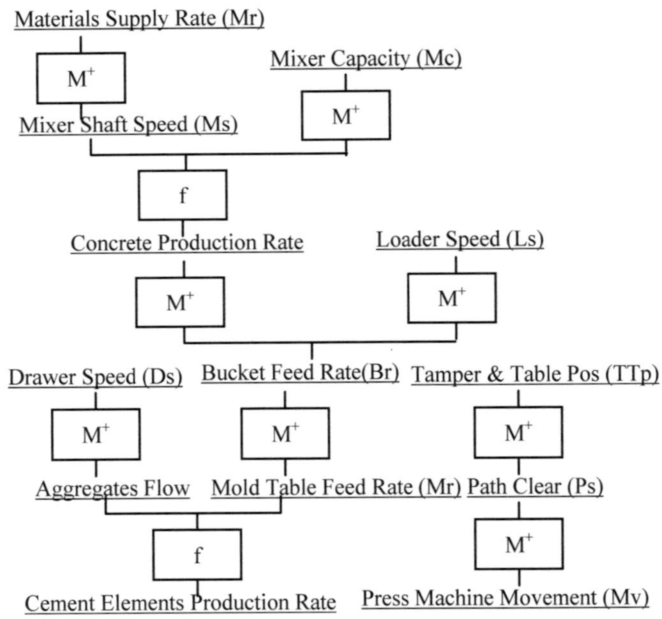

Fig. 19. Partial constraints of the machines system models

The overall behaviour produced from models simulation, is derived from the behaviour of individual components of the system throughout the models structure. This behaviour is presented graphically as Cartesian plots of sequences of time-varying qualitative states. The interactions occurring in the system during the simulation process can be easily analysed and visualised (see Fig. 20).

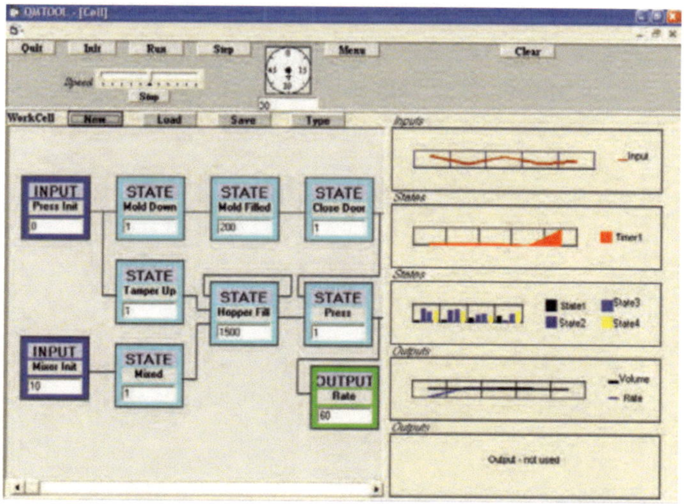

Fig. 20. Partial view of graphical simulation results

The importance of using a model for testing real time control operation algorithms, priori off-line and evaluate it's performance applying alternative solutions back at the design stage, is obvious of the following:

- Describe and analyse the static and dynamic behaviour of machines processes.
- Test and verify the machines overall cooperative functionality.
- Verify the control of each individual machine component.
- Adjust or redefine the design of the overall plant control system early at the specification stage.

Furthermore, using a qualitative approach, the actual productivity abilities of the machines could be estimated on a qualitative basis, closer to human understanding.

5. Implementation

This section describes the generation and application of the control software modules derived from the simulation models.

5.1 Control software implementation

Qualitative machine models were created off-line in order to ensure in safety that machines control and operation within the plant could be established in cooperation quite efficiently. Once the corresponding machine models have been created and tested extensively for their efficient and cooperative control, the overall machines group control system had to be implemented.

A major component of the overall plant operation system is the control software. The control software modules were derived from the creation and implementation of system models. The overall control and actual programming of the machines group is carried out using QMTOOL in conjunction with appropriate Hitachi PLC programming software for EC PLC series, for the implementation of the instructions and PLC download.

The implementation of the control software and the final programming of the central plant control board, as well as the individual PLC unit of the press machine, were realised using

ActGraph software (Actron A.B. Co.). ActGraph allowed the PC to interface with the Hitachi PLC EC series. ActGraph code, in form of a ladder diagram, allows for a final check and then, produces a list of instructions. These PLC instructions are then downloaded for execution in the PLC. A sample of the PLC code and ladder diagram is given in Fig. 21.

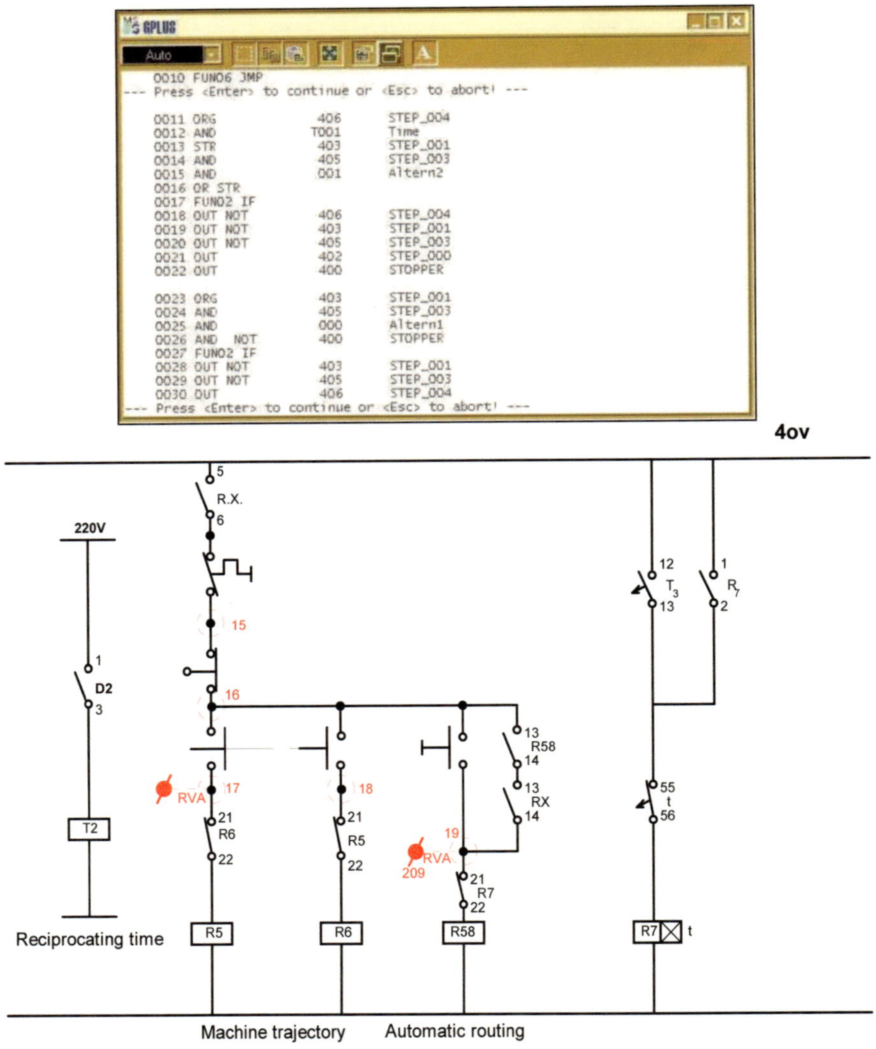

```
 0010 FUN06 JMP
--- Press <Enter> to continue or <Esc> to abort! ---

 0011 ORG          406     STEP_004
 0012 AND          T001    Time
 0013 STR          403     STEP_001
 0014 AND          405     STEP_003
 0015 AND          001     Altern2
 0016 OR STR
 0017 FUN02 IF
 0018 OUT NOT      406     STEP_004
 0019 OUT NOT      403     STEP_001
 0020 OUT NOT      405     STEP_003
 0021 OUT          402     STEP_000
 0022 OUT          400     STOPPER

 0023 ORG          403     STEP_001
 0024 AND          405     STEP_003
 0025 AND          000     Altern1
 0026 AND  NOT     400     STOPPER
 0027 FUN02 IF
 0028 OUT NOT      403     STEP_001
 0029 OUT NOT      405     STEP_003
 0030 OUT          406     STEP_004
--- Press <Enter> to continue or <Esc> to abort! ---
```


Fig. 21. Sample of PLC code and partial view of control diagram

The ladder diagram in Fig. 21, as well as the PLC code listing, are just a sample of the overall control system of the plant machines. In particular, the above are part of the mixer machine control system. Each rung of logic in the diagram (e.g. digital or analog inputs/outputs, contacts, switches, output coils, relays, etc.) corresponds to certain PLC instructions or subroutines, as in the above code listing. In practice, in most of the cases prior to the actual implementation of the operation control modules and creation of the instructions listing, the ladder diagram is being created first. Based on such simple schematic descriptions, the actual code listings are then created and downloaded into the programmable control unit.

6. Conclusion

Since most of the modern concrete elements production plants today are often faced with increasing market demands for further automation, as well as the growing international competition, computer-control systems, teleoperation and automation technology, modelling and simulation tools are some of the technologies and techniques used to acquire the desired functionality in operation control and quality in production. The last decade has seen computer technology applied more widely in industrial production, particularly in manufacturing processes not generally associated with high-technology. Often, such technology was not considered because it was difficult to model manufacturing processes using conventional mathematical modelling tools.

Here, the operation and control of a concrete elements production plant was presented. A qualitative modelling approach has been shown to improve production procedures and manufactured product quality. The creditability of the overall control system was validated using a simulation tool that utilises both conventional numerical methods and more advanced qualitative techniques, in order to deal efficiently with the dynamic processes present in the concrete plant. Qualitative modelling tools and commercially available software were used as tools to aid in the operation and control of concrete elements production machines. Once an optimised control model was obtained, via simulation with QMTOOL, etc., tests were carried out with machines manufacturing concrete elements. The effectiveness of the overall plant control using this approach is defined by the following attributes:

- The ability to describe and analyse the static and dynamic behaviours of machine processes.
- The ability to evaluate the operation of important sub-systems within the machines.
- The ability to easily redefine the design specifications to optimise the machines control.
- The ability to produce a realistic and reliable description of the cooperative plant machines based on qualitative models.
- The ability to plan and test path planning scenarios (e.g. route planning) in safety.
- The ability to reduce the cost of the machines manufacturing and minimise the risk of machines malfunctioning.

7. References

Adam, G. & Grant, E. (1994). QMTOOL - A qualitative modelling and simulation CAD tool for designing automated workcells, *Proceedings of the IEEE Inter. Conf. on Robotics and Automation*, pp. 1141-1146, San Diego

Adiga, S. & Gadre, M. (1990). Object-Oriented software modeling of a flexible manufacturing system. *Journal of Intelligent and Robotic Systems*, 3, 147-165

Chryssolouris, G. (1992). *Manufacturing Systems: Theory and Practice*, Springer-Verlag, New York

Fishwick, P. & Luker, P. (1991). *Qualitative Simulation Modeling and Analysis*, Springer-Verlag, New York

Forbus, K. (1984). Qualitative process theory. *Journal of Artificial Intelligence*, 24, 85-168

Garani, G. & Adam, G. (2007). Qualitative Modelling and Simulation of an Automated Mobile Press Machine, *Proceedings of the 13th IEEE International Conference on Methods and Models in Automation and Robotics*, pp. 1111-1115, Szczecin, Poland

Gutta, M. & Sinha, N. (1996). *Intelligent Control Systems*, IEEE Press, Piscataway

Groumpos, P. & Krauth, J. (1997). Simulation in industrial manufacturing: issues and challenges, *Proceedings of European Conf. on Integration in Manufacturing*, pp. 234-241, Dresden

Hwang, B.; Saif, M. & Jamshidi, M. (1995). Fault detection and diagnosis of a nuclear power plant using artificial neural networks. *Journal of Intelligent and Fuzzy Systems*, 3(3), 197-213

Isayev, I. (1987). *Injection and Compression Molding Fundamentals*, Marcel Dekker, New York

de Kleer, J. & Brown, J. (1984). A qualitative physics based on confluences. *Journal of Artificial Intelligence*, 24, 7-84

Kuipers, B. (1986). Qualitative simulation. *Journal of Artificial Intelligence*, 29, 289-338

Lamperti, G. & Zanella, M. (2003). EDEN: An Intelligent Software Environment for Diagnosis of Discrete-Event Systems. *Applied Intelligence*, 18(1), 55-77

Mak, K.; Lau, H. & Wong, S. (1999). Object-oriented specification of automated manufacturing systems. *Journal of Robotics and Computer Integrated Manufacturing*, 15, 297-312

Marvel, J. & Bloemer, K. (2000). Manufacturing systems, In: *Handbook of Industrial Automation*, R.L. Shell & E.L. Hall, (Eds.), 457-484, Marcel Dekker, New York

Nise, N. (1995). Control *Systems Engineering*, Benjamin/Cummings, Redwood City

Pearce, D.; Grant, E. & Shepherd, B. (1989). A qualitative modelling environment for design and diagnosis of automation, *Proceedings of the 2nd Inter. Conf. on Industrial and Engineering Applications of Artificial Intelligence & Expert Systems*, pp. 192-196, Tullahoma

Rao, P.; Tewari, N. & Kundra, T. (1993). *Computer-Aided Manufacturing*, McGraw-Hill, New York

Reinhart, T. (1987). *Engineered Materials Handbook*. ASM International, Ohio

Shell, R. & Hall, E. (2000). *Handbook of Industrial Automation*, Marcel Dekker, ISBN: 0-8247-0373-1, New York

Shetty, D. & Kolk, R. (1997). *Mechatronics System Design*, PWS Publishing, Boston

Srovnal, V. & Pavliska, A. (2002). Robot Control Using UML and Multi-agent System, *Proceedings of the 6th SCI World Multiconference*, pp. 306-311, Orlando

Trave-Massuyes, L. (1992). Qualitative reasoning over time: history and current prospects. *Journal of The Knowledge Engineering Review*, 7 (1), 1-18

Trybula, W.J. & Goodman, R.L. (1989). Evolution of integrated manufacturing in the 1980s, *Proceedings of the 7th Symposium in Electronic Manufacturing Technology*, pp. 251-256, San Francisco, Sep 1989, IEEE

Zhang, J. ; Roberts, P. & Ellis, J. (1990). Fault diagnosis of a mixing process using deep qualitative knowledge representation of physical behaviour. *Journal of Intelligent and Robotic Systems*, 3, 103-115

16

Operational Amplifiers and Active Filters: A Bond Graph Approach

Gilberto González and Roberto Tapia
University of Michoacan
Mexico

1. Introduction

The most important single linear integrated circuit is the operational amplifier. Operational amplifiers (op-amp) are available as inexpensive circuit modules, and they are capable of performing a wide variety of linear and nonlinear signal processing functions (Stanley, 1994).

In simple cases, where the interest is the configuration gain, the ideal op-amp in linear circuits, is used. However, the frequency response and transient response of operational amplifiers using a dynamic model can be obtained.

The bond graph methodology is a way to get an op-amp model with important parameters to know the performance. A bond graph is an abstract representation of a system where a collection of components interact with each other through energy ports and are place in the system where energy is exchanged (Karnopp & Rosenberg, 1975).

Bond graph modelling is largely employed nowadays, and new techniques for structural analysis, model reduction as well as a certain number of software packages using bond graph have been developed.

In (Gawthrop & Lorcan, 1996) an ideal operational amplifier model using the bond graph technique has been given. This model only considers the open loop voltage gain and show an application of active bonds.

In (Gawthrop & Palmer, 2003), the `virtual earth' concept has a natural bicausal bond graph interpretation, leading to simplified and intuitive models of systems containing active analogue electronic circuits. However, this approach does not take account the type of the op-amp to consider their internal parameters.

In this work, a bond graph model of an op-amp to obtain the time and frequency responses is proposed. The input and output resistances, the open loop voltage gain, the slew rate and the supply voltages of the operational amplifier are the internal parameters of the proposed bond graph model.

In the develop of this work, the Bond Graph model in an Integral causality assignment (BGI) to determine the properties of the state variables of a system is used (Wellstead, 1979; Sueur & Dauphin-Tanguy, 1991). Also, the symbolic determination of the steady state of the variables of a system based on the Bond Graph model in a Derivative causality assignment (BGD) is applied (Gonzalez et al., 2005). Finally, the simulations of the systems represented

by bond graph models using the software 20-Sim by Controllab Products are realized (Controllab Products, 2007).
Therefore, the main result of this work is to present a bond graph model of an op-amp considering the internal parameters of a type of linear integrated circuit and external elements connected to the op-amp, for example, the feedback circuit and the load.
The outline of the paper is as follows. Section 2 and 3 summarizes the background of bond graph modelling with an integral and derivative causality assignment. Section 4 the bond graph model of an operational amplifier is proposed. Also, the frequency responses of the some linear integrated circuits that represent operational amplifier using the proposed bond graph model are obtained. Section 5 gives a comparator circuit using a bond graph model and obtaining the time response. Section 6 presents the proposed bond graph model of an feedback op-amp; the input and output resistances, bandwidth, slew rate and supply voltages of a non-inverting amplifier using BGI and BGD are determined. Section 7 gives the filters using a bond graph model of an op-amp. In this section, we apply the filters for a complex signal in the physical domain. The bond graph model of an op-amp to design a Proportional and Integral (PI) controller and to control the velocity of a DC motor in a closed loop system is applied in section 8. Finally, the conclusions are given in section 9.

2. Bond graph model

Consider the following scheme of a Bond Graph model with an Integral causality assignment (BGI) for a multiport Linear Time Invariant (LTI) system which includes the key vectors of Fig. 1 (Wellstead, 1979; Sueur & Dauphin-Tanguy, 1991).

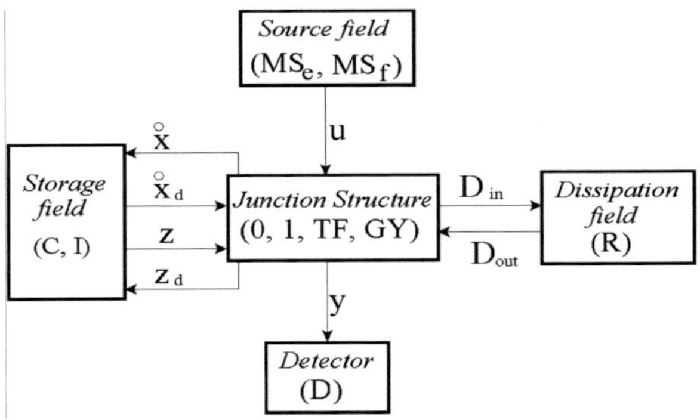

Fig. 1. Key vectors of a bond graph.

In fig. 1, (MS_e, MS_f), (C, I) and (R) denote the source, the energy storage and the energy dissipation fields, (D) the detector and $(0,1,TF,GY)$ the junction structure with transformers, TF, and gyrators, GY.

The state $x(t) \in \Re^n$ and $x_d(t) \in \Re^m$ are composed of energy variables $p(t)$ and $q(t)$ associated with I and C elements in integral causality and derivative causality, respectively, $u(t) \in \Re^p$ denotes the plant input, $y(t) \in \Re^q$ the plant output, $z(t) \in \Re^n$ the co-energy vector, $z_d(t) \in \Re^m$ the derivative co-energy and $D_{in}(t) \in \Re^r$ and $D_{out}(t) \in \Re^r$ are a mixture

of $e(t)$ and $f(t)$ showing the energy exchanges between the dissipation field and the junction structure (Wellstead, 1979; Sueur & Dauphin-Tanguy, 1991).
The relations of the storage and dissipation fields are,

$$z(t) = Fx(t) \tag{1}$$

$$z_d(t) = F_d x_d(t) \tag{2}$$

$$D_{out}(t) = LD_{in}(t) \tag{3}$$

The relations of the junction structure are,

$$\begin{bmatrix} \dot{x}(t) \\ D_{in}(t) \\ y(t) \end{bmatrix} = \begin{bmatrix} S_{11} & S_{12} & S_{13} & S_{14} \\ S_{21} & S_{22} & S_{23} & 0 \\ S_{31} & S_{32} & S_{33} & 0 \end{bmatrix} \begin{bmatrix} x(t) \\ D_{out}(t) \\ u(t) \\ \dot{x}_d(t) \end{bmatrix} \tag{4}$$

$$z_d(t) = -S_{14}^T z(t) \tag{5}$$

The entries of S take values inside the set $\{0, \pm 1, \pm m, \pm n\}$ where m and n are transformer and gyrator modules; S_{11} and S_{22} are square skew-symmetric matrices and S_{12} and S_{21} are matrices each other negative transpose. The state equation is (Wellstead, 1979; Sueur & Dauphin-Tanguy, 1991),

$$\dot{x}(t) = A_p x(t) + B_p u(t) \tag{6}$$

$$y(t) = C_p x(t) + D_p u(t) \tag{7}$$

where

$$A_p = E^{-1}\left(S_{11} + S_{12} M S_{21}\right) F \tag{8}$$

$$B_p = E^{-1}\left(S_{13} + S_{12} M S_{23}\right) \tag{9}$$

$$C_p = \left(S_{31} + S_{32} M S_{21}\right) F \tag{10}$$

$$D_p = S_{33} + S_{32} M S_{23} \tag{11}$$

being

$$E = I_n + S_{14} F_d^{-1} S_{14}^T F \tag{12}$$

$$M = \left(I_n - LS_{22}\right)^{-1} L \tag{13}$$

3. Bond graph in derivative causality assignment

We can use the Bond Graph in Derivative causality assignment (BGD) to solve directly the problem to get A_p^{-1}. Suppose that A_p is invertible and a derivative causality assignment is performed on the bond graph model (Gonzalez et al., 2005). From (4) the junction structure is given by,

$$\begin{bmatrix} z(t) \\ D_{ind}(t) \\ y_d(t) \end{bmatrix} = \begin{bmatrix} J_{11} & J_{12} & J_{13} \\ J_{21} & J_{22} & J_{23} \\ J_{31} & J_{32} & J_{33} \end{bmatrix} \begin{bmatrix} \dot{x}(t) \\ D_{outd}(t) \\ u(t) \end{bmatrix} \tag{14}$$

where the entries of J have the same properties that S and the storage elements in (14) have a derivative causality. Also, D_{ind} and D_{outd} are defined by

$$D_{outd}(t) = L_d D_{ind}(t) \tag{15}$$

and they depend of the causality assignment for the storage elements and that junctions have a correct causality assignment.
From (6) to (13) and (14) we obtain,

$$z(t) = A_p^* \dot{x}(t) + B_p^* u(t) \tag{16}$$

$$y_d(t) = C_p^* \dot{x}(t) + D_p^* u(t) \tag{17}$$

where

$$A_p^* = J_{11} + J_{12} N J_{21} \tag{18}$$

$$B_p^* = J_{13} + J_{12} N J_{23} \tag{19}$$

$$C_p^* = J_{31} + J_{32} N J_{21} \tag{20}$$

$$D_p^* = J_{33} + J_{32} N J_{23} \tag{21}$$

being

$$N = \left(I_n - L_d J_{22}\right)^{-1} L_d \tag{22}$$

The state output equations of this system in integral causality are given by (6) and (7). It follows, from (1), (6), (7), (16) and (17) that,

$$A_p^* = FA_p^{-1} \tag{23}$$

$$B_p^* = -FA_p^{-1}B_p \tag{24}$$

$$C_p^* = C_pA_p^{-1} \tag{25}$$

$$D_p^* = D_p - C_pA_p^{-1}B_p \tag{26}$$

Considering $\dot{x}(t) = 0$, the steady state of a LTI MIMO system defined by

$$x_{ss} = -A_p^{-1}B_pu_{ss} \tag{27}$$

$$y_{ss} = \left(D_p - C_pA_p^{-1}B_p\right)u_{ss} \tag{28}$$

where x_{ss} and y_{ss} are the steady state of the state variables and the output, respectively. In an approach of the BGD, the steady state is determined by

$$x_{ss} = F^{-1}B_p^*u_{ss} \tag{29}$$

$$y_{ss} = D_p^*u_{ss} \tag{30}$$

4. A bond graph model of an operational amplifier

The standard operational amplifier (op-amp) symbol is shown in Fig. 2. It has two input terminals, the inverting (-) input and the noninverting (+) input, and one output terminal. The typical op-amp operates with two Direct Current (DC) supply voltages, one positive and the other negative (Stanley, 1994).

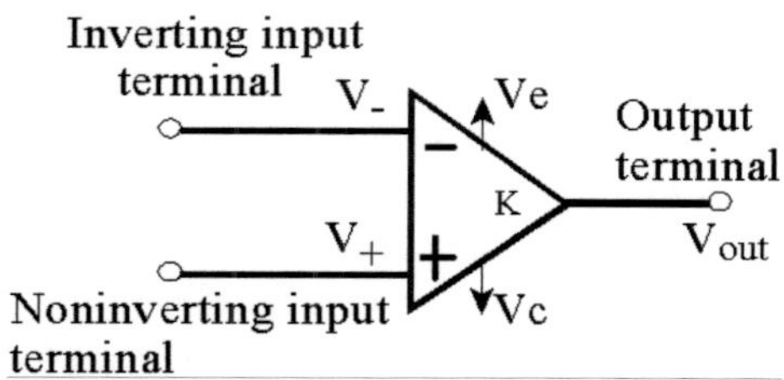

Fig. 2. Operational amplifier symbol.

The complex action of the op-amp results in the amplification of the difference between the voltages at the noninverting, V_+, and the inverting, V_-, inputs by a large gain factor, K, designed open loop gain. The output voltage is,

$$V_{out} = K\left(V_+ - V_-\right) \tag{31}$$

The assumptions of the ideal op-amp are (Barna & Porat, 1989): 1) The input impedance is infinite. 2) The output impedance is zero. 3) The open loop gain is infinite. 4) Infinite bandwidth so that any frequency signal from 0 to ∞ Hz can be amplified without attenuation. 5) Infinite slew rate so that output voltage charges simultaneously with input voltage charges.
The implications of the assumptions are: no current will flow either into or out of either input terminal of the op-amp, also, the voltage at the output terminal does not charge as the loading is varied and finally, from H_3, $V_+ - V_- = \frac{V_{out}}{K}$, if we take the limit when K→∞, note that $V_+ = V_-$, which indicates that the voltages at the two input terminals are forced to be equal in the limit.
The assumptions of an op-amp are not completely true in practice, and to be fully competent in the analysis and design of op-amps circuits, one must be aware of the limitations. Therefore, we propose a more realistic model applicable to DC and low frequencies based on Bond Graph with Intregral causality assignment (BGI), since an op-amp is a multistage amplifier, it can be represented by Fig. 3.

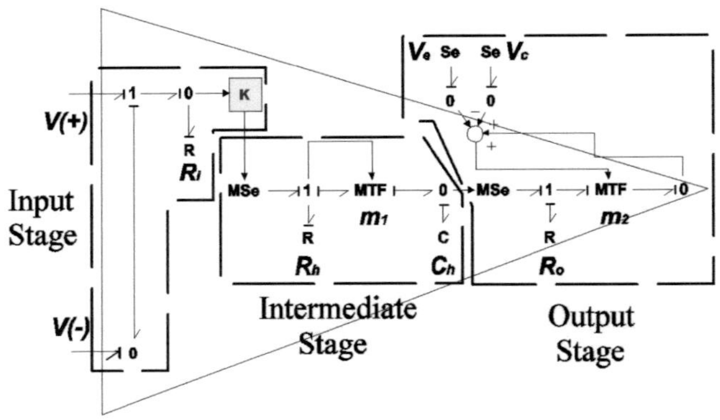

Fig. 3. Bond graph model of an operational amplifier.

The individual stages used in op-amp are separately chosen to develop different amplifier characteristics. Those amplifier characteristics which are determined by a given stage depend on whether it functions as an input stage, intermediate stage or output stage. So, the bond graph model of the op-amp is composed by 3 stages, which are:

- Characteristics of the differential input stage of an operational amplifier are the most critical factors which affect the accuracy of an op-amp in providing voltage gain. Errors effects of following stages are reduced in significance by the gain isolation provided by the first stage. This input stage considers the two input terminals of op-amp, the differential input resistance, denoted as R_i, which is the resistance between the inverting and non-inverting inputs and K is the open loop gain.
- The intermediate stage introduces the frequency compensation of the op-amp using a lag network. Also, using a MTF, the slew rate of the op-amp is considered.
- Following the input and intermediate voltage gain stages of an op-amp, it is desirable to provide impedance isolation from loads. In this way the characteristics of the gain

stages are preserved under load, and adequate signal current is made available to the load. In addition, the output stage provides isolation to the preceding stage and a low output impedance to the load. This stage is formed by the output terminal, the output resistance of the op-amp denoted as R_o and the adjustment of supply voltages, positive voltage V_c and negative voltage V_e, are applied using a MTF element.

The usefulness of the bond graph model of an operational amplifier can be shown, applying this model to $\mu A741$ op-amp by Fairchild Semiconductor Corporation (Stanley, 1994; Gayakward, 2000) and, $TL084$ and $OP27$ by Texas Instruments (Stanley, 1994; Gayakward, 2000) whose data sheets are shown in Table 1.

Op-amp	$\mu A741$	$TL084$	$OP27$
$R_i\,(\Omega)$	2×10^6	10^{12}	6×10^6
$R_o\,(\Omega)$	75	75	70
K	2×10^5	2×10^5	1.8×10^6
$SR\,(V/\mu s)$	0.5	13	2.8
$V_c, V_e\,(V)$	±15	±18	±22

Table 1. Data sheets of $\mu A741$, $TL084$ and $OP27$.

Using the data sheets of an op-amp, the high cutoff frequency of the open loop voltage gain, f_o, is determined. Moreover, the compensation parameters of the bond graph model are defined by

$$f_o = \frac{1}{2\pi R_c C_c} \tag{32}$$

From (32) and the data sheets of the $\mu A741$, $TL084$ and $OP27$ op-amps, the parameters to obtain the frequency response are given in Table 2.

Op-amp	$\mu A741$	$TL084$	$OP27$
$R_h\,(\Omega)$	10^3	10^3	10^3
$C_h\,(F)$	3.06652×10^{-6}	5.3051×10^{-6}	1.9894×10^{-5}

Table 2. Parameters of frequency response.

Substituting the parameters of Tables 1 and 2 to bond graph model of each op-amp, the frequency responses of $\mu A741$, $TL084$ and $OP27$ op-amps are shown in Fig. 4, 5 and 6, respectively.

Note that, the frequency responses of the $\mu A741$, $TL084$ and $OP27$ op-amps are very close respect to the data sheets of these op-amps (Stanley, 1994; Gayakward, 2000). Also, decibel gain is $K_{dB} = 20Log(K)$. The next section an application of the bond graph model of an op-amp to prove the time response is presented.

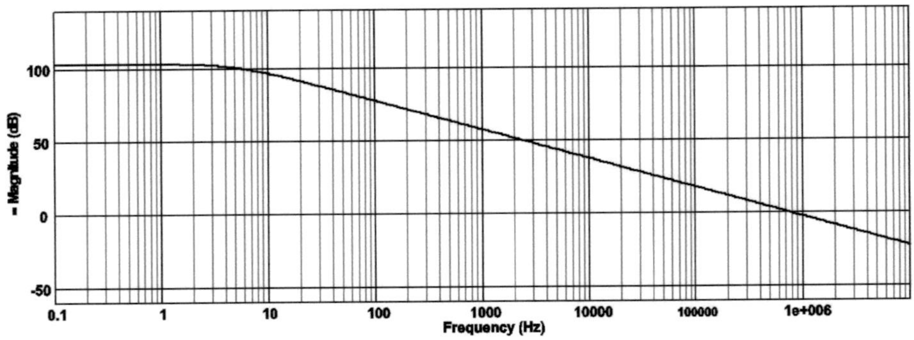

Fig. 4. Frequency response of $\mu A741$ op-amp.

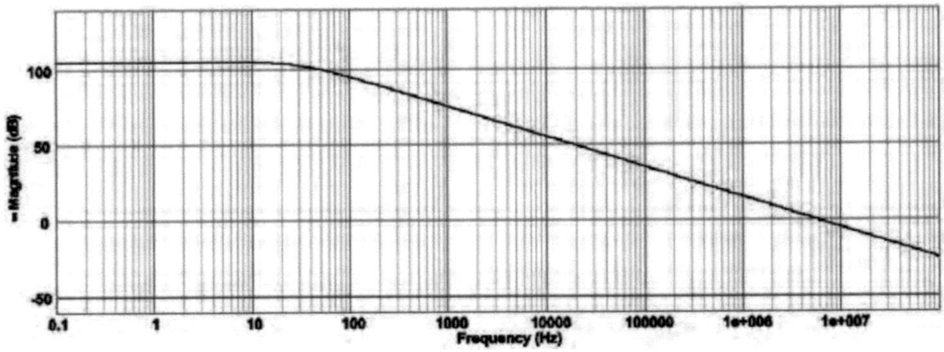

Fig. 5. Frequency response of $TL084$ op-amp.

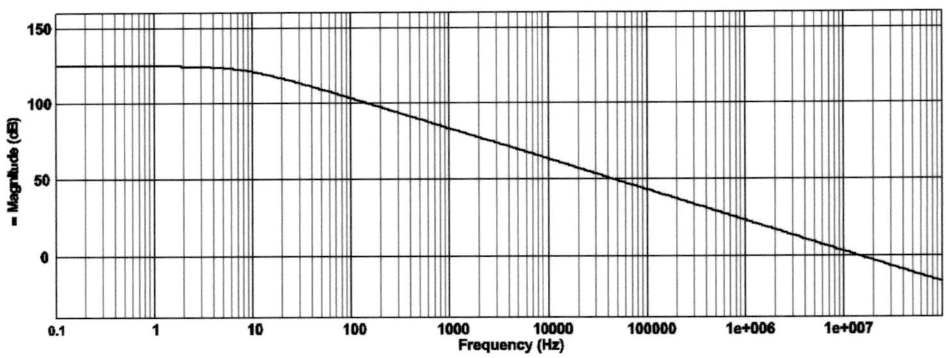

Fig. 6. Frequency response of $OP27$ op-amp.

5. Comparator circuit

Comparator circuits represent to the first class of circuits we have considered that are basically nonlinear in operation. Specifically, comparator circuits produce two or more discrete outputs, each of which is dependent on the input level (Floyd & Buchla, 1999). In this application, the op-amp is used in the open loop configuration with the input voltage on one input and a reference voltage on the other, which is shown in Fig. 7.

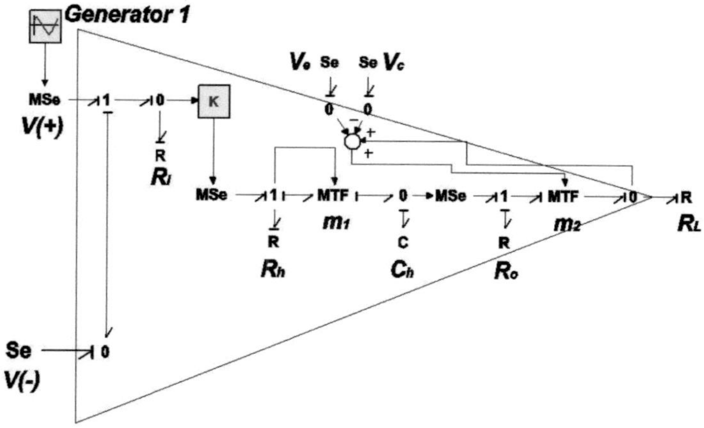

Fig. 7. Bond graph model of a comparator op-amp.

Applying a voltage $v_+(t) = 3\sin(2\pi f_+ t)V$ to the noninverting input, where $f_+ = 0.15Hz$ and $v_- = 1V$ to the inverting input of the bond graph model of Fig. 7. Also, the supply voltages are $V_c = 12V$ and $V_e = -12V$, the time response of the comparator circuit using the $\mu A741$ op-amp is shown in Fig. 8.

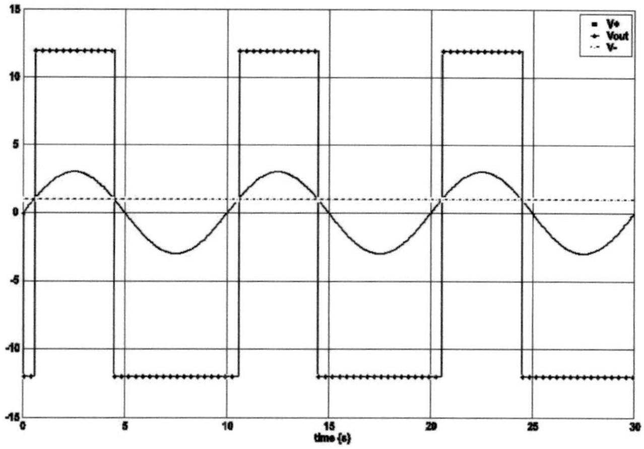

Fig. 8. Time response of the comparator op-amp.

In according with the objective of the comparator circuit, the time response of the Fig. 8 is satisfactory (Stanley, 1994; Gayakward, 2000; Floyd & Buchla, 1999). However, if the frequency of the input signal increases, we have to consider the response of phase shift versus frequency, which is obtained using the proposed bond graph model and is shown in Fig. 9 for $\mu A741$ op-amp phase shift between the input and output signals.

If the noninverting input voltage is $v_+(t) = 0.1\sin(2\pi f_+ t)V$ where $f_+ = 100Hz$, the inverting input voltage is $v_-(t) = 0V$ and, the supply voltages are $V_c = 12V$ and

$V_e = -12V$, then the time response of the comparator circuit using $\mu A741$ op-amp is a square waveform of magnitude $\pm 12V$ and a phase shift of $\theta = -86.8^0$ respect the input signal, which is shown in Fig. 10.

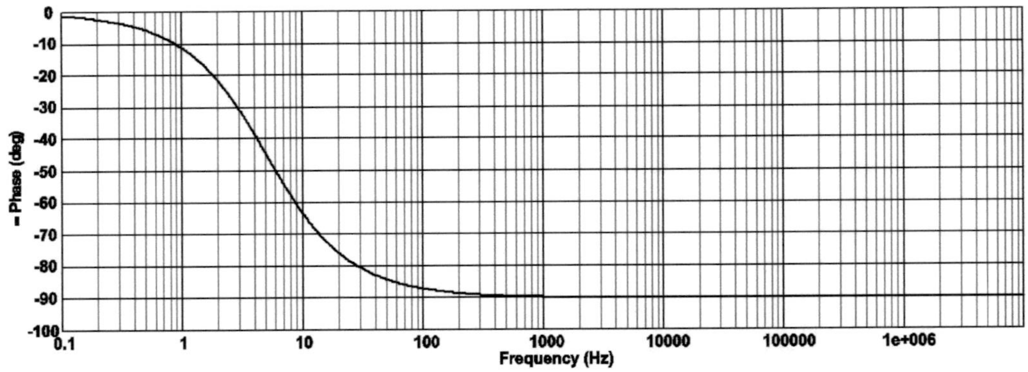

Fig. 9. Phase shift versus frequency of $\mu A741$ op-amp.

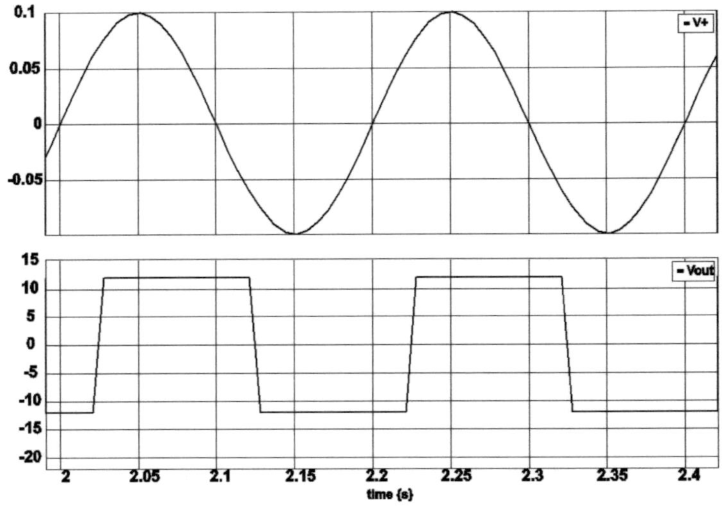

Fig. 10. Time response of comparator with $V_+(t) = 20\sin(200\pi t)$.

The phase shift of the output signal of Fig. 10 can be verified from the following equation, calculating the lag time of the output signal,

$$t = \frac{\theta}{360 f} \tag{33}$$

where θ is the phase shift of the bode plot for $\mu A741$ op-amp is the Fig. 8, and f is the frequency of the input signal. In this case $t = 2.41ms$.

In next section op-amp configurations with negative feedback in the physical domain are proposed.

6. Feedback operational amplifier

An op-amp that uses feedback is called a feedback is called a feedback amplifier. A feedback amplifier is sometimes referred to as a closed loop amplifier because the feedback forms a closed loop between the input and the output. A feedback amplifier essentially consists of two parts: an op-amp and a feedback circuit. The feedback circuit can take any form whatsoever, depending on the intended application of the amplifier. This means that the feedback circuit may be made up of either passive components, active components, or combinations of both (Gayakward, 2000).

A closed loop amplifier can be represented by using two blocks, one for an op-amp and another for a feedback circuit. There are four ways to connect theses two blocks. These connections are classified according to whether the voltage or current is fed back to the input in series or in parallel, as follows: 1) Voltage series feedback, 2) Voltage shunt feedback, 3) Current series feedback and 4) Current shunt feedback (Gayakward, 2000) and (Floyd & Buchla, 1999).

The voltage series feedback configuration is one of the most important because this is commonly used. An in depth analysis of this configuration in the physical domain is presented in this section, computing voltage gain, input resistance, output resistance and the bandwidth.

6.1 A bond graph model of a noninverting amplifier

An op-amp connected in a closed loop configuration as a noninverting amplifier is shown in Fig. 11. The input signal is applied to the noninverting input. A portion of the output is applied back to the inverting input through the feedback network in the physical domain. The BGI and the Bond Graph in a Derivative causality assignment (BGD) are shown in Fig. 11, in order to get the symbolic expressions of the closed loop system in steady state applying the methodology given in section 1.

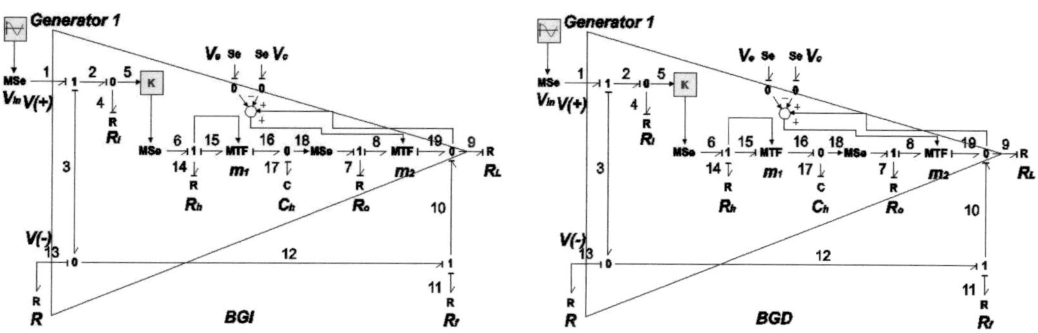

Fig. 11. Bond graph models of a noninverting amplifier.

The closed loop gain, A_{CL}, can be determined using the BGD approach, from (30) we have,

$$A_{CL} = \frac{y_{ss}}{u_{ss}} = D_p^* \tag{34}$$

where y_{ss} and u_{ss} are the steady state values of the output and input, respectively.

We now derive the closed loop gain of the noninverting amplifier using the BGD. The key vectors of BGD are given by,

$$\begin{aligned} x(t) &= q_{17}(t); \dot{x}(t) = f_{17}(t); z(t) = e_{17}(t) \\ u(t) &= e_1(t); y(t) = e_9(t) \\ D_{ind}(t) &= \begin{bmatrix} e_4(t) & e_7(t) & e_9(t) & f_{11}(t) & f_{13}(t) & f_{14}(t) \end{bmatrix} \\ D_{outd}(t) &= \begin{bmatrix} f_4(t) & f_7(t) & f_9(t) & e_{11}(t) & e_{13}(t) & e_{14}(t) \end{bmatrix} \end{aligned} \tag{35}$$

the constitutive relations are,

$$F = \frac{1}{C_h} \tag{36}$$

$$L_d = diag\left\{ \frac{1}{R_i}, \frac{1}{R_o}, R_F, R, R_h \right\} \tag{37}$$

and the junction structure is,

$$J_{21} = \begin{bmatrix} 0 \\ 0 \\ 0 \\ 0 \\ 0 \\ \frac{1}{m} \end{bmatrix}; J_{22} = \begin{bmatrix} 0 & 0 & 0 & 0 & -1 & 0 \\ 0 & 0 & 0 & m_2 & \frac{-K}{m_1} - m_2 & \frac{-1}{m_1} \\ 0 & 0 & 0 & -1 & 1 & 0 \\ 0 & -m & 1 & 0 & 0 & 0 \\ 1 & m_2 & -1 & 0 & 0 & 0 \\ 0 & 0 & 0 & 0 & 0 & 0 \end{bmatrix}; J_{23} = \begin{bmatrix} 1 \\ \frac{K}{m_1} \\ 0 \\ 0 \\ 0 \\ 0 \end{bmatrix}$$

$$J_{12} = \begin{bmatrix} 0 & 0 & 0 & 0 & \frac{-K}{m_1} & \frac{-1}{m_1} \end{bmatrix}; J_{32} = \begin{bmatrix} 0 & 0 & 0 & -1 & 1 & 0 \end{bmatrix} \tag{38}$$

$$J_{13} = \frac{K}{m_1}; J_{11} = J_{31} = J_{33} = 0$$

From (21), (22), (34), (36), (37) and (38), the closed loop gain of the noninverting amplifier is,

$$A_{CL} = \frac{R_L \left[m_2 R_i K \left(R + R_f \right) + m_1 R R_o \right]}{m_1 R_o \Delta + KRm_2 R_L R_i + R_L m_2^2 m_1 \left[R_f \left(R + R_i \right) + RR_i \right]} \tag{39}$$

where $\Delta = \left(R + R_i \right)\left(R_L + R_f \right) + RR_i$

Note that the closed loop gain (39) takes account the internal parameters and the external elements connected to op-amp.
A normal operation of the op-amp using the bond graph model indicates the modules of $MTF's$ are $m_1 = 1$, the slew rate is sufficient of the op-amp, and $m_2 = 1$, the supply voltages allow to obtain the output voltage depending the input voltage and the gain of the op-amp. Considering, $m_1 = 1$, $m_2 = 1$ and $R_o = 0$, we obtain

$$\left(A_{CL}\right)_1 = \frac{R + R_f}{R + \frac{1}{K}\left(R_f + RR_i + \frac{R_f R}{R_i}\right)} \tag{40}$$

Applying the $\lim\limits_{\substack{R_i \to \infty \\ K \to \infty}} \left(A_{CL}\right)_1$, the ideal closed loop gain of this amplifier, $\left(A_{CL}\right)_i$, is determined,

$$\left(A_{CL}\right)_i = 1 + \frac{R_f}{R} \tag{41}$$

The time response of the noninverting amplifier using $\mu A741$ op-amp, $R = 10K\Omega$, $R = 190K\Omega$ and the input signal is $v_i(t) = 0.5\sin(2\pi f_i t)V$ where $f_i = 1KHz$, is shown in Fig. 12.

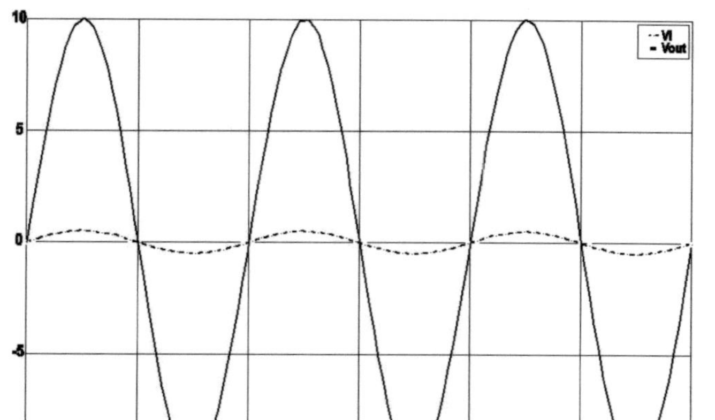

Fig. 12. Time response of the noninverting amplifier.

6.1.1 Input resistance of the noninverting amplifier

The input resistance of the noninverting amplifier can be determined using the BGD of Fig. 11. Considering the output $f_1(t)$, the submatrices J_{31}, J_{32} and J_{33} from (38) are changed by

$$J_{23} = \begin{bmatrix} 1 & 0 & 0 & 0 & 0 & 0 \end{bmatrix}; J_{13} = J_{33} = 0 \tag{42}$$

From (21), (22), (37) and (38) the input resistance is determined by,

$$R_{iF} = \frac{R_o\left[(R+R_i)(R_L+R_f)+RR_i\right]+KRR_LR_i+R_L\left[R_f(R+R_i)+RR_i\right]}{(R+R_f)(R_o+R_L)+R_oR_L} \tag{43}$$

where $(e_1)_{ss}$ and $(f_1)_{ss}$ are the steady state values of the input e_1 and output f_1, respectively.

If $R_o = 0$ we reduce,

$$(R_{iF})_1 = R_i\left(1+\frac{KR}{R+R_f}\right)+\frac{RR_f}{R+R_f} \tag{44}$$

finally, the term $\frac{R_fR}{R+R_f} \ll R_i\frac{KR}{R+R_f}$ hence the ideal input resistance of the noninverting amplifier $(R_{iF})_i$ is defined by,

$$(R_{iF})_i = R_i\left(1+\frac{KR}{R+R_f}\right) \tag{45}$$

The result of (45) indicates that the ideal input resistance of the op-amp with feedback is $\left(1+KR/R+R_f\right)$ times that without feedback. In addition, the equation (43) allows to determine the input resistance of the op-amp considering the internal parameters and external elements for this configuration. Equation (45) can be verified in (Stanley, 1994; Gayakward, 2000).

6.1.2 Output resistance of the noninverting amplifier

Output resistance is the resistance determined looking back into the feedback amplifier from the output terminal. A BGD that allows to obtain the output resistance of a noninverting amplifier is shown in Fig. 13.

The key vectors of the BGD of Fig. 13 are,

$$\begin{aligned} & x(t) = q_{16}(t); \dot{x}(t) = f_{16}(t); z(t) = e_{16}(t) \\ & u(t) = e_1(t); y(t) = f_1(t) \\ & D_{ind}(t) = \begin{bmatrix} e_4(t) & e_7(t) & e_{10}(t) & f_{12}(t) & e_{13}(t) \end{bmatrix} \\ & D_{outd}(t) = \begin{bmatrix} f_4(t) & f_7(t) & f_{10}(t) & e_{12}(t) & f_{13}(t) \end{bmatrix} \end{aligned} \tag{46}$$

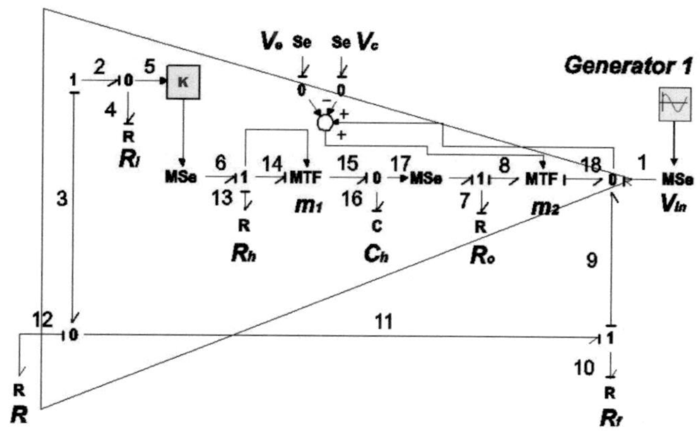

Fig. 13. Derivation of output resistance of a bond graph model of a noninverting amplifier.

the constitutive relations are,

$$L = diag\left\{\frac{1}{R_i}, \frac{1}{R_o}, \frac{1}{R_f}, R, \frac{1}{R_h}\right\} \tag{47}$$

$$F = \frac{1}{C_h} \tag{48}$$

and the junction structure of the BGD is,

$$J_{22} = \begin{bmatrix} 0 & 0 & 0 & -1 & 0 \\ 0 & 0 & 0 & K & -1 \\ 0 & 0 & 0 & 1 & 0 \\ 1 & 0 & -1 & 0 & 0 \\ 0 & 0 & 0 & 0 & 0 \end{bmatrix}; J_{21} = \begin{bmatrix} 0 \\ 0 \\ 0 \\ 0 \\ 1 \end{bmatrix}; J_{21} = J_{32}^T = \begin{bmatrix} 0 \\ -1 \\ -1 \\ 0 \\ 0 \end{bmatrix} \tag{49}$$

$$J_{12} = \begin{bmatrix} 0 & 0 & 0 & -K & -1 \end{bmatrix}; J_{11} = J_{13} = J_{31} = J_{33} = 0$$

Substituting (22), (47), (49) into (21) the output resistance of a noninverting amplifier is obtained,

$$R_{oF} = \frac{(e_1)_{ss}}{(f_1)_{ss}} = \left(D_p^*\right)^{-1} = \frac{R_o\left[R_i\left(R+R_f\right)+RR_f\right]}{R_i\left(R+R_f+KR\right)+RR_f+R_o\left(R+R_i\right)} \tag{50}$$

Calculating $\left(R_{oF}\right)_1 = \lim_{R_i \to \infty} R_{oF}$ we have,

$$\left(R_{oF}\right)_1 = \frac{R_o\left(R+R_f\right)}{R+R_f+KR+R_o} \tag{51}$$

finally, $R_o + R + R_f + KR \approx R + R_f + KR$, the ideal output resistance $\left(R_{oF}\right)_i$ of the noninverting amplifier is given by,

$$\left(R_{oF}\right)_i = \frac{R_o}{1 + \frac{KR}{R + R_f}} \tag{52}$$

This result shows that the ideal output resistance of the noninverting amplifier is $\frac{1}{\left(1 + KR/R + R_f\right)}$ times the output resistance R_o of the op-amp. That is , the output resistance of the op-amp with feedback is much smaller than the output resistance without feedback. In addition (52) can be verified in (Stanley, 1994; Gayakward, 2000).

6.1.3 Bandwidth of the noninverting amplifier

The bandwidth of an amplifier is defined as the band (range) of frequency for which the gain remains constant. Manufacturers generally specify either the gain-bandwidth product or supply open loop gain versus frequency curve for the op-amp (Gayakward, 2000).
Fig. 4 shows the open loop gain versus frequency curve of the $\mu A741$ op-amp. From this curve for a gain of 200,000, the bandwidth is approximately $5Hz$; or the gain-bandwidth product is $1MHz$. On the other extreme, the bandwidth is approximately $1MHz$ when the gain is 1. Hence, the frequency at which the gain equals 1 is known as the unity gain bandwidth (UGB).
Since for an op-amp with a single break frequency f_o, the gain-bandwidth product is constant, and equal to UGB, we can write,

$$UGB = (K)(f_o) = (A_{CL})(f_F) \tag{53}$$

where f_F bandwidth with feedback.
Therefore, the bandwidth of an feedback op-amp is,

$$f_F = \frac{(K)(f_o)}{A_{CL}} \tag{54}$$

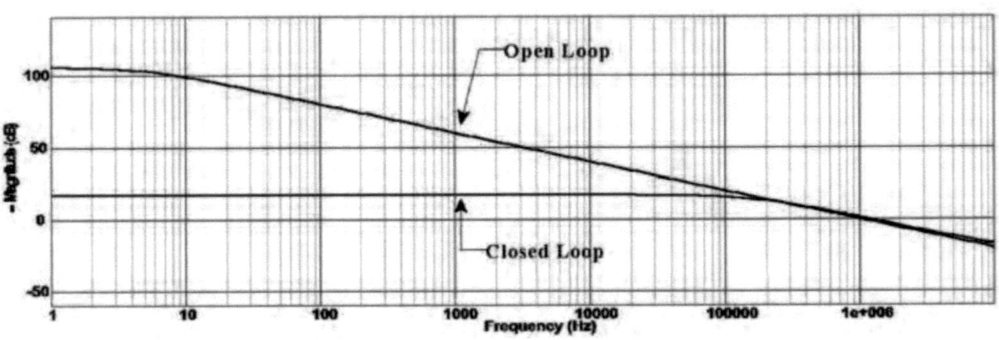

Fig. 14. Frequency response of the noninverting amplifier.

The frequency response of the noninverting amplifier based on BGI of Fig. 11, using $\mu A741$ op-amp, $R = 1K\Omega$, $R_f = 5K\Omega$ and the input signal is $v_i(t) = 1.0\sin(2\pi f_i t)V$ where $f_i = 30KHz$, is shown in Fig. 14.

Note that the frequency response of this amplifier indicates that the closed loop gain is $A_{CL} = 6 = 15.56dB$ until approximately $166KHz$, which is verified from (54).

6.1.4 Slew rate

Another important frequency related parameter of an op-amp is the slew rate. The slew rate is the maximum rate of change of output voltage with respect to time, usually specified in $V/\mu s$. Ideally, we would like an infinity slew rate so that the op-amp's output voltage would change simultaneously with the input. Practical op-amps are available with slew rates from $0.1V/\mu s$ to well above $1000V/\mu s$. The slew rate (SR) can be obtained by,

$$SR = \frac{2\pi f V_p}{10^6} V / \mu s \qquad (55)$$

where f is the input frequency and V_p is the peak value of the output sine wave.

In order to show the effect of the slew rate of an op-amp, the time responses of the noninverting amplifier based on BGI of Fig. 11, using $\mu A741$ and $OP27$ op-amps, $R = 1K\Omega$, $R_f = 5K\Omega$ and the input signal is $v_i(t) = 1.0\sin(2\pi f_i t)V$ where $f_i = 30KHz$, are shown in Fig. 15. The ideal closed gain is then $(A_{CL})_i = 6$.

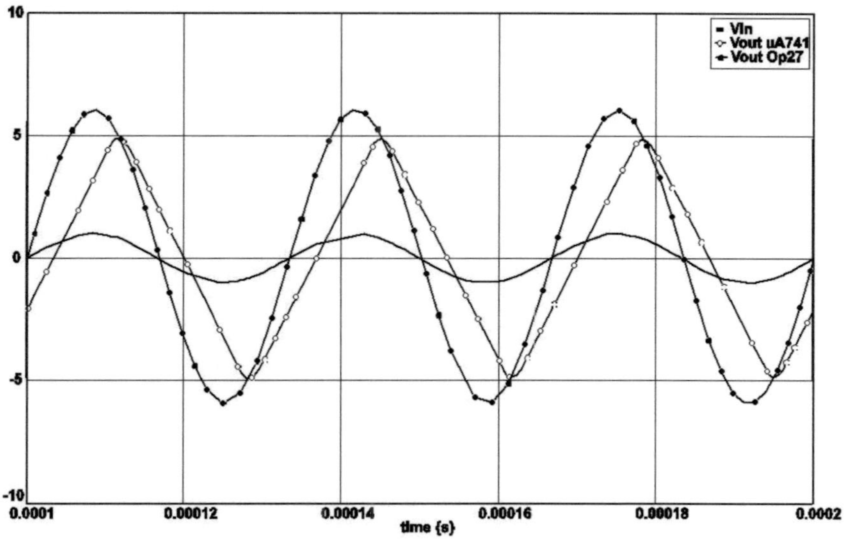

Fig.15. Effect of the slew rate of the noninverting amplifier using $\mu A741$ and $OP27$ op-amps.

From (55), the minimum slew rate of an op-amp with the previous conditions is $SR = 1.13\,V/\mu s$. Therefore, the slew rate of the $OP27$ op-amp, which is $2.8\,V/\mu s$ is enough for the input signal with the given conditions. Fig. 15, shows the output signal of the $\mu A741$ op-amp has distortion because of the slew rate is $0.5\,V/\mu s$.

6.1.5 Supply volages

The most linear integrated circuits, particularly op-amps, use one or more differential amplifier stages, and differential amplifiers require both a positive (V_c) and negative (V_e) power supply for proper operation of the circuit.

The supply voltages of the proposed bond graph model of an op-amp can be tested applying an input signal $v_i(t) = 3\sin(2\pi f_i)t$, $f_i = 30KHz$, $R = 1K\Omega$, $R_f = 5K\Omega$ and $V_c = 12V$ and $V_e = -12V$ to $\mu A741$ op-amp, the time response is shown in Fig. 16.

The ideal closed loop gain is $(A_{CL})_i = 6$, of this form the ideal output signal would be $V_{out}(t) = 18\sin(2\pi f_i)t$. However, the supply voltages of the op-amp are $\pm 12V$, limiting the output signal to this rank of voltage.

Next section, the op-amp integrator that is one the most interesting configurations on a bond graph model is designed.

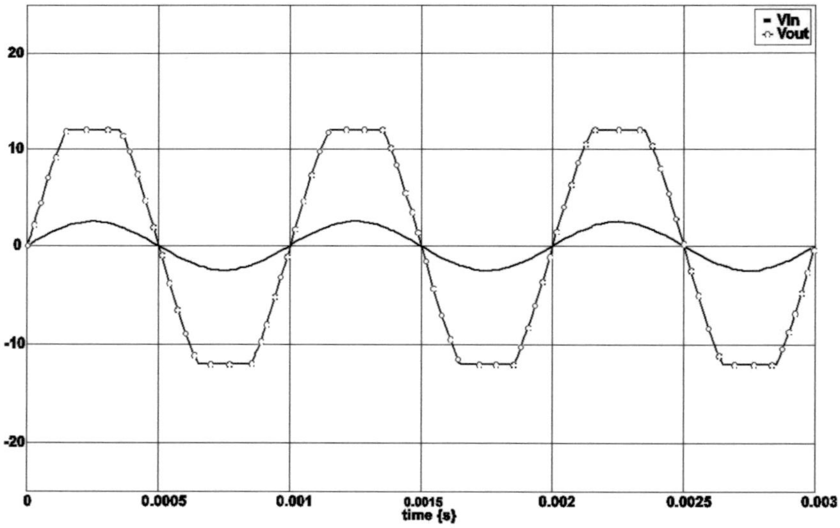

Fig.16. Time response with slew rate and supply voltages using $\mu A741$ op-amp.

6.2 The operational amplifier integrator

An op-amp integrator simulates mathematical integration, which is basically a summing process that determines the total area under the curve of a function (Floyd & Buchla, 1999). A basic integrator on a BGD model is shown in Fig. 17. Notice that the feedback element is a capacitor that forms an RC circuit with the input.

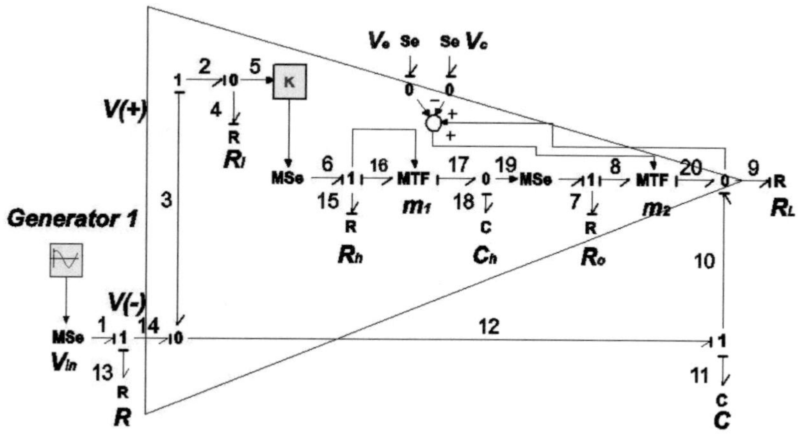

Fig. 17. Bond graphs of an operational amplifier integrator.

In order to determine the transfer function of the op-amp integrator based on bond graph model of Fig. 17, the methodology given in Section 1 is applied. The key vectors are,

$$x(t)=\begin{bmatrix} q_{11}(t) \\ q_{18}(t) \end{bmatrix};\dot{x}(t)=\begin{bmatrix} f_{11}(t) \\ f_{18}(t) \end{bmatrix};z(t)=\begin{bmatrix} e_{11}(t) \\ e_{18}(t) \end{bmatrix};\begin{matrix} u(t)=e_{1}(t) \\ y(t)=e_{9}(t) \end{matrix}$$

$$D_{in}(t)=\begin{bmatrix} e_4(t) & e_7(t) & e_9(t) & f_{13}(t) & e_{15}(t) \end{bmatrix}^T \tag{56}$$

$$D_{out}(t)=\begin{bmatrix} f_4(t) & f_7(t) & f_9(t) & e_{13}(t) & f_{15}(t) \end{bmatrix}^T$$

the constitutive relations are,

$$F=diag\left\{\frac{1}{C},\frac{1}{C_h}\right\} \tag{57}$$

$$L=diag\left\{\frac{1}{R_i},\frac{1}{R_o},\frac{1}{R_L},R,\frac{1}{R_h}\right\} \tag{58}$$

and the junction structure matrix is,

$$S_{22}=\begin{bmatrix} 0 & 0 & 0 & 1 & 0 \\ 0 & 0 & 0 & m_2 & 0 \\ 0 & 0 & 0 & -1 & 0 \\ -1 & -m_2 & 1 & 0 & 0 \\ 0 & 0 & 0 & K & 0 \end{bmatrix};S_{23}=\begin{bmatrix} -1 \\ -m_2 \\ 1 \\ 0 \\ -K \end{bmatrix};S_{21}=\begin{bmatrix} 0 & 0 \\ m_2 & 1 \\ -1 & 0 \\ 0 & 0 \\ 0 & -m_2 \end{bmatrix} \tag{59}$$

$$S_{12}=\begin{bmatrix} 0 & -m & 1 & 0 & 0 \\ 0 & 0 & 0 & 0 & m_1 \end{bmatrix};\begin{matrix} S_{32}=\begin{bmatrix} 0 & 0 & 0 & -1 & 0 \end{bmatrix};S_{33}=1 \\ S_{31}=\begin{bmatrix} -1 & 0 \end{bmatrix};S_{11}=S_{13}=0 \end{matrix}$$

From (8), (13), (57), (58) and (59) the A_p matrix is,

$$A_p = \begin{bmatrix} \frac{-1}{C}\left(R_o + m_2^2 R_L\right)\left(R + R_i\right) & \frac{-1}{C_h}\left(R + R_i\right) m_2 R_L \\ \frac{-1}{C}\left(R_o + m_2^2 R_L\right) m_1 K R R_i & \frac{-m_1}{C_h R_h}\left(\Delta + m_2 K R R_i R_L\right) \end{bmatrix} \tag{60}$$

where $\Delta = R_o\left[R_L\left(R + R_i\right) + R R_i\right] + m_2^2 R R_L R_i$

Substituting (13), (58) (59) into (9), B_p is determined by,

$$B_p = \frac{1}{\Delta}\begin{bmatrix} R_i\left(R_o + m_2^2 R_L\right) \\ \frac{-1}{R_h}\left(m_1 K R_o R_i R_L\right) \end{bmatrix} \tag{61}$$

From (10), (13), (57), (58) and (59) the C_p matrix is,

$$C_p = \frac{1}{\Delta}\begin{bmatrix} \frac{-1}{C}\left(R + R_i\right) R_o R_L & \frac{1}{C_h} m_2 R R_i R_L \end{bmatrix} \tag{62}$$

Finally, substituting (13), (58) and (59) into (11), D_p is given by,

$$D_p = \frac{1}{\Delta} R_o R_i R_L \tag{63}$$

The transfer function of a system represented in space state can be calculated by,

$$G(s) = C_p\left(sI_n - A_p\right)^{-1} B_p + D_p \tag{64}$$

Substituting (60), (61), (62) and (63) into (64), the transfer function of the op-amp integrator of Fig. 17 is,

$$G(s) = \frac{\left(s^2 C C_h R_h R_o + s C R_o m_1^2 - K m_1 m_2\right) R_L R_i}{s^2 C C_h R_h \Delta + s\left(C_h R_h \Delta + C R R_L R_i K m_1 m_2 + C m_1^2 \Delta\right) + m_1^2 \Lambda} \tag{65}$$

where $\Lambda = \left(R + R_i\right)\left(R_o + m_2^2 R_L\right)$.

Considering a normal operation of the op-amp, $m_1 = m_2 = 1$ and $R_o = 0$, we have,

$$G_1(s) = \frac{-1}{s^2 \frac{C C_h R_h R}{K} + s\left[\frac{C_h R_h}{K}\left(\frac{R}{R_i} + 1\right) + CR + \frac{CR}{K}\right] + \frac{1}{K}\left(\frac{R}{R_i} + 1\right)} \tag{66}$$

In addition, applying $\lim_{\substack{R_i \to \infty \\ K \to \infty}} G_1(s)$, the ideal transfer function, $G_i(s)$, is determined by,

$$G_i(s) = \frac{-1}{sRC} \tag{67}$$

Note that, (67) is the typical transfer function of a integral controller. However, the equation (65) is the transfer function of a integral controller based on op-amp and considering their internal parameters and external elements.

The time response of the integrator circuit using $\mu A741$ op-amp and $R = 10\Omega$, $C = 100\mu F$ and $v_i(t) = \sin(2\pi f_i t)V$ where $f_i = 1KHz$ shows in Fig. 18. The output signal proves that the bond graph model of Fig. 18, is an integrator of the input signal.

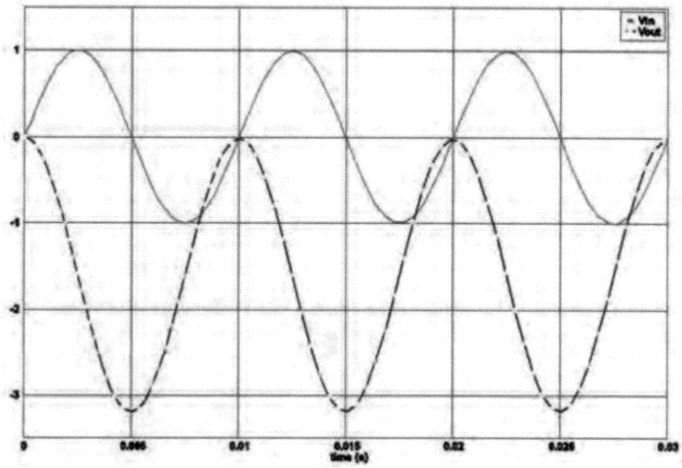

Fig. 18. Time response of the integrator.

The frequency response of the integrator circuit of Fig. 17 is shown in Fig. 19. Note that (67) is represented by Fig. 19.

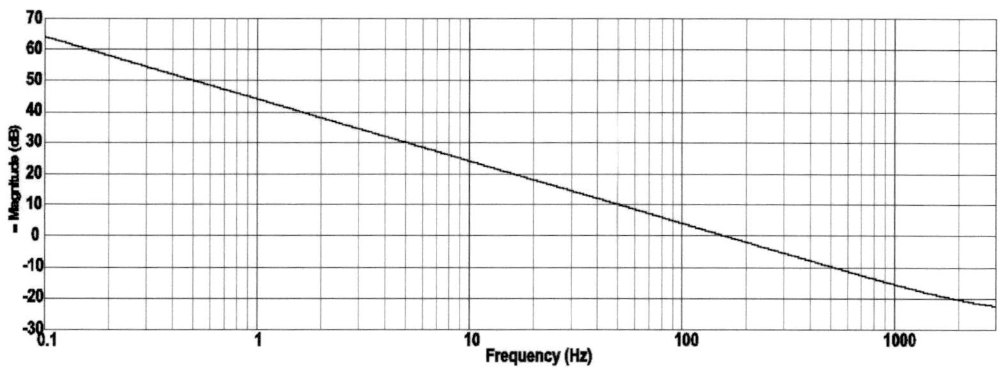

Fig. 19. Frequency response of the integrator circuit.

Next section an important application of the op-amp that is an active filter in the physical domain is proposed.

7. Active filters using bond graph models

An electric filter is often a frequency selective circuit that passes a specified band of frequencies and blocks or attenuates signals of frequencies outside this band. Filters may be classified in a number of ways (Gayakward, 2000):

1. Analog or digital. Analog filters are designed to process analog signals, while digital filters process analog signals using digital techniques.
2. Passive or active. Passive filters use resistors, capacitors and inductors in their construction and the active filters employ transistor or op-amps in addition to resistors and capacitors.

An active filter offers the following advantages over a passive filter: a) Gain and frequency adjustment flexibility. b) No loading problem. c) Cost.

A filter will usually conform to one of four basic response types: low-pass, high-pass, band-pass and band-reject.

7.1 Low-pass filter

A low-pass filter allows only low frequency signals to pass through, while suppressing high-frequency components. The bond graph model of a low-pass filter is shown in Fig. 20.

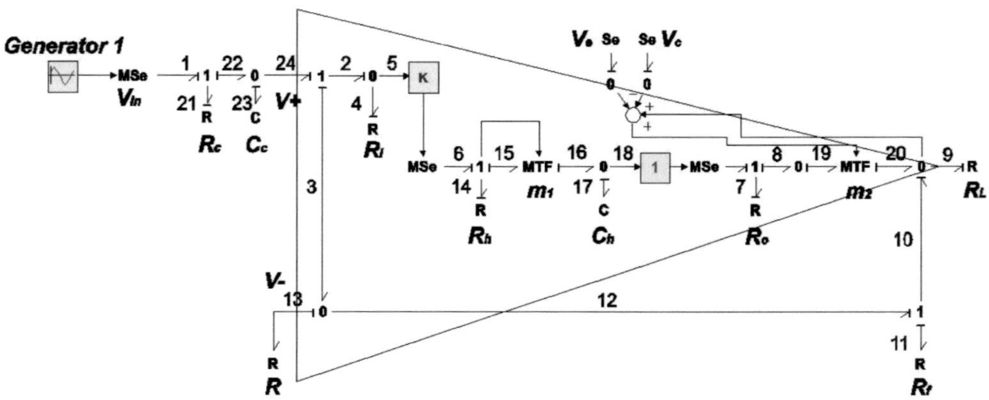

Fig. 20. Bond graph model of a low-pass filter.

The key vectors of the bond graph of Fig. 20 are,

$$x(t) = \begin{bmatrix} q_{17}(t) \\ q_{23}(t) \end{bmatrix}; \dot{x}(t) = \begin{bmatrix} f_{17}(t) \\ f_{23}(t) \end{bmatrix}; z(t) = \begin{bmatrix} e_{17}(t) \\ e_{23}(t) \end{bmatrix}; \begin{matrix} u(t) = e_1(t) \\ y(t) = e_9(t) \end{matrix}$$

$$D_{in}(t) = \begin{bmatrix} e_4(t) & e_7(t) & e_9(t) & f_{11}(t) & f_{13}(t) & e_{14}(t) & e_{21}(t) \end{bmatrix}^T \tag{68}$$

$$D_{out}(t) = \begin{bmatrix} f_4(t) & f_7(t) & f_9(t) & e_{11}(t) & e_{13}(t) & f_{14}(t) & f_{21}(t) \end{bmatrix}^T$$

The constitutive relations of the elements are,

$$F = diag\left\{ \frac{1}{C_h}, \frac{1}{C_e} \right\} \tag{69}$$

$$L = diag\left\{\frac{1}{R_i}, \frac{1}{R_o}, \frac{1}{R_L}, R_f, R, \frac{1}{R_h}, \frac{1}{R_c}\right\} \tag{70}$$

and the junction structure is

$$S_{22} = \begin{bmatrix} 0_{3\times3} & P_1 & \\ -P_1^T & 0_{2\times2} & 0_{7\times2} \\ 0_{2\times3} & P_2 & \end{bmatrix}; S_{21} = \begin{bmatrix} 0 & 1 \\ 1 & 0 \\ & 0_{3\times2} \\ -m_1 & K \\ 0 & -1 \end{bmatrix}$$

$$S_{12} = \begin{bmatrix} 0 & 0_{2\times4} & m_1 & 0 \\ -1 & & 0 & 1 \end{bmatrix}; S_{23} = \begin{bmatrix} 0_{6\times1} \\ 1 \end{bmatrix} \tag{71}$$

$$S_{32} = \begin{bmatrix} 0_{1\times3} & -1 & 1 & 0_{1\times2} \end{bmatrix}; S_{11} = S_{13} = S_{31} = S_{33} = 0$$

where

$$P_1 = \begin{bmatrix} 0 & -1 \\ m_2 & -m_2 \\ -1 & 1 \end{bmatrix}; P_2 = \begin{bmatrix} 0 & -K \\ 0 & 0 \end{bmatrix} \tag{72}$$

From (8), (13), (69), (70) and (71), the A_p matrix of the low-pass filter is,

$$A_p = \begin{bmatrix} \dfrac{-m_1^2}{R_h C_h} - \dfrac{m_1 m_2 KRR_L R_i}{\Delta C_h} & \dfrac{-m_1 K}{R_h C_h} - \dfrac{m_1 RK}{\Delta C_h}\left[R_o\left(R_L + R_f\right) + m_2^2 R_L R_f\right] \\ \dfrac{m_2 RR_L}{\Delta C_h} & \dfrac{-1}{R_c C_c} - \dfrac{1}{\Delta C_h}\left[\left(R + R_f\right)\left(R_o + m_2^2 R_L\right) + R_o R_L\right] \end{bmatrix} \tag{73}$$

where $\Delta = R_o\left[\left(R_L + R_f\right)\left(R + R_i\right) + RR_i\right] + m_2^2\left[RR_L\left(R_f + R_i\right) + R_L R_f R_i\right]$

Substituting (70) and (71) into (13), the B_p matrix is obtained

$$B_p = \begin{bmatrix} 0 & \dfrac{1}{R_c} \end{bmatrix}^T \tag{74}$$

Finally, from (10), (13), (69), (70) and (71), the C_p matrix is

$$C_p = \left[\frac{m_2 R_L}{\Delta C_h} \left[R\left(R_i + R_f\right) + R_i R_f \right] \quad \frac{R R_L R_o}{\Delta C_h} \right] \tag{75}$$

and $D_p = 0$

From (73) to (75), and (64), and considering ideal characteristics of the op-amp, $R_o = 0$, $R_i = \infty$, $K = \infty$ and $R_L = \infty$, the ideal transfer function of the low-pass filter, denoted by $G_i(s)$ is obtained $G_i(s) = \dfrac{A_{CL} / R_c C_C}{s + 1/R_c C_C}$ where $A_{CL} = 1 + \dfrac{R_f}{R}$.

The ideal transfer function of the low-pass filter indicates that on the pass band the gain is almost A_{CL} and the pole of the system is located at the high cutoff frequency f_h defined by $f_h = \dfrac{1}{2\pi C_C R_C}$.

The frequency response of the low-pass filter based on bond graph model using the µA741 op-amp and considering the numerical values of the Table 3 is shown in Fig 21.

R	R_f	R_L	R_c	C_C
$10K\Omega$	$10K\Omega$	$1K\Omega$	$15.9K\Omega$	$1\times10^{-8}F$

Table 3. Numerical values of the low-pass filter.

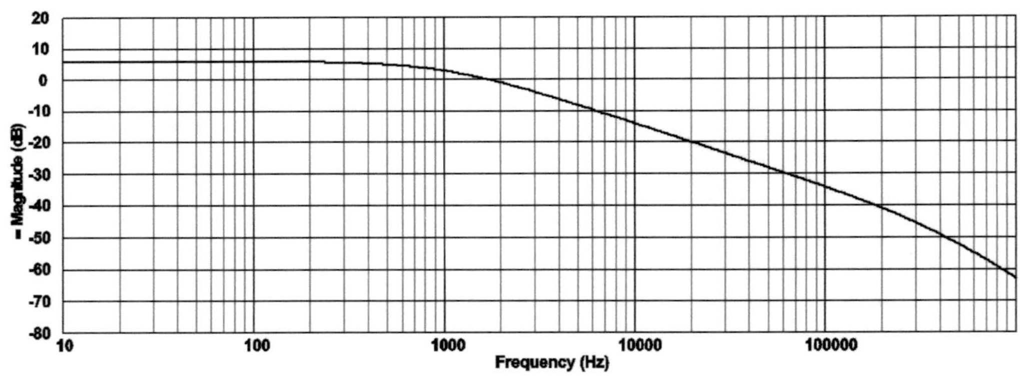

Fig. 21. Frequency response of the low-pass filter.

The Fig 21 shows that $f_h = 1KHz$. Also, we have a first order filter, because the filter has a pole and the rolloff rate of the filter is 20 dB per decade.

7.2 High-pass filter

A high pass filter allows only frequencies above a certain break point to pass through. In other words, it attenuates low frequency components. A first order high-pass filter on bond graph model is shown in Fig. 22.

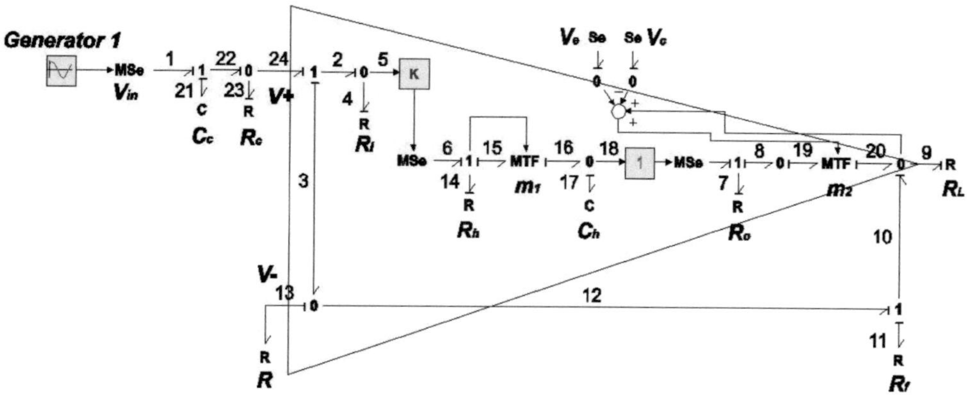

Fig. 22. Bond graph model of a high-pass filter.

The mathematical model of the filter can be determined in the same manner that the low-pass filter. However, for all the remaining filters of this paper, we use the software 20-sim to know the performance of the filter on the physical domain, considering the internal characteristics of the op-amp and the external components connected to the op-amp in order to get the filter type.

Using the same numerical values that the low-pass filter, the frequency response of the filter shows in Fig. 23.

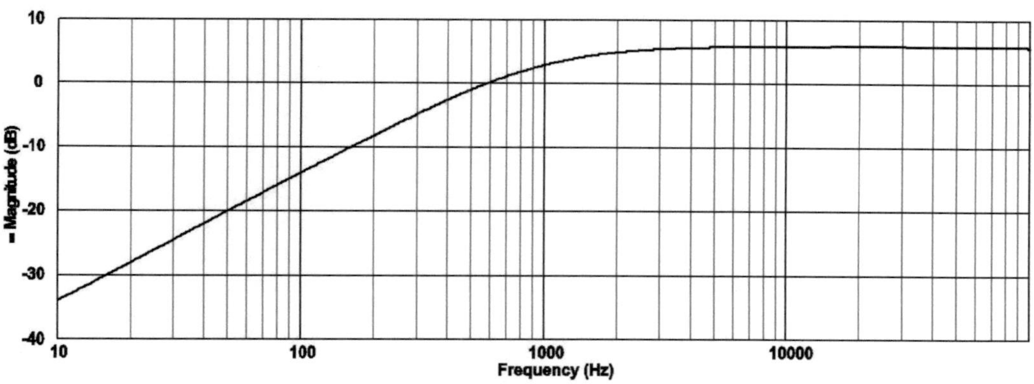

Fig. 23. Frequency response of the high-pass filter.

The Fig. 23 indicates that we have a first order filter and the low cutoff frequency f_L is $1KHz$.

7.3 Band-pass filter

The band-pass filter can be thought of as a combination of high and low pass filters. It allows only frequencies within a specified rang to pass through. In Fig. 24 a band-pass filter on bond graph model is proposed. The characteristic of this filter is a narrow band-pass using multiple feedback .

In order to get the performance of this filter, we use the internal parameters of the $\mu A741$ op-amp given in Tables 1 and 2, and the external components are shown in Table 4.

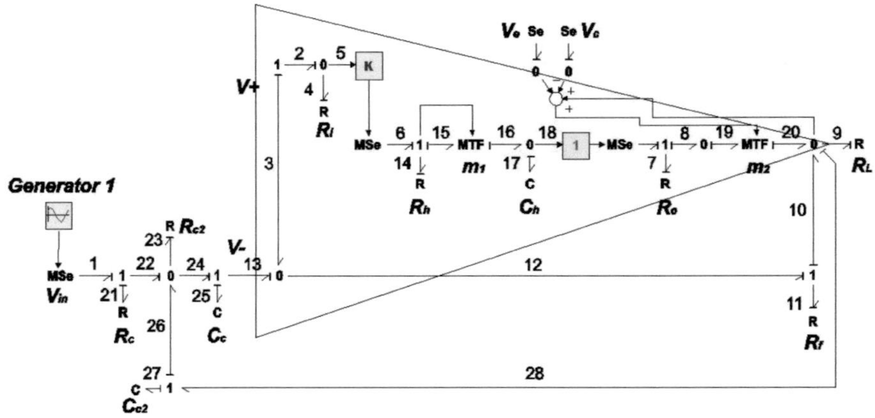

Fig. 24. Bond graph model of a band-pass filter.

R_c	R_f	R_L	R_{c2}	C_c	C_{c2}
$4.77K\Omega$	$100K\Omega$	$10K\Omega$	$0.2K\Omega$	$0.01\mu F$	$0.01\mu F$

Table 4. Numerical values of the external components

The frequency response of the band-pass filter is shown in Fig. 25.

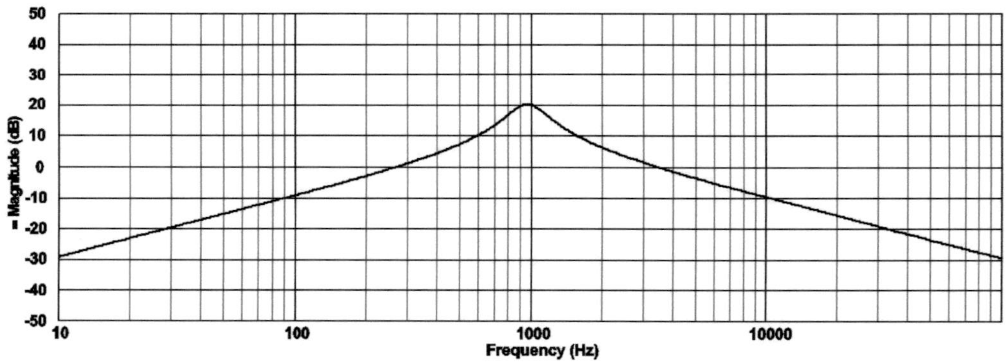

Fig. 25. Frequency response of the band-pass filter.

Note that, the response of the filter allows to pass the frequency component of $1KHz$ with a closed loop gain of 10 and the low and high frequencies respect to $1KHz$ have a small magnitude.

7.4 Band-reject filter

The band-reject filter allows everything to pass through with the exception of a specific range of frequencies. The band-reject filter is often called notch filter, because it is commonly used for the rejection of a single frequency. The Fig. 26 shows this filter on a bond graph model.

Using the parameters of the $\mu A741$ op-amp given on Tables 1 and 2, and the external elements of the op-amp of Fig. 26 are gotten in Table 5, the frequency response of the filter is shown in Fig. 27.

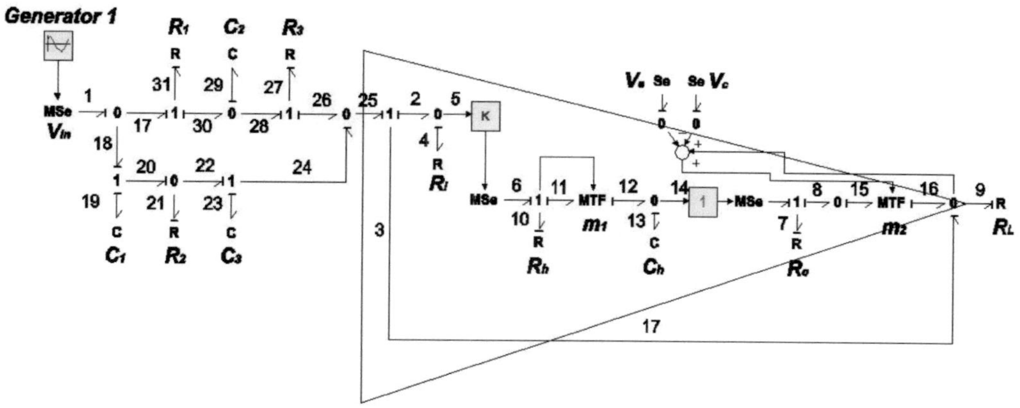

Fig. 26. Bond graph model of a band-reject filter.

R_1	R_2	R_3	R_L	$C_1 = C_3$	C_2
$39K\Omega$	$19.5K\Omega$	$39K\Omega$	$1K\Omega$	$0.068\mu F$	$0.136\mu F$

Table 5. External elements of the band-reject filter.

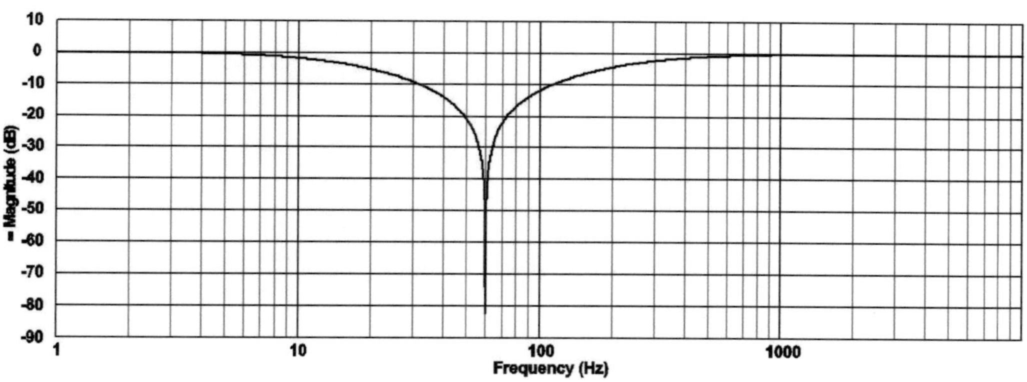

Fig. 27. Frequency response of the band-reject filter.

In Fig. 27, we show that $60Hz$ power line frequency can be attenuated using this filter in the physical domain.

7.5 Applying active filters

A filter is a circuit which inhibits the transfer of a specific range of frequencies. So, we can apply active filters to select a frequency component of a complex signal. An interesting application of filters on bond graph models is shown in Fig. 28 where we have an input signal given by,

$$V_i = 0.1\sin\left[2\pi\left(10Hz\right)t\right] + 0.1\sin\left[2\pi\left(500Hz\right)t\right] + 0.1\sin\left[2\pi\left(20KHz\right)t\right] \quad (76)$$

In Fig. 28, the input is applied to low-pass filter denoted by opamp1, to high-pass filter denoted by opamp2 and to band-pass filter denoted by opamp3.

Also, the external elements of Fig. 28 are obtained on Table 6 and using the parameters of the $\mu A741$ op-amp given on Tables 1 and 2, the frequency responses are shown in Fig. 29.

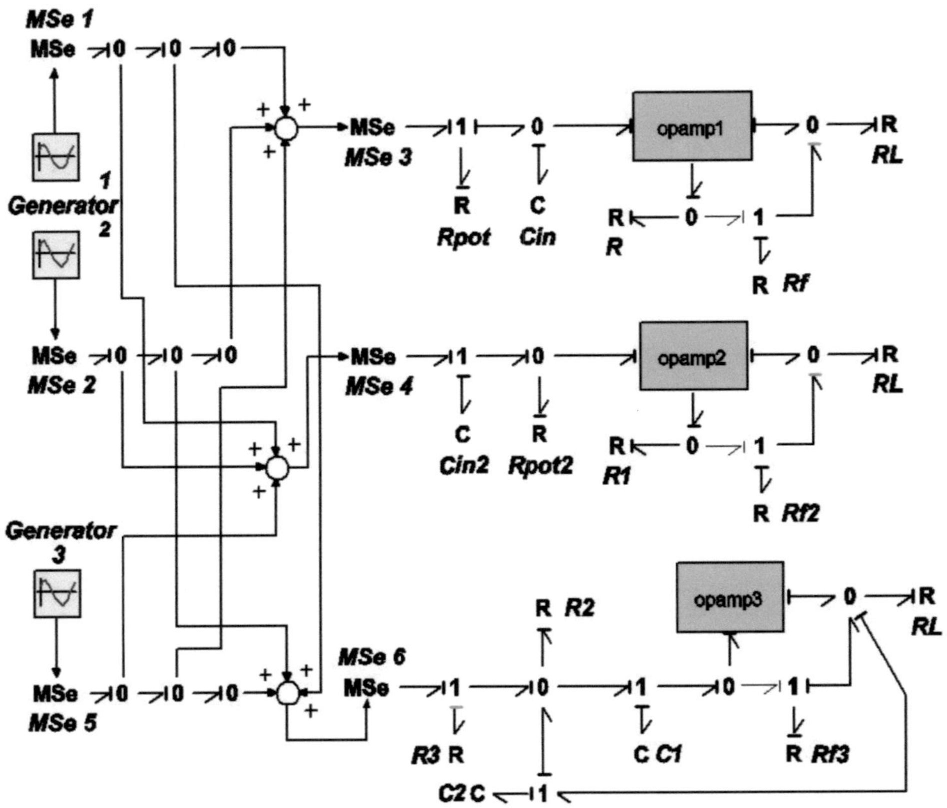

Fig. 28. Compose signal applied to bond graph filters.

$R = R_1$	$R_f = R_{f2}$	C_{in}	R_{pot}
$1M\Omega$	1Ω	$1\mu F$	$15.9K\Omega$
R_3	R_{f3}	$C_1 = C_4 = C_{in2}$	R_2
$95.5K\Omega$	$191K\Omega$	$0.01\mu F$	$5.6K\Omega$

Table 6. External elements of the compose system.

In Fig. 29, the high cutoff frequency is $f_H = 10Hz$ for the low-pass filter, the low cutoff frequency is $f_L = 20KHz$ for the high-pass filter and the center frequency is $f_c = 500Hz$. Finally, the time response of each filter is shown in Fig. 30 and we note that the objective of the filters is successful.

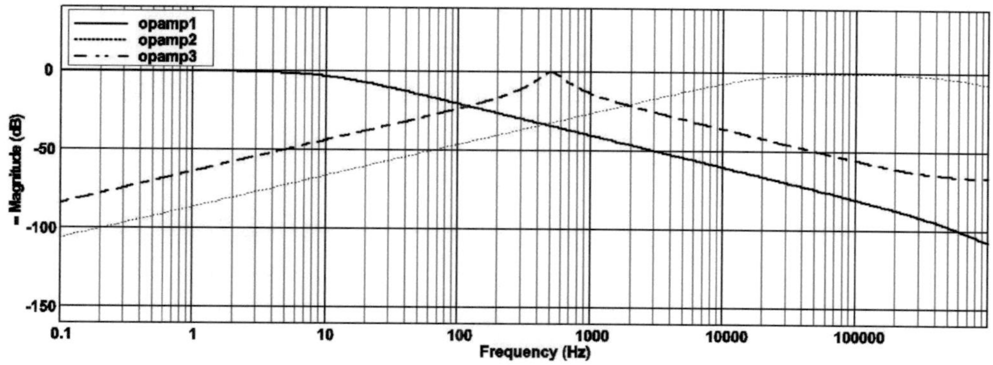

Fig. 29. Frequency response of a complete system.

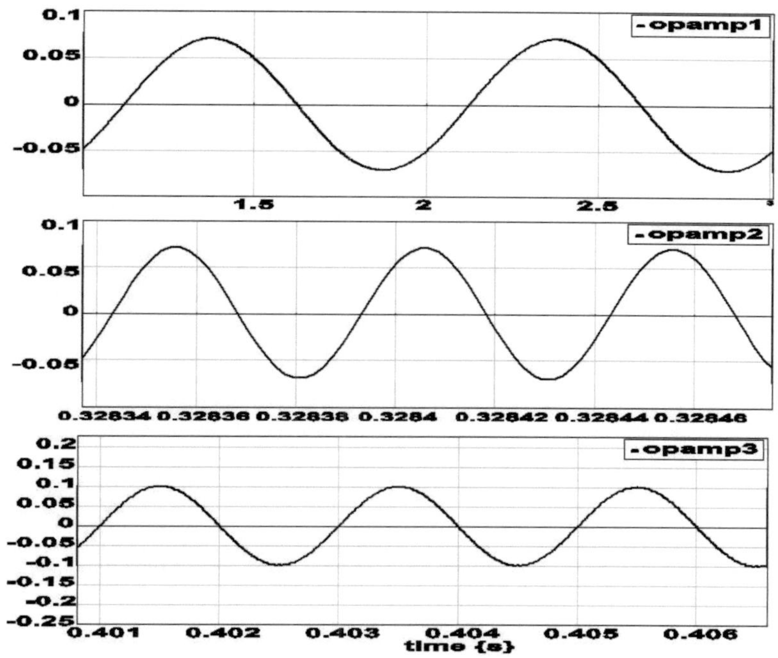

Fig. 30. Time response of the complete system.

Note that the bond graph model of the op-amp to design controllers, analog computers and general linear applications can be applied.

8. Controller based on bond graph model of an operational amplifier

Another important application of operational amplifiers is to implement controllers and can be used to improve the performance of a closed loop system. A proportional and integral (PI) controller designed in the physical domain to control the velocity of a DC motor is applied (Barna & Porat, 1989).

The noninverting and integrator configurations of an op-amp are used to derive the PI controller. Also, the input reference of the system is voltage V_n and on the feedback a element GY to connect the output with the summing junction is applied. The BGI of the closed loop system is shown in Fig. 31.

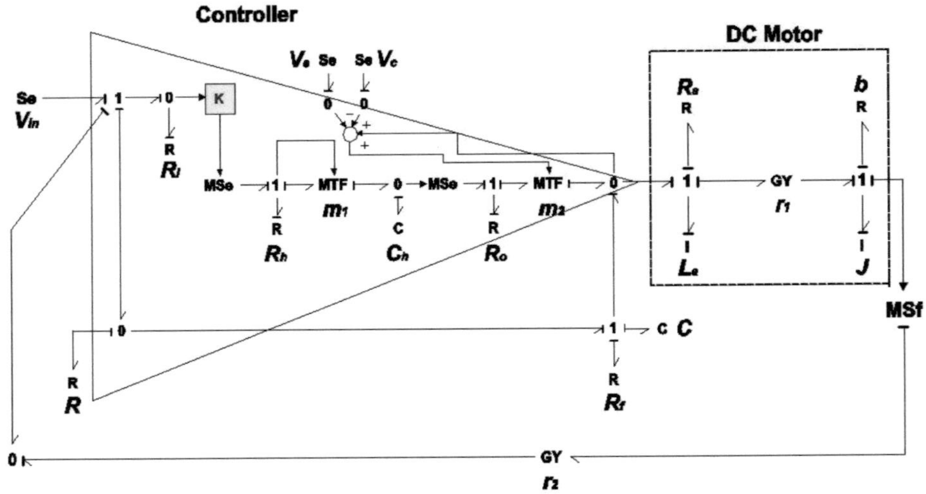

Fig. 31. PI Controller of DC motor on a bond graph model.

The BGI of Fig. 31 can be used to determine the state space representation or the transfer function of the closed loop system. However, in this case we only show the simulation with the objective to test the PI controller connected to DC motor in a closed loop system.

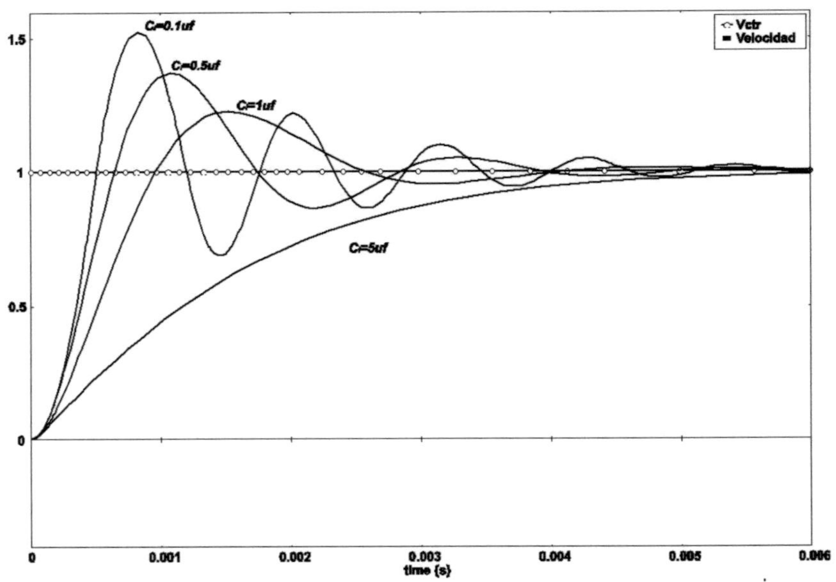

Fig. 32. Time response of the output of the DC motor using a PI controller.

The time response of the output using a $\mu A741$ op-amp, $R = 10K\Omega$, $R_f = 90K\Omega$, $R_a = 2\Omega$, $L_a = 0.01mH$, $J = 0.001Kgm^2$ and $b = 1Nm / rad / s$, is shown in Fig. 32. Note that the PI Controller yields a steady state output equal to input reference of the system and the transient response depends of the parameters of the system and controller.

9. Conclusions

In this work an operational amplifier is shown in a bond graph model. The proposed bond graph takes account the input and output resistances, open loop gain, supply voltages, slew rate and frequency compensation of an operational amplifier. Therefore, an advantage of this model is to determine the performance of applications based on operational amplifiers considering the type of linear integrated circuit to obtain the internal parameters from the data sheets. Finally, open loop and closed loop configurations of the operational amplifier in the physical domain have been shown.

10. References

Arpad Barna and Dan I. Porat, (1989). *Operational Amplifiers*, John Wiley & Sons,ISBN:0-471-63764-5, Canada

C. Sueur, G. Dauphin-Tanguy, (1991), Bond graph approach for structural analysis of MIMO linear systems, *Journal of the Franklin Institute*, vol. 328, no.1 , (55-70).

Dean C. Karnopp, Ronald C. Rosenberg, (1975). *System Dynamics: A Unified Approach*, Wiley, John & Sons,

Forbes T. Brown (2001)., *Engineering System Dynamics*, Marcel Dekker Inc, ISBN:0-8247-0616-1, United States of America.

Gilberto Gonzalez, Dauphin- Tanguy G. Galindo R and De Leon J. (2005), Steady State Error for a Closed Loop Physical System with a Bond Graph Approach, *Proceedings of International Conference on Bond Graph Modeling and Simulation*, pp. 107-112, ISBN:1-56555-287-3, New Orleans, January 2005, SCS.

Norman S. Nise, (2000). *Control Systems Engineering*, John Wiley & Sons, ISBN:970-24-0254-9, United States of America.

Peter Gawthrop, Lorcan Smith (1996)., *Metamodelling*, Prentice-Hall,ISBN:0-13-489824-9, Great Britain.

P.E. Wellstead, (1979). *Physical System Modelling*, Academic Press, ISBN:0-12-744380-0 London.

P. J. Gawthrop and D. Palmer, (2003). A bicausal bond graph representation of operational amplifiers", *Proceedings of the Institution of Mechanical Engineers Part I: Journal Systems and Control Engineering*, Vol. 217

Ramakant A. Gayakward, (2000), *Op-amps and Linear Integrated Circuit*, Prentice Hall, ISBN:0-13-280868-4, United States of America.

Thomas L. Floyd and David Buchla, (1999), *Basic Operational Amplifiers and Linear Integrated Circuits*, Prentice-Hall, ISBN:0-13-082987-0, United States of America.

William D. Stanley, (1994). *Operational Amplifiers with Linear Integrated Circuits*, Maxwell Macmillan International

20-Sim, Controllab Products (2007) B. V., 20-Sim, *http://www.20sim.com/ product/20sim.html*

17

Hypermobile Robots

Grzegorz Granosik
Technical University of Lodz
Poland

1. Introduction

Hypermobile robots belong to the group of hyper-redundant articulated mobile robots. This group can be further divided based on two characteristic features: the way the forward motion of the robot is generated and the activity of its joints, as shown in Table 1.

Propulsion→ Joints↓	External propulsion elements: legs, wheels, tracks	Movement is generated by undulation
Active joints	**Hypermobile robots:** • Koryu-I and Koryu-II (Hirose, 1993) • Snake 2 (Klaassen and Paap, 1999) • Soryu (Takayama and Hirose, 2000) • Millibot Train (Brown et al., 2002) • Moira (Osuka & Kitajima, 2003) • Pipeline Explorer (Schempf et al., 2003) • Omnis family (Granosik et al., 2005) • MAKRO *plus* (Streich & Adria, 2004) • KOHGA (Kamegawa et al., 2004) • JL-I (Zhang et al., 2006) • Wheeeler (Pytasz & Granosik, 2006)	**Snake-like robots:** • Active Cord Mechanism whole family of robots (Hirose, 1993) • Slim Slime Robot (Ohno & Hirose, 2000) • Snake robots by Dr. Gavin Miller (snakerobots.com) • Perambulator-II (Ye et al., 2007)
Passive joints	**Active wheels - passive joints robots:** • Genbu 3 (Kimura & Hirose, 2002)	

Table 1. Articulated mobile robots

Articulated robots can also be divided in other way, as suggested by Robinson and Davies (1999), into three groups: discrete, serpentine and continuum. Most robots are discrete mechanisms constructed from series of rigid links interconnected by discrete joints. In case of robotic manipulators joints are usually one degree of freedom (DOF) but in case of articulated mobile robots we can find 2 and 3 DOF joints more often. Multi degree of freedom joints create naturally spatial devices, which can bend in any direction.

Serpentine robots also utilize discrete joints but combine very short rigid links with a large density of joints. This creates highly mobile mechanisms producing smooth curves, similar to snake. And therefore representatives of this group of robots are also called snake-like robots, as shown in Fig. 1. Some of the hypermobile robots feature very short links relative to the cross section size and also belong to this group.

Fig. 1. Active Cord Mechanism (left) reproduced from (Hirose, 1993), ACM-R3 reproduced from (Mori & Hirose, 2002)

Continuum robots do not contain rigid links and identifiable rotational joints. Instead the structures bend continuously along their length via elastic deformation and produce motion through the generation of smooth curves, similar to the tentacles. The good example of continuum mobile robots is Slim Slime Robot (see Fig. 2).

Fig. 2. Slim Slime Robot reproduced from (Ohno & Hirose, 2000)

In the next part of this paper we present a few major projects of hypermobile robots from around the world, focusing on comparison of design concepts, main features, performance, teleoperation or automated operation techniques. Finally, we present our own hypermobile robot Wheeeler showing design concept, model, simulation results, construction and tests of prototype. In conclusion we summarize this digest with a table showing basic properties of presented robots. We also show advantages and disadvantages of our design and future plans. We hope to show some general ideas on designing, constructing and control of such complex devices as hypermobile robots with many redundant degrees of freedom.

2. History of hypermobile robots

One of the scenarios where hypermobile robots could play the main role is search and rescue. The intensified work in this field was related to the large catastrophes happened in different countries: Kobe earthquake, terrorist attacks on World Trade Center in New York and bomb attacks on trains in London and Madrid. In this application robots are intended to slither into the debris and gather visual information about possible victims. Therefore, it is expected that robot fits small openings, can travel in the rummage of structured

environment and overcome obstacles. The other important application for hypermobile robots are inspection tasks in sewage systems, gas pipes or venting systems.
The first practical realization of a hypermobile robot, called Koryu or KR-I, was introduced by Hirose and Morishima (1990) and later improved with version KR-II (Hirose et al., 1991), as shown in Fig. 3. KR-II was developed with premise that it will be applied as a mobile robot for atomic reactor. It was also considered to be used as a substitution of fireman in rescuing activity: patrolling, gas detection, inspection and to rescue a person. This first hypermobile robot was large and heavy, weighing in at 350 kg. The robot comprised of multiple vertical cylindrical segments on powered wheels (tracks in KR-I) that gave the mechanism a train-like appearance. Vertical joint actuators allow a segment to lift its neighbors up, in order to negotiate steps or span gaps. Each segment of KR-II is equipped with single wheel, arranged so that the unit with wheel on the right side will come after a unit with the wheel on the left side. This single wheel design may seem unbalanced at the first glance but its stability is secured as the segments are linked. Especially, if the vehicle have the zigzag configuration. Moreover, this single wheel design has other advantages:

- as each segment is connected to the body by 2DOF joint it may be seen as having sliding active suspension,
- the adaptability to the steep inclination during traversing can be realized by shifting all wheels on one side up or down in vertical direction,
- in addition, this design doesn't require the differential mechanism of the double wheel structure to permit different speed rotation on curves.

Fig. 3. The Koryu-I (KR-I) robot on the left and KR-II on the right (reproduced from http://www-robot.mes.titech.ac.jp)

These robots inherited all capabilities of earlier developed snake-like robots:

- They can go on irregular terrain with sharp rises and falls and travel a path that winds tightly,
- They can cross over crevasses by holding its body length rigid to act as a bridge,
- In marshy and sandy terrain, it can move by distributing force along its entire body length.

Additional active crawlers or wheels mounted on each segment give further advantages:

- High speed motion - direct propulsion is more effective then undulation,
- High load capacity - simple driving system gives large weight of load to its own weight ratio,
- Good portability by its unitized structure,
- High reliability, because it is made redundant - broken segments can be easily replaced and special segments could be added depending on mission,

- Versatility of the body motion - Koryu can be used not only for "locomotion", but also for "manipulation" - as claim authors (Hirose & Morishima, 1993).

For motion control of the robot with several wheels touching ground the force sensors to detect reaction force were indispensable. To solve the problem, special construction of optical based force sensing was introduced. Such sensors were mounted in both vertical and horizontal axes to control robot among obstacles and on uneven terrain.

More recently, Klaassen and Paap (1999) at the German National Research Center for Information Technology (GMD) developed the Snake2 vehicle, which contains six active segments and a head, as shown in Fig. 4. Each round segment has an array of 12 electrically driven wheels evenly spaced around its periphery. These wheels provide propulsion regardless of the vehicle's roll angle. Segments are interconnected by universal joints actuated by three additional electric motors through strings. Snake2 is an example of a robot that is inspired by the physiological structure of snakes where wheels replace tiny scales observed on the bodies of some real snakes. Snake2 is equipped with six infrared distance sensors, three torque sensors, one tilt sensor, two angle sensors in every segment, and a video camera in the head segment. Snake2 was specifically designed for the inspection of sewage pipes. With segments measuring 18cm in diameter and 13.5cm length Snake2 belongs to the serpentine group.

Fig. 4. Snake2 developed at the GMD

This robot was a successor of the GMD-Snake, typical continuum spatial robot built in a very elastic way to allow flexible bending of the parts (Worst & Linnemann, 1996). However, Authors observed an uncontrolled torsion effect which occurred when the snake lifted some of its parts (to climb on a step). This disadvantage forced them to construct the next generation in a more rigid way using universal joints but leaving rope-based driving system. GMD snakes were the first articulated robots employing CAN bus communication in the distributed control system.

Another hypermobile robot designed for sewer inspection was developed by Scholl et al. (2000) at the Forschungszentrum Informatik (FZI) in Germany. Its segments use only two wheels but the actuated 3-DOF joints allow full control over each segment's spatial orientation. The robot is able to negotiate tight 90° angled pipes and climb over 35 cm high obstacles. One segment and its joint are about 20 cm long each. The sensor suite of this robot is similar to that of Snake2. The development of sewer inspection robots was continued in the joint project MAKRO *plus* (Streich & Adria, 2004).

MAKRO *plus,* is an autonomous service robot that can be used for a whole range of specific duties within a canalization system. Robot has symmetrical construction with head segments on both ends. These segments contain camera, structured light source and ultrasound sensor. Four-level hierarchical control system is proposed to autonomously drive robot inside sewage pipes. The robot's mission is specified by human operator who determines entry and recovery points and downloads map of all pipes and manholes in the inspection area. Then the planning algorithm generates the sequence of actions, which are executed by action controller. In case of obstacle detection, blockage or malfunction, planner automatically finds new set of actions. Robot can be equipped in specialized modules. A chemistry module measures pH levels, conductivity, O_2 and temperature of waste water with the help of a sample probe. When required, samples can be retrieved by the robot for further analysis in a laboratory. A navigation module which can record speed and three fiber optic gyroscopes measure the gradient and direction of the pipes in a canalization system. This helps to support the success of the mission and it is also provides a useful and accurate update for the land registry records, as informs INSPECTOR SYSTEMS Rainer Hitzel GmbH.

Fig. 5. MAKRO *plus* robot for sewer inspection (reproduced from Streich & Adria, 2004)

While wheeled serpentine robots can work well in smooth-walled pipes, more rugged terrain requires tracked propulsion. To this effect Takayama and Hirose (2000) developed the Souryu-I crawler, which consists of three segments, as shown in Fig. 6.

Fig. 6. Souryu from Hirose Lab (reproduced from http://www-robot.mes.titech.ac.jp)

Each segment is driven by a pair of tracks, which, in turn, are all powered simultaneously by a single motor, located in the center segment. Torque is provided to the two distal segments through a rotary shaft and universal joints. Each distal segment is connected to the center segment by a special 2-DOF joint mechanism, which is actuated by two lead screws driven by two electric motors. The robot can move forward and backward, and it can change the orientation of the two distal segments in yaw and pitch symmetrically to the center segment. Coordinated rotations of these joints can generate roll over motion of the robot. One interesting feature is the ability of this robot to adapt to irregular terrain because of the elasticity of its joints. This elasticity is provided by springs and cannot be actively controlled. The newest incarnation - Souryu-II - is designed to separate three bodies easily

so as to make it portable and to make it possible to add segments with special functions. Robot is equipped with camera and batteries, and can be remotely controlled.
A different concept using unpowered joints was introduced by Kimura and Hirose (2002) at the Tokyo Institute of Technology. That robot, called Genbu (see Fig. 7), is probably the only serpentine robot with unpowered joints. The stability of the robot and its high mobility on rough terrain are preserved by large-diameter wheels (220 mm). The control system employs position and torque feedback sensors for the passive but rigid joints. Springs are used to protect the electric motors from impact, although the stiffness of the springs cannot be controlled during operation. Robot was intended mainly for two applications: as a fire-fighting robot to pull a fire hose or as a planetary rover.

Fig. 7. Robot Genbu representing group of active wheels - passive joints robots

Another robot incorporating a combination of passive and active joints as well as independently driven and coupled segments is KOHGA developed by Kamegawa et al. (2004) and shown in Fig. 8. Robot comprises 8 segments of different structure and function: two distal segments have CCD cameras mounted but have no propulsion means, the second units have the right and left crawlers which are driven co-accessibly, the other segments also have the right and left crawlers but independently driven. There is also a variety of joints implemented in this design:

- Two 2DOF joints driven by simple RC servos to control position of heads with cameras,
- Two 2DOF joints with powerful DC motors and linkages to rise two segments on either end, this improves the capability of climbing over obstacles,
- Three 3DOF passive joints interconnecting main driving units, their function is to adjust robot's shape to the environment and efficiently transmit crawler force, they are passive for light weight and simplicity.

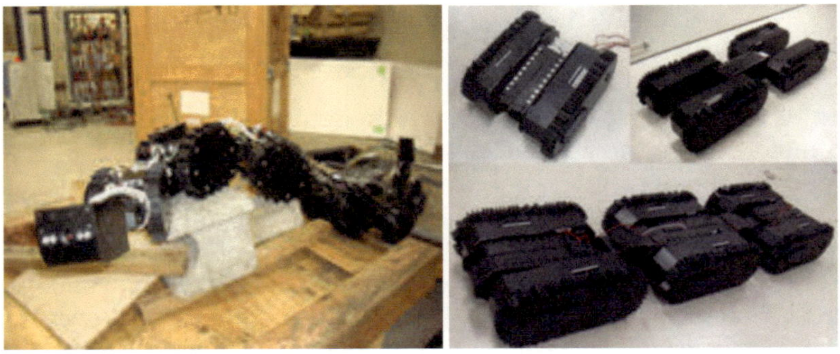

Fig. 8. Robot KOHGA and KOHGA 2 (in a few configurations) from Matsuno Lab. at the University of Electro-Communications

This robot implements a smart design feature: besides a camera in the front segment, there is a second camera in the tail section that can be pointed forward, in the way a scorpion points its tail forward and over-head. This "tail-view" greatly helps teleoperating the robot. Operator is using SONY gamepad as user input and monitor with specially organized video outputs. Authors proposed also algorithm (based on robot kinematics only) to calculate speed of tracks and rotation of joints to realize follow-the-leader control of robot.

KOHGA with its passive joints has an important problem that obstacles can be caught to the joints and then the robot is stuck. To solve this problem, the new reconfigurable version of KOHGA 2 was developed (Miyanaka et al. 2007). The unit structure consists of the crawler-arm-units, the joint-units, the terminal-units and the connecting parts. It can work as a self-contained module or can be connected with other units creating multi-segmented vehicle. Moreover, it can take various forms by the swing motion of the crawler-arms, and avoid various stuck conditions. These crawler-arms can be mounted in two ways: the rotational axes of right and left crawler-arms are alternately attached to the vehicle (called the non-coaxial type), or these axes are attached to the same end of the vehicle (called the coaxial type). Authors have considered several robot configurations, in different stuck-prone conditions, in both high- and low-ceiling environments. They concluded that (1) the ability of the stuck avoidance declines if the number of the connected vehicles is small because the performance of vertical step climbing falls off and (2) that the coaxial type robot is more effective to the stuck avoidance than the non-coaxial type robot.

The concept of joining several small robots into a train to overcome larger obstacles was used by researchers from Carnegie Mellon University in their Millibot Train (Brown et al., 2002). This robot consists of seven electrically driven, very compact segments. The diameter of the track sprockets is larger than the height of each segment, which allows the robot to drive upside-down. Segments are connected by couplers for active connection and disconnection, but the joints have only one DOF. Each joint is actuated by an electric motor with a high-ratio harmonic gear and slip clutch. It provides sufficient torque to lift up the three front segments. The robot has been demonstrated to climb up a regular staircase and even higher steps. However, with only one DOF in each joint the vehicle is kinematically limited.

A serpentine robot that uses tracks for propulsion and pneumatics for joint actuation is MOIRA shown in Fig. 9 (Osuka & Kitajima, 2003). MOIRA comprises four segments, and

Fig. 9. Robot Moira from Osuka Lab.

each segment has two longitudinal tracks on each of its four sides, for a total of eight tracks per segment. All tracks are driven from a single motor through the system of 4 bevel and 4 spiral gears and therefore they move in the same direction. With tracks on each side robot is insensitive for rollovers and with additionally cone shaped distal segments robot can dig into the debris with obstacles touching it from all sides. The 2-DOF joints between segments are actuated by pneumatic cylinders. Although with pneumatic cylinders MOIRA can lift up its segments high enough to overcome obstacles, it can also decrease stiffness of actuators to nicely conform to the ground, but we think that with very long joints this design is prone to getting stuck on some narrow obstacles. Robot is controlled from the specially designed control box containing 3 joysticks and several switches. There is also view from nose CCD camera transmitted via USB.

The newest construction from NREC (National Robotics Engineering Center) is Pipeline Explorer - robot designed and built for inspection of live gas pipelines (Schempf et al., 2003). This robot, shown in Fig. 10, has a symmetric architecture. A seven-element articulated body design houses a mirror-image arrangement of locomotor (camera) modules, battery carrying modules, and support modules, with a computing and electronics module in the middle. The robot's computer and electronics are protected in purged and pressurized housings. Segments are connected with articulated joints: the locomotor modules are connected to their neighbors with pitch-roll joints, while the others - via pitch-only joints. These specially designed joints allow orientation of the robot within the pipe, in any direction needed.

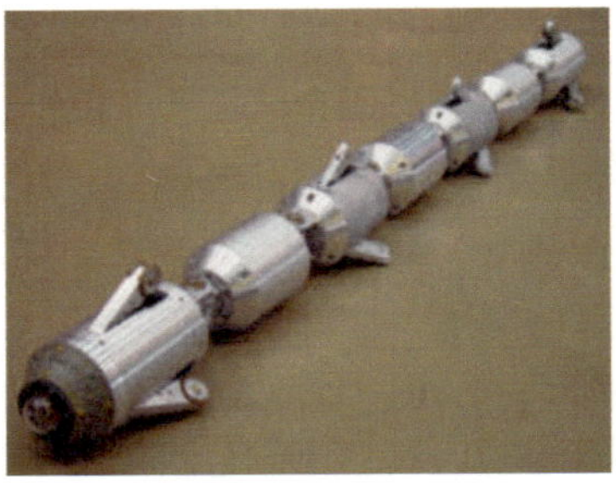

Fig. 10. Pipeline Explorer from NREC (reproduced from http://www.rec.ri.cmu.edu/projects/explorer)

The locomotor module houses a mini fish-eye camera, along with its lens and lighting elements. The camera has a 190-degree field of view and provides high-resolution color images of the pipe's interior. The locomotor module also houses dual drive actuators designed to allow for the deployment and retraction of three legs equipped with custom-molded driving wheels. The robot can sustain speeds of up to four inches per second. It is fully untethered (battery-powered, wirelessly controlled) and can be used in explosive underground natural gas distribution pipelines. Construction of robot naturally limits its application to pipes of certain diameters.

From 2002 to 2005 researchers from the Mobile Robotics Lab at the University of Michigan introduced the whole family of hypermobile robots called Omnis, shown in Fig. 11. In the OmniPede, the first one, they introduced three innovative functional elements: (1) propulsion elements (here: legs) evenly located around the perimeter of each segment; (2) pneumatic power for joint actuation; and (3) a single so called "drive shaft spine" that transfers mechanical power to all segments from a single drive motor (Long et al., 2002). From the study of the OmniPede, and from the observed shortcomings of this legged propulsion prototype, they derived important insights about the design of serpentine robots. These insights led to the development of the far more practical "OmniTread"

serpentine robot (Granosik et al., 2005). The OmniTread design offers two fundamentally important advantages over its predecessor and, in fact, over all other serpentine robots described in the scientific literature to date. These features are: maximal coverage of all sides of all segments with propulsion elements, joint actuation with pneumatic bellows. We believe that the bellows-based joint actuators used in OmniTread have a substantial advantage over a cylinder-based design, as discussed in Granosik & Borenstein (2005).
This robot passed extended tests at SouthWest Research Institute in Texas showing excellent performance on the send and rock testbeds as well as in the underbrush. It can climb obstacles 2.5 times higher then itself and span trenches almost half of own length. The latest version of the OmniTread is called OT-4 as it can fit through a hole 4 inches (10 cm) in diameter (Borenstein et al., 2006). The OT-4 is even more versatile then its predecessors, with onboard power sources (both electric and pneumatic) it can operate up to one hour, with wireless communication is completely tetherless, with clutches can precisely control power consumption, and with additional flipper-tracks can easily overcome the knife-edge hole obstacle and climb almost 5 times its own height. The detailed information on performance of all members of the Omnis family can be found in (Granosik et al., 2007).

Fig. 11. The Omnis family of hypermobile robots from University of Michigan: OmniPede (upper left), OmniTread (lower left), OT-4 (right)

Another example of reconfigurable hypermobile robot was developed by Zhang et al. (2006). The JL-I system, shown in Fig. 12, consists of three identical modules; actually each module is an entire robotic system that can perform distributed activities. Vehicles have a form of crawlers with skid-steering ability. To achieve highly adaptive locomotion capabilities, the robot's serial and parallel mechanisms form an active joint, enabling it to change its shape in three dimensions. A docking mechanism enables adjacent modules to connect or disconnect flexibly and automatically. This mechanical structure and the control system are intended to ensure optimal traction for assembled robot. Each module is an autonomous mobile robot capable of performing basic tasks such as search and navigation. In order to achieve all these functions, the control system of the robot is based on distributed architecture with wireless connection to the base station. This flexible system with several identical modules which can work separately or simultaneously when assembled, required hierarchical software, based on the multi-agent behavior-based concept. Robot showed ability to climb steps, span gaps and recover from any rollover situation.

Fig. 12. Reconfigurable robot JL-I developed by Zhang et al. (2006)

3. Wheeeler project

Our project is focused on precise modeling and simulation of hypermobile robot in a testing environment, and eventually building it in as simple as possible way to verify a high level control concept. As we observed from the literature review, most of the hypermobile robots presented to date lack the autonomy or intuitive teleoperation, or this autonomy is limited to very specific environment of operation. Although, every robot has some control system but in most cases they employ multi DOF joysticks (Osuka & Kitajima, 2003) or sophisticated user interfaces (Baker & Borenstein, 2006), or require more then one operator. Our goal is to simplify teleoperation of these robots and increase their applicability. We consider articulated mobile robot propelled on wheels and therefore called - Wheeeler. We start with precise modeling of Wheeeler and designing the most intuitive user interface to control it. Then we show some mechanical details of suspension system and proof-of-concept prototype containing 3 identical segments built with many off-the-shelf components used in RC models technology.

3.1 Modeling and simulation

In this stage of a project we have used Webots PRO simulation software to model robot and working environment (Michel, 2004). Applying masses, inertias, friction coefficients and damping made model and simulation very realistic (see Fig. 13). Webots relies on ODE (Open Dynamics Engine) to perform accurate physics simulation and uses OpenGL graphics.

We assumed that robot will contain 7 identical segments interconnected by 2DOF joints allowing pitch and yaw rotations. Each segment has its own drive and suite of sensors including: 4 distance sensors facing up, down, left and right; encoder on main motor, 3 axis accelerometer and single axes gyro. We also assumed position feedback from joints and vision feedback from two cameras mounted on both ends of robot. With these two cameras robot will have advantages similar to Kohga robot providing operator with view from the nose camera and perspective view from behind and above the robot when tail of Wheeler is lifted in scorpion-like manner.

Fig. 13. Model of Wheeeler in Webots PRO simulator (Pytasz & Granosik, 2006)

In simulation environment we have access to information from all sensors. This data is processed by robot controller and streamed to the client-operator. CORBA framework has been used as communication layer. The choice was made because of its portability and flexibility and detailed explanation can be found in (Pytasz & Granosik 2007). With robot development and sensory suite extension the larger amount of data had to be transferred over network, including:

- control commands to robot,
- sensor data from robot,
- video streaming.

The selected mechanism allows for easy extension of communication features, decreasing probability of programming errors to occur. The same data structures and transport mechanisms as used in simulation will be verified in real robot.

Inter-segment joints working in vertical direction have a range of movement close to ±90, in horizontal it is a little over ±45. These ranges combined with short segments and zigzag posture of robot (e.g. as shown in Fig. 14) can compensate for lack of all side tracks (known from Moira or OmniTread). When rotation of upper wheels is opposite to the lower wheels robot is able to enter pipes, shafts, or low ceiling environments.

Fig. 14. Zigzag configuration of Wheeeler for working in pipes, shafts and low ceiling environments.

3.2 Mechanical concept

Designing Wheeeler we tried to take the best features of other hypermobile robots but we have also borne in mind that mechanical construction has to be simple. Impressed with behavior of Genbu - even with passive joints this wheeled robot can evade stuck situations, and envisaging easy method of driving two wheels on the common axel, we decided to use light-weight plastic wheels known from Monster Truck models (see Fig. 15). With big wheels, larger then segment's interior robot can easily ride upside down. The driving module uses single RC servo motor and bevel gear to transmit rotation directly to both wheels. We decided not to use differential mechanism to reduce weight and simplify transmission system. Moreover, for off-road vehicles it is much better to have the same speed and torque on both wheels to ensure grip on rocks or send, even though skidding will appear on the curves.

Fig. 15. Proof-of-concept prototype of Wheeeler – 3 segments (out of planned 7 segments) connected with 2 DOF joints

Hypermobile robots should conform to the terrain compliantly, so that as many driving segments as possible are in contact with the ground at all times to provide effective propulsion. Based on the literature review in the previous section and as shown in Table 4 there are, in general, three methods of adapting of articulated mobile robots to the rugged terrain. They are: active control of joints of the robot, passive joints and naturally compliant joints. The first method requires exact sensing of contact forces between propulsion means and the ground. Based on these measurements in each segment, control algorithm has to adapt joint position accordingly.

In case of robot Koryu the impedance control is proposed (Hirose & Morisima, 1993). It was shown that based on force sensing in both vertical and horizontal direction robot can follow the curvature of the ground and surmount higher, vertical obstacles.

For motion control of robot Makro: like branching into pipes, overcoming obstacles and driving at the bottom of the sewer, combination of 2D inclinometers (or 2 axes accelerometers) with joint angles sensing was proposed.

Active connection mechanism of Souryu introduces special elasticity. Rolling deformation is generated by the vehicle's own dead weight and does not interfere with proper operation of other DOF in joint thanks to combination of soft and hard springs. This elasticity also absorbs impacts. Pitch and yaw are also secured from impacts by additional springs.

In the robot Kohga full 3 DOF passive joints are used in the middle part of the robot - 4 central segments are interconnected by combination of freely rotating universal joint and

additional roll joint. This design allows the robot to adjust its shape corresponding to irregular surfaces, so that the driving force can be transmitted to the ground more effectively. The units, which are connected with passive joint, are controlled by driving the right and left crawlers independently instead of manipulating the joint.
Pneumatically driven joints of Moira and Omnis robots employ natural compliance of pneumatic springs. The advantage of using pneumatic springs instead of earlier mentioned solutions is possibility of controlling their stiffness actively. Regulating the level of pressures in chambers of the cylinders (driving Moira's joints) or in each of 4 bellows constituting Integrated Joint Actuator of OmniTread (or OT-4) changes spatial compliance of this joint. Therefore, theses robots can nicely conform to rock beds when joints go limp and a second later they can span gaps after pumping pressure up. Of course, the drawback of this solution is need of additional (pneumatic) source of power - increasing weight and noise.
We decided to combine active and stiff joints with passive suspension system in each segment and soft tires. Driving module (described earlier) is mounted in the base of the segment of Wheeeler rotationally in such a way, that it can rotate ±10° over longitudinal axis of the robot. This angle is measured with rotary potentiometer. Axis of wheels is supported by two ball-bearings in the funnel, which at ends is connected with the body of segment using 4 springs (Granosik et al., 2008).
We are very pleased with the behavior of Wheeeler's passive suspension, which helps to travel in an uneven terrain, as shown in Fig. 15, preserving continuous contact with ground for all wheels of the robot. Even for obstacles as high as half of wheel's diameter, springs allow each segment to conform to the ground and provide good grip for all tires.
In Fig. 16 we can see the behavior of springs depending on the position of wheel with respect to the floating platform. If wheel is lifted up by an obstacle springs extend as shown on the left part of Fig. 16, while springs on the wheel which is lower are compressed (right part).

Fig. 16. Close view of springs in passive suspension of Wheeeler during riding over obstacle

3.3 Electronics

In order to control all the sensors envisioned in Wheeeler and in order to simply mechanical fit into the segment we have designed and built specialized controller based on the AT90CAN128 (Atmel), as shown in Fig. 17. We have chosen this processor for the fast AVR structure and relatively high processing power, as for 8-bit controllers. Additionally, in-system programming from Atmel offers reprogramming of each processor of the system directly through CAN bus. This will simplify development procedure of the robot's lowest level software. Local controllers are augmented with all necessary peripherials: 3-axis accelerometers LIS3LV02DL (STMicroelectronics), single axis gyroscope ADIS16100 (Analog Devices), quadrature counters LS7366R (LSI/CSI) and IR distance sensors GP2D120 (Sharp). Functionality of controller can be further extended through serial communication interfaces: CAN, SPI, I2C and RS232. CAN bus is used as a main communication means for data acquisition and robot control.

Fig. 17. Local controller mounted on each segment of Wheeeler

3.4 Controller

Local controllers are daisy-chained along robot's body and connected to the main controller realized on PC104 computer, as shown in Fig. 18. This main controller gathers data from robot and forwards to operators station via wireless link. It will also be used to transfer video signal. In the opposite direction, control orders comes from operator, they are being analyzed in main controller and distributed to local ones. We are planning that main controller will be also responsible for basic autonomous behavior of Wheeeler.

At first, basic teleoperation with only a visual feedback was introduced. Communication was unidirectional, allowing client (operator) send one of the following instructions:

- new angular velocity of the axle of specified segment,
- new position of the horizontal or vertical joint of a segment,
- stop all segments.

This form of control would be very inconvenient in a real application; therefore a simple propagation algorithm for angular position of joints was introduced. This algorithm is usually referred as follow the leader approach and is most often used to control serpentine and snake-like robots (Choset & Henning, 1999). However, this method requires very strong assumption that we know exact value of robot's speed with reference to the ground. Unfortunately, in most cases where hypermobile robots are intended to operate this condition is not fulfilled due to slippage, skidding on rocks or hitting obstacles. To improve operation of hypermobile robot among obstacles we are combining accelerometers' readings with potential field method based on the measurements of distances from each segment to the nearest obstacle. Using accelerometers we can detect wheel slippage and correct velocity accordingly. Using IR sensors we can check surroundings of the robot in four directions: up, down, left and right, and correct robot's trajectory according to these measurements.

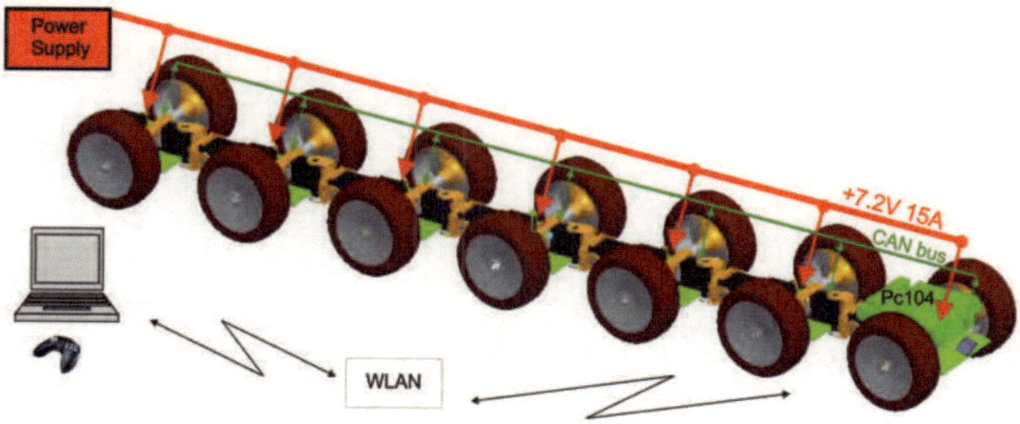

Fig. 18. Wheeler control structure

3.5 Tests

After building the proof-of-concept version of Wheeeler, consisting of 3 segments, we have made some preliminary tests to verify robot's behaviour, power consumption and performance. Results are presented in the following tables. Table 2 compares speed of the robot on the flat terrain (carpet) and supply current measured for three levels of supply voltage. Table 3 shows the current consumption during driving on the inclined steel flat surface (measurement for two inclinations and three voltage levels).

Supply voltage [V]	Speed of robot [cm/s]	Starting current [A]	Nominal current [A]
5	32.2	1.7	0.7
6	40.0	1.7	0.7
7	46.0	2.3	0.9

Table 2. Performance of 3 segment Wheeeler on flat terrain

Inclination [deg]	Supply voltage [V]	Starting current [A] Going up (down)	Nominal current [A] Going up (down)
16.2	5	2.6 (1.5)	1.4 (0.3)
	6	2.7 (1.6)	1.5 (0.3)
	7	2.8 (1.6)	1.7 (0.5)
21.3	5	2.6	2.0 (0.2)
	6	2.7	2.0 (0.3)
	7	2.8	2.0 (0.4)

Table 3. Power consumption of 3 segment Wheeeler on inclined surface

4. Conclusion

We have made an extended literature review in order to analyze methodologies used in designing and building hypermobile robots. We have also included our own experience in this field coming from Omnis project and recent Wheeeler development. The most important information of each hypermobile robot is summarized in Table 4.

Feature \ Robot	KR-II	Makro	Souryu	Kohga	Moira	OmniTread	OT-4	JL-I	Wheeeler
Number of segments	7	5	3	8	4	5	7	3	3 (7)
Length [cm]	330	160	116	205	143	127	94	105	55.5 (129)
Height [cm]	108	18	13.5	13.5	15	18.6	8.2	15	11.5
Width [cm]	46	20.3	17.5	18	15	18.6	8.2	25	21
Weight [kg]	320	30	10.2	18	18	13.6	4	21	2.7 (7)
Joints	2DOF, active electric	3DOF active electric	3DOF active electric	2DOF active electric, 3DOF passive	2DOF active pneumatic	2DOF active pneumatic	2DOF active pneumatic	3DOF active electric	2DOF active electric
Propulsion	wheels	wheels	treads	treads	treads	treads	treads	treads	wheels
No of propulsion means per unit	1	2	2	2	8	8	8	2	2
Speed [cm/s]	50	60	NA	5	20	10	15	18	40
Adapting to rugged terrain	Active control of joint	Active control of joint	Passivity in joint	Passive joints	Natural compliance	Natural compliance	Natural compliance	NA	Spring suspension
Max slope to travel [deg]	38	27	NA	30	34	30	40	40	21
Types of operation	Remote control	Remote control, some autonomy	Remote control,	Remote control, gamepad CAC	Remote control	Remote control, 2 gamepads	Remote control, 3 gamepads	NA	Remote control, gamepad CAC
Max height of obstacle [cm] % of robot height	38 35	35 194	42 300	15 11	38 253	46 247	40 488	28 187	12 104
Rollover sensitivity	One side only	One side only	Upside down	Upside down	Four sides, insensitive	Four sides, insensitive	Four sides, insensitive	Upside down	Upside down
Low ceiling operation	Very limited	Limited	Limited	Limited	Unlimited	Unlimited	Unlimited	Limited/ possible	Limited/ possible

Table 4. Basic properties of hypermobile robots, CAC – computer aided control, NA – information not available

5. Acknowledgement

This work was partially financed by The Ministry of Science and Higher Education under grant No **3 T11A 024 30**. Author is grateful to Dr. Krzysztof Mianowski for mechanical design and to Mr. Michał Pytasz for his work on the control system of Wheeeler.

6. References

Baker, J. & Borenstein, J. (2006). The Joysnake A Haptic Operator Console for High-Degree-of-Freedom Robots. *2006 International Joint Topical Meeting: "Sharing Solutions for Emergencies and Hazardous Environments,"* February 12-15, Salt Lake City, Utah, USA

Blitch, J.G. (2003). Adaptive Mobility for Rescue Robots, *Proc. of SPIE. Sensors, and Command, Control, Communications, and Intelligence (C3I) Technologies for Homeland Defense and Law Enforcement II*, vol. 5071, pp. 315–321.

Brown, H.B. Jr.; Vande Weghe, J.M.; Bererton, C.A. & Khosla, P.K. (2002). Millibot trains for enhanced mobility, *IEEE/ASME Transactions on Mechatronics*, Vol. 7, Issue 4, pp. 452-461.

Borenstein, J.; Hansen, M.G. & Nguyen, H. (2006). The OmniTread OT-4 Serpentine Robot for Emergencies and Hazardous Environments, *2006 Int. Joint Topical Meeting: "Sharing Solutions for Emergencies and Hazardous Environments,"* February 2006, Salt Lake City, Utah, USA.

Choset H. & Henning W. (1999). A Follow-the-Leader Approach to Serpentine Robot Motion Planning, *ASCE Journal of Aerospace Engineering*, available on-line http://www.ri.cmu.edu/pubs/pub_2863.html.

Granosik, G. & Borenstein, J. (2004) Minimizing Air Consumption of Pneumatic Actuators in Mobile Robots, *Proc. IEEE Int. Conference on Robotics and Automation*, New Orleans, pp. 3634-3639.

Granosik, G.; Hansen, M. & Borenstein, J. (2005). The OmniTread Serpentine Robot for Industrial Inspection and Surveillance. *Industrial Robots International Journal, Special Issue on Mobile Robots*, vol. IR32-2, pp. 139-148, March 18th, 2005.

Granosik, G. & Borenstein, J. (2005). Integrated Joint Actuator for Serpentine Robots, *IEEE/ASME Transactions on Mechatronics*, Vol. 10, pp. 473-481, October 2005.

Granosik, G.; Borenstein, J. & Hansen, M.G. (2007). Serpentine Robots for Industrial Inspection and Surveillance, In: *Industrial Robotics. Programming, Simulation and Applications*, Low Kin Huat (Ed.), pp. 633-662, Published by the plV pro literatur Verlag, ISBN 3-86611-286-6, Germany

Granosik G., Mianowski K. & Pytasz M. (2008). Design and control of Wheeeler - hypermobile inspection robot, *Submitted to International Journal of Intelligent Control and Systems*

Hirose, S. (1993). *Biologically Inspired Robots (Snake-like Locomotor and Manipulator)*, Oxford University Press.

Hirose, S. & Morishima, A. (1990). Design and Control of a Mobile Robot With an Articulated Body, *The International Journal of Robotics Research*, Vol. 9, No. 2, pp. 99-113.

Hirose, S.; Morishima, A.; Tukagosi S.; Tsumaki T. & Monobe, H. (1991). Design of Practical Snake Vehicle: Articulated Body Mobile Robot KR-II, *Fifth Int. Conference on Advanced Robotics, 'Robots in Unstructured Environments'*, Vol. 1, pp 833 -838.

Hirose, S. & Morishima, A. (1993). Impedance Control of Articulated Body Mobile Robot "Koryu", *Proc. IEEE/RSJ Int. Conf. on Intelligent Robots and Systems*, pp.1786-1790

Kamegawa, T.; Yamasaki, T.; Igarashi, H. & Matsuno, F. (2004). Development of the Snake-like Rescue Robot KOHGA, *Proc. IEEE Int. Conference on Robotics and Automation*, New Orleans, LA, April, pp. 5081-5086.

Kimura, H. & Hirose, S. (2002). Development of Genbu: Active wheel passive joint articulated mobile robot, *Proc. IEEE/RSJ Int. Conference on Intelligent Robots and System*, Vol.1, pp. 823 -828.

Klaassen, B. & Paap, K.L. (1999). GMD-SNAKE2: A Snake-Like Robot Driven by Wheels and a Method for Motion Control, *Proc. IEEE Int. Conference on Robotics and Automation*, Detroit, MI, May 10-15, pp. 3014-3019.

Long, G.; Anderson, J.; Borenstein, J. (2002). The OmniPede: A New Approach to Obstacle Traversion. *Proc. IEEE Int. Conf. on Robotics and Automation*, USA, pp. 714-719.

Michel. O. (2004). WebotsTM: Professional Mobile Robot Simulation. *International Journal of Adavnced Robotic Systems*, vol. 1, No. 1, ISSN 1729-8806, pp. 39–42.

Miyanaka, H.; Wada, W.; Kamegawa, T.; Sato, N.; Tsukui, S.; Igarashi, H & Matsuno, F. (2007). Development of an unit type robot "KOHGA2" with stuck avoidance ability, *Proc. 2007 IEEE International Conference on Robotics and Automation*, pp. 3877-3882, Roma, Italy, 10-14 April 2007

Mori, M. & Hirose, S. (2002). Three-dimensional serpentine motion and lateral rolling by active cord mechanism ACM-R3, *IEEE/RSJ International Conference on Intelligent Robots and System*, pp. 829-834 vol.1.

Ohno, H. & Hirose, S. (2000). Study on slime robot (proposal of slime robot and design of slim slime robot), *Proc. IEEE/RSJ Int. Conference on Intelligent Robots and Systems*, (IROS 2000), pp 2218-2223, Vol 3.

Osuka, K. & Kitajima, H. (2003). Development of Mobile Inspection Robot for Rescue Activities: MOIRA, *Proc. IEEE/RSJ Int. Conference on Intelligent Robots and Systems*, Las Vegas, Nevada, pp. 3373-3377.

Paap, K.L.; Christaller, T.; Kirchner, F. (2000). A robot snake to inspect broken buildings, *Proc. IEEE/RSJ Int. Conference on Intelligent Robots and Systems*, pp. 2079-2082.

Pytasz M. & Granosik G. (2006). Modelling of Wheeeler – hyper mobile robot, (in polish) In: *Postępy Robotyki. Sterowanie, percepcja i komunikacja.* Tchoń K. (Ed.), pp. 275-284. Wydawnictwa Komunikacji i Łączności, Warszawa, ISBN: 83-206-1628-X

Pytasz M. & Granosik G. (2007). Applying CORBA technology for the teleoperation of Wheeeler, In: *Robot Motion and Control 2007 in the "Lecture Notes in Control and Information Sciences"*, Kozłowski K. (Ed.), series of the Springer Verlag, London 2007, pp. 311-318, ISBN-13: 978-1-84628-973-6

Schempf, H.; Mutschler, E.; Goltsberg, V.; Skoptsov, G.; Gavaert, A. & Vradis, G. (2003). Explorer: Untethered Real-time Gas Main Assessment Robot System, *Proc. of Int. Workshop on Advances in Service Robotics, ASER'03*, Bardolino, Italy.

Scholl, K.U.; Kepplin, V.; Berns, K.; Dillmann, R. (2000). Controlling a multi-joint robot for autonomous sewer inspection, *Proc. IEEE Int. Conference on Robotics and Automation, ICRA '00*, vol.2, pp. 1701-1706.

Streich, H. & Adria, O. (2004). Software approach for the autonomous inspection robot MAKRO. *Proc. IEEE Int. Conference on Robotics and Automation*, New Orleans, LA, USA, pp. 3411-3416.

Takayama, T. & Hirose, S. (2000). Development of Souryu-I connected crawler vehicle for inspection of narrow and winding space, *26th Annual Conference of the IEEE Industrial Electronics Society, IECON 2000*, vol.1, pp 143-148.

Worst, R.; Linnemann, R.; (1996). Construction and operation of a snake-like robot, *Proc. IEEE Int. Joint Symposia on Intelligence and Systems*, 4-5 Nov. 1996, pp. 164 – 169

Ye, S.; Ma, S.; Li, B.; Liu, H. & Wang, H. (2007). Development of a 3D Snake-like Robot: Perambulator-II, *Proc. of the 2007 IEEE Int. Conference on Mechatronics and Automation*, August 5 - 8, Harbin, China

Zhang, H.; Wang, W; Deng, Z.; Zong, G & Zhang, J. (2006). A Novel Reconfigurable Robot for Urban Search and Rescue, *International Journal of Advanced Robotic Systems*, Vol. 3, No. 4, pp. 359-366, ISSN 1729-8806

18

Time-Scaling of SISO and MIMO Discrete-Time Systems

Bogdan Grzywacz
Szczecin University of Technology
Poland

1. Introduction

Finally the paper deals with the solution of the following problem:
Let signals $y_1(iT), ..., y_q(iT)$ (elements of output vector $\boldsymbol{y}(iT)$) be responses of MIMO discrete-time system to the input signals $u_1(iT),..,u_q(iT)$ (elements of input vector $\boldsymbol{u}(iT)$). Determine discrete-time excitations $u_{A1},\ldots\ldots,u_{Aq}$ (elements of vector $\boldsymbol{u_A}$) scaling the system responses to the required forms $y_1(iA^{-1}T),\ldots,y_q(iA^{-1}T)$, where A is positive number called "time scale coefficient", T–reference sample time, i–sample number.
If $A>1$, then system responses are speeded up comparing them to reference responses $y_1(iT),..., y_q(iT)$. Putting $0<A<1$ one slows the responses down. The perfect scaling of system makes, that moments of appearances of consecutive amplitudes belonging to the reference responses $y_1(iT),..., y_q(iT)$ are "controlled" according to value of A. The scaling of system responses yields transparent representations in time and frequency domains. Thus, the time-scaling seems to be useful tool for speeding the system responses up, or slowing them down, if forms of reference responses satisfy technical needs. Let us note, that perfect scaling of stable system conserves its stability.
The methods presented in current Chapter can be applied for time-scaling of responses of continuous-time systems on the basis of respective discrete–time models. Thus, the considered methods can be treated as alternative solutions to those for time-scaling of continuous–time systems (Durnas & Grzywacz, 2001; Durnas & Grzywacz, 2002; Grzywacz, 2006). Of course, there are other ways of application of time-scaling techniques, like those, for example, presented in (Moya at al., 2002; Respondek & Pogromsky, 2004), where problem of synthesis of controllers and observers for certain classes of non-linear plants has been solved. In current Chapter we do not deal with time-scaling in this meaning.

2. The idea of method for SISO systems

2.1 Slowing the system response down

Let us consider the class of SISO nonlinear, discrete-time systems of order n defined for sample time T by state equations system:

$$x_1(i+1) = x_2(i)$$

$$x_2(i+1) = x_3(i)$$

$$\dots\dots\dots\dots \tag{1}$$

$$x_n(i+1) = f[\, x_1(i),\ x_2(i),\ \dots,\ x_{n-1}(i)\,] + u(i)$$

$$y(i) = F\,[b_0\, x_1(i)\ + b_1\, x_2(i) + \dots\ b_{n-1}\, x_n(i)\,]$$

where $x_1(i)$, $x_2(i)$,..., $x_n(i)$ - components of state vector $\boldsymbol{x}(i)$, f and F represent static nonlinear functions, $u(i)$ - system input, $y(i)$ - system output, i - sample number. In particular case, if $F\,[.] = b_0\, x_1(i) + b_1\, x_2(i) + \dots + b_{n-1}\, x_n(i)$ and $f(.\,) = -\,(a_o\, x_1(i) + + a_1\, x_2(i) + \dots + a_{n-1}\, x_n(i))$, the system (1) becomes to linear one given by transfer function:

$$G(z) = \frac{b_{n-1}z^{n-1} + \dots + b_1 z + b_0}{z^n + a_{n-1}z^{n-1} \dots + a_1\ z + a_0} \tag{2}$$

The simplified scheme of system (1) is shown in Fig.1. In order to slow system response down α times (α positive integer number), we can join the element z^{-k}, where $k=(\alpha-1)$, to the all single unit delay elements z^{-1} belonging to the system shown in Fig. 1 (i.e. each z^{-1} in "primary" structure is replaced by $z^{-(k+1)}$). Additionally, if we substitute the reference excitation $u(iT)$ with the new one $u(iT')$, where $T' = \alpha T$, then both above modifications change the system response to the form $y(iT')$. This means, that form of reference response $y(iT)$ is conserved perfectly. If system (1) represents real plant or its model which is used to calculation of signal for plant control, then "internal" modification of structure in Fig. 1 cannot be done. Thus, the time-scaling of system in Fig. 1 has to be done by suitable forming of its excitation $u(i)$, without modification of its internal structure.

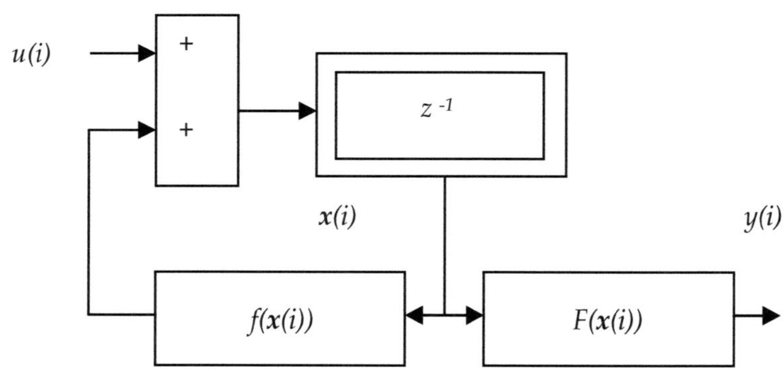

Fig. 1. The simplified scheme of system (1): z^{-1} - chain of unit delay elements, $\boldsymbol{x}(i)$ –state vector with components representing outputs of single delay elements, F and f - static nonlinear functions, u -input, y - output.

To solve the task of scaling one can try to do reconfiguration of modified structure like in Fig. 1 (that containing elements $z^{-(k+1)}$ instead of z^{-1}) to the structure shown in Fig. 2, where SYSTEM represents "primary" structure shown in Fig. 1 (from before any modification). The relevant calculations allow to express the operation realized by "INPUT" corrector in the form:

$$G_z(z) = \frac{b_{n-1}z^{nk+n-k-1} + b_{n-2}z^{nk+n-2k-2} + \cdots + b_1 z^{k+1} + b_o}{b_o z^{nk} + b_1 z^{nk+1} + \cdots + b_{n-2}z^{nk+n-2} + b_{n-1}z^{nk+n-1}} \tag{3}$$

The output signal of „FEEDBACK" corrector is formed as it follows: components of state vector $\boldsymbol{x}(i)$ are passed through the transfer function $(G_z(z))^{-1}$. This creates auxiliary signals $x'_1(z) = [(G_z(z))^{-1} x_1(z)]$, ..., $x'_n(z) = [(G_z(z))^{-1} x_n(z)]$. Then, on the basis of signals $x'_1(i)$, ..., $x'_n(i)$ one can create signal $u_f(i)$ according to formula:

$$u_f(i) = f\,[x'_1(i - n\,k),\ x'_2(i-(n-1)\,k),...,x'_n(i - k)] \tag{4}$$

Note, that operation (4) processes the delayed signals $x'_1(i)$, ...,$x'_n(i)$. Next signal $u_f(i)$ has to be passed through the transmittance $G_z(z)$. Its output signal is $u_{fG}(i)$. Finally, the output signal $U_f(i)$ of "FEDDBACK" corrector which "fits" for scheme shown in Fig. 2. is composed using expression:

$$U_f(i) = u_{fG}(i)\ -\ f[x_1(i),\ x_2(i),\ ...,\ x_{n-1}(i)\ ] \tag{5}$$

The input signal of structure shown in Fig.2 ought to be $u(iT')$, which means, that one has to repeat the form of reference input signal of system shown in Fig. 1 (i.e. $u(iT)$ for $A^{-1} = \alpha = 1$), however the consecutive amplitudes of signal $u(iT')$ are changed now at moments (iT'). Let us note, that both systems (those in Fig. 1 and Fig. 2) operate with the same sample time T. If order of denominator of $G_z(z)$ is higher than order of nominator, then we can use function $G'_z(z) = (z^d\ G(z))$ instead of $G(z)$, where d represents the difference between denominator order and nominator order. This "deviation" does not affect the form of output signal. It is merely shifted forwards d samples T.

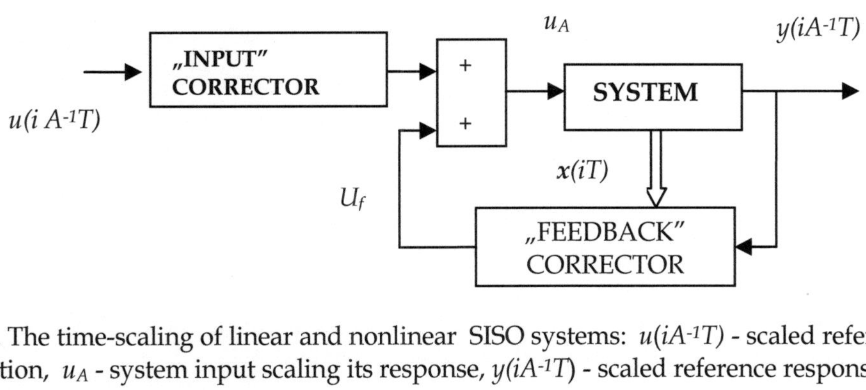

Fig. 2. The time-scaling of linear and nonlinear SISO systems: $u(iA^{-1}T)$ - scaled reference excitation, u_A - system input scaling its response, $y(iA^{-1}T)$ - scaled reference response $y(iT)$, $\boldsymbol{x}(iT)$ - system state vector.

Example A. Let us consider the second order system (6) belonging to class (1):

$$x_1(i+1) = x_2(i)$$

$$x_2(i+1) = f\,[\,x_1(i),\, x_2(i)\,] + u(i) \tag{6}$$

$$y(i) = F\ [b_0\, x_1(i) + b_1\, x_2(i)\ ]$$

where $f\,(.) = -0.72\, x_1(i) + 0.5\,(x_2(i))^3$, $F(.) = |\,2x_1(i) + 5x_2(i)\,|$.

The response of system (6) to signal $u(i) = 1(i)$ for $T = 1$s is shown in Fig. 3. Let us assume, that form of that response fulfils the technical needs, however it is "too speedy" and should be slowed down 2 times. Hence A=0.5, n=2, $\alpha = 2$ k=1, b_0=2, b_1= 5. Putting k=1, n=2 to (3) one obtains the INPUT corrector (see Fig. 2) in the form:

$$G_z(z) = \frac{5z^2 + 2}{5z^3 + 2z^2} \tag{7}$$

To design FEEDBACK corrector we have to use $(G_z(z))^{-1}$. Inversion of $G(z)$ yields transfer function with order of numerator higher than order of denominator. However, this is only the apparent difficulty. Instead of $G(z)$ we can put the invertible transfer functions $G_z'(z) = [z\, G_z(z)]$ with identical orders of nominator and denominator to the FEEDBACK and INPUT correctors. This "deviation" does not affect the form of output signal. It is merely shifted forward one sample time period T.

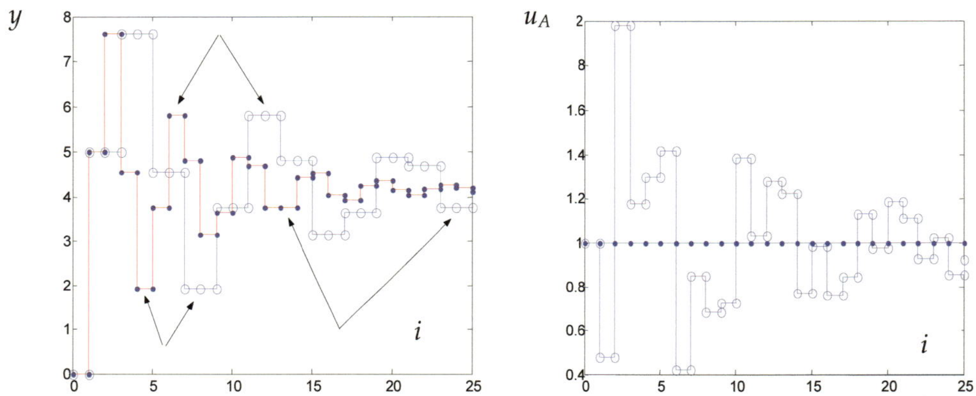

Fig. 3. **Left position:** the reference response of system (6) to signal $u(i)$= $1(i)$ – curve distinguished by "." - and response of system (6) obtained as output signal of structure in Fig. 2 – curve distinguished by "o". Note, that consecutive amplitudes of both responses are identical (compare chosen referring amplitudes indicated by arrows). **Right position:** reference input signal $u(i) = 1(i)$ and input signal $u_A(i)$ of system (6) when included to structure in Fig. 2 as SYSTEM.

The FEEDBACK corrector (see Fig. 2) for system (6) and assumed values of A, k, n can be defined by means of $G_z'(z) = [z\, G(z)]$ and nonlinear functions

$$u_f(i) = f[x'_1(i-2), x'_2(i-1)] = -0.72\, x'_1(i-2) + 0.5(x'_2(i-1))^3$$

$$U_f(i) = u_{fG}(i) - f[x_1(i), x_2(i)] \tag{8}$$

where signal $u_{fG}(i)$ is generated by passing of signal $u_f(i)$ through the transfer function $G_z'(z)$. The simulations carried out for structure like in Fig. 2 and data referring to current example yield results shown in Fig. 3. We can observe, that described above algorithm allows to design the INPUT and FEEDBACK correctors which guarantee the perfect result of scaling.

2.2 Speeding the system response up

Let model (1) be used for calculation of system input signal which speeds its reference response up A times (A - positive integer). If primary model (1) as well as system excitations are defined for sample time T, then one cannot speed its response up without shortening of sample time. We can treat, that operator z^{-1} associated with sample time T can be expressed as $z^{-1} = Z^{-A}$, where Z^{-1} refers to delay $T' = A^{-1}T$. Thus, we can imagine, that each unit delay z^{-1} of "primary" structure in Fig. 1 is substituted by Z^{-A}. The described transformations of primary model (1) make, that modified structure operates with sample time T', although system model (1) has been defined for sample time T. Now, if we remove $k = (A\text{-}1)$ elements Z^{-1} from each single "cell" $z^{-1} = Z^{-A}$, then we obtain structure like in Fig. 1, where operators z^{-1} are replaced with Z^{-1}. If we put scaled signal $u(iT')$ to input of that modified structure (instead of primary $u(iT)$), then response of modified system will be speeded up A-times and form of reference output (from before the described modification) will be conserved. However, dealing with discrete-time models of real plants used for calculations of signals for control purposes we cannot manipulate "inside" of structure modeling the plant and all manipulations ought to be done "externally" in relation to plant model "interior".

To solve the problem of scaling by synthesis of suitable input signal we can try to do reconfiguration of modified structure like in Fig.1 (that containing Z^{-1} instead of z^{-1}) to the structure shown in Fig. 2, where SYSTEM represents the "primary" structure shown in Fig.1 from before modifications described above. Like in case taken into account in Section 2.1 the current task can be solved similarly, due to equivalent transformations of modified structure aimed at separation of its subsystem, which obtains the form of "primary" system, that shown in Fig. 1, with unit delays z^{-1} replaced by chain of A single delays Z^{-1}. The equivalent transformations are based on property $Z^{-1} = z^{-1} Z^{k}$, where $k = (A\text{-}1)$. The calculations allow to define the following operation realized by "INPUT" corrector:

$$G_z(Z) = \frac{b_o Z^{nk} Z^{o} + b_1 Z^{(n-1)k} Z^{2A} + ... + b_{n-1} Z^{k} Z^{2A(n-1)}}{b_o + b_1 Z^{k+1} + ... + b_{n-1} Z^{(n-1)(k+1)}} \qquad (9)$$

The output signal of „FEEDBACK" corrector can be generated as it follows: the shifted forward components of state vector, those corresponding to sample time T, i.e. $x_1(i+nk)$, $x_2(i+(n-1)k),...,x_n(i+k)$ should be passed through the transfer function $(G_z(Z))^{-1}$. This operation yields the signals $x'_1(i+nk)$, $x'_2(i+(n-1)\,k),...,x'_n(i+k)$ respectively. Using these auxiliary signals one can form signal $u_f(i)$:

$$u_f(i) = f\,[x'_1(i + n\,k),\ x'_2(i + (n-1)\,k),....,x'_n(i + k)] \qquad (10)$$

Note, that shifted forwards components of vector x are available, because they are generated as output signals of "former" delay elements Z^{-1} creating chain of delays used for assembling the model (1) or can be generated by delaying of "former" state variables associated with model (1). Next signal $u_f(i)$ has to be passed through the transfer function $G_z(Z)$. Let output signal of $G_z(Z)$ be denoted by $u_{fG}(i)$. Finally, the output signal $U_f(i)$ of "FEDDBACK" corrector (see Fig. 2) is composed using formula :

$$U_f(i) = u_{fG}(i) - f[x_1(i),\ x_2(i),\ ...,\ x_{n-1}(i)\ ] \qquad (11)$$

The described rules allow to scale exactly the output y, if SYSTEM "pretends" operation with sample time T (because of substitution $z^{-1} = Z^{-A}$) and its real sample time is $T'=(A^{-1}T)$. It is obvious, that one cannot speed up the reference output $y(iT)$, conserving its consecutive amplitudes, if system sample time is still T. However, dependently of A, we can remove every second, or every third, etc. amplitudes from reference sequence $y(iT)$ and consecutive remaining amplitudes generate with sample time T. This way can be treated as simplified one for speeding the SYSTEM response up (some amplitudes of reference response are not repeated), if sample time T of primary SYSTEM cannot be shortened. To obtain simplified result of speeding of reference response up we can use signal u_A (Fig. 2) which is generated exactly like it was described above for SYSTEM operating with sample time T'. However, signal u_A determined for T' should be passed through the "ZOH" (zero order hold) element defined for sample time T. Then output signal of "ZOH" operation should be put as excitation to input of "primary" SYSTEM, i.e. that operating with sample time T. It means, that SYSTEM operating with T' in structure like in Fig. 2 should be treated now as calculation model of real primary SYSTEM operating with the sample time T.

Example B. Let us consider once more the second order system (6). The reference response of system (6) to signal $u(i) = 1(i)$ for T =1 has been shown in Fig. 3. Let us assume, that form of considered response fulfills the technical needs, however it is "too slow" and should be speeded up 2 times. Hence A=2, n=2, k=1, b_0=2, b_1= 5. Putting k=1, n=2 to (9) one obtains the INPUT corrector (see Fig. 2) in the form:

$$G_z(Z) = \frac{5Z^3 + 2Z}{5Z^2 + 2} \tag{12}$$

To avoid of processing of transfer function with higher order of nominator than order of denominator we can use transfer function $G_z'(Z) = [Z^{-1} G_z(Z)]$ with identical orders of nominator and denominator. This "deviation" does not affect the form of time-scaled output signal. It is merely shifted backwards one sample period T'. The FEEDBACK corrector (Fig. 2) for system (6) and assumed values A,k,n can be defined by means of $G_z'(Z)=[Z^{-1} G_z(Z)]$ and nonlinear functions:

$$u_f(i)=f[x'_1(i+2),x'_2(i+1)]= - 0.72\, x'_1(i+2) + 0.5(x'_2(i+1))^3$$

$$U_f(i) = u_{fG}(i) - f[x_1(i),\ x_2(i)] \tag{13}$$

where signal $u_{fG}(i)$ is generated by passing the signal $u_f(i)$ through the transfer function $G_z'(Z)$. The scheme of system for speeding the response of system (6) is shown in Fig. 4. The exemplary simulation results are shown in Fig. 5.

The result of simplified scaling of system (6) is shown in Fig. 5 as well (see lowest position). This result has been obtained by passing of signal u_A generated in system shown in Fig. 4 through the "ZOH" operation defined for primary sample time T. After that, the output of "ZOH" operation has been used as excitation of primary SYSTEM (6), that defined for sample time T.

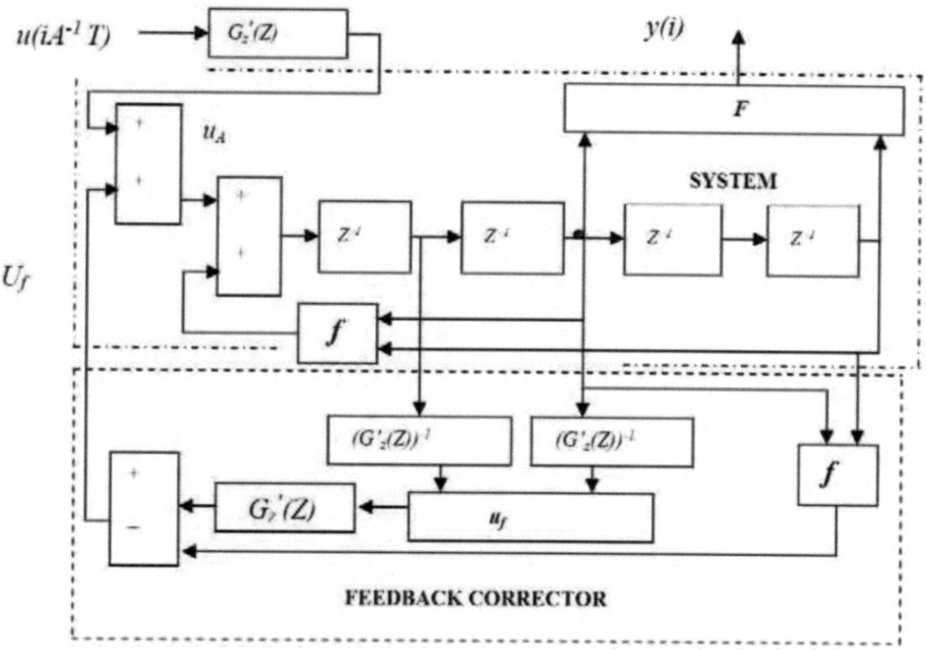

Fig. 4. The scaling of system (6) according to Fig. 2 and matter of ***Example B***. Note, that primary delays T (for z^{-1}) are substituted with the two delays $T' = 0.5\ T$, where T' refers to operator Z^{-1}.

2.3 Generalization

The considerations in previous Sections have been carried out for A being fraction with numerator equal to one (for slowing the response down) or A being integer number (for speeding the response up). The identical reasoning can be repeated, if each operator of primary unit delay z^{-1} in system shown in Fig.1 is substituted with the chain of α operators Z^{-1} associated with delay $T'=T/\alpha$ and next each single unit delay $z^{-1}=Z^{-\alpha}$ is substituted with ($Z^{-\alpha}$ $Z^{-\beta}$) for slowing the response or with ($Z^{-\alpha}$ Z^{β}), where $\beta < \alpha$, for speeding the response. All farther transformations aimed at separation of primary system structure (from before scaling) can be done exactly like it has been described in previous Sections. Thus, it is easy way of scaling if one needs to slow the response down [$(\alpha+\beta)/\alpha$] times or speed it up [$\alpha/(\alpha-\beta)$] times. Of course, the obtained final structure (like in Fig. 2) has to be supplied with scaled reference excitation u.

Looking for other possibilities of scaling of discrete-time systems we can adjust algorithms for scaling of continuous-time systems (Durnas & Grzywacz, 2001; Durnas & Grzywacz, 2002; Grzywacz, 2006). The system (1) can be or can be treated as it would be the discrete-time model of certain continuous-time system. So, one can determine the continuous-time model associated with system (1). Then obtained model can be scaled like continuous-time system. Finally, the respective scheme for scaling of continuous-time model can be transformed back into discrete-time scheme. We must honestly admit, that scaling via continuous-time representation does not guarantee the same consecutive amplitudes of discrete-time output signals for variety of values of A. Nevertheless, we can treat this way as determination of approximate solution.

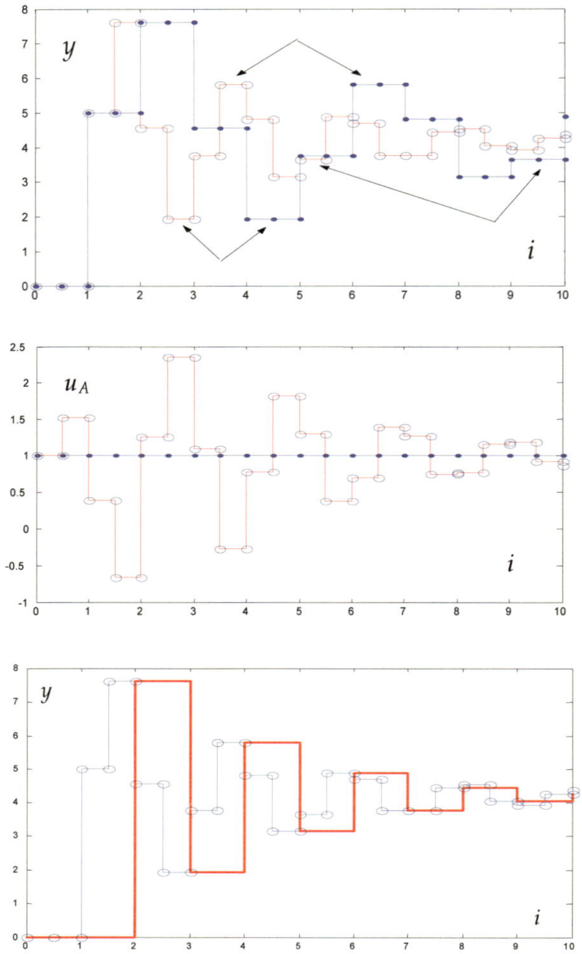

Fig. 5. **Upper figure**: the reference response of system (6) to signal $u(i)=1(i)$ - curve distinguished by "**.**" - and the speeded response of system (6) obtained as output signal of structure in Fig. 4 - curve distinguished by "o". Note, that consecutive amplitudes of both responses are identical (compare chosen referring amplitudes indicated by arrows). **Below**: reference input $u(i)=1(i)$ and input signal $u_A(i)$ of system (6) when included to structure in Fig. 4 (or in Fig. 2) as SYSTEM. **The lowest position**: the speeded response of system (6) obtained as output of structure in Fig. 4 - curve distinguished by "o" - and simplified result of scaling with sample time T - heavy line. Note, that every second amplitude of perfectly scaled output $y(iT')$ is equal to respective amplitude of simplified result of scaling for sample time T.

3. Time-scaling of MIMO systems

Let us assume, that MIMO system can be modelled by "V" structure (Chen, 1983) shown in Fig. 6, where V_{mj} are linear or nonlinear operations processing the input or output signals respectively. To scale the "V" structure one has to replace its SISO elements V_{mj} (Fig. 6) by respective SISO structures shown in Fig. 2 (where V_{mj} has to be treated as "SYSTEM" - see Fig. 2 - and elements V_{Imj}, V_{Fmj} represent operations of associated INPUT corrector and FEEDBACK one respectively). After the above modification of primary "V" structure one can arrange the set of equivalent scheme transformations aimed at separation of primary "V" structure. This goal can be achieved and signals u_{A1}, u_{A2} scaling the outputs y_1, y_2 can be generated by equipping the system with external correction loops. It means, that internal structure of system is not affected. If the reference signals $u_1(iT)$, $u_2(iT)$ exciting the system (see Fig. 6, Fig.7) are substituted with signals u_{A1}, u_{A2}:

$$u_{A1} = V_{I11}\,(u_1(i\,A^{-1}\,T) + V_{A21}(y_2)) + V_{F11}\,(x_{11}, y_1) - V_{21}(y_2)$$

$$u_{A2} = V_{I22}\,(u_2(i\,A^{-1}\,T) + V_{A12}(y_1)) + V_{F22}\,(x_{22}, y_2) - V_{12}(y_1) \quad (14)$$

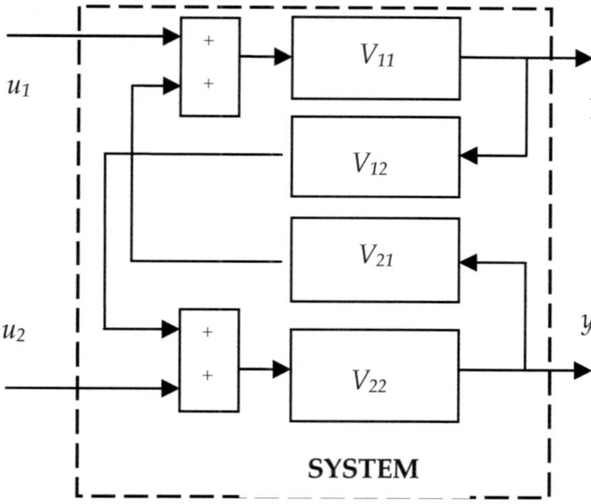

Fig. 6. The exemplary V-structure for 2 inputs and 2 outputs.

then system responses to these signals will be $y_1(iT')$ and $y_2(iT')$, instead of $y_1(iT)$ and $y_2(iT)$ from before correction. Thus, the system output signals are scaled perfectly. The operations realised by INPUT correctors associated with elements V_{11} and V_{22} (see Fig. 2) have been denoted in (14) by V_{I11}, V_{I22}. The operations realised by FEEDBACK correctors associated with V_{11} and V_{22} have been denoted by V_{F11}, V_{F22}. The operations responsible for interaction (Fig. 6) are denoted by V_{21}, V_{12}. The time-scaled interaction operations V_{21} and V_{12} are denoted by V_{A21} and V_{A12} (if, for example, $r_1(iT)=V_{21}(y_2(iT))$, then $r_1(iT')=V_{A21}(y_2(iT'))$). Finally, the state vectors chosen for V_{11} and V_{22} are denoted by $x_{11}(i)$, $x_{22}(i)$. If necessary, one can generalise (14) to the form covering the required number of inputs and outputs:

$$u_{A\,m} = V_{I\,mm}\,(\,u_m(iA^{-1}T) + \sum_{\substack{j=1\\ j\neq m}}^{q} V_{A\,jm}(y_j)\,) + V_{F\,mm}\,(x_{mm}, y_m) - \sum_{\substack{j=1\\ j\neq m}}^{q} V_{jm}(y_j), \quad m=1,..,q, \quad j=1,..,q \quad (15)$$

The generalization (15) is applicable, if SISO components of "V" model of MIMO system can be scaled in structure shown in Fig. 2. This means, that presented rules of scaling for SISO systems can be useful for scaling of MIMO systems.

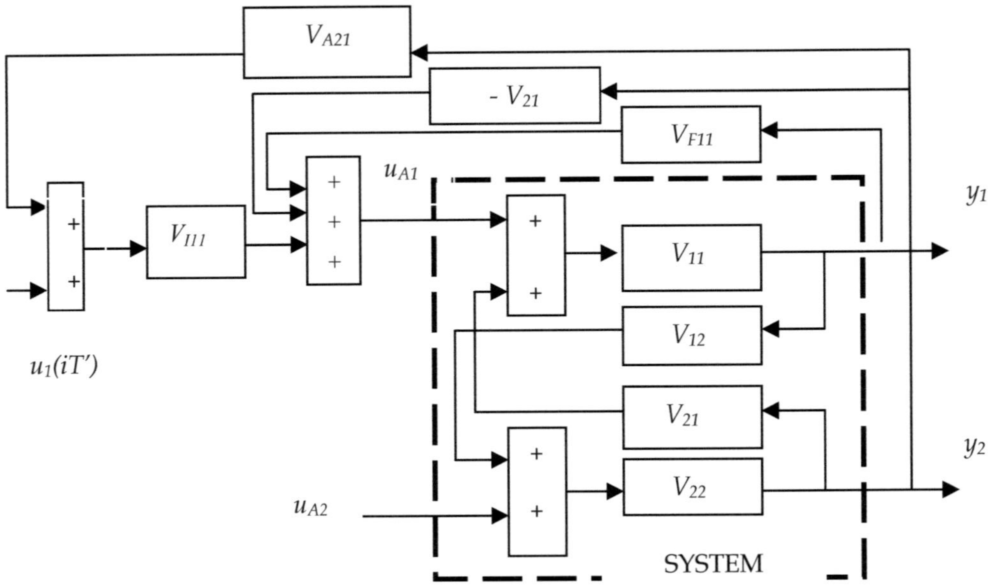

Fig. 7. The synthesis of signal u_{A1} for scaling of SYSTEM output signal y_1 . To avoid the illegibility of scheme the sub-structure generating signal u_{A2} has not been attached. Note, that effect of time-scaling has been achieved without modification of internal structure of SYSTEM.

Example C. For simplicity, let us consider the linear, continuous-time MIMO system where

$$V_{11}(s) = [6\, s^2 + s + 1]^{-1}, \qquad V_{22}(s) = [12\, s^2 + 4s + 1]^{-1},$$

$$V_{21}(s) = -10\, s^2, \qquad V_{12}(s) = -5s^2 . \tag{16}$$

Let us assume, that forms of system responses $y_1(t)$, $y_2(t)$ to excitations $u_1(t)$, $u_2(t)$ fulfil technical needs and ought to be conserved. However, they are too "fast" and $y_1(t)$, $y_2(t)$ have to be slowed down 2 times (A=0.5). Moreover, let us assume, that one cannot change the system parameters. The solution of this task can be found using the idea of time-scaling, for example, by processing the discrete-time V-model of system. Using Tustin's transform one obtains:

$$V_{11}(z)=0.0833\, T^2 (z^2+10\, z+1)\, (M_{11}(z))^{-1}, \quad V_{22}(z)= 0.0833\, T^2 (z^2+10\, z+1)\, (M_{22}(z))^{-1},$$

$$V_{21}(z)= -120\, T^{-2} (z^2-2z+1)(z^2+10z+1)^{-1}, \qquad V_{12}(z)= -60\, T^{-2} (z^2-2z+1)(z^2+10z+1)^{-1}, \tag{17}$$

where :

$$M_{11}(z) = (6+0.5T+0.0833T^2)\, z^2 + (0.8333T^2-12)\, z + 0.0833\, T^2 - 0.5T - 6,$$

$$M_{22}(z) = (12+2T+0.0833T^2)\, z^2 + (0.8333T^2 - 24)\, z + 0.0833T^2 - 2T - 12.$$

The responses of system discrete model for sample time T=1s are shown in Fig. 8. The excitations of system have been obtained using (14). The elements $V_{mj}(z)$ of structure in Fig. 6 have been scaled according to rules described in Section 2.1.

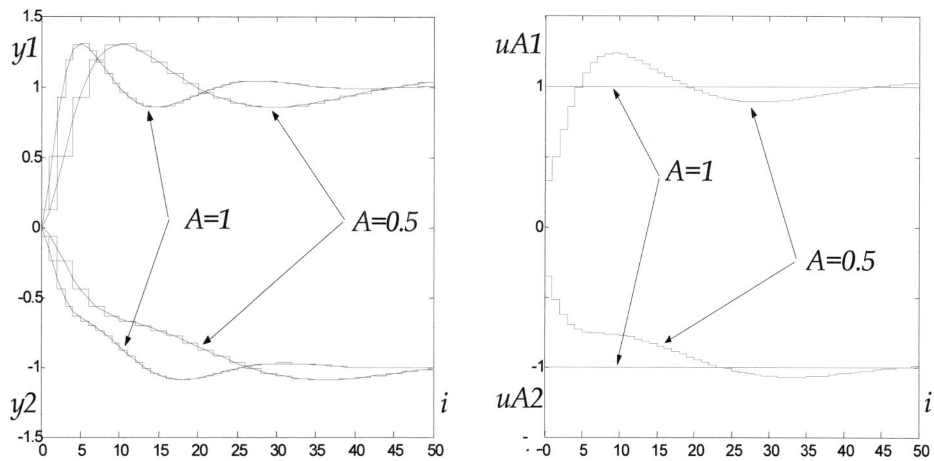

Fig 8. Result of scaling of outputs $y_1(t)$, $y_2(t)$ (solid lines – responses of system to excitations u_{A1},u_{A2}, staircase lines- responses of discrete-time model of system) and discrete-time signals u_{A1}, u_{A2} supplying system .

4. Conclusions

1. The scaling of SISO systems is realised by equipping them with INPUT and FEEDBACK correctors (Fig. 2). It makes, that external loops process the system output signal as well as system state variables and internal structure of system is not affected.
2. The scaling of MIMO system is based on its "V" model and can be implemented, if linear and nonlinear SISO elements of this model can be scaled using SISO structure shown in Fig. 2.
3. The presented algorithms can be successfully applied to discrete-time models of continuous-time systems (see Example C). Thus, the discrete-time algorithms can occur helpful for time-scaling of responses of continuous–time systems.
4. The perfect scaling of stable system conserves its stability. Furthermore, the frequency representations of signals and systems after scaling can be immediately determined on the basis of reference representations (from before scaling).
5. The considerable number of parameters representing system and associated signals in time domain and frequency domain can be treated as invariant while system dynamic properties are changed according to rules of time scaling. This advantageous feature allows to design the advanced control algorithms which conserve the crucial parameters characterising the control process (overshoots, steady state errors, stability margins, etc.) if plant responses have to be slowed down or speeded up. The control algorithms using idea of time-scaling process the plant state variables. That is why the well known MFC structure can be advised for implementation purposes (Durnaś & Grzywacz, 2001; Durnaś & Grzywacz, 2002; Grzywacz, 2006).

6. The attractive area of applications of idea of time-scaling seems to be that dealing with algorithms for control of robot drives. If displacements along *x,y,z* - axes are scaled with the same *A,* then forms of space trajectories of robot movement for various *A* are identical (they do not depend on speed of robot movement).

5. References

Chen Hui, L. (1983). *General Decoupling Theory of Multivariable Process Control Systems.* 1983, Springer - Verlag, Berlin - New York.

Durnaś, M. & Grzywacz, B. (2001). Application of idea of time-scaling to synthesis of linear and non-linear control systems. Proc. 7th IEEE *Int. Conf. Methods and Models in Automation and Robotics,* pp. 284 - 290, ISBN 83-88764-75-6, Międzyzdroje, Poland, August 2001.

Durnaś, M. & Grzywacz, B. (2002). Application of idea of time-scaling to control of nonlinear plants represented by cascade consisting of Wiener and Hammerstein models. Proc. 8th IEEE *Int. Conf. Methods and Models in Automation and Robotics,* pp. 1263 -1268, ISBN 83-88764-51-9, Szczecin, Poland, September 2002.

Grzywacz, B. (2006). The Time-Scaling of Responses of MIMO Systems. *Proc. of 13 IEEE Mediterranean Electrotechnical Conference MELECON,* pp. 429 - 432, ISBN 1 4244 0088 0, Malaga, Spain, May 2006.

Moya, P.; Ortega, R.; Netto, M. & Praly, L. (2002). Application of Nonlinear Time-Scaling for Robust Controller Design of Reaction System. *International Journal of Robust and Nonlinear Control,* Vol.12, 2002, pp. 57 – 69, ISSN 1049 - 8923.

Respondek, W.; Pogromsky, A. & Nimejer, H. (2004). Time–scaling for observer design with linearizable error dynamics. *Automatica,* Vol. 40, No. 40, February 2004, pp. 277 – 285, ISSN 0005 – 1098.

19

Models of Continuous-Time Linear Time-Varying Systems with Fully Adaptable System Modes

Miguel Ángel Gutiérrez de Anda, Arturo Sarmiento Reyes[1],
Roman Kaszyński and Jacek Piskorowski[2]
[1]Instituto Nacional de Astrofísica, Óptica y Electrónica
[2]Szczecin University of Technology
[1]Mexico
[2]Poland

1. Introduction

Linear time-varying (LTV) models have a niche of their own in the representation of systems whose behaviour may be fairly approximated as linear but whose parameters are not constant or when their behaviour shows some other properties not displayed by linear time-invariant (LTI) models. LTV models have been applied successfully in a wide range of problems ranging from system modelling and control (see, for instance, Benton & Smith, 2005; Kim et al., 2005; Vaishya & Singh, 2001) or electronic circuit design (Darabi et al., 2004) to less common applications such as the modelling of soil carbon dynamics (Martin et al., 2007) or the analysis of the stability of oscillatory (bio)chemical systems (Zak et al., 2005).

A common problem found in systems science and which is relevant for automation techniques and robotics is the proper identification of the parameters present in a given system. For this kind of problems, methods have been derived for the identification of LTV dynamics (see, for instance, Lortie & Kearney, 2001). However, in particular applications where it is required to estimate in real time the parameters of a given plant with LTV behaviour and there is limited computing power for this purpose, it would be desirable to resort to another less expensive scheme.

A traditional scheme used to identify certain parameters of a given system is depicted in Figure 1. In this scheme, the output of the system under investigation x is compared to the output of the adaptive filter y and the difference e is used to tune the filter. Traditionally, the filter is based on an algorithm implemented on a suitable computing platform and adequate interfacing circuitry. However, nothing precludes the implementation of such a filter using analogue techniques which may lead to the synthesis of systems for analogue computing (Cowan et al., 2006). Nowadays circuit design techniques are advanced enough to synthesise in a rather convenient way all kinds of static and dynamic linear and nonlinear functions without relying in implementations comprising several operational amplifiers, resistors, capacitors and multipliers and working with low power consumption indexes and relatively high speed processing capabilities (Mulder et al., 1998). For instance, a second-order low-pass filter whose bandwidth depends linearly on the bias current I_o is depicted in Figure 2 (Frey, 1993). It is even possible to perform with such techniques quite advanced signal processing functions like, for instance, generation of wavelet bases (Haddad et al., 2005).

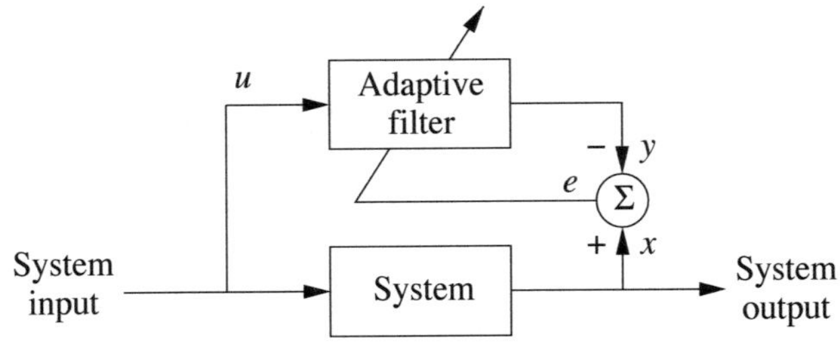

Figure 1. Parameter identification using adaptive filter

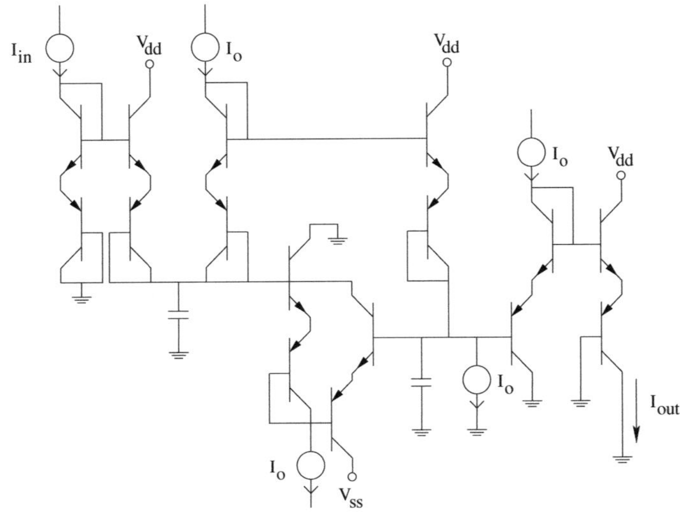

Figure 2. A second-order low-pass filter implemented with log-domain techniques (Frey, 1993).

In this chapter, a strategy to formulate continuous-time dynamical LTV systems with a prescribed dynamical behaviour will be proposed. Without any loss of generality, the strategy proposed will be first used to derive the model of a second-order LTV system with fully configurable modes. Such a model may be used to implement, for instance, an adaptive filter for system identification purposes together with an appropriate tuning scheme or may even be used for analogue computing (Cowan et al., 2006). Furthermore, the proposed model is guaranteed to have a stable behaviour provided that certain system constraints may be observed.

The rest of this chapter is organised as follows: in Section 2, a model for a second-order LTV system which may accept fast variations in its parameters without compromising its stability will be derived. In Section 3, the stability properties of the proposed model will be assessed. The properties of the new model will be compared with previous work done by the authors. The behaviour of the new model will be further validated through simulations in Section 4. Finally, some concluding remarks will be given in Section 5.

2. Synthesis of continuous-time LTV models of n-th order

Without any loss of generality, consider the second-order LTV differential equation

$$x''(t) + a_1(t)x'(t) + a_0(t)x(t) = 0 \tag{1}$$

where x(t) is a scalar function depending on the time variable t with a prescribed dynamical behaviour and $a_0(t)$ and $a_1(t)$ are also scalar functions of the time variable t which serve as time-varying coefficients of (1).
It is desired that the behaviour of x(t) in (1) may resemble the behaviour of the scalar function y(t) arising from the following LTI equation:

$$y''(t) + 2\xi\omega y'(t) + \omega^2 y(t) = 0 \tag{2}$$

where ξ is the damping parameter and ω is the undamped natural frequency associated to (2).
The general solution of (2) is given by

$$y(t)= C_1 e^{\omega(-\xi + (\xi^2-1)^{1/2})t} + C_2 e^{\omega(-\xi - (\xi^2-1)^{1/2})t} \tag{3}$$

where C_1 and C_2 are arbitrary constants. The general solution of x(t) in (1) should resemble the behaviour of the solution of (2). However, the parameters ξ and ω presented in (3) must be in general time-varying.
A possible solution is that x(t) is composed by a linear combination of two modes of the form

$$x_1(t) = e^{\int \omega(t)(-\xi(t) + (\xi^2(t)-1)^{1/2})dt} \tag{4}$$

$$x_2(t) = e^{\int \omega(t)(-\xi(t) - (\xi^2(t)-1)^{1/2})dt} \tag{5}$$

The proposed modes for (1) are now defined in terms of time-varying parameters. These solutions may be used to determine the coefficients $a_1(t)$ and $a_0(t)$ which are required in (1) to have the specified dynamic behaviour.
In order to obtain the time-varying coefficients of (1) from a set of known solutions, a linear algebraic system of equations has to be solved. Substitution of (4) and (5) in (1) leads to the following set of linear algebraic equations which may be solved for $a_1(t)$ and $a_0(t)$

$$\begin{bmatrix} x_1'(t) & x_1(t) \\ x_2'(t) & x_2(t) \end{bmatrix} \begin{bmatrix} a_1(t) \\ a_0(t) \end{bmatrix} = \begin{bmatrix} -x_1''(t) \\ -x_2''(t) \end{bmatrix} \tag{6}$$

The solution of (6) is guaranteed to exist since $x_1(t)$ and $x_2(t)$ are linearly independent functions. After solving (6) using (4) and (5), the following expressions for $a_1(t)$ and $a_0(t)$ are obtained

$$a_1(t) = \xi(t)[\, 2\omega(t) - \xi'(t)(\xi^2(t) -1)^{-1}\,] - \omega(t)\omega^{-1}(t) \tag{7}$$

$$a_0(t) = \omega(t)[\, 2\omega(t) - \xi'(t)(\xi^2(t) -1)^{-1}\,] \tag{8}$$

It should be noticed that other definitions for the modes of (1) could have been proposed which may resemble the dynamic behaviour of (2) when the time-varying parameters of (1) reach a constant value. Such a pair of modes would be, for instance

$$x_1(t) = e^{\omega(t)\,(-\xi(t) + (\xi^2(t)-1)^{1/2})} \tag{9}$$

$$x_2(t) = e^{\omega(t)\,(-\xi(t) - (\xi^2(t)-1)^{1/2})} \tag{10}$$

However, such a choice would give a very complicated formulation of the functions $a_1(t)$ and $a_0(t)$ in (1).

In general, the method used for the determination of $a_1(t)$ and $a_0(t)$ for (1) may be applied to determine the time-varying coefficients $a_i(t)$, i =0, 1,...,n − 1 of the n-th order differential LTV equation of the form

$$x^{(n)}(t) + a_{n-1}(t)x^{(n-1)}(t) + a_{n-2}(t)x^{(n-2)}(t)...+ a_1(t)x'(t) + a_0(t)x(t) = 0 \tag{11}$$

provided that n linearly independent solutions $x_i(t)$, i = 1, 2,...,n are known. In this case, the time-varying coefficients $a_i(t)$ will be the solutions of the following system of algebraic equations

$$\begin{bmatrix} x_1^{(n-1)}(t) & x_1^{(n-2)}(t) & \dots & x_1'(t) & x_1(t) \\ x_2^{(n-1)}(t) & x_2^{(n-2)}(t) & \dots & x_2'(t) & x_2(t) \\ \dots & \dots & \dots & \dots & \dots \\ x_{n-1}^{(n-1)}(t) & x_{n-1}^{(n-2)}(t) & \dots & x_{n-1}'(t) & x_{n-1}(t) \\ x_n^{(n-1)}(t) & x_n^{(n-2)}(t) & \dots & x_n'(t) & x_n(t) \end{bmatrix} \begin{bmatrix} a_{n-1}(t) \\ a_{n-2}(t) \\ \dots \\ a_1(t) \\ a_0(t) \end{bmatrix} = \begin{bmatrix} -x_1^{(n)}(t) \\ -x_2^{(n)}(t) \\ \dots \\ -x_{n-1}^{(n)}(t) \\ -x_n^{(n)}(t) \end{bmatrix}$$

In this particular case, the existence of the solutions of this system of equations is guaranteed to exist since the solutions $x_i(t)$ are linearly independent and therefore their Wronksian will be different from zero for all t. In the formulation of a model with set of fully configurable modes, and depending on the expected dynamics of the system to be modelled, the modes given in expressions (4) and (5) are excellent candidates to represent a couple of complex conjugate poles whose exact locations are not known. On the other hand, the function $x(t) = e^{-\int\sigma(t)dt}$ with $\sigma(t) > 0$ may be used to represent a real pole located in the left plane. As it will be seen soon, the proposed functions represent the best alternative to build a system based on equation (11) with complex dynamical behaviour.

In previous work (Kaszyński, 2003; Jaskula, & Kaszyński, 2004; Piskorowski, 2006), the following equation was proposed for defining a new class of low-pass time-varying filters

$$x''(t)+2\xi(t)\omega(t)x'(t)+ \omega^2(t)x(t) = \omega^2(t)u(t) \tag{12}$$

where $u(t)$ is the signal to be filtered, $x(t)$ represents the output signal and $\xi(t)$ and $\omega(t)$ represent time-varying parameters. If the coefficients of (12) are compared to the coefficients defined in (7) and (8) for (1), it can be concluded that the system defined in (1) will approximate the behaviour of (12) when the maximum magnitude of the logarithmic derivative of function $\omega(t)$ and the maximum magnitude of function $\xi'(t)/(\xi^2(t) - 1)$ are small compared to $2\xi(t)\omega(t)$ and $\omega(t)$, respectively. In other words, $\xi(t)$ and $\omega(t)$ have to vary slowly.

3. Stability properties of the proposed model

The stability properties of (1) when $a_1(t)$ and $a_0(t)$ are defined according to (7) and (8) are determined solely by the modes used in the formulation of these coefficients. In the general case (i.e. when time-varying parameters $\xi(t)$ and $\omega(t)$ vary arbitrarily), a suitable measure of the stability of the modes given in (4) and (5) can be obtained if their Lyapunov exponents are computed. The Lyapunov exponents L_1 and L_2 associated to modes $x_1(t)$ and $x_2(t)$ in (4) and (5) are given by

$$L_1 = \lim_{t\to\infty} \sup t^{-1} \ln |x_1(t)| = \lim \mathrm{Re}\, t^{-1} \int \omega(t) \left[-\xi(t) + \left(\xi^2(t) - 1\right)^{1/2} \right] dt \quad (13)$$

$$L_2 = \lim_{t\to\infty} \sup t^{-1} \ln |x_2(t)| = \lim \mathrm{Re}\, t^{-1} \int \omega(t) \left[-\xi(t) - \left(\xi^2(t) - 1\right)^{1/2} \right] dt \quad (14)$$

In order to assure the stability of (1), $L_1 < 0$ and $L_2 < 0$. Therefore, it suffices that the real part of those time averages remains negative. This means that function $\xi(t)$ may take arbitrary negative values and the stability of the system will be still guaranteed, provided that the average value of $\omega(t)\,[-\xi(t) \pm (\xi^2(t) - 1)^{1/2}]$ is negative over the whole time interval in which (1) is operating. This gives added flexibility when implementing a control for modulating $\xi(t)$ and $\omega(t)$ according to a predefined rule.
An important issue behind the proposed model in (1) is the possibility that it might be bounded-input bounded-output (BIBO) stable when the right hand of (1) contains a non-zero term. In order to guarantee this type of stability, it suffices that the homogeneous response of (1) is exponentially asymptotically stable and that the coefficients $a_0(t)$ and $a_1(t)$ are bounded for all t (Anderson & Moore, 1969). In this case, both conditions are satisfied and therefore the proposed model has BIBO stability. The proposed modes in expressions (4) and (5) have exponential asymptotic stability provided that $\omega(t)$ and $\xi(t)$ remain positive for all t. In order to guarantee the boundedness of the coefficients of (1), $\omega(t)$ hast to be different from zero for all t, whereas $\xi(t)$ has to be different from 1 for all t.
In the particular case of the system governed by equation (11), the considerations given in (Anderson & Moore, 1969) to guarantee its BIBO stability when the right hand of (11) is non-zero are also applicable. It should be noticed that if the dynamics of the system should include a real pole in the left plane whose location is not known, function $x(t) = e^{-\int \sigma(t) dt}$ has also exponential asymptotic stability provided that $\sigma(t) > 0$ for all t. Moreover, the average value of $\sigma(t)$ will define the Lyapunov exponent associated to that solution.
The results obtained so far should be compared against previous work. In (Kaszyński, 2003), the following conditions for assuring the stability of (12) were given

$$\omega(t) > 0 \quad (15)$$

$$\xi(t) > 0 \quad (16)$$

$$|\omega'(t)| < |2\xi(t)\omega^2(t)| \quad (17)$$

Such conditions were obtained using the second Lyapunov method. Conditions (15) and (16) are sufficient in (1) to ensure stability for all t. With these conditions, it is guaranteed that the arguments of the integrals in (13) and (14) are always negative, and therefore the

Lyapunov exponents computed in this way will be also negative. Condition (17) imposes an additional constraint on (12): in order to ensure stability, $\omega(t)$ may not be varied above the limit imposed by the product $2\xi(t)\omega^2(t)$, thus limiting the tunability range of this parameter. System (1) with coefficients $a_1(t)$ and $a_0(t)$ as defined in (7) and (8) does not show the shortcoming described above.
To further demonstrate that the dynamics of (1) and (12) are different, the sum of the Lyapunov exponents will be computed. According to (Nemytskii & Stepanov, 1989), the sum of the Lyapunov exponents ν of a regular n-th order LTV system of the form (11) is given by

$$\nu = - \lim_{t\to\infty} \sup t^{-1} \int_0^t a_{n-1}(\tau)\, d\tau \quad (18)$$

If the coefficient associated to the $x'(t)$ term of (12) is compared to (7), it will be verified that the only way to make the sum of Lyapunov exponents equal for both systems is forcing the product $2\xi(t)\omega(t)$ to be the same in both systems and cancelling the time variations of $\xi(t)$ and $\omega(t)$. This means that if the sum of Lyapunov exponents for (1) and (12) is meant to be the same, both systems must be LTI and have the same set of eigenvalues.

4. Performance evaluation

In order to verify the stability properties of the proposed model, its response will be tested for a predefined test signal (a step function). Therefore, $x(t)$ will be estimated numerically from the following equation

$$x''(t) + a_1(t)x'(t) + a_0(t)x(t) = a_0(t)u(t) \quad (19)$$

where coefficients $a_1(t)$ and $a_0(t)$ are defined as in (7) and (8) and $u(t)$ is the step function. The obtained response will be compared to the response obtained from a reference LTI system and from the LTV filter based on equation (12) subject to the same parameter variation. It will be assumed that the LTI reference filter is a second-order lowpass Butterworth filter with poles located on $-5 \pm 5j$. Furthermore, it will be assumed that $\omega(t)$ and $\xi(t)$ are given by the following expressions

$$\omega(t) = [50+50e^{-40t} + 100e^{-20t}]^{1/2} \quad (20)$$

$$\xi(t) = (10 + 10\, e^{-20t})/2\omega(t) \quad (21)$$

Although it has been already demonstrated a long time ago that the eigenvalues obtained from an arbitrary LTV system by means of the well-known characteristic equation for LTI systems do not convey any valid information regarding the stability properties of the system or its solution (Vinogradov, 1952), with the definition given for $\omega(t)$ and $\xi(t)$ in (20) and (21) the instantaneous location of the roots of the characteristic equation associated to (12) is modulated exponentially in time from $-10 \pm 10j$ at $t = 0$ to $-5 \pm 5j$ within a relatively short time interval. With a time constant of 0.05 seconds for the modulation factor, the roots associated to the characteristic equation of (12) should be very close to the poles of the reference LTI system after 0.2 seconds.
The simulated responses obtained in Mathematica for the LTI reference system, the filter described based on (12) and the proposed LTV model are depicted in Figure 3. From the

simulation results it can be seen that the responses of both LTV systems become identical to the response of the LTI reference system as t increases. Although the response generated by (12) rises faster compared to the response generated by (19), the proposed model produces a smaller overshoot.

In Figure 4, the response to the step function of the systems defined by (19) and (12) is depicted. In this particular case, it was assumed that ω(t) and ξ(t) were varied according to the following relations

$$\omega(t) = [50 + 90 \sin(10\pi t) + 40.5 \sin^2(10\pi t)]^{1/2} \tag{22}$$

$$\xi(t) = [10 + 9 \sin(10\pi t)]/ 2\omega(t) \tag{23}$$

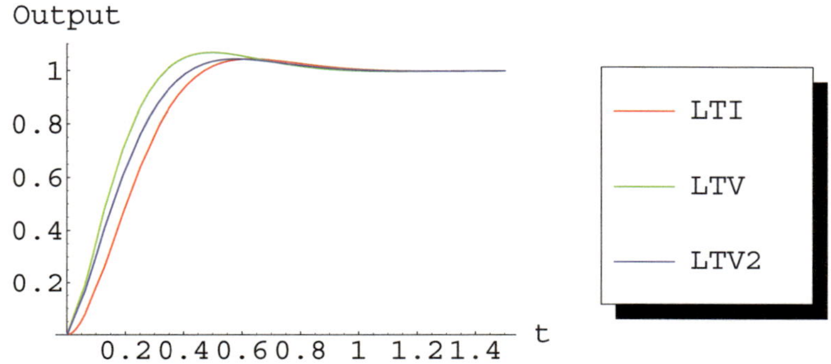

Figure 3. Responses of (12) and (19) to a step response with an exponential variation of ω(t) and ξ(t). In this figure, the acronym LTV stands for the response of (12) whereas the acronymLTV2 stands for the response of (19)

With the chosen variation parameters for ω(t) and ξ(t), the roots of the characteristic equation associated to (12) will vary periodically according to the following relation

$$p_{1,2} = -5 \pm 5j + (-4.5 \pm 4.5j) \cos(10\pi t) \tag{24}$$

where p_1 and p_2 stand for the roots of the characteristic equation of (12). With this variation scheme, the condition given in (17) for (12) is not valid anymore. However, in the case of (19), the stability measures given in (13) and (14) for equation (1) ($L_1 = L_2 = -5$), the exponential asymptotic nature of its homogeneous response and the boundedness of its coefficients guarantee that the output of (19) will be bounded (Anderson & Moore, 1969). Given that (12) is expected to show an unstable behaviour, backward differentiation formulae were chosen to solve numerically equations (19) and (12). From the results of the simulation it can be seen that both LTV systems reach in a finite time their steady-state behaviour. However, the system described by (12) displays a somewhat larger overshoot before it reaches steady-state behaviour.

It is noteworthy to consider the role of the scaling coefficient of the input function u(t) in equations (12) and (19). According to condition (17), the output of equation (12) should be unstable if the coefficients given in expressions (23) and (24) are considered. However, the simulation results of Figure 4 show that the output of the filter described by equation (12) is stable. If the scaling coefficient of the input function u(t) present in equation (12) is removed and the following equation is instead considered

$$x''(t) + 2\xi(t)\omega(t)x'(t) + \omega^2(t)x(t) = u(t) \quad (25)$$

it is possible to demonstrate that the stability condition given in (17) is indeed broken.

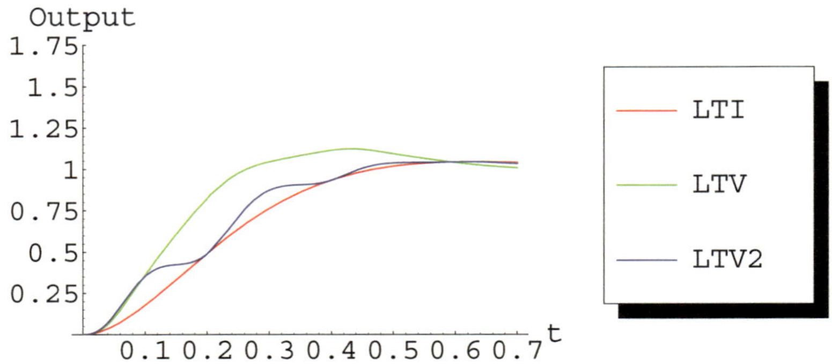

Figure 4. Responses of (12) and (19) to a step response with a periodic variation of ω(t) and ξ(t).

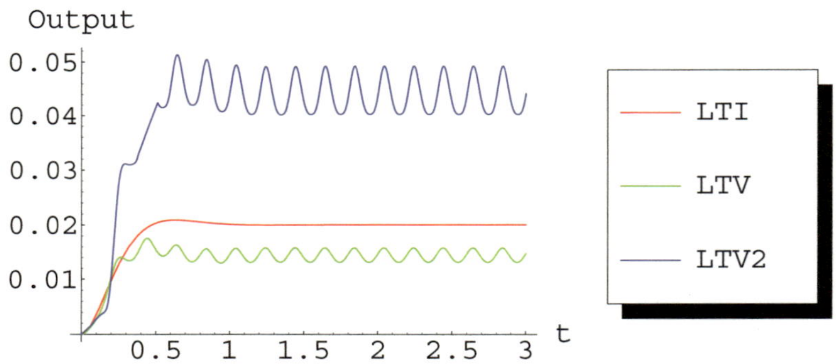

Figure 5. Responses of (25) and (26) to a step response with a periodic variation of ω(t) and ξ(t)

In Figure 5, the response of equation (25) with periodic coefficients ω(t) and ξ(t) as defined in (23) and (24) to a unit step function is depicted. This response is compared to the response of the LTV differential equation

$$x''(t) + a_1(t)x'(t) + a_0(t)x(t) = u(t) \quad (26)$$

and to the response of the lowpass filter described by the following LTI differential equation

$$x''(t) + 50x'(t) + 10x(t) = u(t) \quad (27)$$

In expression (26), coefficients $a_0(t)$ and $a_1(t)$ are defined as given in (8) and (7). From Figure 5 it may be noticed that the responses of equations (25) and (26) are oscillatory and do not track the input function u(t). In this case, function u(t) is assumed to be a step function.

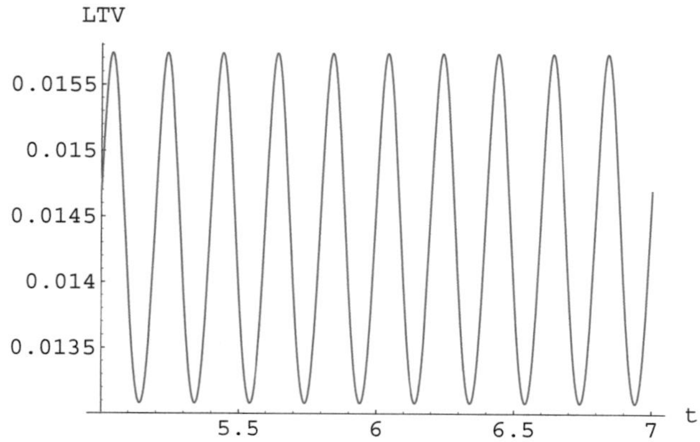

Figure 6. Time series considered for the output of (25)

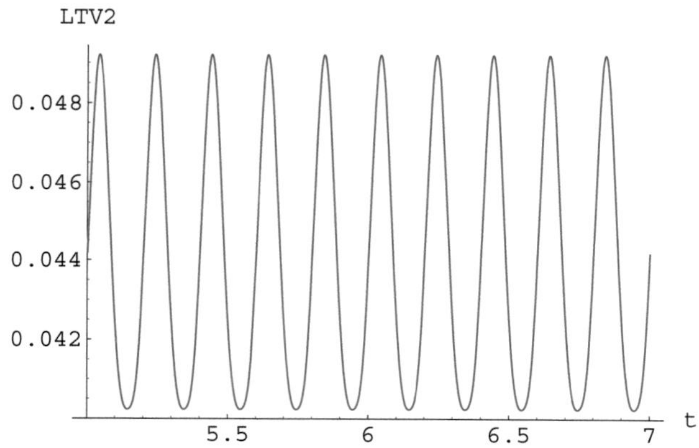

Figure 7. Time series considered for the output of (26)

A detailed analysis of a portion of the time series obtained from (25) and (26) gives more information on the results obtained through simulation with Mathematica. The time series considered for analysis appear in Figures 6 and 7. In a first attempt, Lyapunov exponents may be determined to establish the nature of the behaviour displayed by the systems represented by equations (25) and (26). However, given the periodic character of their time series, other methods should be used to assess the stability of (25) and (26) (Sprott, 2003).

In order to determine whether the stability condition given in (17) is broken or not for equation (25), the power spectra of the time series considered should be obtained. According to (Sigeti, 1995), the power spectrum of a given signal with positive Lyapunov exponents has an exponential high-frequency falloff relationship. Such characteristic in the frequency domain is due to the fact that the function which defines the signal under consideration has singularities in the complex plane when the time variable t is seen as a complex variable and not as a real one (Sigeti, 1995). When the Fourier transform is computed for such a signal, the singularities must be avoided in the complex plane through an adequate integration path and in this way exponential terms appear on its associated Fourier transform (Sigeti, 1995). In the presence of noise, the exponential frequency falloff relationship will be noticeable up to a given frequency and afterwards it will decay as a power of f^{-n} where f is the frequency and n a natural number (Lipton & Dabke, 1996). These phenomena are also observable in chaotic systems as well, independently of the appearance of attractors or not in their dynamic behaviour (van Wyk &. Steeb, 1997). When there are no singularities in the complex variable t present in a given signal and in the absence of noise, its power spectrum will decay at high frequencies as a power of f^{-n} as well (Sigeti & Horsthemke, 1987).

Frequency (Hz)	Magnitude
0	2.86448×10^{-2}
5	1.32849×10^{-3}
10	8.75641×10^{-5}
15	2.82938×10^{-6}
20	4.9275×10^{-8}
25	1.02782×10^{-9}

Table 1. Discrete power spectrum for the output of equation (25)

Frequency (Hz)	Magnitude
0	8.78076×10^{-2}
5	4.50563×10^{-3}
10	8.13031×10^{-4}
15	5.94339×10^{-5}
20	7.58989×10^{-6}
25	2.38456×10^{-6}
30	8.0822×10^{-7}
35	3.04263×10^{-7}
40	1.23233×10^{-7}
45	5.27326×10^{-8}
50	2.35502×10^{-8}
55	1.08831×10^{-8}
60	5.1718×10^{-9}

Table 2. Discrete power spectrum for the output of equation (26)

Given that the numerical solutions obtained for equations (25) and (26) are periodic, their power spectra turn out to be discrete. In Tables 1 and 2 the magnitude of the harmonic components of the responses computed via Mathematica has been tabulated. The data given in Table 1 was used to obtain the best fit in Mathematica using routine NonlinearFit[ ] for expressions

$$y = A_1 e^{B_1 f} \tag{28}$$

and

$$y = A_2 f^{B_2} \tag{29}$$

where A_1, A_2, B_1 and B_2 are fitting parameters. If the data given in Table 1 is considered from f = 15 Hz for the fitting process, the constants A_1 and B_1 which fit best expression (28) are equal to 0.535465 and -0.810056 respectively. With the same data, the constants obtained for the best fit of expression (29) are $A_2 = 175010$ and $B_2 = -9.17964$. In Figure 8 expressions (28) and (29) are plotted together with the original data and it can be seen that the exponential curve matches better the obtained data from equation (25) at high frequencies. The same procedure was carried out with the data presented in Table 2. The coefficients obtained for expression (28) were $A_1 = 0.0244961$ and $B_1 = -0.401458$ whereas for expression (29) the coefficients were $A_2 = 10292.2$ and $B_2 = -7.00509$. From Figure 9 it can be seen that

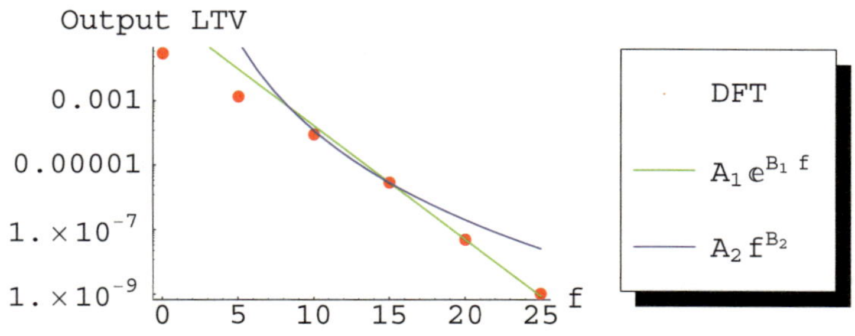

Figure 8. Power spectrum obtained for the time series of (25)

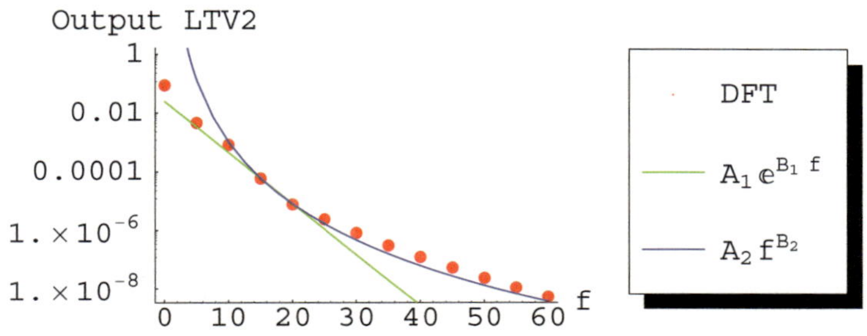

Figure 9. Power spectrum obtained for the time series of (26)

expression (29) gives the best fit for the data obtained from equation (26) at frequencies greater than 15 Hz. Given that condition (17) is broken, it can be thus safely concluded that the response obtained from equation (26) is *unstable* when ω(t) and ξ(t) are defined as given in expressions (23) and (24). In the case of equation (26), under the same conditions, it turns out that its response is bounded. The response of equation (26) is *bounded* for a bounded input because the conditions given in (Anderson & Moore, 1969) for BIBO stability are enforced.

5. Conclusions

In this chapter, a strategy for the formulation of a LTV scalar dynamical system with predefined dynamic behaviour was presented. Moreover, a model of a second-order LTV system whose dynamic response is fully adaptable was presented. It was demonstrated that the proposed model has a exponentially asymptotically stable behaviour provided that a set of stability constraints are observed. Moreover, it was demonstrated that the obtained system is BIBO stable as well. Finally, it was shown via simulations that the response of the proposed model reaches with a smaller overshoot its steady-state response compared to the response of a LTV lowpass filter proposed previously.

6. References

Anderson, B. & Moore, J. (1969). "New results in linear system stability," SIAM Journal of Control, vol. 7, no. 3, pp. 398–414.

Benton, R.E & Smith, D. (2005). "A static-output-feedback design procedure for robust emergency lateral control of a highway vehicle," *IEEE Transactions on Control Systems Technology*, vol. 13, no. 4, pp. 618- 623.

Cowan G.E.R.; Melville, R.C.; & Tsividis, Y.P. (2006) "A VLSI analog computer/digital computer accelerator," *IEEE Journal of Solid-State Circuits*, vol. 41, no. 1, pp. 42–53.

Darabi, H.; Ibrahim, B. Rofougaran A. (2004). "An analog GFSK modulator in 0.35-µm CMOS," *IEEE Journal of Solid-State Circuits*, vol. 39, no. 12, pp. 2292–2296.

Frey, D.R. (1993). "Log-domain filtering: an approach to current-mode filtering," *IEE Proceedings G: Circuits, Devices and Systems*, vol. 43, no. 6, pp. 403–416.

Haddad, S.A.P.; Bagga, S. & Serdijn, W.A. (2005). "Log-domain wavelet bases," *IEEE Transactions on Circuits and Systems I -Regular Papers*, vol. 52, no. 10, pp. 2023–2032.

Jaskula, M. & Kaszyński, R. (2004). "Using the parametric time-varying analog filter to average evoked potential signals," *IEEE Transactions on Instrumentation and Measurement*, vol. 53, no. 3, pp. 709–715.

Kaszyński, R (2003). "Properties of analog systems with varying parameters [averaging/low-pass filters]," in *Proceedings of the 2003 International Symposium on Circuits and Systems 2003*, vol. 1, pp. 509–512.

Kim, W.; Lee, D.-J.; & Chung, J. (2005). "Three-dimensional modelling and dynamic analysis of an automatic ball balancer in an optical disk drive," *Journal of Sound and Vibration*, vol. 285, pp. 547–569.

Lipton, J.M. & Dabke, K.P. (1996)."Reconstructing the state space of continuous time chaotic systems using power spectra," *Physics Letters A*, vol. 210, pp. 290–300.

Lortie, J.M. & Kearney, R.E. (2001). "Identification of physiological systems: estimation of linear time-varying dynamics with non-white inputs and noisy outputs," *Medical and Biological Engineering and Computing*, vol. 39, pp. 381–390, 2001.

Martin, M.P.; Cordier, S.C.; Balesdent, J. & Arrouays D. (2007). "Periodic solutions for soil carbon dynamics equilibriums with time-varying forcing variables," *Ecological modelling*, vol. 204, no. 3-4, pp. 523-530.

Mulder, J.; Serdijn, W.A.; van der Woerd, A. & van Roermund, A.H.M. (1998). *Dynamic translinear and log-domain circuits: analysis and synthesis*, Kluwer Academic Publishers, Dordrecht,The Netherlands.

Nemytskii, V.V. & Stepanov, V.V. (1989). *Qualitative theory of differential equations*, Dover, NewYork, 1989.

Piskorowski, J. (2006). "Phase-compensated time-varying Butterworth filters," *Analog Integrated Circuits and Signal Processing*, vol. 47, no. 2, pp. 233–241.

Sigeti, D.E. (1995). "Exponential decay of power spectra at high frequency and positive Lyapunov exponents," *Physica D*, vol. 82, pp. 136–153.

Sigeti, D. & Horsthemke, W. (1987). "High-frequency power spectra for systems subject to noise," Physical Review A, vol. 35, no. 5, pp. 2276–2282.

Sprott, J.C. (2003). *Chaos and time-series analysis*, Oxford University Press, Oxford.

Vaishya, M.& Singh R. (2001). "Sliding friction-induced nonlinearity and parametric effects in gear dynamics," *Journal of Sound and Vibration*, vol. 248, pp. 671–694.

van Wyk, M.A. &. Steeb, W.-H. (1997). *Chaos in Electronics*, Kluwer, Dordrecht, the Netherlands.

Vinogradov, R.E. (1952), "On a criterion for instability in the sense of A.M. Lyapunov for solutions of linear systems of differential equations," *Dokl. Akad. Nauk SSSR*, vol. 84, no. 2.

Zak, D.E.; Stelling, J. & Doyle III, F.J. (2005). "Sensitivity analysis of oscillatory (bio)chemical systems," *Computers and Chemical Engineering*, vol. 29, pp. 663–673.

20

Directional Change Issues in Multivariable State-feedback Control

Dariusz Horla
Poznan University of Technology,
Institute of Control and Information Engineering,
Department of Control and Robotics
ul. Piotrowo 3a, 60-965 Poznan
Poland

1. Introduction

Control limits are ubiquitous in real world, in any application, thus taking them into consideration is of prime importance if one aims to achieve high performance of the control system. One can abide constraints by means of two approaches – the first case is to impose constraints directly at the design of the controllerwhat usually leads to problemswith obtaining explicit forms (or closed-form expressions) of control laws, apart from very simple cases, e.g. quadratic performance indexes. The other approach is based on assuming the system is linear and having imposed constraints on the controller output (designed for unconstrained case – bymeans of optimisation, using Diophantine equations, etc) one has to introduce necessary amendments to the control system because of, possibly, active constraints (Horla, 2004a; Horla, 2007d; Öhr, 2003; Peng et al., 1998).

When internal controller states do not correspond to the actual signals present in the control systems because of constraints, or in general – nonlinearity at controller output, then such a situation is referred in the literature as windup phenomenon (Doná et al., 2000; Horla, 2004a; Öhr, 2003). It is obvious that due to not taking control signal constraints into account during the controller design stage, one can expect inferior performance because of infeasibility of computed control signals.

Many methods of anti-windup compensation are known from the single-input single-output framework, but a few work well enough in the case of multivariable systems (Horla, 2004a; Horla, 2004b; Horla, 2006a; Horla, 2006b; Horla, 2006c; Horla, 2007a; Horla, 2007b; Horla, 2007c; Horla, 2007d; Öhr, 2003; Peng et al., 1998; Walgama & Sternby, 1993). For multivariable systems have additional feature – windup phenomenon is tightly connected with directional change phenomenon in the control vector due to different implementations of constraints, affecting in this way the direction of the computed control vector. Even for a simple amplitude-constrained case, the constrained control vector $\underline{u}_t$ may have a different direction than a computed control vector $\underline{v}_t$. The situation is even more complicated for amplitude and rate-constrained system, where for additional requirements, e.g. keeping constant direction, there may be no appropriate control action to be taken (Horla, 2007d).

Apart from windup and directional change phenomena one can expect to obtain inferior performance because of problems with (dynamic) decoupling, especially when the plant does not have equal numbers of control signals and output signals (Albertos & Sala, 2004; Maciejowski, 1989). In such a case, control direction corresponds not only to input principal directions (or maximal directional gain of the transfer function matrix), but also to the degree of decoupling, and by altering it one achieve better decoupling (though not in all cases).

Directional change has been discussed in (Öhr, 2003; Walgama and Sternby, 1993), where the first description of the problemwas given, connections in between anti-windup compensation and directional change has been made. A review of multivariable anti-windup compensators has been included in (Horla, 2007b; Peng et al., 1998; Walgama & Sternby, 1993) with basic analysis of the topic.

Windup phenomenon (thus decoupling and directional change) are tightly connected with industrial applications are crucial when control laws are to be applied. Many papers treated application of anti-windup compensation (AWC) in areas as motor drives, paper machine headbox or hydraulic drives control. But they lack in understanding what is the connection in between directional change and AWC.

To recapitulate, when control limits are taken into consideration, the presence of windup phenomenon requires certain actions to compensate it, i.e., to retrieve the correspondence of the internal controller states with its (vector) output. Heuristic modifications feeding back to the controller the portion of controls changed by nonlinearity are performed by a posteriori antiwindup compensators and a priori AWCs enable windup phenomenon avoidance (i.e., a priori compensation) by generating feasible control actions only (Doná et al., 2000; Horla, 2006a; Horla, 2006b).

Having avoided generation of infeasible control actions one avoids windup phenomenon in a priori manner, and implicitly eliminates windup phenomenon that would inevitably take place had control limits not been taken into consideration first.

The chapter aims to focus on directional change issues (and, simultaneously, anti-windup compensation) in multivariable state-feedback controller with a priori anti-windup compensator for systems given in state-space form. The problem is presented through the framework of linear matrix inequalities (LMIs). Imposing only amplitude constraints on the control vector results in LMI conditions, but taking rate constraints into consideration results in nonsymmetric matrix inequality, that is transformed into LMI by making certain assumptions, as in (Horla, 2007a).

2. Control vector constraints and directional change

Let us suppose that amplitude constraints are imposed on the input signals of two-input plant. Depending on the method of imposing constraints one can observe directional change, illustrated in Fig. 1a in the case of cut-off saturation that is not present when saturation is performed according to imposed constraints (dashed lines) with *constant* direction, Fig. 1b.

The situation is more complicated when rate constraints are taken into consideration. Let $\mathcal{D}_\alpha$ denote the set of all feasible control vectors due to amplitude constraints and $\mathcal{D}_\beta$ denote the set of all feasible control vectors due to rate constraints. If $\mathcal{D}_\alpha \cap \mathcal{D}_\beta \neq 0$ than constrained

input vector is feasible. The aim is to constrain the control vector so that as much of its primal information is kept with minimum directional change (Horla, 2007c).
Let the computed control vector violate amplitude constraints and have the property that its amplitude-constrained companion does not violate rate constraints, i.e. $\underline{u}_t \in \mathscr{D}_\beta$ (see Fig. 2a). The necessary condition here for control direction to be preserved is as above, for such a case only two sets: a point $(\underline{u}_{1,t}, \underline{u}_{2,t})$ in the plane and $\mathscr{D}_\beta$ have a common part.

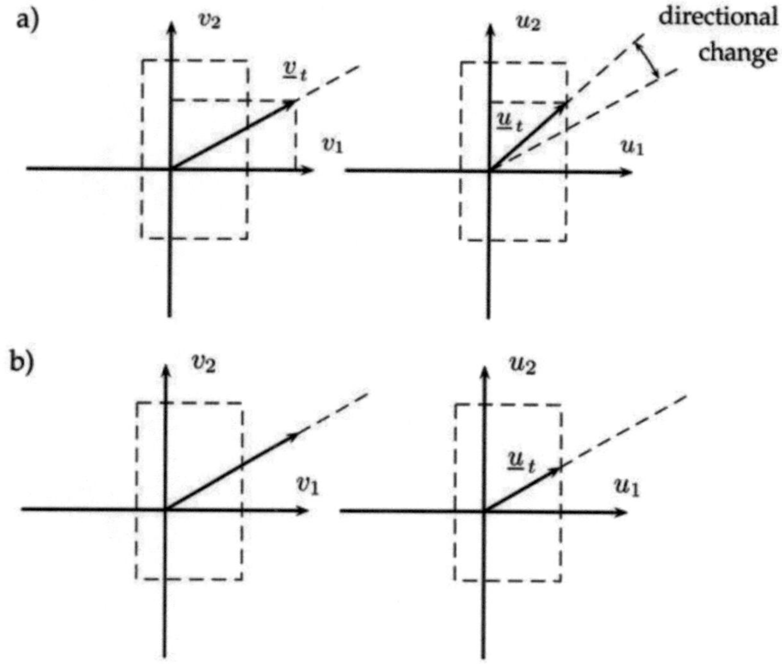

Fig. 1. a) direction-changing, b) direction-preserving saturation (left: control vector before saturation, right: after saturation)

When the point on the end of direction-preserved, amplitude-constrained, computed control vector and $\mathscr{D}_\beta$ do not have a common part, than it is impossible to generate feasible control actions with both amplitude and rate constraints imposed so that direction of the computed control vector is sustained. This is depicted in Figure 2b, where the only constrained control vector lies „as close as possible" to the computed control vector satisfies $\underline{u}_t \in \mathscr{D}_\alpha \cap \mathscr{D}_\beta$ and $\underline{u}_t \in b(\mathscr{D}_\beta)$ (boundary of $\mathscr{D}_\beta$). When rate constraints are violated, one has to treat them either as secondary constraints (to be omitted) or introduce soft rate constraints instead of hard rate constraints (Maciejowski, 1989).

3. Directional change phenomenon, an example

Let two-input two-output system be not coupled and both loops be driven by separate controllers (with no cross-coupling). The systemoutput y_t is to track reference vector comprising two sinusoid waves, what corresponds to drawing a circular shape in the (y_1, y_2) plane.

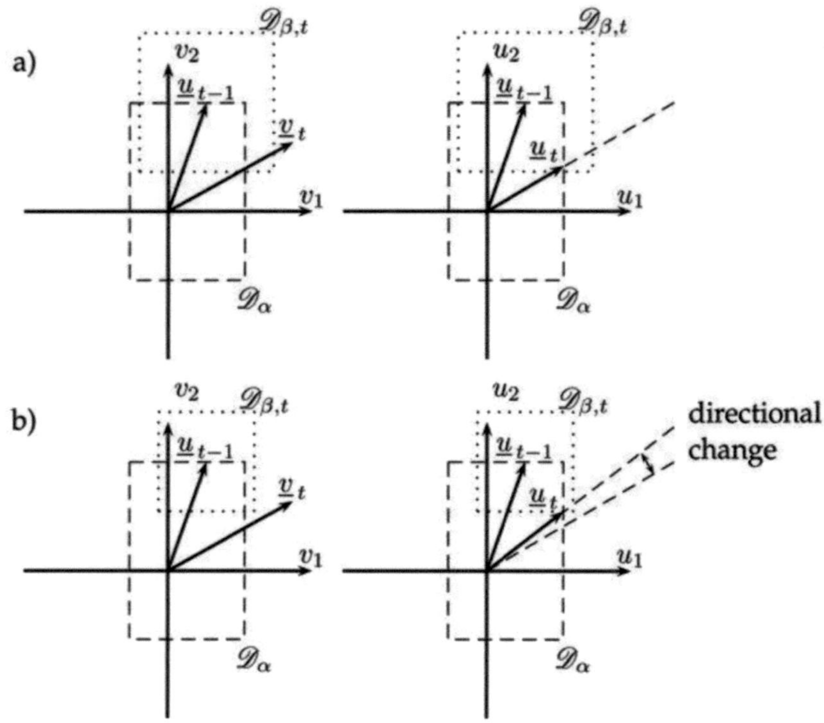

Fig. 2. a) direction-preserved saturation, b) saturation with directional change

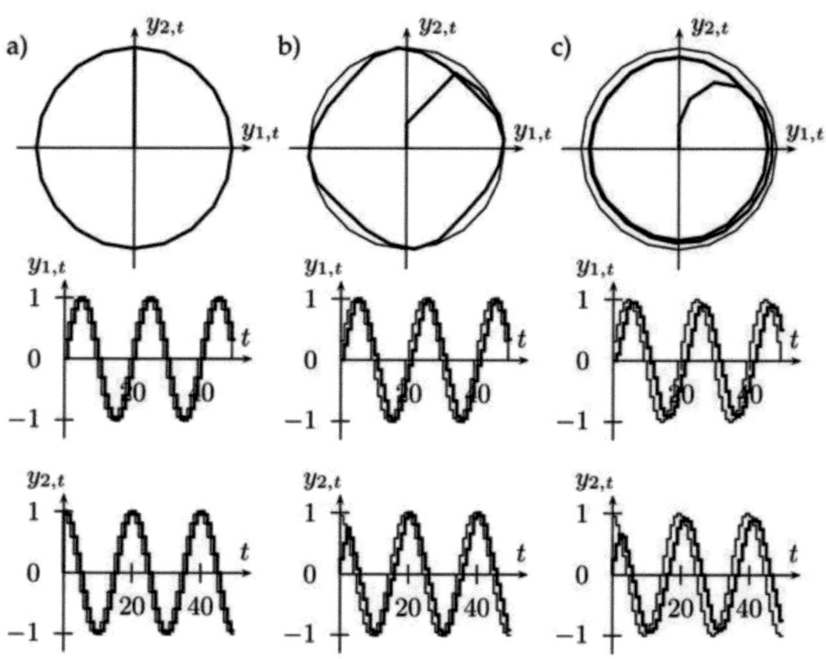

Fig. 3. a) unconstrained system, b) cut-off saturation, c) direction-preserving saturation

As it can be seen in the Fig. 3a, the unconstrained system performs best, whereas in the case of cut-off saturation imposed on both elements of control vector (Fig. 3b) the tracking performance is poor. This is because of directional change in controls that changes proportions between its components. In the application for, e.g., shape-cutting, performance of the system from Fig. 3c (direction-preserving saturation) is superior. Furthermore, in order to achieve such a performance the system must be perfectly decoupled at all times (Horla, 2007b; Öhr, 2003).

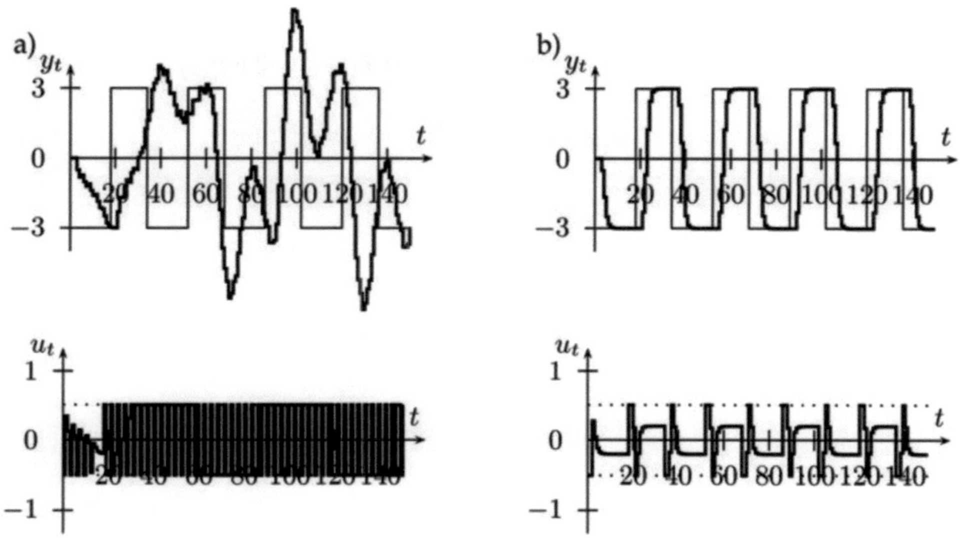

Fig. 4. results from closed-loop system a) without AWC, b) with AWC

4. Anti-windup compensation, an example

An example action of AWC is shown in Figure 4, where for hard constraints imposed on the control signal and pole-placement controller it is impossible to ensure tracking properties if windup phenomenon is left uncompensated. On the other hand, by performing compensation, the control signal is desaturated and is not prone to consecutive resaturations, operating in a period of time in a linear zone.

5. How to understand windup phenomenon in multivariable systems – literature remarks

The problem of windup phenomenon in multivariable systems with its connection to directional change in controls has rarely been addressed in the literature. The only valuable remark concerning directional change is in (Walgama and Sternby, 1993):

Solving the windup phenomenon problem does not mean that constrained control vector is of the same direction as computed control vector.

On the other hand, avoiding directional change in control enables one to avoid windup phenomenon.

In further parts of this chapter, it will be described where the latter description holds.

6. Considered plant model

The directional change issues are discussed for state-feedback control law that has been derived for shifted-input $\underline{u}_t^s \in \mathscr{R}^m$ and shifted-output $\underline{y}_t^s \in \mathscr{R}^p$ plant in the CARMA structure, taking into account the offset resulting from the current set-point vector for plants without integration (in a steady-state)

$$A(q^{-1})\underline{y}_t^s = B(q^{-1})\underline{u}_{t-d}^s, \tag{1}$$

represented in state-space representation for non-shifted (original) inputs and outputs:

$$\underline{x}_{t+1} = A\underline{x}_t + B\underline{u}_{t-d}, \tag{2}$$

$$\underline{y}_t = C\underline{x}_t, \tag{3}$$

with

$$A = \begin{bmatrix} -A_1 & I & \cdots & 0 \\ \cdots & \cdots & \cdots & 0 \\ -A_{n-1} & \cdots & \cdots & I \\ -A_n & \cdots & \cdots & 0 \end{bmatrix}, \tag{4}$$

$$B = [B_1^T, \dots, B_n^T]^T, \tag{5}$$

$$C = [I, 0, \dots, 0]^T ., \tag{6}$$

$$A(q^{-1}) = I + A_1 q^{-1} + \cdots + A_n q^{-n}, \tag{7}$$

$$B(q^{-1}) = B_1 + B_2 q^{-1} + \cdots + B_{n-1} q^{-n}. \tag{8}$$

The aim of state-feedback controller is to track a given reference vector $\underline{r}_t \in \mathscr{R}^p$ with plant output vector $\underline{y}_t^s$ minimising certain performance index. The offset previouslymentioned:

$$\underline{x}_t^s = \underline{x}_t + \underline{x}_\infty, \tag{9}$$

$$\underline{u}_t^s = \underline{u}_t + \underline{u}_\infty, \tag{10}$$

$$\underline{y}_t^s = \underline{y}_t + \underline{y}_\infty, \tag{11}$$

where for plants without integral terms

$$\underline{x}_\infty = (I - A)^{-1} B\underline{u}_\infty, \tag{12}$$

$$\underline{y}_{\infty} = \underline{r}_t, \quad (13)$$

with $\underline{u}_{\infty} \in \mathscr{R}^m$ being the control vector value assuring tracking in steady state, i.e.

$$\boldsymbol{A}(1)\underline{r}_t = \boldsymbol{B}(1)\underline{u}_{\infty}. \quad (14)$$

For plants comprising integral terms there is no need to shift states because $\underline{u}_{\infty} \neq \underline{0}$ holds. In the case of $m \neq p$, the control vector offset results from (14) by means of pseudoinverse.
The considered state-feedback controller enables one to constrain the part of $\underline{u}_t$ which is related to the answer of the plant to non-zero initial conditions at instant t, which subsequently corresponds to the current values of reference vector. In other words, it enables constraining the absolute value of the elements of $\underline{u}_t^s$ that are above absolute value of $\underline{u}_{\infty}$.
In order to fully analyze the directional change phenomenon interplay with AWC, rate vector constraints $\Delta \underline{u}_t = \underline{u}_t - \underline{u}_{t-1}$ are also to be taken into account here (Horla, 2007c; Horla, 2007a).

7. State-feedback controller

At each time instant the optimal state-feedback matrix is generated (Horla, 2006b)

$$\boldsymbol{F}_t^{\star} : J_t(\boldsymbol{F}_t^{\star}) = \inf_{\boldsymbol{F}_t \in \mathscr{D}(J_t)} \{J_t(\boldsymbol{F}_t)\}, \quad (15)$$

assuming that $\underline{r}_t$ is of constant value $\underline{r}$, $\underline{u}_t = \boldsymbol{F}_t \underline{x}_t$, state vector is perfectly measured and constraints are imposed on the control vector. The set $\mathscr{D}$ denotes all $\boldsymbol{F}_s$, for which the performance index J_t is of finite value.
At each time instant the optimisation procedure of $\boldsymbol{F}_t^{\star}$ is performed for current values of reference vector, and at the next instant the procedure is repeated again.
The performance index

$$J_t = \sum_{i=t}^{\infty} \left(\|\underline{x}_i\|^2_{\boldsymbol{Q}_1} + \|\underline{u}_i\|^2_{\boldsymbol{R}_1} \right), \quad (16)$$

is a quadratic function and is minimised subject to $\boldsymbol{F}_t$, with state-feedback control law $\underline{u}_t = \boldsymbol{F}_t \underline{x}_t$. As it has been already said, plant state is fully accessible (if not, one can perform estimation on the basis of the separation theorem).
In order to minimise the performance index (16), its upper bound is to be found. Let the following Lyapunov function be given

$$V(\underline{x}_t) = \underline{x}_t^T \boldsymbol{P} \underline{x}_t, \quad (17)$$

with positive definite $\boldsymbol{P} > 0$, and $V(\underline{0}) = 0$. Having assumed that at each time instant t holds

$$V(\underline{x}_{t+1}) - V(\underline{x}_t) \leqslant -\left(\underline{x}_t^T \boldsymbol{Q}_1 \underline{x}_t + \underline{u}_t^T \boldsymbol{R}_1 \underline{u}_t \right), \quad (18)$$

which left - and right-hand side sum from $t = t$ to $t = \infty$ satisfies

$$-V(\underline{x}_t) \leqslant -J_t\,, \tag{19}$$

the performance index (16) is bounded from above with

$$J_t \leqslant V(\underline{x}_t)\,, \tag{20}$$

from where using (17) one obtains

$$J_t \leqslant \underline{x}_t^T \boldsymbol{P} \underline{x}_t\,. \tag{21}$$

Minimisation of the quadratic form $\underline{x}_t^T\ \boldsymbol{P}\ \underline{x}_t$, with $\boldsymbol{P} > 0$, on the basis of Schur complement for $\underline{x}_t^T\ \boldsymbol{P}\underline{x}_t \leq \gamma$ is equivalent to linear matrix inequality (LMI) (Boyd et al., 1994; Boyd and Vandenberghe, 2004)

$$\begin{aligned} &\min\ \gamma \\ &\text{s.t.}\ \begin{bmatrix} 1 & \star \\ \underline{x}_t & \boldsymbol{Q} \end{bmatrix} \geqslant 0 \end{aligned} \tag{22}$$

for $\gamma > 0$ and $\boldsymbol{Q} = \gamma \boldsymbol{P}^{-1}$.
Having substituted (17) into (18)

$$\underline{x}_{t+1}^T \boldsymbol{P} \underline{x}_{t+1} - \underline{x}_t^T \boldsymbol{P} \underline{x}_t \leqslant -\left(\underline{x}_t^T \boldsymbol{Q}_1 \underline{x}_t + \underline{u}_t^T \boldsymbol{R}_1 \underline{u}_t\right)\,, \tag{23}$$

using (2), and putting $\underline{u}_t = \boldsymbol{F}\,\underline{x}_t$ one can write

$$((\boldsymbol{A}+\boldsymbol{B}\boldsymbol{F})\underline{x}_t)^T \boldsymbol{P}\,((\boldsymbol{A}+\boldsymbol{B}\boldsymbol{F})\underline{x}_t) - \underline{x}_t^T \boldsymbol{P}\underline{x}_t + \underline{x}_t^T \boldsymbol{Q}_1 \underline{x}_t + (\boldsymbol{F}\underline{x}_t)^T \boldsymbol{R}_1\,(\boldsymbol{F}\underline{x}_t) \leqslant 0 \tag{24}$$

which negative-definiteness is equivalent to

$$(\boldsymbol{A}+\boldsymbol{B}\boldsymbol{F})^T \boldsymbol{P}\,(\boldsymbol{A}+\boldsymbol{B}\boldsymbol{F}) - \boldsymbol{P} + \boldsymbol{F}^T \boldsymbol{R}_1 \boldsymbol{F} + \boldsymbol{Q}_1 \leqslant 0\,. \tag{25}$$

Putting $\boldsymbol{P} = \gamma \boldsymbol{Q}^{-1}$ post- and pre-multiplying with $\boldsymbol{Q}^T$ and $\boldsymbol{Q}$, and putting $\boldsymbol{Y} = \boldsymbol{F}\boldsymbol{Q}$, the inequality can be rewritten as

$$\boldsymbol{Q} - \frac{1}{\gamma}\boldsymbol{Y}^T \boldsymbol{R}_1 \boldsymbol{Y} - \frac{1}{\gamma}\boldsymbol{Q}^T \boldsymbol{Q}_1 \boldsymbol{Q} - (\boldsymbol{A}\boldsymbol{Q}+\boldsymbol{B}\boldsymbol{Y})^T \boldsymbol{Q}^{-1} (\boldsymbol{A}\boldsymbol{Q}+\boldsymbol{B}\boldsymbol{Y}) \geqslant 0\,. \tag{26}$$

Applying the Schur complement again one obtains

$$\begin{aligned} &\begin{bmatrix} \boldsymbol{Q} - \frac{1}{\gamma}\boldsymbol{Y}^T \boldsymbol{R}_1 \boldsymbol{Y} - \frac{1}{\gamma}\boldsymbol{Q}^T \boldsymbol{Q}_1 \boldsymbol{Q} & \star \\ \boldsymbol{A}\boldsymbol{Q}+\boldsymbol{B}\boldsymbol{Y} & \boldsymbol{Q} \end{bmatrix} \geqslant 0\,, \\ &\begin{bmatrix} \boldsymbol{Q} & \star \\ \boldsymbol{A}\boldsymbol{Q}+\boldsymbol{B}\boldsymbol{Y} & \boldsymbol{Q} \end{bmatrix} - \frac{1}{\gamma}\begin{bmatrix} \boldsymbol{Q}^T \boldsymbol{Q}_1 \boldsymbol{Q} + \boldsymbol{Y}^T \boldsymbol{R}_1 \boldsymbol{Y} & \star \\ 0 & 0 \end{bmatrix} = \\ &= \begin{bmatrix} \boldsymbol{Q} & \star \\ \boldsymbol{A}\boldsymbol{Q}+\boldsymbol{B}\boldsymbol{Y} & \boldsymbol{Q} \end{bmatrix} - \frac{1}{\gamma}\begin{bmatrix} \boldsymbol{Q}^T \boldsymbol{Q}_1^{1/2} & \boldsymbol{Y}^T \boldsymbol{R}_1^{1/2} \\ 0 & 0 \end{bmatrix}\begin{bmatrix} \boldsymbol{Q}_1^{1/2}\boldsymbol{Q} & 0 \\ \boldsymbol{R}_1^{1/2}\boldsymbol{Y} & 0 \end{bmatrix} = \\ &= \begin{bmatrix} \boldsymbol{Q} & \star \\ \boldsymbol{A}\boldsymbol{Q}+\boldsymbol{B}\boldsymbol{Y} & \boldsymbol{Q} \end{bmatrix} - \begin{bmatrix} \boldsymbol{Q}^T \boldsymbol{Q}_1^{1/2} & \boldsymbol{Y}^T \boldsymbol{R}_1^{1/2} \\ 0 & 0 \end{bmatrix}\begin{bmatrix} \gamma \boldsymbol{I} & 0 \\ 0 & \gamma \boldsymbol{I} \end{bmatrix}^{-1}\begin{bmatrix} \boldsymbol{Q}_1^{1/2}\boldsymbol{Q} & 0 \\ \boldsymbol{R}_1^{1/2}\boldsymbol{Y} & 0 \end{bmatrix} \geqslant 0\,. \end{aligned} \tag{27}$$

Having applied the Schur complement again, the optimal control law minimising (17) is given as

$$\underline{u}_t = F_t \underline{x}_t, \tag{28}$$

with (time index has been omitted)

$$F = YQ^{-1}, \tag{29}$$

where $Q > 0$ and Y are solutions of

$$\min \quad \gamma \tag{30}$$

$$\text{s.t.} \quad \begin{bmatrix} 1 & \star \\ \underline{x}_t & Q \end{bmatrix} \geqslant 0, \tag{31}$$

$$\begin{bmatrix} Q & \star & \star & \star \\ AQ+BY & Q & \star & \star \\ Q_1^{1/2}Q & 0 & \gamma I & \star \\ R_1^{1/2}Y & 0 & 0 & \gamma I \end{bmatrix} \geqslant 0. \tag{32}$$

One can also take symmetrical control vector constraints into account. Let

$$\|\underline{u}_t\|_{\max} = \max_i |u_{t,i}|,$$

$1 \leq i \leq m$, with $\underline{u}_t \in \mathscr{R}^m$. If there exist γ, Q, Y, satisfying (30)–(32), than there holds

$$\|\underline{x}_t\| \leqslant \rho,$$

and every state $\|\underline{x}_{t+j}\| \leqslant \rho \ (j > 0)$ lies inside the invariant ellipsoid $\varepsilon_P = \{\underline{z} : \|\underline{z}\|_P \leqslant \rho\}$, with $\rho = \|\underline{x}_t\|_P$ for invariant reference vector (Horla, 2007a; Horla, 2006b).

Imposing symmetrical constraints on amplitudes of elements of $\underline{u}_t$ is equivalent to imposing constraints on

$$\|\underline{u}_t\|_{\max} = \|F\underline{x}_t\|_{\max} = \|YQ^{-1}\underline{x}_t\|_{\max} \leqslant \max_{\underline{x}\in\varepsilon} \|YQ^{-1}\underline{x}\|_{\max}, \tag{33}$$

or

$$\|\underline{u}_t\|_{\max} \leqslant \max_{\underline{x}\in\varepsilon} \|YQ^{-1}\underline{x}\|_{\max} = \max_i (YQ^{-1}Y^T)_{ii}. \tag{34}$$

Than imposing different constraints on each of the elements of control vector is equivalent to LMI

$$\begin{bmatrix} \Lambda_\alpha & \star \\ Y^T & Q \end{bmatrix} \geqslant 0, \tag{35}$$

Where $\Lambda_\alpha = \text{diag}\{\alpha_1^2, \ldots, \alpha_m^2\}$ is a diagonal matrix comprising squares of amplitude constraints of $u_{1,t}, \ldots, u_{m,t}$ on its diagonal.

The amplitudes of elements of the control vector $\underline{u}_t$ are constrained if the above LMI is added to the set of LMIs (30)–(32).
The presented state-feedback control law stabilises the closed-loop system, guaranteed by the existence of invariant ellipsoid describing $V(\underline{x}_t)$ with fully known plant and constant reference vector.
In a similar manner, one can impose rate of changes constraints. If $\underline{x}_t \approx \underline{x}_{t-1}$ is a state-vector of approximately constant value, or in a steady-state, than

$$\Delta\underline{u}_t = \boldsymbol{F}\underline{x}_t - \boldsymbol{F}_{t-1}\underline{x}_{t-1} = (\boldsymbol{F} - \boldsymbol{F}_{t-1})\underline{x}_t, \tag{36}$$

where $\boldsymbol{F}_{t-1}$ is a matrix computed at previous sample and $\boldsymbol{F}$ is the sought matrix computed at the current time instant.
As it has been stated in (Horla, 2007a), imposing symmetrical constraints on rates of elements of $\underline{u}_t$ is equivalent to imposing constraints on

$$\|\Delta\underline{u}_t\|_{\max} \leqslant \max_{\underline{x}\in\varepsilon} \|(\boldsymbol{Y}\boldsymbol{Q}^{-1} - \boldsymbol{F}_{t-1})\underline{x}\|_{\max}, = \max_i (\boldsymbol{Y}\boldsymbol{Q}^{-1}\boldsymbol{Y}^T - \boldsymbol{F}^\star)_{ii} \tag{37}$$

where $\boldsymbol{F}^\star = \boldsymbol{F}_{t-1}\boldsymbol{Y}^T$ should be a symmetrical matrix.
Assuming that $\boldsymbol{F}_{t-1}\boldsymbol{Y}^T = \boldsymbol{F}_{t-1}\boldsymbol{Y}_{t-1}^T$ hold, one can obtain approximate rough rate constraint as

$$\|\Delta\underline{u}_t\|_{\max} \leqslant \max_i (\boldsymbol{Y}\boldsymbol{Q}^{-1}\boldsymbol{Y}^T - \boldsymbol{F}_{t-1}\boldsymbol{Y}_{t-1}^T)_{ii}, \tag{38}$$

or as LMI

$$\begin{bmatrix} \boldsymbol{\Lambda}_\beta + \boldsymbol{F}_{t-1}\boldsymbol{Y}_{t-1}^T & \star \\ \boldsymbol{Y}^T & \boldsymbol{Q} \end{bmatrix} \geqslant 0, \tag{39}$$

where $\boldsymbol{\Lambda}_\beta = \mathrm{diag}\{\beta_1^2, \ldots, \beta_m^2\}$ is a diagonal matrix comprising squares of rate constraints of $u_{1,t}, \ldots, u_{m,t}$ on its diagonal.
The rates of elements of the control vector $\underline{u}_t$ are constrained if the above LMI is added to the set of LMIs (30)–(32).

8. Performance index, evaluation of directional change

Evaluation of control performance that is coupled with anti-windup compensation requires following indices to be introduced:

$$J_1 = \frac{1}{N}\sum_{i=1}^{p}\sum_{t=1}^{N} |r_{i,t} - y_{i,t}|, \tag{40}$$

$$J_2 = \frac{1}{N}\sum_{i=1}^{p}\sum_{t=1}^{N} (r_{i,t} - y_{i,t})^2, \tag{41}$$

$$\overline{\varphi}_1 = \frac{1}{N}\sum_{t=1}^{N} |\varphi(\underline{v}_t) - \varphi(\underline{u}_t)| \quad [^\circ], \tag{42}$$

$$\overline{\varphi}_2 = \frac{1}{N}\sum_{t=1}^{N}(\varphi(\underline{v}_t) - \varphi(\underline{u}_t))^2, \tag{43}$$

where (40) corresponds to mean absolute tracking error of p outputs, (42) is a mean absolute direction change in between computed and constrained control vector, and φ denotes angle measure. In the case of m = 3, φ corresponds to absolute angle measure (in which case there is no need to decide its direction).

9. Plant models for simulation studies

The considered plants are taken with delay d = 1 and are cross-coupled (values of control offset have been given for reference signals of amplitude 3, where in the case of P3 the last amplitude of reference signal is zero):

- P1 (m = 2, p = 2)

$$\boldsymbol{A} = \left[\begin{array}{cc|c} -0.80 & 0.10 & \\ -0.40 & 1.00 & \boldsymbol{I} \\ \hline 0.49 & 0.10 & \\ -0.10 & -0.25 & \boldsymbol{0} \end{array}\right], \boldsymbol{B} = \begin{bmatrix} 1.0 & 0.3 \\ 0.5 & 0.8 \\ 0.0 & 0.0 \\ 0.0 & 0.0 \end{bmatrix}.$$

- P2 (m = 3, p = 2)

$$\boldsymbol{A} = \left[\begin{array}{cc|c} -0.80 & 0.10 & \\ -0.40 & 1.00 & \boldsymbol{I} \\ \hline 0.49 & 0.10 & \\ -0.10 & -0.25 & \boldsymbol{0} \end{array}\right], \boldsymbol{B} = \begin{bmatrix} 1.0 & 0.2 & 0.3 \\ 0.5 & 0.3 & 0.8 \\ 0.0 & 0.0 & 0.0 \\ 0.0 & 0.0 & 0.0 \end{bmatrix}.$$

- P3 (m = 2, p = 3)

$$\boldsymbol{A} = \left[\begin{array}{ccc|c} 0.7 & 0.0 & -0.1 & \\ 0.1 & 0.8 & -0.2 & \boldsymbol{I} \\ -0.1 & 0.0 & 0.8 & \\ \hline 0.1 & 0.0 & 0.0 & \\ 0.0 & -0.1 & 0.0 & \boldsymbol{0} \\ 0.0 & 0.0 & -0.5 & \end{array}\right], \boldsymbol{B} = \begin{bmatrix} 1.0 & 0.1 \\ 0.2 & 1.0 \\ 0.5 & -0.1 \\ 0.0 & 0.0 \\ 0.0 & 0.0 \\ 0.0 & 0.0 \end{bmatrix}.$$

10. Simulation studies

The performed simulations present anti-windup compensation performance for three different plants and hard constraints imposed on the components of the control vector.

There are two systems simulated and depicted in the Figure 5, namely systemwith amplitude constraints only and with added rate constraints, clipping only a part of the rates of changes in order to enable a comparison. From Table 1 it is visible that for this case of system with equal number of inputs and outputs, thus possible for dynamic decouplingwith time-varying state-feedback control law, introducing additional constraints causes performance indices to increase (i.e. there is more windup phenomenon in the system) and, simultaneously it causes more severe directional change.

This is because of the fact that one-step-ahead cannot foresee future changes of reference signals, nor can assure perfect decoupling. Since imposed constraints alter the direction of unconstrained control vector, directional change is necessary to alter the coupling in the system, in order to achieve better control performance.

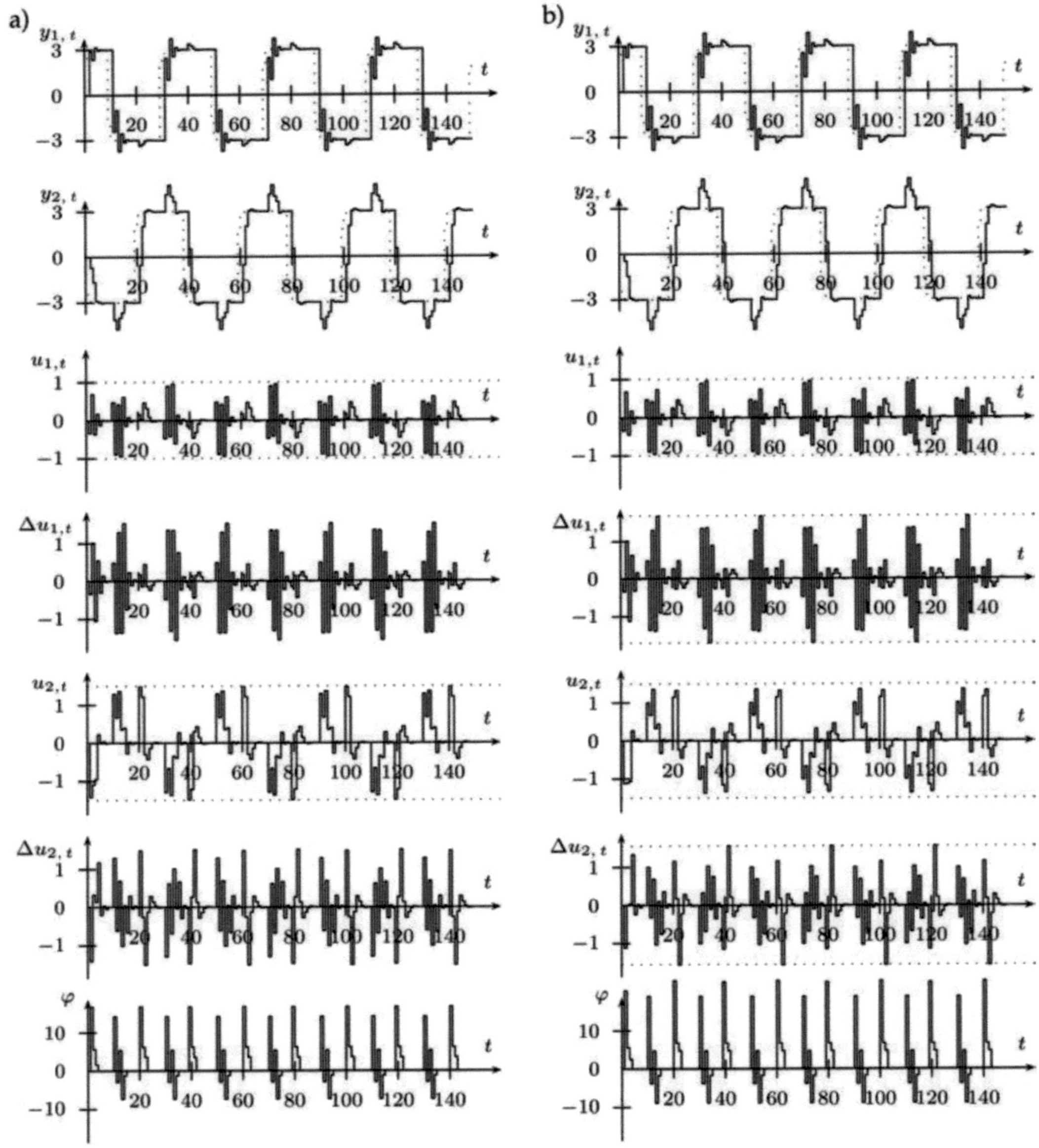

Fig. 5. P1: a) $\alpha_1 = 1.0$, $\alpha_2 = 1.5$, $\beta_1 = \beta_2 = \infty$, b) $\alpha_1 = 1.0$, $\alpha_2 = 1.5$, $\beta_1 = 1.7$, $\beta_2 = 1.5$)

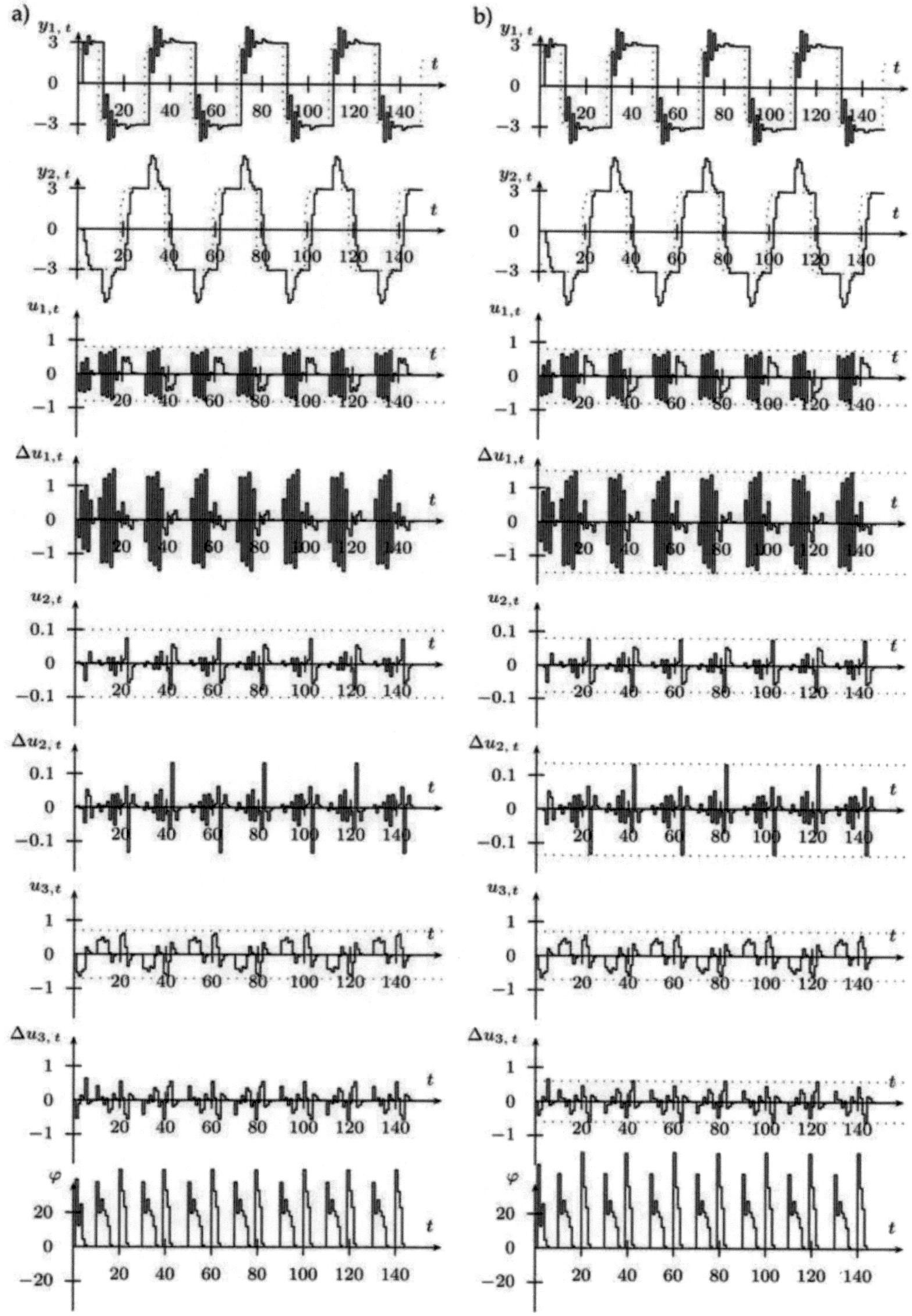

Fig. 6. P2: a) $\alpha_1 = 0.8$, $\alpha_2 = 0.1$, $\alpha_3 = 0.7$, $\beta_1 = \beta_2 = \beta_3 = \infty$, b) $\alpha_1 = 0.8$, $\alpha_2 = 0.1$, $\alpha_3 = 0.7$, $\beta_1 = 1.5$, $\beta_2 = 0.14$, $\beta_3 = 0.6$)

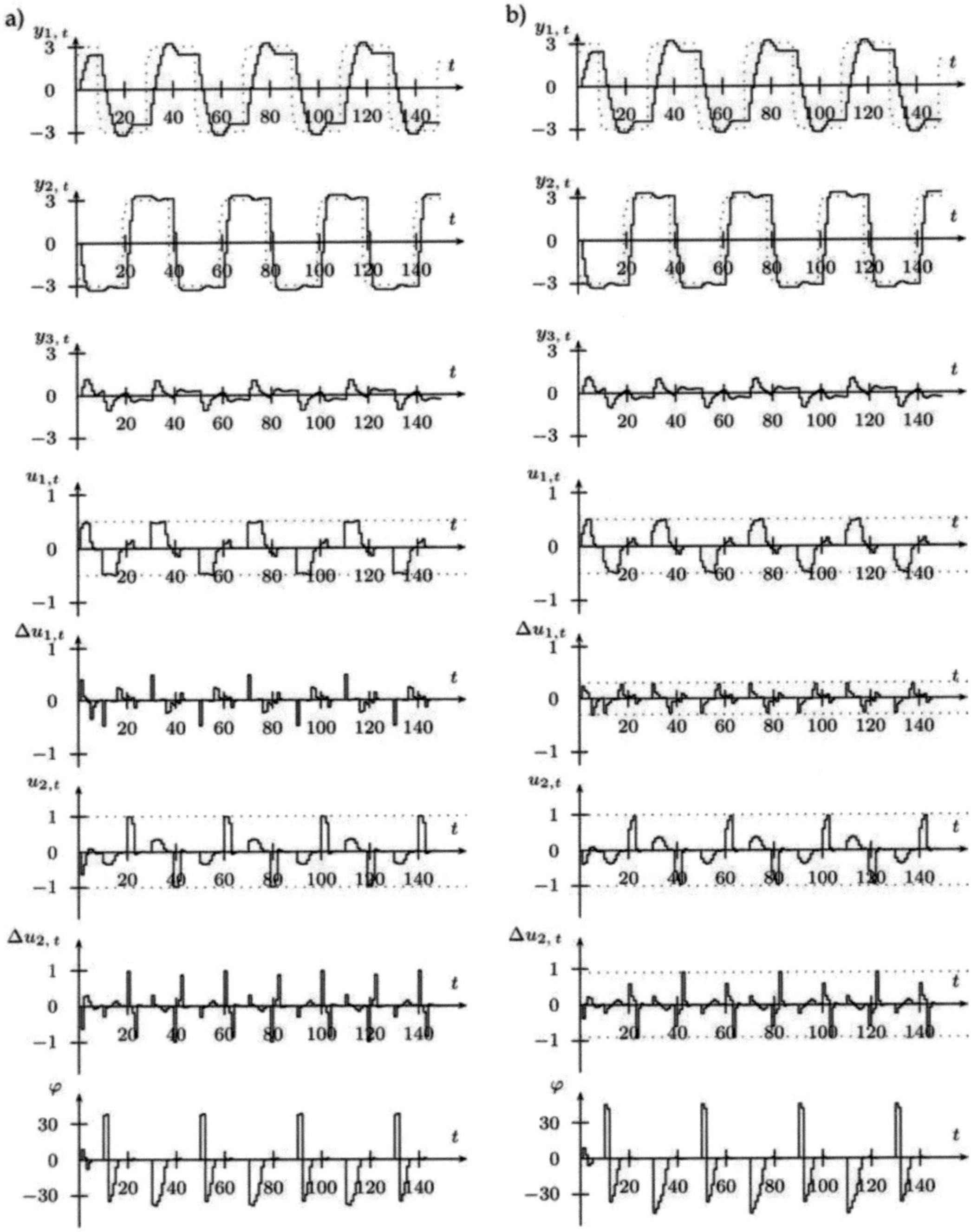

Fig. 7. P3: a) $\alpha_1 = 1.0$, $\alpha_2 = 1.5$, $\beta_1 = \beta_2 = \infty$, b) $\alpha_1 = 1.0$, $\alpha_2 = 1.5$, $\beta_1 = 0.3$, $\beta_2 = 0.9$)

P1a	$i=1$	$i=2$
J_{i1}	2.0997	5.0601
J_{i2}	2.2919	5.9127
J_i	4.3916	10.9728

P2a	$i=1$	$i=2$
J_{i1}	2.1408	5.3081
J_{i2}	2.4300	7.0549
J_i	4.5708	12.3630

P3a	$i=1$	$i=2$
J_{i1}	1.6947	3.4929
J_{i2}	2.2419	5.5571
J_{i3}	0.3613	0.2092
J_i	4.2979	9.2592

P1b	$i=1$	$i=2$
J_{i1}	2.1103	5.1055
J_{i2}	2.3239	6.1269
J_i	4.4342	11.2324

P2b	$i=1$	$i=2$
J_{i1}	2.1386	5.3000
J_{i2}	2.4353	7.1140
J_i	4.5739	12.4140

P3b	$i=1$	$i=2$
J_{i1}	1.7133	3.5442
J_{i2}	2.2101	5.5040
J_{i3}	0.3548	0.1982
J_i	4.2782	9.2464

	P1a	P2a	P3a
$\overline{\varphi}_1$	2.8383	11.7238	7.9377
$\overline{\varphi}_2$	31.2958	347.2096	250.0595

	P1b	P2b	P3b
$\overline{\varphi}_1$	3.5644	12.7296	8.8754
$\overline{\varphi}_2$	52.9696	434.2473	310.9078

Table 1. Performance indices: a) without, b) with rate constraints

In the case of plant with greater number of control inputs than plant outputs (P2), Figure 6, it is visible that in comparison with P1 the directional change is more severe, because of three components of control vector changing in time. There are more degrees or freedom (ways in which control vector may very in time, it varies in space to be exact, instead as previously in plane), thus it is necessary to alter its direction in order to improve decoupling. Once again performance indexes tend to increase with rate constraints added.

For the last plant considered, P3, it is obvious that since the number of control inputs is deficient in comparison with plant outputs, direction of control vector corresponds to good tracking performance, thus having introduced rate constraints it should not be altered excessively. By comparison of directional change indices and performance indices for P3 it is visible that by introducing rate constraints one can avoid bumps in control signals, what leads to better tracking.

11. Concluding remarks

Solving the windup phenomenon problem does not have to mean that constrained control vector is of the same direction as computed control vector if cross-coupling is present in the control system. The presented state-feedback control law by avoiding generation of infeasible control actions compensated windup phenomenon in a priori manner, though as it can be seen, directional change is present in the system in order to assure better decoupling.

On the other hand, avoiding directional change in control enables one to avoid windup phenomenon if and only in the plant is perfectly decoupled or is not coupled at all. The latter due to the constraints is hardly ever met, and if the application of some control law does no require to preserve direction of control vector (what might correspond to, e.g., keeping proportions in between control signals), one should allow directional change to take place. This will both improve anti-windup compensation performance and plant decoupling.

12. References

Albertos, P. and Sala, A. (2004). *Multivariable Control Systems.* Springer-Verlag, London, United Kingdom.

Boyd, S., Ghaoui, L. E., Feron, E., and Balakrishnan, V. (1994). *Linear Matrix Inequalities in System and Control Theory.* Society for Industrial and AppliedMathematics, Philadelphia, United States of America, 3rd edition.

Boyd, S. and Vandenberghe, L. (2004). *Convex Optimization.* Cambridge University Press, United Kingdom.

Doná, J. D., Goodwin, G., and Seron, M. (2000). Anti-windup and model predictive control: Reflections and connections. *European Journal of Control,* 6(5):455–465.

Horla, D. (2004a). Anti-windup compensators (in Polish). *Studies in Automation and Information Technology,* 28/29:35–52.

Horla, D. (2004b). Direction alteration of control vector and anti-windup compensation for multivariable systems (in Polish). *Studies in Automation and Information Technology,* 28/29:53–68.

Horla, D. (2006a). LMI-based multivariable adaptive predictive controller with anti-windup compensator. In *Proceedings of the 12th IEEE International Conference MMAR,* pages 459- 462, Miedzyzdroje.

Horla, D. (2006b). Multivariable state-feedback control with windup phenomenon avoidance. In *Proceedings of the 18th ICSS,* pages 143–146, Coventry.

Horla, D. (2006c). Standard vs. LMI approach to a convex optimisation problem in multivariable predictive control task with a priori anti-windup compensator. In *Proceedings of the 18th ICSS,* pages 147–152, Coventry.

Horla, D. (2007a). Close-to-optimal adaptive multivariable state-feedback controller with a priori anti-windup compensator. In *Proceedings of the 13th IEEE IFAC International Conference on Methods and Models in Automation and Robotics,* pages 363–368, Szczecin.

Horla, D. (2007b). Directional change and windup phenomenon. In *Proceedings of the 4th IFAC International Conference on Informatics in Control Automation and Robotics,* pages CD-ROM, Angers, France.

Horla, D. (2007c). Directional change for rate-constrained systems with anti-windup compensation. In *Proceedings of the 16th International Conference on Systems Science,* volume 1, pages 122–131, Wrocław.

Horla, D. (2007d). Optimised conditioning technique for a priori anti-windup compensation. In *Proceedings of the 16th International Conference on Systems Science,* pages 132–139, Wrocław, Poland.

Maciejowski, J. (1989). *Multivariable Feedback Design.* Addison-Wesley Publishing Company, Cambridge, United Kingdom.

Öhr, J. (2003). *Anti-windup and Control of Systems withMultiple Input Saturations: Tools, Solution and Case Studies.* PhD thesis, Uppsala University, Uppsala, Sweden.

Peng, Y., Vranˇci´c, D., Hanus, R., and Weller, S. (1998). Anti-windup designs for multivariable controllers. *Automatica,* 34(12):1559–1565.

Walgama, K. and Sternby, J. (1993). Contidioning technique for multiinput multioutput processes with input saturation. *IEE Proceedings-D,* 140(4):231–241.

21

A Smith Factorization Approach to Robust Minimum Variance Control of Nonsquare LTI MIMO Systems

Wojciech P. Hunek and Krzysztof J. Latawiec
Institute of Control and Computer Engineering
Department of Electrical, Control and Computer Engineering
Opole University of Technology
Poland

1. Introduction

The minimum phase systems have ultimately been redefined for LTI discrete-time systems, at first SISO and later square MIMO ones, as those systems for which minimum variance control (MVC) is asymptotically stable, or in other words those systems who have 'stable' zeros, or at last as 'stably invertible' systems. The redefinition has soon been extended to nonsquare discrete-time LTI MIMO systems (Latawiec, 1998; Latawiec et al., 2000) and finally to nonsquare continuous-time systems (Hunek, 2003; Latawiec & Hunek, 2002), giving rise to defining of new 'multivariable' zeros, i.e. the so-called control zeros. Control zeros are an intriguing extension of transmission zeros for nonsquare LTI MIMO systems. Like for SISO and square MIMO systems, control zeros are related to the stabilizing potential of MVC, and, in the input-output modeling framework considered, are generated by (poles of) a generalized inverse of the 'numerator' polynomial matrix $B(.)$. Originally, the unique, so-called T-inverse, being the minimum-norm right or least-squares left inverse involving the regular (rather than conjugated) transpose of the polynomial matrix, was employed in the specific case of full normal rank systems (Hunek, 2002; Latawiec, 2004). The associated control zeros were later called by the authors 'control zeros type 1' (Latawiec, 2004; Latawiec et al., 2004), as opposed to an infinite number of 'control zeros type 2' generated by the myriad of possible polynomial matrix inverses, even those called τ- and σ-inverses also involving the unique minimum-norm or least-squares inverses (Latawiec, 2004; Latawiec et al., 2005b). Transmission zeros, if any, are included in the set of control zeros; still, we will discriminate between control zeros and transmission zeros. In the later, new 'inverse-free' MVC design approach based on the extreme points and extreme directions method (Hunek, 2007; Hunek & Latawiec, 2006), it was possible to design a pole-free inverse of the polynomial matrix $B(.)$ so that no control zeros did appear. Well, except when transmission zeros are present, in which case the extreme points and extreme directions method does not hold. In the current important result of the authors, the Smith factorization of the polynomial matrix $B(.)$ can lead to its pole-free inverse, when there are no transmission zeros. Well, provided that the applied inverse is just the T-inverse, the intriguing result bringing us back to the origin of the introduction of control zeros. And in case of any other inverse of Smith-factorized $B(.)$ we end up with control zeros.

The remainder of this paper is organized as follows. System representations are reviewed in Section 2. Section 3 presents the problem of minimum variance control for discrete-time LTI MIMO systems. Section 4 describes the new approach to MVC design, confirming the Davison's theory of minimum phase systems and indicates the role of the control zeros in robust MVC-related designs. A simple simulation example of Section 5 indicates favorable properties of the new method in terms of its contribution to robust MVC design. New results of the paper are summarized in the conclusions of Section 6.

2. System representations

Consider an n_u-input n_y-output LTI discrete- or continuous-time system with the input $u(t)$ and the output $y(t)$, described by possibly rectangular transfer-function matrix $G \in \mathbf{R}^{n_y \times n_u}(p)$ in the complex operator p, where $p = z$ or $p = s$ for discrete-time or continuous-time systems, respectively. The transfer function matrix can be represented in the *matrix fraction description* (MFD) form $G(p) = A^{-1}(p)B(p)$, where the left coprime polynomial matrices $A \in \mathbf{R}^{n_y \times n_y}[p]$ and $B \in \mathbf{R}^{n_y \times n_u}[p]$ can be given in form $A(p) = p^n I + ... + a_n$ and $B(p) = p^m b_0 + ... + b_m$, respectively, where n and m are the orders of the respective matrix polynomials. An alternative MFD form $G(p) = \widetilde{B}(p)\widetilde{A}^{-1}(p)$, involving right coprime $\widetilde{A} \in \mathbf{R}^{n_y \times n_y}[p]$ and $\widetilde{B} \in \mathbf{R}^{n_u \times n_y}[p]$, is also tractable here but in a less convenient way (Latawiec, 1998). Algorithms for calculation of the MFDs are known (Rosenbrock, 1970; Wolowich, 1974) and software packages in the MATLAB's Polynomial Toolbox® are available. Unless necessary, we will not discriminate between $\underline{A}(p^{-1}) = I + ... + \underline{a}_n p^{-n}$ and $A(p) = p^n \underline{A}(p^{-1})$, nor between $\underline{B}(p^{-1}) = \underline{b}_0 + ... + \underline{b}_m p^{-m}$ and $B(p) = p^m \underline{B}(p^{-1})$. In the sequel, we will assume for clarity that $B(p)$ is of full normal rank; a more general case of $B(p)$ being of non-full normal rank can be easily tractable (Latawiec, 1998). Let us finally concentrate on the case when normal rank of $B(p)$ is n_y ('symmetrical' considerations can be made for normal rank n_u). Now, for discrete-time systems we have $\underline{A}(z^{-1}) = z^{-n}A(z) = I + ... + \underline{a}_n z^{-n}$ and $\underline{B}(z^{-1}) = z^{-m}B(z) = \underline{b}_0 + ... + \underline{b}_m z^{-m}$, with $G(z) = A^{-1}(z)B(z) = = z^{-d}\underline{A}^{-1}(z^{-1})\underline{B}(z^{-1})$, where $d = n - m$ is the time delay of the system. The analyzed MFD form can be directly obtained from the AR(I)X/AR(I)MAX model of a system $\underline{A}(q^{-1})y(t) = = q^{-d}\underline{B}(q^{-1})u(t) + [\underline{C}(q^{-1})/\underline{D}(q^{-1})]v(t)$, where q^{-1} is the backward shift operator, $y(t) \in \mathbf{R}^{n_y}$, $u(t) \in \mathbf{R}^{n_u}$ and $v(t) \in \mathbf{R}^{n_y}$ are the output, input and uncorrelated zero-mean disturbance, respectively, in (discrete) time t; A and B as well as A and $C \in \mathbf{R}^{n_y \times n_y}[z]$ are relatively prime polynomial matrices, with $\underline{C}(z^{-1}) = \underline{c}_0 + ... + \underline{c}_k z^{-k}$ and $k \le n$, and the $\underline{D}$ polynomial in

z^{-1}-domain is often equal to $1-z^{-1}$ (or to n_y-identity matrix in discrete-time MVC considerations).

The familiar Smith-McMillan form $S_M(p)$ (Kaczorek, 1998) of $G(p)$ (as a special case of the MFD factorization (Desoer & Schulman, 1974)) is given by $G(p)=U_0(p)S_M(p)V_0(p)$, where $U_0 \in \mathbf{R}^{n_y \times n_y}[p]$ and $V_0 \in \mathbf{R}^{n_u \times n_u}[p]$ are unimodular and the pencil $S_M \in \mathbf{R}^{n_y \times n_u}(p)$ is of the form

$$S_M(p)=\begin{bmatrix} M_{r\times r} & 0_{r\times(n_u-r)} \\ 0_{(n_y-r)\times r} & 0_{(n_y-r)\times(n_u-r)} \end{bmatrix} \tag{1}$$

with $M(p)=\text{diag}(\varepsilon_1/\psi_1,\varepsilon_2/\psi_2,...,\varepsilon_r/\psi_r)$, where $\varepsilon_i(p)$ and $\psi_i(p)$, $i=1,...,r$ (with r being the normal rank of $G(p)$), are monic coprime polynomials such that $\varepsilon_i(p)$ divides $\varepsilon_{i+1}(p)$, $i=1,...,r-1$, and $\psi_i(p)$ divides $\psi_{i-1}(p)$, $i=2,...,r$. The particular Smith form is given by the appropriate pencil $S(p)$, with $M(p)=\text{diag}(\varepsilon_1,\varepsilon_2,...,\varepsilon_r)$ often associated with *Smith zeros* or *transmission zeros*. The polynomials $\varepsilon_i(p)$ are often called the *invariant factors* of $G(p)$ and their product $\varepsilon(p)=\Pi_1^r\,\varepsilon_i(p)$ is sometimes referred to as the *zero polynomial* of $G(p)$.

Extend the discrete-time system input-output description to the form accounting for additive disturbances

$$\underline{A}(q^{-1})y(t)=q^{-d}\underline{B}(q^{-1})u(t)+\underline{C}(q^{-1})v(t) \tag{2}$$

where $u(t)$ and $y(t)$ are the input and output vectors, respectively, $v(t)$ is the zero-mean uncorrelated disturbance vector, d is the time delay and $\underline{A}(q^{-1})$, $\underline{B}(q^{-1})$ and $\underline{C}(q^{-1})$ are the appropriate matrix polynomials (in the backward shift operator q^{-1}) of orders n, m and k, respectively. As usual, we assume that the leading coefficient of $\underline{A}(q^{-1})$ is equal to the identity matrix. Assume that $\underline{A}(q^{-1})$ and $\underline{B}(q^{-1})$ as well as $\underline{A}(q^{-1})$ and $\underline{C}(q^{-1})$ are left coprime, with $\underline{B}(q^{-1})$ and (stable) $\underline{C}(q^{-1})$ being of full normal rank n_y. For the general purposes and for duality with the continuous-time case, we use here the ARMAX model, even though it is well known that the $\underline{C}(q^{-1})$ polynomial matrix of disturbance parameters is usually in control engineering practice unlikely to be effectively estimated (and is often used as a control design, observer polynomial matrix instead).

In the sequel, we proceed with discrete-time systems only but all the results are available for continuous-time systems as well (Hunek, 2003; Hunek & Latawiec, under review; Latawiec, 2004; Latawiec & Hunek, 2002; Latawiec et al., 2004).

3. Closed-loop minimum variance control

Consider a right-invertible system described by equation (2) and assume that the observer (or disturbance-related) polynomial $\underline{C}(q^{-1})=\underline{c}_0+\underline{c}_1q^{-1}+...+\underline{c}_kq^{-k}$ has all roots inside the unit disk. (Note: Similar results can be obtained for left-invertible systems.)

Then the general MVC law, minimizing the performance index

$$\min_{u(t)} E\left\{ \left[y(t+d) - y_{ref}(t+d)\right]^{\mathrm{T}} \left[y(t+d) - y_{ref}(t+d)\right] \right\} \tag{3}$$

where $y_{ref}(t+d)$ and $y(t+d) = \underline{\widetilde{C}}^{-1}(q^{-1})[\underline{\widetilde{F}}(q^{-1})\underline{B}(q^{-1})u(t) + \underline{\widetilde{H}}(q^{-1})y(t)] + \underline{F}(q^{-1})v(t)$ (Hunek, 2003; Hunek, 2007; Hunek & Latawiec, 2006; Hunek & Latawiec, under review; Latawiec, 2004) are the output reference/setpoint and the stochastic output predictor, respectively, is of form

$$u(t) = \underline{B}^{\mathrm{R}}(q^{-1})\underline{\widetilde{F}}^{-1}(q^{-1})\left[\underline{\widetilde{C}}(q^{-1})y_{ref}(t+d) - \underline{\widetilde{H}}(q^{-1})y(t)\right] \tag{4}$$

The appropriate $n_y \times n_y$-polynomial matrices $\underline{\widetilde{F}}(q^{-1}) = I_{n_y} + \underline{\widetilde{f}}_1 q^{-1} + \ldots + \underline{\widetilde{f}}_{d-1} q^{-d+1}$ and $\underline{\widetilde{H}}(q^{-1}) = \underline{\widetilde{h}}_0 + \underline{\widetilde{h}}_1 q^{-1} + \ldots + \underline{\widetilde{h}}_{n-1} q^{-n+1}$ are computed from the polynomial matrix identity (called Diophantine equation)

$$\underline{\widetilde{C}}(q^{-1}) = \underline{\widetilde{F}}(q^{-1})\underline{A}(q^{-1}) + q^{-d}\underline{\widetilde{H}}(q^{-1}) \tag{5}$$

with

$$\underline{\widetilde{C}}(q^{-1})\underline{F}(q^{-1}) = \underline{\widetilde{F}}(q^{-1})\underline{C}(q^{-1}) \tag{6}$$

where $\underline{F}(q^{-1}) = I_{n_y} + \underline{f}_1 q^{-1} + \ldots + \underline{f}_{d-1} q^{-d+1}$, $\underline{\widetilde{C}}(q^{-1}) = \underline{\widetilde{c}}_0 + \underline{\widetilde{c}}_1 q^{-1} + \ldots + \underline{\widetilde{c}}_k q^{-k}$ and I_{n_y} denotes the n_y-identity matrix.

For right-invertible systems the symbol $\underline{B}^{\mathrm{R}}(q^{-1})$ denotes three possible classes of minimum-norm right T-, τ- and σ-inverses of the polynomial matrix $\underline{B}(q^{-1})$ (Hunek, 2003; Latawiec, 2004; Latawiec et al., 2004; Latawiec et al., 2005b; Latawiec et al., 2003). Like with transmission zeros for SISO and square MIMO systems, poles of the right inverse $\underline{B}^{\mathrm{R}}(q^{-1})$ have been defined as *control zeros* (Hunek, 2003; Hunek, 2007; Hunek & Latawiec, 2006; Hunek & Latawiec, under review; Latawiec, 1998; Latawiec, 2004; Latawiec et al., 2000; Latawiec & Hunek, 2002; Latawiec et al. 2005a; Latawiec et al., 2004; Latawiec et al., 2005b; Latawiec et al., 2003). The minimum-norm right inverse was used in the unique T-inverse to generate a unique set of control zeros type 1 for right-invertible systems (Hunek, 2003; Latawiec, 2004; Latawiec & Hunek, 2002; Latawiec et al., 2003).
However, the formula (4) can be treated as a solver of the MVC-related matrix polynomial equation

$$\underline{B}(q^{-1})u(t) = \underline{y}(t) \tag{7}$$

where $\underline{y}(t) = \underline{\widetilde{F}}^{-1}(q^{-1})\left[\underline{\widetilde{C}}(q^{-1})y_{ref}(t+d) - \underline{\widetilde{H}}(q^{-1})y(t)\right]$ (Latawiec, 2004). When analyzing possible solutions to equation (7) we have introduced new classes of inverses of polynomial matrices, that is a finite number of τ-inverses and an infinite number of σ-inverses (Latawiec, 2004; Latawiec et al., 2004; Latawiec et al., 2005b), all surprisingly employing the unique minimum-norm right inverse. The τ- and σ-inverses contribute to generation of what has been referred to as control zeros type 2 (Latawiec, 2004; Latawiec et al., 2004; Latawiec et al., 2005b). It is interesting to note that transmission zeros make a subset of control zeros.

4. New approach to MVC design

In an attempt to essentially reduce the computational burden of the extreme points and extreme directions method we introduce yet another effective (and much simpler) approach to the MVC design, in which we make use of the equality (Hunek, 2007; Hunek & Latawiec, 2006)

$$\underline{B}(q^{-1})\underline{B}^{\mathrm{R}}(q^{-1}) = I \tag{8}$$

Consider an LTI n_u-input n_y-output system described by the ARMAX model (2). Put $w = q^{-1}$ and factorize $B(w)$ to the Smith form $B(w) = U(w)S(w)V(w)$, where $U(w)$ and $V(w)$ are *unimodular*. Now, $B^{\mathrm{R}}(w) = V^{-1}(w)S^{\mathrm{R}}(w)U^{-1}(w)$, with determinants of $U(w)$ and $V(w)$ being independent of w, that is possible instability of an inverse polynomial matrix $B^{\mathrm{R}}(w)$ being related to $S^{\mathrm{R}}(w)$ only. Amazingly, applying the minimum-norm right T-inverse $S_0^{\mathrm{R}}(w) = S(w)^{\mathrm{T}}[S(w)S(w)^{\mathrm{T}}]^{-1}$ guarantees that no control zeros except transmission zeros appear in the inverse $S^{\mathrm{R}}(w)$. (Employing any other inverses, e.g. τ- or σ-inverses, causes the control zeros to appear in $S^{\mathrm{R}}(w)$ in addition to transmission zeros.) This intriguing result has been confirmed in a number of simulations but no formal proof exists, so far. The result confirms the value of the Smith factorization on the one hand, and the T-inverse on the other.

5. Simulation example

Consider the three-input and two-output unstable system described by noise-free deterministic part of model (2) with $\underline{B}(q^{-1}) = \begin{bmatrix} 2+3.8q^{-1} & 2q^{-1} & 1 \\ 4q^{-1} & 1+1.9q^{-1} & 1 \end{bmatrix}$, $\underline{A}(q^{-1}) = 500 + 570q^{-1} + 19q^{-2}$ and $d = 2$. The control zeros type 1, obtained on a basis of T-inverse of $\underline{B}(q^{-1})$, determine unstable MVC or perfect control of the system. Besides, it is very difficult to find stable MVC/perfect control on the basis of τ- and σ-inverses with control zeros type 2 associated. Since the system has one (stable) transmission zero at $z = 0.1$, it is impossible to employ the extreme points and extreme directions method. Therefore, we apply our new method of Section 4. Now, after substitution $w = q^{-1}$ and after Smith factorization we obtain $U(w)=\begin{bmatrix}1 & 0\\ 1 & 1\end{bmatrix}$, $S(w)=\begin{bmatrix}1 & 0 & 0\\ 0 & w-10 & 0\end{bmatrix}$, $V(w)=\begin{bmatrix}3.8w+2 & 2w & 1\\ 0.2 & -0.1 & 0\\ 0 & -1 & 0\end{bmatrix}$

and finally

$$u(t)=\begin{bmatrix}0 & 5 & -0.5\\ 0 & 0 & -1\\ 1 & -10-19q^{-1} & 1+3.9q^{-1}\end{bmatrix}\begin{bmatrix}1 & 0\\ 0 & \dfrac{1}{q^{-1}-10}\\ 0 & 0\end{bmatrix} \cdot\begin{bmatrix}1 & 0\\ -1 & 1\end{bmatrix}\underline{\widetilde{F}}^{-1}(q^{-1})\left[y_{ref}(t+d)-\underline{\widetilde{H}}(q^{-1})y(t)\right] \quad (9)$$

with specific forms of $\underline{\widetilde{F}}^{-1}(q^{-1})$ and $\underline{\widetilde{H}}^{-1}(q^{-1})$ not presented here due to their mathematical complexity. Now, for $y1_{ref}=1$, $y2_{ref}=1.5$ the outputs remain at the setpoint for $t\geq d=2$ under the stabilizing perfect control, whose plots $u_1(t)$, $u_2(t)$ and $u_3(t)$ according to equation (9) are shown in Fig. 1. For clarity, we have chosen to show the performance of (noise-free) perfect control rather than MVC.

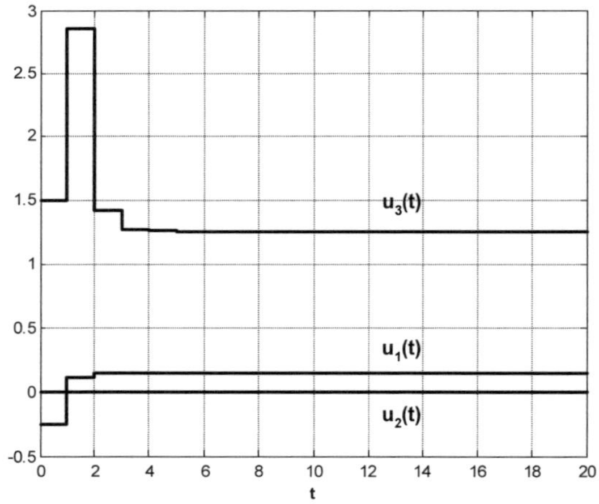

Fig. 1. Perfect control plots for the specific example

Remark. However, the Smith factorization approach undeniably contributes to the robust MVC design, in the majority cases the application of the control zeros can give much better results (Hunek, under review), giving rise to the extension of the Davison's theory of minimum phase systems (Davison, 1983). Unfortunately, there exists no formal proof of the above statement and it has been left for future research.

6. Conclusions

The Smith factorization approach to the robust minimum variance control has been presented in this paper. The new method appears much better than others, designed by authors, namely those based on the extreme points and extreme directions method and second one called minimum-energy. Firstly, it is computationally much simpler and secondly, it works also for the case when transmission zeros are (nongenerically) present in the nonsquare system. Strange enough, the presented method should operate on the T-inverse exclusively and any other inverse applied gives rise to the appearance of control zeros. What is also strange, applying the T-inverse directly to the polynomial $B(.)$ (rather than to its Smith-factorized form) inevitably ends up with control zeros. Finally, the new approach confirms the Davison's theory and indicates the need of the introduction of the complementary control zeros theory.

7. References

Davison, E. J. (1983). Some properties of minimum phase systems and 'squared-down' systems. *IEEE Trans. Auto. Control*, Vol. AC-28, No. 2, 1983, pp. 221-222.

Desoer, C. A. & Schulman, J. D. (1974). Zeros and poles of matrix transfer functions and their dynamical interpretation. *IEEE Trans. Circuits & Systems*, Vol. CAS-21, No. 1, 1974, pp. 3-8.

Hunek, W. P. (2003). *Control zeros for continuous-time LTI MIMO systems and their application in theory of circuits and systems (in Polish)*, Ph.D. thesis, Opole University of Technology, Department of Electrical, Control and Computer Engineering, Opole.

Hunek, W. P. (2007). A robust approach to the minimum variance control of LTI MIMO systems. *Emerging Technologies, Robotics and Control Systems*, Vol. 2, 2007, pp. 133-138, ISBN: 978-88-901928-9-5; also in *International Journal of Factory Automation, Robotics and Soft Computing*, Vol. 2, 2007, pp. 191-196, ISSN: 1828-6984.

Hunek, W. P. (to be published). Towards robust minimum variance control of nonsquare LTI MIMO systems. *Archives of Control Sciences*.

Hunek, W. P. & Latawiec, K. J. (2006). An inverse-free approach to minimum variance control of LTI MIMO systems, *Proceedings of 12th IEEE International Conference on Methods and Models in Automation and Robotics (MMAR'2006)*, pp. 373-378, Międzyzdroje, Poland, August 2006.

Hunek, W. P. & Latawiec, K. J. (under review). Minimum variance control of discrete-time and continuous-time LTI MIMO systems - a new unified framework. *Control and Cybernetics*.

Kaczorek, T. (1998). *Vectors and Matrices in Automatic Control and Electrical Engineering (in Polish)*, WNT, Warszawa.

Latawiec, K. J. (1998). *Contributions to Advanced Control and Estimation for Linear Discrete-Time MIMO Systems*, Opole University of Technology Press, ISSN: 1429-6063, Opole.

Latawiec, K. J. (2004). *The Power of Inverse Systems in Linear and Nonlinear Modeling and Control*, Opole University of Technology Press, ISSN: 1429-6063, Opole.

Latawiec, K. J.; Bańka, S. & Tokarzewski, J. (2000). Control zeros and nonminimum phase LTI MIMO systems. *Annual Reviews in Control*, Vol. 24, 2000, pp. 105-112; also in *Proceedings of the IFAC World Congress*, Vol. D, pp. 397-404, Beijing, P.R. China, 1999.

Latawiec, K. J. & Hunek, W. P. (2002). Control zeros for continuous-time LTI MIMO systems, *Proceedings of 8th IEEE International Conference on Methods and Models in Automation and Robotics (MMAR'2002)*, pp. 411-416, Szczecin, Poland, September 2002.

Latawiec, K. J.; Hunek, W. P. & Adamek, B. (2005a). A new uniform solution of the minimum variance control problem for discrete-time and continuous-time LTI MIMO systems, *Proceedings of 11th IEEE International Conference on Methods and Models in Automation and Robotics (MMAR'2005)*, pp. 339-344, Międzyzdroje, Poland, August-September 2005.

Latawiec, K. J.; Hunek, W. P. & Łukaniszyn, M. (2004). A new type of control zeros for LTI MIMO systems, *Proceedings of 10th IEEE International Conference on Methods and Models in Automation and Robotics (MMAR'2004)*, pp. 251-256, Międzyzdroje, Poland, August-September 2004.

Latawiec, K. J.; Hunek, W. P. & Łukaniszyn, M. (2005b). New optimal solvers of MVC-related linear matrix polynomial equations, *Proceedings of 11th IEEE International Conference on Methods and Models in Automation and Robotics (MMAR'2005)*, pp. 333-338, Międzyzdroje, Poland, August-September 2005.

Latawiec, K. J.; Hunek, W. P.; Stanisławski, R. & Łukaniszyn, M. (2003). Control zeros versus transmission zeros intriguingly revisited, *Proceedings of 9th IEEE International Conference on Methods and Models in Automation and Robotics (MMAR'2003)*, pp. 449-454, Międzyzdroje, Poland, August 2003.

Rosenbrock, H. H. (1970). *State-space and Multivariable Theory*, Nelson-Wiley, New York.

Wolowich, W. A. (1974). *Linear Multivariable Systems*, Springer-Verlag, New York.

22

The Wafer Alignment Algorithm Regardless of Rotational Center

HyungTae Kim, HaeJeong Yang and SungChul Kim
Korea Institute of Industrial Technology
South Korea

1. Introduction

Semiconductor manufacturers prefer automatic machines due to quality, productivity and effectiveness. Compared with other industries, the semiconductor industry has automized the individual steps of a process to a relatively high level. Most of the operators usually learn about wafer placement rather than the principle of the process. But the manual systems do not know the placement of a wafer, so operators should set the initial conditions for the process. Wafer alignment is an operation for correcting the current wafer position in the system coordinate until the wafer is located at the target position. The wafer position varies after loading, so alignment steps are required.

Manual alignment systems need the operators' help every time the wafer is loaded and is actually a time-consuming process, that lowers manufacturing productivity and raises costs. So, automatic alignment can save these time and costs. If the machines have automatic alignment function, wafer processes can be connected automatically. Operators then would only have to check and monitor the processing situation, and fix a problem when it arises. Therefore, one operator can operate more machines, and would not be required to have high process skills. Fig. 1 shows the concept of wafer alignment in the dicing process.

Passive alignment is related with mechanical structures which persist into external forces without any actuators. A self-constrained mechanism is developed by Choi. When axial force is exerted on a stage, grooves beneath the stage generate internal stress which prevents from moving the stage (Choi et al., 1999). Pyramid and groove mechanism make stacking force under external stress (Slocum & Weber, 2003).

Active alignment skill using sensors and actuators is applied widely in semiconductor manufacturing process. Anderson's method (Anderson et al, 2004) is based on cross-relation between a defined template and an inspected image. He segmented the pixels around a peak and interpolated under sub-pixel level. Misalignment can be detected by Moire effect and laser beam. PZT actuators are applied to remove misalignment in lithography (Fan et al., 2006). Machine vision is a common device to detect misalignment in wafer aligment (Hong & Fang, 2002).

We have developed an algorithm for wafer alignment. This alignment algorithm was derived from rigid body transformation or object transformation. The algorithm was based on the simultaneous motion of x-y-θ axes in 2D space. A 2-step algorithm has a simple form which can be written by 2×2 matrix operations. The magnitude of misalignment was reduced in base of macro and micro inspection data(Kim et al., 2004). The matrix was expanded with 4×4, and θ was included in the equation. So, the alignment variables of x-y-θ can be calculated within one equation(Kim et al, 2004), (Kim et al, 2006). The manufacturing condition which was varied to be ideal conditions, affected the quality of alignment. Sometimes the misalignment did not become zero after only macro-micro alignment. In this case, the problem can be solved by iterative alignment equation, which is similar to numerical algorithms(Kim et al, 2007). The convergence speed of the iteration can be controlled by the convergence constant. This constant can prevent numerical vibration. The convergence analysis method, similar to a numerical method, is proposed(Kim et al, 2006). We tried to obtain the exact solution in these studies, but they found that the solutions can be obtained from an estimated equation. The idea in this study came from the estimated method. The equation could be simplified by making a few assumptions of the wafer alignment condition. The derived formula did not have the terms for rotational center, which was impossible to measure exactly. The alignment results showed that the performance of the proposed algorithm was similar to the exact solution, and that the error convergence speed can be controlled.

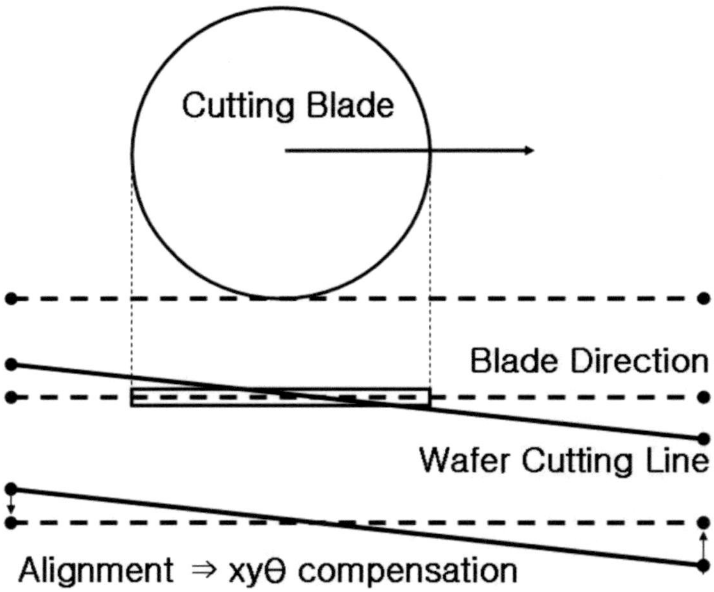

Fig. 1. Concept of wafer alignment in dicing process

2. Review of 2D alignment model

2.1 Coordinate transformation for alignment(Kim et al, 2004)

The machine coordinate in the alignment system has three variables - x, y and θ. Let be the P(x,y) original coordinate, and P′(x′,y′) be the transformed coordinate. The each coordinate can be shown as follows

$$P = (x \;\; y \;\; \theta \;\; 1)^T \quad P' = (x' \;\; y' \;\; \theta' \;\; 1)^T \quad P = (C_x \;\; C_y \;\; 0 \;\; 0)^T \tag{1}$$

The alignment space is on 2D, the alignment procedure carries out translation and rotational motion. The movement can be described by rigid body transformation and the coordinate after the motion can be calculated simply by multiplying matrices. The notation of the translational matrix usually has a 'T', the rotational matrix has an 'R' and the center of rotation has a 'C'. Then the transformation is formulated by equation (2).

$$P' = T\{R(P-C)+C\} \tag{2}$$

TR matrices in the wafer alignment system can be derived as equations (3) and (4), which are 4 × 4 matrices.

$$T = \begin{bmatrix} 1 & 0 & 0 & \Delta x \\ 0 & 1 & 0 & \Delta y \\ 0 & 0 & 1 & 0 \\ 0 & 0 & 0 & 1 \end{bmatrix} \tag{3}$$

$$R = \begin{bmatrix} \cos\Delta\theta & -\sin\Delta\theta & 0 & 0 \\ \sin\Delta\theta & \cos\Delta\theta & 0 & 0 \\ 0 & 0 & 1 & \Delta\theta \\ 0 & 0 & 0 & 1 \end{bmatrix} \tag{4}$$

2.2 Basic alignment algorithm(Kim et al, 2006)

The wafer has marks for alignment. The ideal mark position P_t is stored when the wafer is perfectly aligned. Misalignment is calculated from the current position P_c. The vision system inspects the location of the mark on the screen. These mark positions can be defined as follows.

$$P_t = (x_t \;\; y_t \;\; \theta_t \;\; 1)^T \;\; P_c = (x_c \;\; y_c \;\; \theta_c \;\; 1)^T \tag{5}$$

When the current position of the mark is deviated from the ideal one, the resulting displacement can be defined as 4. The mark position in the machine can be obtained from the target position and the displacement by equation (6).

$$P_c \approx P_t + \Delta = (x_c + \Delta x, y_c + \Delta y, \theta_c + \Delta\theta, \;\; 1)^T \tag{6}$$

If the current position is compensated with an arbitrary value $\alpha = (\alpha_x, \alpha_y, \alpha_\theta, 0)$, the mark will be located at the target position. So, an alignment algorithm f(x) can be written by equation (7).

$$f(P_c,\alpha) - P_t = 0 \tag{7}$$

f(Pc,α) can be replaced with the equation from the rigid body transformation. The result is shown as (8). The T and R have the unknown compensation variable for the current position.

$$T\{R(P_c - C) + C\} - P_t = 0 \tag{8}$$

The plus direction between the mathematical coordinate and vision can be reverse, and the relation can be written by vision direction matrix D_v whose diagonal terms have a value of either +1 or -1 and the other terms are zero.

$$T\{R(P_t + D_v\Delta - C) + C\} - P_t = 0 \tag{9}$$

The direction problem can occur between the math coordinate and the machine, and the machine direction matrix D_m has the similar characteristics as D_v.

$$\beta = D_m\alpha \quad \beta = (\beta_x \ \ \beta_y \ \ \beta_\theta \ \ 1)^T \tag{10}$$

The unknown α can be calculated from the equation, and (11) and (12) are the exact solution in the case when two points are inspected to align a line.

$$\begin{aligned} \alpha_{xn} &= x_{tn}\text{-}C_x\text{-}(x_{cn}\text{-}C_x)\cos\theta_n + (y_{cn}\text{-}C_y)\sin\theta_n \\ \alpha_{yn} &= y_{tn}\text{-}C_y\text{-}(x_{cn}\text{-}C_x)\sin\theta_n\text{-}(y_{cn}\text{-}C_y)\cos\theta_n \end{aligned} \tag{11}$$

$$\tan\alpha_\theta = \frac{(x_{c1} - x_{c2})(y_{t1} - y_{t2}) - (y_{c1} - y_{c2})(x_{t1} - x_{t2})}{(x_{t1} - x_{t2})(x_{c1} - x_{c2}) + (y_{t1} - y_{t2})(y_{c1} - y_{c2})} \tag{12}$$

3. Centerless model

3.1 Simplification

The equations (11) and (12) are the exact solution, but estimated solutions have been used for many numerical problems. Some variables can be erased by geometric relations and alignment conditions. Fig. 2 shows the general condition for wafer alignment in the dicing process. First, angular misalignment in the process is within ±2°, which means sin α ≈ α and cos α ≈ 1. the equation (11) can be written as follows

$$\begin{aligned} \alpha_{xn} &= x_{tn}\text{-}x_{cn} + (y_{cn}\text{-}C_y)\sin\alpha_{\theta n} = -\Delta_{xn} + (y_{cn}\text{-}C_y)\alpha_{\theta n} \\ \alpha_{yn} &= y_{tn}\text{-}y_{cn}\text{-}(x_{cn}\text{-}C_x)\sin\alpha_{\theta n} = -\Delta_{yn} - (x_{cn}\text{-}C_x)\alpha_{\theta n} \end{aligned} \tag{13}$$

Second, inspection is carried out at two points, and the compensation value is the average, $\alpha=(\alpha_1+\alpha_2)/2$. And the inspection points are axis-symmetric at the rotational center, $2C_x-(x_{c1}+x_{c2})=0$. Another assumption is that the mark position is defined near the rotational center, $2C_y-(y_{c1}+y_{c2}) = 0$. Therefore, the equation (13) can be expressed as (14).

$$\begin{aligned} \alpha_{xn} &= -(\Delta_{x1} + \Delta_{x2})/2 \\ \alpha_{yn} &= -(\Delta_{y1} + \Delta_{y2})/2 \end{aligned} \tag{14}$$

The x-stroke of two points is actually constant, $l=x_{t2}-x_{t1}\approx x_{c2}-x_{c1}$ because the x variation by misalignment is much smaller than the moving stroke. The y-stroke of two points is actually zero, $y_{t2} - y_{t1} = 0$. Equation (15) is derived from these relations.

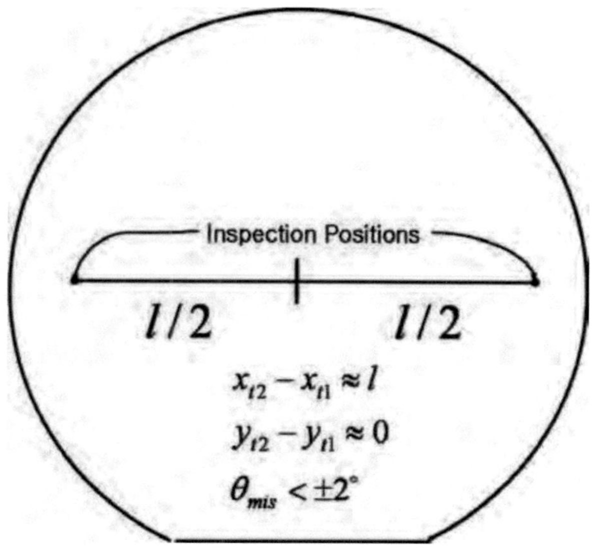

Fig. 2. General conditions for wafer alignment

$$\tan\alpha_\theta \approx \alpha_\theta = \frac{(\Delta_{y2} - \Delta_{y1})}{l} \tag{15}$$

The derived equations are much simpler and have no center terms for rotation. Considering the wafer alignment system, there are three centers, as shown Fig. 3: rotational center, wafer center, and chuck center. The positions of these three centers are different, but cannot be measured exactly or cannot be fixed at the same position. Centerless algorithm cannot give an exact solution, but an estimated one, so the iteration step is necessary.

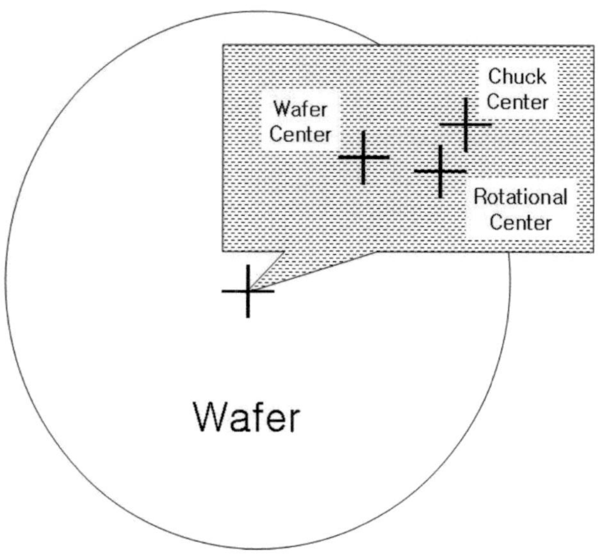

Fig. 3. Different Centers on alignment table

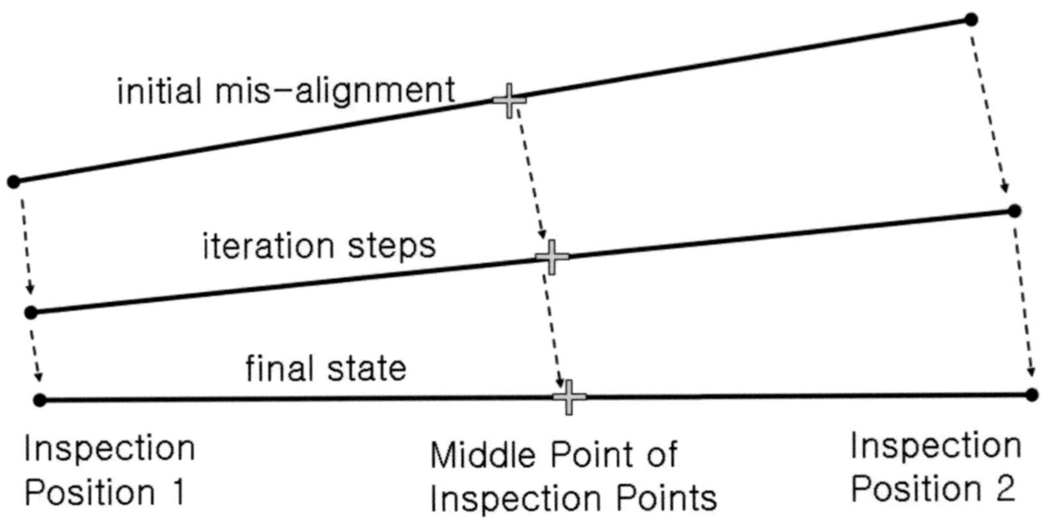

Fig. 4. Concept of movement for the points in alignment

The equation can be explained in another way. Fig. 4 shows the virtual alignment procedure. The inspection positions are located at both ends of the lines, and the middle point can represent the inspection points. The misalignment of the middle point can be estimated from the average of the misalignment on the two points. And the compensation value of the middle point is approximately equal to the magnitude of the misalignment, and the result can be written as (14) and (15).

3.2 Iteration and convergence

The alignment properties are estimated, and it is possible that the misalignment cannot be zero after the first alignment. And manufacturing conditions can vary and are different from the ideal condition. The alternative is the iterative alignment, which is carried out until the misalignment decreases under tolerance level. Compensation values are added to the current position, and the i-th step of the alignment can be written as equation (16). It is necessary to control convergence speed, and the convergence constant is defined as η.

$$ {}^{i+1}P_c = {}^{i}P_c + \eta \times {}^{i}\beta \tag{16} $$

Misalignment can be defined as the magnitude of the deviation, as shown in (17). The iteration is terminated when the misalignment becomes smaller than tolerance ε.

$$ \left| {}^{i}\Delta \right| = \sqrt{\frac{(\Delta_{x1}^2 + \Delta_{x2}^2) + (\Delta_{y1}^2 + \Delta_{y2}^2)}{2}} < \varepsilon \tag{17} $$

As the automatic alignment proceeds, the numerical position on the machine is compensated. The magnitude of the compensation value β will decrease by the number of iterations. γ is defined as the total amount of the compensation or difference between initial position and current position. The γ will be converged to an arbitrary value if the alignment is done well.

$$ {}^{i+1}\gamma = {}^{i}\gamma + \eta \times {}^{i}\beta = {}^{i}P_c - {}^{0}P_c \tag{17} $$

Fig. 5. Photo of automatic wafer dicing machine

4. Experiment

4.1 Dicing machine

The algorithm was tested on the wafer dicing machine. The machine had 4 axes - x, y, z and θ . Because the z axis is actually used only for cutting action, it was excluded for alignment. Each axis is composed of a ball-screw and LM guide. The axes were accurate to the micro-level. Fig. 5 shows a picture of the dicing machine, and table 1 shows its specifications. The align mark was inspected with a PCI frame grabber, which has 0.1 sub-pixel accuracy. Two cameras were connected to the frame grabber. Very small lenses were attached to the cameras, which had same magnifications because of the align patterns.

contents	name/axis	specification
resolution	x	1μm
	y	0.2μm
	θ	2.0 x10^{-4}deg
linear scale	y	10000ps/mm
pitch	x	10mm/rev
	y	4mm/rev
	θ	1/100(harmonic driver)
motor	x	10000ps
	y	20000ps
	θ	18000ps
backlash	x	7μm
	y	0μm
camera	model	Sony XC-HR50
	pixel	640×480
	FOV	1.31mm×0.98mm
	exposure	20ms
frame grabber	model	Cog8501
	Precision	0.1 sub-pixel
	library	Vision Pro 3.5

Table 1. Specification of Machine

4.2 Procedure

First, a wafer was aligned manually to get a standard pattern on an inspected image. The shape of align pattern in the experiment was the cross mark. The machine was moved to search for the best pattern of a high-quality image. The image of the mark and training results were stored. The inspection positions were defined at the mechanical positions when the align pattern was located at the center of the screen. The inspection positions were defined for dicing lines of $\theta = 0°$ and $\theta = 90°$.

After the position definition, the wafer was released from the table and placed again manually to give random errors. The system began aligning from 0 ° alignment, and then it proceeded to 90° alignment. The magnifications of the lenses were the same, and the macro-alignment had no meaning. Three lines were aligned for 0 °, and ten for 90 °. The deviations were stored at each inspection points. The compensation values were obtained from the deviation. The system axes were compensated by these values, so the inspection positions were also changed. The inspection and compensation were iterated until the misalignment was under 1.0 pixel. The convergence constant η was varied from 0.5 to 1.5 without releasing the wafer. The experiment was repeated for 15 cases of mark locations on the vision screen, as shown in the previous report.

5. Result

Wafers were aligned successfully for the 15 cases. One of the cases is shown in this paper. The variation of γ's is shown in Fig. 6 - Fig. 11. The horizontal axis of the plots was the number of iterations, and the vertical axis was the compensation value. The thick-black line, called 'org' is the result obtained by the use of the original equation before the simplification. The convergent path was varied by η, and the convergent speed can be controlled. When the η increased, the path showed a bigger overshoot and sharp edges. This kind of trend always occurred when the value was above 1.0. This also makes the alignment time longer. When the η drcreases, the path showed a smooth shape and longer alignment time. This trend always occurred when the η was below 1.0. There was no overshoot for this case. The original equation provided the fastest convergence for a case, but the result showed that the simplified equation was also effective for application. The best value for γ_x was 1.1, but that of γ_y was 1.0. The response of the best case was delayed about 1.0 step for the case of the original equation.

6. Conclusion

The proposed equation for wafer alignment was derived from object transformation and simplified with some assumptions made. The alignment algorithm had the iteration terms with the convergence constant. The algorithm was applied to a dicing machine. After setup, the wafers were placed manually, and aligned with the proposed algorithm. The iteration was terminated until the measured misalignment became below 1.0 vision pixel. The convergence constant η varied from 0.5 to 1.5 for each case. For all 15 cases, the alignment was finished. The result showed that the simplified algorithm converged slower than the original equation. But the delay was about 1.0 step according to the convergent constant. When the η was above 1.0, the response curve had an overshoot and sharp edges. But the curve had smoothness and slower response when the η was below 1.0. The alignment algorithm was simple so that it can be applied to PLC-base systems.

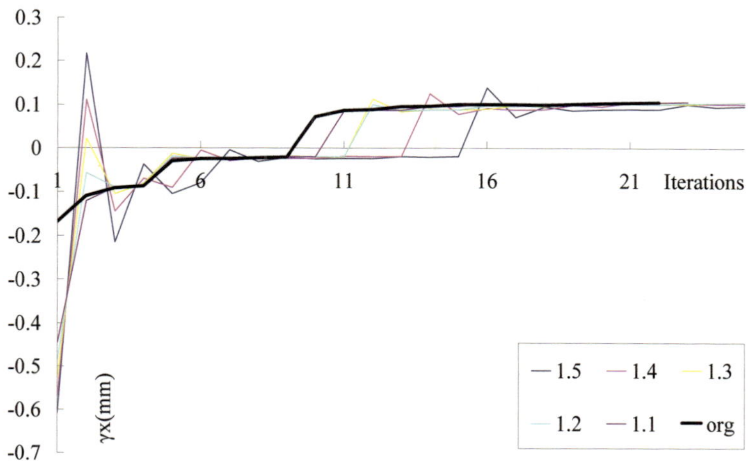

Fig. 6. Variation of γ_x by iteration (γ_x=1.1-1.5)

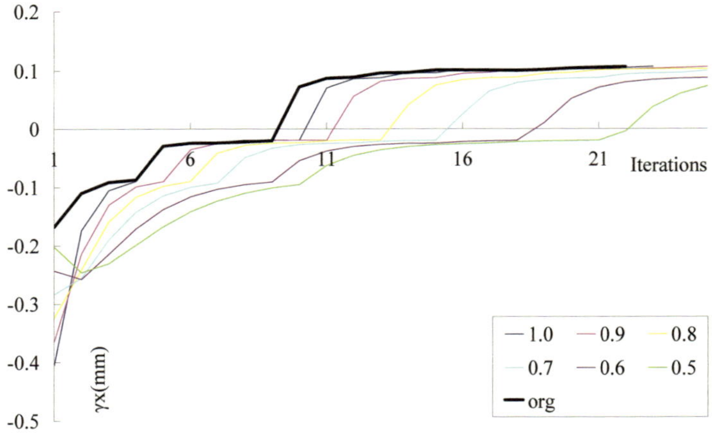

Fig. 7. Variation of γ_x by iteration (γ_x=0.5-1.0)

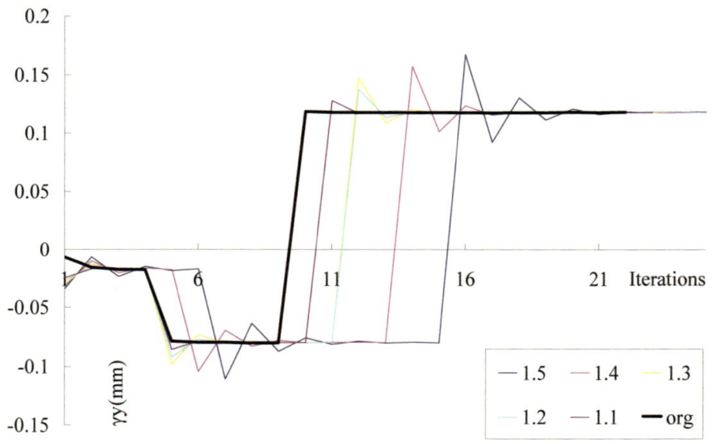

Fig. 8. Variation of γ_y by iteration (γ_y=1.1-1.5)

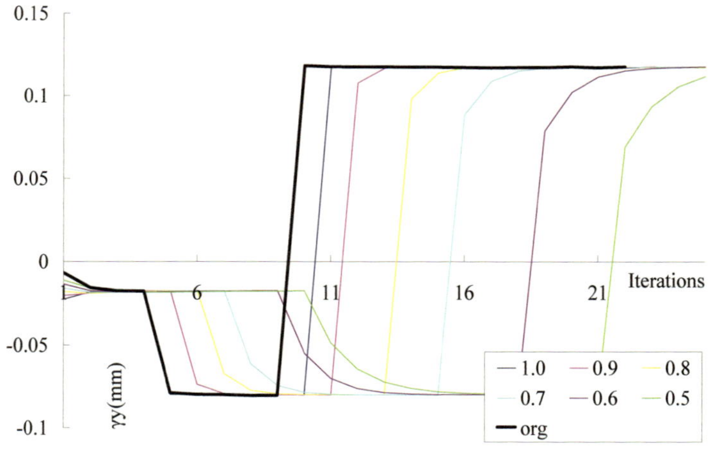

Fig. 9. Variation of γ_y by iteration (γ_y=0.5-1.0)

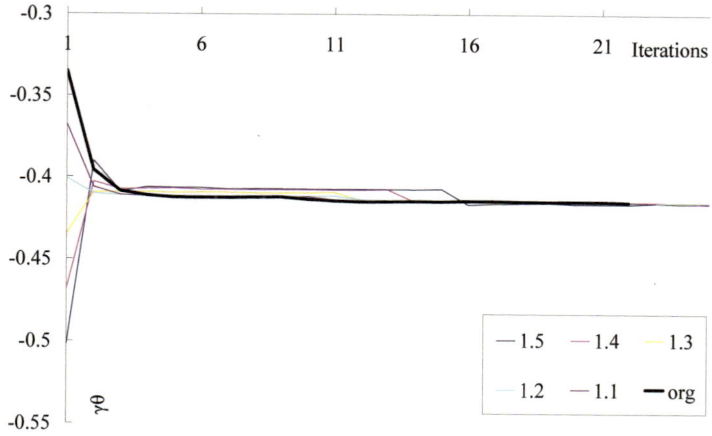

Fig. 10. Variation of γ_θ by iteration (γ_θ=1.1-1.5)

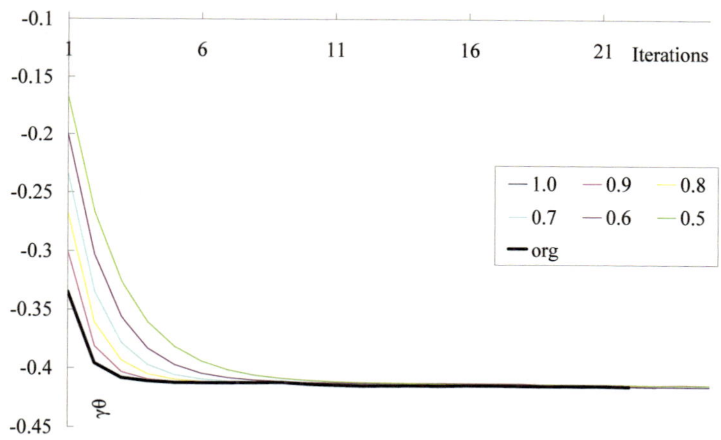

Fig. 11. Variation of γ_θ by iteration (γ_θ=0.5-1.0)

8. References

Choi, M. H.; Koh, H. J. , Yoon, E. S., Shin, K. C. & Song, K. C., (1999) Self-Aligning Silicon Groove Technology Platform for the Low Cost Optical Module, *Proceedings of Electronic Components and Technology Conference,* pp. 1140-1144, ISBN 0-7803-5231-9, San Diego, June 1999, IEEE, CA

Slocum, A.H. & Weber, A.C. (2003). Precision passive mechanical alignment of wafers. *Journal of Microelectromechanical Systems,* Vol. 12, No. 6, (Dec. 2003) pp. 826-834, ISSN 1057-7157

Anderson, E. H.; Ha, D. & Liddle, J. A. (2004) Sub-pixel alignment for direct-write electron beam lithography. *Microelectronic Engineering,* Vol. 73-74, (June 2004) pp. 74-79, ISSN 0167-9317

Fan, X.; Zhang, H., Liu, S. Hu, X. & Jia, K. (2006) NIL - A low cost and high throughput MEMS fabrication method compatible with IC manufacturing technology. *Microelectronics Journal,* Vol. 37, No. 2, (Feb 2006) pp. 121-126, ISSN 0026-2692

Hong, S. & Fang, M. (2002) A Hybrid Image Alignment System for Fast Precise Pattern Localization. *Real-Time Imaging,* Vol. 8, No. 1, (Feb. 2002) 23-33, ISSN 1077-201

Kim, H. T.; Song, C. S. & Yang, H. J., (2004) 2-step algorithms for automatic alignment. *Microelectronics Reliability,* Vol.44, No.6, (July 2004) pp. 1165-1179, ISSN 0026-2714

Kim, H. T.; Song, C. S. & Yang, H. J. (2004) Matrix form of automatic alignment algorithm in 2D space, *Proceedings of the IEEE International Conference on Mechatronics,* pp. 465-469, ISBN 0-7803-8599-3, Istanbul, June 2004, IEEE, Turkey

Kim, H. T.; Song, C. S. & Yang, H. J. (2006) Algorithm for automatic alignment in 2D space by object transformation, *Microelectorics Reliability,* Vol.46, No.1, (Jan. 2006) pp. 100-108, ISSN 0026-2714

Kim, H. T.; Yang, H. J. & Baek, S. Y. (2007) Iterative algorithm for automatic alignment by object transformation, *Microelectorics Reliability,* Vol. 47, No. 6, (June 2007) pp. 972-985, ISSN 0026-2714

Kim, H. T. ; Yang H. J. & Kim, S. C., (2006) Convergence analysis of wafer alignment algorithm based on object transformation, Proceedings of the IEEE International Conference on Industrial Electorics Application, pp.1690-1695, ISBN 0-7803-9514-X, Singapore, May 2006, Singapore